Contents

PREFACE   vii

INTRODUCTION   1

Part I   **THE SOCIAL CONTEXT IN WHICH SCIENTIFIC KNOWLEDGE IS PRODUCED**   5

Gerald Holton, *On the Psychology of Scientists, and Their Social Concerns*   9

Marguerite Holloway, *A Lab of Her Own*   25

Natalie Angier, *Women Join the Ranks of Science but Remain Invisible at the Top*   35

Shirley Tilghman, *Science vs. The Female Scientist*   40

Shirley Tilghman, *Science vs. Women: A Radical Solution*   43

Bruno Latour and Steve Woolgar, *An Anthropologist Visits the Laboratory*   46

Part II   **THE EMPIRICAL BASIS OF SCIENTIFIC KNOWLEDGE**   65

Karl Popper, *The Problem of the Empirical Basis*   75

Norwood Russell Hanson, *Observation*   81

Steven Shapin, *Pump and Circumstance: Robert Boyle's Literary Technology*   100

Ann Oakley, *Interviewing Women: A Contradiction in Terms*   117

Andy Pickering, *Against Putting the Phenomena First: The Discovery of the Weak Neutral Current*   135

Part III   THE VALIDATION OF SCIENTIFIC KNOWLEDGE   153

Rudolph Carnap, *The Confirmation of Laws and Theories*   **164**

Karl Popper, *Science: Conjectures and Refutations*   **176**

Pierre Duhem, *Physical Theory and Experiment*   **187**

Imre Lakatos, *Falsification and the Methodology of Scientific
Research Programmes*   **195**

Thomas Kuhn, *Objectivity, Value Judgment, and Theory Choice*   **212**

Ruth Hubbard, *Have Only Men Evolved?*   **225**

Helen Longino, *Can There Be a Feminist Science?*   **243**

**Part IV   THE HISTORICAL DEVELOPMENT OF
SCIENTIFIC KNOWLEDGE   253**

Carl Hempel, *Explanation in Science*   **261**

Paul Oppenheim and Hilary Putnam, *Unity of Science as a Working Hypothesis*   **267**

Karl Popper, *The Rationality of Scientific Revolutions*   **286**

Thomas Kuhn, *The Function of Dogma in Scientific Research*   **301**

Thomas Kuhn, *The Nature and Necessity of Scientific Revolutions*   **316**

Larry Laudan, *Dissecting the Holist Picture of Scientific Change*   **327**

**Part V   REALISM VERSUS ANTI-REALISM: THE ONTOLOGICAL
IMPORT OF SCIENTIFIC KNOWLEDGE   339**

Grover Maxwell, *The Ontological Status of Theoretical Entities*   **348**

Bas van Fraassen, *Arguments Concerning Scientific Realism*   **355**

Ernan McMullin, *A Case for Scientific Realism*   **369**

Arthur Fine, *The Natural Ontological Attitude*   **386**

Evelyn Fox Keller, *Critical Silences in Scientific Discourse:
Problems of Form and Re-Form*   **397**

Michael R. Gardner, *Realism and Instrumentalism in Pre-Newtonian Astronomy*   **410**

Ian Hacking, *Experimentation and Scientific Realism*   **428**

Scientific Knowledge
Basic Issues in the Philosophy of Science

Second Edition

Janet A. Kourany
University of Notre Dame

Wadsworth Publishing Company
I(T)P® An International Thomson Publishing Company

Belmont, CA • Albany, NY • Bonn • Boston • Cincinatti • Detroit • Johannesburg • London • Madrid
Melbourne • Mexico City • New York • Paris • Singapore • Tokyo • Toronto • Washington

Editor: *Peter Adams*
Assistant Editor: *Kerri Abdinoor*
Editorial Assistant: *Kelly Bush*
Marketing Manager: *Dave Garrison*
Project Editor: *John Walker*
Print Buyer: *Stacey Weinberger*
Production: *Dovetail Publishing Services*
Copy Editor: *Dovetail Publishing Services*
Illustrations: *Dovetail Publishing Services*
Cover Design: *Norman Baugher*
Printer: *Malloy Lithographing*

Printed in the United States of America
1 2 3 4 5 6 7 8 9 10

For more information, contact Wadsworth Publishing Company, 10 Davis Drive, Belmont, CA 94002, or electronically
at http://www.thomson.com/wadsworth.html

International Thomson Publishing Europe
Berkshire House 168-173
High Holborn
London, WC1V 7AA, England

International Thomson Editores
Campos Eliseos 385, Piso 7
Col. Polanco
11560 México D.F. México

Thomas Nelson Australia
102 Dodds Street
South Melbourne 3205
Victoria, Australia

International Thomson Publishing Asia
221 Henderson Road
#05-10 Henderson Building
Singapore 0315

Nelson Canada
1120 Birchmount Road
Scarborough, Ontario
Canada M1K 5G4

International Thomson Publishing Japan
Hirakawacho Kyowa Building, 3F
2-2-1- Hirakawacho
Chiyoda-ku, Tokyo 102, Japan

International Thomson Publishing GmbH
Königswinterer Strasse 418
53227 Bonn, Germany

International Thomson Publishing Southern Africa
Building 18, Constantia Park
240 Old Pretoria Road
Halfway House, 1685 South Africa

Library of Congress Cataloging-in-Publication Data
Kourany, Janet A.
    Scientific knowledge : basic issues in the philosophy of science / Janet A. Kourany. — 2nd. ed.
      p.   cm.
    Includes bibliographic references
    ISBN 0-534-52530-X
    1. Science—Philosophy.   I. Kourany, Janet A.
Q175.3.S327   1997
501—dc21   97-43411
                                      CIP

To my Mother and Father
Whose love and support are now sorely missed

Preface

The current scene in philosophy of science is as riddled with controversy as it was in 1987, when the first edition of this book appeared. Indeed, philosophers of science still disagree not only about the nature of science but also about the aims and methods of philosophy of science itself. Since 1987, however, the field of philosophy of science has undergone significant changes.

First, a new field of science studies has attained prominence, the sociology of scientific knowledge, concerned with the social explanation of even the technical aspects of scientific activity and knowledge. Philosophers of science, as a result, have been interested in the relationship between such new "social constructivist" analyses of science and more traditional analyses within the so-called "logic of science."

Second, and relatedly, philosophers and historians of science, as well as anthropologists and sociologists of science, have been focusing attention on the experimental aspects of science. Up until now, experiments have been treated by philosophers and others simply as vehicles to develop and test scientific theories. Now this very "theory-directed" characterization of science is coming into question as new historical case studies and current anthropological work disclose that experimentation has an important developmental "life of its own" independent of theory.

And third, feminist critiques within, especially, the biological and social sciences, as well as feminist work within philosophy and history of science, have drawn attention to various gender dimensions of science—to, for example, the historical (as well as ongoing) exclusion of women from the most important activities in science, and the inadequate treatment of women, and females in general, within the content and methods of science. In this case philosophers of science *should be*, but by and large have not been, concerned with the repercussions of these gender dimensions of science on more traditional analyses within the philosophy of science.

This second edition of *Scientific Knowledge* takes full note of these recent developments in philosophy of science, integrating them with the more traditional positions and approaches of the first edition. As before, the most basic issues in the philosophy of science are explored without any attempt to minimize prevailing controversies. And as before, the attempt is made to include essays that presuppose no special scientific or philosophical (for example, formal logic) background on the part of the reader, and explanatory material is included in the introductions to further assist the reader. But the changes in the field of philosophy of science over the last ten years have occasioned a total replacement of the first two sections of the book, and changes in other sections as well. In addition, nearly all of the essays carried over from the first edition have been re-edited, and new articles have been added, to enable readers to more easily grasp and reflect on the central questions involved. Finally, a more coherent and more interesting picture of philosophy of science is drawn, since all issues are now connected from the outset to the realism/anti-realism controversy, the focal point of the book and the subject of the final section. This new edition thus provides a clearer and more unified, as well as a more up-to-date, understanding of philosophy of science.

Many philosophers of science have offered kind words of encouragement over the years, and many have shared their experiences and suggestions as well, and this has meant a great deal to me. Foremost among these individuals is my Notre Dame colleague Ernan McMullin. I would also like to thank Tad Beckman of Harvey Mudd College, Douglas Cannon of the University Puget Sound, and Brian Clayton of Gonzaga University for their reviews. They offered much useful advice. Wadsworth philosophy editor Peter Adams has shown superhuman patience and good cheer through many delays, and much understanding and encouragement as well. Jon Peck, who supervised the production of the book, took care of many thorny details and admirably kept things on schedule. Finally, Jim Sterba has contributed the 360 degree, comprehensive kind of support that only a combination partner/philosophy colleague knows how to provide.

Janet A. Kourany
University of Notre Dame

INTRODUCTION

PHILOSOPHY OF SCIENCE: AN OVERVIEW

Are the sciences moving toward a unified account of the world, or are the pictures of reality they provide becoming ever more disparate? Do scientists have any reason to believe that current scientific theories are true when all the scientific theories of the past have turned out to be false? Is there anything that especially distinguishes current theories from past ones? How can scientists test a scientific theory about entities and processes no one can observe? These are some of the questions philosophers have raised about science that we shall deal with in this book.

Why are philosophers so interested in science? On the simplest level, such interest reflects the traditional concern of philosophy with the nature of reality and the foundations and limits of human knowledge. But the answer goes deeper than this, and it affects more than just philosophy. The knowledge science provides is immensely impressive, and this knowledge has had a profound impact on our lives. Indeed, the noted historian of science Herbert Butterfield has said, of the Scientific Revolution that was instrumental in bringing this knowledge into existence:

> . . . It outshines everything since the rise of Christianity and reduces the Renaissance and Reformation to the rank of mere episodes. . . . It changed

the character of men's habitual mental operations even in the conduct of
the nonmaterial sciences, while transforming the whole diagram of the
physical universe and the very texture of human life itself★.

Small wonder that science inspires a deep interest among philosophers.

But science inspires an equally deep interest among the representatives of other
disciplines as well. Philosophers want to explore the general characteristics of science that most directly relate to its function as a knowledge-producing activity,
such as the nature and reliability of its empirical basis, the nature of its validation
procedures using this basis, its patterns of development, and the truth-status of its
theories. Historians want to know exactly how the concepts, methods, and goals
of science have reached their present state of development; what particular factors brought about crucial changes in these at various times and places; and what
particular social and economic forces promoted or inhibited these changes. Psychologists want to analyze what types of individuals engage in this enterprise;
what relationship their personality characteristics and motivation have to their
research styles; and what psychological processes characterize their research.
Sociologists want to understand how far, and in what ways, such individuals are
influenced by the social and cultural contexts in which they work, to what extent a society's presuppositions mold the findings of scientific research.

These various approaches to science—the philosophical, the historical, the
psychological, and the sociological—are not independent of one another. Alternative philosophical views regarding the nature of theory-testing have shaped alternative sociological views regarding the influence of social factors on scientists'
acceptance or rejection of theories. In turn, completed sociological research in
this area will test and refine those philosophical views. Similarly, historical data
have suggested philosophical views regarding general patterns of scientific development, which might help in the construction of more adequate historical narratives. Historical data might also be used to test psychological or sociological
hypotheses regarding science. For example, the detailed diaries of experimental
investigations, hypotheses, speculations, plans, and incidental observations left by
the nineteenth-century English physicist Michael Faraday have been used to test
psychological hypotheses regarding scientific inference. Successful psychological
or sociological hypotheses might, in turn, disclose the relevance of factors not
previously noted when gathering historical data or constructing historical narratives, thereby yielding more successful historical research.

A completely adequate picture of science will emerge only with the integration of these different approaches to science. Unfortunately, such a picture is still
a long way off. We now lack even the separate approaches themselves in an adequate state of development. What's more, deep controversies exist in the philosophy of science, the history of science, the sociology of science, and the
psychology of science—and none more so than in the philosophy of science.
The controversies relate not only to particular views on particular questions but
also to the methods that should be used in answering those questions and even,

★Butterfield, Herbert T., *The Origins of Modern Science, 1300–1800*, pp. 7–8,
New York: Macmillan, 1957.

on occasion, to the relative importance of the questions themselves. In the sections that follow we shall explore some of the most basic questions in the philosophy of science today, making no attempt to minimize either the controversies that surround them or the connections they have with questions in the psychology, the sociology, or the history of science.

The main question on which we shall focus throughout this text is the so-called scientific realism/anti-realism question, that is, the question whether scientific knowledge provides us with true representations of the world (the scientific realist position) or only with representations that are useful for various purposes, such as for prediction and control of the environment (the scientific anti-realist position). This is a question on which many people have definite views. Indeed, science courses, textbooks, and journals, as well as the more popular sources of information about science, frequently reflect the perspective that the currently held theories in science are true, or at least approximately true, and people who learn about science from these sources (scientists and non-scientists alike) tend to think and act accordingly. But few people have thought about the realism/anti-realism question in any detail, much less arrived at cogent reasons for their views. Nevertheless the question is an important one. Scientists' positions on it, for example, can affect how they do science. Scientists who believe that scientific theories are only useful formalisms, rather than true representations of the world, are sometimes more able than other scientists to distance themselves from established ways of thinking (which are only useful formalisms, after all) and come up with radically new ways of seeing the world. On the other hand, scientists who believe that scientific theories are true representations of the world are sometimes more motivated than other scientists to develop deeper, more comprehensive theories to explain the phenomena in which they are interested, even in cases in which existing theories allow them to predictively deal with the phenomena in an effective way. Non-scientists' beliefs in realism or anti-realism can manifest themselves in significant ways as well. For example, a clash between accepted scientific views and accepted religious views frequently elicits a dismissal (or at least a reinterpretation) of the religious views from realists, while anti-realists can maintain beliefs in both sets of views without any problems.

We shall take up the realism/anti-realism question in detail in Part V, where we consider a variety of approaches to it together with their supporting rationales. But the realism/anti-realism question will also connect with, and interconnect, every other question with which we deal.

In part I we shall look into the nature of the scientists and scientific communities that produce our scientific knowledge, the organization of their research laboratories and information networks, their social hierarchies, and the like. This will give us a concrete picture of the science with which we shall be dealing more abstractly in later parts of the book. It will also prepare us to consider whether this social context of science shapes scientific knowledge in such a way as to allow it to be, or preclude it from being, a true representation of the world.

In Part II we shall consider the nature of the empirical basis of scientific knowledge—that is, the nature of the "facts" by which the theories of science are tested and judged acceptable or unacceptable. We shall wonder whether this empirical basis of scientific knowledge is trustworthy enough and secure enough to establish the truth of the theories it supports.

In Part III we shall investigate the testing process itself—the validation procedures used by scientists to establish scientific knowledge. Here we shall wonder whether the procedures are powerful enough to establish truth.

In Part IV we shall investigate the track record of science—the kind of historical development typically found in mature scientific fields. We shall wonder whether science's historical development gives us reason to think that science has achieved, or is moving toward, truth.

Part V will then integrate these various strands of the realism/anti-realism controversy, further clarifying the controversy and the options available.

By the time you reach the end of this book, then, you will have investigated the most basic issues in the philosophy of science, witnessed the kinds of controversies that surround them, and traced their interrelations. But you will not have been given a connected set of answers, a well-developed, well-articulated philosophy of science. That you will have to provide for yourself. May you have great success in your venture.

PART I

THE SOCIAL CONTEXT IN WHICH SCIENTIFIC KNOWLEDGE IS PRODUCED

What are scientists like? Do they come from every background? What do their day-to-day laboratory activities actually look like? Philosophy of science is, above all, about the knowledge scientists produce, and the experimental and logical/mathematical ways they produce it. The nature of the producers themselves is widely thought to be irrelevant. But might the producers leave their mark on their productions in science just as they do in other enterprises, so that an understanding of them is necessary for a full understanding of those productions? If we do not investigate scientists at the outset, we shall never know. If we do investigate them, we shall gain, at the very least, a helpfully concrete introduction to the science that will be dealt with more abstractly in the sections to come.

So what *are* scientists like? We are certainly all aware of the standard picture: unemotional, logical types, impersonal to the core; detached from the everyday and the mundane and isolated from their fellows, their attention riveted to their research; always seeking order, structure, simplicity, and always optimistic about the prospects of their success. But how much truth is there to this picture? In "On the Psychology of Scientists, and Their Social Concerns," Gerald Holton lays out the social science research supporting this standard picture of scientists, and sketches in further details in accordance with the results of that research. He also confronts a serious shortcoming of scientists highlighted by this picture: that insofar as they seek order and simplicity in their research ventures, and insofar as they are detached from the everyday and the mundane, they fail to deal with complex societal problems in that research. The effect that this shortcoming in scientists has on scientific knowledge is grave indeed:

> . . . the *lack of relevant scientific knowledge* in such "pure" fields as physics, chemistry, or biology is among the central causes of almost any major societal problem—whether in nutrition, population, pollution, mental health, occupational disease, and so on. (For example, a better understanding of the physics, chemistry, and biology of the detailed processes of conception is still fundamental to the formulation of sounder strategies for dealing with over-population and family planning.) (p. 9)

Because the picture Holton sketches guides the selection (including self-selection), training, and socialization of scientists, this picture and the attendant shortcoming of scientists tend to be self-perpetuating. However, the consequent limitations in scientific knowledge to which he draws attention are not inevitable, and he concludes his essay with various strategies for changing the situation.

The picture of scientists that Holton offers us—logical, unemotional, impersonal, detached from the everyday, etc.—makes scientists look exceedingly masculine. Should this be surprising? After all, Holton's findings, as he admits, come from research done only on men scientists. But there is more to it than this. As Marguerite Holloway ("A Lab of Her Own"), Natalie Angier ("Women Join the Ranks of Science But Remain Invisible at the Top"), and Shirley Tilghman ("Science vs. the Female Scientist" and "Science vs. Women—A Radical Solution") make clear, the enterprise these scientists are engaged in, modern Western science, has been controlled by men from the start. In the past the control took such obvious forms as denying women with scientific talents access to universities and other centers of scientific learning, denying them all but menial research roles, and denying them membership in prestigious scientific academies and professional organizations. More recently men's control of Western science has taken subtler forms: restrictive admissions quotas for undergraduate and graduate women students, or deliberate recruitment and selection by (masculine) gender; less financial assistance for women students; research positions for women with inferior workspace and equipment and pay, and with little authority or possibility of advancement; exclusion of women from the most important scientific meetings and collaborations and information networks, and restricted access to prestigious scientific academies; and a system of expectations and rewards structured for the lives that men traditionally have led, free of family responsibilities. What's more, the way in which the scientific enterprise is controlled by men has been deemed appropriate by most of society, in large part based upon "documentation" from the (male) scientific establishment that women lack the requisite mental and physical capabilities to engage in it. Small wonder that the characteristics of scientists and masculinity are so closely matched.

Despite the significant obstacles women have confronted in science, they have been involved in it from the beginning, and, Holloway makes clear, they have made significant contributions to it. If women scientists were studied as men have been in the research Holton describes—and the start is now being made— would our picture of scientists and science look different? Holloway indicates that the answer may be "yes," though it is still too early to tell. But if the answer *is* "yes," and women have been distinctive scientists and made distinctive contributions to science, then that is all the more reason to rid science of the obstacles that have historically confronted women scientists. Holloway, Angier, and Tilghman discuss various ways of doing this.

In the last essay of Part I, "An Anthropologist Visits the Laboratory," Bruno Latour and Steve Woolgar describe not the general characteristics of scientists, but their day-to-day behavior in their natural habitat: a scientific laboratory (in this case, one of the laboratories at the Salk Institute for Biological Sciences). The vantage point in this essay is that of an "outsider"—an anthropological observer—trying to make sense of, and communicate to other outsiders, scientists' activities in terms outsiders can understand. Thus we are told that the main objective in the laboratory observed is the production of scientific papers. (During the time the laboratory was observed a paper was produced on the average of every ten days, at an average cost of from $30,000 to $60,000 each.) We are told about, and even shown, via a map of the laboratory together with photographs of the different areas shown in the map, the detailed processes that go into the production of these papers. At the same time, we are shown how dependent the production of these papers is on various kinds of technical apparatus and routinized practices, manufacturing skills and the results of past research in other scientific fields. Finally, we are provided with graphic illustration of some of the themes touched on by Holton, Holloway, Angier, and Tilghman. For example, all the women pictured in the photographs are either secretaries or assistants ("technicians"), whereas all the principle investigators ("doctors") are men. The doctors are architecturally positioned at the center of the laboratory, in their own offices amid books and articles and their own writing activities. They are insulated by partitions from the concrete experimental activities and experiences of the technicians at "the bench," and even from the outside world (the doctors' offices are windowless). And the production of papers involves successive stages of abstraction and simplification of the piles of results brought on a daily basis from the bench.

As we noted in the introduction, the focus of this book is the scientific realism/anti-realism question, the question whether scientific knowledge provides us with true representations of the world, or only with representations that are useful for various purposes—for example, for prediction and control of the environment. As interesting and helpful as the readings of Part I are, how do they relate to this question? We shall have to await the sections to come for well-delineated relations to be visible, but glimmerings of relations should already be apparent. Thus, if, as Holton suggests, scientists fail to deal with complex societal problems in their research due to their distinctive psychological characteristics, then how can scientific knowledge provide us with useful (but not true) representations of the world? On the other hand, if, as Holloway, Angier, and Tilghman suggest, science has been controlled by men from the start, and there is reason to think that women might do science differently from men, with different results, then how can scientific knowledge provide us with true representations of the world rather than with representations that simply reflect its male producers? Again, Latour and Woolgar, from their anthropological perspective, see the scientific knowledge applied and produced in the laboratory they observed as like the knowledge—that is, the culture and mythology and beliefs—applied and produced by other tribes observed by other anthropologists. But if this perspective is adequate, then how can scientific knowledge provide us with true representations of the world, rather than simply with representations of the world on a par with any other representations produced by any other group of people?

Of course, the accounts provided by Holton, Holloway, Angier, Tilghman, and Latour and Woolgar deal only with the social context of science. In consequence, they leave out such cruciallyimportant features of science as the nature of scientists' knowledge claims, their basis in logic and experience, and the record of their successes. To pursue our realism/anti-realism question responsibly, we must deal with these features as well, and integrate them into the terrain covered in Part I. This we shall do in Parts II, III, and IV.

GERALD HOLTON

On the Psychology
of Scientists, and Their
Social Concerns

Scientific Optimism and Its Costs

There is much discussion these days on ethical problems of scientific advance, the social responsibility of scientists, the participation of scientists in public policy discussions, and the need to bring the scientist and "citizen" together to clarify their mutual expectations. These worthy moves seem to depend on harnessing the natural scientific optimism of academic researchers in the service of their societal concerns. At first glance, these qualities appear to be natural allies—the former reigning inside the laboratory and the latter outside—and we might therefore expect them to be allied in some way, perhaps even stemming from a common trait that, if nurtured, would make both flourish equally.

I suspect, however, that on the contrary we may be dealing with characteristics that, at least for the large majority of scientists in academe, are inherently antithetical. It is perhaps not an accident that scientific optimism is as old as science itself, whereas examples of societal con-

cerns on the part of scientists acting *as* scientists are much more recent. Another clue is that basic researchers in the physical and biological sciences have only rarely looked for their puzzles among the predicaments of society, even though it is not difficult to show that the *lack of relevant scientific knowledge* in such "pure" fields as physics, chemistry, or biology is among the central causes of almost any major societal problem—whether in nutrition, population, pollution, mental health, occupational disease, and so on. (For example, a better understanding of the physics, chemistry, and biology of the detailed processes of conception is still fundamental to the formulation of sounder strategies for dealing with overpopulation and family planning.)

On this point, of course, scientists will defend themselves at once with some clarity and much passion. They will say the discoverers of the laws of thermodynamics that allowed the design of efficient machines, taking over burdens previously carried on the backs of men and animals, were not motivated by anguish

From *The Scientific Imagination* by Gerald Holton, © 1978 by Cambridge University Press. Reprinted by permission of the publisher.

over the lot of humanity, nor would such motivation have likely led to the discoveries. It is not a lack of compassion but the nature of science itself that requires us to take the circuitous route of research. Sentimentality will lead not to humanitarian advance but to bad science.

A great deal of this argument is undoubtedly just. Yet what Whitehead called the "celibacy of the intellect" also becomes apparent there. Pessimism about the efficacy of societal concerns, rarely tested, has deeper roots in the psychology of scientists—a subject rarely considered when hopes are voiced for "science-and-society" links. It seems to me that the best way to begin to understand the sources of that pessimism is to look at the opposite side of the coin. A comment attributed to Anne Roe comes to mind: On looking back at her long and distinguished studies on the psychology of scientists, she is said to have commented that the one thing all of these very different people had in common was an *unreasonable amount of optimism* concerning the ultimately successful outcome of their research. Whereas the stereotype of the humanists is that of a rearguard group, gallantly holding up the flag of a civilization that is now being destroyed by barbarians, the scientists tend to feel that the most glorious period in intellectual history is about to dawn, and *they* will be there to make it happen. As C. P. Snow has said, they have the future in their bones. In truth, everyone who has done something basic in science treasures these memorable periods of individual euphoria when one has found a problem—one that may be tormenting in its subtlety, and all too slow to crack open—but at least one that promises to be delimitable, "analyzable," *solvable*, and therefore worthy of throwing one's whole being into it.

This hopeful, most absorbing and rewarding aspect of scientific research—and also another side to which I shall soon turn—is, however, precisely in opposition to the demands of an outer-directed humanism that, one may assume, is at the base of a person's societal concerns. Indeed, the psychodynamic vectors that

propel a scientist into the bright world of solvable problems often turn out, on examination, to have components originating in the flight from the dark world of anguished compromises and makeshift improvisations that commonly characterize the human situation. (To a large degree this is undoubtedly true also for humanists and other scholars. But that is suspiciously easy to assert, and one therefore hopes that the kind of research results I shall summarize for the case of scientists will some day soon be done for the other groups.)

The whole dilemma has never been put better than in a passage in Einstein's writings of which I have long been fond.[1] He was considering who these people are who aspire to live in the "Temple of Science," and acknowledged first of all that they are mostly "rather odd, uncommunicative, solitary fellows, who despite these common characteristics resemble one another really less than the host of the banished." And then he asked:

> What led them into the Temple? The answer is not easy to give, and can certainly not apply uniformly. To begin with, I believe with Schopenhauer that one of the strongest motives that lead persons to art and science is flight from the everyday life, with its painful harshness and wretched dreariness, and from the fetters of one's own shifting desires. One who is more finely tempered is driven to escape from personal existence and to the world of objective observing and understanding. This motive can be compared with the longing that irresistibly pulls the town dweller away from his noisy, cramped quarters and toward the silent, high mountains, where the eye ranges freely through the still, pure air and traces the calm contours that seem to be made for eternity.
>
> With this negative motive there goes a positive one. Man seeks to form for himself, in whatever manner is suitable for him, a simplified and lucid image of the world, and so to overcome the world of experience by

striving to replace it to some extent by this image. This is what the painter does, and the poet, the speculative philosopher, the natural scientist, each in his own way. Into this image and its formation, he places the center of gravity of his emotional life, in order to attain the peace and serenity that he cannot find within the narrow confines of swirling, personal experience.

What a splendid image: science as self-transcendence, as an act of lifting oneself into a purer state of being! Eloquent support for this view is not difficult to find. James Clark Maxwell confessed in his inaugural lecture at Cambridge (1871):

When the action of the mind passes out of the intellectual state, in which truth and error are the alternatives, into the more violently emotional states of anger and passion, malice and envy, fury and madness; the student of science, though he is obliged to recognise the powerful influence which these wild forces have exercised on mankind, is perhaps in some measure disqualified from pursuing the study of this part of human nature.

But then how few of us are capable of deriving profit from such studies. We cannot enter into full sympathy with these lower phases of our nature without losing some of that antipathy to them which is our surest safeguard against a reversion to a meaner type, and we gladly return to the company of those illustrious men [of science] who by aspiring to noble ends, whether intellectual or practical, have risen above the region of storms into a clearer atmosphere, where there is no misrepresentation of opinion, nor ambiguity of expression, but where one mind comes into closest contact with another at the point where both approach nearest to the truth.

There we have indeed a clarion call to move to the high, pure empyrean where one can work undisturbed on what counts for science, while at the same time (and, it would seem, as a necessary consequence) withdrawing from the scene of mankind's problems and concerns.[2]

There are, to be sure, also other sources for scientific optimism. One is what Boris Kuznetsov[3] has called "epistemological optimism": Most scientists feel there is no *ignorabimus* to be feared, that at least in principle knowledge can be gained indefinitely, without limits. Even the occasional mountainous obstacle will turn into a monument to a memorable victory. Remember the "physics of despair" which, Max Planck confessed, drove him to the quantum, or Niels Bohr's allegiance to the aphorism that "truth lies in the abyss." When the idea of Laplace's deterministic supreme mind failed, it led not to disaster and demoralization, but to Heisenberg's even more fruitful indeterminism. *There* is ignorance one can live with— so unlike the "narrow confines of swirling, personal experience," by its very nature ever unrequited, unsolved, unconquerable, unyielding to reductionistic subdivision into "simplified and lucid," manageable reconstruction.

Even as the laboratory is a microcosm for harnessing the puzzle of phenomena captured within its walls, the uses made of the scientific findings by others, unknown and far away, but presumably for the alleviation of the sorry conditions of human life, is the macroscopic equivalent. The one is the scientific imperative, the other the technological imperative. Both are powered by the same optimistic dynamism. William James in his lectures on pragmatism in 1906 recognized the proper scale of that ambition when he noted that the division between *optimists* (that is, the type he also characterized as rationalistic, intellectual, idealistic, and monistic) and *pessimists* to hinge on nothing less than the most far-reaching matters: "There are unhappy men who think the salvation of the world impossible. Theirs is the doctrine known as pessimism. Optimism in turn would be the doctrine that thinks the world's salvation inevitable"—although, one must add in the case of the scientist, inevitable not by his direct intervention but rather as a by-product, through the working out of the consequences of his ideas by others who will follow him.

At least until lately it has been taken for granted that science and optimism are virtually synonymous throughout modern society, that somehow both the doing and the findings of science will be for the good of mankind—for science's own sake, for its antimetaphysical and liberating philosophical message, for its eventual technological fruits. We know that these beliefs are now held far more widely in the "second" and "third" worlds, both of which endorse science as a path to a better society, than they are held in our own world. The public's ambivalence about the beneficence of science and technology is amply documented[4]—now that the impact of science, medicine, and technology is larger and more visible than ever before, it also is more worrisome and confusing to the wider public.

Of course, not all scientists have been hiding from the swirling fortunes of public discussion. On the time scale of history, social responsibility and other social concerns as a topic of active introspection by even a small percentage of practicing scientists is a recent notion, largely a post-Hiroshima conception; yet there are already some honorable institutional inventions and landmarks—from the founding of the Federation of Atomic Scientists and the appeals of Leo Szilard and James Franck in 1945 to the Asilomar Conference on Recombinant DNA Research (1975). Other achievements for which research scientists can take a large share of the credit and which must at least be mentioned include the Pugwash movement, the Committee on Science and Public Policy (COSPUP) of the National Academy of Sciences, the codes of ethics now adopted or under discussion among scientific societies, the relevant activities of the National Institutes of Health (NIH) including the institutionalization of concern with experimentation on human subjects, the AAAS Committee on Ethics and Science, and the development

within NSF and NEH of programs for the study of the ethical and human values impact of science and technology. These institutions, and the few real statesmen of science we *do* have now, are evidence of goodwill and—one fervently hopes—of a reservoir of talent and interest among hitherto uncommitted scientists.

But there's the rub. The vast majority of working scientists in fact are quite happy to leave the discussion of societal concerns to the small minority. Most in the silent majority and even some in the vocal minority, although willing to tolerate such discussions up to a point, would not go as far as to make such concerns a matter of personal, active participation. I would estimate that the fraction of scientists in the U.S. active in such matters (e.g., helping to formulate or administer science policy on matters of explicit societal concerns or even writing or teaching occasionally on the topic) is of the order of 1 percent.

On the assumption that scientists will have to be involved in larger numbers, we thus come to the crucial questions: Do the public's expressions of ambivalence with respect to science, together with the existence of a core of concerned scientists, constitute harbingers of a substantial increase in the participation of scientists on issues where science and societal concerns come together? Or, on the contrary, could it be that we have already gathered up the largest fraction of that small minority of scientists which is susceptible to such considerations—that from now on we shall find it ever harder to add more recruits from the ranks of working physical and biological scientists? To use an analogy from physics, does there exist some inherent barrier so high and wide that the small quantum leakage through it cannot be expected to become much larger?

I believe the more pessimistic of these two possibilities is closer to the truth. We shall have to face the possibility that for the large majority of scientists euphoric personal commitment to and pursuit of science *as currently fostered and understood*, and the hoped-for societal concerns needed on the part of professionals in today's world, are at bottom orthogonal or possibly even largely antithetical traits—antithetical both in terms of the psychodynamics of the majority of individual scientists *and* in terms of the social structure of science as a profession. A chief aim in this chapter will be to scrutinize and juxtapose widely scattered data now in the literature, and to see what causal connection may exist among the personal-psychological, institutional, and sociopolitical factors in the scientific profession that have fostered the current state. We shall find some evidence that the selection, training, and socialization of scientists are biased in just the direction where the requirements of a code of explicit, personal societal concern are least easy to fulfill.

We may not have to go as far as believing seriously the anguished exclamation of Albert Szent-Györgyi, who was recently quoted to have advised: "If any student comes to me and says he wants to be useful to mankind and go into research to alleviate human suffering, I advise him to go into charity instead. Research wants real egotists who seek their own pleasure and satisfaction, but find it in solving the puzzles of nature."[5] However, it may be true that, for many, scientific work, as shaped by present practices and images and from a very early point in the career, is now perceived by the scientists themselves as being located at one end of a seesaw, rising only at the cost of paying correspondingly less attention to practical societal concerns. I shall argue that a better understanding of the psychodynamics of young scientists and of the institutional pressures on them is needed to show us how to bring out more of the socially aware side of scientists than we thought was needed in our golden age of innocence, so recently past.

Stereotypes and Prototypes

Making due allowance for the fact that the study of personality and character structure is not one of the "hard" sciences, the way to

begin is to look at what data there are concerning the raw material, the scientists themselves. How flexible is their frame of thought and behavior? How willing are they to struggle with opinions and beliefs that, in the nature of the case, are inherently unprovable, or with problems that are inherently resistant to simplification, or even to moderately satisfactory solutions? How able are they to deal with the problems that are inherently resistant to simplification, or even to moderately satisfactory solutions? How able are they to deal with the personal stresses and strains that are part of any participation in serious debates on such unverifiable and unyielding problems as societal concerns?

There are a few useful published studies on the psychology of scientists. Some are retrospective analyses on groups of children and young persons who later become scientists; some are on samples of adult members of the profession; and a very few are individual psychohistorical case studies of scientists such as Newton, Darwin, Einstein, and Fermi. Most of the studies that have been made focus a great deal on what may be called the *styles* of creative scientists, the kind of behavior they exhibit fairly consistently.[6] It is easy enough to list the main features that define scientific style as commonly understood at present; the point to keep in mind is, however, that this common understanding is shared not only among the scientists themselves but also, in about the same terms, among the wider public. Thus, on the basis of a survey of the existing literature in the field, B. T. Eiduson concluded: "Scientists as a group seem to be caught up in the same stereotypes that the public holds about them, *and, in fact, the researchers seem to have been drawn into science by some of the same fantasies and stereotypes.*"[7]

1. The scientist typically insists that in written reports of work—from students' laboratory write-ups to the papers we referee and the textbooks we write—the individual traces of the personal self be attenuated as far as that can be done. Hence the impersonal style of the

scientist, for which there are only few counterexamples. The aim is to make one's work seem "objective," repeatable by anyone, or, as Louis Pasteur said, *inevitable*. This is part of the scientist's value of "other-orientation," to use Talcott Parsons's term, and at the same time is another way of transcending the world of personal experience. Through the analyses of Robert K. Merton and others we know that disputes and priority fights exist as intense undercurrents. But their importance is generally disavowed by scientists, as are the deep thematic presuppositions underlying apparently "neutral" presentations.

This eradication of individualistic elements from publication is of course exceedingly functional insofar as it helps to minimize personal disputes of the unresolvable kind and removes interpersonal obstacles to consensus. But it is also seen as responding to the epistemological demands of science itself. With typical succinctness, Einstein summarized this view of reality in a manner that shows how the concept of the individual self sinks into the shadows: "Physics is an attempt conceptually to grasp reality as it is thought independently of its being observed. In this sense one speaks of 'physical reality.'"[8]

2. The second, related commandment of the scientific ethos, as commonly understood, is to be logical, not emotional. Statements that fall into areas with a large component of not easily verifiable or of falsifiable content are frowned upon, and issues dealing with ethical conflict, responsibility, or even long-range prediction of the technological applications of scientific findings are therefore not expected to be raised in scientific meetings. Mere opinions, preferences, emotions, and instincts must be repressed, and even the exhilarating flights of intuitive imagination must be recast in deductive style to be respectable.

3. Errors or unlikely hypotheses are to be avoided at all cost, not least because the scientific community is far less tolerant or forgiving on that score than almost any other group. A batting average of only, say, 0.500 would not look good at all in this league. One is taught to repeat, verify, and repeat again before going public, not the least to avoid endangering one's dignity and credibility in the experimental field.

4. The desired outcome is the simple, not the complex. One aspires to economy of thought and uses Occam's Razor to help achieve it. Therefore in most cases, and for most scientists, the reductionistic strategy is far safer than a synthesis-seeking one. The main charm of work in a physical or biological science is that it ideally permits one to formulate statements of simple lawfulness that is the very opposite of the complexity characterizing most social questions and interactions.

5. As with the content of science itself, the setting in which one does one's science is ideally as removed from interpersonal disputes as possible. (This is a significant point to which we shall return.) As the psychologist David C. McClelland put it with ample research documentation, "Scientists avoid interpersonal contact," and "scientists avoid and are disturbed by complex human emotions, perhaps particularly interpersonal aggression."[9] Even recent changes in the self-identification of young scientists only reinforce this old theme:

> There is evidence, however, that differences in the way science is being practiced today are accompanied by certain differences in the identifications that scientists have with other scientists. An example of this changing trend is the researcher's shying away from identification with the "great but maladjusted" or "eccentric" scientist. Reverence for forefathers whose outstanding minds were sometimes housed in very peculiar and odd personalities still exists, and yet the newer scientists seem consciously to be dissociating themselves from peculiar and difficult associates or students, knowing full well that they may be thus shutting themselves off from some very creative

workers in their own laboratory. These men nowadays prefer to depend for progress on well-organized, smooth-running, large-scale operations, whose stability demands the minimum of interpersonal relationships, especially disturbed ones.[10]

A paradigmatic hero who fits most of these five traits superbly and who remains one of the widely admired scientists and role models is Enrico Fermi—ever "cool" and rational, virtually always right, generous in sharing his intellectual self, always focused on the pioneer problems of physics of the day, finding the unraveling simplicity in the most surprising yet convincing way but also, to very nearly the end of his life, studiously avoiding participation in any of the political or science-society questions that raged through both history and science in his time.[11] The hero among most scientists is clearly *not*, say, a Leo Szilard—as "hot" as Fermi was "cool," also a superb scientist by spreading himself over many fields from physics to biology to cybernetics, fond of speculative and daring proposals, and above all deeply and successfully occupied with the need to make his life and influence count in matters concerning the impact of science and technology on political (national and international), ethical, and social problems. Fermi and Szilard may be seen as prototypes that define two extremes of the range of models of scientific behavior, one widely accepted, admired, and imitated, the other regarded with a certain affection but deeply appreciated by only a relative few.

We shall leave them for a time. For the moment we should note that the *differences* between these or any other scientists are not accounted for in the public stereotypes of working scientists. The same problem adheres to some of the psychoanalytical studies of scientists, for example, that of Lawrence Kubie,[12] who held that their work can be coordinated with symptoms of what Kubie called "masked neurosis." The psychoanalytical perspective invites (perhaps all too readily) the construction

of parallels between the prototypical behavior of scientists (as well as other scholars) and that of the obsessive-compulsive personality type.[13] If one believed the parallelism fully, it would raise the insuperable puzzle how and why scientists for the most part do in fact preserve themselves sufficiently to be as effective as they are, as both professionals and human beings. Yet there are perhaps certain analogous characteristics:

(a) There is narrow, intensely focused attention, almost constant concentration on one area within which the more creative persons roam freely. (The powers of concentration in scientists such as Gauss were legendary. At moments they have amounted to voluntary sensory deprivation—for example, Fermi reported that he had failed altogether to hear the blast of the atomic bomb at the Alamogordo test because he was working on a problem of measuring the intensity of the blast by a simple, improvised method.) Attention is diverted and dedicated to the high drama and wonderful entertainment going on in one's own brain.

(b) One is driven to succeed and therefore keeps away from situations that are unlikely to yield success. There is a tense deliberateness to clear up puzzles and ambiguities or to remove the threat of the unknown, and restless intellectual (or physical) activity.

(c) One is preoccupied with control, with the need for order and structure that extends from regularity of schedule to ready acceptance of authority outside one's own field of expertise.

(d) And finally, there is only a limited need or ability to deal with affective experience, hence—as we have noted—the avoidance of open battle and other social risks. (One remembers Newton's remark that he would be rid of that litigious lady, Natural Philosophy, promising in a letter to Oldenburg during the controversy following his early work on optics, "I will resolutely bid adieu to it eternally, except what I do for my own private satisfaction"; and later: "I desire to decline being involved in such troublesome and insignificant disputes."

Findings of Sociological-Psychological Studies

Emile Durkheim warned, "Every time that a social phenomenon is *directly* explained by a psychological phenomenon, we may be sure that the explanation is false."[14] But one need not demand the exclusion of other than psychological causes, or the acceptance of the framework of orthodox psychoanalytic theory, or the postulation of parallels with obsessive-compulsive types, and yet allow the possibility that the scientific-societal polarization many scientists seem to experience may well have psychological roots. In the absence of one clearly fruitful framework, the safest entry point for the time being seems to be through a study of the results of the more sociological-psychological investigation.

Despite all the changes in the profession, a major classic of this kind is still Anne Roe's *The Making of a Scientist*,[15] published over two decades ago. A clinical psychologist, she studied the careers of sixty-four leading, male, U.S.-born scientists (in the biological, physical, and social sciences), concentrating on the most eminent in each field. Separately, her findings within this group were checked to some degree against a larger sample of more ordinary scientists. Her chief aim was to study the relation between vocation and personality structure. In an earlier study on artists, she had discovered that definite and "very direct relationships [exist] . . . between what and how the man painted and what sort of person he was and what sort of problems he had." As to scientists, she significantly found that "although such relationships pertain among them also, they are usually much more obscure and the technique of reporting scientific results serves rather to hide the man than to display him."

Her findings do not add up to a profile of part-time social reformers, nor does the total pattern seem altogether unfamiliar to the nonspecialist or in drastic conflict with the popular stereotype. Not unexpectedly, curiosity about a special area, to the exclusion of all else, was the chief characteristic, evidently transcending even the intense devotion to work (that was also found among her group of artists) and the willingness to select one variable for study, holding the rest constant where possible. "There is probably no more important factor in the achievement of this group of [physical] scientists than the depth of their absorption in their work." This trait is of course of high utility because, as Roe understands, it is unlikely that one can achieve anything of great value if one does not dedicate oneself deeply, even passionately to the work.[16]

A whole set of her other findings is naturally correlated. The age at marriage was rather late for that group—twenty-seven years on the average. (The divorce rate among physical and biological scientists was markedly below average, 5 percent among the physicists and 15 percent among the biologists in her sample.) She found her scientists often to be working right through a seven-day week and during sleepless nights. Even when they engaged in sports, it was preferably individual rather than team play. Significantly, only four in her study group of sixty-four leading scientists "played any active part in political or civic organizations." Most of the physicists and biologists "disliked social occasions" and avoided them "as much as possible." Only three out of sixty-four were seriously concerned with organized religion. Far more than the rest of the population, her scientists came from families where "value is placed [on learning] *for its own sake* . . . not just for economic or social rewards." A decisive event in their career choice was early research experience or, even before that, "the discovery of the possibility of finding out things for oneself." One might say that their first and most interesting scientific discovery may have been their own selves.

Many of the scientists had "quite specific and fairly strong feelings of personal isolation" when they were children. A strikingly low number of theoretical physicists, only three out of twelve, reported that they had "good health and normal physical development" as children. Loneliness or the existence of very few friends was commonly reported by both the physicists and biologists. A main hobby during childhood was solitary reading. "Many of them [physicists and biologists] were slow to develop socially and to go out with girls." Whereas this was painful to some, it did not seem "to matter enough to most of them to do anything about it." "There is a characteristic pattern of growing up among biologists and physical scientists . . . The pattern is that of the rather shy boy, sometimes with intense personal interests, usually intellectual or mechanical, who plays with one or two like-minded companions rather than with a gang, and who does not start dating until well into college years." Even then, dating may be a very secondary matter. "This is in great contrast to the social scientists . . ."

None of the scientists, particularly the physicists, liked business. "The extreme competitiveness, the indifference to fact, the difficulty of doing things personally, all were distasteful to them." Coming now closer to the finding reported also earlier, Roe notes that "the biologists and physicists . . . are strongly inclined to keep away from intense emotional situations as much as possible." On the basis of the Thematic Apperception Test, she reports that "none of these groups is particularly aggressive."

Summing up, she finds that with all the variety in her subjects, "there are patterns, patterns in their life histories, patterns of intellectual abilities, patterns of personality structure, which are more characteristic of scientists than they are of people at large . . ." The lack of early and continued attention to societal concerns is part of that general pattern, both of life history, of work, and of personality structure.[17] She contrasts this with the ancient stereotype that the "scientist is a completely altruistic being, devoting himself selflessly to the pursuit of truth, solely in order to contribute to the welfare of humanity." To be sure, from World War II on, "scientists are being forced to consider the social repercussions of their work," and, she agrees, it is "an excellent thing both for them and for society." But the characteristics of early career development and personality formation show the built-in obstacles to the easy fulfillment of that hope.

Roe's study was perhaps the first popularly noted, scientific psychological work that bore out by research results the long-suspected basic dichotomy implied for many in their choice between a scientific career and a career that concerns itself with the world of personal relations. In later studies, Roe accumulated the evidence for a powerful generalization that has proved to be of value for other career-development studies: "Apparently one of the earliest differentiations, if not the first one, in the orientation of attention is between persons and nonpersons."[18]

This fundamental perception of a thematic antithesis, also familiar from other psychological studies, was bolstered and documented by subsequent research, perhaps most strikingly by the study of William W. Cooley and Paul R. Lohnes. . . They found that the polarization of general interests, which has also been called the "people-versus-thing" (or "people-versus-ideas") polarization, is

> the earliest trait for which there is fairly solid research evidence . . . The distinction is whether the boy's primary orientation is toward people or toward science-technology. This orientation first appears in student talk about vocations somewhere around fifth or sixth grade, when the student passes from the fantasy to the interest stage in his career development. In interest inventories this basic orientation shows up as interest in the various science, technology, mechanical scales *versus* interest in areas

which involve more people contact, business, humanistic or cultural concerns. This is the earliest variable on which we find we can classify careers, and thus in our [career development] tree structure this variable defines the two branches at the first level of branching.[19]

No matter that counterexamples exist among one's colleagues, and no matter how skeptical one may be about the methodologies in some psychometric studies, the solemn warning implied in the findings of Cooley and Lohnes seems to me sufficiently bolstered by other careful research, such as that of James A. David,[20] and must be taken seriously. The "people" versus "thing" potential is undoubtedly connected functionally to differences in styles of effective thinking and feeling—for example, those modes, means, and ends that are fundamentally logical, experimental, invariance- and simplicity-seeking, versus those that are predominantly affective, intuitive, and ambiguity-tolerating. But the danger appears to be that such predominant preferences, which can be made to coexist tolerably, are allowed to degenerate into polar opponents that tend to become mutually exclusive. The "interests" that show up early in these interest inventories are, at this time in history, still cast and perhaps nurtured in ways that permit a young person all too easily to make the "people" versus "thing" choice—and a whole set of institutions, in education, guidance, and peer group support, is designed to help make a choice, and to make it comfortable enough to live with it. Moreover, as those of us can attest who have worked hard to modify the present institutional context—for example, by inventing and injecting a combination of scientific, humanistic, and cultural concerns into the educational system for young people, or by trying to bring to the attention of scientists and humanists alike the ethical and human value implications of science—such efforts must all overcome an immense amount of disbelief, resistance, or

hostility. Indeed, the chief obstacles are those professionals in decision-making positions who have "made it" precisely by sticking to their early choice between things and people on reaching the bifurcation of interests and who are now successfully barricaded behind that self-chosen barrier. Here lies the crux of the problem of interesting more people in "people-*and*-thing" subjects such as research on the public policy or the ethical impacts of science.

In a study of seventy-nine eminent scientists, Warren O. Hagstrom stressed that a key element of internal social control in science is peer recognition.[21] It is essential to keep in mind that the risk of ostracism or isolation is difficult to bear for scientists, who depend greatly on a somewhat distant and abstract form of peer approval. As the scientific community is presently constituted, preoccupation with social action invites just such risks, at least before one is amply fortified with professional honors. Receiving adequate recognition is less likely when traditional role behavior is violated. One must therefore have a clear mandate before one introduces major changes into such a carefully structured social entity, for anything that isolates a scientist tends to lower his reputation and productivity greatly. . . .

This finding invites a comment on the obvious fact that more than a few good scientists have nevertheless chosen to go into positions of political prominence and power and that a few have even done a very good job of it by any standard. This fact however does not cancel the pervasive declarations of disapproval or even contempt among scientists (though not without ambivalence) when the suggestion comes up of participating in affairs having to do with public policy or political power.[22] Evidence of the dismay many scientists have experienced in participating in or merely watching the essential business of rendering scientific advice on politically sensitive matters is not difficult to find. Case studies in the weekly "News and Comments" section of the magazine *Science* or in J. Primack and F. von Hippel, *Advice and Dissent*,[23] and Philip Boffey, *The Brain Bank of America*,[24] contain enough "horrors" to discourage precisely some of the most sensitive and creative scientists from participation. Of course this is not the intent of the authors of these important publications, and they would be the first to urge that it would be entirely counterproductive to turn the battle over to the hardened politicos and bishops—to be found among scientists as in any other academic group—who are ever willing to shoulder the necessary tasks all by themselves.

In looking for a theoretical basis for distinguishing between the careers of scientists and nonscientists, Cooley comes on a significant point: "Outside of the emphasis upon the superior abilities of scientists, introversion is perhaps the most frequently cited 'personal characteristic of scientists.'" Cooley hastens to reassure us that "although scientists are far less interested in dealing with people in their day-to-day work, their concern for humanity and human rights appears to be no different from that of the other groups studied."[25] Cooley's remark on the scientist's "concern" is not presented as a research finding, and I would like to think of it as a hopeful perception of a trait to be nurtured, even if it starts out as something of an abstraction. In the extreme case it reminds one again of the scientist who remains one of the best role models, not the least for his ability of frank self-assessment. Einstein wrote:

> My passionate sense of social justice and social responsibility has always contrasted oddly with my pronounced lack of need for direct contact with human beings and human communities. I am truly a "lone traveler" and have never belonged to my country, my home, my friends, or even my immediate family, with my whole heart; in the face of all these ties, I have never lost a sense of distance and need for solitude—feelings which increase with the years. One becomes sharply aware, but without regret,

of the limits of mutual understanding and consonance with other people. No doubt, such a person loses some of his innocence and unconcern; on the other hand, he is largely independent of the opinions, habits, and judgments of his fellows and avoids the temptation to build his inner equilibrium upon such insecure foundations.[26]

Conclusions

Still other studies could be discussed here if space allowed, and we would find again and again confirmation of the general picture that we have obtained here concerning the interaction between the research scientists' cognitive characteristics, developmental and background characteristics, and personality patterns. By way of summary, some conclusions and caveats:

1. Optimism and human goodwill are well-known personality characteristics of scientists. But the optimism about the role and eventual success of science is quite possibly correlated with a pessimism or skepticism about the chance of doing much personally to guide human affairs. As a rule, a scientist's goodwill seems to be held abstractly (and is expected by others so to be held in their stereotypical image of scientists), rather than being acted out operationally in the sphere of social interactions—except, it should always be emphasized, in the area of collaboration among scientists themselves (in laboratories, teams, student-teacher exchanges, and so on), which is generally as humane as one is apt to find anywhere else.

2. The coherence of a scientist's identity, as presently constituted and reinforced by social role models and by educational and other institutions, may well depend on this antithetical casting of scientific optimism and wider social concerns.

3. Whether it is psychologically or socially imposed, an early choice seems to be made between people and things as antithetical entities when young people reach certain branching

points in the career tree. The stereotypes associated with these choices are shared by scientists and nonscientists alike and are thereby reinforced. The system is "in resonance," with personality traits and institutional settings supporting one another. . . .

4. We must remember Thoreau's remark: "Winter, with its ice and snow, is not an evil to be cured." My intention has not been to deplore or castigate or moralize. Nor do I think lecturing at scientists about social responsibility, ethics, and morals will do much to shift the mean value of the response curve of scientists toward more societal concerns. A head-on attack of trying to increase the average score on some "social interest" scales is surely doomed to failure. Rather, I want to fasten on an essential fact that is often not stressed sufficiently: that there is here, as in all natural populations, a *spread*, a normal or quasi-Gaussian-type distribution.

Imagine a bell-shaped curve in a plane where the horizontal axis indicates the present degree of responsiveness of physical and biological scientists to societal concerns. The highest vertical point on the curve indicates the most probable value for this population. (From all we have heard so far, this peak is likely to occur to the left, at fairly low values along the horizontal scale, compared with the curve for others—nonscientists, for example.) Educational systems, professional societies, and other social institutions tend to be designed so as to "resonate" with the mean or most probable value of a characteristic on which the institution depends. Normally, it is feedback from the peak value that stabilizes a system.

Different scientists are of course located on different parts of the bell-shaped curve; a Fermi would presumably appear near the low, left end, and a Leo Szilard or a Linus Pauling on the other wing, near the high end. This perception suggests some strategies for change. One is to increase the amount of feedback coupling of the system at the "Szilard end"—for example, most simply by beginning to make

teachers, guidance counselors, and scientists at their more accessible moments (e.g., during attendance at professional scientific meetings) more aware of the mere *existence* of the right wing of the curve, the historical existence of successful scientists who, in their very lives, exhibited the possibility of combining *rather than choosing between* people and things. The public "image" of scientists often needs correction; thus Madame Curie's reported remark "Science deals with things, not people" has to be supplemented by her own dedicated participation in groups such as the League of Nations Committee on Intellectual Cooperation. Another strategy is structuring opportunities so that participation is possible or choices are confronted within the setting of a professional society. The formation of the Forum on Physics and Society within the American Physical Society is a relevant example of such an institutional development. The availability of mid-career opportunities (such as fellowships or seminars) also needs to be enlarged greatly for scientists who are ready for and interested in the interactions between science and the world of human affairs.

5. This is not the place for a detailed discussion of strategies to bring about major changes by changes in the classroom, or even to summarize all the likely "first-aid" tactics, but some points are so clear that they must at least be mentioned. Particularly at the precollege level we need more large-scale curriculum innovations opposing the pervasive dichotomy that Cooley and Lohnes (among many others) quite rightly identified as interest in the various sciences versus interest in areas which involve humanistic and cultural concerns. One way is to put at least an effective modicum of history of science, epistemology, and discussion of the social impact of science and technology right into the educational material used in the science classes. This was a chief motivation for those of us who have worked on one such program.[27] Other educational experiments along these lines, difficult though they may be to

execute in detail, include more positive and more aggressive college-level programs designed to encourage actively what has been called "double literacy." I have no fear that such arrangements will scare off from a science career those who, for good reasons of their own, must do science as their flight to the pure empyrean. I do expect that the mere visibility of the option, properly presented, can attract to science a latent population, including socially concerned persons who, given the current self-image of the scientist, would normally not think of science as their proper career field. Scientists (and nonscientists) now surely need also more exposure to substantial discussions of the ethical and human value impacts of science and technology. The flight of most members of a profession to the high empyrean, where they can work peacefully on purely scientific problems, isolated from the turmoil of real life, was perhaps quite appropriate at an earlier stage of science; but in today's world it is a luxury we cannot afford.

It may, of course, turn out that we must settle for the "see-saw" for many if not most of the productive research scientists. High scientific (or any scholarly) performance is often obtained at the cost of low social involvement, and the very identity formation of the scientist may depend on his carving out a manageable portion of the world for himself and reducing, therefore, his ties with the rest. This is the classic model, and, so far, educators not only have not resisted it but have built it into their assumptions. We clearly can no longer do this, and we must try to do something about it. As an educator and optimist, I have a professional affirmation that education will find in the "Szilard" tail of the curve, not Szilards—because that would be too much to hope for—but at least people who have enough of the Szilard component to meliorate the stern demands of science. I place much hope in finding incentives that will influence students to do excellent science and yet to be interested actively in societal concerns, or at the very least to be able to work together and sympathize with those who do.

6. A further strategy is this: Since it is not likely that the mean value of the distribution can be shifted by converting those now on the low, left wing of the curve, we must try to add to the population of the right, high wing of the curve by increased visibility and effectiveness, in addition to increased recruitment. By a kind of affirmative-action process, the members at that end of the spectrum should be given more than their usual low share in matters such as filling leadership positions in professional societies (as the American Chemical Society did a few years ago in electing Alan C. Nixon as its president, the American Physical Society in electing V. Weisskopf and W. Panofsky, and Margaret Mead's election to the presidency of the AAAS).

7. I believe it is reasonable to hope that the scientists' fear of the intractibility and seamless quality of societal problems—which has made the flight to simpler models of the world functional and reasonable—can be shown, in sufficiently many interesting instances, not to be borne out by the facts. Except in biomedical areas, we have had few pioneers willing to map out plausible routes to the kernel of scientific ignorance at the center of complex societal difficulties.[28] Nor has there been adequate financial support for work that is unlikely to give early results. Hence the attitude of the profession may be a self-fulfilling fear. But once even a few scientists have dared to identify and successfully worked on such essential questions, the bridge will become progressively more firm, more visible, more traveled, and more plausible. Eventually, the fear of unavoidable failure should be deprived of its rational component. Much is at stake here, and much depends on the generation of a few prototypical successes.

8. Finally, we need more research on this whole topic. In this period of rapid change we need to know far more up-to-date facts. . . . The methodology of research has also been

much improved since the days when many of the data still used today were obtained.

There have been a host of other significant changes as well. Consider the situation with respect to women in science. As was evident from my summaries, most of the available data on scientists are on males in the United States; there has been an outstanding lack of research and useful results on women scientists.[29] Cooley and Lohnes had to confide:[30] "If we ever hoped to develop a theory of careers that would apply to both sexes, the experience of wrestling with the follow-up data has disabused us of that notion . . . We have done very little with the problem of female career development, either empirically or theoretically. The Project TALENT girls, in their development toward womanhood, are a challenge we haven't really met." And again: "We subscribe to the suggestion of Roe and of Super that the career process for women needs to be conceptualized differently and researched differently than for men. The process is probably more complex and difficult to study for women . . ."

. . . It is a testable hypothesis that the new influx of young women into science who are coming from outside the older, stereotypical population may yield more representatives from the right, high wing of the bell-shaped curve referred to earlier—at least if they find role models and other support to encourage the trend.

It is evident that a whole spectrum of interesting research problems suggests itself in the still very obscure area called the psychology of scientists. How is it really possible that such a human enterprise as science, in the hands of such a diversity of people, does in fact yield relatively invariant information? How do the various and perhaps contradictory elements in the psyche of the scientist somehow function together to produce a body of work that transcends the individual's limitations? More understanding of matters of this kind will help us in the task of fusing native scientific optimism and mature societal concerns among scientists.

Notes

1. A. Einstein, "Motiv de Forschens," republished in English translation in Sonja Bargmann, trans. and rev., *Ideas and Opinions of Albert Einstein* (New York: Crown Publishers, Inc., 1954), pp. 224–27. The somewhat revised translation used here is from G. Holton, *Thematic Origins of Scientific Thought: Kepler to Einstein* (Cambridge, Mass.: Harvard University Press, 1973), pp. 376–78 (hereafter cited as *Thematic Origins*).

2. An implied claim of moral superiority of the scientist engaged in pure research without direct commercial applications can be discerned in other confessions of this sort. Thus, writing about the university physicist, a scientist in the 1920s said, "Financially his lot is not a wealthy one, nor socially is he high . . . [but close] to nature and by it closer and closer every day to the Almighty God who made him, what matters it to the physicist if the days be dull or neighboring man uncouth? His soul is more or less aloof from mortal strife" (R. Hamer, *Science 61* [1925]: 109–10; quoted by S. Weart, *Nature 262* [July 1, 1976]: 15).

3. B. Kuznetsov, "Nonclassical Science and the Philosophy of Optimism," in R. McCormmach, ed., *Historical Studies in the Physical Sciences*, (Princeton, N.J.: Princeton University Press, 1975), 4: 192–231.

4. For example, G. Holton and W. A. Blanpied, eds., *Science and Its Public: The Changing Relationship* (Boston: D. Reidel Publishing Co., 1976); also the *Newsletters* of the Harvard University Program on Public Conceptions of Science (now the *Newsletter on Science, Technology and Human Values*). . . .

5. A. Szent-György, *American Journal of Physics 43*, no. 5 (1975): 427.

6. Marshall Bush, in an interesting essay, "Psychoanalysis and Scientific Creativity," abridged and reprinted in Bernice T. Eiduson and Linda Beckman, eds., *Science as a Career Choice* (New York: Russell Sage Foundation, 1973), pp. 243–57 . . . does find useful generalizations to hold. See also F. Barron, *Creative Person and Creative Process* (New York: Holt, 1969), ch. 9.

7. B. T. Eiduson, "Psychological Aspects of Career Choice and Development in the Research Scientist," in *Science as a Career Choice*, p. 15; italics supplied.

8. A. Einstein, "Autobiographical Notes," in P.A. Schilpp, ed., *Albert Einstein: Philosopher-Scientist* (New York: Harper and Brothers, 1959), p. 81.

9. D. C. McClelland, "On the Psychodynamics of Creative Physical Scientists" (1962), reproduced in

abridged form in *Science as a Career Choice*, pp. 187–95. The quotations are from pp. 188 and 189, respectively.

10. Eiduson, op. cit. (n. 7), p. 15. . . .

11. The only trait not fully matched in the list given earlier is Fermi's "familial" and close personal relations with those who worked with him. . . .

12. L. S. Kubie, "Some Unresolved Problems of the Scientific Career," *American Scientist* 41 (1953): 596–613, and 42 (1954): 104–12. See also L. S. Kubie, "The Fostering of Creative Scientific Productivity," *Daedalus* 91 (1962): 304 ff.

13. For example, in David Shapiro, *Neurotic Styles* (New York: Basic Books, 1965), as cited in D. J. Taylor, "Enrico Fermi: The Psychology of Scientific Style" (unpublished doctoral thesis, Yale University School of Medicine, 1975). Taylor asks the interesting question why there have been so few psychoanalytic studies on scientists ever since Sigmund Freud's theories of neurosis.

He notes that Freud published studies of many creative persons—philosophers, artists, writers— but never of a scientist other than himself (though the work on Leonardo perhaps came close); moreover, the work of those who followed Freud has had largely the same bias. It may well be because science, of which Freud thought psychoanalysis to be a special example, was considered by Freud to be endowed with "impersonal" objectivity and therefore that there was a relative paucity of emotional goals and of fantasies in the work of scientists. Only in *other* fields would the subjectivity of the creators show itself sufficiently for them to be interesting subjects for scientific (i.e., psychoanalytic) studies.

Ironically, the claims of psychoanalysis to scientific status were long denied by other scientists. Einstein, for one, was quite skeptical; see his exchanges with Freud, for example, in O. Nathan and H. Norden, eds., *Einstein on Peace* (New York: Schocken Books, 1960), pp. 185–88. The reluctance of scientists to this day, by and large, to take interest in the psychological study of the scientific imagination itself is also relevant.

14. E. Durkheim, *The Rules of Sociological Method* (Glencoe, Ill.: The Free Press, 1950; originally 1895), p. 104.

15. Anne Roe, *The Making of a Scientist* (New York: Dodd, Mead & Co., 1952).

16. I have discussed the coherence of intellect and character in the case of highly achieving scientists in Chapter 10 of *Thematic Origins*. Many of the findings of Roe (n. 15) are of course parallel to others, made over the years.

17. Additional Support was provided later from the Project TALENT data bank, computed in 1968. . . .
See also M. Bush, in *Science as a Career Choice*, pp. 244–45; J. A. Chambers, in *Science as a Career Choice*, p. 350; and M. J. Moravcsik, "Motivation of Physicists," *Physics Today* 20 (October 1975): 9. . . .

18. Anne Roe, *The Psychology of Occupations* (New York: John Wiley & Sons, 1956), p. 319. See also the research results in Anne Roe and Marvin Siegelman, *The Origin of Interests*, American Personnel and Guidance Association Inquiry Study No. 1 (Washington, D.C.: APGA, 1964), particularly pp. 3–7, 45, 64–67.

19. W. W. Cooley and Paul R. Lohnes, *Predicting Development of Young Adults*, Project TALENT, 5-year Follow-up Studies, Interim Report 5 (Palo Alto, Calif.: Project TALENT, American Institutes for Research, and Pittsburgh: School of Education, University of Pittsburgh, 1968), p. 4.44. The cited passage has further references to supporting work, that is, that of Roe and Siegelman, op. cit. (n. 18); W. W. Cooley, *Career Development of Scientists: An Overlapping Longitudinal Study, Cooperative Research Project No. 436* (Cambridge: Graduate School of Education, Harvard University, 1963); and D. E. Super et al., *The Psychology of Careers* (New York: Harper & Row, 1957). . . .

20. J. A. David, *Undergraduate Career Decisions* (Chicago: Aldine Publishing Co., 1965), especially pp. 10–13, 50–63, 132–39, 152–65. See also, for example, Bernice T. Eiduson, *Scientists, Their Psychological World* (New York: Basic Books, 1962). Her story of forty research scientists reports their "chief interest in childhood" in descending order as follows: reading, 33; science, 23; sports, 22; artistic, 16; mechanical, 7; social, 4.

Among other publications, the following contain interesting work along similar lines: Robert S. Albert, "Toward a Behavioral Definition of Genius," *American Psychologist* 30 (1975): 140–51 (includes a good bibliography); Charles C. Gillispie, "Remarks on Social Selection as a Factor in the Progressiveness of Science," *American Scientist* 56 (1968): 439–50; Howard E. Gruber, Glenn Terrell, and Michael Wertheimer, eds., *Contemporary Approaches to Creative Thinking* (New York: Atherton Press, 1962), especially the essay by Allen Newell, J. C. Shaw, and Herbert A. Simon, "The Processes of Creative Thinking," pp. 63–119; Liam Hudson, *Contrary Imaginations* (London: Pelican, 1966); Ian I. Mitroff, *The Subjective Side of Science* (Amsterdam: Elsevier, 1974); Ian I. Mitroff and Ralph H. Kilman,

"On Evaluating Scientific Research: The Contribution of the Psychology of Science," *Technological Forecasting and Social Change* 8 (1975): 163–74; Michael Mulkay, "Some Aspects of Cultural Growth in the Natural Sciences," *Social Research* 36 (1969): 22–52; and Barry F. Singer, "Toward a Psychology of Science," *American Psychologist* 26 (1971): 1010–15 (includes a good bibliography).

21. Cf. W. O. Hagstrom, *The Scientific Community* (New York: Basic Books, 1965).

22. See, for example, the discussion in Bernice T. Eiduson, "Scientists as Advisors and Consultants in Washington," *Science and Public Affairs, Bulletin of the Atomic Scientists* 22 (1966): 26–31. She cites a typical reaction of a scientist to the "Washington Experience": "I was becoming a government committee figure. I was really big business. I found myself doing unpleasant things with people I despised and even before I knew it, I was finding myself trying to rival them. Then I realized I was really selling out my soul to them; and that if I were going to do this, I might as well go into the Hollywood business, or do something else that would be more interesting and profitable.

"This attitude came to me one day when, at a committee meeting . . . a man leaned over the table, and said to me, 'Is this what we went to college for?' I felt nauseous, and almost had a blackout, and decided to get out right then and there . . . It's an emotionally revolting and emotionally draining experience, and I've done my duty."

23. J. Primack and F. von Hippel, *Advice and Dissent* (New York: Basic Books, 1974).

24. Philip Boffey, *The Brain Bank of America* (New York: McGraw-Hill Book Company, 1975).

25. Cooley, op cit. (n. 19), p. 108.

26. Albert Einstein, in *Ideas and Opinions* (n. 1), p. 9.

27. See the discussion of the program in Chapter 11 [of *The Scientific Imagination*].

28. I have intentionally not been dealing with "applied research" or "development," where existing scientific knowledge is put to use. The benefits one expects from these efforts is different from what one may expect from basic scientific research and researchers who are able to go beyond the barriers of current ignorance on fundamental matters.

29. See H. Zuckerman and J. R. Cole, "Women in American Science," *Minerva* 13 (1975): 82–102; and two useful earlier studies: Roe and Siegelman, op. cit., n. 18; and H. S. Astin, *The Woman Doctorate in America* (New York: Russell Sage Foundation, 1966). . . .

30. Cooley and Lohnes, op. cit. (n. 19), pp. 1.29, 4.42. See also p. 4.48. . . .

MARGUERITE HOLLOWAY

A Lab of Her Own

There is no one story to tell about women in science. C. Dominique Toran-Allerand just received tenure—after 20 years at Columbia University, after watching male peers enjoy promotion, after listening to colleagues laugh when she requested recommendations. "They thought I was joking," explains the neuroscientist, who studies the role of hormones in brain development, with light bitterness in her voice. "People generally did not believe I did not have tenure."

Cheryl Ann Butman, a tenured biological oceanographer at the Woods Hole Oceanographic Institution, moves clothes at midnight from a backpack, unemptied since her return from a Gordon Conference, into a canvas bag. In four hours she will leave on a cruise to place research equipment on the ocean floor. Downstairs, Bradford Butman, branch chief of the U.S. Geological Survey in Woods Hole, washes dishes. He is just back from a meeting. The race against time is interrupted when Dylan, their two-year-old, has a nightmare. The evening is remarkable only in that both scientists are home. "Once Brad met me at the airport, handed Dylan to me and then got on a plane himself," Butman recalls.

Kay Redfield Jamison, a psychiatrist at the Johns Hopkins University School of Medicine who studies creativity and manic-depressive illness, would rather not talk about problems that women may encounter. "The system is a harsh one, but it is for men as well," she asserts. "In the end, you just have to get your work done. How many women really spend much time thinking about these things?"

Some find it hard to avoid doing so. A researcher at a prestigious women's college describes being told to "go knit or do whatever it is you women do" when she asked for comments on her grant application to the National Institutes of Health.

The experiences of these scientists and the challenges they face are as varied as the women themselves and as the research they do. Which is perhaps why the fight that women wage so that they and their daughters can practice science remains unfinished. Although their struggle to enter and to advance in this overwhelmingly male-dominated field parallels the struggles of women in other professions, science seems a uniquely well fortified bastion of sexism. "How shocking it is that there are any women in science at all," remarks Sandra

Harding, a philosopher at the University of Delaware.

Despite speeches, panels and other efforts at consciousness-raising, women remain dramatically absent from the membership of the informal communities and clubs that constitute the scientific establishment. Only 16 percent of the employed scientists and engineers in this country are female. At a finer level of detail, the numbers of women in different disciplines and positions are so low that a recitation of the statistics sounds like a warped version of "The Twelve Days of Christmas": 1 percent of working environmental scientists, 2 percent of mechanical engineers, 3 percent of electrical engineers, 4 percent of medical school department directors, 5 percent of physics Ph.D.'s, 6 of close to 300 tenured professors in the country's top 10 mathematics departments, and so on.

"There is still so much to be done," rues Jane Z. Daniels, director of women's programs at the National Science Foundation (NSF). "The traditional areas of science for women are still those areas where there is the most growth. There is not a lot of change in physics, geology and engineering. Those are the ones where the stereotypes have been preserved." Other fields are not quite so male heavy. Forty-one percent of working biologists and life scientists are women. Nearly half of all psychology and neuroscience graduate students are female. According to the American Chemical Society, women constituted 17 percent of their members in 1991, up from 8 percent in 1975.

Regardless of their field, women scientists typically earned salaries that are about 25 percent lower than those paid to men in the same positions, they are twice as likely to be unemployed and they are rarely promoted to high positions (in 1989, 7 percent of tenured faculty in the sciences were female). Women report less encouragement from their peers and supervisors, less mentoring and help with professional advancement as well as greater isolation and harassment.

These conditions persist despite more than two decades of efforts to redress an imbalance

that was brought to light in large part by the women's movement. In the past 20 years an array of federal and other educational programs have sought to attract women into science. These attempts gained some momentum in 1988, when a congressional study announced that the U.S. would need more than half a million scientists and engineers by the year 2010. As men were dropping out of science, women and members of minority groups were seen as possible replacements.

The cumulative attention has brought about some gains. In 1989 women received 27.8 percent of the doctorates in science and engineering, whereas in 1966 only 8 percent of such degrees were awarded to women. The NSI recently found that differences in science scores between girls and boys on some standardized tests had decreased. The U.S. Equal Employment Opportunity Commission has also documented an increase in the number of female full professors.

"I have never seen a period in history where they are trying to encourage women so much," notes Londa Schiebinger, a historian of science at Pennsylvania State University. "But I think what is extremely interesting is that there is all this funding and this goodwill, and they are still dropping like flies." Attrition has increasingly led many observers to examine the culture of science for clues about why so few women stay in the field. What, if anything, ask the researchers, is it about science that continues to exclude or deter women from remaining in research?

"They have been attempting to get more women into science, trying to fix the women, give them enough science courses, prevent them from falling behind," Schiebinger, who wrote *The Mind Has No Sex? Women in the Origins of Modern Science.* "But we can't fix the girls, we have to fix science, get it to be something they want to do. We have to look deeply into the culture of science and see what is turning women off."

Peering into the scientific establishment to pinpoint the origins of the problem—why so few women?—reveals both the mysterious and the obvious. Throughout the centuries, for no cogent reason, women have been excluded from most aspects of professional and political life. And the majority of fields have until recently remained male. Within this larger tradition of sexism, there are some clear explanations for the absence of women in science. From the moment they begin to be socialized, most girls are directed away from science. This subtle and overt deterrence can be seen in the educational system and is fortified by the perceptions of many male scientists that women simply should not be scientists.

It is not that there have historically been no women in science. Only nine women may have been awarded a Nobel Prize as opposed to more than 300 men, but there are many unsung women who have made vital contributions in all fields. In the past decade or so, historians have increasingly begun to describe these mostly invisible participants. In 1982 Margaret W. Rossiter, a historian of science at Cornell University, published a lengthy account of American women who did science before 1940. "People said the book would not be very long, because there were no women of consequence. They were wrong," says Rossiter, who is working on her next tome: women in science from 1945 to 1972. Although many workers were tucked away as assistants and technicians, their contributions were invaluable. She found many of them hidden in footnotes in books about male scientists.

Other researchers have traced the roots of the scientific establishment's attitude toward women. Each period of history and each culture are, of course, characterized by a different prevailing view, but there is no shortage of "documentation" by males of the physical and mental inferiority of women. In the late 1880s, following a series of studies on the small size of women's brains—and, not insignificantly, their enormous pelvic bones, all the better to bear children with—a friend of Charles Darwin's summed up that illustrious scientist's view of women's intellectual powers: "It must take

many centuries for heredity to produce the missing five ounces of the female brain."

The emergence of the modern scientific establishment appears to have institutionalized many of these perceptions. Historian David F. Noble of York University in Toronto argues that the first universities were monastic, organized by the Christian church, and thus excluded women. In his book *A World without Women: The Christian Clerical Culture of Western Science*, he discusses how this segregation persisted in the academies and institutions that arose with modern science. The Royal Society was established in 1662 and did not admit women until 1945. Before then, as Schiebinger notes, the only woman in the Royal Society was a skeleton in the anatomy collection. Today 2.9 percent of the "fellows" are female.

Some institutions have better records, but by and large, women were not made to feel at

Academic Rank of Doctoral Scientists, 1990

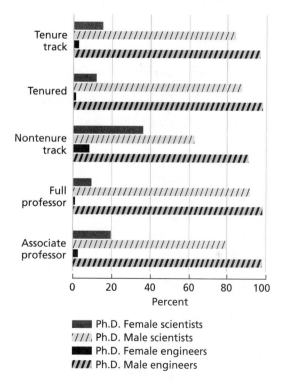

- ▓ Ph.D. Female scientists
- ⁄⁄⁄ Ph.D. Male scientists
- ■ Ph.D. Female engineers
- ⁄⁄⁄ Ph.D. Male engineers

Source: National Science Foundation; the statistics are for U.S.

home in the inner sanctum of science and were denied access to traditional training. Beatrix Potter, for instance, was an accomplished mycologist—in fact, she was the first person to report on the symbiotic aspects of lichen and to catalogue the fungi of the British Isles. But Potter was not allowed to join any professional scientific societies because of her sex. So, fortunately for English-speaking children and their parents, she turned to writing and illustrating children's books. The 1880 official minutes from "The Misogynist Dinner of the American Chemical Society," unearthed by Rossiter, are part of the same tradition.

It is the vestiges of these attitudes and the impenetrability of the elite social institutions that most frustrate female scientists still. The National Academy of Sciences currently has only 70 female members, out of 1,750 living scientists. "There is still resentment between the old guard and women," says Betty M. Vetter, executive director of the Commission on Professionals in Science and Technology. She adds bluntly, "It will change when they die."

Doctorates awarded to women, by field, in 1989

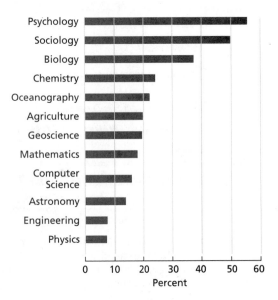

Source: National Science Foundation; the statistics are for U.S.

By maintaining a male majority, many institutions perpetuate the status quo, preventing women from participating in forums where important contacts are made. Women "don't get invited to write as many book chapters, and they don't get a chance to network as much. It is not a question of a more or less collaborative style," comments Christina L. Williams, a neuroscientist at Barnard College. "You do what you can do. You can't get yourself invited to things if you don't get invited."

Studies have found that meetings organized by men usually have a male majority—no matter what the percentage of women in the field. Only 24 percent of the speakers at past meetings of the American Society for Cell Biology, which is roughly 50 percent female, were women, even when the conferences were organized by women, notes Susan Gerbi, president of the society. When men organized the conferences, less than 10 percent were female. "It is not men sitting around saying, 'Don't invite women,'" Williams explains. "It is done blindly, and it is just that there is no concerted effort. A lot of the people in power in science are still men."

Another place where similar discrimination may occur is on editorial boards. Staff at many scientific publications remains mostly male and has shown a tendency to accept more male-authored papers or to invite men to do review articles. It is not clear, however, that selection of papers would change if editorial boards were more sexually balanced. A study conducted in the early 1980s asked 180 men and 180 women to rate comparable papers. One third of the papers was supposedly written by John T. McKay, another third by Joan T. McKay and the final series by J. T. McKay. Both the women and men gave the "John T." papers the highest score. Whatever the cause, Harriet Zuckerman of the Andrew W. Mellon Foundation and Jonathan R. Cole of Columbia have found that women tend to publish 30 percent fewer papers than do their male colleagues in the first 12 or so years of their careers. The disparity increases over time.

One controversial solution to making meetings more reflective of the work force, thereby spreading the wealth of information and contacts, is affirmative action. Last year the NSF announced it would not fund conferences unless a number of women proportionate to the number in the field were invited. "You hope it is not going to lead to less qualified women being asked," Williams says. "But there is no reason that it should. There are plenty of good women out there in all fields."

Opinions about affirmative action are, inevitably, mixed. An editorial in *Nature* bemoaned the NSF's new "quota" policy. "There is no evidence that sex is related to success in scientific research," the editors wrote, "and no inherent justification for holding women out for special treatment as part of a formal policy carrying the bludgeon of budgets." Many female scientists also view legislative remedies with some skepticism. "I personally do not want any favors because I am a woman. I want to be competitive on a gender-free basis," Toran-Allerand says. Her view echoes that of many female scientists, in particular those who struggled through the system before it was subjected to feminist scrutiny. Many of those who succeeded, including Nobel laureates Gertrude Belle Elion and Rita Levi-Montalcini, did not want special attention as women in science—they just desperately wanted to do their science.

Toran-Allerand, who was the only woman in both her medical school class and residency, attributes some of this to a double standard for women. "In the past, women were really an intellectual elite. You had to be slightly crazy if you wanted to go do that in that kind of environment," she comments. A woman "who interviewed me at Yale said I had to realize that the women had to be perfect. There were so few women; they could not tolerate any imperfection. The imperfections in the men would be accepted because there were so many of them that they would even out over the population."

With more women in science, such pressures have been alleviated—to a point. Many

scientists and educators have noted that scientific institutions are not the only source of discouragement for women: the educational system does not foster a love of science in girls (for that matter, however, it has not been wildly successful in recent years with boys either). Most teachers of kindergarten through eighth grade are women, and many are not well versed in science. They do not serve as effective role models for young girls interested in science. In addition, many stereotypes—of scientists as nerds, as mad and as male—persist. "The basic idea is that if you are a woman interested in science, you are gender confused," notes Catherine J. Didion, executive director of the Association for Women in Science.

Research by the American Association of University Women has found that at all educational levels, boys receive more attention than do girls in the classroom. The effect is independent of the teacher's sex. Adults also encourage boys to be assertive in answering questions and expressing opinions. Therefore, a young woman who pursues a career in

Science Ph.D.'s by employment sector

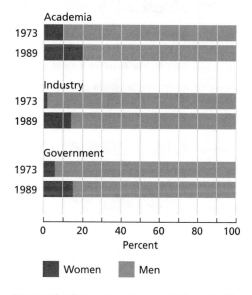

Source: National Science Foundation; the statistics are for U.S.

science needs a particularly strong endowment of mettle.

Girls are told in myriad ways that they are not as good at mathematics as boys are. This social myth has no foundation in reality. Researchers have found that girls often do as well as boys in math in elementary and junior high school. Yet girls hear "quite early that higher math is for boys," Vetter notes. "Girls are not taught to put themselves forward to get into that group of precocious math kids. You have to push yourself forward, but girls are not encouraged to do that."

Exploiting this perception of feminine math anxiety, the toy manufacturer Mattel last year made a Barbie doll that said, "Math class is tough." The company deleted the statement from the doll's voice track after several women's groups protested. (The NCF's Daniels points out that the pink Lego building blocks designed for girls do not send the right message either.)

A distinct irony surrounds the issue of women and mathematics. Mathematics was at times considered a woman's subject. Schiebinger describes the English *Ladies' Diary*, published between 1704 and 1841, which encouraged women to perfect their "Arithmetick, Geometry, Trigonometry . . . Algebra . . . and all other Mathematical Sciences." It goes to show that "when the rules of society change, the girls perform just as well as the boys," remarks Mildred S. Dresselhaus, professor of electrical engineering and physics at the Massachusetts Institute of Technology. "If they act as though they are interested, they get very discouraging signals. I got my share of those, too, I suppose. But I went to an all-girls school, and there I did not know that girls were not supposed to study math."

In addition to discouragement, women cite boredom as the reason that they stopped studying science. Many experts are trying to find new ways of teaching girls and women to maintain interest. Sue V. Rosser, director of women's studies and professor of family and preventive medicine at the University of South Carolina, has found that women tend to be interested in a problem or a question if it has some context or social relevance or the solution produces some benefit. They also respond to a challenge better if the process of meeting it is framed as a collaboration rather than a competition. "Men, in general, find that a technological fix in and of itself is enough," she explains. Rosser and many others have designed successful teaching methods that harness these insights. Re-forming questions and experiments appears to have an unexpected boon: it captures the imagination of male students as well.

An NSF study of questions for National Assessment of Educational Progress tests reached the same conclusion. When math problems have some social implication, girls do better. On the other hand, boys' scores on tests of verbal ability, which are traditionally lower than those of girls, improve if the excerpts describe sports or science. Ellen Spertus, a graduate student in computer science at M.I.T., observes that computer games in which the objective is,

Median annual salaries at the doctoral level, 1989

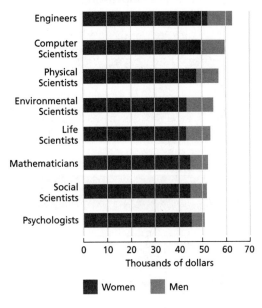

Thousands of dollars

■ Women   ■ Men

Source: National Science Foundation; the statistics are for U.S.

say, to prevent a meteor from hitting the planet are often more likely to interest girls than are games in which the players are supposed to slaughter invading aliens.

Changes in testing and in school curriculums, however, may not be sufficient to hold women in science. Sometimes as many as half of the first-year female college students are interested in science and engineering, yet at some point in their academic careers, their attrition rate exceeds that of the male students. Certain universities and colleges as well as the Association for Women in Science have sought to combat this tendency by establishing mentoring programs.

In 1990, for instance, Dartmouth College set up internships to give as many as 75 female students experience in a laboratory, to demystify science and to introduce them to scientists. "They get to see what is going on in science first-hand, that scientists are not all geeky, that they are very regular people who make mistakes and have to do things over again," according to Mary Pavone, director of the women in science project.

Initially, many of the participants do not think the program is necessary. "They come here freshman year and see that the numbers of men and women in introductory science courses are fairly even—they don't see what happens; they don't see the filter. By junior year, they look around their classes, and all of a sudden a light goes on," Pavone says. The number of women majoring in science at Dartmouth was up in 1993, but it is not clear that the project is responsible.

At the doctoral level the situation becomes more difficult. Women have a higher attrition rate than do men before they enter Ph.D. programs; they are about 15 percent less likely to finish their degrees. "You have to have someone on the faculty who wants you," says C. Megan Urry, chief of the research support branch at the National Aeronautics and Space Administration's Space Telescope Science Institute. Science is ultimately a guild, in which a master passes on skills and professional touch to apprentices. For reasons of ancient tradition and contemporary culture, those apprentices are predominantly male. "No one ever told me what was going on. The men are getting a lot of help, and the male advisers are helping them write. The women don't get it much," Urry says.

A combination of institutional changes, including mentoring programs, educational reforms and affirmative action strategies, has traditionally been perceived as the means for bringing women into science and keeping them there. These approaches address the problem illustrated by the often strange metaphors that have been used to explain why there are so few women in science or in any other field: the pipeline is leaking, the glass ceiling has not cracked, women are stuck on the bottom rung of the ladder.

But a growing number of observers are questioning the fundamental and long-term success of these efforts. Feminist thinkers, including Schiebinger and Rosser as well as Brown University biologist Anne Fausto-Sterling and Harvard University professor emerita Ruth Hubbard, take a more radical position. They believe the whole edifice—plumbing, ceiling and ladder—has to be reconstructed. "My view is that getting women into science is not just being nicer to them at younger ages,

Bachelor's degrees: 1966–1990

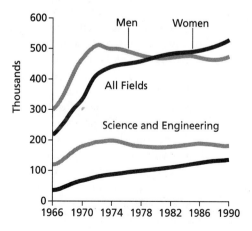

Source: National Science Foundation; the statistics are for U.S.

although that is important. But we really have to rethink our whole notion of what science is and how it functions," says Fausto-Sterling, author of *Myths of Gender: Biological Theories about Women and Men.*

Fausto-Sterling and others are examining how scientific knowledge in the West has been shaped by social mores and by the white male culture that has directed it. The scrutiny is not well received by many in the scientific community. "Scientists think this is not very important," says Harding, who wrote *Whose Science? Whose Knowledge?* "But our conceptions of how we think about the history of science shape how we are doing science now. We want to learn from the past. If we have distorted views, we should understand them."

Perhaps the most prickly issue that some of these thinkers have raised is whether women and men approach science differently and, if they do, whether differences in style account for the low numbers of women attracted to science. Most of the discussion was initiated by Evelyn Fox Keller's 1983 book about Nobel laureate Barbara McClintock. In *A Feeling for the Organism: The Life and Work of Barbara McClintock,* Keller suggests that McClintock's unusual insights into genetics were shaped by intuition, by a more stereotypically "female" approach. The fires have been stoked by other researchers, among them Doreen Kimura, a psychologist at the University of Western Ontario. Her work shows distinctly different patterns of male and female mentation with respect to solving problems and framing intellectual challenges [see "Sex Differences in the Brain," by Doreen Kimura; *Scientific American,* September 1992].

Many scientists think this idea of difference has some validity in the biological sciences in particular. "There is a strong argument that when you bring women in, they look at what the female [subjects] are doing," Schiebinger notes. "So far we have found these examples only for sciences where there is sex involved." Perhaps the best example of this view is the work of Jane Goodall, Dian Fossey and Birute

Galdikas, anthropologists who revolutionized understanding of the primates by changing the way animals were observed, by following individuals. "They looked at female-female interactions and saw new behaviors," Rosser explains.

Rosser has her own example. She recalls that when she first taught animal behavior she asked the class to examine Siamese fighting fish: What were the reactions of males to males, to self and to females? The exercise never included female reactions to females or to males. Sandra Steingraber, a Bunting Fellow at Radcliffe and Harvard, studied dioramas of white-tailed deer in natural history museums and found that the males were always depicted in a warriorlike stance, about to defend a doe and fawn. In reality, Steingraber says, does and bucks unite only to mate. Does and fawns stay together only until they begin to compete for food. The dioramas, an educational tool, were shaped by the anthrocentric and anthropomorphic social vision of the men who designed them.

If it is true that women can bring a different perspective, feminist scholars argue, that is all the more reason to encourage women, minorities and people from diverse cultures to practice science. "I think there is a lot of validity to the idea that women do things differently, not from a biological basis but from a sociological perspective. There is a clash between women's and men's cultures," Schiebinger says. "Women and men are not interchangeable parts. They act in very different ways, and it seems to me that that carries over into the professional world. It brings an enriching perspective."

Anecdotal reports suggest that many women organize their laboratories differently, in a less hierarchical fashion, than do their male colleagues. "I don't think I think differently in terms of questions, because I have been trained," says Kathie L. Olsen, a program director at the NSF. "The difference is in the daily operation in the laboratory and in terms of how I interact with people." Ruth Ginzberg, a philosopher at Wesleyan University in Connecticut, has observed the same phenomenon in other fields, such as business. "For a long time, women were not thought of as good managers. Then somebody decided that perhaps women might have a different management style. Women were not rising in the ranks, because they were doing things differently—not because they were doing it less well."

Other differences have also been found. Studies of men and women interacting in groups suggest that women are interrupted more frequently, that their contributions are more often attributed to men in the group and that they are less comfortable with antagonistic discussions. "The problem is that women are being judged by men in a system set up by men that basically reflects their standards and criteria," Urry maintains. "Some of that has not to do with excellence in science but with style."

Whereas many female scientists agree that women and men may act differently, the idea that this variation translates into a different way of doing science remains sticky. "I find this topic a bit difficult," Dresselhaus admits. "Spending a lot of time on this doesn't do credit to women in fields with few women. In medicine, say, gynecology, women may have a different approach. But if you are resolving a flow equation, there is not a woman's way or a man's way: there is the way the air flows around an airplane wing—it just flows around the wing."

There is a lack of very solid evidence for the proposition, Zuckerman concurs. In an unpublished study the sociologist and her colleagues found that sex differences were minor with respect to how scientists think about and describe their work. The criteria were how they chose their research topics and the significance of the research they were doing. "Gender is not a good predictor of difference," Zuckerman says. "Science is supposed to be attentive to evidence, and there is a lack of it here. These are matters about which people feel very strongly."

Some female scientists also see such perceptions of difference as potentially dangerous.

"We would all be better off if we could forget about gender altogether," says Deborah M. Gordon, an animal behaviorist at Stanford University and one of very few women studying social insects. "It is hard for young women starting out to hear that they are different. They should hear that everyone will have to work hard to be a good scientist. They should be thinking about how to do their work as best they can, not how their work is channeled by gender."

Many scientists believe individual variations are so great that they outweigh those between men and women. "I am an adamant feminist about a lot of these issues, but this one I get sort of riled by," Williams states. "People approach science differently, so to categorize a woman's versus a man's approach would be difficult. It is not that it does not exist, it is just that there are many styles of doing science."

Yet by questioning the culture of science, many feminist scientists and scholars claim to be broadening this repertoire of styles. In their view, such enrichment will ultimately lead to a more thorough science and a better society. Some such thinkers have suggested that research priorities may shift as a consequence. "A lot of physics has been defense related, and many women left it for that reason," Didion explains. "At the minimum, the way that science would be communicated would be different, not necessarily the science itself."

Medicine has already changed in some ways as a result of the growing number of women researchers and practitioners. Women's health is receiving more funding and attention. Conclusions based on white male patients are no longer being blindly applied to female or minority patients. A recent study in the *New England Journal of Medicine* concluded that female patients who have female doctors were twice as likely to receive Pap smears and mammograms.

"These are not just women's issues," Didion declares. The contemporary culture of science "is not only not good for women, it is not good for many men." In particular, raising a family has been seen as incompatible with a successful scientific career. Women are often perceived to be less committed if they want to have children—although Zuckerman and Cole found that married women and mothers publish as many papers as single and childless women [see "Marriage, Motherhood and Research Performance in Science," by J. R. Cole and H. Zuckerman; *Scientific American*, February 1987].

Nevertheless, without support at the institution where they work or from their spouses, women are more likely to drop out of science to have children. "Early career time is when women raise children, and organizations have to make it doable," Dresselhaus says. "I know in my own career it was awfully hard in those years. I had four children. I got help from my husband and hired a baby-sitter. But many people made totally unreasonable demands on me—it was almost humanly impossible to do what I was being asked to do."

Dresselhaus's success at maintaining her career and family is unusual. "The fact remains that science, like professional life in general, has been organized around the assumption that society need not reproduce itself—or that scientists are not among those involved in reproduction," Schiebinger notes wryly. The American Chemical Society, for example, found that 37 percent of female chemists older than 50 years had no children; only 9 percent of the men older than 50 were childless.

Moreover, 43 percent of women had relocated because of a change in the employment of a spouse. Only 7 percent of the men had relocated. For that reason, many female and male scientists—and people in all fields—support more flexible work time, family leave and child care legislation.

"These professions have evolved around the lives of men who could be professionals around the clock and spend little time on anything else," Hubbard says. "In science, it is certainly ridiculous to the extent that there is this notion that if you don't work 24 hours a day, nature is going to run away. It won't. It will still be there next year, unless we louse it up."

Gordon of Stanford would like to see universities organized in such a way that they could provide jobs to both partners of a married couple. "They are set up for men whose wives went with them, but the world is not like that anymore," Gordon observes.

All these considerations, from legislation to more subtle changes in the culture of science, will not ensure that more women or minorities will study or stay in science. Many scientists describe the situation as a catch-22: more women will enter the field only when there are more women in it. And, they say, the only way out of the conundrum is to change society's attitudes toward women—and men.

Such changes require continued vigilance, especially now that the anticipated job shortage has not materialized. To some, the existing economic malaise portends a loss of ground that women and members of minorities have gained in science. For others, it bodes well. "We are being forced to recognize that people do not have the money to throw at the problems, but that may be a blessing in disguise because people are going to have to do something," Didion asserts.

As for the old guard, the best thing that could happen is "that they get terribly fond of a granddaughter who is very interested in science," Vetter says. "It is possible to change people for their granddaughters."

NATALIE ANGIER

Women Join the Ranks of Science but Remain Invisible at the Top

The National Academy of Sciences announced its annual roll of new members this month, bestowing a highly coveted honor on a small group of American researchers. But of the 60 American scientists elected to the academy this year, only 6 are women. Some women in science take little satisfaction in the academy's election results.

"I think it's a disgusting percentage," said Dr. Susan E. Leeman, a neuroscientist at the University of Massachusetts Medical School in Worcester who was one of the newly chosen members. "I'm very proud and pleased to have been elected, but 6 out of 60? Isn't that amazing."

Since 1970, only a trickle of women—at most half a dozen in any one year—have won election to the academy, even though the number of eligible candidates would seem to have steadily increased.

According to the National Research Council, the percentage of Ph.D. scientists who are women doubled from 10 percent in 1973 to 20 percent in 1989. . . . And if scientists with all types of degrees, from master's to medical, are taken into account, women today make up almost one-third of the total.

Dr. Peter Raven, the academy's home secretary and the official in charge of conducting elections, said that the academy was trying hard to recruit younger members and hence more who are women. But the continuing scarcity of female academy members is one facet of a larger issue: women have been swelling the lower and middle ranks of science for years, yet still have not managed to pierce the upper scientific strata in anything beyond token numbers.

The problem is hardly limited to science, of course, but if science is a profession where advancement depends solely on the merit of an individual's ideas, the barriers to women might be expected to be lower than in other walks of life.

But in extensive interviews with women at all stages of their scientific careers and in a broad variety of disciplines, the researchers insisted that in fact some of the difficulties they encountered were peculiar to their trade, and that certain characteristics of the scientific culture were likelier to impede women's progress than to propel it.

Among those characteristics is the extreme insularity of science, and the need to be at the center of the rumor mill if one is to hear of vital new results before competitors do.

Women said that because they were often excluded from the most important scientific meetings and collaborations, they were frequently left out of the gossip loop. They also said they were given far fewer chances to present their findings and ideas to powerful audiences of their peers, a key method for winning converts and scientific influence.

Other women objected to the raw fisticuffs style that so many researchers adopt in their dissections of one another's results, intelligence, and all-round scientific and personal worthiness.

"The legal barriers to progress have been removed," said Dr. Londa Schiebinger a history professor at Pennsylvania State University in University Park and the author of *The Mind Has No Sex?* about the history of women in science. "The most visible barriers are gone. So what we're left with are the things that aren't very well perceived. And these are things that can be hard to talk about, not only because they're unquantifiable, but because they evoke a lot of hostility when you mention them to men."

To be sure, many women pointed out that progress had been great since the days when women were forbidden to observe at telescopes or to accompany male researchers on field studies, and some expressed great optimism that the changes would continue to proceed smartly.

"If you go back 20 years, it was hard then for women to get a job at entry levels," said Dr. Mildred Dresselhaus, an engineer and solid state physicist who has been on the faculty of Massachusetts Institute of Technology since 1960. "I think that's turned around recently very significantly. I think we're in an era now where men are sensitized and they want to give women an equal shot." Yet Dr. Dresselhaus admitted that "when push comes to shove, what people say and what they do don't always agree."

Despite the greater opportunities in the lower ranks, women remain poorly represented in the upper echelons.

Far fewer women than men hold tenured professorships in science, and fewer still are heads of their departments. Women make up only 3 percent of the physics faculty members in the United States, and about 2 percent of the engineering faculty.

The record in the life sciences like biology and biomedicine is somewhat better, with 22 percent of all faculty members in biology being women. But even here a quarter of them fall into categories, like "research associate" or "staff scientist," that offer no chance of tenure. By comparison, fewer than 10 percent of male biologists are in positions that are not on a tenure track.

Even as full professors, women almost never run the sort of large laboratories that earn multimillion-dollar Federal grants and give them visibility.

"When women get tenure, they're often secluded in their little cubbyhole, doing their own little thing," said Dr. Leeman. "As they age, they're not put on committees of power, they don't participate in allocation of resources, the division of space or the direction an institution is going in."

Women's salaries reflect the age-related discrepancies in power. The National Science Foundation has found that although women and men command roughly the same salaries at entry-level positions in science, differences in annual raises soon have an impact. After a decade of laboring full time in science, men earn 25 percent to 35 percent more than women do. And while male scientists' salaries continue to rise until retirement, women's peak before age 50, and then either stagnate, or even drop.

The reasons for the failure of women to break through science's traditional glass ceiling, or even to touch it with upstretched arms, are a complex mix of the obvious and the elusive. Many said it was partly a result of their being the ones who bear and care for children. Combining motherhood and science is particularly hard, they said, because the mechanics of research experiments often require all-night vigils that cannot be interrupted. And several studies have shown that the majority of married female scientists are married to other scientists, who themselves are tethered to the laboratory for days upon nights and thus may have trouble contributing much to child care.

But others argues that far subtler factors than maternity come into play in keeping women from the scientific forefront. Some of the researchers said that beliefs about women's innate inferiority to men in mathematics and abstract reasoning still held strong sway over some male scientists, even when the particular women have, through their achievements, proved themselves to be extremely skilled in math.

Dr. Vera C. Rubin, a scientist at the department of terrestrial magnetism at the Carnegie Institution in Washington, recently reviewed figures showing how, for several years in a row, male mathematicians received a proportionately higher number of fellowships to support their graduate work relative to the pool of men and women who applied.

In 1990, for example, 134 men applied for the fellowships, and 21 got them. But of the 56 women who applied, only 1 received the support.

From her own long-term experience as a professor and administrator, Dr. Rubin knew that by the time they were in graduate school, all but the most talented female mathematicians had been weeded out, and she was dismayed by the differences in grant awards. Her distress only mounted when she discussed her findings with a few men.

"I went up to several male mathematicians, including my son, Carl, who's quite eminent in his field," she said. "I presented them with the numbers and asked, 'Can you believe this?' They all said, "Well, the men must be better than the women.' That was all there was to it. And my son is married to a mathematician!"

Others attributed the barriers facing women to the singular dynamics of the scientific subculture, and the differences between the myth of the scientist and the reality.

Politics and business may demand a certain conformity in appearance, behavior and mindset from their participants, making it particularly difficult for women to blend into the male backdrop. But science is supposedly a haven for the misfits and the eccentrics of society. By the old stereotype, scientists are eggheaded loners who stare into microscopes or telescopes with such single-mindedness that they could not be expected to notice another person's presence, let alone the person's sex.

But as women and men quickly learn during their training, science in fact is one of the most gregarious of trades. Many scientific enterprises require extensive collaborations between teams of researchers. And men still seem to feel more comfortable collaborating with men than with women.

"There is a lot of friendship and social interactions that go on at the scientific level, and a lot of important information is exchanged in those interactions," said Dr. Elaine Fuchs, professor of molecular and cell biology at the University of Chicago. "You may be at a complete disadvantage in your ability to do good science if you can't get inside information. And though in an ideal world it would be otherwise, men usually feel more chummy with other men."

The difficulties of collaborating are multiplied by the extraordinarily international texture of science. Foreign scientists flock here in huge numbers, and when male researchers come from conservative nations like Japan, Middle Eastern countries and India, they may be even more reluctant to collaborate with women than are American scientists.

Many women complained that they were often excluded from the all-important conference circuit, a crucial route to scientific prominence. Meetings are where researchers exchange their latest findings long before the information is disseminated in scientific journals. But many female scientists believe that when conference organizers put together their roster of speakers, deciding who are the most respected elders, or the hottest young turks, or the most amusing raconteurs, women seem to come to mind rarely.

"Women appear invisible to men," said Dr. Margaret Davis, a professor of ecology at the University of Minnesota in Minneapolis who herself often organizes conferences. "If you ask men for the names of seminar or symposium speakers, the names you get back from them are almost invariable male. If you ask women, you get both male and female names."

At the biggest skin cancer meeting of the year, held last month in New York, all but 1 of the 47 researchers on the program were men, even though the field of dermatology research is known to have a number of outstanding female investigators.

When asked why he thought women were largely omitted from the program, Dr. Darrell S. Rigel of the New York University School of Medicine, a conference participant, said he thought it was an act of benign neglect on the part of the conference coordinators. He then hastened to add that the ratio would be different at a skin cancer meeting that he and his colleagues had organized.

"We've got lots of women on our panel," he said. But on checking the exact number, he laughed nervously. "Oh, wait a minute," he said. "Only 2 out of 28. Hmm. It never occurred to me. I just don't choose people on the basis of gender. But this does raise my consciousness."

Women who are invited to speak encounter other difficulties. Many complain that they are subjected to a level of scrutiny not accorded their male peers, and that withering scrutiny does not come from the men alone.

"When I listen to somebody talk, I tend to find fault with the way a woman speaks more than with a man," said Dr. Marjorie Oettinger, who recently got her doctorate at the Whitehead Institute for Biomedical Research and is already becoming quite well known for her successes in the field of immunology. "If she sounds aggressive, or whiny, or ditzy or schoolmarmish, I notice. I always feel bad about that, but I know I'm more sensitized to how a woman is presenting herself."

Their fear of being unduly criticized may prompt many women to forgo the podium altogether, although it is on the stage where scientists often do the best job of wooing others to believe in their genius and their vision.

"Young women won't talk on a subject unless they really know it and are totally prepared," said Dr. Florence Haseltine of the National Institute for Child Health and Development in Bethesda, Md., who frequently organizes seminars. "They'll say, 'I don't know, I don't feel qualified to do that.' Men will talk about anything. If you ask a man to speak, he'll almost never turn you down."

Another aspect of the scientific culture that can alienate women is its brutality. Scientists often engage in scathing intellectual brawls where they try to demolish the other's results and reasonings, with little regard for the niceties of social etiquette. Women often feel uncomfortable with the demand that they up the insult ante if their research is to be believed.

"Scientists can be like schoolyard toughs," said Dr. Caroline Porco, a planetary scientist at the University of Arizona in Tucson who has been appointed head of NASA's Cassini spacecraft mission, scheduled to fly past Saturn in the early 21st century. "I grew up as the only girl with four brothers, but still I wasn't prepared for what I encountered at Stanford when I went there in 1974, as a graduate student. You'd present your results, and somebody would say, 'How did you get here? Why are you wasting my time? If you had half a brain you could have done that calculation.'"

What is more, said Dr. Porco, if she had had the inclination to respond in kind, "the guys would probably say, 'She's a pushy bitch.'"

Many researchers, men and women alike, said that the greatest changes would probably come with the efforts of women themselves—women like Dr. Christiane Nüsslein-Volhard, a renowned fruit-fly geneticist at the Max Planck Institute in Tubingen and a woman of boundless verve and intelligence. For the past 15 years. Dr. Nüsslein-Volhard has attracted young women from around the world to her laboratory, and those women have in turn become powerhouses in the fruit-fly genetics at the great universities, both here and abroad.

As a result, the study of how the tiny insect develops from fertilization to completion is now dominated by women. "Oh, there are plenty of guys around like me," said Dr. Claude Desplan, a fruit-fly expert at Rockefeller University in New York. "It's a big field, and one of the most exciting fields, and a lot of people are jumping on it. But many, many of the best people are women, and nearly all of them have trained with Christiane."

SHIRLEY M. TILGHMAN

Science

vs.

The Female Scientist

In the last two years, we have witnessed a flurry of concern over the under-representation of women and minorities in science and engineering. The concern does not arise from a belated appreciation that women and minorities have been denied access to careers in science. Rather it comes from projections of a significant shortfall in scientists around the turn of the century, caused, at least in part, by the reduced number of white males choosing scientific careers.

This reminds me of the explanation given by a president of an all-male university for why he favored coeducation. He explained that unless the institution admitted women, it would no longer be able to compete for the best male students, who were being attracted to co-ed campuses. The inclusion of women, in his eyes, was a solution to a problem.

Likewise, today women and minorities are viewed as one solution to a manpower problem in the sciences. Despite the base underpinnings of the motive, this may be a unique opportunity to bring about a greater participation of women and minorities in science. In fact, many universities have commissioned studies on improving recruiting and retention of women students and faculty in science and engineering. Programs abound in government and the philanthropic community to encourage the inclusion of women and minorities.

What are the realistic prospects for these endeavors? First, we need to understand what has stood in the way of women in science.

You can look at the last 20 years in two ways, depending on whether you are an optimist or pessimist. The optimist sees that between 1966 and 1988, the percentage of women receiving science, medical or engineering degrees increased dramatically. In 1966, 23 percent of the bachelor's degrees in science were awarded to women; by 1988, that figure had risen to 40 percent. Women now compose 38 percent of medical school enrollments. As for science doctorates, women earned 9 percent of the total in 1966 and 27 percent in 1988.

The first thing a pessimist would find in the same 20-year span is that the increase in women in scientific and medical careers has not been steady. Most of the increase came in the 1970's, with very little progress after 1982. The second thing a pessimist would note is that the women who have been trained are not in leadership positions in proportion to their representation in the field. The most common response to this is that enough time has not passed for women graduates to have acquired the appropriate seniority. But this is not the case.

Finally, the pessimist would point out that the increases are the average of highly disparate disciplines and hide large differences between fields. For example, in psychology women receive more than half of new doctorates, while in engineering they earn just 7 percent. If you look carefully, almost no progress has been made in increasing the number of women practicing physics, mathematics and engineering in the last 50 years.

Physics and mathematics are clearly at one extreme. In the life sciences, a slightly different dynamic is at work. Fifty percent of bachelor's degrees in biology are awarded to women. There is a drop in graduate and medical schools, where 35 to 40 percent of the graduating classes are female.

Only then do women begin to disappear from the system. By almost every measure, postgraduate women in the life sciences are faring less well than their male colleagues. If one takes as a measure of success those who have reached the status of principal investigator of a

National Institutes of Health grant, just 19 percent are women. Where are the other 19 percent who received M.D.'s and Ph.D.'s? They are in non-tenure-track positions in which they often cannot compete for research funds.

What the different experiences of women in the physical and life sciences tell us is that multiple forces are at work to retard the rate at which women enter the scientific work force. Yet I believe that the common thread is the role that culture plays in determining career choices for women.

The cultural issues begin with the low expectations that our education system sets on the performance of females in science, especially in physics and math. This culminates in the hierarchical culture of the laboratory, which evolved in the absence of females. This notion that cultural biases are at the basis of the problem is sobering, as cultures are difficult to change. However, if we indeed have to change the culture, we need to understand its underpinnings and where the pressure points lie.

Let's begin with education. A study by Joan Girgus for the Pew Charitable Trust Science Education Program revealed that differences in the two sexes can be detected as early as 9 years of age, when girls report fewer science-related experiences, such as looking through a telescope. By 13, girls are less likely than boys to read science articles and books, watch science shows or have science hobbies. The cues girls receive in these formative years are not always subtle. Mattel Inc. recently marketed a Barbie doll that says, "I hate math!" when poked in the stomach. I shudder to think what Ken says back!

Another example comes from the experience of a young assistant professor at Princeton. In high school, she obtained the highest grades in science. Shortly before graduation, her principal called her in and asked if she would be willing to forgo the traditional science award so that the second-ranked student, a male, could receive it. The explanation was that he would be better able to use it, as he was headed for a career in science. To the principal, it was inconceivable that this young woman would also consider such a career.

These are shocking stories, the more so because they occurred in the 1980's and 1990's, not the 1950's. This failure of our society, particularly our educators, to equate women with careers in science, and the propensity to discount their achievements when they persist with this ambition lies at the heart of the problem.

In universities, the trend of discouraging women from science careers continues. The number of declared freshmen science majors of both sexes is three times the number who will actually graduate with a degree in science or engineering. However, the percentage decline is greater for women than men. The only exception to this is instructive: women's colleges lose far fewer of their science undergraduates to other fields. Surely this is telling us that in an environment that places high expectations on women's achievement, women flourish in science.

When questioned about their experiences as science majors, women at co-ed colleges complain of feelings of isolation in a large class of males, of being ignored by faculty and of not being taken seriously. Women who begin college well-qualified and strongly motivated lose their self-esteem.

I think the difference between the numbers who overcome these hurdles in the physical vs. the biological sciences is directly attributable to the number of women practicing each discipline. It is slowly becoming accepted that women make good biologists, and consequently women are no longer discouraged from following this path. Put another way, the rich tend to get richer. All but the most determined women will tend to gravitate to the environment which is most positive and rewarding, and that tends to be where other women have already led the way.

SHIRLEY M. TILGHMAN

Science vs. Women:
A Radical Solution

Science, like all human activity, has its individual cultural milieu. The culture of science evolved in a period when it was being practiced exclusively by men, and that has greatly influenced the outcome. It is a men's game and it continues to be played by men's rules.

Although we would like to believe that scientists are driven by a desire to understand some aspect of the natural world, in fact they are also driven by a desire for personal recognition. Sociologists of science like Robert Merton have identified this need for personal recognition as a motivating force in science. This can lead to behavior which is, at the very least, unattractive: aggressive attacks on competitors, secrecy, sometimes even prevarication.

Linda Wilson, president of Radcliffe and a chemist, recently raised a firestorm by suggesting that the fierce rivalries and ruthless competition among scientists was incompatible with the inclusion of women and minorities in science. She predicted that there will be little change in women's participation until scientific decorum changes. The predictable reaction from men was to extol aggression as the fuel that drives the enterprise and to argue that any attempt to civilize scientific discourse will be its undoing.

Feminists have generally had two responses to this issue. On one side, it has been acknowledged that aggression is a necessary quality for a scientist and that we should be encouraging it in our female students. The opposite view is that women should and will stay out of science so long as it is practiced in such a distasteful way. I find the latter position unappealing at best: ceding the playing field to males will lead to no change. My response is, as much as possible, to encourage my female students to be verbal, confident and curious.

The second cultural aspect that dramatically affects the prospects for women's participation in science careers is the jealous demands on our time. A friend of mine once described science as a black hole, prepared to suck up whatever proportion of your life that you allow it. This complete devotion to science was fostered in the culture of the 50's in which women stayed home and raised families while their husbands conquered the secrets of the universe.

When women began to enter science careers in the 1940's and 1950's, they were expected to renounce any intention of having a family. This is the ultimate un-level playing field, one that persists to this day. Women have paid a terrible price for the success they have realized in the last 20 years. Study after study of all fields, not just science, document that women have forgone marriage and children for their success.

The problem of reconciling a scientific career with some semblance of a normal life is exacerbated by the tenure system. A woman is usually 30 years of age before assuming an assistant professorship at a university, which puts her tenure decision at age 35 to 36. Thus her critical scientific years, in which she is establishing her reputation, and her peak reproductive years coincide. This is a dirty trick. Many in my own generation chose to forgo childbearing until the security of tenure had been granted, only to find that their biological clock had stopped ticking.

Institutions are beginning to grapple with this problem, with different solutions. Some have initiated programs allowing women to have one or more years before the tenure decision to compensate for the time lost in childbearing. Others have adopted policies to allow both fathers and mothers to take this option.

I favor an even more radical solution: abolish tenure entirely, in favor of rolling appointments that are reviewed regularly. Tenure is no friend to women. It does not protect them from institutional discrimination. Rather it rigidifies their career path when they need maximum flexibility.

Ultimately we must solve this conflict between work and family if we hope to increase the participation of women in science. The alternative is to accept that women will never reach parity or continue to pay an unequal price for their success.

It is not sufficient to improve child care, though that is certainly a worthy short-term goal. And I would not advocate a society in which our children are raised by efficient and subsidized surrogate parents. Rather I would like to create a workplace in which our roles in our families and in society are equally valued. I have sat through too many late-night sessions at scientific meetings listening to my male colleagues brag about their busy schedules and long absences from home.

Science will never be a 9-to-5 profession. It just doesn't work that way. There will always be the astrophysicist who has to spend weeks at a telescope on a mountain in Hawaii, the geologist who runs when the volcano blows, the biologist who has to give injections every three hours round the clock.

On the other hand, I don't believe that science must be practiced to the exclusion of all other human activity. The system I object to confuses quantity with quality. It is not the number of hours you work that determines your contributions to science: it is the quality of your insights and your creativity. The distinction between quantity and quality needs to be continually pointed out, and I suspect that it is going to take women to do it. Most important, we must begin by declaring it loud and clear to our students, who still fear that the two are the same.

What are the prospects for changing the cultural milieu to make it more hospitable for women? There is only one solution and that is the recruitment of more women into science. Numbers really matter. When women reach a critical mass in a field, the cultural barriers naturally begin to slip away.

I would suggest that the greatest change will come in institutions that focus in the short term on the senior faculty level. University faculties are extraordinarily hierarchical, and the graduate students and assistant professors at the bottom of the totem pole are very vulnerable. They are excluded from the most serious decisions on hiring and promotion, and often find it difficult to have their voices heard when they are included in decisions.

When women at the lowest level are vocal, they are too often dismissed as strident. Senior women, on the other hand, participate in all aspects of decision-making, and their presence in senior-level deliberations acts as a brake on the more egregious forms of discrimination. They provide the example to young students and faculty that women can have successful science careers. By acting as mentors, they can interpret not just the science, but the scientific culture.

Focusing on the hiring and retention of senior women is clearly not a national solution: there just aren't enough senior women in most fields of science. But it is a solution for institutions eager to change rapidly, and to take a leadership role.

The reason we care so much about this subject is that science is an extraordinary profession. I know of few other professions where the excitement that brought you to the field in the first place is sustained over so many years. It would be a tragedy to exclude women from all this fun.

BRUNO LATOUR AND STEVE WOOLGAR

An Anthropologist
Visits the Laboratory

When an anthropological observer enters the field, one of his most fundamental preconceptions is that he might eventually be able to make sense of the observations and notes which he records. This, after all, is one of the basic principles of scientific enquiry. No matter how confused or absurd the circumstances and activities of his tribe might appear, the ideal observer retains his faith that some kind of a systematic, ordered account is attainable. For a total newcomer to the laboratory, we can imagine that his first encounter with his subjects would severely jeopardise such faith. The ultimate objective of systematically ordering and reporting observations must seem particularly illusory in the face of the barrage of questions which first occur to him. What are these people doing? What are they talking about? What is the purpose of these partitions or these walls? Why is this room in semidarkness whereas this bench is brightly lit? Why is everybody whispering? What part is played by the animals who squeak incessantly in anterooms?

But for our partial familiarity with some aspects of scientific activity and our ability to draw upon a body of common sense assumptions, a flood of nonsensical impressions would follow the formulation of these questions. Perhaps these animals are being processed for eating. Maybe we are witnessing oracular prophecy through the inspection of rats' entrails. Perhaps the individuals spending hours discussing scribbled notes and figures are lawyers. Are the heated debates in front of the blackboard part of some gambling contest? Perhaps the occupants of the laboratory are hunters of some kind, who, after patiently lying in wait by a spectrograph for several hours, suddenly freeze like a gun dog fixed on a scent.

Such speculations and the questions which give rise to them appear nonsensical precisely because we as observers do presuppose some knowledge of what the laboratory could be doing. For example, it is possible to imagine the purpose of walls and partitions without ever having set foot in a laboratory. We attempt to make sense not by bracketing our familiarity with the setting but by using features which we perceive as common both to the setting and to our knowledge or previous experience. Indeed, it would be difficult to provide any sensible account of the laboratory without recourse to our taken-for-granted familiarity with some aspects of science.

Clearly, then, the observer's organisation of questions, observations, and notes is inevitably constrained by cultural affinities. Only a limited set of questions is relevant and hence sensible. In this sense, the notion of a *total* newcomer is unrealisable in practice. At another extreme, an observer's total reliance on scientists' versions of laboratory life would be unsatisfactory. A description of science cast entirely in terms used by scientists would be incomprehensible to outsiders. The adoption of scientific versions of science would teach us little that is new about science in the making; the observer would simply reiterate those accounts provided by scientists when they conduct guided tours of their laboratory for visitors.

In practice, observers steer a middle path between the two extreme roles of total newcomer (an unattainable ideal) and that of complete participant (who in going native is unable usefully to communicate to his community of fellow observers). This is not to deny, of course, that at different stages throughout his research he is severely tempted towards either extreme. His problem is to select a principle of organisation which will enable him to provide an account of the laboratory sufficiently distinct from those given by scientists themselves and yet of sufficient interest to both scientists and readers not familiar with biology. In short, the observer's principle of organisation should provide an Ariadne's thread in a labyrinth of seeming chaos and confusion.

In this chapter, we follow the trials and tribulations of a fictional character, "the observer,"[1] in his attempts to use the notion of literary inscription[2] as a principle for organizing his initial observations of the laboratory.

Literary Inscription

Although our observer shares the same broad cultural knowledge as scientists, he has never seen a laboratory before and has no knowledge of the particular field within which laboratory members are working. He is enough of an insider to understand the general purpose of walls, chairs, coats, and so on, but not enough to know what terms like TRF, Hemoglobin, and "buffer" mean. Even without knowledge of these terms, however, he can not fail to note the striking distinction between two areas of the laboratory. One area of the laboratory (section B on Figure 1) contains various items of apparatus, while the other (section A) contains only books, dictionaries, and papers. Whereas in section B individuals work with apparatus in a variety of ways: they can be seen to be cutting, sewing, mixing, shaking, screwing, marking, and so on; individuals in section A work with written materials: either reading, writing, or typing. Furthermore, although occupants of section A, who do not wear white coats, spend long periods of time with their white-coated colleagues in section B, the reverse is seldom the case. Individuals referred to as doctors read and write in offices in section A while other staff, known as technicians, spend most of their time handling equipment in section B.

Each of sections A and B can be further subdivided. Section B appears to comprise two quite separate wings: in the wing referred to by participants as the "physiology side" there are both animals and apparatus: in the "chemistry side" there are no animals. The people from one wing rarely go into the other. Section A can also be subdivided. On the one hand, there are people who write and engage in telephone conversations; on the other hand, there are those who type and dial telephone calls. This division, like the others, is marked by partitions. In one area (the library) eight offices surround the perimeter of a conference room with table, chairs, and a screen. In the other area ("the secretariat") there are typewriters and people controlling the flow of telephone calls and mail.

What is the relationship between section A ("my office," "the office," "the library") and section B ("the bench")? Consulting the map he has drawn, our observer tries to imagine another institution or setting with a similar division. It is hard to call to mind any factory or administrative organisation which has a similar set up. If, for example, it was a factory, we might expect the office space (section A) to be much smaller. If it was some kind of administrative agency, the bench space (section B) would be entirely superfluous. Although the relation between the two wings of the office space is common to many productive units, the special relation between office space and bench space is sufficient to distinguish the laboratory from other productive units. This is apparent on two counts. Firstly, at the end of each day, technicians bring piles of documents from the

bench space through to the office space. In a factory we might expect these to be reports of what has been processed and manufactured. For members of this laboratory, however, these documents constitute what is yet to be processed and manufactured. Secondly, secretaries post off papers from the laboratory at an average rate of one every ten days. However, far from being *reports* of what has been produced in the factory, members take these papers to be the *product* of their unusual factory. Surely, then, if this unit merely processes paper work, it must be some sort of administrative agency? Not so: even a cursory look at the papers shows that the figures and diagrams which they contain are the very same documents produced in section B a few days or weeks previously.

It occurs to our observer that he might be able to make sense of laboratory activity ac-

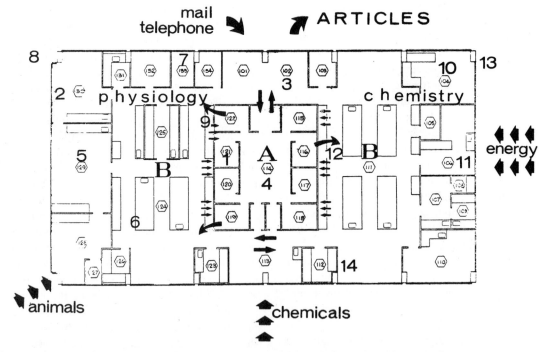

Figure 1   Map of the laboratory showing partitions and the main flows described in the text. The numbers on the map correspond to the photographs in this essay. The map shows the extent to which the differences between sections A and B, and between the chemistry and physiology wings, are reinforced by the architectural layout of the laboratory

Photograph 1   An office desk: the juxtaposition of literatures

cording to one very simple principle. For him, the scene shown in Photograph 1, represents the prototype of scientific work in the laboratory: a desk belonging to one of the inhabitants of the office space (referred to as the doctors) is covered with paperwork. On the left is an opened issue of *Science*. To the right is a diagram which represents a tidied or summarised version of data sheets lying further to the right. *It is as if two types of literature are being juxtaposed:* one type is printed and published outside the laboratory; the other type comprises documents produced within the laboratory, such as hastily drawn diagrams and files containing pages of figures. Beneath the documents at the centre of the desk lies a draft. Just like the drafts of a novel or a report, this draft is scribbled, its pages heavy with corrections, question marks, and alterations. Unlike most novels however, the text of the draft is peppered with references, either to other papers, or to diagrams, tables or documents ("as shown in figure . . . ," "in table . . . we can see that . . . "). Closer inspection of the material lying on the desk (Photograph 1) reveals, for example, that the opened issue of *Science* is cited in the draft. Part of the argument contained in a *Science* article is said in the draft to be unrepeatable by virtue of what is contained in documents lying to the right of the desk. These documents are also cited in the draft. The desk thus appears to be

the hub of our productive unit. For it is here that new drafts are constructed by the juxtaposition of two sources of literature, one originating outside and the other being generated within the laboratory.

It is no surprise to our observer to learn that scientists read published material. What surprises him more is that a vast body of literature emanates from within the laboratory. How is it that the costly apparatus, animals, chemicals, and activities of the bench space combine to produce a written document, and why are these documents so highly valued by participants?

After several further excursions into the bench space, it strikes our observer that its members are compulsive and almost manic writers. Every bench has a large leatherbound book in which members meticulously record what they have just done against a certain code number. This appears strange because our observer has only witnessed such diffidence in memory in the work of a few particularly scrupulous novelists. It seems that whenever technicians are not actually handling complicated pieces of apparatus, they are filling in blank sheets with long lists of figures; when they are not writing on pieces of paper, they spend considerable time writing numbers on the sides of hundreds of tubes, or pencilling large numbers on the fur of rats. Sometimes they use coloured papertape to mark beakers or to index different rows on the glossy surface of a surgical table. The result of this strange mania for inscription is the proliferation of files, documents, and dictionaries. Thus, in addition to the Oxford dictionary and the dictionary of known peptides, we can also find what might be called material dictionaries. For example, Photograph 2 shows a refrigerator which houses racks of samples, each of which bears a label with a ten-figure code number. Similarly, in another part of the laboratory, a vast supply of chemicals has been arranged in alphabetical order on shelves from which technicians can select and make use of appropriate

Photograph 2   Refrigerator containing racks of samples

Photograph 3   In the secretariat: typing the final product

substances. A more obvious example of these material dictionaries is the collection of reprints (Photograph 3, background) and thousands of files full of data sheets, each of which also has its own code number. Quite apart from these labelled and indexed collections is the kind of paperwork (such as invoices, pay cheques, inventory schedules, mail files, and so on) which can be found in most modern productive units.

When the observer moves from the bench space to the office space, he is greeted with yet more writing. Xeroxed copies of articles, with words underlined and exclamation marks in the margins, are everywhere. Drafts of articles in preparation intermingle with diagrams scribbled on scrap paper, letters from colleagues and reams of paper spewed out by the computer in

the next room; pages cut from articles are glued to other pages; excerpts from draft paragraphs change hands between colleagues while more advanced drafts pass from office to office being altered constantly, retyped, recorrected, and eventually crushed into the format of this or that journal. When not writing, the occupants of section A scribble on blackboards (Photograph 4) or dictate letters, or prepare slides for their next talk.

Our anthropological observer is thus confronted with a strange tribe who spend the greatest part of their day coding, marking, altering, correcting, reading, and writing. What then is the significance of those activities which are apparently not related to the marking, writing, coding, and correcting? Photograph 5, for example, shows two young women handling some rats. Despite the protocol sheet to the right, the numbered tubes on the rack and the clock in the foreground which controls the rhythm of the assay, the women themselves are neither writing nor reading. The woman on the left is injecting a liquid with a syringe and withdrawing another liquid with another syringe which she then passes on to the other woman; the second woman then empties the syringe into a tube. It is only then that writing takes over: the time and tube number is carefully recorded. In the

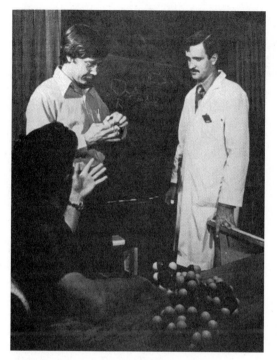

Photograph 4   Discussion in the office space

Photograph 6   A bioassay: at the bench

meantime animals have been killed and various materials, such as ether, cotton, pipettes, syringes, and tubes have been used. What then is the point of killing these animals? How does the consumption of materials relate to the writing activity? Even the careful monitoring of the contents of the rack (Photograph 6)

Photograph 5   A bioassay: the preparatory stage

makes the situation no clearer to our observer. Over a period of several days, tubes are arranged in rows, other liquids are added, the mixtures are shaken and eventually removed for refrigeration.

Periodically, the routine of manipulation and rearrangement of tubes is interrupted. The samples extracted from rats are put into one of the pieces of apparatus and undergo a radical transformation: instead of modifying or labelling the samples, the machine produces a sheet of figures (Photograph 7). One of the participants tears the sheet from the machine's counter and, after scrutinising it carefully, arranges for the disposal of the tubes. In other words, the same tubes which had been carefully handled for a week, which had cost time and effort to the tune of several hundred dollars, were now regarded as worthless. The focus of attention shifted to a sheet of figures. Fortunately, our observer was quite used to finding such absurd and erratic behavior in

Photograph 7   A bioassay: output from the gamma counter

the subjects of his studies. Relatively unperturbed, therefore, he braced himself for his next surprise.

It was not long in coming. The sheet of figures, taken to be the end result of a long assay, was used as the input to a computer (Photograph 8). After a short time, the computer printed out a data sheet and it was this, rather than the original sheet of figures, which was regarded as the important product of the operation. The sheet of figures was merely filed alongside thousands like it in the library. Nor was the series of transformations yet complete. Photograph 9 shows a technician at work on several data sheets produced by the computer. Soon after this photograph was taken, she was called into one of the offices to show the product of her labours: a single elegant curve carefully drawn on graph paper. Once again, the focus of attention shifted: the computer data sheets were filed away and it was the peaks and slopes of the curve which excited comment from participants in their offices: "how striking," "a well differentiated peak," "it goes down quite fast," "this spot is not very different from this one." A few days later, the observer could see a neatly redrawn version of the same curve in a paper sent out for possible publication. If accepted, this same figure would be seen by others when they read the article and it was more than likely that the same figure would eventually sit on some other desk as part

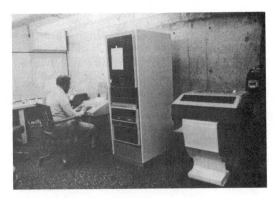

Photograph 8   The computer room

Photograph 9   Cleaning up the data

of a renewed process of literary juxtaposition and construction.

The whole series of transformations, between the rats from which samples are initially extracted and the curve which finally appears in publication, involves an enormous quantity of sophisticated apparatus (Photograph 10). By contrast with the expense and bulk of this apparatus, the end product is no more than a curve, a diagram, or a table of figures written on a frail sheet of paper. It is this document, however, which is scrutinised by participants for its "significance" and which is used as "evidence" in part of an argument or in an article. Thus, the main upshot of the prolonged series of transformations is a document which, as will become clear, is a crucial resource in the construction of a "substance." In some situations, this process is very much shorter. In the chemistry wing in particular, the use of certain pieces of apparatus makes it easy to get the impression that substances directly provide their own "signatures" (Photograph 11). While participants in the office space struggle with the writing of new drafts, the laboratory around them is itself a hive of writing activity. Sections of muscle, light beams, even shreds of blotting paper activate various recording equipment. And the scientists themselves base their own writing on the written output of the recording equipment.

It is clear, then, that particular significance can be attached to the operation of apparatus which provides some kind of written output. Of course, there are various items of apparatus in the laboratory which do not have this function. Such "machines" transform matter between one state and another. Photograph 12, for example, shows a rotary evaporator, a centrifuge, a shaker, and a grinder. By contrast, a number of other items of apparatus, which we shall call "inscription devices,"[3] transform pieces of matter into written documents. More exactly, an inscription device is any item of apparatus or particular configuration of such items which can transform a material substance into a figure or diagram which is directly usable by one of the members of the office space. As we shall see later, the particular arrangement of apparatus can have a vital significance for the production of a useful inscription. Furthermore, some of the components of such a configuration are of little consequence by themselves. For example, the counter shown in Photograph 7 is not itself an inscription device since its output is not directly usable in an argument. It does, however, form part of an inscription device known as a bioassay.[4]

An important consequence of this notion of inscription device is that inscriptions are regarded as having a direct relationship to "the original substance." The final diagram or curve thus provides the focus of discussion about properties of the substance. The intervening material activity and all aspects of what is often

Photograph 10 The nuclear magnetic resonance spectrometer

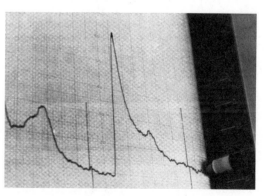

Photograph 11 Traces from the automatic amino acid analyser

Photograph 12   The chemistry section

Photograph 13   View from the laboratory roof

a prolonged and costly process are bracketed off in discussions about what the figure means. The process of writing articles about the substance thus takes the end diagram as a starting point. Within the office space, participants produce articles by comparing and contrasting such diagrams with other similar diagrams and with other articles in the published literature.

At this point, the observer felt that the laboratory was by no means quite as confusing as he had first thought. It seemed that there might be an essential similarity between the inscription capabilities of apparatus, the manic passion for marking, coding, and filing, and the literary skills of writing, persuasion, and discussion. Thus, the observer could even make sense of such obscure activities as a technician grinding the brains of rats, by realising that the eventual end product of such activity might be a highly valued diagram. Even the most complicated jumble of figures might eventually end up as part of some argument between "doctors." For the observer, then, the laboratory began to take on the appearance of a system of literary inscription.

From this perspective, many hitherto strange occurrences fell into place. Many other types of activity, although superficially unrelated to the literary theme, could be seen as means of obtaining inscriptions. For example, the energy

inputs (Photograph 13) represented intermediary resources to be consumed in the process of ensuring that inscription devices functioned properly. By also taking into account the supply of animals and chemicals, it was clear that a cycle of production which ended in a small folder of figures might have cost several thousand dollars. Similarly, the technicians and doctors who comprised the work force represented one further kind of input necessary for the efficient operation of the inscription devices and for the production and dispatch of articles. . . .

The Culture of the Laboratory

To those familiar with the work of the laboratory, the above account will have little to say that is new. For an anthropologist, however, the notion of literary inscription is still problematic. As we said earlier, our observer has an intermediary status: while the broad cultural values which he shares with the scientists facilitate some familiarity with the commonplace objects and events in the laboratory, he is unwilling solely to rely on scientists' own versions of the way the laboratory operates. One consequence of his intermediary status is that his account so far has failed to satisfy any one audience. It could be said, for example, that in portraying scientists as readers and writers he has said nothing of the *substance* of their reading and writing. Indeed, our observer incurred the considerable anger of members of the laboratory, who resented their representation as participants in some literary activity. In the first place, this failed to distinguish them from any other writers. Secondly, they felt that the important point was that they were writing *about* something, and that this something was "neuroendocrinology." Our observer experienced the depressing sensation that his Ariadne's thread had led him up a blind alley. . . .

Articles about Neuroendocrinology

Our observer noticed that when asked by a total stranger, members of the laboratory replied that they worked (or were) "in neuroendocrinology." They went on to explain that neuroendocrinology was the result of a hybridisation which had taken place in the 1940s between neurology, described as the science of the nervous system, and endocrinology, the science of the hormonal system. It occurred to our observer that such location "in a field" facilitated the correspondence between a particular group, network, or laboratory and a complex mixture of beliefs, habits, systematised knowledge, exemplary achievements, experimental practices, oral traditions, and craft skills. Although referred to as the "culture" in anthropology, this latter set of attributes is commonly subsumed under the term paradigm when applied to people calling themselves scientists.[5] Neuroendocrinology seemed to have all the attributes of a mythology: it had had its precursors, its mythical founders, and its revolutions (Meites et al., 1975). In its simplest version, the mythology goes as follows: After World War II it was realised that nerve cells could also secrete hormones and that there is no nerve connection between brain and pituitary to bridge the gap between the central nervous system and the hormonal system. A competing perspective, designated the "hormonal feedback model" was roundly defeated after a long struggle by participants who are now regarded as veterans (Scharrer and Scharrer, 1963). As in many mythological versions of the scientific past, the struggle is now formulated in terms of a fight between abstract entities such as models and ideas. Consequently, present research appears based on one particular conceptual event, the explanation of which only merits scant elaboration by scientists. The following is a typical account: "In the 1950s there was a sudden crystallization of ideas, whereby a number of scattered and apparently unconnected results suddenly made sense and were intensely gathered and reviewed." . . .

After his first few days in the setting, our observer was no longer told about neuroendocrinology. Instead, daily concerns focussed on a different set of specific cultural values which, although from time to time talked about as being in neuroendocrinology, appeared to constitute a distinct culture. . . . Our criteria for identifying this specific culture is not simply that a specialty represents a subset of a larger discipline. . . . We use culture to refer to the set of arguments and beliefs to which there is a constant appeal in daily life and which is the object of all passions, fears, and respect. Participants in our laboratory said that they were dealing with "substances called releasing factors" (for popular accounts, see Guillemin and Burgus, 1972; Schally et al., 1973; Vale, 1976). When they presented their work to scientifically informed outsiders, they formulated their efforts as attempting "to isolate, characterize, synthesise and understand the modes of action of releasing factors. "This is the brief that distinguishes them from their other colleagues in neuroendocrinology. It is also their cultural trait, their particularity, and their horizon of work and achievement. The general mythology provides them with the tenet that the brain controls the endocrine system, and

Table 1

First Programme (isolation of new substance)	31 papers	15% of total
Second Programme: Total (analogs and functions)	78 papers	37% of total
Task One (analogs)	—	—
Task Two (structure function)	52 papers	24% of total
Task Three (clinical)	19 papers	9% of total
Task Four (basic chemistry)	7 papers	3% of total
Third Programme (mode of actions)	47 papers	22% of total
Technical Papers	20 papers	9% of total
General Articles	27 papers	13% of total
Others	10 papers	5% of total
Total	213 papers	

they share this with a large cultural group of neuroendocrinologists. Specific to their own culture, however, is an additional postulate that "control by the brain is mediated by discrete chemical substances, so called releasing factors, which are of a peptidic nature" (Meites, 1970). Their skills, working habits, and the apparatus at their disposal are all organised around one specific material (the hypothalamus), which is deemed especially important for the study of releasing factors. . . .

. . . Our observer should now be able to discern several distinct lines of activity in the laboratory, each of which corresponds to a specific type of article which is finally produced. For each type he should be able to identify the individuals concerned, their location in the laboratory, the technicians who assist, the inscription devices employed, and the type of outside literature to which their work relates. Three main lines of article production, referred to by participants as "programmes," could be clearly differentiated at the time of the study. As can be seen from Table 1, they do not contribute equally to the overall output of the laboratory, nor do they have the same cost and subsequent impact. By examining the three

programmes in some detail, our observer hoped to be able to specify which characteristics of activity were peculiar to this laboratory.

The *first* type of article written in this laboratory concerned *new natural* substances in the hypothalamus. . . . A substance is obtained by superimposing two sets of inscriptions, one from a recording device known as an assay in the physiology side of the laboratory and the other from "purification cycles" carried out in the chemistry side. Since the assay and purification cycle are inscription devices common to all three programmes, we shall describe them in some detail.

Despite the many different types of activity referred to as assays (for example, the bioassay, the *in vitro* and *in vivo* assays, direct or indirect assays, radioimmunological or biological assays) they are all based on the same principle (Rodgers, 1974). A recording mechanism (such as a myograph, a gamma counter, or a simple rating sheet) is connected up to an organism (either a cell, a muscle, or a whole animal) so as to produce an easily readable trace. A substance with a known effect on the organism is then administered to the organism as a control. The effect on the organism is inscribed and its recorded trace is taken as a baseline. An unknown substance is then administered and its effect recorded. The result is a recorded *difference* between two traces, a difference about which simple perceptive judgments ("it is the same," "it goes up," "there is a peak") can be made. If there is a difference, it is taken as the sign of an "activity" in the unknown substance. Since the central objective of the culture is to define any activity in terms of a discrete chemical entity, the unknown substance is taken to the other side of the laboratory for tests in the second main type of inscription device, the purification cycle.

The goal of the purification cycle is to isolate the entity which is believed to have caused the recorded difference between two traces. Samples of brain extract are subjected to a series of *discriminations* (Anonymous, 1974). This entails the use of some stationary material (such as a gel or a piece of blotting paper) as a selective sift which delays the gradual movement of a sample of brain extract. (This movement can be variously due to gravity, electric forces, or cellular binding—Heftmann, 1967.) As a result of this process, samples are transformed into a large number of fractions, each of which can be scrutinised for physical properties of interest. The results are recorded in the form of several peaks on graph paper. Each of these peaks represents a discriminated fraction, one of which may correspond to the discrete chemical entity which caused an activity in the assay. In order to discover whether the entity is present, the fractions are taken back to the physiology section of the laboratory and again take part in an assay. By superimposing the result of this last assay with the result of the previous purification, it is possible to see an overlap between one peak and another. If the overlap can be repeated, the chemical fraction is referred to as a "substance" and is given a name.

Ideally, this shuttle between the assay (Photograph 5) and the purification cycle (Photograph 14) ends with the identification of an "isolated" substance. This is almost never the

case, however, because most of the differences between activities in the assay disappear when the assay is repeated. The postulated substance CRF, for example, has been shuttling to and fro in six laboratories since 1954. . . . Even when differences between activities do not disappear, the entity can often no longer be traced after a few steps of purification. . . . The elimination of these elusive and transitory substances (known as "artefacts") is the main concern of the tribe. Although the details of the elimination process are extremely complex, the general principle is simple.

Since most competitors' claims to have an "isolated" substance are put into quotation marks, it follows that the assertion that an entity is "isolated" depends primarily on the operation of local criteria. When this claim has been made within the laboratory, the chemical fraction breaks out of the shuttle between assay

Photograph 14 Fractionating columns

and purification and switches to another circuit of operations. This new circuit comprises an inscription device known as an Amino Acid Analyser (AAA), which automatically records the effects of the isolated sample on a series of other chemical "reagents" and allows this effect to be directly read in terms of certain letters of the amino acid vocabulary. Thus, the inscription of the substance is decipherable in letters, such as, for example, Glu, Pyro, His, rather than just in terms of peaks, spots, and slopes. However, this is not the end of the matter. By this stage, each component amino acid is known; but the particular order of the amino acids has not yet been determined. To do this, the previous samples are taken to another room, where there are expensive inscription devices handled by full-time "Ph.D. holders." The two main inscription devices, the "mass spectrometer" and the "Edmann degradation sequence," provide written spectra and diagrams which allow the specification of the configuration of amino acids which are present in the substance. These are great and rare moments in the work of the first programme. The determination of structure constitutes the most exciting and exhausting periods of work, which are remembered vividly by participants many years after. . . .

The concern of a *second* main programme in the laboratory is to reconstruct substances (whose structure has already been determined), using amino acids supplied by the chemical industry, and to evaluate their activity. The main objective of this programme is to produce artificially reconstructed substances, known as analogs, with properties which, because they are different from the original substances, will facilitate their use in medicine or physiology. The second research programme can be divided into four tasks. The first task is the chemical production of analogs. Instead of buying analogs or obtaining them from another investigator, the laboratory can supply substances relatively cheaply in its own inhouse chemical section. The production of analogs is largely mechanised, using apparatus such as the peptide automatic synthetizer. Many of the analytical inscription devices (such as the mass spectrometer, the amino acid analyser, or the nuclear magnetic resonance spectrometer) which are used in the original purification of a substance are also used in its artificial reconstruction. In the second programme, however, these inscription devices are used to monitor the reconstruction process rather than to produce new information. The second task concerns so-called "structure function relationships." Using a number of slightly different analogs, physiologists try to identify connections between bioassay effects and combinations of analogs which give rise to them. For example, the natural substance which inhibits the release of a substance called growth hormone, is a fourteen amino acid structure. By substituting a right-handed form for the left-handed form of the amino acid at the eighth position, a more potent substance is obtained. This has major implications for the treatment of diabetes. Consequently, the outcome of these kinds of trial and error operations, which make up 24 percent of published papers, are of special interest to funding agencies and to the chemical industry (Latour and Rivier, 1977). A third task, which makes up to 9 percent of published papers, concerns the determination of structure function relationships in the effect of substances on humans. Most of the papers which result from this work are written in collaboration with clinicians. The aim is to devise analogs which most nearly match the natural substances required for clinical purposes. It would be desirable, for example, to devise an analog of LRF which would inhibit the release of LH instead of triggering it. This would make possible the production of a much better contraceptive pill than at present and thus represents a highly prized (and highly funded) research objective. The fourth and last task, which makes up only 3 percent of total research output, comprises research in collaboration with fundamental chemists on the configuration of molecules which make up the substance. The role of the laboratory in this work is mainly the provision of material, but the results are nevertheless very important for studies of "structure-function relationships."[6] As in the third task, first authors of papers resulting from this fourth task are based outside the laboratory.

So far we have discussed two main programmes: the isolation of new natural substances on the one hand and their reproduction by synthesis on the other. A *third* programme is said by participants to be aimed at understanding the mechanisms by which different substances interact. This work is carried out in the physiology section of the laboratory using bioassays. A variety of different trails, ranging from those generating crude behavioural responses to those which record the rate of DNA synthesis following hormonal contact, are used to try and access how substances react together.

In terms of published papers, these three programmes accounted respectively for 15 percent, 37 percent, and 22 percent of the total output from the laboratory between 1970 and 1976. It is rarely the case, however, that participants refer to the programme in which they are working. The specification and particular arrangement of apparatus does not in itself correspond to the self-perceptions of work which they hold. Rather than saying, "I am doing purification," for example, they are much more likely to say, "I am purifying substance X." It is not purification in general which concerns them, but "the isolation of CRF": it is not the synthesis of analogs, but the study of "DTRP8SS." Furthermore, objectives of each programme change in the course of a few months. Our notion of programme is thus inadequate in that it is merely an intermediary device which our observer has used in becoming familiar with his setting. On the other hand, our observer now knows what distinguishes this laboratory from others and which papers are written on the basis of particular combinations of staff and inscription devices. . . .

The "Phenomenotechnique"

. . . It would be wrong to contrast the material with conceptual components of laboratory activity. The inscription devices, skills, and machines which are now current have often featured in the past literature of *another field*. Thus, each sequence of actions and each routinised assay has at some stage featured as the object of debate in another field and has been the focus of several published papers. The apparatus and craft skills present in one field thus embody the end results of debate or controversy in some other field and make these results available within the walls of the laboratory. It is in this sense that Bachelard (1953) referred to apparatus as "reified theory." The inscription device provides inscriptions which can be used to write papers or to make points in the literature on the basis of a transformation of established arguments into items of apparatus. This transformation, in turn, allows the generation of new inscriptions, new arguments and potentially new items of apparatus. . . . When, for example, a member of the laboratory uses a computer console (Photograph 8), he mobilises the power of both electronics and statistics. When another member handles the NMR spectrometer (Photograph 10) to check the purity of his compounds, he is utilising spin theory and the outcome of some twenty years of basic physics research. Although Albert knows little more than the general principles of spin theory, this is sufficient to enable him to handle the switchboard of the NMR and to have the power of the theory working to his advantage. When others discuss the spatial structure of a releasing factor, they implicitly make use of decades of research in elementary chemistry. Similarly, a few principles of immunology and a general knowledge of radioactivity are sufficient to benefit from these two sciences when using the radioimmunoassay in the quest for a new substance (Yalow and Berson, 1971). Every move in the laboratory thus relies in some way on other scientific fields. . . . By borrowing well-established knowledge, and by incorporating it in pieces of furniture or in routine operational sequences, the laboratory can harness the enormous power of tens of other fields for its own purposes.

However, the accumulation of material theories and practices from other fields itself depends on certain manufacturing skills. For example, the mere existence of a discipline such as nuclear physics does not in itself ensure the presence of a beta-counter in the laboratory. Clearly, the use of such equipment presupposes their manufacture. Without Merrifield's invention, for example, there would be no solid phase synthesis and no way of automating peptide synthesis (Merrifield, 1965; 1968). But even without a company like Beckmann, there would still be a prototype at the Rockefeller Institute where it was invented and this could be used by other scientists. Apart from the automatic pipette, a simple time-saving device, both the principle and basic prototype of all the other apparatus used in the laboratory originated in other scientific laboratories. However, industry plays an important role in designing, developing, and making these scientific prototypes available to a larger public, as is clear if we imagine that there were only one or two existing prototypes of each item of new equipment. In this case, scientists would have to travel vast distances and there would be a dramatic fall in the rate of production of papers. The transformation of Merrifield's original prototype into the marketable, self-contained reliable, and compact item of equipment sold under the name of Automatic Peptide Synthesizer, is a measure of the debt of the laboratory to technological skills (Anonymous, 1976). If inscription devices are the reification of theories and practices, the actual pieces of equipment are the marketed forms of these reifications.

The material layout of the laboratory has been constructed from items of apparatus, many of which have long and sometimes controversial histories. Each item of apparatus has combined with certain skills to form specific devices, the styluses and needles of which scratch the surface of sheets of graph paper. The string of events to which each curve owes its very existence is too long for any observer, technician, or scientist to remember. And yet each step is crucial, for its omission or mishandling can nullify the entire process. Instead of a "nice curve," it is all too easy to obtain a chaotic scattering of random points of curves which cannot be replicated. To counter these catastrophic possibilities, efforts are made to routinise component actions either through technicians' training or by automation. Once a string of operations has been routinised, one can look at the figures obtained and quietly forget that immunology, atomic physics, statistics, and electronics actually made this figure possible. Once the data sheet has been taken to the office for discussion, one can forget the several weeks of work by technicians and the hundreds of dollars which have gone into its production. After the paper which incorporates these figures has been written, and the main result of the paper has been embodied in some new inscription device, it is easy to forget that the construction of the paper depended on material factors. The bench space will be forgotten, and the existence of laboratories will fade from consideration. Instead, "ideas," "theories," and "reasons" will take their place. Inscription devices thus appear to be valued on the basis of the extent to which they facilitate a swift transition from craft work to ideas. The material setting both makes possible the phenomena and is required to be easily forgotten. . . .

Documents and Facts

Thus far, our observer has begun to make sense of the laboratory in terms of a tribe of readers and writers who spend two-thirds of their time working with large inscription devices. They appear to have developed considerable skills in setting up devices which can pin down elusive figures, traces, or inscriptions in their craftwork, and in the art of persuasion. The latter skill enables them to convince others that what they do is important, that what they say is true, and that their proposals are worth funding. They are so skillful, indeed, that they manage to convince others not that they are being convinced but that they are simply following a consistent line of interpretation of available evidence. Others are persuaded that they are not persuaded, that no mediations intercede between what is said and the truth. They are so persuasive, in fact, that within the confines of their laboratory it is possible to forget the material dimensions of the laboratory, the bench work, and the influence of the past, and to focus only on the "facts" that are being pointed out. Not surprisingly, our anthropological observer experienced some dis-ease in handling such a tribe. Whereas other tribes believe in gods or complicated mythologies, the members of this tribe insist that their activity is in no way to be associated with beliefs, a culture, or a mythology. Instead, they claim to be concerned only with "hard facts." The observer is puzzled precisely because his informants insist that everything is straightforward. Moreover, they argue that if he were a scientist himself, he would understand this. Our anthropologist is sorely tempted by this argument. He has begun to learn about the laboratory, he has read lots of papers and can recognise different substances. Furthermore, he begins to understand fragments of conversation between members. His informants begin to sway him. He begins to admit that there is nothing strange about this setting and nothing which requires explanation in terms other than those of informants' own accounts. However, in the back of his mind there remains a nagging question. How can we account for the fact that in any one year, approximately one and a half million dollars is spent to enable twenty-five people to produce forty papers?

Apart from the papers themselves, of course, another kind of product provides the means for generating documents in other laboratories. As we said above, two of the main objectives of this laboratory are the purification of natural substances and the manufacture of analogs of known substances. Frequently, purified fractions and samples of synthetic substances are sent to investigators in other laboratories. Each analog is produced at an average cost of $1,500, or $10 per milligram, which is much lower than the market value of these peptides. Indeed, the market value of all peptides produced by the laboratory would amount to $1.5 million, the same as the total budget of the laboratory. In other words, the laboratory could pay for its research by selling its analogs. However, the quantities, the number, and the nature of the peptides actually produced by the laboratory are such that there is no market for 99 percent of them. Moreover, nearly all the peptides (90 percent) are manufactured for internal consumption and are not available as output. The actual output (for example, 3.2 grams in 1976) is potentially worth $130,000 at market value, and although it cost only $30,000 to produce, samples are sent free of charge to outside researchers who have been able to convince one of the members of the laboratory that his or her research is of interest. Although members of the laboratory do not require their names to appear on papers which report work resulting from the use of these samples, the ability to provide rare and costly analogs is a powerful resource. If, for example, only a few micrograms were made available, this would effectively prevent the recipient from carrying out sufficient investigations to make a discovery . . .[7] Purified substances and rare antisera are also considered valuable assets. When, for example, a participant talks about leaving the group, he often expresses concern about the fate of the antiseras, fractions, and samples for which he has been responsible. It is these, together with the papers he has produced, that represent the riches needed by a participant to enable him to settle elsewhere and write further papers. He is likely to find similar inscription devices elsewhere, but not the idiosyncratic antisera that permit a specific radioimmunoassay to be run.

Besides samples, the laboratory also produces skills in the members of a workforce who from time to time leave the laboratory to work elsewhere. Here again, the skill is only a means to the end of publishing a paper.

The production of papers is acknowledged by participants as the main objective of their activity. . . .

The Publication List

The range and scope of papers produced by the laboratory is indicated by a list kept and updated by participants. We used those items listed between 1970 and 1976. Although referred to by participants as the "publication list," a number of articles were included which had not in fact been published.[8]

Let us classify output according to the channel chosen by investigators. Fifty percent consisted of "regular" papers. Such items comprised several pages and were published in professional journals. Twenty percent of the output comprised abstracts submitted to professional congresses. A further 16 percent comprised solicited contributions to meetings, only half of which found their way into print as conference proceedings. Participants also contributed chapters to edited collections of papers, which made up 14 percent of the total output.

Another way of classifying papers is by the literary "genre" of articles. Differences in genre were defined both in terms of formal characteristics (such as the size, style, and format of each article) and by the nature of the audience. For example, 5 percent of all papers were addressed to lay audiences, such as lay readers of *Scientific American*, *Triangle*, and *Science Year* or to physicians for whom a simplified account of recent progress in biology is available in articles, such as those in *Clinician*, *Contraception*, or *Hospital Practice*. Although a relatively minor output in terms of quantity, this genre fulfills an important public relations function in that

such articles can be useful in the long-term acquisition of public funds. A second genre, which made up 27 percent of total output, addressed scientists working outside the releasing factors field. Sample titles included: "Hypothalamus Releasing Hormones," "Physiology and Chemistry of the Hypothalamus," and "Hypothalamic Hormones: Isolation, Characterisation and Structure Function." The details of specific substances and assays or of the relations between them were rarely discussed in these kinds of articles, which could be found most frequently in advanced textbooks, reference books, nonspecialised journals, book reviews, and invited lectures. The information in these articles was often utilised by students or by colleagues in outside fields. Such papers are both incomprehensible to laymen and unremarkable to colleagues within the field of releasing factors. They simply summarize the state of the art for scientists outside the field. A third genre, which made up 13 percent of the total output, included titles such as: "Luteinizing Releasing Factor and Somatostatin Analogs: Structure Function Relationships," "Biological Activities of SS," and "Chemistry and Physiology of Ovine and Synthetic TRF and LRF." These articles were specialised to the extent that they made little sense outside the specialty. They were characterised by an unusually high number of coauthors (5.7 compared with an average of 3.8 for all papers) and were usually presented at professional meetings within the field such as the Endocrine Society Meetings and Peptide Chemistry Symposia. Articles in this third genre enabled colleagues to catch up on the latest available information. Lastly, a genre which made up 55 percent of the total output comprised highly specialised articles as indicated by the following example titles: "(Gly) 2LRF and Des His LRF. The synthesis purification and characterisation of two LRF analogs antagonists to LRF" and "Somatostatin inhibits the release of acetylcholine induced electrically in the myenteric plexus."

Such articles, which aimed to convey minute pieces of information to a select band of insiders, were published mainly in journals such as *Endocrinology* (18 percent), *BBRC* (10 percent), and *Journal of Medical Chemistry* (10 percent). Whereas papers falling within the first and second genres were thought to be important in a teaching context, only those articles in the latter two genres (the insider reviews and specialised articles) were regarded by members of the laboratory as containing new information.

By dividing the annual budget of the laboratory by the number of articles published (and at the same time discounting those articles in the laymen's genre), our observer calculated that the cost of producing a paper was $60,000 in 1975 and $30,000 in 1976. Clearly, papers were an expensive commodity! . . .

Conclusion

. . . By pursuing the notion of literary inscription, our observer has been able to pick his way through the labyrinth. He can now explain the objectives and products of the laboratory in his own terms, and he can begin to understand how work is organised. . . . He can see that both main sections (A and B) of the laboratory are part of the same process of literary inscription. The so-called material elements of the laboratory are based upon the reified outcomes of past controversies which are available in the published literature. As a result, it is these same material elements which allow papers to be written and points to be made. Furthermore, the anthropologist feels vindicated in having retained his anthropological perspective in the face of the beguiling charms of his informants: they claimed merely to be scientists discovering facts; he doggedly argued that they were writers and readers in the business of being convinced and convincing others. Initially this had seemed a moot or even absurd standpoint, but now it appeared far more reasonable. The problem for participants was to persuade read-

ers of papers (and constituent diagrams and figures) that its statements should be accepted as fact. To this end rats had been bled and beheaded, frogs had been flayed, chemicals consumed, time spent, careers had been made or broken, and inscription devices had been manufactured and accumulated within the laboratory. This, indeed, was the very raison d'être of the laboratory. By remaining steadfastly obstinate, our anthropological observer resisted the temptation to be convinced by the facts. Instead, he was able to portray laboratory activity as the organisation of persuasion through literary inscription. Has the anthropologist himself been convincing? Has he used sufficient photographs, diagrams, and figures to persuade his readers not to qualify his statements . . ., and to adopt his assertions that a laboratory is a system of literary inscription? . . .

Notes

1. We stress that "the observer" is a fictional character so as to draw attention to the process whereby we are engaged in constructing an account. The essential similarity of our procedures for constructing accounts and those used by laboratory scientists in generating and sustaining facts will become clear in the course of our discussion.
2. The notion of inscription as taken from Derrida (1977) designates an operation more basic than writing (Dagognet, 1973). It is used here to summarize all traces, spots, points, histograms, recorded numbers, spectra, peaks, and so on. See below.
3. See note 2.
4. This notion of inscription device is sociological by nature. It allows one to describe a whole set of occupations in the laboratory, without being disturbed by the wide variety of their material shapes. For example, a "bioassay for TRF" counts as *one* inscription device even though it takes five individuals three weeks to operate and occupies several rooms in the laboratory. Its salient feature is the final production of a figure. . . .
5. Our observer was well aware of the popularisation of the term due to Kuhn (1970) and of the subsequent debates over its ambiguity and significance for models of scientific development (see, for example, Lakatos and Musgrave, 1970).

6. The observer would be told, for example, that "when a chemist shows the spatial configuration of somatostatin is such that a particular amino acid is very exposed on the outside of the molecular structure; it may be that by replacing or protecting it, some new activity will be observed."

7. These calculations are only approximate: they are based on the overall budget of the laboratory as computed from grant applications. The activation of the laboratory cost about one million dollars. This was simply to connect the space to the rest of the institute (Photograph 1); buying the equipment on the general market cost approximately $300,000 a year; Ph.D. holders earn an average of $25,000 a year, while for technicians the figure is nearer $19,000 a year. The total wage bill tops half a million dollars a year. The total budget of the laboratory is one and a half million dollars a year.

8. The advantage of a well-kept publication list is that it includes every item produced by the group, including rejected articles, unpublished lectures, abstracts, and so on. The following figures are intended to convey an idea of the scale of article production. Of course, only a stable laboratory can provide a reliable publication list.

References

Anonymous (1974) "Sephadex: Gel Filtration in Theory and Practice." Uppsala: Pharmacia.
———— (1976) B.L.'s interview. Oct. 19. Dallas.
Bachelard, G. (1953) *Le matérialisme rationnel*. Paris: P.U.F.
Dagognet , F. (1973) *Ecriture et iconographie*. Paris: Vrin.
Derrida, J. (1977) *Of Grammatology*. Baltimore: Johns Hopkins University Press.
Guillemin, R. and Burgus, R. (1972) "The hormones of the hypothalamus." *Scientific American* 227(5): pp. 24–33.
Heftmann, E. [ed.] (1967) *Chromatography*. New York: Van Nostrand Reinhold.
Kuhn, T. (1970) *The Structure of Scientific Revolutions*. Chicago: University of Chicago Press.
Lakatos, I. & Musgrave, A. (1970) *Criticism and the Growth of Knowledge*. Cambridge: Cambridge University Press.
Latour, B. and Rivier, J. (1977, forthcoming) "Sociology of a molecule."
Meites, J. [ed.] (1970) *Hypophysiotropic Hormones of the Hypothalamus*. Baltimore: Williams and Wilkins.
————, Donovan B., and McCann, S. (1975) *Pioneers in Neuroendocrinology*. New York: Plenum Press.
Merrifield, R. B. (1965) "Automated synthesis of peptides." *Science* 150 (8; Oct.): pp. 178–189.
———— (1968) "The automatic synthesis of proteins." *Scientific American* 218 (3): pp. 56–74.
Rodgers, R. C. (1974) *Radio Immuno Assay Theory for Health Care Professionals*. Hewlett Packard.
Schally, A. V., Arimura, A., and Kastin, A. J. (1973) "Hypothalamic regulatory hormones." Science 179 (Jan. 26): pp. 341–350.
Scharrer, E. and Scharrer, B. (1963) *Neuroendocrinology*. New York: Columbia University Press.
Vale, W. (1976) "Messengers from the Brain." *Science Year* 1976. Chicago: F.E.E.C.
Yalow, R. S. and Berson, S. A. (1971) "Introduction and general consideration." In E. Odell and O. Daughaday (eds.) *Principles of Competitive Protein Binding Assays*. Philadelphia: J. B. Lippincott.

PART II

THE EMPIRICAL BASIS OF SCIENTIFIC KNOWLEDGE

Does scientific knowledge provide us with true representations of the world (the scientific realist position), or only with representations that are useful for various purposes, such as for prediction and control of the environment (the scientific anti-realist position)? The answer to this question will depend heavily on the nature of the empirical basis of scientific knowledge—that is, the "facts" by which the theories of science are tested and judged acceptable or unacceptable—and the nature of the testing procedures themselves. In this part we shall investigate the empirical basis of scientific knowledge. In the next part we shall investigate the testing procedures.

It would seem as though the empirical basis of scientific knowledge should pose no problems for scientific realism. After all, scientific knowledge purports to be knowledge of the empirical world, the world we observe every day. So, if the empirical basis of scientific knowledge merely includes reports of those observations, then the empirical basis of scientific knowledge should provide us with true representations of the world. Of course two conditions must be met:

1. The reports of observations must express only what is directly observed. They must not go beyond what is directly observed, or else they will say more than can be justified by those observations.

2. What is directly observed must correspond to what is there in the world, as measured by what other people also observe. It must contain nothing that is personal or subjective or idiosyncratic.

If the empirical basis of scientific knowledge satisfies both of these conditions, then it should provide us with true representations of the world. And if scientific knowledge includes only this basis and the claims (e.g., theories) that can be supported on this basis, then scientific knowledge should provide us with true representations of the world as well.

But *does* the empirical basis of scientific knowledge satisfy both of these conditions? Consider, for example, part of Nobel prize winner Barbara McClintock's description of what she observed when studying the meiotic cycle of *Neurospora* (the process of two consecutive cell divisions by which the number of chromosomes is reduced from the diploid (paired) number found in somatic cells to the haploid (unpaired) number found in gametes):

> The major thing I found out was that in the perithecium [fruiting body], where the asci [oval sacs containing the sexual zygotes] are going to be found, you get fusion of the nuclei from the two parents. Now what happens is that these nuclei go into prophase [the initial stage of the process, during which chromosomes appear within the nucleus and undergo pairing] and then fuse following the prophase. There is a big nucleolus [a dense body residing in the nucleus, containing RNA and protein], and I could see that these chromosomes moved toward one another and began their synapses [pairing]. But they were tiny, tiny little chromosomes. After they synapsed, they began to elongate—about fifty times what they were. As they elongated they got fatter, but they looked like railroad tracks. At this very elongated stage, I could determine chromomere patterns [darkly staining granules found at consistent locations along chromosomes] and so forth. Then they went into a diffuse stage [diplotene, the stage in which pairs of chromatids derived from paired chromosomes begin to separate from each other except at certain points of connection where interchange occurs ("crossing over")], which I felt sure was the stage when crossing over was occurring. But I couldn't see anything well with the light microscope. They came out of it suddenly and went into diakinesis [the final stage in prophase following diplotene] and a metaphase of the first meiotic division very rapidly after this long period of being in diplotene. Then from that state on, from the stage of actual fusion of the two nuclei with the chromosomes intact, they remain in the chromosomes stage. . . . (Quoted in Evelyn Fox Keller, *A Feeling for the Organism: The Life and Work of Barbara McClintock* (New York: W.H. Freeman and Company, 1983), p. 116)

If the above report of her observations expresses only what McClintock directly observed (condition 1), and if what she directly observed corresponded to what was there in the world, as measured by what other people also observed (condition 2), then the above report of her observations provides us with a true representation of the world. But were these conditions satisfied in this case, and are they generally satisfied in scientific research? The readings of this part suggest negative answers to these questions, and thereby pose for us a variety of sceptical challenges to scientific realism. Let us see what these challenges amount to.

Popper's Challenge

To begin with, Karl Popper denies that condition 1 is satisfied. In "The Problem of the Empirical Basis," he suggests that "basic statements" like the ones in Mc-Clintock's report, that is, statements that describe "immediate experience," are inherently more general than the experiences that call them forth. "An 'immediate experience' is *only once* 'immediately given'; it is unique." (p. 76) Statements, on the other hand, statements like "There is a big nucleolus . . . ," are associated with an indefinite number and variety of such unique immediate experiences.

Think of all the different experiences associated with the much more familiar statement "Here is a glass of water," (Popper's example). What I see over time from different vantage points, what I see (and feel) if I touch it, bounce a ball off it, tip it, drop it, etc. If any of these experiences does not come to pass after the appropriate action is taken—if, for example, a ball "goes through" the glass rather than bounces off it—then I may be led to take back the statement "Here is a glass of water." Its acceptance, in short, depends upon the availability of all these experiences. Comparable things can be said of McClintock's statement, and the different experiences associated with it occasioned by different actions on the part of an observer. As a result, basic statements like the ones in her report cannot be justified by what McClintock directly observed, since *at best* what she directly observed constitutes too small a base of evidence for them.

But the situation is actually more desperate than this according to Popper. Basic statements like the ones in her report cannot be justified by what McClintock directly observed, since only *statements* can enter into justificatory relations with other statements. "Experiences can *motivate a decision*, and hence an acceptance or a rejection of a statement, but a basic statement cannot be *justified* by them—no more than by thumping the table." (p. 78) As a result, the empirical basis of scientific knowledge is constituted for Popper by decisions to accept particular basic statements. These decisions are motivated by experiences like Mc-Clintock's, but not justified by them. The empirical basis of scientific knowledge is not arbitrary for all that, according to Popper. Because every basic statement in it, though unjustified by experience, is nonetheless testable by other basic statements should questions arise. McClintock's statements are testable, for example, by other statements about her staining techniques and other statements about the functioning of her microscope and in some cases the process of testing is actually carried out, so that some basic statements are corroborated (or else, falsified) by other basic statements. Popper points out, however, that because the process of testing basic statements by means of other basic statements cannot go on forever, it must end with the acceptance within the empirical basis of scientific knowledge of testable but untested and experientially unjustified basic statements.

Hanson's Challenge

In "Observation," Norwood Russell Hanson disagrees in significant ways with Popper. For Hanson, observational reports like McClintock's given above *do* express only what is directly observed, and hence, *are* justified by what is directly observed. For Hanson, unlike Popper, that is to say, condition 1 *is* satisfied by the empirical basis of scientific knowledge.

Hanson's reasoning goes like this. When McClintock said, for example, "There is a big nucleolus, and I could see that these chromosomes moved toward one another and began their synapses," there is no reason to think that she was confused, or that she was giving a misleading account of her experience. There is no reason to think that she saw only (very insufficient!) *evidence* for a nucleolus and chromosomes, only vague patches of color or whatever, and *hypothesized* that they were a nucleolus and chromosomes. (Compare the very different: "Then they went into a diffuse stage, which I felt sure was the stage when crossing over was occurring. But I couldn't see anything well with the light microscope.") Similarly, *you* simply *see* the words on this page; you do not see something else that you *interpret* to be these things.

Of course, it takes knowledge to see these things. A young child cannot see what you see here when you see words and sentences and she sees but marks and lines. The child must first learn what the marks mean; she must first learn how to read. Only then will her visual field be organized in ways that reflect that linguistic knowledge. In the same way, McClintock did not initially see all the things she reported. When she first started work on *Neurospora* all she could see, and all anyone else could see, was disorder. The entire meiotic cycle lacked any description. After working with *Neurospora*, however, she could pick out the chromosomes easily.

> I found that the more I worked with them the bigger and bigger [they] got, and when I was really working with them I wasn't outside, I was down there. I was part of the system. I was right down there with them, and everything got big. I even was able to see the internal parts of the chromosomes—actually everything was there." (Quoted in Evelyn Fox Keller, *Reflections on Gender and Science* (New Haven: Yale University Press, 1985), p. 165)

With the knowledge McClintock had acquired, the chromosomes were now to be seen, not only by her but with her instruction, by others as well. Her knowledge had shaped her perception and the perception of others. Indeed, that knowledge was then there in the seeing for them. Those without that knowledge, however, remained blind to what she saw.

Thus, for Hanson, observational reports like McClintock's express only what is directly observed, because what is directly observed has already been shaped by such information. Indeed, if scientists' observations were not shaped in this way by their knowledge, then nothing scientists observed would ever be relevant to what they know, and nothing they know could ever have significance for what they observe. But this means that, for Hanson, condition 1 is satisfied by the empirical basis of scientific knowledge, but condition 2 is not. For what McClintock directly observed did *not* correspond to what other people observed, since what McClintock directly observed was shaped by *her* knowledge, and what other people observed was shaped by theirs. And aside from those scientists instructed by her, these "knowledges" were quite different. In his essay, in fact, Hanson takes up cases of scientists with different training, different theories—different "knowledge"—seeing different things when looking at the same objects, and, as a consequence, giving different observational reports.

Shapin's Challenge

But there are plenty of cases in which scientists have different training, different theories—different knowledge—and yet give or accept *the same* observational reports. Such cases of scientists sharing an empirical basis for their diverse research projects despite their theoretical differences, and even exploring those differences by way of this basis, are of fundamental importance to the scientific enterprise. It is with such cases, however, that Hanson's account of observation cannot cope. Might these shared observational reports in the midst of theoretical differences indicate that the reports express only what is directly observed, where what is directly observed is shared as well? Might they indicate, that is, that conditions 1 and 2 are satisfied by the empirical basis of scientific knowledge after all? In "Pump and Circumstance: Robert Boyle's Literary Technology," Steven Shapin takes up one such case of shared observational reports, those relating to Robert Boyle's researches in pneumatics in the late 1650s and early 1660s. But he suggests with it that there is no reason to suppose that conditions 1 and 2 are satisfied. How does he do this?

According to Shapin, few of Boyle's contemporaries were present at Boyle's experiments. Furthermore, few of his contemporaries were able to replicate Boyle's experiments for themselves, because few of them had the necessary funds to purchase equipment like Boyle's—and precious little such equipment was available for purchase in any case—and fewer still had the necessary skills and understanding to make the equipment function the way Boyle did. As a result, the experimental results that Boyle observed and reported were observed by very few others. Nevertheless, Boyle's contemporaries did accept Boyle's observational reports, not because his reports expressed what these individuals directly observed, but because of the carefully crafted way he *expressed* his reports (his "literary technology"). Boyle's plain style of writing, the modesty he displayed, his confidence in the facts he reported, the wealth of circumstantial details he included, the naturalistic pictures of his apparatus and experiments that he placed alongside his text, the accounts of unexpected outcomes and problems with apparatus and unsuccessful experiments he also included, convinced his contemporaries to accept his observational reports. Boyle's "material technology" and "social technology," connected to his literary technology—that is to say, Boyle's specially contrived experimental apparatus and new social practices designed for the emerging scientific community of the seventeenth century—also functioned as tools for getting Boyle's contemporaries to accept his observational reports. For Shapin, in short, shared observational reports at the dawn of modern science did not indicate that conditions 1 and 2 were satisfied by the empirical basis of scientific knowledge.

The circumstances that prevailed in the seventeenth century *still* prevail. After all, the number of individuals who directly take part in, or directly observe, any contemporary scientific experiment is *still* a very small proportion of the scientific community, much less society in general. The opportunities for replicating such an experiment are *still* frequently limited (think of the many years and many millions of dollars that individual experiments in many parts of science require!). The literary, material, and social technologies that Boyle put in place back in the seventeenth century (or technologies very much like them) are *still* functioning as tools for getting the scientific community and society at large to accept the observational reports that result from these experiments. So shared observational reports even in the context of theoretical difference certainly do *not* indicate that conditions 1 and 2 are satisfied by the empirical basis of scientific knowledge.

Oakley's Challenge

But surely, you will now insist impatiently, surely Boyle and those who attended or replicated his experiments, or any of the other established scientists of that time, could represent other individuals when they made their observations and gave their reports. And surely the same can be said of these scientists' modern-day counterparts as well. Surely we are all constituted in the same way, all interchangeable potential producers of scientific knowledge, and what distinguishes scientists from the rest is just a generally higher level of intelligence and training to help them do this better.

It is just here, however, that the issues raised by Ann Oakley in "Interviewing Women: A Contradiction in Terms" intervene. We are *not* all constituted in the same way, Oakley would say. We are a group very diverse in gender and race and class and political outlook and a host of other respects potentially relevant to the production of scientific knowledge. But Boyle and those of his colleagues at the center of the scientific enterprise back in the seventeenth century as well as their modern-day counterparts are *not* a very diverse group. Those who have controlled the modern scientific enterprise from its beginning have tended to be upper or middle class white men quite homogeneous in other respects as well. And this may mean that such individuals cannot adequately represent the broader society when they make their observations and give their reports.

Consider the case of Ann Oakley and her sociological research with new mothers reported in "Interviewing Women: A Contradiction in Terms." According to Oakley, the traditional aim of interviewing, as of other survey methods in social research, is to gather data about people, data that are both amenable to statistical treatment and relevant to social theory. As a consequence, the interviews that are part of a research project are supposed to be conducted in such a way that the personalities, beliefs, and values of the various interviewers, as well as other "local features" of the interview situations, do not affect—do not "bias"—the data obtained. To be sure, interviewers are supposed to show no reactions to interviewees' comments, are supposed to dodge interviewees' questions about themselves (the interviewers) and their views, are supposed to refrain from emotional involvement with interviewees and their problems—are supposed to be, in short, detached, unemotional, disinterested, and objective. In-deed, Oakley suggests that a power hierarchy is set up as an essential part of such a research process: "It is important to note that while the interviewer must treat the interviewee as an object or data-producing machine which, when handled correctly will function properly, the interviewer herself/himself has the same sta-tus from the point of view of the person/people, institution or corporation con-ducting the research. Both interviewer and interviewee are thus depersonalized participants in the research process," and both are used to achieve the personal goals of researchers. (p. 120)

As a feminist woman sociologist interviewing women during their transition to motherhood, however, Oakley found herself unable to engage in this objecti-fying, exploitative—this "masculine"—mode of research. Indeed, as a feminist woman sociologist, Oakley aimed to document women's own accounts of their lives in an effort to give the subjective situation of women greater visibility, both in sociology and in society. This meant that Oakley had to become, in her inter-views, a data-gathering instrument for those whose lives were being researched, women, rather than a data-gathering instrument for the theoretical concerns of herself and other researchers. And it meant that she had to gather her data, not in a hierarchical way, but in a way that engaged her subjects and herself in a joint and mutually-beneficial enterprise. Thus, Oakley followed such non-standard procedures as answering her subjects' questions as honestly and fully as she could. And she refrained from exploiting either her subjects or the information they gave her ("For instance, if the interview clashed with the demands of housework and motherhood I offered to, and often did, help with the work that had to be done." (p. 126)). As a result, nearly three-quarters of the women interviewed felt that being interviewed had affected them in a positive way—that it had led them to reflect on their experiences more than they would otherwise have done, for example, or had reduced the level of their anxiety or reassured them of their nor-mality—and no one felt that being interviewed had affected her in a negative way. And far from Oakley's feminist mode of interviewing yielding biased data, it yielded better results, in terms of the quality and depth of information gathered, than the traditional mode of interviewing. Indeed, interviewees showed a sincere interest in Oakley and her research, just as Oakley, in her research, showed a sin-cere interest in them and their experiences.". . . [I]n most cases, the goal of find-ing out about people through interviewing is best achieved when the relationship of interviewer and interviewee is non-hierarchical and when the interviewer is prepared to invest his or her own personal identity in the relationship." (p. 123)

According to Oakley, in short, the men who had played a central role in de-veloping sociological research agendas did not represent her aims and methods as a feminist woman researcher in the interviewing procedures they established. Nor, consequently, did they represent her when they made their observations and wrote up their reports using those interviewing procedures. Might the male-controlled scientific research establishment fail to represent the aims and meth-ods, and hence observations and observation reports, of other researchers than Ann Oakley in other specialties than sociology? Interestingly, though Barbara McClintock claimed to be neither a feminist nor a practitioner of anything but gender-neutral research, her approach to her subject matter was as non-standard as Oakley's and, in fact, bore a striking resemblance to it. Like Oakley and unlike most of her colleagues in biology, McClintock focused on the peculiarities of individuals rather than the repeatable properties of large groups. And she sought not to exert power over these individuals, to reduce them to simplicity in an effort to predict and control their behavior. Instead, she sought to "listen to" them, to know them in minute detail so as to understand and appreciate their complexity and diversity. Again, like Oakley and unlike her colleagues, McClintock did not take a detached, unemotional, disinterested stance toward the subjects of her research. Rather, McClintock identified with them; her vocabulary is consistently one of affection, of kinship, of empathy. Thus, McClintock explained:

> No two plants are exactly alike. They're all different, and as a consequence, you have to know that difference. I start with the seedling, and I don't want to leave it. I don't feel I really know the story if I don't watch the plant all the way along. So I know every plant in the field. I know them intimately, and I find it a great pleasure to know them. (Quoted in Keller, *A Feeling for the Organism*, p. 198)

Finally, like Oakley and unlike her colleagues, McClintock was enabled to make her novel contributions to scientific knowledge by her intimate personal relationship with the subjects of her research. It may be, then, that what is directly observed and how it is described is a function not only of what is there but also of the various sensitivities that observers bring to a situation. Such sensitivities will be conditioned by how the observers have been socialized, their status and roles in and out of the family, their political outlooks, theoretical commitments, and the like. But if this is the case, then what is observed and how it is described will not correspond to, and hence, not be represented by, what other people with other sensitivities observe and describe.

Pickering's Challenge

Oakley's challenge makes it sound as though what is observed and reported is a purely individual affair. What the last reading of Part II, Andy Pickering's "Against Putting the Phenomena First: The Discovery of the Weak Neutral Current," makes clear, however, is that what is observed and/or how it is described is at least as much a community affair as an individual one. To show this, Pickering considers what went into the discovery of weak neutral current in the early 1970s.

According to Pickering, essentially the same bubble chamber and electronic neutrino experiments were performed in the 1960s and then again in the early 1970s, with comparable results. But the 1960s' experiments were seen as showing that weak neutral current does not exist, whereas the 1970s' experiments were seen as constituting its discovery. Since the experimentally-produced phenomena were largely the same each time, and many of the participants were the same as well, Pickering looks to other factors to explain the discrepancy. What he finds is that the set of assumptions used by participants to interpret their experimental results had changed over the period in question, a change due mostly to changes in theoretical particle physics. Whereas the theories actively being de-

veloped in the 1960s required the non-existence of neutral current, the theories of most interest in the 1970s required its existence. In the 1970s, pressure was thus exerted on the experimental particle physics community by the theoretical particle physics community to find evidence of neutral current. At the same time, motivation was strong in the experimental particle physics community to find such evidence. Weak neutral current would provide experimental particle physicists with an exciting new phenomenon that could be explored using existing techniques or ones easily developed. The result was that experimental particle physicists reinterpreted negative experimental outcomes from the 1960s and 1970s in such a way as to disclose such evidence "As a real phenomenon, the weak neutral current was a bonanza for theorists and experimenters alike and the acceptance
of novel interpretative practices was a small price to pay." (p. 150) And so it was paid.

The conclusion Pickering draws from his case study is that experimental scientists are not engaged in uncovering an empirical basis of scientific knowledge largely set by the world, in an effort to test, and ultimately judge acceptable or unacceptable, the theoretical hypotheses that theoretical scientists develop. Instead, experimental scientists *collaborate with theorists* in the *production* of this empirical basis of scientific knowledge. But this again means that the empirical basis of scientific knowledge fails to satisfy the conditions 1 and 2 that we set out at the start.

Summary

We have been concerned with the empirical basis of scientific knowledge in the attempt to determine whether scientific knowledge provides us with true representations of the world (the scientific realist position), or only with representations that are useful for various purposes, such as for prediction and control of the environment (the scientific anti-realist position). We noted at the outset that if the empirical basis of scientific knowledge satisfies two conditions, then it will provide us with true representations of the world; and that if scientific knowledge includes only this basis and the claims (e.g., theories) that can be supported on this basis, then scientific knowledge will provide us with true representations of the world as well. The two conditions were that:

1. The observation reports included in the empirical basis must express only what is directly observed. They must not go beyond what is directly observed, or else they will say more than can be justified by those observations.

2. What is directly observed must correspond to what is there in the world, as measured by what other people also observe. It must contain nothing that is personal or subjective or idiosyncratic.

The authors in this part seriously challenge the view that the empirical basis of scientific knowledge satisfies conditions 1 and 2, and thereby, seriously challenge the view of scientific realism itself. Regarding condition 1, Popper argues that scientists' observation reports, being statements, inherently go beyond what is included in direct observation and, in any case, can be justified only by other statements, not by direct observation. Shapin adds that scientists' observation reports have been accepted not because the reports express what has been directly observed, but because of the way the reports have been expressed, the instrumentation that has been used in coming to assert them, and the like. And Pickering adds that scientists' observation reports reflect the interpretative practices in effect at the time of the reports, and changes with changes in those practices even when the content of observation stays the same. Regarding condition 2, Hanson argues that what is directly observed depends upon an observer's theories and knowledge and training, and changes with changes in these. In consequence, what is directly observed will vary from observer to observer, depending on the observer's theories and knowledge and training. And Oakley suggests that an observer's gender and political outlook (and perhaps also class, race, and ethnicity) can affect the observer's research goals and methods, and thereby, the observer's observational data as well. In consequence, one scientist's observational data need not correspond to other scientists' observational data.

What conclusions follow from these challenges of Popper, Hanson, Shapin, Oakley, and Pickering? Do they show that scientific realism is unacceptable? You will be able to decide only after you have carefully read and analyzed the selections that follow. But keep in mind that the challenges our authors pose to realism are not always compatible with each other. We have already seen, for example, that Popper's and Hanson's are not. At best, therefore, you will need to make choices among them, or to modify some in light of others. Keep in mind, as well, that the challenges of some of our authors—for example, Shapin, Oakley, and Pickering—are developed using specific cases in specific scientific fields. You will need to decide whether the points they make are nonetheless applicable to other cases in other scientific fields. Finally, keep in mind that the satisfying of conditions 1 and 2 by the empirical basis of scientific knowledge is only a *sufficient* condition for the truth of the empirical basis, not a *necessary* condition. That is to say, if the empirical basis of scientific knowledge *does* satisfy conditions 1 and 2, then, as we said at the outset, it will provide us with true representations of the world. But if the empirical basis of scientific knowledge does *not* satisfy conditions 1 and 2, then it may or may not provide us with true representations of the world. Truth is then not precluded, nor is it assured. In that case, however, we will need a different argument to show that the empirical basis of scientific knowledge provides us with true representations of the world.

KARL POPPER

The Problem of
the Empirical Basis

Perceptual Experiences as
Empirical Basis: Psychologism

The doctrine that the empirical sciences are reducible to sense-perceptions, and thus to our experiences, is one which many accept as obvious beyond all question. However, this doctrine . . . is here rejected. . . . I do not wish to deny that there is a grain of truth in the view that mathematics and logic are based on thinking, and the factual sciences on sense-perceptions. But what is true in this view has little bearing on the epistemological problem. And indeed, there is hardly a problem in epistemology which has suffered more severely from the confusion of psychology with logic than this problem of the basis of statements of experience.

The problem of the basis of experience has troubled few thinkers so deeply as Fries.[1] He taught that, if the statements of science are not to be accepted *dogmatically*, we must be able to *justify* them. If we demand justification by reasoned argument, in the logical sense, then we

are committed to the view that *statements can be justified only by statements*. The demand that *all* statements are to be logically justified (described by Fries as a "predilection for proofs") is therefore bound to lead to an *infinite regress*. Now, if we wish to avoid the danger of dogmatism as well as an infinite regress, then it seems as if we could only have recourse to *psychologism, i.e.* the doctrine that statements can be justified not only by statements but also by perceptual experience. Faced with this *trilemma*—dogmatism *vs.* infinite regress *vs.* psychologism—Fries, and with him almost all epistemologists who wished to account for our empirical knowledge, opted for psychologism. In sense-experience, he taught, we have "immediate knowledge": by this immediate knowledge, we may justify our "mediate knowledge"—knowledge expressed in the symbolism of some language. And this mediate knowledge includes, of course, the statements of science.

Usually the problem is not explored as far as this. . . . It is taken for granted that empirical

Reprinted from *The Logic of Scientific Discovery* by Karl Popper by permission of the estate of Karl Popper.

scientific statements "speak of our experiences." For how could we ever reach any knowledge of facts if not through sense-perception? Merely by taking thought a man cannot add an iota to his knowledge of the world of facts. Thus perceptual experience must be the sole "source of knowledge" of all the empirical sciences. All we know about the world of facts must therefore be expressible in the form of statements *about our experiences.* Whether this table is red or blue can be found out only by consulting our sense-experience. By the immediate feeling of conviction which it conveys, we can distinguish the true statement, the one whose terms agree with experience, from the false statement, whose terms do not agree with it. Science is merely an attempt to classify and describe this perceptual knowledge, these immediate experiences whose truth we cannot doubt; *it is the systematic presentation of our immediate convictions.*

This doctrine founders in my opinion. . . . For we can utter no scientific statement that does not go far beyond what can be known with certainty "on the basis of immediate experience." (This fact may be referred to as the "transcendence inherent in any description.") Every description uses *universal* names (or symbols, or ideas); every statement has the character of a theory, of a hypothesis. The statement, "Here is a glass of water" cannot be verified by any observational experience. The reason is that the *universals* which appear in it cannot be correlated with any specific sense-experience. (An "immediate experience" is *only once* "immediately given"; it is unique.) By the word "glass," for example, we denote physical bodies which exhibit a certain *law-like behavior,* and the same holds for the word "water." Universals cannot be reduced to classes of experiences. . . .

The Objectivity of the Empirical Basis

I propose to look at science in a way which is slightly different from that favoured by the various psychologistic schools: I wish to *distinguish*

sharply between objective science on the one hand, and "our knowledge" on the other.

I readily admit that only observation can give us "knowledge concerning facts," and that we can (as Hahn says) "become aware of facts only by observation."[2] But this awareness, this knowledge of ours, does not justify or establish the truth of any statement. I do not believe, therefore, that the question which epistemology must ask is, ". . . on what does our *knowledge* rest? . . . or more exactly, how can I, having had the *experience S,* justify my description of it, and defend it against doubt?"[3] . . . In my view, what epistemology has to ask is, rather: how do we test scientific statements by their deductive consequences?[4] And *what kind* of consequences can we select for this purpose if they in their turn are to be inter-subjectively testable?

By now, this kind of objective and non-psychological approach is pretty generally accepted where logical or tautological statements are concerned. Yet not so long ago it was held that logic was a science dealing with mental processes and their laws—the laws of our thought. On this view there was no other justification to be found for logic than the alleged fact that we just could not think in any other way. A logical inference seemed to be justified because it was experienced as a necessity of thought, as a feeling of being compelled to think along certain lines. In the field of logic, this kind of psychologism is now perhaps a thing of the past. Nobody would dream of justifying the validity of a logical inference, or of defending it against doubts, by writing beside it in the margin the following . . . sentence. ". . . In checking this chain of inferences today, I experienced an acute feeling of conviction."

The position is very different when we come to *empirical statements of science.* Here everybody believes that these are grounded on experiences such as perceptions. . . . Yet whether statements of logic are in question or statements of empirical science, I think the answer is the same: our *knowledge,* which may be described vaguely as a system of *dispositions,* and which may be of concern to psychology, may be in both cases linked with feelings of belief or of conviction: in the one case, perhaps, with the feeling of being compelled to think in a certain way; in the other with that of "perceptual assurance." But all this interests only the psychologist. It does not even touch upon problems like those of the logical connections between scientific statements, which alone interest the epistemologist. . . .

There is only one way to make sure of the validity of a chain of logical reasoning. This is to put it in the form in which it is most easily testable: we break it up into many small steps, each easy to check by anybody who has learnt the mathematical or logical technique of transforming sentences. If after this anybody still raises doubts then we can only beg him to point out an error in the steps of the proof, or to think the matter over again. In the case of the empirical sciences, the situation is much the same. Any empirical scientific statement can be presented (by describing experimental arrangements, etc.) in such a way that anyone who has learned the relevant technique can test it. If, as a result, he rejects the statement, then it will not satisfy us if he tells us all about his feelings of doubt or about his feelings of conviction as to his perceptions. What he must do is to formulate an assertion which contradicts our own, and give us his instructions for testing it. If he fails to do this we can only ask him to take another and perhaps a more careful look at our experiment, and think again. . . .

The Relativity of Basic Statements: Resolution of Fries's Trilemma

Every test of a theory, whether resulting in its corroboration or falsification, must stop at some basic statement or other which we *decide to accept*. If we do not come to any decision, and do not accept some basic statement or other, then the test will have led nowhere. But considered from a logical point of view, the situation is never such that it compels us to stop

at this particular basic statement rather than at that, or else give up the test altogether. For any basic statement can again in its turn be subjected to tests, using as a touchstone any of the basic statements which can be deduced from it with the help of some theory, either the one under test, or another. This procedure has no natural end. Thus if the test is to lead us anywhere, nothing remains but to stop at some point or other and say that we are satisfied, for the time being.

It is fairly easy to see that we arrive in this way at a procedure according to which we stop only at a kind of statement that is especially easy to test. For it means that we are stopping at statements about whose acceptance or rejection the various investigators are likely to reach agreement. And if they do not agree, they will simply continue with the tests, or else start them all over again. If this too leads to no result, then we might say that the statements in question were not inter-subjectively testable, or that we were not, after all, dealing with observable events. . . .

Just as a logical proof has reached a satisfactory shape when the difficult work is over, and everything can be easily checked, so, after science has done its work of deduction or explanation, we stop at basic statements which are easily testable. Statements about personal experiences . . . are clearly *not* of this kind; thus they will not be very suitable to serve as statements at which we stop. . . .

What is our position now in regard to Fries's trilemma, the choice between dogmatism, infinite regress, and psychologism? [*Cf.* page 75] The basic statements at which we stop, which we decide to accept as satisfactory, and as sufficiently tested, have admittedly the character of *dogmas*, but only in so far as we may desist from justifying them by further arguments (or by further tests). But this kind of dogmatism is innocuous since, should the need arise, these statements can easily be tested further. I admit that this too makes the chain of deduction in principle infinite. But this kind of "*infinite regress*" is also innocuous since in our theory there is no question of trying to prove any statements by means of it. And finally, as to *psychologism*: I admit, again, that the decision to accept a basic statement, and to be satisfied with it, is causally connected with our experiences—especially with our *perceptual experiences*. But we do not attempt to *justify* basic statements by these experiences. Experiences can *motivate a decision*, and hence an acceptance or a rejection of a statement, but a basic statement cannot be *justified* by them—no more than by thumping the table.

Theory and Experiment

Basic statements are accepted as the result of a decision or agreement; and to that extent they are conventions. The decisions are reached in accordance with a procedure governed by rules. Of special importance among these is a rule which tells us that we should not accept *stray basic statements*—i.e. logically disconnected ones—but that we should accept basic statements in the course of testing *theories*; of raising searching questions about these theories, to be answered by the acceptance of basic statements.

Thus the real situation is quite different from the one visualized by the naïve empiricist. . . . He thinks that we begin by collecting and arranging our experiences, and so ascend the ladder of science. . . . But if I am ordered: "Record what you are now experiencing" I shall hardly know how to obey this ambiguous order. Am I to report that I am writing; that I hear a bell ringing; a newsboy shouting; a loudspeaker droning; or am I to report, perhaps, that these noises irritate me? And even if the order could be obeyed: however rich a collection of statements might be assembled in this way, it could never add up to a *science*. A science needs points of view, and theoretical problems.

Agreement upon the acceptance or rejection of basic statements is reached, as a rule, on the occasion of *applying* a theory; the agree-ment, in fact, is part of an application which puts the theory to the test. Coming to an agreement upon basic statements is, like other kinds of applications, to perform a purposeful action, guided by various theoretical considerations. . . .

All these considerations are important for the epistemological *theory of experiment*. The theoretician puts certain definite questions to the experimenter, and the latter, by his experiments, tries to elicit a decisive answer to these questions, and to no others. All other questions he tries hard to exclude. . . . Thus he makes his test with respect to this one question ". . . as sensitive as possible, but as insensitive as possible with respect to all other associated questions. . . . Part of this work consists in screening off all possible sources of error"[5] . . . Theory dominates the experimental work from its initial planning up to the finishing touches in the laboratory.[6]

This is well illustrated by cases in which the theoretician succeeded in predicting an observable effect which was later experimentally produced; perhaps the most beautiful instance is de Broglie's prediction of the wave-character of matter, first confirmed experimentally by Davisson and Germer.[7] It is illustrated perhaps even better by cases in which experiments had a conspicuous influence upon the progress of theory. What compels the theorist to search for a better theory, in these cases, is almost always the experimental *falsification* of a theory, so far accepted and corroborated: it is, again, the outcome of tests guided by theory. Famous examples are the Michelson-Morley experiment which led to the theory of relativity, and the falsification, by Lummer and Pringsheim, of the radiation formula of Rayleigh and Jeans, and of that of Wien, which led to the quantum theory. Accidental discoveries occur too, of course, but they are comparatively rare. . . .

Thus . . . basic statements are not justifiable by our immediate experiences, but are, from the logical point of view, accepted by an act, by a free decision. (From the psychological point of view this may perhaps be a purposeful and well-adapted reaction.)

This important distinction, between a *justification* and a *decision*—a decision reached in accordance with a procedure governed by rules—might be clarified, perhaps, with the help of an analogy: the old procedure of trial by jury.

The *verdict* of the jury (*vere dictum* = spoken truly), like that of the experimenter, is an answer to a question of fact (*quid facti?*) which must be put to the jury in the sharpest, the most definite form. But what question is asked, and how it is put, will depend very largely on the legal situation, *i.e.* on the prevailing system of criminal law (corresponding to a system of theories). By its decision, the jury accepts, by agreement, a statement about a factual occurrence—a basic statement, as it were. The significance of this decision lies in the fact that from it, together with the universal statements of the system (of criminal law) certain consequences can be deduced. In other words, the decision forms the basis for the *application* of the system; the verdict plays the part of a "true statement of fact." But it is clear that the statement need not be true merely because the jury has accepted it. This fact is acknowledged in the rule allowing a verdict to be quashed or revised.

The verdict is reached in accordance with a procedure which is governed by rules. These rules are based on certain fundamental principles which are chiefly, if not solely, designed to result in the discovery of objective truth. They sometimes leave room not only for subjective convictions but even for subjective bias. Yet even if we disregard these special aspects of the older procedure and imagine a procedure based solely on the aim of promoting the discovery of objective truth, it would still be the case that the verdict of the jury never justifies, or gives grounds for, the truth of what it asserts.

Neither can the subjective convictions of the jurors be held to justify the decision reached; although there is, of course, a close causal connection between them and the decision reached—a connection which might be stated by psychological laws; thus these convictions may be called the "motives" of the decision. The fact that the convictions are not justifications is connected with the fact that different rules may regulate the jury's procedure (for example, simple or qualified majority). This shows that the relationship between the convictions of the jurors and their verdict may vary greatly.

In contrast to the verdict of the jury, the *judgment* of the judge is "reasoned"; it needs, and contains, a justification. The judge tries to justify it by, or deduce it logically from, other statements: the statements of the legal system, combined with the verdict that plays the role of initial conditions. This is why the judgment may be challenged on logical grounds. The jury's decision, on the other hand, can only be challenged by questioning whether it has been reached in accordance with the accepted rules of procedure; *i.e.* formally, but not as to its content. (A justification of the content of a decision is significantly called a "motivated report," rather than a "logically justified report.")

The analogy between this procedure and that by which we decide basic statements is clear. It throws light, for example, upon their relativity, and the way in which they depend upon questions raised by the theory. In the case of the trial by jury, it would be clearly impossible to *apply* the "theory" unless there is first a verdict arrived at by decision; yet the verdict has to be found in a procedure that conforms to, and thus applies, part of the general legal code. The case is analogous to that of basic statements. Their acceptance is part of the application of a theoretical system; and it is only this application which makes any further applications of the theoretical system possible.

The empirical basis of objective science has thus nothing "absolute" about it. Science does not rest upon solid bedrock. The bold structure of its theories rises, as it were, above a swamp. It is like a building erected on piles.

The piles are driven down from above into the swamp, but not down to any natural or "given" base; and if we stop driving the piles deeper, it is not because we have reached firm ground. We simply stop when we are satisfied that the piles are firm enough to carry the structure, at least for the time being.

Notes

1. J.F. Fries, *Neue oder anthropologische Kritik der Vernunft* (1828 to 1831).
2. H. Hahn, *Logik, Mathematik und Naturerkennen*, in *Einheitswissenschaft* 2, 1933, pp. 19 and 24.
3. Cf. Carnap, for instance, *Scheinprobleme in der Philosophie*, 1928, p. 15 (no italics in the original).
4. At present, I should formulate this question thus. How can we best *criticize* our theories (our hypotheses, our guesses), rather than defend them against doubt? Of course, *testing* was always, in my view, part of *criticizing*. . . .
5. H. Weyl, *Philosophie der Mathematik und Naturwissenschaft*, 1927, p. 113; English Edition: *Philosophy of Mathematics and Natural Science*, Princeton, 1949, p. 116.
6. I now feel that I should have emphasized in this place a view which can be found elsewhere in the book [*The Logic of Scientific Discovery*] (for example in the fourth and the last paragraphs of section 19). I mean the view that observations, and even more so observation statements and statements of experimental results, are always *interpretations* of the facts observed; that they are *interpretations in the light of theories*. . . .
7. The story is briefly and excellently told by Max Born in *Albert Einstein, Philosopher-Scientist*, edited by P. A. Schilpp, 1949, p. 174. There are better illustrations, such as Adams's and Leverrier's discovery of Neptune, or that of Hertzean waves.

NORWOOD RUSSELL HANSON

Observation

Were the eye not attuned to the Sun,
The Sun could never be seen by it.

GOETHE

A

Consider two microbiologists. They look at a prepared slide; when asked what they see, they may give different answers. One sees in the cell before him a cluster of foreign matter: it is an artefact, a coagulum resulting from inadequate staining techniques. This clot has no more to do with the cell, *in vivo*, than the scars left on it by the archaeologist's spade have to do with the original shape of some Grecian urn. The other biologist identifies the clot as a cell organ, a "Golgi body." As for techniques, he argues: "The standard way of detecting a cell organ is by fixing and staining. Why single out this one technique as producing artefacts, while others disclose genuine organs?"

The controversy continues.[1] It involves the whole theory of microscopical technique; nor is it an obviously experimental issue. Yet it affects what scientists say they see. Perhaps there is a sense in which two such observers do not see the same thing, do not begin from the same data, though their eyesight is normal and they are visually aware of the same object.

Imagine these two observing a Protozoon— *Amoeba*. One sees a one-celled animal, the other a non-celled animal. The first sees *Amoeba* in all its analogies with different types of single cells: liver cells, nerve cells, epithelium cells. These have a wall, nucleus, cytoplasm, etc. Within this class *Amoeba* is distinguished only by its independence. The other, however, sees *Amoeba*'s homology not with single cells, but with whole animals. Like all animals *Amoeba* ingests its food, digests and assimilates it. It excretes, reproduces and is mobile—more like a complete animal than an individual tissue cell.

This is not an experimental issue, yet it can affect experiment. What either man regards as significant questions or relevant data can be determined by whether he stresses the first or the last term in "unicellular animal."

Some philosophers have a formula ready for such situations: "Of course they see the same thing. They make the same observation since they begin from the same visual data. But they interpret what they see differently. They

From *Patterns of Discovery* by Norwood Russell Hanson, pp. 4–30, © 1958, 1965 by Cambridge University Press. Reprinted by permission of Cambridge University Press.

construe the evidence in different ways." The task is then to show how these data are moulded by different theories or interpretations or intellectual constructions.

Considerable philosophers have wrestled with this task. But in fact the formula they start from is too simple to allow a grasp of the nature of observation within physics. Perhaps the scientists cited above do not begin their inquiries from the same data, do not make the same observations, do not even see the same thing? Here many concepts run together. We must proceed carefully, for wherever it makes sense to say that two scientists looking at x do not see the same thing, there must always be a prior sense in which they do see the same thing. The issue is, then, "Which of these senses is most illuminating for the understanding of observational physics?"

These biological examples are too complex. Let us consider Johannes Kepler: imagine him on a hill watching the dawn. With him is Tycho Brahe. Kepler regarded the sun as fixed: it was the earth that moved. But Tycho followed Ptolemy and Aristotle in this much at least: the earth was fixed and all other celestial bodies moved around it. *Do Kepler and Tycho see the same thing in the east at dawn?*

We might think this an experimental or observational question, unlike the questions "Are there Golgi bodies?" and "Are Protozoa one-celled or non-celled?" Not so in the sixteenth and seventeenth centuries. Thus Galileo said to the Ptolemaist ". . . neither Aristotle nor you can prove that the earth is *de facto* the centre of the universe. . .".[2] "Do Kepler and Tycho see the same thing in the east at dawn?" is perhaps not a *de facto* question either, but rather the beginning of an examination of the concepts of seeing and observation.

The resultant discussion might run:

"Yes, they do."
"No, they don't."
"Yes, they do!"
"No, they don't!". . .

That this is possible suggests that there may be reasons for both contentions. Let us consider some points in support of the affirmative answer.

The physical processes involved when Kepler and Tycho watch the dawn are worth noting. Identical photons are emitted from the sun; these traverse solar space, and our atmosphere. The two astronomers have normal vision; hence these photons pass through the cornea, aqueous humour, iris, lens and vitreous body of their eyes in the same way. Finally their retinas are affected. Similar electro-chemical changes occur in their selenium cells. The same configuration is etched on Kepler's retina as on Tycho's. So they see the same thing.

Locke sometimes spoke of seeing in this way: a man sees the sun if his is a normally-formed retinal picture of the sun. Dr. Sir W. Russell Brain speaks of our retinal sensations as indicators and signals. Everything taking place behind the retina is, as he says, "an intellectual operation based largely on non-visual experience . . .".[3] What we *see* are the changes in the *tunica retina*. Dr. Ida Mann regards the macula of the eye as itself "seeing details in bright light," and the rods as "seeing approaching motor-cars." Dr. Agnes Arber speaks of the eye as itself seeing.[4] Often, talk of seeing can direct attention to the retina. Normal people are distinguished from those for whom no retinal pictures can form: we may say of the former that they can see whilst the latter cannot see. Reporting when a certain red dot can be seen may supply the occulist with direct information about the condition of one's retina.[5]

This need not be pursued, however. These writers speak carelessly: seeing the sun is not seeing retinal pictures of the sun. The retinal images which Kepler and Tycho have are four in number, inverted and quite tiny.[6] Astronomers cannot be referring to these when they say they see the sun. If they are hypnotized, drugged, drunk or distracted they may not see the sun, even though their retinas register its image in exactly the same way as usual.

Seeing is an experience. A retinal reaction is only a physical state—a photochemical excitation. Physiologists have not always appreciated the differences between experiences and physical states. People, not their eyes, see. Cameras, and eye-balls, are blind. Attempts to locate within the organs of sight (or within the neurological reticulum behind the eyes) some nameable called "seeing" may be dismissed. That Kepler and Tycho do, or do not, see the same thing cannot be supported by reference to the physical states of their retinas, optic nerves or visual cortices: there is more to seeing than meets the eyeball.

Naturally, Tycho and Kepler see the same physical object. They are both visually aware of the sun. If they are put into a dark room and asked to report when they see something—anything at all—they may both report the same object at the same time. Suppose that the only object to be seen is a certain lead cylinder. Both men see the same thing: namely this object—whatever it is. It is just here, however, that the difficulty arises, for while Tycho sees a mere pipe, Kepler will see a telescope, the instrument about which Galileo has written to him.

Unless both are visually aware of the same object there can be nothing of philosophical interest in the question whether or not they see the same thing. Unless they both see the sun in this prior sense our question cannot even strike a spark.

Nonetheless, both Tycho and Kepler have a common visual experience of some sort. This experience perhaps constitutes their seeing the same thing. Indeed, this may be a seeing logically more basic than anything expressed in the pronouncement "I see the sun" (where each means something different by "sun"). If what they meant by the word "sun" were the only clue, then Tycho and Kepler could not be seeing the same thing, even though they were gazing at the same object.

If, however, we ask, not "Do they see the same thing?" but rather "What is it that they both see?," an unambiguous answer may be forthcoming. Tycho and Kepler are both aware of a brilliant yellow-white disc in a blue expanse over a green one. Such a "sense-datum" picture is single and uninverted. To be unaware of it is not to have it. Either it dominates one's visual attention completely or it does not exist.

If Tycho and Kepler are aware of anything visual, it must be of some pattern of colours. What else could it be? We do not touch or hear with our eyes, we only take in light. This private pattern is the same for both observers. Surely if asked to sketch the contents of their visual fields they would both draw a kind of semicircle on a horizon-line. They say they see the sun. But they do not see every side of the sun at once; so what they really see is discoid to begin with. It is but a visual aspect of the sun. In any single observation the sun is a brilliantly luminiscent disc, a penny painted with radium.

So something about their visual experiences at dawn is the same for both: a brilliant yellow-white disc centred between green and blue colour patches. Sketches of what they both see could be identical—congruent. In this sense Tycho and Kepler see the same thing at dawn. The sun appears to them in the same way. The same view, or scene, is presented to them both.

In fact, we often speak in this way. Thus the account of a recent solar eclipse:[7] "Only a thin crescent remains; white light is now completely obscured; the sky appears a deep blue, almost purple, and the landscape is a monochromatic green . . . there are the flashes of light on the disc's circumference and now the brilliant crescent to the left. . . ." Newton writes in a similar way in the *Opticks*: "These Arcs at their first appearance were of a violet and blue Colour, and between them were white Arcs of Circles, which . . . became a little tinged in their inward Limbs with red and yellow. . . ."[8] Every physicist employs the language of lines, colour patches, appearances, shadows. In so far as two normal observers use this language of the same event, they begin from the same data: they are making the same observation. Differences between them must arise in the interpretations they put on these data.

Thus, to summarize, saying that Kepler and Tycho see the same thing at dawn just because their eyes are similarly affected is an elementary mistake. There is a difference between a physical state and a visual experience. Suppose, however, that it is argued as above—that they see the same thing because they have the same sense-datum experience. Disparities in their accounts arise in *ex post facto* interpretations of what is seen, not in the fundamental visual data. If this is argued, further difficulties soon obtrude.

B

Normal retinas and cameras are impressed similarly by figure 1.[9] Our visual sense-data will be the same too. If asked to draw what we see, most of us will set out a configuration like figure 1.

Do we all see the same thing? Some will see a perspex cube viewed from below. Others will see it from above. Still others will see it as a kind of polygonally-cut gem. Some people see only criss-crossed lines in a plane. It may be seen as a block of ice, an aquarium, a wire frame for a kite—or any of a number of other things.

Do we, then, all see the same thing? If we do, how can these differences be accounted for?

Here the "formula" re-enters: "These are different *interpretations* of what all observers see in common. Retinal reactions to figure 1 are virtually identical; so too are our visual sense-data, since our drawings of what we see will have the same content. There is no place in the seeing for these differences, so they must lie in the interpretations put on what we see."

This sounds as if I do two things, not one, when I see boxes and bicycles. Do I put differ-

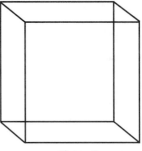

Figure 1

ent interpretations on figure 1 when I see it now as a box from below, and now as a cube from above? I am aware of no such thing. I mean no such thing when I report that the box's perspective has snapped back into the page.[10] If I do not mean this, then the concept of seeing which is natural in this connexion does not designate two diaphanous components, one optical, the other interpretative. Figure 1 is simply seen now as a box from below, now as a cube from above; one does not first soak up an optical pattern and then clamp an interpretation on it. Kepler and Tycho just see the sun. That is all. That is the way the concept of seeing works in this connexion.

"But," you say, "seeing figure 1 first as a box from below, then as a cube from above, involves interpreting the lines differently in each case." Then for you and me to have a different interpretation of figure 1 just *is* for us to see something different. This does not mean we see the same thing and then interpret it differently. When I suddenly exclaim "Eureka—a box from above," I do not refer simply to a different interpretation. (Again, there is a logically prior sense in which seeing figure 1 as from above and then as from below is seeing the same thing differently, i.e., being aware of the same diagram in different ways. We can refer just to this, but we need not. In this case we do not.)

Besides, the word "interpretation" is occasionally useful. We know where it applies and where it does not. Thucydides presented the facts objectively; Herodotus put an interpretation on them. The word does not apply to everything—it has a meaning. Can interpreting always be going on when we see? Sometimes, perhaps, as when the hazy outline of an agricultural machine looms up on a foggy morning and, with effort, we finally identify it. Is this the "interpretation" which is active when bicycles and boxes are clearly seen? Is it active when the perspective of figure 1 snaps into reverse? There was a time when Herodotus was half-through with his interpretation of the Graeco-Persian wars. Could there be a time when one is half-through interpreting figure 1 as a box from above, or as anything else?

"But the interpretation takes very little time—it is instantaneous." Instantaneous interpretation hails from the Limbo that produced unsensed sensibilia, unconscious inference, incorrigible statements, negative facts and *Objektive*. These are ideas which philosophers force on the world to preserve some pet epistemological or metaphysical theory.

Only in contrast to "Eureka" situations (like perspective reversals, where one cannot interpret the data) is it clear what is meant by saying that though Thucydides could have put an interpretation on history, he did not. Moreover, whether or not an historian is advancing an interpretation is an empirical question: we know what would count as evidence one way or the other. But whether we are employing an interpretation when we see figure 1 in a certain way is not empirical. What could count as evidence? In no ordinary sense of "interpret" do I interpret figure 1 differently when its perspective reverses for me. If there is some extraordinary sense of word it is not clear, either in ordinary language, or in extraordinary (philosophical) language. To insist that different reactions to figure 1 *must* lie in the interpretations put on a common visual experience is just to reiterate (without reasons) that the seeing of *x*

must be the same for all observers looking at *x*.

"But 'I see the figure as a box' means: I am having a particular visual experience which I always have when I interpret the figure as a box, or when I look at a box. . . ." ". . . if I meant this, I ought to know it. I ought to be able to refer to the experience directly and not only indirectly. . . ."[11]

Ordinary accounts of the experiences appropriate to figure 1 do not require visual grist going into an intellectual mill: theories and interpretations are "there" in the seeing from the outset. How can interpretations "be there" in the seeing? How is it possible to see an object according to an interpretation? "The question represents it as a queer fact; as if something were being forced into a form it did not really fit. But no squeezing, no forcing took place here."[12]

Consider now the reversible perspective figures which appear in textbooks on Gestalt psychology: the tea-tray, the shifting (Schröder) staircase, the tunnel. Each of these can be seen as concave, as convex, or as a flat drawing.[13] Do I really see something different each time, or do I only interpret what I see in a different way? To interpret is to think, to do something; seeing is an experiential state.[14] The different ways in which these figures are seen are not due to different thoughts lying behind the visual reactions. What could "spontaneous" mean if these reactions are not spontaneous? When the staircase "goes into reverse" it does so spontaneously. One does not think of anything special; one does not think at all. Nor does one interpret. One just sees, now a staircase as from above, now a staircase as from below.

The sun, however, is not an entity with such variable perspective. What has all this to do with suggesting that Tycho and Kepler may see different things in the east at dawn? Certainly the cases are different. But these reversible perspective figures are examples of different things being seen in the same configuration, where this difference is due neither to differing visual pictures, nor to any "interpretation" superimposed on the sensation.

Some will see in figure 2 an old Parisienne, others a young woman (à la Toulouse-Lautrec).[15] All normal retinas "take" the same picture; and our sense-datum pictures must be the same, for even if you see an old lady and I a young lady, the pictures we draw of what we see may turn out to be geometrically indistinguishable. (Some can see this *only* in one way, not both. This is like the difficulty we have after finding a face in a tree-puzzle; we cannot thereafter see the tree without the face.)

When what is observed is characterized so differently as "young woman" or "old woman," is it not natural to say that the observers see different things? Or must "see different things" mean only "see different objects"? This is a primary sense of the expression, to be sure. But is there not also a sense in which one who cannot see the young lady in figure 2 sees something different from me, who sees the young lady? Of course there is.

Similarly, in Köhler's famous drawing of the Goblet-and-Faces[16] we "take" the same retinal/cortical/sense-datum picture of the configuration; our drawings might be indistinguishable. I see a goblet, however, and you see two men staring at one another. Do we see the same thing? Of course we do. But then again we do not. (The sense in which we *do* see the same thing begins to lose its philosophical interest.)

I draw my goblet. You say "That's just what I saw, two men in a staring contest." What steps must be taken to get you to see what I see? When attention shifts from the cup to the faces does one's visual picture change? How? What is it that changes? What could change? Nothing optical or sensational is modified. Yet one sees different things. The organization of what one sees changes.

How does one describe the difference between the *jeune fille* and the *vieille femme* in figure 2? Perhaps the difference is not describable:

Figure 2

it may just show itself. That two observers have not seen the same things in figure 2 could show itself in their behaviour. What is the difference between us when you see the zebra as black with white stripes and I see it as white with black stripes? Nothing optical. Yet there might be a context (for instance, in the genetics of animal pigmentation), where such a difference could be important.

A third group of figures will stress further this organizational element of seeing and observing. They will hint at how much more is involved when Tycho and Kepler witness the dawn than "the formula" suggests.

What is portrayed in figure 3? Your retinas and visual cortices are affected much as mine are; our sense-datum pictures would not differ. Surely we could all produce an accurate sketch of figure 3. Do we see the same thing?

I see a bear climbing up the other side of a tree. Did the elements "pull together"/cohere/organize, when you learned this?[17] You

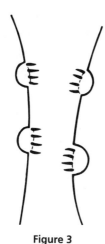

Figure 3

might even say with Wittgenstein "it has not changed, and yet I see it differently . . ."[18] Now, does it not have ". . . a quite particular 'organization'"?

Organization is not itself seen as are the lines and colours of a drawing. It is not itself a line, shape, or a colour. It is not an element in the visual field, but rather the way in which elements are appreciated. Again, the plot is not another detail in the story. Nor is the tune just one more note. Yet without plots and tunes details and notes would not hang together. Similarly the organization of figure 3 is nothing that registers on the retina along with other details. Yet it gives the lines and shapes a pattern. Were this lacking we would be left with nothing but an unintelligible configuration of lines.

How do visual experiences become organized? How is seeing possible?

Consider figure 4 in the context of figure 5:

Figure 4

The context gives us the clue. Here some people could not see the figure as an antelope. Could people who had never seen an antelope, but only birds, see an antelope in figure 4?

In the context of figure 6 the figure may indeed stand out as an antelope. It might even be urged that the figure seen in figure 5 has no similarity to the one in figure 6 although the two are congruent. Could anything be more opposed to a sense-datum account of seeing?

Of a figure similar to the Necker cube (figure 1) Wittgenstein writes, "You could imagine [this] appearing in several places in a text-book. In the relevant text something different is in question every time: here a glass cube, there an inverted open box, there a wire frame of that shape, there three boards forming a solid angle. Each time the text supplies the interpretation of the illustration. But we can also see the illustration now as one thing, now as another. So we interpret it, and see it as we interpret it."[19]

Consider now the head-and-shoulders in figure 7:

The upper margin of the picture cuts the brow, thus the top of the head is not shown. The point of the jaw, clean shaven and brightly illuminated, is just above the geometric center of the picture. A white mantle . . . covers the right shoulder. The

Figure 5

Figure 6

right upper sleeve is exposed as the rather black area at the lower left. The hair and beard are after the manner of a late mediaeval representation of Christ.[20]

The appropriate aspect of the illustration is brought out by the verbal context in which it appears. It is not an illustration of anything determinate unless it appears in some such context. In the same way, I must talk and gesture around figure 4 to get you to see the antelope when only the bird has revealed itself. I must provide a context. The context is part of the illustration itself.

Such a context, however, need not be set out explicitly. Often it is "built into" thinking, imagining and picturing. We are set[21] to appreciate the visual aspect of things in certain ways. Elements in our experience do not cluster at random.

Figure 7

A trained physicist could see one thing in figure 8: an X-ray tube viewed from the cathode. Would Sir Lawrence Bragg and an Eskimo baby see the same thing when looking at an X-ray tube? Yes, and no. Yes—they are visually aware of the same object. No—the *ways* in which they are visually aware are profoundly different. Seeing is not only the having of a visual experience; it is also the way in which the visual experience is had.

At school the physicist had gazed at this glass-and-metal instrument. Returning now, after years in University and research, his eye lights upon the same object once again. Does he see the same thing now as he did then? Now he sees the instrument in terms of electrical circuit theory, thermodynamic theory, the theories of metal and glass structure, thermionic emission, optical transmission, refraction, diffraction, atomic theory, quantum theory and special relativity.

Contrast the freshman's view of college with that of his ancient tutor. Compare a man's first glance at the motor of his car with a similar glance ten exasperating years later.

"Granted, one learns all these things," it may be countered, "but it all figures in the interpretation the physicist puts on what he sees. Though the layman sees exactly what the physicist sees, he cannot interpret it in the same way because he has not learned so much."

Is the physicist doing more than just seeing? No; he does nothing over and above what the layman does when he sees an X-ray tube. What are you doing over and above reading these words? Are you interpreting marks on a page? When would this ever be a natural way of speaking? Would an infant see what you see here, when you see words and sentences and he sees but marks and lines? One does nothing beyond looking and seeing when one dodges bicycles, glances at a friend, or notices a cat in the garden.

"The physicist and the layman see the same thing," it is objected, "but they do not make

Figure 8

the same thing of it." The layman can make nothing of it. Nor is that just a figure of speech. I can make nothing of the Arab word for *cat*, though my purely visual impressions may be indistinguishable from those of the Arab who can. I must learn Arabic before I can see what he sees. The layman must learn physics before he can see what the physicist sees.

If one must find a paradigm case of seeing it would be better to regard as such not the visual apprehension of colour patches but things like seeing what time it is, seeing what key a piece of music is written in, and seeing whether a wound is septic.[22]

Pierre Duhem writes:

Enter a laboratory; approach the table crowded with an assortment of apparatus, an electric cell, silk-covered copper wire, small cups of mercury, spools, a mirror mounted on an iron bar; the experimenter is inserting into small openings the metal ends of ebony-headed pins; the iron oscillates, and the mirror attached to it throws a luminous band upon a celluloid scale; the forward-backward motion of this spot enables the physicist to observe the minute oscillations of the iron bar. But ask him

what he is doing. Will he answer "I am studying the oscillations of an iron bar which carries a mirror"? No, he will say that he is measuring the electric resistance of the spools. If you are astonished, if you ask him what his words mean, what relation they have with the phenomena he has been observing and which you have noted at the same time as he, he will answer that your question requires a long explanation and that you should take a course in electricity.[23]

The visitor must learn some physics before he can see what the physicist sees. Only then will the context throw into relief those features of the objects before him which the physicist sees as indicating resistance.

This obtains in all seeing. Attention is rarely directed to the space between the leaves of a tree, save when a Keats brings it to our notice.[24] (Consider also what was involved in Crusoe's seeing a vacant space in the sand as a footprint.) Our attention most naturally rests on objects and events which dominate the visual field. What a blooming, buzzing, undifferentiated confusion visual life would be if we all arose tomorrow with attention capable of dwelling only on what had heretofore been overlooked.[25]

The infant and the layman can see: they are not blind. But they cannot see what the physicist sees; they are blind to what he sees.[26] We may not hear that the oboe is out of tune, though this will be painfully obvious to the trained musician. (Who incidentally, will not hear the tones and *interpret* them as being out of tune, but will simply hear the oboe to be out of tune. We simply see what time it is; the surgeon simply sees a wound to be septic; the physicist sees the X-ray tube's anode overheating.) The elements of the visitor's visual field, though identical with those of the physicist, are not organized for him as for the physicist; the same lines, colours, shapes are apprehended by both, but not in the same way. There are indefinitely many ways in which a constellation of lines, shapes, patches, may be seen. *Why* a visual pattern is seen differently is a question for psychology, but *that* it may be seen differently is important in any examination of the concepts of seeing and observation. Here, as Wittgenstein might have said, the psychological is a symbol of the logical.

You see a bird, I see an antelope; the physicist sees an X-ray tube, the child a complicated lamp bulb; the microscopist sees coelenterate mesoglea, his new student sees only a gooey, formless stuff. Tycho and Simplicius see a mobile sun, Kepler and Galileo see a static sun.[27]

It may be objected, "Everyone, whatever his state of knowledge, will see figure 1 as a box or cube, viewed as from above or as from below." True; almost everyone, child, layman, physicist, will see the figure as box-like one way or another. But could such observations be made by people ignorant of the construction of box-like objects? No. This objection only shows that most of us—the blind, babies, and dimwits excluded—have learned enough to be able to see this figure as a three-dimensional box. This reveals something about the sense in which Simplicius and Galileo do see the same thing (which I have never denied): they both see a brilliant heavenly body. The schoolboy and the physicist both see that the X-ray tube will smash if dropped. Examining how observers see different things in *x* marks something important about their seeing the same thing when looking at *x*. If seeing different things involves having different knowledge and theories about *x*, then perhaps the sense in which they see the same thing involves their sharing knowledge and theories about *x*. Bragg and the baby share no knowledge of X-ray tubes. They see the same thing only in that if they are looking at *x* they are both having some visual experience of it. Kepler and Tycho agree on more: they see the same thing in a stronger sense. Their visual fields are organized in much the same way. Neither sees the sun about to break out in a grin, or about to crack into ice cubes. (The baby is not "set" even against these eventualities.) Most people today see the same thing at dawn in an even stronger sense: we share much knowledge of the sun. Hence Tycho and Kepler see different things, and yet they see the same thing. That these things can be said depends on their knowledge, experience, and theories.

Kepler and Tycho are to the sun as we are to figure 4, when I see the bird and you see only the antelope. The elements of their experiences are identical; but their conceptual organization is vastly different. Can their visual fields have a different organization? Then they can see different things in the east at dawn.

It is the sense in which Tycho and Kepler do not observe the same thing which must be grasped if one is to understand disagreements within microphysics. Fundamental physics is primarily a search for intelligibility—it is philosophy of matter. Only secondarily is it a search for objects and facts (though the two endeavours are as hand and glove). Microphysicists seek new modes of conceptual organization. If that can be done the finding of new entities will follow. Gold is rarely discovered by one who has not got the lay of the land.

To say that Tycho and Kepler, Simplicius and Galileo, Hooke and Newton, Priestley and Lavoisier, Soddy and Einstein, De Broglie and Born, Heisenberg and Bohm all make the same observations but use them differently is too easy.[28] It does not explain controversy in research science. Were there no sense in which they were different observations they could not be used differently. This may perplex some: that researchers sometimes do not appreciate data in the same way is a serious matter. It is important to realize, however, that sorting out differences about data, evidence, observation, may require more than simply gesturing at observable objects. It may require a comprehensive reappraisal of one's subject matter. This may be difficult, but it should not obscure the fact that nothing less than this may do.

C

There is a sense, then, in which seeing is a "theory-laden" undertaking. Observation of x is shaped by prior knowledge of x. Another influence on observations rests in the language or notation used to express what we know, and without which there would be little we could recognize as knowledge. This will be examined.[29]

I do not mean to identify seeing with *seeing as*. Seeing an X-ray tube is not seeing a glass-and-metal object as an X-ray tube.[30] However, seeing an antelope and seeing an object as an antelope have much in common. Something of the concept of seeing can be discerned from tracing uses of "seeing . . . as . . ." Wittgenstein is reluctant[31] to concede this, but his reasons are not clear to me. On the contrary, the logic of "seeing as" seems to illuminate the general perceptual case.[32] Consider again the footprint in the sand. Here all the organizational features of *seeing as* stand out clearly, in the absence of an "*object*." One can even imagine cases where "He sees it as a footprint" would be a way of referring to another's apprehension of what actually is a footprint. So, while I do not identify, for example, Hamlet's seeing of a camel in the clouds with his seeing of Yorick's skull, there is still something to be learned about the latter from noting what is at work in the former.

There is, however, a further element in seeing and observation. If the label "seeing as" has drawn out certain features of these concepts, "seeing that . . ." may bring out more. Seeing a bear in figure 3 was to see that were the "tree" circled we should come up behind the beast. Seeing the dawn was for Tycho and Simplicius to see that the earth's brilliant satellite was beginning its diurnal circuit around us, while for Kepler and Galileo it was to see that the earth was spinning them back into the light of our local star. Let us examine "seeing that" in these examples. It may be the logical element which connects observing with our knowledge, and with our language.

Of course there are cases where the data are confused and where we may have no clue to guide us. In microscopy one often reports sensations in a phenomenal, lustreless way: "it is green in this light; darkened areas mark the broad end . . ." So too the physicist may say: "the needle oscillates, and there is a faint streak near the neon parabola. Scintillations appear on the periphery of the cathodescope . . ." To deny that these are genuine cases of seeing, even observing, would be unsound, just as is the suggestion that they are the *only* genuine cases of seeing.

These examples are, however, overstressed. The language of shapes, colour patches, oscillations and pointer-readings is appropriate to the unsettled experimental situation, where confusion and even conceptual muddle may dominate. The observer may not know what he is seeing: he aims only to get his observations to cohere against a background of established knowledge. This seeing is the goal of observation. It is in these terms, and not in terms of "phenomenal" seeing, that new inquiry proceeds. Every physicist forced to observe his data as in an oculist's office finds himself in a special, unusual situation. He is obliged to forget what he knows and to watch events like a child. These are non-typical cases, however spectacular they may sometimes be.

First registering observations and then casting about for knowledge of them gives a simple model of how the mind and the eye fit together. The relationship between seeing and the corpus of our knowledge, however, is not a simple one.

What is it to see boxes, staircases, birds, antelopes, bears, goblets, X-ray tubes? It is (at least) to have knowledge of certain sorts. (Robots and electric eyes are blind, however efficiently they react to light. Cameras cannot see.) It is to see that, were certain things done to objects before our eyes, other things would result. How should we regard a man's report that he sees x if we know him to be ignorant of all x-ish things? Precisely as we would regard a four-year-old's report that he sees a meson shower. "Smith sees x" suggests that Smith could specify some things pertinent to x. To see an X-ray tube is at least to see that, were it dropped on stone, it would smash. To see a goblet is to see something with concave interior. We may be wrong, but not always—not even usually. Besides, deceptions proceed in terms of what is normal, ordinary. Because the world is not a cluster of conjurer's tricks, conjurers can exist. Because the logic of "seeing that" is an intimate part of the concept of seeing, we sometimes rub our eyes at illusions.

"Seeing as" and "seeing that" are not components of seeing, as rods and bearings are parts of motors: seeing is not composite. Still, one *can* ask logical questions. What must have occurred, for instance, for us to describe a man as having found a collar stud, or as having seen a bacillus? Unless he had had a visual sensation and knew what a bacillus was (and looked like) we would not say that he had seen a bacillus, except in the sense in which an infant could see a bacillus. "Seeing as" and "seeing that," then, are not psychological components of seeing. They are logically distinguishable elements in seeing-talk, in our concept of seeing.

To see figure 1 as a transparent box, an ice-cube, or a block of glass is to see that it is six-faced, twelve-edged, eight-cornered. Its corners are solid right angles; if constructed it would be of rigid, or semi-rigid material, not of liquescent or gaseous stuff like oil, vapour or flames. It would be tangible. It would take up space in an exclusive way, being locatable here, there, but at least somewhere. Nor would it cease to exist when we blinked. Seeing it as a cube is just to see that all these things would obtain.

This is knowledge: it is knowing what kind of a thing "box" or "cube" denotes and something about what materials can make up such an entity. "Transparent box" or "glass cube" would not express what was seen were any of these further considerations denied. Seeing a bird in the sky involves seeing that it will not suddenly do vertical snap rolls; and this is more than marks the retina. We could be wrong. But to see a bird, even momentarily, is to see it in all these connexions. As Wisdom would say, every perception involves an aetiology and a prognosis.[33] . . .

"Seeing that" threads knowledge into our seeing; it saves us from re-identifying everything that meets our eye; it allows physicists to observe new data as physicists, and not as cameras. We do not ask "What's that?" of every passing bicycle. The knowledge is there in the seeing and not an adjunct of it. (The pattern of threads is there in the cloth and not tacked on to it by ancillary operations.) We rarely catch ourselves tacking knowledge on to what meets the eye. Seeing this page as having an opposite side requires no squeezing or forcing, yet nothing optical guarantees that when you turn the sheet it will not cease to exist. This is but another way of saying that ordinary seeing is corrigible, which everybody would happily concede. The search for incorrigible seeing has sometimes led some philosophers to deny that anything less than the incorrigible is seeing at all.

Seeing an object x is to see that it may behave in the ways we know x's do behave: if the object's behaviour does not accord with what we expect of x's we may be blocked from seeing it as a straight-forward x any longer. Now we rarely see dolphin as fish, the earth as flat, the heavens as an inverted bowl or the sun as our satellite. ". . . [W]hat I perceive as the dawning of an aspect is not a property of the object, but an internal relation between it and other objects.[34] To see in figure 8 an X-ray tube is to see that a photo-sensitive plate placed below it will be irradiated. It is to see that the target will get extremely hot, and as it has no water-jacket it must be made of metal with a high melting-point—molybdenum or tungsten. It is to see that at high voltages green fluorescence will appear at the anode. Could a physicist see an X-ray tube without seeing that these other things would obtain? Could one see something as an incandescent light bulb and fail to see that it is the wire filament which "lights up" to a white heat? The answer may sometimes be "yes," but this only indicates that different things can be meant by "X-ray tube" and "incandescent bulb." Two people confronted with an *x* may mean different things by *x*. Must their saying "I see *x*" mean that they see the same thing? A child could parrot "X-ray tube," or "Kentucky" or "Winston," when confronted with the figure above, but he would not see that these other things followed. And this is what the physicist does see.

If in the brilliant disc of which he is visually aware Tycho sees only the sun, then he cannot but see that it is a body which will behave in characteristically "Tychonic" ways. These serve as the foundation for Tycho's general geocentric-geostatic theories about the sun. They are not imposed on his visual impressions as a tandem interpretation: they are "there" in the seeing. (So too the interpretation of a piece of music is there in the music. Where else could it be? It is not something superimposed upon pure, unadulterated sound.)

Similarly we see figure 1 as from underneath, as from above, or as a diagram of a rat maze or a gem-cutting project. However construed, the construing is there in the seeing. One is tempted to say "the construing *is* the seeing." The thread and its arrangement *is* the fabric, the sound and its composition *is* the music, the colour and its disposition *is* the painting. There are not two operations involved in my seeing figure 1 as an ice-cube; I simply see it as an ice-cube. Analogously, the physicist sees an X-ray tube, not by first soaking up reflected light and then clamping on interpretations, but just as you see this page before you.

Tycho sees the sun beginning its journey from horizon to horizon. He sees that from some celestial vantage point the sun (carrying with it the moon and planets) could be watched circling our fixed earth. Watching the sun at dawn through Tychonic spectacles would be to see it in something like this way.

Kepler's visual field, however, has a different conceptual organization. Yet a drawing of what he sees at dawn could be a drawing of exactly what Tycho saw, and could be recognized as such by Tycho. But Kepler will see the horizon dipping, or turning away, from our fixed local star. The shift from sunrise to horizon-turn is analogous to the shift-of-aspect phenomena already considered; it is occasioned by differences between what Tycho and Kepler think they know.

These logical features of the concept of seeing are inextricable and indispensable to observation in research physics. Why indispensable? That men do see in a way that permits analysis into "seeing as" and "seeing that" factors is one thing; "indispensable," however, suggests that the world must be seen thus. This is a stronger claim, requiring a stronger argument. Let us put it differently: that observation in physics is not an encounter with unfamiliar and unconnected flashes, sounds and bumps, but rather a calculated meeting with these as flashes, sounds and bumps of a particular kind—this might figure in an account of what observation is. It would not secure the point that observation could not be otherwise. This latter type of argument is now required: it must establish that an alternative account would be not merely false, but absurd. To this I now turn.

D

Fortunately, we do not see the sun and the moon as we see the points of colour and light in the oculist's office; nor does the physicist see his laboratory equipment, his desk, or his hands in the baffled way that he may view a cloud-chamber photograph or an oscillograph pattern. In most cases we could give further information about what sort of thing we see. This might be expressed in a list: for instance, that *x* would break if dropped, that *x* is hollow, and so on.

To see figure 3 as a bear on a tree is to see that further observations are possible; we can imagine the bear as viewed from the side or from behind. Indeed, seeing figure 3 as a bear is just to have seen that these other views could all be simultaneous. It is also to see that certain observations are not possible: for example, the bear cannot be waving one paw in the air, nor be dangling one foot. This too is "there" in the seeing.

"Is it a question of both seeing and thinking? Or an amalgam of the two, as I should almost like to say?" Whatever one would like to say, there is more to seeing figure 3 as a bear than optics, photochemistry or phenomenalism can explain.[35]

Notice a logical feature: "see that" and "seeing that" are always followed by "sentential" clauses. The addition of but an initial capital letter and a full stop sets them up as independent sentences. One can see an ice-cube, or see a kite as a bird. One cannot see that an ice-cube, nor see that a bird. Nor is this due to limitations of vision. Rather, one may see that *ice-cubes can melt*; that *birds have "hollow" bones*. Tycho and Simplicius see that *the universe is geocentric*; Kepler and Galileo see that *it is heliocentric*. The physicist sees that *anode-fluorescence will appear in an X-ray tube at high voltages*. The phrases in italics are complete sentential units.

Pictures and statements differ in logical type, and the steps between visual pictures and the statements of what is seen are many and intricate. Our visual consciousness is dominated by pictures; scientific knowledge, however, is primarily linguistic. Seeing is, as I should almost like to say, an amalgam of the two—pictures and language. At the least, the concept of seeing embraces the concepts of visual sensation and of knowledge.

The gap between pictures and language locates the logical function of "seeing that." For vision is essentially pictorial, knowledge fundamentally linguistic. Both vision and knowledge are indispensable elements in seeing; but differences between pictorial and linguistic representa-

tation may mark differences between the optical and conceptual features of seeing. This may illuminate what "seeing that" consists in.

Not all the elements of statement correspond to the elements of pictures: only someone who misunderstood the uses of language would expect otherwise. There is a "linguistic" factor in seeing, although there is nothing linguistic about what forms in the eye, or in the mind's eye. Unless there were this linguistic element, nothing we ever observed could have relevance for our knowledge. We could not speak of significant observations: nothing seen would make sense, and microscopy would only be a kind of kaleidoscopy. For what is it for things to make sense other than for descriptions of them to be composed of meaningful sentences?

We must explore the gulf between pictures and language, between sketching and describing, drawing and reporting. Only by showing how picturing and speaking are different can one suggest how "seeing that" may bring them together; and brought together they must be if observations are to be *significant or noteworthy*.

Knowledge here is of what there is, as factually expressed in books, reports, and essays. How to do things is not our concern. I know how to whistle; but could I express that knowledge in language? Could I describe the taste of salt, even though I know perfectly well how salt tastes? I know how to control a parachute—much of that knowledge was imparted in lectures and drills, but an essential part of it was not *imparted* at all; it was "got on the spot." Physicists rely on "know-how," on the "feel" of things and the "look" of a situation, for these control the direction of research. Such imponderables, however, rarely affect the corpus of physical truths. It is not Galileo's insight, Newton's genius and Einstein's imagination which have *per se* changed our knowledge of what there is: it is the true things they have said. "Physical knowledge," therefore, will mean "what is reportable in the texts, reports and discussions of physics." We are concerned with *savoir*, not *savoir faire*.[36]

The "foundation" of the language of physics, the part closest to mere sensation, is a series of statements. Statements are true or false. Pictures are not at all like statements: they are neither true nor false; retinal, cortical, or sense-datum pictures are neither true nor false. Yet what we see can determine whether statements like "The sun is above the horizon" and "The cube is transparent," are true or false. Our visual sensations may be "set" by language forms; how else could they be appreciated in terms of what we know? Until they *are* so appreciated they do not constitute observation: they are more like the buzzing confusion of fainting or the vacant vista of aimless staring through a railway window. Knowledge of the world is not a *montage* of sticks, stones, colour patches and noises, but a system of propositions.

Figure 8 asserts nothing. It could be inaccurate, but it could not be a lie. This is the wedge between pictures and language.

Significance, relevance—these notions depend on what we already know. Objects, events, pictures, are not intrinsically significant or relevant. If seeing were just an optical-chemical process, then nothing we saw would ever be relevant to what we know, and nothing known could have significance for what we see. Visual life would be unintelligible; intellectual life would lack a visual aspect. Man would be a blind computer harnessed to a brainless photoplate.[37]

Pictures often copy originals. All the elements of a copy, however, have the same kind of function. The lines depict elements in the original. The arrangement of the copy's elements shows the disposition of elements in the original. Copy and original are of the same logical type; you and your reflexion are of the same type. Similarly, language might copy what it describes.[38]

Consider figure 3 alongside "The bear is on the tree," The picture contains a bear-element and a tree-element. If it is true to life, then in the original there is a bear and a tree. If the

sentence is true *of* life, then (just as it contains "bear" and "tree") the situation it describes contains a bear and a tree. The picture combines its elements, it mirrors the actual relation of the bear and the tree. The sentence likewise conjoins "bear" and "tree" in the schema "The ——— is on the ———." This verbal relation signifies the actual relation of the real bear and the real tree. Both picture and sentence are true copies: they contain nothing the original lacks, and lack nothing the original contains. The elements of the picture stand for (represent) elements of the original: so do "bear" and "tree." This is more apparent when expressed symbolically as $b \, R \, t$, where b = bear, t = tree and R = the relation of being on.

By the arrangement of their elements these copies show the arrangement in the original situation. Thus figure 3, "The bear is on the tree," and "$b \, R \, t$" show what obtains with the real bear and the real tree; while "The tree is on the bear," and "$t \, R \, b$," and a certain obvious cluster of lines do not show what actually obtains.

The copy is of the same type as the original. We can sketch the bear's teeth, but not his growl, any more than we could see the growl of the original bear. Leonardo could draw Mona Lisa's smile, but not her laugh. Language, however, is more versatile. Here is a dissimilarity between picturing and asserting which will grow to fracture the account once tendered by Wittgenstein, Russell and Wisdom. Language can encapsulate scenes and sounds, teeth and growls, smiles and laughs; a picture, or a gramophone, can do one or the other, but not both. Pictures and recordings stand for things by possessing certain properties of the original itself. Images, reflections, pictures and maps duplicate the spatial properties of what they image, reflect, picture or map; gramophone recordings duplicate audio-temporal properties. Sentences are not like this. They do not stand for things in virtue of possessing properties of the original; they do not *stand for* anything. They can state what is, or could be, the case. They can be used to make assertions, convey descriptions, supply narratives, accounts, etc., none of which depend on the possession of some property in common with what the statement is about. We need not write "THE BEAR is bigger than ITS CUB" to show our meaning.

Images, reflexions, pictures and maps in fact copy originals with different degrees of strictness. A reflexion of King's Parade does not copy in the same sense that a charcoal sketch does, and both differ from the representation of "K.P." on a map of Cambridge and from a town-planner's drawing. The more like a reflexion a map becomes, the less useful it is as a map. Drawings are less like copies of originals than are photographs. Of a roughly sketched ursoid shape one says either "That's a bear" or "That's supposed to be a bear." Similarly with maps. Of a certain dot on the map one says either "This is Cambridge" or "This stands for Cambridge."

Language copies least of all. There are exceptional words like "buzz," "tinkle" and "toot," but they only demonstrate how conventional our languages and notations are. Nothing about "bear" looks like a bear; nothing in the sound of "bear" resembles a growl. That b-e-a-r can refer to bears is due to a convention which co-ordinates the word with the object. There is nothing dangerous about a red flag, yet it is a signal for danger. Of figure 3 we might say "There is a bear." We would never say this of the word "bear." At the cinema we say "It's a bear," or "There's K.P."—not "That stands for a bear," or "That denotes K.P." It is words that denote; but they are rarely like what they denote.

Sentences do not show, for example, bears climbing trees, but they can state that bears climb trees. Showing the sun climbing into the sky consists in representing sun and sky and arranging them appropriately. Stating that the sun is climbing into the sky consists in referring to the sun and then characterizing it as climbing into the sky. The differences between

representing and referring, between arranging and characterizing—these are the differences between picturing and language-using.

These differences exist undiminished between visual sense-data and basic sentences. Early logical constructionists were inattentive to the difficulties in fitting visual sense-data to basic sentences. Had they heeded the differences between pictures and maps, they might have detected greater differences still between pictures and language. One's visual awareness of a brown ursoid patch is logically just as remote from the utterance "(I am aware of a) brown, ursoid patch now," as with any of the pictures and sentences we have considered. The picture is of x; the statement is to the effect that x. The picture shows x; the statement refers to and describes x. The gap between pictures and language is not closed one millimetre by focusing on sense-data and basic sentences.

The prehistory of languages need not detain us. The issue concerns differences between *our* languages and *our* pictures, and not the smallness of those differences at certain historical times. Wittgenstein is misleading about this: ". . . and from [hieroglyphic writing] came the alphabet without the essence of representation being lost."[39] This strengthened the picture theory of meaning, a truth-functional account of language and a theory of atomic sentences. But unless the essence of representation had been lost, languages could not be used in speaking the truth, telling lies, referring and characterizing.

Not all elements of a sentence do the same work. All the elements of pictures, however, just represent. A picture of the dawn could be cut into small pictures, but sentences like "The sun is on the horizon" and "I perceive a solaroid patch now" cannot be cut into small sentences. All the elements of the picture show something; none of the elements of the sentences state anything. "Bear!" may serve as a statement, as may "Tree!" from the woodcutter, or "Sun!" in eclipse-observations. But "the," "is" and "on" are not likely ever to behave as statements.

Pictures are of the picturable. Recordings are of the recordable. You cannot play a smile or a wink on the gramophone. But language is more versatile: we can describe odours, sounds, feels, looks, smiles and winks. This freedom makes type-mistakes possible: for example, "They found his pituitary but not his mind," "We surveyed his retina but could not find his sight." Only when we are free from the natural limitations of pictures and recordings can such errors occur. They are just possible in maps; of the hammer and sickle which signifies Russia on a school map, for instance, a child might ask "How many miles long is the sickle?" Maps with their partially conventional characters must be read (as pictures and photographs need not be); yet they must copy.

There is a corresponding gap between visual pictures and what we know. Seeing bridges this, for while seeing is at the least a "visual copying" of objects, it is also more than that. It is a certain sort of seeing of objects: seeing that if x were done to them y would follow. This fact got lost in all the talk about knowledge arising from sense experience, memory, association and correlation. Memorizing, associating, correlating and comparing mental pictures may be undertaken *ad indefinitum* without one step having been taken towards scientific knowledge, that is, propositions known to be true. How long must one shuffle photographs, diagrams and sketches of antelopes before the statement "antelopes are ungulates" springs forth?

When language and notation are ignored in studies of observation, physics is represented as resting on sensation and low-grade experiment. It is described as repetitious, monotonous concatenations of spectacular sensations, and of school-laboratory experiments. But physical science is not just a systematic exposure of the senses to the world; it is also a way of thinking about the world, a way of forming conceptions. The paradigm observer is not the man who sees and reports what all normal observers see and report, but the man who sees in familiar objects what no one else has seen before.[40]

Notes

1. Cf. The papers by Baker and Gatonby in *Nature*, 1949–present [1958].
2. Galileo, *Dialogue Concerning the Two Chief World Systems* (California, 1953), "The First Day", p. 33.
3. Brain, *Recent Advances in Neurology* (with Strauss) (London, 1929), p. 88. . . .
4. Mann, *The Science of Seeing* (London, 1949), pp. 48–49. Arber, *The Mind and the Eye* (Cambridge, 1954). . . .
5. Kolin: "An astigmatic eye when looking at millimeter paper can accommodate to see sharply either the vertical lines or the horizontal lines" (*Physics* (New York, 1950), pp. 570ff.).
6. Cf. Whewell, *Philosophy of Discovery* (London, 1860), "The Paradoxes of Vision".
7. From the B.B.C. report, 30 June 1954.
8. Newton, *Opticks*, Bk. II, Part I. . . .
9. This famous illusion dates from 1832, when L. A. Necker, the Swiss naturalist, wrote a letter to Sir David Brewster describing how when certain rhomboidal crystals were viewed on end the perspective could shift in the way now familiar to us. Cf. *Phil. Mag.* III, no. 1 (1832), 329–37, especially p. 336. It is important to the present argument to note that this observational phenomenon began life not as a psychologist's trick, but at the very frontiers of observational science.
10. Wittgenstein, *Philosophical Investigations* (Blackwell, Oxford,1953). p. 214.
11. Ibid. p. 194 (top).
12. Ibid. p. 200.
13. This is *not* due to eye movements, or to local retinal fatigue. Cf. Flugel, *Brit. F. Psychol.* VI (1913), 60; *Brit. F. Psychol.* V (1913), 357. Cf. Donahue and Griffiths, *Amer. F. Psychol.* (1931), and Luckiesh, *Visual Illusions and their Applications* (London, 1922). Cf. also Pierce, *Collected Papers* (Harvard, 1931), 5, 183. . . .
14. Wittgenstein, *Phil. Inv.* p. 212.
15. From Boring, *Amer. F. Psychol.* XLII (1930), 444 and cf. Allport, *Brit. F. Psychol.* XXI (1930), 133; Leeper, *F. Genet. Psychol.* XLVI 91935), 41; Street, *Gestalt Completion Test* (Columbia Univ., 1931); Dees and Grindley, *Brit. F. Psychol.* (1947).
16. Köhler, *Gestalt Psychology* (London, 1929). Cf. His *Dynamics in Psychology* (London, 1939).
17. This case is different from figure 1. Now I can help a "slow" percipient by tracing in the outline of the bear. In figure 1 a percipient either gets the perspectival arrangement, or he does not, though even here Wittgenstein makes some suggestions as to how one might help; cf. *Tractatus*, 5. 5423, last line.

18. Wittgenstein, *Phil. Inv.* p. 193. . . .

19. Ibid. p. 193. . . . Cf. Also Wittgenstein, *Tractatus*, 2. 0123.

20. P. B. Porter, *Amer. F. Psychol.* LXVII (1954), 550.

21. Writings by Gestalt psychologists on "set" and "Aufgabe" are many. Yet they are overlooked by most philosophers. A few fundamental papers are: Külpe, *Ber. I Kongress Exp. Psychol., Gessen* (1904); Bartlett, *Brit. F. Psychol.* VIII (1916), 222; George, *Amer. F. Psychol.* XXVIII (1917), 1; Fernberger, *Psychol. Monogr.* XXVI (1919), 6; Zigler, *Amer. F. Psychol.* XXXI (1920), 273; Boring, *Amer. F. Psychol.* XXXV (1924), 301; Wilcocks, *Amer. F. Psychol.* XXXVI (1925), 324; Gilliland, *Psychol. Bull.* XXIV (1927), 622; Gottschaldt, *Psychol. Forsch.* XII (1929), 1; Boring, *Amer. F. Psychol.* XLII (1930), 444; Street, *Gestalt Completion Test* (Columbia University, 1931); Ross and Schilder, *F. Gen. Psychol.* X (1934), 152; Hunt, *Amer. F. Psychol.* XLVII (1935), 1; Süpola, *Psychol. Monogr.* XLVI (1935), 210, 27; Gibson, *Psychol. Bull.* XXXVIII (1941), 781; Henle, *F. Exp. Psychol.* XXX (1942), 1; Luchins, *F. Soc. Psychol.* XXI (1945), 257; Wertheimer, *Productive Thinking* (1945); Russell Davis and Sinha, *Quart. F. Exp. Psychol.* (1950); Hall, *Quart. F. Exp. Psychol.* 11 (1950), 153.

   Philosophy has no concern with fact, only with conceptual matters (cf. Wittgenstein, *Tractatus*, 4. 111); but discussions of perception could not but be improved by the reading of these twenty papers.

22. Often "What do you see?" only poses the question "Can you identify the object before you?". This is calculated more to test one's knowledge than one's eyesight.

23. Duhem, *La Théorie Physique* (Paris, 1914), [see Part III, p.187]

24. Chinese poets felt the significance of "negative features" like the hollow of a clay vessel or the central vacancy of the hub of a wheel (cf. Waley, *Three Ways of Thought in Ancient China* (London, 1939), p. 155).

25. Infants are indiscriminate; they take in spaces, relations, objects and events as being of equal value. They still must learn to organize their visual attention. The camera-clarity of their visual reactions is not by itself sufficient to differentiate elements in their visual fields. Contrast Mr. W. H. Auden who recently said of the poet that he is "bombarded by a stream of varied sensations which would drive him mad if he took them all in. It is impossible to guess how much energy we have to spend every day in not-seeing, not-hearing, not-smelling, not-reacting."

26. Cf. "He was blind to the *expression* of a face. Would his eyesight on that account be defective?" (Wittgenstein, *Phil. Inv.* p. 210) and "Because they seeing see not; and hearing they hear not, neither do they understand" (Matt. Xiii. 10–13).

27. Against this Professor H. H. Price has argued: "Surely it appears to both of them to be rising, to be moving upwards, across the horizon . . . they both see a moving sun: they both see a round bright body which appears to be rising." Philip Frank retorts: "Our sense observation shows only that in the morning the distance between horizon and sun is increasing, but it does not tell us whether the sun is ascending or the horizon is descending . . ." (*Modern Science and Its Philosophy* (Harvard, 1949), p. 231). Precisely. For Galileo and Kepler the horizon drops; for Simplicius and Tycho the sun rises. This is the difference Price misses, and which is central to this essay.

28. This parallels the too-easy epistemological doctrine that all normal observers see the same things in *x*, but interpret them differently.

29. Cf. The important paper by Carmichael, Hogan and Walter, "An Experimental Study of the Effect of Language on the Reproduction of Visually Perceived Form," *F. Exp. Psychol.* XV (1932), 73–86. . . . Cf. also Wittgenstein, *Tractatus*, 5. 6; 5. 61.

30. Wittgenstein, *Phil. Inv.* p. 206.

31. "'Seeing as . . .' is not part of perception. And for that reason it is like seeing and again not like" (ibid. p. 197).

32. "All seeing is seeing as . . . if a person sees something at all it must look like something to him . . ." (G. N. A. Vesey, "Seeing and Seeing As," *Proc. Aristotelian Soc.* (1956), p. 114.)

33. "Is the pinning on of a medal merely the pinning on of a bit of metal?" (Wisdom, "Gods", *Proc. Aristotelian Soc.* (1944–45)).

34. Wittgenstein, *Phil. Inv.* p. 212. Cf. *Tractatus* 2. 0121. Cf. also Helmholtz, *Phys. Optik*, vol. III, p. 18.

35. Wittgenstein, *Phil. Inv.* p. 197.

36. "'Knowing' it means only: being able to describe it" (Wittgenstein, *Phil. Inv.* p. 185).

37. Cf. Kant: "Intuition without concepts is blind. . . . Concepts without intuition are empty." Indeed how is "interpretation" of a *pure* visual sense-datum possible?

38. Cf. Wittgenstein, *Tractatus*, 2. 1–2, 2 and 3–3. 1.

39. Ibid. 4. 016.

40. "'Natural Philosophy' . . . lies not in discovering facts, but in discovering new ways of thinking about them. The test which we apply to these ideas is this—do they enable us to fit the facts to

each other?" Bragg, "The Atom," in *The History of Science* (London, 1948), p. 167.

"Orderly arrangement is the task of the scientist. A science is built out of facts just as a house is built out of bricks. But a mere collection of facts cannot be called a science any more than a pile of bricks can be called a house" (Poincaré, *Foundations of Science* (Science Press, Lancaster, Pa., 1946), p. 127). "An object is frequently not seen *from not knowing how to see it*, rather than from any defect in the organ of vision . . . [Herschel said] "I will prepare the apparatus, and put you in such a position that [Fraunhofer's dark lines] shall be visible, and yet you shall look for them and not find them: after which, while you remain in the same position, I will instruct you *how to see them*, and you shall see them, and not merely wonder you did not see them before, but you shall find it impossible to look at the spectrum without seeing them'" (Babbage, *The Decline of Science in England* (R. Clay, London, 1830)).

STEVEN SHAPIN

Pump and Circumstance:
Robert Boyle's
Literary Technology

The production of knowledge and the communication of knowledge are usually regarded as distinct activities. In this paper I shall argue to the contrary: speech about natural reality is a means of generating knowledge about reality, of securing assent to that knowledge, and of bounding domains of certain knowledge from areas of less certain standing. I shall attempt to display the conventional status of specific ways of speaking about nature and natural knowledge, and I shall examine the historical circumstances in which these ways of speaking were institutionalized. Although I shall be dealing with communication within a scientific community, there is a clear connection between this study and the analysis of scientific popularization. The popularization of science is usually understood as the extension of experience from the few to the many. I argue here that one

of the major resources for generating and validating items of knowledge within the scientific community under study was this same extension of experience from the few to the many: the creation of a scientific public. The etymology of some of our key terms is apposite: if a *community* is a group sharing a common life, *communication* is a means of making things common.

The materials selected to address this issue come from episodes of unusual interest to the history, philosophy and sociology of science. Robert Boyle's experiments in pneumatics in the late 1650s and early 1660s represent a revolutionary moment in the career of scientific knowledge. In his *New Experiments Physico-Mechanical* (1660) and related texts of the early Restoration, Boyle not only produced new knowledge of the behavior of air, he exhibited the proper experimental means by which legitimate knowledge was to be generated and evaluated. And he did so against the background of alternative programmes for the production of knowledge, the proponents of which subjected Boyle's recommended methods to explicit criticism. What was at issue in the controversies over Boyle's air-pump experiments during the 1660s was the question of how claims were to be authenticated as knowledge. What was to count as knowledge, or "science"? How was this to be distinguished from other epistemological categories, such as "belief" and "opinion"? What degree of certainty could be expected of various intellectual enterprises and items of knowledge? And how could the appropriate grades of assurance and certainty be secured?[1]

These were all practical matters. In the setting of early Restoration England there was no one solution to the problem of knowledge which commanded universal assent. The technology of producing knowledge had to be built, exemplified and defended against attack. The categories of knowledge and their generation that seem to us self-evident and unproblematic were neither self-evident nor unproblematic in the 1660s. The foundations of knowledge were not matters merely for philosophers' reflections; they had to be constructed and the propriety of their foundational status had to be argued. The difficulties that many historians evidently have in recognizing this work of construction arise from the very success of that work: to a very large extent we live in the conventional world of knowledge-production that Boyle and his colleagues amongst the experimental philosophers laboured to make safe, self-evident and solid.

Robert Boyle sought to secure universal assent by way of the experimental *matter of fact*. About such facts one could be highly certain; about other items of natural knowledge more circumspection was indicated. Boyle was, therefore, an important actor in the probabilist

and fallibilist movement of seventeenth-century England. Before *circa* 1660, as Hacking and Shapiro have shown, the designations of "knowledge" and "science" were rigidly distinguished from "opinion."[2] Of the former one could expect the absolute certainty of *demonstration*, exemplified by logic and geometry. The goal of physical science had been to attain to this kind of certainty that compelled assent. By contrast, the English experimentalists of the mid-seventeenth century increasingly took the view that all that could be expected of physical knowledge was *probability*, thus breaking down the radical distinction between "knowledge" and "opinion." Physical hypotheses were provisional and revisable; assent to them was not necessary, as it was to mathematical demonstration; and physical science was, to varying degrees, removed from the realm of the demonstrative. The probabilistic conception of physical knowledge was not regarded as a regrettable retreat from more ambitious goals; it was celebrated by its proponents as a wise rejection of failed dogmatism. The quest for necessary and universal assent to physical propositions was seen as improper and impolitic.

If universal assent was not to be expected of explanatory constructs in science, how, then, was proper science to be founded? Boyle and the experimentalists offered the *matter of fact*. The fact was the item of knowledge about which it was legitimate to be "morally certain." A crucial boundary was drawn around the domain of the factual, separating it from those items which might be otherwise and from which absolute and permanent certainty should not be expected. Nature was like a clock: man could be certain of its effects, of the hours shown by its hands; but the mechanism by which these effects were produced, the clock-work, might be various.

It is in the understanding of how matters of fact were produced and how they came to command universal assent that historians have tended to succumb to the temptations of self-evidence.[3] It is the purpose of this paper to display the processes by which Boyle constructed experimental matters of fact and thereby produced the conditions in which assent could be mobilized.

The Mechanics of Fact-Making

Boyle proposed that matters of fact be generated by a multiplication of the witnessing experience. An experience, even of an experimental performance, that was witnessed by one man alone was not a matter of fact. If that witness could be extended to many, and in principle to all men, then the result could be constituted as a matter of fact. In this way, the matter of fact was at once an epistemological and a social category. The foundational category of the experimental philosophy, and of what counted as properly grounded knowledge generally, was an artefact of communication and of whatever social forms were deemed necessary to sustain and enhance communication. I argue that the establishment of matters of fact utilized three technologies: a *material technology* embedded in the construction and operation of the air-pump; a *literary technology* by means of which the phenomena produced by the pump were made known to those who were not direct witnesses; and a *social technology* which laid down the conventions natural philosophers should employ in dealing with each other and considering knowledge-claims.[4] Given the concerns of this paper, I shall be devoting most attention to Boyle's literary technology: the expository means by which matters of fact were established and assent mobilized. Yet the impression should not be given that we are dealing with three distinct technologies: each embedded the others. For example, experimental practices employing the material technology of the air-pump crystallized particular forms of social organization; desired forms of social organization were dra-

matized in the exposition of experimental findings; the literary reporting of air-pump performances provided an experience that was said to be essential to the propagation of the material technology or even to be a valid substitute for direct witness. In studying Boyle's literary technology we are not, therefore, talking about something which is merely a "report" of what was done elsewhere; we are dealing with a most important form of experience and the means for extending and validating experience.

The Material Technology of the Air-Pump

We start by noting the obvious: Boyle's matters of fact were *machine-made*. In his terminology, performances using the air-pump counted as "unobvious" or "elaborate" experiments, contrasted to either the "simple" observation of nature or the "obvious" experiments involved in reflecting upon common artefacts like the gardener's watering-pot. The air-pump (or "pneumatic engine") constructed for Boyle in 1659 (largely by Robert Hooke) was indeed an elaborate bit of scientific machinery (see Figure 1). It consisted of a glass "receiver" of about 30-quarts volume, connected to a brass "cylinder" ("3") within which plied a wooden piston or "sucker" ("4"). The aim was to evacuate the receiver of atmospheric air and thus to achieve a working vacuum. This was done by manually operating a pair of valves: on the downstroke, valve "S" (the stop-cock) was opened and valve "R" was inserted; the sucker was then moved down by means of a rack-and-pinion device ("5" and "7"). On the upstroke, the stop-cock was closed, the valve "R" removed, and a quantity of air drawn into the cylinder was expelled. This operation was repeated many times until the effort of moving the sucker became too great, at which point a working vacuum was deemed to have been attained. Great care had to be taken to ensure that the pump was sealed against leakage, for example at the juncture of receiver and cylinder and around the sides of the sucker. Experi-

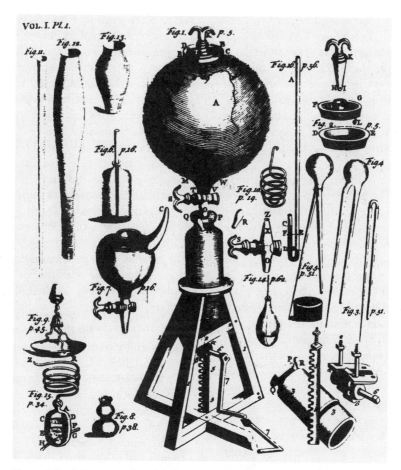

Figure 1 Boyle's pump of 1660 (Source: from Boyle's *New Experiments Physico-Mechanical*, op. cit. note 1)

mental apparatus could be placed into the receiver through an aperture at the top of the receiver ("B-C"), for instance a barometer or simple Torricellian apparatus. The machine was then ready to produce matters of fact. Boyle used the pump to generate phenomena which he interpreted in terms of "the spring of the air" (its elasticity) and the weight of the air (its pressure).

Boyle's air-pump was, as he said, an "elaborate" device; it was also temperamental (difficult to operate properly) and very expensive: the air-pump was seventeenth-century "Big Science." To finance its construction on an individual basis it helped mightily to be a son of the Earl of Cork. Other natural philosophers, almost as well supplied with cash, shied away from the cost of having one built, and a major justification for founding scientific societies in the 1660s and afterwards was the collective financing of the instruments upon which the experimental philosophy was deemed to depend. Air-pumps were not widely distributed in the 1660s. They were scarce commodities: Boyle's original machine was quickly presented to the Royal Society of London; he had one or two re-designed instruments built for him by 1662, operating mainly in Oxford; Christiaan Huygens had one made in The Hague in 1661; there was one at the Montmor Academy in Paris; there was probably one at Christ's College, Cambridge by the mid-1660s, and Henry Power may have possessed one in Halifax from 1661. So far as can be found out, these were all the air-pumps that existed in the decade after their invention.

Thus, air-pump technology posed a problem of access. If knowledge was to be produced using this technology, then the numbers of philosophers who could produce it were limited. Indeed, in Restoration England this restriction was one of the chief recommendations of "elaborate" experimentation: knowledge could no longer legitimately be generated by alchemical "secretists" and sectarian "enthusiasts" who claimed individual and unmediated inspiration from God. Experimental knowledge was to be tempered by collective labour and disciplined by artificial devices. The very intricacy of machines like the air-pump allowed philosophers, it was said, to discern which cause, amongst the many possible, might be responsible for observed effects. This was something, in Boyle's view, that the gardener's pot could not do. However, access to the machine had to be opened up if knowledge-claims were not to be regarded as mere individual opinion and if the machine's matters of fact were not to be validated on the bare say-so of an individual's authority. How was this special sort of access to be achieved?

Witnessing Science

In Boyle's programme the capacity of experiments to yield matters of fact depended not only upon their actual performance but essentially upon the assurance of the relevant community that they had been so performed. He therefore made an important distinction between actual experiments and what are now termed "thought experiments." If knowledge

was to be empirically based, as Boyle and other English experimentalists insisted it should, then its experimental foundations had to be attested to by eye-witnesses. Many phenomena, and particularly those alleged by the alchemists, were difficult to credit; in which cases Boyle averred "that they that have seen them can much more reasonably believe them, than they that have not."[5] The problem with eye-witnessing as a criterion for assurance was one of discipline. How did one police the reports of witnesses so as to avoid radical individualism? Was one obliged to credit a report on the testimony of any witness whatever?

Boyle insisted that witnessing was to be a collective enterprise. In natural philosophy, as in criminal law, the reliability of testimony depended crucially upon its multiplicity:

> For, though the testimony of a single witness shall not suffice to prove the accused party guilty of murder; yet the testimony of two witnesses, though but of equal credit …shall ordinarily suffice to prove a man guilty; because it is thought reasonable to suppose, that, though each testimony single be but probable, yet a concurrence of such probabilities, (which ought in reason to be attributed to the truth of what they jointly tend to prove) may well amount to a moral certainty, i.e. such a certainty, as may warrant the judge to proceed to the sentence of death against the indicted party.[6]

And Thomas Sprat, defending the reliability of the Royal Society's judgements in matters of fact, inquired

> whether, seeing in all Countreys, that are govern'd by Laws, they expect no more, than the consent of two, or three witnesses, in matters of life, and estate; they will not think they are fairly dealt withall, in what concerns their *Knowledg*, if they have the concurring Testimonies of *threescore or an hundred*.[7]

The thrust of the legal analogy should not be

missed. It was not just that one was multiplying authority by multiplying witnesses (although this was part of the tactic); it was that right *action* could be taken, and seen to be taken, on the basis of these collective testimonies. The action concerned the positive giving of assent to matters of fact. The multiplication of witness was an indication that testimony referred to a true state of affairs in nature. Multiple witnessing was counted as an active, and not just a descriptive, licence. Does it not force the conclusion that such and such an action was done (a specific trial), and that subsequent action (offering assent) was warranted?

In experimental practice one way of securing the multiplication of witnesses was to perform experiments in a social space. The "laboratory" was contrasted to the alchemist's closet precisely in that the former was said to be a public and the latter a private space. The early air-pump trials were routinely performed in the Royal Society's ordinary public rooms, the machine being brought there specially for the occasion. In reporting upon his experimental performances Boyle commonly specified that they were "many of them tried in the presence of ingenious men," or that he made them "in the presence of an illustrious assembly of virtuosi (who were spectators of the experiment)."[8] Boyle's collaborator Robert Hooke worked to codify the Society's procedures for the standard recording of experiments: the register was "to be sign'd by a certain Number of Persons present, who have been present, and Witnesses of all the said Proceedings, who, by Sub-scribing their Names, will prove undoubted Testimony..."[9] And Sprat described the role of the "Assembly" in "resolv[ing] upon the matter of *Fact*" by collectively correcting individual idiosyncracies of observation and judgement.[10] In reporting experiments that were particularly crucial or problematic, Boyle named his witnesses and stipulated their qualifications. Thus, the experiment of the original air-pump trials that was

"the principal fruit I promised myself from our engine" was conducted in the presence of "those excellent and deservedly famous Mathematic Professors, Dr. *Wallis*, Dr. *Ward*, and Mr. *Wren*...., whom I name, both as justly counting it an honour to be known to them, and as being glad of such judicious and illustrious witnesses of our experiment..." Another important experiment was attested to by Wallis "who will be allowed to be a very competent judge in these matters." And in his censure of the alchemists Boyle generally warned natural philosophers not "to believe chymical experiments...unless he, that delivers that, mentions his doing it upon his own particular knowledge, or upon the relation of some credible person, avowing it upon his own experience." Alchemists were recommended to name the putative author of these experiments "upon whose credit they relate" them.[11] The credibility of witnesses followed the taken-for-granted conventions of that setting for assessing individuals' reliability and trustworthiness: Oxford professors were accounted more reliable witnesses than Oxfordshire peasants. The natural philosopher had no option but to rely for a substantial part of his knowledge on the testimony of witnesses; and, in assessing that testimony, he (no less than judge or jury) had to determine their credibility. This necessarily involved their moral constitution as well as their knowledgeableness, "for the two grand requisites, of a witness [are] the knowledge he has of the things he delivers, and his faithfulness in truly delivering what he knows." Thus, the giving of witness in experimental philosophy transmitted the social and moral accounting systems of Restoration England.[12]

Another important way of multiplying witnesses to experimentally produced phenomena was to facilitate their replication. Experimental protocols could be reported in such a way as to enable readers of the reports to perform the experiments for themselves, thus ensuring distant but direct witnesses. Boyle elected to publish several of his experimental series in the form of letters to other experimentalists or potential experimentalists. The *New Experiments* of 1660 was written as a letter to his nephew Lord Dungarvan; the various tracts of the *Certain Physiological Essays* of 1661 were written to another nephew Richard Jones; the *History of Colours* of 1664 was originally written to an unspecified friend. The purpose of this form of communication was explicitly to proselytize. The *New Experiments* was published so "that the person I addressed them to might, without mistake, and with as little trouble as possible, be able to repeat such unusual experiments...." The *History of Colours* was designed "not barely to relate [the experiments], but... to teach a young gentleman to make them."[13] Boyle wished to encourage young gentlemen to "addict" themselves to experimental pursuits and, thereby, to multiply both experimental philosophers and experimental facts.

Replication, however, rarely succeeded, as Boyle himself recognized. When he came to prepare the *Continuation of New Experiments* seven years after the original air-pump trials, Boyle admitted that, despite his care in communicating details of the engine and of his procedures, there had been few successful replications:

> ... in five or six years I could hear but of one or two engines that were brought to be fit to work, and of but one or two new experiments that had been added by the ingenious owners of them...[14]

This situation had not notably changed by the mid-1670s. In the seven or eight years after the *Continuation*, Boyle said that he heard "of very few experiments made, either in the engine I used, or in any other made after the model thereof." By this time a note of despair began to appear in Boyle's statements concerning the replication of his air-pump experiments. He

> was more willing to set down divers things with their minute circumstances; because I

was of opinion, that probably many of these experiments would be never either re-examined by others, or re-iterated by myself. For though they may be easily read... yet he, that shall really go about to repeat them, will find it no easy task.[15]

The Literary Technology of Virtual Witnessing

The third way by which witnesses could be multiplied is far more important than the performance of experiments before direct witnesses or the facilitating of actual replication: it is what I shall call "virtual witnessing." The technology of virtual witnessing involves the production in a reader's mind of such an image of an experimental scene as obviates the necessity for either its direct witness or its replication. Through virtual witnessing the multiplication of witnesses could be in principle unlimited. It was therefore the most powerful technology for constituting matters of fact. The validation of experiments, and the crediting of their outcomes as matters of fact, necessarily entailed their realization in the laboratory of the mind and the mind's eye. What was required was a technology of trust and assurance that the things had been done and done in the way claimed.

The technology of virtual witnessing was not different in kind to that used to facilitate actual replication. One could deploy the same linguistic resources in order to encourage the physical replication of experiments or to trigger in the reader's mind a naturalistic image of the experimental scene. Of course, actual replication was to be preferred, for this eliminated reliance upon testimony altogether. Yet, because of natural legitimate suspicion amongst those who were neither direct witnesses nor replicators, a greater degree of assurance was required to produce assent in virtual witnesses. Boyle's literary technology was crafted to secure this assent.

Prolixity and Iconography

In order to understand how Boyle deployed his literary technology of virtual witnessing we have to reorientate some of our common ideas about the status of the scientific *text*. We usually think of an experimental report as a narration of some prior visual experience: it points to sensory experience that lies behind the text. This is correct. However, we should also appreciate that the text itself constitutes a visual source. It is my task here to see how Boyle's texts were constructed so as to provide a source of virtual witness that was agreed to be reliable. The best way to fasten upon the notion of the text as this kind of source might be to start by looking at some of the pictures that Boyle provided alongside his prose.

Figure 1, for example, is an engraving of his original air-pump, appended to the *New Experiments*. Producing these kinds of images was an expensive business in the mid-seventeenth century and natural philosophers used them sparingly. As we see, Figure 1 is not a schematized line-drawing but an attempt at detailed naturalistic representation, complete with the conventions of shadowing and cut-away sections of parts. This is not a picture of the "idea" of an air-pump but of a particular existing air-pump. The same applies to Boyle's pictorial representations of his particular pneumatic experiments: in one, we are shown a mouse lying dead in the receiver; in another, images of the experimenters. Boyle devoted great attention to the manufacture of these engravings, sometimes consulting directly with artist and engraver, sometimes by way of Hooke. Their role was to be a supplement to the imaginative witness provided by the words in the text. In the *Continuation* Boyle expanded upon the relationships between the two sorts of exposition. He told his readers that "they who either were versed in such kind of studies or have any peculiar facility of imagining, would well enough conceive my meaning only by words," but others required visual assistance. He apologized for the relative poverty of the images, "being myself absent from the engraver for a good part of the time he was at work, some of the cuts were misplaced, and not graven in the plates.[16]

Thus, visual representations, few as they necessarily were in Boyle's texts, were mimetic devices. By virtue of the density of *circumstantial* detail that could be conveyed through the engraver's laying of lines, the images imitated reality and gave the viewer a vivid impression of the experimental scene. The sort of naturalistic images that Boyle favoured provided a greater density of circumstantial detail than would have been proffered by more schematic representations. The images served to announce that "this was really done" and that it was done in the way stipulated; they allayed distrust and facilitated virtual witnessing. Therefore, understanding the role of pictorial representations offers a way of appreciating what Boyle was trying to achieve with his literary technology.

In the introductory pages of the *New Experiments*, Boyle's first published experimental findings, he directly announced his intention to be "somewhat prolix." His excuses were three-fold: first delivering things "circumstantially" would, as we have already seen, facilitate replication; second, the density of circumstantial details was justified by the fact that these were "new" experiments, with novel conclusions drawn from them: it was therefore necessary that they be "circumstantially related, to keep the reader from distrusting them"; third, circumstantial reports such as these offered the possibility of virtual witnessing. As Boyle said, "these narratives [are to be] as standing records in our new pneumatics, and [readers] need not reiterate themselves an experiment *to have as distinct an idea of it*, as may suffice them to ground their reflexions and speculations upon."[17] If one wrote an experimental report in the correct way, the reader could take on trust that these things happened. Further, it would be as if that reader had been present at the proceedings. He would be recruited as a witness and be put in a position where he could validate experimental phenomena as matters of fact. Therefore, attention to the writing of experimental reports was of equal importance to doing the experiments themselves.

In the late 1650s Boyle devoted himself to laying down the rules for the literary technology of the experimental programme. Stipulations about how to write proper scientific prose are dispersed throughout his experimental reports of the 1660s, but he also composed a special tract on the subject of "experimental essays." Here Boyle offered extended apologia for his "prolixity": "I have," he understated, "declined that succinct way of writing"; he had sometimes "delivered things, to make them more clear, in such a multitude of words, that I now seem even to myself to have in divers places been guilty of verbosity..." Not just his "verbosity" but also Boyle's ornate sentence-structure, with appositive clauses piled on top of each other, was, he said, part of a plan to convey circumstantial details and to give the impression of verisimilitude:

> ...I have knowingly and purposely transgressed the laws of oratory in one particular, namely, in making sometimes my periods [i.e., complete sentences] or parentheses over-long: for when I could not within the compass of a regular period comprise what I thought requisite to be delivered at once, I chose rather to neglect the precepts of rhetoricians, than the mention of those things, which I thought pertinent to my subject, and useful to you, my reader.[18]

Elaborate sentences, with circumstantial details encompassed within the confines of one grammatical entity, might mimic that immediacy and simultaneity of experience afforded by pictorial representations.

Boyle was endeavouring to constitute himself as a reliable purveyor of experimental testimony and to offer conventions by means of which others could do likewise. The provision of circumstantial details of experimental scenes was a way of assuring readers that real experiments had yielded the findings stipulated. It was also necessary, in Boyle's view, to offer readers circumstantial accounts of *failed* experiments. This performed two functions: first, it allayed anxieties in those neophyte experimentalists whose expectations of success were not immediately fulfilled; second, it assured the reader that the relator was not willfully suppressing inconvenient evidence, that he was in fact being faithful to reality. Complex and circumstantial accounts were to be taken as undistorted mirrors of complex experimental performances, in which a wide range of contingencies might influence outcomes. So, for example, it was not legitimate to hide the fact that air-pumps sometimes did not work properly or that they often leaked: "...I think it becomes one, that professeth himself a faithful relator of experiments not to conceal" such unfortunate contingencies.[19] It is, however, vital to keep in mind that the contingencies proffered in Boyle's circumstantial accounts represent a selection of possible contingencies. There was not, nor can there be, any such thing as a report which notes all circumstances which might affect an experiment. Circumstantial, or stylized, accounts do not, therefore, exist as pure forms but as publicly acknowledged moves towards or away from the reporting of contingencies.

The Modesty of Experimental Narrative

The ability of the reporter to multiply witnesses depended upon readers' acceptance of him as a provider of reliable testimony. It was the burden of Boyle's literary technology to assure his readers that he was such a man as should be believed. He therefore had to find the means to make visible in the text the accepted tokens of a man of good faith. One technique has just been discussed: the reporting of experimental failures. A man who recounted unsuccessful experiments was such a man whose objectivity was not distorted by his interests. Thus, the literary display of a certain sort of morality was a technique in the making of matters of fact. A man whose narratives could be credited as mirrors of reality was a "modest man"; his reports should make that modesty visible.

Boyle found a number of ways of displaying modesty. One of the most straightforward was the use of the form of the experimental essay. The essay (that is, the piece-meal reporting of experimental trials), was explicitly contrasted to the natural philosophical system. Those who wrote entire systems were identified as "confident" individuals, whose ambition extended beyond what was proper or possible. By contrast, those who wrote experimental essays were "sober and modest men," "diligent and judicious" philosophers, who did not "assert more than they can prove." This practice cast the experimental philosopher into the role of intellectual "under-builder," or even that of "a drudge of greater industry than reason." This was, however, a noble character, for it was one that was freely chosen to further "the real advancement of true natural philosophy" rather than personal reputation.[20] The public display of this modesty was an exhibition that concern for individual celebrity did not cloud judgement and distort the integrity of one's reports. In this connection it is absolutely crucial to remember who it was that was portraying himself as a mere "under-builder." He was the son of the Earl of Cork, and everyone knew that very well. Thus, it was plausible that such modesty could have a noble character, and Boyle's presentation of self as a role model for experimental philosophers was powerful.

Another technique for displaying modesty was Boyle's professedly "naked way of writing." He would eschew a "florid" style; his object was to write "rather in a philosophical than a rhetorical strain." This plain, puritanical, unadorned (yet convoluted) style was identified as *functional*. It served to exhibit, once more, the

philosopher's dedication to community service rather than to his personal reputation. Moreover, the "florid" style to be avoided was a hindrance to the clear provision of virtual witness: it was, Boyle said, like painting "the eye-glasses of a telescope."[21]

The most important literary device Boyle employed for demonstrating modesty acted to protect the fundamental epistemological category of the experimental programme: the matter of fact. There were to be appropriate moral postures, and appropriate modes of speech, for epistemological items on either side of the crucial boundary that separated matters of fact from the locutions used to account for them: theories, hypotheses, speculations, and the like. Thus, Boyle told his nephew,

> in almost every one of the following essays I...speak so doubtingly, and use so often, *perhaps, it seems, it is not improbable*, and such other expressions, as argue a diffidence of the truth of the opinions I incline to, and that I should be so shy of laying down principles, and sometimes of so much as venturing at explications.

Since knowledge of physical causes was only "probable," this was the correct moral stance and manner of speech, but things were otherwise with matters of fact, and here a confident mode was not only permissible but necessary:

> ...I dare speak confidently and positively of very few things, except of matters of fact.[22]

It was necessary to speak confidently of matters of fact because, as the foundations of proper philosophy, they required protection. And it was proper to speak confidently of matters of fact, because they were not of one's own making; they were, in the empiricist model, discovered rather than invented. As Boyle told one of his adversaries, experimental facts can "make their own way" and "such as were very probable, would meet with patrons and defenders..."[23] The separation of modes of speech, and the ability of facts to make their own way, was made visible on the printed page. In *New Experiments* Boyle said he intended to leave "a conspicuous interval" between his narratives of experimental findings and his occasional "discourses" upon their interpretation. One might then read the experiments and the "reflexions" separately.[24] Indeed, the construction of Boyle's experimental essays makes manifest the proper balance between the two categories: *New Experiments* consists of a sequential narrative of 43 pneumatic experiments; *Continuation* of 50; and the second part of *Continuation* of an even larger number of disconnected experimental observations, only sparingly larded with interpretative locutions.

The confidence with which one ought to speak about matters of fact extended to stipulations about the proper use of authorities. Citations of other writers should be employed to use them not as "judges, but as witnesses," as "certificates to attest matters of fact." If this practice ran the risk of identifying the experimental philosopher as an ill-read philistine, it was, however, necessary: "...I could be very well content to be thought to have scarce looked upon any other book than that of nature."[25] The injunction against citing of authorities performed a significant function in the mobilization of assent to matters of fact. It was a way of displaying that one was aware of the workings of the Baconian "Idols" and was taking measures to mitigate their corrupting effects on knowledge-claims. A disengagement between experimental narrative and the authority of systematists served to dramatize the author's lack of preconceived expectations and, especially, of theoretical investments in the outcome of experiments. For example, Boyle several times insisted that he was an innocent of the great theoretical systems of the seventeenth century. In order to reinforce the primacy of experimental findings, "I had purposely refrained from acquainting myself thoroughly

with the entire system of either the Atomical, or the Cartesian, or any other whether new or received philosophy..." And, again, he claimed that he had avoided a systematic acquaintance with the systems of Gassendi, Descartes, and even of Bacon, "that I might not be prepossessed with any theory or principles..."[26]

Boyle's "naked way of writing," his professions and displays of humility, and his exhibition of theoretical innocence all complemented each other in the establishment and the protection of matters of fact. They served to portray the author as a disinterested observer and his accounts as unclouded and undistorted mirrors of nature. Such an author gave the signs of a man whose testimony was reliable. Hence, his texts could be credited and the number of witnesses to his experimental narratives could be multiplied indefinitely.

Scientific Discourse and the Community

I have said that the matter of fact was a social as well as an intellectual category. And I have argued that Boyle deployed his literary technology so as to make virtual witnessing a practical option for the validation of experimental performances. I want in this section to examine the ways in which Boyle's literary technology dramatized the social relations proper to a community of experimental philosophers. Only by establishing right rules of discourse between individuals could matters of fact be generated and defended, and only by constituting these matters of fact into the agreed foundations of knowledge could a moral community of experimentalists be created and sustained. Matters of fact were to be produced in a public space: a particular space in which experiments were collectively performed and directly witnessed and an abstract space constituted through virtual witnessing. The problem of producing this kind of knowledge was, therefore, the problem of maintaining a certain form of discourse and a certain form of social solidarity. In the following sections I will discuss the ways in which Boyle's literary technology worked to create and maintain this social solidarity amongst experimental philosophers.

The Linguistic Boundaries of the Experimental Community

In the late 1650s and early 1660s, when Boyle was formulating his experimental and literary practices, the English experimental community was still in its infancy. Even with the founding of the Royal Society, the crystallization of an experimental community centered on Gresham College, and the network of correspondence organized by Henry Oldenburg, the experimental programme was far from securely institutionalized. Criticisms of the experimental way of producing physical knowledge emanated from English philosophers (notably Hobbes) and from Continental writers committed to rationalist methods and to the practice of physics as a demonstrative discipline. Experimentalists were made into figures of fun on the Restoration stage: Thomas Shadwell's *The Virtuoso* dramatized the absurdity of weighing the air, and scored most of its good jokes by parodying the convoluted language of Sir Nicholas Gimcrack (Boyle). The practice of experimental philosophy, despite what numerous historians have assumed, was not overwhelmingly popular in Restoration England. In order for experimental philosophy to be established as a legitimate activity, several things needed to be done. First, it required *recruits*: experimentalists had to be enlisted as neophytes, and converts from other forms of philosophical practice had to be obtained. Second, the social role of the experimental philosopher and the linguistic practices appropriate to an experimental community needed to be defined and publicized.[27] What was the proper nature of discourse in such a community? What were the linguistic

signs of competent membership? And what uses of language could be taken as indications that an individual had transgressed the conventions of the community?

The entry fee to the experimental community was to be the communication of a candidate matter of fact. In *The Sceptical Chymist*, for instance, Boyle extended an olive-branch even to the alchemists. The solid experimental findings produced by some alchemists could be sifted from the dross of their "obscure" speculations. Since the experiments of the alchemists (and of the Aristotelians) frequently "do not evince what they are alleged to prove," the former could be accepted into the experimental philosophy by stripping away the theoretical language with which they happened to be glossed. As Carneades (Boyle's mouthpiece) said,

> ...your hermetic philosophers present us, together with divers substantial and noble experiments, theories, which either like peacocks feathers make a great shew, but are neither solid nor useful; or else like apes, if they have some appearance of being rational, are blemished with some absurdity or other, that, when they are attentively considered, make them appear ridiculous.[28]

Thus, those alchemists who wished to be incorporated into a legitimate philosophical community were instructed what linguistic practices could secure their entry. The same principles were laid down with respect to any practitioner: "let his opinions be never so false, his experiments being true, I am not obliged to believe the former, and am left at liberty to benefit myself by the latter."[29] By arguing that there was only a contingent, not a necessary, connection between the language of matters of fact and theoretical language, Boyle was defining the linguistic terms upon which existing communities could join the experimental enterprise. They were liberal terms, which might serve to maximize potential membership....

Linguistic Boundaries within the Experimental Community

Just as linguistic categories were used to manage entry to the experimental community, distinctions between the language of facts and that of theories were deployed to regulate discourse within it. . . .

The vital difference between matters of fact and all other epistemological categories was the degree of assent one might expect of them. To an authenticated matter of fact all men will assent. In Boyle's system that was taken for granted because it was through the technologies that multiplied witness that matters of fact were constituted. General assent was what made matters of fact, and general assent was therefore mobilized around matters of fact. With "hypotheses," "theories," "conjectures," and the like, the situation was quite different. These categories threatened that assent which could be crystallized in the institution of the matter of fact. Thus, the linguistic conventions of Boyle's experimental programme separated speech appropriate to the two categories as a way of drawing the boundaries between that about which one was to expect certainty and assent and that about which one could expect uncertainty and divisiveness. The idea was not to eliminate dissent or to oblige men to agree to all items in natural philosophy (as it was for Hodges); rather, it was to manage dissent and to keep it within safe bounds. An authenticated matter of fact was treated as a mirror of nature; a theory, by contrast, was clearly man-made and could, therefore, be contested. Boyle's linguistic boundaries acted to segregate what could be disputed from what could not. The management of dispute in experimental philosophy was crucial to protecting the foundations of knowledge.

Manners in Dispute

Since natural philosophers were not to be compelled to give assent to all items of knowledge, dispute and controversy was to be expected. How should this be dealt with? The problem of conducting dispute was a matter of intense practical concern in early Restoration science. During the Civil War and Interregnum the divisiveness of "enthusiasts," sectarians and hermeticists threatened to bring about radical individualism in philosophy. Nor did the various sects of Peripatetic natural philosophers display a public image of a stable and united intellectual community. Unless the new experimental community could exhibit a broadly-based consensus and harmony within its own ranks, it was unreasonable to expect it to secure the legitimacy within Restoration culture that its leaders desired. Moreover, that very consensus was vital to the establishment of matters of fact as the foundational category of the new practice.

By the early 1660s Boyle was in a position to give concrete exemplars of how disputes ought to be conducted; three critics published their responses to his *New Experiments*, and he replied to each one: Linus, Hobbes and Henry More. But even before he had been engaged in dispute, Boyle laid down a set of rules for how controversies were to be handled by the experimental philosopher. For example, in *A Proëmial Essay* (composed 1657), Boyle insisted that disputes should be about findings and not about persons. It was proper to take a hard view of reports which were inaccurate but most improper to attack the character of those who rendered them: "for I love to speak of persons with civility, though of things with freedom." The *ad hominem* style must at all costs be avoided, for the risk was that of making foes out of mere dissenters. This was the key point: potential contributors of matters of fact, however wrong they may be, must be treated as possible converts to the experimental philosophy. If, however, they were bitterly treated, they would be lost to the cause and to the community whose size and consensus validated matters of fact:

> And as for the (very much too common) practice of many, who write, as if they thought railing at a man's person, or wran-

gling about his words, necessary to the confutation of his opinions; besides that I think such a quarrelsome and injurious way of writing does very much misbecome both a philosopher and a Christian, methinks it is as unwise, as it is provoking. For if I civilly endeavour to reason a man out of his opinions, I make myself but one work to do, namely, to convince his understanding; but, if in a bitter or exasperating way I oppose his errors, I increase the difficulties I would surmount, and have as well his affections against me as his judgment: and it is very uneasy to make a proselyte of him, that is not only a dissenter from us, but an enemy to us. . . .[30]

Scientific Knowledge and Exposition: Conclusions

I have shown that three technologies were involved in the production and validation of Boyle's experimental matters of fact: the material, the literary and the social. Although I have concentrated here upon the literary technology, I have also suggested that the three technologies are not distinct: the working of each depends upon and incorporates the others. I want now briefly to develop that point by showing how each technology contributes to a common strategy for constituting matters of fact.

What makes a fact different from an artefact is that the former is not perceived to be man-made. What men make, men may unmake, but a matter of fact is taken to be the very mirror of nature. To identify the role of human agency in the making of an item of knowledge is to identify the possibility of its being otherwise. To shift agency on to natural reality is to stipulate the grounds for universal assent. Each of the three technologies works to achieve the appearance of matters of fact as *given* items: each functions as an objectifying resource.

Take for example, the role of the air-pump in the production of matters of fact. As I have noted, pneumatic facts were machine-made. The product of the pump was not, as it is for the modern scientific machines studied by Latour, an "inscription": it was a visual experience that had to be transformed into an inscription by a witness.[31] However, the air-pump of the 1660s has this in common with the gamma counter of the present-day neuroendocrinological laboratory: it stands between the perceptual competences of a human being and natural reality itself. A "bad" observation taken from a machine need not be ascribed to cognitive or moral faults in the human being, nor is a "good" observation his personal product. It is the machine that has generated the finding. A striking instance of this usage arose in the 1660s when Christiaan Huygens offered a matter of fact produced by his pump which appeared to conflict with one of Boyle's central explanatory resources. Boyle did not impugn Huygens's integrity or his perceptual and cognitive competences. Instead, he suggested that the fault lay with the machine: "[I] question not his Ratiocination, but only the staunchness of his pump."[32] The machine constitutes a resource that may be used to factor out human agency in the intellectual product: "It is not I who says this; it is the machine that speaks," or "it is not your fault; it is the machine's."

Boyle's social technology constituted an objectifying resource by making the production of knowledge visible as a collective enterprise: "it is not I who says this; it is all of us." As Sprat insisted, collective performance and collective witness served to correct the natural working of the "idols": the faultiness, the idiosyncrasy or the bias of any individual's judgement and observational ability. The Royal Society advertised itself as a "union of eyes, and hands"; the space in which it produced its experimental knowledge was stipulated to be a *public space*. It was public in a very precisely defined and very rigorously policed sense: not everyone could come in; not everyone's testimony was of equal worth; not everyone was equally able to influence the official voice of the institution. Nevertheless, what Boyle was proposing, and what the Royal Society was endorsing, was a crucially important *move towards* the public constitution and validation of knowledge. The contrast was, on the one hand, with the private work of the alchemists, and, on the other, with the individual dictates of the systematical philosophers.

In the official formulation of the Royal Society, the production of experimental knowledge commenced with individuals' acts of seeing and believing, and was completed when all individuals voluntarily agreed with one another about what had been seen and ought to be believed. This freedom to speak had to be protected by a special sort of discipline. Radical individualism—each individual setting himself up as the ultimate judge of knowledge —would destroy the conventional basis of knowledge, while the disciplined collective social structure of the experimental language game would create and sustain that factual basis. Thus, the experimentalists were on guard against "dogmatists" and "tyrants" in philosophy, just as they abominated "secretists" who produced their knowledge-claims in a private space. No one man was to have the right to lay down what was to count as knowledge. Legitimate knowledge was objective insofar as it was produced by the collective, and agreed to voluntarily by those who comprised the collective. The objectification of knowledge proceeded through displays of the communal basis of generation and evaluation. Human coercion was to have no visible place in the experimental way of life.

It was the function of the literary technology to create that communal way of life, to bound it, and to provide the forms and conventions of social relations within it. The literary technology of virtual witnessing supplemented the public space of the laboratory by extending a valid witnessing experience to all readers of the text. The boundaries stipulated by Boyle's linguistic practices acted to keep that community from fragmenting and served to protect items of knowledge to which one could expect universal assent from items which produced divisiveness. Similarly, Boyle's stipulations concerning proper manners in dispute worked to guarantee that social solidarity which generated assent to matters of fact and to rule out of order those imputations which would undermine the moral integrity of the experimental way of life.

I have attempted to display these linguistic practices in the making, and, within restrictions of space, I have alluded to sources of seventeenth-century opposition to these practices. It is important to understand two things about these ways of expounding scientific knowledge and securing assent: that they are historical constructions and that there have been alternative practices. It is particularly important to understand this because of the problems of givenness and self-evidence that attend the institutionalization and conventionalization of these practices. Just as the three technologies operate to create the illusion that matters of fact are not man-made, so the institutionalized and conventional status of the scientific discourse that Boyle helped to produce makes the illusion that scientists' speech about natural reality is simply a reflection of that reality. In this instance, and in others like it, the historian has two major tasks: to display the man-made nature of scientific knowledge, and to account for the illusion that this knowledge is *not* man-made. It is one of the recommendations of the sociology of knowledge perspective that analysts often attempt to accomplish these two tasks in the same exercise.

In the late twentieth century scientific papers are rarely, if ever, written with the depth of circumstantial detail which Boyle's reports contained. Why might this be? The answer to this question leads us to the study of linguistic aspects of scientific institutionalization and differentiation. In discussing the characteristics of a *Denkkollektiv*, Ludwik Fleck noted that such a group cultivates "a certain exclusiveness both formally and in content":

> A thought commune becomes isolated formally, but also absolutely bonded together, through statutory and customary arrangements, sometimes a separate language, or at least special terminology...
> The optimum system of a science, the ultimate organization of its principles, is completely incomprehensible to the novice [or, Fleck might have added, to any non-member].[33]

Fleck was suggesting that the linguistic conventions of a body of practitioners constitute an answer to the question "Who may speak?" The language of an institutionalized and specialized scientific group is removed from ordinary speech, and from the speech of scientists belonging to another community, both as a sign and as a vehicle of the group's special and bounded status. Not everyone may speak; the ability to speak entails the mastering of special linguistic competences; and the use of ordinary speech is taken as a sign of non-membership and non-competence. Such a group gives linguistic indications that the generation and validation of its knowledge does not require the mobilizing of belief, trust and assent outwith its own social boundaries. (Yet, when external support or subvention is required, special *occasional* modes of speech may be resorted to, including the various languages of "popularization.")

By contrast, Boyle's circumstantial reporting was a means of involving a wider community and soliciting its participation in the making of factual experimental knowledge. His circumstantial language was a way of bringing readers into the experimental scene, indeed of making the reader an actor in that scene. The reader was to be shown not just the products of experiments but their mode of construction and the contingencies affecting their performance, *as if he were present.* Boyle aimed to accomplish this, not by inventing a totally novel language

(although it was novel to the natural philosophical community of the time), but, it could be argued, by incorporating aspects of ordinary speech and lay techniques of validating knowledge-claims. The language of early Restoration experimental science was, in this sense, a public language. And the use of this public language was, in Boyle's work, essential to the creation of both the knowledge and the social solidarity of the experimental community. Trust and assent had to be won from a public that might crucially deny trust and assent.

Notes

1. R. Boyle, "New Experiments Physico-Mechanical, touching the Spring and Weight of the Air...," in Boyle, *Works*, ed. T. Birch, 6 Vols. (London, 1772), Vol. I, pp. 1–117. (All subsequent references to Boyle's writings are to this edition and will be cited as *RBW*.)
2. I. Hacking, *The Emergence of Probability: A Philosophical Study of Early Ideas about Probability, Induction and Statistical Inference* (Cambridge: Cambridge University Press, 1975), esp. Chapters 3–5; B.J. Shapiro, *Probability and Certainty in Seventeenth-Century England: A Study of the Relationships between Natural Science, Religion, History, Law and Literature* (Princeton, NJ: Princeton University Press, 1983), esp. Chapter 2.
3. This is especially evident in historians' treatment (or lack thereof) of criticisms of seventeenth-century experimentalism by philosophers who denied both the central role of experimental procedures and the foundational status of the matter of fact....
4. By using "technology" to refer to social and literary practices, as well as to hardware, I wish to stress that all three are *knowledge-producing tools.*
5. Boyle, "Two Essays, Concerning the Unsuccessfulness of Experiments," in *RBW*, Vol. I, pp. 318–53, at p. 343 (orig. publ. 1661); Boyle, "Sceptical Chymist," [in *RBW*, Vol. I, pp. 458–586, at] 486....
6. Boyle, "Some Considerations about the Reconcileableness of Reason and Religion," in *RBW*, Vol. IV, pp. 151–91, at p. 182 (orig. publ. 1675); ...
7. T. Sprat, *History of the Royal Society* (London, 1667), 100.
8. Boyle, "New Experiments," op. cit. note 1, 1; Boyle, "The History of Fluidity and Firmness,"

in *RBW*, Vol;. I, pp. 377–442, at p. 410 (orig. publ. 1661); . . .

9. R. Hooke, *Philosophical Experiments and Observations* (London, 1726), pp. 27–28.

10. Sprat, op. cit. note 7, pp. 98–99; see also Shapiro, op. cit. note 2, pp. 21–22.

11. Boyle, "New Experiments," op. cit. note 1, pp. 33–34; Boyle, "A Discovery of the Admirable Rarefaction of Air . . .," in *RBW*, Vol. III, pp. 496–500, at p. 498 (orig. publ. 1671); Boyle, "Sceptical Chymist," op. cit. note 5, p. 460.

12. Boyle, "The Christian Virtuoso," in *RBW*, Vol. V, pp. 508–40, at p. 529 (orig. publ. 1690); see also Shapiro, op. cit. note 2, Chapter 5 (esp. 179). . . .

13. M. Boas [Hall], *Robert Boyle and Seventeenth-Century Chemistry* (Cambridge: Cambridge University Press, 1958), pp. 40–41; Boyle, "New Experiments," op. cit. note 1, 2; Boyle, "The Experimental History of Colours," in *RBW*, Vol. I, pp. 662–778, at p. 633 (orig. publ. 1663). Cf. p. 664, where certain "easy and recreative experiments, which require but little time, or charge, or trouble in the making" were recommended to be tried by ladies. Richard Jones was the "Pyrophilus" to whom other essays were addressed.

14. Boyle "A Continuation of New Experiments Physico-Mechanical, touching the Spring and Weight of the Air," in *RBW*, Vol. III, pp. 175–276, at p. 176.

15. Boyle, "A Continuation of New Experiments, Physico-Mechanical . . . The Second Part," in *RBW*, Vol. IV, pp. 505–93, at p. 505, 507 (orig. publ. 1680).

16. Boyle, "Continuation of New Experiments," op. cit. note 14, p. 178.

17. Boyle, "New Experiments," op. cit. note 1, 1–2 (emphases added).

18. Boyle, ["A Proëmial Essay . . . with Some Considerations Touching Experimental Essays in General" in *RBW*, Vol. 1, pp. 299–318, (orig. publ. 1661)] pp. 305–06; cf. Boyle, "New Experiments," op. cit. note 1, 1: R. S. Westfall, "Unpublished Boyle Papers relating to Scientific Method," *Annals of Science*, Vol. 12 (1956), pp. 63–73, pp. 103–17.

19. Boyle, "New Experiments," op. cit. note 1, p. 26. For an example of Boyle reporting an experimental failure, see ibid., pp. 69–70.

20. Boyle, "Proëmial Essay," op. cit. note 18, pp. 300–01, p. 307; cf. "Sceptical Chymist,"

op. cit. note 5, pp. 469–70, p. 486, p. 584. Several of the less modest personalities of seventeenth-century English science were individuals who lacked the gentle birth that routinely enhanced the credibility of testimony: e.g., Hobbes, Hooke, Wallis and Newton.

21. Boyle, "Proëmial Essay," op. cit. note 18, p. 318, p. 304.

22. Boyle, "Proëmial Essay," op. cit. note 18, p. 307 (emphases in original).

23. Boyle, "An Hydrostatical Discourse, Occansioned by the Objections of the Learned Dr. Henry Morse," in *RBW*, Vol. 3, pp. 596–628 (orig. publ. 1672).

24. Boyle, "New Experiments," op. cit. note 1, 2.

25. Boyle, "Proëmial Essay," op. cit. note 18, p. 313, p. 317.

26. Boyle, "Some Specimens of an Attempt to Make Chymical Experiments Useful to Illustrate the Notions of the Corpuscular Philosophy. The Preface," in *RBW*, Vol. I, pp. 354–59, at p. 355 (orig. publ. 1661); Boyle, "Proëmial Essay," op. cit. note 18, p. 302. On the corrupting effects of "preconceived hypothesis or conjecture," see Boyle, "New Experiments," op. cit. note 1, p. 47; . . .

27. This is not intended as an exhaustive catalogue of the measures necessary for institutionalization. Obviously, patronage was required and alliances had to be forged with existing powerful institutions.

28. Boyle, "Sceptical Chymist," op. cit. note 5, esp. p. 468, p. 513, p. 550, p. 584.

29. Boyle, "Proëmial Essay," op. cit. note 18, p. 303.

30. Boyle, "Proëmial Essay," op. cit. note 18, p. 312.

31. B. Latour and S. Woolgar, *Laboratory Life: The Social Construction of Scientific Facts* (Beverly Hills, Calif.: Sage, 1979), Chapter 2 [reprinted in Part I, p 48] . . .

32. Boyle to R. Moray, July 1662, in [Christiaan Huygens, *Oeuvres complètes*, 22 Vols. (The Hague: M. Nijhoff, 1888–1950)], Vol. IV, pp. 217–20; cf. Boyle, ["A Defence of the Doctrine touching the Spring and Weight of the Air . . . against the Objections of Franciscus Linus," in *RBW*, Vol. I, pp. 118–185], pp. 152–53.

33. L. Fleck, *Genesis and Development of a Scientific Fact*, trans. F. Bradley and T. J. Trenn, eds Trenn and R. K. Merton (Chicago: The University of Chicago Press, 1979), p. 103, p. 105 (orig. publ. In German, 1935).

ANN OAKLEY

Interviewing Women:
A Contradiction in Terms

Interviewing is rather like marriage: everybody knows what it is, an awful lot of people do it, and yet behind each closed front door there is a world of secrets. Despite the fact that much of modern sociology could justifiably be considered "the science of the interview" (Benney and Hughes, 1970, p. 190), very few sociologists who employ interview data actually bother to describe in detail the process of interviewing itself. The conventions of research reporting require them to offer such information as how many interviews were done and how many were not done; the length of time the interviews lasted; whether the questions were asked following some standardised format or not; and how the information was recorded. Some issues on which research reports do not usually comment are: social/personal characteristics of those doing the interviewing; interviewees' feelings about being interviewed and about the interview; interviewers' feelings about interviewees; and quality of interviewer-interviewee interaction; hospitality offered by interviewees to interviewers; attempts by interviewees to use interviewers as sources of information; and the extension of interviewer-interviewee encounters into more broadly-based social relationships.

I shall argue....that social science researchers' awareness of those aspects of interviewing which are "legitimate" and "illegitimate" from the viewpoint of inclusion in research reports reflect their embeddedness in a particular research protocol. This protocol assumes a predominantly masculine model of sociology and society. The relative undervaluation of women's models has led to an unreal theoretical characterisation of the interview as a means of gathering sociological data which cannot and does not work in practice. This lack of fit between the theory and practice of interviewing is especially likely to come to the fore when a feminist interviewer is interviewing women (who may or may not be feminists).

Interviewing: a Masculine Paradigm?

Let us consider first what the methodology textbooks say about interviewing. First, and most obviously, an interview is a way of finding out about people. "If you want an answer, ask a question.... The asking of questions is the main source of social scientific information about everyday behaviour" (Shipman, 1972, p. 76). According to Johan Galtung (1967, p. 149):

> The survey method.... has been indispensable in gaining information about the human conditions and new insights in social theory.
>
> The reasons for the success of the survey method seem to be two:
>
> (1) *theoretically relevant* data are obtained
>
> (2) they are amenable to *statistical treatment*, which means (a) the use of the powerful tools of correlation analysis and multivariate analysis to test substantive relationships, and (b) the tools of statistical tests of hypotheses about generalizability from samples to universes.

Interviewing, which is one[1] means of conducting a survey is essentially a conversation, "merely one of the many ways in which two people talk to one another" (Benney and Hughes, 1970, p. 191), but it is also, significantly, an *instrument* of data collection: "the interviewer is really a tool or an instrument"[2] (Goode and Hatt, 1952, p. 185). As Benney and Hughes express it, (1970, pp. 196–97):

> Regarded as an information-gathering tool, the interview is designed to minimise the local, concrete, immediate circumstances of the particular encounter—including the respective personalities of the participants—and to emphasise only those aspects that can be kept general enough and demonstra-

ble enough to be counted. As an encounter between these two particular people the typical interview has no meaning; it is conceived in a framework of other, comparable meetings between other couples, each recorded in such fashion that elements of communication in common can be easily isolated from more idiosyncratic qualities.

Thus an interview is "not simply a conversation. It is, rather, a pseudo-conversation. In order to be successful, it must have all the warmth and personality exchange of a conversation with the clarity and guidelines of scientific searching" (Goode and Hatt, 1952, p. 191). This requirement means that the interview must be seen as "a specialised pattern of verbal interaction—initiated for a specific purpose, and focussed on some specific content areas, with consequent elimination of extraneous material" (Kahn and Cannell, 1957, p. 16).

The motif of successful interviewing is "be friendly but not too friendly." For the contradiction at the heart of the textbook paradigm is that interviewing necessitates the manipulation of interviewees as objects of study/sources of data, but this can only be achieved via a certain amount of humane treatment. If the interviewee doesn't believe he/she is being kindly and sympathetically treated by the interviewer, then he/she will not consent to be studied and will not come up with the desired information. A balance must then be struck between the warmth required to generate "rapport" and the detachment necessary to see the interviewee as an object under surveillance; walking this tightrope means, not surprisingly, that "interviewing is not easy" (Denzin, 1970, p. 186), although mostly the textbooks do support the idea that it *is* possible to be a perfect interviewer and both to get reliable and valid data and make interviewees believe they are not simple statistics-to-be. It is just a matter of following the rules.

A major preoccupation in the spelling out of the rules is to counsel potential interviewers about where necessary friendliness ends and unwarranted involvement begins. Goode and Hatt's statement on this topic quoted earlier, for example, continues (1952, p. 191):

> Consequently, the interviewer cannot merely lose himself[3] in being friendly. He must introduce himself as though beginning a conversation but from the beginning the additional element of respect, of professional competence, should be maintained. Even the beginning student will make this attempt, else he will find himself merely "maintaining rapport," while failing to penetrate the clichés of contradictions of the respondent. Further he will find that his own confidence is lessened, if his only goal is to maintain friendliness. He is a professional researcher in this situation and he must demand and obtain respect for the task he is trying to perform.

Claire Selltiz and her colleagues give a more explicit recipe. They say (1965, p. 576):

> The interviewer's manner should be friendly, courteous, conversational and unbiased. He should be neither too grim nor too effusive; neither too talkative nor too timid. The idea should be to put the respondent at ease, so that he[4] will talk freely and fully. . . . [Hence,] A brief remark about the weather, the family pets, flowers or children will often serve to break the ice. Above all, an informal, conversational interview is dependent upon a thorough mastery by the interviewer of the actual questions in his schedule. He should be familiar enough with them to ask them conversationally, rather than read them stiffly; and he should know what questions are coming next, so there will be no awkward pauses while he studies the questionnaire.

C.A. Moser, in an earlier text, (1958, pp. 187–88, 195) advises of the dangers of "over-rapport."

Some interviewers are no doubt better than others at establishing what the psychologists call "rapport" and some may even be too good at it—the National Opinion Research Centre Studies[5] found slightly less satisfactory results from the . . . . sociable interviewers who are "fascinated by people" . . . . there is something to be said for the interviewer who, while friendly and interested does not get too emotionally involved with the respondent and his problems. Interviewing on most surveys is a fairly straightforward job, not one calling for exceptional industry, charm or tact. What one asks is that the interviewer's personality should be neither over-aggressive nor over-sociable. Pleasantness and a business-like nature is the ideal combination.

"Rapport," a commonly used but ill-defined term, does not mean in this context what the dictionary says it does ("a sympathetic relationship," *O.E.D.*) but the acceptance by the interviewee of the interviewer's research goals and the interviewee's active search to help the interviewer in providing the relevant information. The person who is interviewed has a passive role in adapting to the definition of the situation offered by the person doing the interviewing. The person doing the interviewing must actively and continually construct the "respondent" (a telling name) as passive. Another way to phrase this is to say that both interviewer and interviewee must be "socialised" into the correct interviewing behaviour (Sjoberg and Nett, 1968, p. 210):

> it is essential not only to train scientists to construct carefully worded questions and draw representative samples but also to educate the public to respond to questions on matters of interest to scientists and to do so in a manner advantageous for scientific analysis. To the extent that such is achieved, a common bond is established between interviewer and interviewee. [However,] It is not enough for the scientist to understand

the world of meaning of his informants; if he is to secure valid data via the structured interview, respondents must be socialised into answering questions in proper fashion.

One piece of behaviour that properly socialised respondents do not engage in is asking questions back. Although the textbooks do not present any evidence about the extent to which interviewers do find in practice that this happens, they warn of its dangers and in the process suggest some possible strategies of avoidance: "Never provide the interviewee with any formal indication of the interviewer's beliefs and values. If the informant[6] poses a question . . . . parry it" (Sjoberg and Nett, 1968, p. 212). "When asked what you mean and think, tell them you are here to learn, not to pass any judgement, that the situation is very complex" (Galtung 1967, p. 161). "If he (the interviewer) should be asked for his views, he should laugh off the request with the remark that his job at the moment is to get opinions, not to have them" (Selltiz *et al.*, 1965, p. 576), and so on. Goode and Hatt (1952, p. 198) offer the most detailed advice on this issue:

What is the interviewer to do, however, if the respondent really wants information? Suppose the interviewee does answer the question but then asks for the opinions of the interviewer. Should he give his honest opinion, or an opinion which he thinks the interviewee wants? In most cases, the rule remains that he is there to obtain information and to focus on the respondent, not himself. Usually, a few simple phrases will shift the emphasis back to the respondent. Some which have been fairly successful are "I guess I haven't thought enough about it to give a good answer right now," "Well, right now, your opinions are more important than mine," and "If you really want to know what I think, I'll be honest and tell you in a moment, after we've finished the interview." Sometimes the diversion can be accomplished by a head-shaking gesture

which suggests "That's a hard one!" while continuing with the interview. In short, the interviewer must avoid the temptation to express his own views, even if given the opportunity.

Of course the reason why the interviewer must pretend not to have opinions (or to be possessed of information the interviewee wants) is because behaving otherwise might "bias" the interview. "Bias" occurs when there are systematic differences between interviewers in the way interviews are conducted, with resulting differences in the data produced. Such bias clearly invalidates the scientific claims of the research, since the question of which information might be coloured by interviewees' responses to interviewers' attitudinal stances and which is independent of this "contamination" cannot be settled in any decisive way.

The paradigm of the social research interview prompted in the methodology textbooks does, then, emphasise (a) its status as a mechanical instrument of data-collection; (b) its function as a specialised form of conversation in which one person asks the questions and another gives the answers; (c) its characterisation of interviewees as essentially passive individuals, and (d) its reduction of interviewers to a question asking and rapport-promoting role. Actually, two separate typifications of the interviewer are prominent in the literature, though the disjunction between the two is never commented on. In one the interviewer is "a combined phonograph and recording system" (Rose, 1945, p. 143); the job of the interviewer "is fundamentally that of a reporter, not an evangelist, a curiosity-seeker, or a debater" (Selltiz *et al.*, 1965, p. 576). It is important to note that while the interviewer must treat the interviewee as an object or data-producing machine which, when handled correctly will function properly, the interviewer herself/himself has the same status from the point of view of the person/people, institution or corporation conducting the research. Both interviewer and interviewee are thus deperson-alised participants in the research process.

The second typification of interviewers in the methodology literature is that of the inter-viewer as psychoanalyst. The interviewer's re-lationship to the interviewee is hierarchical and it is the body of expertise possessed by the in-terviewer that allows the interview to be suc-cessfully conducted. Most crucial in this exercise is the interviewer's use of non-direc-tive comments and probes to encourage a free association of ideas which reveals whatever truth the research has been set up to uncover. Indeed, the term "nondirective interview" is derived directly from the language of psy-chotherapy and carries the logic of inter-viewer-impersonality to its extreme (Selltiz *et al.*, 1965, p. 268):

> Perhaps the most typical remarks made by the interviewer in a nondirective interview are: "You feel that ..." or "Tell me more" or "Why?" or "Isn't that interesting?" or simply "Uh huh." The nondirective inter-viewer's function is primarily to serve as a catalyst to a comprehensive expression of the subject's feelings and beliefs and of the frame of reference within which his feelings and beliefs take on personal significance. To achieve this result, the interviewer must create a completely permissive atmosphere, in which the subject is free to express him-self without fear of disapproval, admonition or dispute and without advice from the interviewer.

Sjoberg and Nett spell out the premises of the free association method (1968, p. 211):

> the actor's (interviewee's) mental condition (is) .... confused and difficult to grasp. Fre-quently the actor himself does not know what he believes; he may be so "immature" that he cannot perceive or cope with his own subconscious thought patterns .... the interviewer must be prepared to follow the interviewee through a jungle of meander-

ing thought ways if he is to arrive at the person's true self.

It seems clear that both psychoanalytic and mechanical typifications of the interviewer and, indeed, the entire paradigmatic represen-tation of "proper" interviews in the methodol-ogy textbooks, owe a great deal more to a masculine social and sociological vantage point than to a feminine one. For example, the para-digm of the "proper" interview appeals to such values as objectivity, detachment, hierarchy and "science" as an important cultural activity which takes priority over people's more indi-vidualised concerns. Thus the errors of poor interviewing comprise subjectivity, involve-ment, the "fiction"[7] of equality and an undue concern with the ways in which people are not statistically comparable. This polarity of "proper" and "improper" interviewing is an al-most classical representation of the widespread gender stereotyping which has been shown, in countless studies, to occur in modern indus-trial civilisations (see for example Bernard, 1975, part I; Fransella and Frost, 1977; Grif-fiths and Saraga, 1979; Oakley, 1972; Sayers, 1979). Women are characterised as sensitive, intuitive, incapable of objectivity and emo-tional detachment and as immersed in the busi-ness of making and sustaining personal relationships. Men are thought superior through their capacity for rationality and sci-entific objectivity and are thus seen to be pos-sessed of an instrumental orientation in their relationships with others. Women are the ex-ploited, the abused; they are unable to exploit others through the "natural" weakness of al-truism—a quality which is also their strength as wives, mothers and housewives. Conversely, men find it easy to exploit, although it is most important that any exploitation be justified in the name of some broad political or economic ideology ("the end justifies the means").

Feminine and masculine psychology in pa-triarchal societies is the psychology of subordi-nate and dominant social groups. The tie between women's irrationality and heightened sensibility on the one hand and their materially disadvantaged position on the other is, for example, also to be found in the case of ethnic minorities. The psychological characteristics of subordinates "form a certain familiar cluster: submissiveness, passivity, docility, dependency, lack of initiative, inability to act, to decide, to think and the like. In general, this cluster includes qualities more characteristic of children than adults—immaturity, weakness and helplessness. If subordinates adopt these characteristics, they are considered well adjusted" (Miller, 1976, p. 7). It is no accident that the methodology textbooks (with one notable exception) (Moser, 1958)[8] refer to the interviewer as male. Although not all interviewees are referred to as female, there are a number of references to "housewives" as the kind of people interviewers are most likely to meet in the course of their work (for example Goode and Hatt, 1952, p. 189). Some of what Jean Baker Miller has to say about the relationship between dominate and subordinate groups would appear to be relevant to this paradigmatic interviewer-interviewee relationship (Miller, 1976, pp. 6–8):

> A dominant group, inevitably, has the greatest influence in determining a culture's overall outlook—its philosophy, morality, social theory and even its science. The dominant group, thus, legitimizes the unequal relationship and incorporates it into society's guiding concepts. . . .
>
> Inevitably the dominant group is the model for "normal human relationships." It then becomes "normal" to treat others destructively and to derogate them, to obscure the truth of what you are doing by creating false explanations and to oppose actions toward equality. In short, if one's identification is with the dominant group, it is "normal" to continue in this pattern. . . .
>
> It follows from this that dominant groups generally do not like to be told about or

even quietly reminded of the existence of inequality. "Normally" they can avoid awareness because their explanation of the relationship becomes so well integrated *in other terms*; they can even believe that both they and the subordinate group share the same interests and, to some extent, a common experience. . . .
>
> Clearly, inequality has created a state of conflict. Yet dominant groups will tend to suppress conflict. They will see any questioning of the "normal" situation as threatening; activities by subordinates in this direction will be perceived with alarm. Dominants are usually convinced that the way things are is right and good, not only for them but especially for the subordinates. All morality confirms this view and all social structure sustains it.

To paraphrase the relevance of this to the interviewer-interviewee relationship we could say that: interviewers define the role of interviewees as subordinates; extracting information is more to be valued than yielding it; the convention of interviewer-interviewee hierarchy is a rationalisation of inequality; what is good for interviewers is not necessarily good for interviewees.

Another way to approach this question of the masculinity of the "proper" interview is to observe that a sociology of feelings and emotion does not exist. Sociology mirrors society in not looking at social interaction from the viewpoint of women (Smith, 1979; Oakley, 1974, chapter 1). While everyone has feelings, "Our society defines being cognitive, intellectual or rational dimensions of experience as superior to being emotional or sentimental. (Significantly, the terms 'emotional' and 'sentimental' have come to connote excessive or degenerate forms of feeling.) Through the prism of our technological and rationalistic culture, we are led to perceive and feel emotions as some irrelevancy or impediment to getting things done." Hence their role in interviewing.

But "Another reason for sociologists' neglect of emotions may be the discipline's attempt to be recognised as a 'real science' and the consequent need to focus on the most objective and measurable features of social life. This coincides with the values of the traditional 'male culture'" (Hochschild, 1975, p. 281).

Getting involved with the people you interview is doubly bad: it jeopardises the hard-won status of sociology as a science and is indicative of a form of personal degeneracy.

Women Interviewing Women: or Objectifying Your Sister

Before I became an interviewer I had read what the textbooks said interviewing ought to be. However, I found it very difficult to realise the prescription in practice, in a number of ways which I describe below. It was these practical difficulties which led me to take a new look at the textbook paradigm. In the rest of this chapter the case I want to make is that when a feminist interviews women: (1) use of prescribed interviewing practice is morally indefensible; (2) general and irreconcilable contradictions at the heart of the textbook paradigm are exposed; and (3) it becomes clear that, in most cases, the goal of finding out about people through interviewing is best achieved when the relationship of interviewer and interviewee is non-hierarchical and when the interviewer is prepared to invest his or her own personal identity in the relationship.

Before arguing the general case I will briefly mention some relevant aspects of my own interviewing experience. I have interviewed several hundred women over a period of some ten years, but it was the most recent research project, one concerned with the transition to motherhood, that particularly highlighted problems in the conventional interviewing recipe. Salient features of this research were that it involved repeated interviewing of a sample of women during a critical phase in their lives (in fact 55 women were interviewed four times; twice in pregnancy and twice afterwards and the average total period of interviewing was 9.4 hours.) It included for some[9] my attendance at the most critical point in this phase: the birth of the baby. The research was preceded by nine months of participant observation chiefly in the hospital setting of interactions between mothers or mothers-to-be and medical people. Although I had a research assistant to help me, I myself did the bulk of the interviewing—178 interviews over a period of some 12 months.[10] The project was my idea[11] and the analysis and writing up of the data was entirely my responsibility.

My difficulties in interviewing women were of two main kinds. First, they asked me a great many questions. Second, repeated interviewing over this kind of period and involving the intensely personal experiences of pregnancy, birth and motherhood, established a rationale of personal involvement I found it problematic and ultimately unhelpful to avoid.

Asking Questions Back

Analysing[12] the tape-recorded interviews I had conducted, I listed 878 questions that interviewees had asked me at some point in the interviewing process. Three-quarters of these (see Table 1) were requests for information (e.g., "Who will deliver my baby?" "How do you cook an egg for a baby?"). Fifteen per cent were questions about me, my experiences or attitudes in the area of reproduction ("Have you got any children?" "Did you breast feed?"); 6 per cent were questions about the research ("Are you going to write a book?" "Who pays

Table 1 *Questions interviewees asked (total 878), Transition to Motherhood Project (percentages)*

Information requests	76
Personal questions	15
Questions about the research	6
Advice questions	4

Table 2 *Interviewees' requests for information (total 664), Transition to Motherhood Project (percentages)*

Medical procedures	31
Organisational procedures	19
Physiology of reproduction	15
Baby care/development/feeding	21
Other	15

you for doing this?"), and 4 per cent were more directly requests for advice on a particular matter ("How long should you wait for sex after childbirth?" "Do you think my baby's got too many clothes on?"). Table 2 goes into more detail about the topics on which interviewees wanted information. The largest category of questions concerned medical procedures: for example, how induction of labour is done, and whether all women attending a particular hospital[13] are given episiotomies. The second-largest category related to infant care or development: for example, "How do you clean a baby's nails?" "When do babies sleep through the night?" Third, there were questions about organisational procedures in the institutional settings where antenatal or delivery care was done; typical questions were concerned with who exactly would be doing antenatal care and what the rules are for husbands' attendance at delivery. Last, there were questions about the physiology of reproduction; for example "Why do some women need caesareans?" and (from one very frightened mother-to-be) "Is it right that the baby doesn't come out of the same hole you pass water out of?"

It would be the understatement of all time to say that I found it very difficult to avoid answering these questions as honestly and fully as I could. I was faced, typically, with a woman who was quite anxious about the fate of herself and her baby, who found it either impossible or extremely difficult to ask questions and receive satisfactory answers from the medical staff with whom she came into contact, and

who saw me as someone who could not only reassure but inform.[14] I felt that I was asking a great deal from these women in the way of time, co-operation and hospitality at a stage in their lives when they had every reason to exclude strangers altogether in order to concentrate on the momentous character of the experiences being lived through. Indeed, I *was* asking a great deal—not only 9.4 hours of interviewing time but confidences on highly personal matters such as sex and money and "real" (i.e., possibly negative or ambivalent) feelings about babies, husbands, etc. I was, in addition, asking some of the women to allow me to witness them in the highly personal act of giving birth. Although the pregnancy interviews did not have to compete with the demands of motherhood for time, 90 per cent of the women were employed when first interviewed and 76 per cent of the first interviews had to take place in the evenings. Although I had timed the first postnatal interview (at about five weeks postpartum) to occur after the disturbances of very early motherhood, for many women it was nevertheless a stressful and busy time. And all this in the interests of "science" or for some book that might possibly materialise out of the research—a book which many of the women interviewed would not read and none would profit from directly (though they hoped that they would not lose too much).

The Transition to Friendship?

In a paper on "Collaborative Interviewing and Interactive Research," Laslett and Rapoport (1975) discuss the advantages and disadvantages of repeated interviewing. They say (p. 968) that the gain in terms of collecting more information in greater depth than would otherwise be possible is partly made by "being responsive to, rather than seeking to avoid, respondent reactions to the interview situation and experience." This sort of research is deemed by them "interactive." The principle of a hierarchical relationship between interviewer and interviewee is not adhered to and "an attempt is made to generate a collaborative approach to the research which engages both the interviewer and respondent in a joint enterprise." Such an approach explicitly does not seek to minimise the personal involvement of the interviewer but as Rapoport and Rapoport (1976, p. 31) put it, relies "very much on the formulation of a relationship between interviewer and interviewee as an important element in achieving the quality of the information....required."[15]

As Laslett and Rapoport note, repeated interviewing is not much discussed in the methodological literature: the paradigm is of an interview as a "one-off" affair. Common sense would suggest that an ethic of detachment on the the interviewer's part is much easier to maintain where there is only one meeting with the the interviewee (and the idea of a "one-off" affair rather than a long-term relationship is undoubtedly closer to the traditional masculine world view I discussed earlier).

In terms of my experience in the childbirth project, I found that interviewees very often took the initiative in defining the interviewer-interviewee relationship as something which existed beyond the limits of question-asking and answering. For example, they did not only offer the minimum hospitality of accommodating me in their homes for the duration of the interview: at 92 per cent of the interviews I was offered tea, coffee or some other drink; 14 per cent of the women also offered me a meal on at least one occasion. As Table 1 suggests, there was also a certain amount of interest in my own situation. What sort of person was I and how did I come to be interested in this subject?

In some cases these kind of "respondent" reactions were evident at the first interview. More often they were generated after the second interview and an important factor here was probably the timing of the interviews. There was an average of 20 weeks between interviews 1 and 2, an average of 11 weeks between interviews 2 and 3 and an average of 15 weeks between interviews 3 and 4. Between the first two interviews most of the women were very busy. Most were still employed and had the extra work of preparing equipment/clothes/a room for the baby—which sometimes meant moving house. Between interviews 2 and 3 most were not out at work and, sensitised by the questions I had asked in the first two interviews to my interest in their birth experience, probably began to associate me in a more direct way with their experiences of the transition to motherhood. At interview 2 I gave them all a stamped addressed postcard on which I asked them to write the date of their baby's birth so I would know when to recontact them for the first postnatal interview. I noticed that this was usually placed in a prominent position (for example on the mantlepiece), to remind the woman or her husband to complete it and it probably served in this way as a reminder of my intrusion into their lives. One illustration of this awareness comes from the third interview with Mary Rosen, a 25-year-old exhibition organiser: "I thought of you after he was born, I thought she'll *never* believe it—a six-hour labour, a 9 lb 6 oz baby and *no* forceps—and all without an epidural, although I had said to you that I wanted one." Sixty two per cent of the women expressed a sustained and quite detailed interest in the research; they wanted to know its goals, any proposed methods for disseminating its findings, how I had come to think of it in the first place, what the attitudes of doctors I had met or collaborated with were to it and so forth. Some of the women took the initiative in contacting me to arrange the second or a subsequent interview, although I had made it clear that I would get in touch with them. Several rang up to report particularly important pieces of information about their antenatal care—in one case a distressing encounter with a doctor who told a woman keen on natural childbirth that this was "for animals: in this hospital we give epidurals"; in another case to tell me of an ultrasound result that changed the expected date of delivery. Several also got in touch to correct or add to things they had said during an interview—for instance, one contacted me several weeks after the fourth interview to explain that she had had an emergency appendicectomy five days after my visit and that her physical symptoms at the time could have affected some of her responses to the questions I asked.

Arguably, these signs of interviewees' involvement indicated their acceptance of the goals of the research project rather than any desire to feel themselves participating in a personal relationship with me. Yet the research was presented to them as *my* research in which I had a personal interest, so it is not likely that a hard and fast dividing line between the two was drawn. One index of their and my reactions to our joint participation in the repeated interviewing situation is that some four years after the final interview I am still in touch with more than a third of the women I interviewed. Four have become close friends, several others I visit occasionally, and the rest write or telephone when they have something salient to report such as the birth of another child.

A Feminist Interviews Women

Such responses I have described on the part of the interviewees to participation in research, particularly that involving repeated interviewing, are not unknown, although they are almost certainly under-reported. It could be suggested that the reason why they were so pronounced in the research project discussed here is because of the attitudes of the interviewer—i.e., the women were reacting to my own evident wish for a relatively intimate and non-hierarchical relationship. While I was careful not to take direct initiatives in this direction, I certainly set out to convey to the people whose co-operation I was seeking the fact that I did not intend to exploit either them or the information they gave me. For instance, if the interview clashed with the demands of

housework and motherhood I offered to, and often did, help with the work that had to be done. When asking the women's permission to record the interview, I said that no one but me would ever listen to the tapes; in mentioning the possibility of publications arising out of the research I told them that their names and personal details would be changed and I would, if they wished, send them details of any such publications, and so forth. The attitude I conveyed could have had some influence in encouraging the women to regard me as a friend rather than purely as a data-gatherer.

The pilot interviews, together with my previous experience of interviewing women, led me to decide that when I was asked questions I would answer them. The practice I followed was to answer all personal questions and questions about the research as fully as was required. For example, when two women asked if I had read their hospital case notes I said I had, and when one of them went on to ask what reason was given in these notes for her forceps delivery, I told her what the notes said. On the emotive issue of whether I experienced childbirth as painful (a common topic of conversation) I told them that I did find it so but that in my view it was worth it to get a baby at the end. Advice questions I also answered fully but made it clear when I was using my own experiences of motherhood as the basis for advice. I also referred women requesting advice to the antenatal and childbearing advice literature or to health visitors, GPs, etc. when appropriate—though the women usually made it clear that it was my opinion in particular they were soliciting. When asked for information I gave it if I could or, again, referred the questioner to an appropriate medical or non-medical authority. Again, the way I responded to interviewees' questions probably encouraged them to regard me as more than an instrument of data-collection.

Dissecting my practice of interviewing further, there were three principal reasons why I decided not to follow the textbook code of ethics with regard to interviewing women. First, I did not regard it as reasonable to adopt a purely exploitative attitude to interviewees as sources of data. My involvement in the women's movement in the early 1970s and the rebirth of feminism in an academic context had led me, along with many others, to re-assess society and sociology as masculine paradigms and to want to bring about change in the traditional cultural and academic treatment of women. "Sisterhood," a somewhat nebulous and problematic, but nevertheless important, concept,[16] certainly demanded that women re-evaluate the basis of their relationships with one another.

The dilemma of a feminist interviewer interviewing women could be summarised by considering the practical application of some of the strategies recommended in the textbooks for meeting interviewee's questions. For example, these advise that such questions as "Which hole does the baby come out of?" "Does an epidural ever paralyse women?" and "Why is it dangerous to leave a small baby alone in the house?" should be met with such responses from the interviewer as "I guess I haven't thought enough about it to give a good answer right now," or "a head-shaking gesture which suggests 'that's a hard one'" (Goode and Hatt, quoted above). Also recommended is laughing off the request with the remark that "my job at the moment is to get opinions, not to have them" (Selltiz *et al.*, quoted above).

A second reason for departing from conventional interviewing ethics was that I regarded sociological research as an essential way of giving the subjective situation of women greater visibility not only in sociology, but, more importantly, in society, than it has traditionally had. Interviewing women was, then, a strategy for documenting women's own accounts of their lives. What *was* important was not taken-for-granted sociological assumptions about the role of the interviewer but a new awareness of the interviewer as an instrument for promoting a sociology for women[17]—that is, as a tool for

making possible the articulated and recorded commentary of women on the very personal business of being female in a patriarchal capitalist society. Note that the formulation of the interviewer role has changed dramatically from being a data-collecting instrument for researchers to being a data-collecting instrument for those whose lives are being researched. Such a reformulation is enhanced where the interviewer is also the researcher. It is not coincidental that in the methodological literature the paradigm of the research process is essentially disjunctive, i.e., researcher and interviewer functions are typically performed by different individuals.

A third reason why I undertook the childbirth research with a degree of scepticism about how far traditional precepts of interviewing could, or should, be applied in practice was because I had found, in my previous interviewing experiences, that an attitude of refusing to answer questions or offer any kind of personal feedback was not helpful in terms of the traditional goal of promoting "rapport." A different role, that could be termed "no intimacy without reciprocity," seemed especially important in longitudinal in-depth interviewing. Without feeling that the interviewing process offered some personal satisfaction to them, interviewees would not be prepared to continue after the first interview. This involves being sensitive not only to those questions that are asked (by either party) but to those that are not asked. The interviewee's definition of the interview is important.

The success of this method cannot, of course, be judged from the evidence I have given so far. On the question of the rapport established in the Transition to Motherhood research I offer the following cameo:

A.O.: "Did you have any questions you wanted to ask but didn't when you last went to the hospital?"

M.C.: "Er, I don't know how to put this really. After sexual intercourse I had some bleeding, three times, only a few drops and I didn't tell the hospital because I didn't know how to put it to them. It worried me first off, as soon as I saw it I cried. I don't know if I'd be able to tell them. You see, I've also got a sore down there and a discharge and you know I wash there lots of times a day. You think I should tell the hospital; I could never speak to my own doctor about it. You see I feel like this but I can talk to you about it and I can talk to my sister about it."

More generally the quality and depth of the information given to me by the women I interviewed can be assessed in *Becoming a Mother* (Oakley, 1979), the book arising out of the research which is based almost exclusively on interviewee accounts.

So far as interviewees' reactions to being interviewed are concerned, I asked them at the end of the last interview the question, "Do you feel that being involved in this research—my coming to see you—has affected your experience of becoming a mother in any way?" Table 3 shows the answers.

Nearly three-quarters of the women said that being interviewed had affected them and the three most common forms this influence

took were in leading them to reflect on their experiences more than they would otherwise have done; in reducing the level of their anxiety and/or in reassuring them of their normality; and in giving a valuable outlet for the verbalisation of feelings. None of those who thought being interviewed had affected them regarding this affect as negative. There were many references to the "therapeutic" effect of talking: "getting it out of your system." (It was generally felt that husbands, mothers, friends, etc., did not provide a sufficiently sympathetic or interested audience for a detailed recounting of the experiences and difficulties of becoming a mother.) It is perhaps important to note here that one of the main conclusions of the research was that there is a considerable discrepancy between the expectations and the reality of the different aspects of motherhood—pregnancy, childbirth, the emotional relationship of mother and child, the work of childrearing. A dominant metaphor used by interviewees to describe their reactions to this hiatus was "shock." In this sense, a process of emotional recovery is endemic in the normal transition to motherhood and there is a general need for some kind of "therapeutic listener" that is not met within the usual circle of family and friends.

On the issue of co-operation, only 2 out of 82 women contacted initially about the research actually refused to take part in it,[18] making a refusal rate of 2 per cent which is extremely low. Once the interviewing was under way only one woman voluntarily dropped out (because of marital problems); an attrition from 66 at interview 1 to 55 at interview 4 was otherwise accounted for by miscarriage, moves, etc. All the women who were asked if they would mind me attending the birth said they didn't mind and all got in touch either directly or indirectly through their husbands when they started labour. The postcards left after interview 2 for interviewees to return after the birth were all completed and returned.

Table 3 *"Has the research affected your experience of becoming a mother?"* *(percentages)*

No	27
Yes:	73
Thought about it more	30
Found it reassuring	25
A relief to talk	25
Changed attitudes/behaviour	7

*Percentages do not add up to 100% because some women gave more than one answer.

Is a "Proper" Interview Ever Possible?

Hidden amongst the admonitions on how to be a perfect interviewer in the social research methods manuals is the covert recognition that the goal of perfection is actually unattainable: the contradiction between the need for "rapport" and the requirement of between-interview comparability cannot be solved. For example, Dexter 1956, p. 156) following Paul (1954), observes that the pretence of neutrality on the interviewer's part is counterproductive: participation demands alignment. Selltiz *et al.* (1965, p. 583) says that

> Much of what we call interviewer bias can more correctly be described as interviewer *differences*, which are inherent in the fact that interviewers are human beings and not machines and that they do not work identically.

Richardson and his colleagues in their popular textbook on interviewing (1965, p. 129) note that

> Although gaining and maintaining satisfactory participation is never the primary objective of the interviewer, it is so intimately related to the quality and quantity of the information sought that the interviewer must always maintain a dual concern: for the quality of his respondent's participation and for the quality of the information being sought. Often.... these qualities are independent of each other and occasionally they may be mutually exclusive.

It is not hard to find echoes of this point of view in the few accounts of the actual process of interviewing that do exist. For example, Zweig, in his study of *Labour, Life and Poverty*, (1949, pp. 1–2)

> dropped the idea of a questionnaire or formal verbal questions.... instead I had casual talks with working-class men on an absolutely equal footing ...

> I made many friends and some of them paid me a visit afterwards or expressed a wish to keep in touch with me. Some of them confided their troubles to me and I often heard the remark: "Strangely enough, I have never talked about that to anybody else." They regarded my interest in their way of life as a sign of sympathy and understanding rarely shown to them even in the inner circle of their family. I never posed as somebody superior to them, or as a judge of their actions but as one of them.

Zweig defended his method on the grounds that telling people they were objects of study met with "an icy reception" and that finding out about other peoples' lives is much more readily done on a basis of friendship than in a formal interview.

More typically and recently, Marie Corbin, the interviewer for the Pahls' study of *Managers and Their Wives*, commented in an Appendix to the book of that name (Corbin, 1971, pp. 303–5):

> Obviously the exact type of relationship that is formed between an interviewer and the people being interviewed is something that the interviewer cannot control entirely, even though the nature of this relationship and how the interviewees classify the interviewer will affect the kinds of information given.... simply because I am a woman and a wife I shared interests with the other wives and this helped to make the relationship a relaxed one.

Corbin goes on:

> In these particular interviews I was conscious of the need to establish some kind of confidence with the couples if the sorts of information required were to be forthcoming.... In theory it should be possible to establish confidence simply by courtesy towards and interest in the interviewees. In practice it can be difficult to spend eight hours in a person's home, share their meals

and listen to their problems and at the same time remain polite, detached and largely uncommunicative. I found the balance between prejudicing the answers to questions which covered almost every aspect of the couples' lives, establishing a relationship that would allow the interviews to be successful and holding a civilised conversation over dinner to be a very precarious one.

Discussing research on copper mining on Bougainville Island, Papua New Guinea, Alexander Mamak describes his growing consciousness of the political context in which research is done (1978, p. 176):

as I became increasingly aware of the unequal relationship existing between management and the union, I found myself becoming more and more emotionally involved in the proceedings. I do not believe this reaction is unusual since, in the words of the well known black sociologist Nathan Hare, "If one is truly cognizant of adverse circumstances, he would be expected, through the process of reason, to experience some emotional response."

And, a third illustration of this point, Dorothy Hobson's account of her research on housewives' experiences of social isolation contains the following remarks (1978, pp. 80–1):

The method of interviewing in a one-to-one situation requires some comment. What I find most difficult is to resist commenting in a way which may direct the answers which the women give to my questions. However, when the taped interview ends we usually talk and then the women ask me questions about my life and family. These questions often reflect areas where they have experienced ambivalent feelings in their own replies. For example, one woman who said during the interview that she did not like being married, asked me how long I had been married and if I liked it. When I told her how long I had

been married she said, "Well I suppose you get used to it in time, I suppose I will." In fact the informal talk after the interview often continues what the women have said during the interview.

It is impossible to tell exactly how the women perceive me but I do not think they see me as too far removed from themselves. This may partly be because I have to arrange the interviews when my own son is at school and leave in time to collect him.[19]

As Bell and Newby (1977, pp. 9–10) note "accounts of doing sociological research are at least as valuable, both to students of sociology and its practitioners, as the exhortations to be found in the much more common textbooks on methodology." All research is political, "from the micropolitics of interpersonal relationships, through the politics of research units, institutions and universities, to those of government departments and finally to the state"—which is one reason why social research is not "like it is presented and prescribed in those texts. It is definitely more complex, messy, various and much more interesting" (Bell and Encel, 1978, p. 4). The "cookbooks" of research methods largely ignore the political context of research, although some make asides about its "ethical dilemmas": "Since we are all human we are all involved in what we are studying when we try to study any aspect of social relations" (Stacey, 1969, p. 2); "frequently researchers, in the course of their interviewing, establish rapport not as scientists but as human beings; yet they proceed to use this humanistically gained knowledge for scientific ends, usually without the informants' knowledge" (Sjoberg and Nett, 1968, pp. 215–16).

These ethical dilemmas are generic to all research involving interviewing for reasons I have already discussed. But they are greatest where there is least social distance between the interviewer and interviewee. Where both share the same gender socialisation and critical life-experiences, social distance can be minimal.

Where both interviewer and interviewee share membership of the same minority group, the basis for equality may impress itself even more urgently on the interviewer's consciousness. Mamak's comments apply equally to a feminist interviewing women (1978, p. 168):

> I found that my academic training in the methodological views of Western social science and its emphasis on "scientific objectivity" conflicted with the experiences of my colonial past. The traditional way in which social science research is conducted proved inadequate for an understanding of the reality, needs and desires of the people I was researching.

Some of the reasons why a "proper" interview is a masculine fiction are illustrated by observations from another field in which individuals try to find out about other individuals—anthropology. Evans-Pritchard reported this conversation during his early research with the Nuers of East Africa (1940, pp. 12–13):

I: "Who are you?"

Cuol: "A man."

I: "What is your name?"

Cuol: "Do you want to know my *name*?"

I: "Yes."

Cuol: "You want to know *my* name?"

I: "Yes, you have come to visit me in my tent and I would like to know who you are."

Cuol: "All right, I am Cuol. What is your name?"

I: "My name is Pritchard."

Cuol: "What is your father's name?"

I: "My father's name is also Pritchard."

Cuol: "No, that cannot be true, you cannot have the same name as your father."

I: "It is the name of my lineage. What is the name of your lineage?"

Cuol: "Do you want to know the name of my lineage?"

I: "Yes."

Cuol: "What will you do with it if I tell you? Will you take it to your country?"

I: "I don't want to do anything with it. I just want to know it since I am living at your camp."

Cuol: "Oh well, we are Lou."

I: "I did not ask you the name of your tribe. I know that. I am asking you the name of your lineage."

Cuol: "Why do you want to know the name of my lineage?"

I: "I don't want to know it."

Cuol: "Then why do you ask me for it? Give me some tobacco."

I defy the most patient ethnologist to make headway against this kind of opposition [concluded Evans-Pritchard].

Interviewees are people with considerable potential for sabotaging the attempt to research them. Where, as in the case of anthropology or repeated interviewing in sociology, the research cannot proceed without a relationship of mutual trust being established between interviewer and interviewee the prospects are particularly dismal. This inevitably changes the interviewer/anthropologist's attitude to the people he/she is studying. A poignant example is the incident related in Elenore Smith Bowen's[20] *Return to Laughter* when the anthropologist witnesses one of her most trusted informants dying in childbirth (1956, p. 163):

> I stood over Amara. She tried to smile at me. She was very ill. I was convinced these women could not help her. She would die. She was my friend but my epitaph for her would be impersonal observations scribbled in my notebook, her memory preserved in an anthropologist's file: "Death (in childbirth)/Cause: witchcraft/Case of Amara." A lecture from the past reproached me: "The anthropologist cannot, like the chemist or biologist, arrange controlled experiments. Like the astronomer, his mere presence

produces changes in the data he is trying to observe. He himself is a disturbing influence which he must endeavour to keep to the minimum. His claim to science must therefore rest on a meticulous accuracy of observations and on a cool, objective approach to his data."

A cool, objective approach to Amara's death?

One can, perhaps, be cool when dealing with questionnaires or when interviewing strangers. But what is one to do when one can collect one's data only by forming personal friendships? It is hard enough to think of a friend as a case history. Was I to stand aloof, observing the course of events?

Professional hesitation meant that Bowen might never see the ceremonies connected with death in childbirth. But, on the other hand, she would see her friend die. Bowen's difficult decision to plead with Amara's kin and the midwives in charge of her case to allow her access to Western medicine did not pay off and Amara did eventually die.

An anthropologist has to "get inside the culture"; participant observation means "that . . . the observer participates in the daily life of the people under study, either openly in the role of researcher or covertly in some disguised role" (Becker and Geer, 1957, p. 28). A feminist interviewing women is by definition both "inside" the culture and participating in that which she is observing. However, in these respects the behaviour of a feminist interviewer/researcher is not extraordinary. Although (Stanley and Wise, 1979, pp. 359–61)

Descriptions of the research process in the social sciences often suggest that the motivation for carrying out substantive work lies in theoretical concerns . . . . the research process appears a very orderly and coherent process indeed. . . . The personal tends to be carefully removed from public statements; these are full of rational argument [and] careful discussion of academic points. [It can equally easily be seen that] all research is "grounded," because no researcher can separate herself from personhood and thus from deriving second order constructs from experience.

A feminist methodology of social science requires that this rationale of research be described and discussed not only in feminist research but in social science research in general. It requires, further, that the mythology of "hygienic" research with its accompanying mystification of the researcher and the researched as objective instruments of data production be replaced by the recognition that personal involvement is more than dangerous bias—it is the condition under which people come to know each other and to admit others into their lives.

Notes

1. I am not dealing with others, such as self-administered questionnaires, here since not quite the same framework applies.
2. For Galtung (1967, p. 138) the appropriate metaphor is a thermometer.
3. Most interviewers are, of course, female.
4. Many "respondents" are, of course, female.
5. See Hyman *et al.* (1955).
6. This label suggests that the interviewer's role is to get the interviewee to "inform" (somewhat against his/her will) on closely guarded and dangerous secrets.
7. Benney and Hughes (1970) discuss interviewing in terms of the dual conventions or "fictions" of equality and comparability.
8. Moser (1958, p. 185) says, "since most interviewers are women I shall refer to them throughout as of the female sex."
9. I attended six of the births.
10. What I have to say about my experience of interviewing relates to my own experience and not that of my research assistant.
11. I am grateful to the Social Science Research Council for funding the research and to Bedford College, London University, for administering it.
12. The interviews were fully transcribed and the analysis then done from the transcripts.
13. The women all had their babies at the same London maternity hospital.
14. I had, of course, made it clear to the women I was

interviewing that I had no medical training, but as I have argued elsewhere (Oakley, 1981b) mothers do not see medical experts as the only legitimate possessors of knowledge about motherhood.

15. It is, however, an important part of the Rapoports' definition of "interactive research" that psychoanalytic principles should be applied in analysing processes of "transference" and "counter-transference" in the interviewer-interviewee relationship.

16. See Mitchell and Oakley (1976) and Oakley (1981a) on the idea of sisterhood.

17. See Smith (1979).

18. Both these were telephone contacts only. See Oakley (1980), chapter 4, for more on the research methods used.

19. Hobson observes that her approach to interviewing women yielded no refusals to co-operate.

20. Elenore Smith Bowen is a pseudonym for a well-known anthropologist.

References

Becker, H. S. and Geer, B. (1957), "Participant Observation and Interviewing: A Comparison? *Human Organisation*, vol. XVI, pp. 28–32.

Bell, C. and Encel, S. (eds) (1978), *Inside the Whale*, Pergamon Press, Oxford.

Bell, C. and Encel, S. (1978), "Introduction" to Bell and Encel (eds), *Inside the Whale*, Pergamon Press, Oxford.

Bell, C. and Newby, H. (1977), *Doing Sociological Research*, Allen & Unwin, London.

Benney, M. and Hughes, E.C. (1970), "Of Sociology and the Interview" in N.K. Denzin (ed.), *Sociological Methods: A Source Book*, Butterworth, London.

Bernard, J. (1975), *Women, Wives, Mothers*, Aldine, Chicago.

Bowen, E. S. (1956), *Return to Laughter*, Gollancz, London.

Corbin, M. (1971), "Appendix 3" in J. M. and R. E. Pahl, *Managers and Their Wives*, Allen Lane, London.

Denzin, N. K. (ed.) (1970), *Sociological Methods: A Source Book*, Butterworth, London.

Denzin, N.K. (1970), "Introduction: Part V" in N. K. Denzin (ed.), *Sociological Methods: A Source Book*, Butterworth, London.

Dexter, L. A. (1956), "Role Relationships and Conceptions of Neutrality in Interviewing," *American Journal of Sociology*, vol. LX14, pp. 153–7.

Evans-Pritchard, E.E. (1940), *The Nuer*, Oxford University Press, London.

Fransella, F. and Frost, K. (1977), *On Being a Woman*, Tavistock, London.

Galtung, J. (1967), *Theory and Methods of Social Research*, Allen & Unwin, London.

Goode, W. J. and Hatt, P. K. (1952), *Methods in Social Research*, McGraw Hill, New York.

Griffiths, D. and Saraga, E. (1979), "Sex Differences and Cognitive Abilities: A Sterile Field of Enquiry" in O. Hartnett *et al.* (eds), *Sex Role Stereotyping*, Tavistock, London.

Hartnett, O., Boden, G. and Fuller, M. (eds) (1979), *Sex-Role Stereotyping*, Tavistock, London.

Hobson, D. (1978), "Housewives: Isolation as Oppression" in Women's Studies Group, Centre for Contemporary Cultural Studies, *Women Take Issue*, Hutchinson, London.

Hochschild, A. R. (1975), "The Sociology of Feeling and Emotion: Selected Possibilities" in M. Millman and R. M. Kanter (eds), *Another Voice: Feminist Perspectives on Social Life and Social Science*, Anchor Books, New York.

Hyman, H. H. *et al.* (1955), *Interviewing in Social Research*, University of Chicago Press.

Kahn, R. L. and Cannell, L. F. (1957), *The Dynamics of Interviewing*, John Wiley, New York.

Laslett, B. and Rapoport, R. (1975), "Collaborative Interviewing and Interactive Research," *Journal of Marriage and the Family*, November, pp. 968–77.

Mamak, A. F. (1978), *Nationalism, Race-Class Consciousness and Social Research on Bougainville Island, Papua, New Guinea*, in C. Bell and S. Encel (eds), *Inside the Whale*, Pergamon Press, Oxford.

Miller, J. B. (1976), *Toward a New Psychology of Women*, Beacon Press, Boston.

Mitchell, J. and Oakley, A. (1976), "Introduction" in J. Mitchell and A. Oakley (eds), *The Rights and Wrongs of Women*, Penguin, Harmondsworth.

Moser, C. A. (1958), *Survey Methods in Social Investigation*, Heinemann, London.

Oakley, A. (1972), *Sex, Gender and Society*, Maurice Temple Smith, London.

Oakley, A. (1974), *The Sociology of Housework*, Martin Robertson, London.

Oakley, A. (1979), *Becoming a Mother*, Martin Robertson, Oxford.

Oakley, A. (1980), *Women Confined: Towards a Sociology of Childbirth*, Martin Robertson, Oxford.

Oakley, A. (1981a), *Subject Women*, Martin Robertson, Oxford.

Oakley, A. (1981b), "Normal Motherhood: An Exercise in Self-Control," in B. Hutter and G. Williams (eds), *Controlling Women*, Croom Helm, London.

Paul, B. (1954), "Interview Techniques and Field Relationships" in A. C. Kroeber (ed.), *Anthropology Today*, University of Chicago Press.

Rapoport, R. and Rapoport, R. (1976), *Dual Career Families Reexamined*, Martin Robertson, London.

Richardson, S.A. *et al.* (1965), *Interviewing: Its Forms and Functions*, Basic Books, New York.

Rose, A. M. (1945), "A Research Note on Experimentation in Interviewing," *American Journal of Sociology*, vol. 51 pp. 143–4.

Sayers, J. (1979), *On the Description of Psychological Sex Differences* in O. Hartnett *et al.* (eds), *Sex Role Stereotyping*, Tavistock, London.

Selltiz, C. Jahoda, M., Deutsch, M. and Cook, S.W. (1965), *Research Methods in Social Relations*, Methuen, London.

Shipman, M. D. (1972), *The Limitations of Social Research*, Longman, London.

Sjoberg, G. and Nett, R. (1968), *A Methodology for Social Research*, Harper & Row, New York.

Smith, D. E. (1979), "A Sociology for Women" in J. A. Sherman and E. T. Beck (eds), *The Prism of Sex*, University of Wisconsin Press, Madison.Stacey, M. (1969), *Methods of Social Research*, Pergamon, Oxford.

Stanley, L. and Wise, S. (1979), "Feminist Research, Feminist Consciousness and Experiences of Sexism," *Women's Studies International Quarterly*, vol. 2, no. 3, pp. 359–79.

Zweig, F. (1949), *Labour, Life and Poverty*, Gollancz, London.

ANDY PICKERING

Against Putting the Phenomena First: The Discovery of the Weak Neutral Current

The discovery of a new natural phenomenon, the so-called "weak neutral current," was reported in July 1973 by a group of European elementary particle physicists. The existence of this phenomenon was seen as constituting the first item of empirical support for a class of quantum field theories known as "gauge theories." Since these theories have subsequently come to dominate the thinking of particle physicists, the discovery of the neutral current represents a major landmark in the development of the field. As such, it has already caught the attention of several historians, philosophers and sociologists of science. . . .

My aim in returning to this topic is to situate the production and reception of the discovery claim within the wider context of contemporary experimental and theoretical work in elementary particle physics, and to attempt to draw some general conclusions from the picture which emerges. The theme of my analysis is that *behind every phenomenon lies a set of practices*, and before beginning the historical account I want to explain what I mean by this.

My explanation pertains directly to the historiography rather than the philosophy of science but, as I hope will become clear, the former has interesting implications for the latter.

Let me begin by sketching out the characteristics of a style of historical writing which I call "the scientist's account."[1] The distinguishing feature of the scientist's account is that the primary explanatory load is put upon natural phenomena: these *come first* and are used to explain scientists' experimental and theoretical practice. Thus, for example, scientists' histories of the discovery of the weak neutral current take it for granted that the neutral current exists as part of the furniture of the world. The discovery of this phenomenon is therefore treated as an observation of the world made with essentially unproblematic and transparent experimental techniques. The actual discovery experiment is presented as a "closed," perfectly well understood, system that yielded data commanding universal assent. A further consequence of taking natural phenomena for granted is that experiment, in the scientist's

From *Studies in History and Philosophy of Science*, Vol. 15, Number 2, (1984) pp. 85–117, Copyright © Pergamon Press Ltd. Reprinted by permission.

account, is treated as entirely separate from theory, and can hence be seen as the ultimate arbiter of theoretical validity: theories stand or fall on their relative success in accounting for the observed phenomena. Thus the present popularity of gauge theory is ascribed to its ability to explain the existence and properties of the weak neutral current and other novel phenomena.[2]

...[H]istorians have had some difficulty in seeing their way past the key element of the scientist's account: few of them have been able fully to escape from the scientist's habit of *putting the phenomena first*, of using natural phenomena to explain scientific practice.... Typically, historians ask why one scientist *succeeded* in observing some historically-accepted phenomenon while others *failed*, and experiment continues to be treated as an independent arbiter of theory. Rarely is the ability of experiment alone to establish the existence of natural phenomena consistently questioned.

That historians should continue to follow scientists in putting the phenomena first is, I would argue, an unsatisfactory state of affairs for two reasons. Firstly: because the historian's methods are not appropriate to adjudicating upon the reality of natural phenomena. One can, for example, sift through the documentary record of particle physics for as long as one likes without coming across a weak neutral current. What one will find is a record of practices, a record of what scientists were *doing*. This leads me to my second and more constructive reason for believing that historians should not put the phenomena first: namely, that to do so leads one to take for granted scientific practices which are interestingly problematic. In this account of the history of the neutral current I therefore put practice, which is accessible to the historian's methods, first—rather than the phenomenon, which is not. I argue that the reality of the weak neutral current was the *upshot* of particle physicists' practices, and not the reverse.

The analysis proceeds in two stages. Firstly, I argue that it is not useful to regard the dis-

covery experiment as a closed system. In contrast, I show that the experiment is more appropriately conceptualised as being performed upon an imperfectly-understood, "open" system. I argue that the discovery claim was grounded in experimental interpretative practices which were themselves problematic, and that the acceptability of those interpretative practices therefore hinged upon the acceptability of the phenomenon they produced. The interpretative practices and the natural phenomenon stood or fell together. This observation apparently points to a self-defeating circularity or arbitrariness in empirical research, by virtue of which experimenters are free to report whatever phenomena they choose. However, the second stage of the analysis shows that the arbitrariness is illusory. There I argue that the acceptability of the weak neutral current (and hence of the associated interpretative practices) was determined by the opportunities its existence offered for *future* experimental *and* theoretical practice in particle physics. Quite simply, particle physicists accepted the existence of the neutral current because they could see how to ply their trade more profitably in a world in which the neutral current was real. The key idea here is that of a symbiotic relationship between experimenters and theorists, the two distinct professional groupings within particle physics. I show that by accepting the existence of the neutral current each group could put itself in a position where the practice of the other constituted both justification and subject matter for its own practice. The argument is, then, that the reality of the neutral current and the acceptability of the experimenters' interpretative practice were both consequences of the achievement of such a symbiosis.

We can now turn to the history of the weak neutral current. The next section of the paper presents the necessary conceptual background and discusses theoretical and experimental approaches to weak interaction physics in the 1960s. This sets the scene for the first stage of the analysis. The discovery experiment is reviewed, focusing upon the interpretative practice of the experimenters and contrasting it with routines developed in earlier generations of similar experiments. A parallel discussion is also given of a contemporary American experiment which had an important bearing upon the discovery process. Two further sections carry through the second stage of the analysis. They review the significance of the neutral current discovery for the development of existing traditions of experimental and theoretical research in particle physics and emphasize the importance of the rapidly changing theoretical context within which the discovery experiment was situated. The paper concludes with a discussion of the general features which emerge from this study.

The Weak Interaction and Neutrino Physics

Particle physicists think in terms of three fundamental forces of nature, known, in order of increasing strength, as the weak, the electromagnetic and the strong interaction. Associated with this classification of forces is a two-fold division of types of elementary particles. Most particles, such as the neutron and proton, experience all three forces and are known as "hadrons," but a handful of particles are immune to the strong force and are known as "leptons." In the period under consideration just four leptons were believed to exist: the electron, the muon and two species of neutrinos. The electron and muon are electrically charged and thus experience both the electromagnetic and weak forces. The neutrinos, however, are electrically neutral and are therefore unique amongst elementary particles in experiencing only the weak force.

It is the properties of the weak force which concern us here. In the 1950s and 1960s information on the weak interaction came from observation of characteristic weak decays of

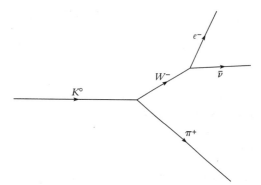

Figure 1   Charged-current decay.

hadrons, nuclear β-decay being prototypical. This information was systematised in a theoretical model of the weak interactions known as the "V–A" theory which was first written down by various authors in 1958. In the present context, the most significant feature of the V–A theory was that it embodied the empirical observation that weak interactions were mediated solely by "charged currents": "neutral currents" were believed not to exist. The distinction between charged and neutral currents is best explained in terms of the diagrams of weak decay processes shown in Figures 1 and 2.

These figures show conceivable weak decay modes of a well-known hadron called the

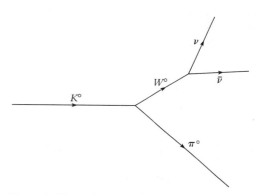

Figure 2   Neutral-current decay.

K-meson. In Figure 1, the electrically neutral *K*-meson decays to a positively charged pi-meson by a emitting a negatively charged "*W*" particle, the hypothetical carrier of the weak force. The *W* in turn decays into an electron and an antineutrino. Because the *W* carries a non-zero electric charge this is known as a charged-current event. In Figure 2, the *K*-meson emits an electrically-neutral *W* particle and, if observed, this would therefore be called a neutral-current decay. But, as I have noted, all of the hadronic decays observed in the 1950s and 1960s could be interpreted in terms of charged *W*'s: no neutral-current type decays were observed.

In 1959, it was pointed out that besides the observation of hadronic decays there was another way to investigate the properties of the weak interactions: namely, to fire a beam of neutrinos at a target and to see what happened. Because neutrinos experience only the weak force, such experiments promised to reveal the properties of that force in a much clearer way than decay experiments (which were complicated by strong and electromagnetic effects). It was also apparent that the experiments would be very difficult: the weak force being indeed weak, intense neutrino beams and very large detectors would be needed in order to stand a chance of being able to observe any effects whatsoever.

Despite this evident difficulty, neutrino experiments got underway in the early 1960s at the world's two major particle physics laboratories—the Brookhaven National Laboratory on Long Island in the U.S.A. and CERN, the joining European Laboratory located in Switzerland just outside Geneva. I will return to these 1960s neutrino experiments later, but for the moment the point to note is that their results were taken as confirmation of the contemporary V–A theory; in particular, it remained part of physics lore that there was no weak neutral current—only charged-current events were reported from these experiments.

The Gargamelle Experiment

While the first rounds of neutrino experiments were in progress in the 1960s, a group of French physicists led by André Lagarrigue were building an enormous bubble chamber which they called Gargamelle. It was with Gargamelle that the first evidence for the existence of the weak neutral current was discovered; and to begin the account of the discovery I must first explain what a bubble chamber is and how it is used.

A bubble chamber is basically a tank full of superheated liquid, held under pressure to prevent it from boiling. When a beam of particles, such as neutrinos, is fired into the tank, the pressure is released and small bubbles begin to form along the tracks of electrically charged particles. These tracks are then photographed and subsequently analysed for the information they yield on the particle interactions or "events" which have taken place within the liquid. Figure 3 shows a typical bubble chamber photographed in which the white lines are interpreted as charged-particle tracks (the large circular blobs are reference marks on the walls of the chamber).

The point of using a very large bubble chamber like Gargamelle was that it would present more material for neutrinos to interact with, and to further increase the interaction rate, Gargamelle was designed to be filled with a very dense liquid (freon) rather than the more usual hydrogen. The active volume of Gargamelle was cylindrical in shape, 4.8 m long and 1.88 m in diameter, containing 18 tonnes of freon; and this volume was enclosed within 1000 tonnes of ancillary equipment (the chamber body, equipment for controlling the temperature and pressure of the freon, a large electromagnet, and so on).

Gargamelle was installed at CERN during 1971, where the photographs it produced were analysed by a team of more than 50 physicists, drawn from CERN and six European univer-

Figure 3   Photograph of an event in Gargamelle. (Reproduced by permission of CERN.)

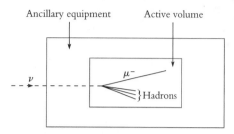

Figure 4   Charged-current event in Gargamelle: the electrically-neutral neutrino converts into a negatively-charged muon, as if it had emitted a charged *W*-particle.

neutral current, which they submitted for publication in July 1973. There they reported that having examined a total of 290,000 photographs the group had found around 100 genuine neutral-current events (and around 400 charged-current events). But the word to stress here is "genuine": concealed within it is the interpretative practice of the CERN experimenters, to which we can now turn.

Neutron Background

The principal problem which the Gargamelle group faced in claiming to have discovered neutral currents went as follows. Neutrinos are electrically neutral and therefore leave no tracks in bubble chambers. Thus the primary indication that an event recorded on film is due to a neutrino is the apparent absence of any

sities. Analysis of Gargamelle film produced when the chamber was exposed to a neutrino beam began in early 1972. It was soon observed that although the majority of interesting photographs corresponded to charged-current events—in which the electrically-neutral neutrino converted to a negatively-charged muon, as in Figure 4—some of them were apparently due to neutral-current interactions—in which the neutrino emerged unscathed, as in Figure 5.

Photographs of the type represented in Figure 5 were to form the basis of the experimenters' claim to have discovered the weak

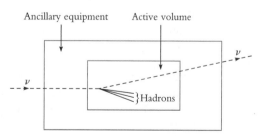

Figure 5   Neutral-current event: the neutrino emerges intact, as if it had emitted an electrically-neutral *W*-particle.

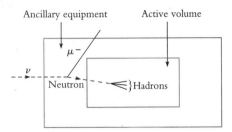

Figure 6 Neutron-background event: a neutron is produced in a charged-current neutrino event in the ancillary equipment, and enters the active volume where it gives rise to an apparent neutral-current event.

cause in the shape of an incoming charged-particle track.[3] However, there are believed to be many species of electrically-neutral particles, all of which can, like neutrinos, enter a bubble chamber unseen and there give rise to events of just the same form as neutrino-induced events. The most obvious example of a neutrino-mimicking particle in the Gargamelle experiment was the neutron, and it was apparent to the experimenters that: (a) neutrons must be produced by the incident neutrino beam in the large amount of ancillary material surrounding the active volume of Gargamelle; and (b) some of these neutrons would penetrate into the active volume and there induce spurious neutral-current type events, as shown in Figure 6.

Between early 1972 and mid-1973 members of the Gargamelle collaboration spent an increasing amount of time persuading themselves and preparing to persuade others that this "neutron background," as it was called, could not account for all of the neutral current events on the film. I want now to discuss the ways in which they attempted to do this. My aim will be to demonstrate the fragility—the lack of compelling force—of their interpretative practice, both as a matter of principle and as a matter of historical fact. I will then highlight this fragility by contrasting the interpretative prac-

tice of the Gargamelle experimenters with that of earlier neutrino experimenters at CERN.

The best estimates of the neutron background in the Gargamelle experiment came from what are known as "Monte Carlo" computer simulations. The inputs to these simulations were: the characteristics of the neutrino beam; the probabilities that a neutrino would produce a neutron in its interaction with matter; the probabilities of various kinds of possible interactions of neutrons with matter; and the matter distribution of Gargamelle and its ancillary equipment. Supplied with this information, the outputs of the computer programmes were estimates of the number of neutrons entering the chamber and of their interactions therein. And the conclusion of such analyses was, according to the Gargamelle group, that only around 10% of their neutral current candidates could be ascribed to neutron background: the remaining 90% were genuine manifestations of the weak neutral current. Hence their claim to have observed a real new phenomenon.

Now, if one examines the details of these Monte Carlo simulations the potential for counter-argument becomes evident. In general terms this potential derived from the scale of the simulation being attempted. The 18 tonne active volume of Gargamelle was surrounded by 1000 tonnes of ancillary equipment; and since the neutrino event rate was believed to be proportional to the mass of the target, this implied that for each event taking place within the active volume there would be around 50 outside it. The task of first trying to describe all of the conceivable unseen interactions and of then evaluating what repercussions these would have within the active volume, was daunting, to say the least. (So daunting, in fact, as to deter anyone from taking such attempts seriously in the pre-Gargamelle era, as we shall see below.)

In more specific terms, let me just note four points of possible counter-argument concerning the most definitive Gargamelle Monte Carlo.

Details of the characteristics of the incoming neutrino beam were a crucial input: these characteristics could only be inferred from indirect measurements, and neither the measurements nor the chain of inference based upon them were publicly available.

Similarly crucial were the probabilities of the production of neutrons by neutrinos. These were not known in advance: "reasonable" estimates were fed into the programme, normalised to a very few (27) so-called "associated star" events found in the Gargamelle film.

The relevant parameters for the interaction of neutrons and protons with atomic nuclei were not experimentally known. They were therefore deduced from a very limited set of measurements on proton—proton collisions using a very simple model of the nucleus.

In performing the calculations, an idealised geometry of the apparatus was assumed, while large unexpected effects in particle physics have often been ascribed to apparently unimportant details of the configuration of equipment.

This is not intended as an extensive list of the assumptions implicit in the neutron-background simulations, and neither is it intended to imply that there was anything improper or unusual in experimenters making such assumptions. My object here is simply to demonstrate that assumptions were made which could legitimately be questioned: one can easily imagine a determined critic taking issue with some or all of these assumptions. Moreover, even if all of the assumptions were granted, it remained the case that they were the input not to an analytic calculation, but to an extremely complex numerical simulation. The details of such simulations are enshrined in machine code and are therefore inherently unpublished and not independently verifiable. Thus the sceptic could legitimately accept the input to the calculation but continue to doubt its output.

It is clear, then, that the interpretative practice of the Gargamelle experimenters was, in principle, far from absolutely compelling of assent.[4] And the members of the group were not unaware of this; that is why several of them worked for more than a year to try to make the Monte Carlos as convincing as possible. But it is significant to note that even within the Gargamelle collaboration the degree of conviction was never absolute. In the early stages of analysis many were highly sceptical and it is a matter of record that at least one leading Gargamelle experimenter felt that the analysis was still inadequate when the discovery was made public in July 1973. And indeed, it seems clear that the decision of the group as a whole to publish the claim at that time was influenced as much by priority concerns and the forthcoming conference season as by the conviction that the analysis was watertight. A group of American researchers performing a neutrino experiment at the newly operational National Accelerator Laboratory (NAL—now known as Fermilab) near Chicago, had let it be known that they too were finding evidence for neutral currents, and were also intending to report their discovery during the summer.

A further indication of the lack of compulsive force of the Gargamelle group's interpretative practices came in the winter of 1973. By this time the NAL experimenters had made changes to their apparatus and had concluded that neutral currents did not in fact exist. This result was transmitted to CERN, where the Gargamelle experimenters came under great pressure, from both the physicists and management of CERN, to either improve their result or retract it. Their position was not strengthened when CERN physicist Jack Steinberger—a veteran of the first neutrino experiment at Brookhaven, though not a member of the Gargamelle team—made public his own Monte Carlo simulations, which indicated that a substantial fraction of the

Gargamelle neutral-current events could be interpreted as neutron background.

The debate over the Gargamelle team's interpretative practices was finally more-or-less closed in the spring of 1974, but again it is significant to note that this cannot be ascribed to any new compelling quality of their neutron background calculations. The turning point came when the American experimenters revised their own Monte Carlo simulations and, for the second time, decided that they had indeed found evidence for neutral currents.

It seems reasonable therefore to assert that as a matter of principle and as a matter of historical fact the interpretative practices of the Gargamelle group were not beyond legitimate doubt. Put simply, in 1973 and early 1974 particle physicists both inside and outside the Gargamelle group did not treat the neutron-background calculations as compelling assent. Assent to the practices implied assent to the existence of the weak neutral current, but any physicist dissenting from the latter could quite legitimately question the former. Interpretative practice and natural phenomenon stood or fell together. I will return to this point shortly, but first it will be useful to digress briefly into the pre-history of the Gargamelle experiment—the CERN neutrino bubble chamber experiments of the 1960s.

Bubble Chamber Neutrino Experiments in the 1960s

During the 1960s three bubble chamber neutrino experiments were carried out, all at CERN between the years of 1963 and 1967, and many of the participants in these experiments went on to become principals of the Gargamelle experiment. In the present context, the reports on the 1960s experiments are interesting in that they reveal a quite different set of interpretative practices, which supported a quite different phenomenal world, from that of Gargamelle. The phenomenal world of

neutrino physics in the 1960s was that of the V–A theory which, as noted above, included charged currents but not neutral currents. And it is clear from the documents of the time that CERN experimenters in the 1960s therefore *equated* the considerable number of neutral-current type events which they observed to the neutron background of their experiments. Neutral-current type events were treated as a *measure* of the neutron background and this measure was used to estimate the background contribution to the observed charged-current event rate.

To illustrate how this procedure worked, let me refer to the most detailed analysis of the neutrino runs from 1963 to 1965 which was made by E.C.M. Young. Under the heading "Neutron Background Estimation," Young noted:

> In the phenomenological classification of events recorded in the chamber, neutral events with at least one lepton candidate (i.e. non-interacting particle) are classified as ν or $\bar{\nu}$ [neutrino or antineutrino] candidates. Neutral events without lepton candidates [i.e. possible neutral-current events] are taken as neutron-induced background.[5]

Having thus arrived at an operational definition of the neutron background, Young went on to estimate the rate at which neutron-induced events would produce a pi-meson which would be misidentified as a muon, and hence make a spurious contribution to the measured charged-current event rate.

The most extensive discussion of the background problem in the third CERN neutrino experiment, carried out in 1967, was given by G. Myatt in 1969.[6] He noted that in the 1967 experiment "a considerable number of neutral events were found which had no μ^- [muon] candidate"—i.e., neutral-current type events—and then continued directly: "It is interesting to speculate on the origin of these neutrons."[7] The equation between neutral-current type events and neutron background was made as simply as that.

Perhaps the most interesting point to note here is that, even in the 1960s, this equation was not above question. Young, for example, attempted a detailed estimate of the neutron flux in the earlier neutrino runs and concluded that most, but not all, of the observed neutral-current type events could be ascribed to this source. Left unaccounted for were around 150 neutral-current type events, to be compared with around 570 positively identified charged-current events: a ratio of roughly one neutral-current even to every four charged-current events—the same as that which was later reported from Gargamelle.

Thus it is clear that the interpretative practice of the 1960s—the equation of neutral-current events with neutron background—is not only questionable with scientific hindsight, but it was questionable even in contemporary terms. Nonetheless the 1960s experimenters put their faith in the phenomenon—the non-existence of the weak neutral current—and took this as a yardstick against which to evaluate estimates of the neutron background. The estimates which were actually made failed this test, and it remained a fact of nature, embedded in the interpretative practices of neutrino experimenters, that neutral currents did not exist.

We see, then, that central to the CERN neutrino bubble chamber experiments in the 1960s and in the 1970s were disparate sets of interpretative practices; that neither set of practices was above dispute; and that, nevertheless, each set of practices supported a distinctive and socially-accepted phenomenal world.

I now want to discuss briefly the American neutrino experiment, which has so far been mentioned only in passing, in order to show that similar comments apply to it and its predecessors. We can then turn to the central question of this paper: can one understand why one constellation of interpretative practices and natural phenomena was displaced by the other in the early 1970s?

The HPW Experiment

In 1972 a new particle accelerator came into operation at the National Accelerator Laboratory in the United States. It was by far the most powerful accelerator then in existence (providing particle beams around ten times as energetic as those available at CERN and Brookhaven) and one of the first experiments to get under way there was a neutrino experiment, mounted by a collaboration of physicists drawn from the Universities of Harvard, Pennsylvania and Wisconsin. This was the experiment which was held first to confirm, then to deny, and then to confirm the Gargamelle discovery, and it is this experiment which I want to discuss here.

The Harvard-Pennsylvania-Wisconsin (HPW) experiment was not a bubble chamber experiment like Gargamelle; it was an electronic experiment. That is, the active detecting elements registered the passage of charged tracks by electronic means, rather than by the physical formation of bubbles as in a bubble chamber.

Electronic detectors and bubble chambers were, by the early 1970s, well-established alternative techniques for particle detection, and their relative virtues and shortcomings were well-known. As far as the extraction of detailed information on individual particle interactions was concerned, bubble chamber photographs, which provided an accurate record of individual tracks, had the edge over the relatively coarse-grained electronic detectors. On the other hand, economic considerations dictated that electronic detectors could be constructed which were much more massive than any feasible bubble chamber. This latter was an especially important consideration in neutrino physics—in which the most direct way to increase the very low detection rate was to increase the mass of the detector. Thus each type of detector had its merits and electronic and bubble chamber neutrino experiments grew up in parallel during the 1960s.[8] I will first outline the salient features of the early electronic neutrino experiments, in order to bring out a major difference of experimental practice which distinguished them from the HPW experiment. I will then review the interpretive practices involved in the HPW experiment itself.

We saw in the preceding section that in the 1690s bubble chamber neutrino experiments it was standard practice to equate neutral-current type events to an uninteresting neutron background. Much the same can be said of 1960s electronic experiments, except that here the interpretative assumption was actually built into the experimental apparatus from the beginning. The relevant point to note is that electronic detectors have a further advantage over bubble chambers which has not yet been mentioned: through an appropriate combination of hardware and electronic logic circuits they can be designed to register only a subset, with specified characteristics, of the particle interactions which take place within them.[9] The 1960s electronic neutrino experimenters exploited this advantage in order to obtain a "clean" signal of neutrino events. They reasoned, in accordance with the standard V–A theory, that any genuine neutrino interaction would be a charged-current even leading to the production of a muon. Neutrino-induced events could therefore be distinguished from the uninteresting neutron background precisely by counting only those events in which muons were produced. This reasoning was then built into the apparatus itself, which was so designed as to only register events when at least one muon was produced. In this way, the experimenters obtained a relatively clean signal of neutrino events but, of course, they simultaneously guaranteed that they could never find any evidence of the existence of neutral currents— for the simple reason that the mark of a neutral current event would be the absence of muon production.

For reasons which will be discussed in the following section, the HPW experimenters abandoned this aspect of the standard practice of electronic neutrino experiment. They arranged their logic circuits so that their counters were triggered by the production of hadrons. This enabled them to try to determine whether or not muons were produced in association with these hadrons, and hence whether or not there was an appreciable neutral-current signal.

The HPW experiment began running at Fermilab in early 1972 and a highly complex sequence of events ensued. These have been reviewed at length by Peter Galison, and I will report here only the main features of Galison's account as they bear upon the arguments of this paper.[10] In its first months of operation the new Fermilab accelerator operated intermittently, but by early 1973 the HPW experimenters had gathered sufficient data to convince some of them, at least, that neutral currents existed. But, as in the case of the Gargamelle experiment, this conclusion was by no means watertight. The principal interpretative problem in the HPW experiment was "escaping muons" and went as follows. The HPW apparatus was divided into two parts: a front section, where hadron showers produced in neutrino interactions were detected and a rear section, designed to detect any muons produced in association with the hadrons. Any muonless event, in which the rear section of the apparatus failed to detect a particle, was thus a candidate neutral-current event. Unfortunately, the apparatus was long and thin and it was quite conceivable that muons produced by charged-current events in the front section of the detector could escape from the sides of the apparatus before reaching the rear section. These fugitive muons would not register their presence in the muon-detecting rear section, and hence run-of-the-mill charged-current events could mimic neutral-current events.

To try to rule out this explanation of the neutral-current signal, the HPW experimenters, like the Gargamelle group, performed Monte Carlo simulations of muon production by neutrinos in the front section of their apparatus. The upshot of these calculations was that escaping muons could not account for the observed neutral-current signal. This news was communicated to CERN where, as we have seen, it contributed to the decision of the Gargamelle group to publish their findings; and it was submitted for publication by the HPW group shortly afterwards.

Here, then, we see the first steps towards the establishment of a new interpretative practice, consistent with the existence of the weak neutral current, in electronic neutrino experiment. Once again, though, even the experimenters themselves did not treat this novel interpretative practice as having any compulsory force. Certain of the leading members of the HPW collaboration distrusted Monte Carlo simulations, on the general grounds which I outlined above in connection with the CERN experiment.[11] Furthermore, a new set of neutrino data taken by HPW in mid-1973 showed a much smaller neutral-current signal than had been found in previous, lower energy data.

The HPW group therefore decided to improve their experiment and hold their initial publication in abeyance (by not responding to the referees' comments). They modified their apparatus so that the rear section would subtend a larger solid angle with respect to the front. The object here was to catch more muons and thus to reduce the escaping muon problem and the consequent dependence upon Monte Carlo simulations. The experimenters took more data with this new detector configuration and by late 1973 they had concluded that the neutral-current signal was very much smaller than that reported from CERN, possibly being zero. This news was communicated to CERN, where it precipitated the already-noted crisis of confidence in the Gargamelle result, and a paper was drafted at Fermilab to the effect that no significant evidence for the existence of the weak neutral current was to be found.

However, the HPW experimenters had by that time become aware of a further point of fragility in their interpretative arguments: hadron "punch through." This problem concerned the fact that in the first version of the experiment the front and rear portions of the detector were separated by 4 feet of iron, while in the second version this had been reduced to 13 inches of steel. The function of this steel was to stop hadrons entering the muon detector—according to contemporary expectations, muons but not hadrons would be able to penetrate 13 inches or more of steel and hence any particle registered in the rear section of the detector could be assumed to be a muon. There remained, however, the possibility that this assumption was wrong: that hadrons could "punch through" 13 inches of steel, even if 4 feet of iron was too much for them. In this case, hadrons produced in the front section might penetrate the steel barrier and be identified as muons in the rear section: in other words, neutral-current events, with no genuine muon, could mimic charged-current events.

To prove that the weak neutral current did not exist, the HPW group had to argue that hadron punch-through could not account for the observed neutral-current signal. Here they faced a problem very similar to that encountered by the Gargamelle group in estimating their neutron background: the relevant parameters of hadron interactions wee known only poorly, if at all. The American experimenters were thus obliged to copy their European counterparts in making "reasonable" assumptions and theoretical extrapolations from what little was known.

The initial estimate of punch through indicated a penetration rate for hadrons of around 13%—insufficient to account for the number of "muons" registered in the muon-detecting rear section of the apparatus—and this estimate was the basis of the draft publication reporting the absence of neutral currents. More detailed estimates were subsequently made, which first disagreed amongst themselves, but then bean to move upwards. By early 1974 the estimated rate of hadron punch through had doubled, with the effect that the HPW collaboration could now report a neutral current event rate in broad agreement with that found at Gargamelle.

At this point the American experimenters decided to go ahead with publication of their first 1973 paper which reported the sighting of the weak neutral current and two further publications to the same effect on the data taken with the new detector configuration quickly followed. The second version of the 1973 paper, which reported the apparent absence of neutral currents was, of course, discarded.

By early 1974, then, the HPW experimenters had put themselves in a position whereby their findings could be seen as confirmation of those from Gargamelle. The price which they paid for this was the same as that paid by the European bubble chamber physicists: the abandonment of the 1960s interpretative practice, which made neutral currents non-existent by definition, and the adoption of a new interpretative practice in its place. In the case of the HPW experiment this practice had first one and then two new elements. The initial HPW publication, on the earliest version of the experiment, depended crucially upon Monte Carlo simulation of muon production in the detector—simulations which several of the experimenters themselves distrusted. The dependence on the muon-production Monte Carlos was reduced (but not removed) in the second version of the experiment, but, as we have seen, the replacement of 4 feet of iron by 13 inches of steel made manifest a second set of assumptions, this time concerning hadron punch through. Like the muon Monte Carlos, estimates of punch through depended upon "reasonable" assumptions concerning physical quantities which were a priori unknown. Nonetheless, if one accepted the estimates of the escaping-muon and punch-through rates as they stood in early 1974, then one could conclude that the weak-neutral current indeed existed.

Thus, in both branches of neutrino physics—bubble chamber and electronic experiments—the pattern was the same. The 1960s order, in which distinctive interpretative practices supported the non-existence of the neutral current, was displaced in the early 1970s by a new conjunction of practice phenomenon. We can now go on to look at the wider, theoretical, context in which neutrino experiments were situated, in order to discuss the dynamics of this change.

Electroweak Unification

By the late 1970s, the existence and properties of the weak neutral current had come to be regarded as well-established and the interpretative practices of the Gargamelle and HPW experimenters had become institutionalised in succeeding generations of neutrino experiments. From this secure vantage point, particle physicists paused to reflect upon the circumstances of the discovery itself. In the present context, most interesting aspect of these reflections was the frequency with which it was noted that evidence for the existence of the neutral current had been there all the time, even before Gargamelle. Thus, in 1979, a leading neutrino experimenter observed:

> In retrospect, it is likely that events due to neutral currents had been seen as early as 1967. Data from the CERN heavy-liquid bubble chamber... showed a surprisingly large number of events with hadrons in the final state, but with no visible muon. The calculations of neutron and pion-initiated backgrounds were so uncertain as to render the observed number of events inconclusive. In 1967 there was *little pressure* to rectify these uncertainties. Five years later the *theoretical climate* had changed dramatically, so that there were persistent but cautious efforts to conclusively resolve whether such events were actually anomalous.[12]

A leading theorist put the matter more forcefully when he noted that neutral currents could well have been reported from the neutrino experiments of the 1960s, but that the experimenters had only begun to reconsider their interpretative practices when "theorists all over the world really started screaming for neutral currents."[13] In the remainder of this paper I want to analyse why theorists began screaming for neutral currents and how and why their appeals became translated into experimental practice.

To begin: what were the theorists screaming about? They were screaming about a class of theoretical models known as unified electroweak gauge theories. The prototype for this class of models was the Weinberg-Salam model, first published by Steven Weinberg in 1967 (Abdus Salam independently published a similar model in 1968). The Weinberg-Salam model had two especially interesting features. Firstly, it unified the weak and electromagnetic interactions, representing them as manifestations of a single, underlying, "electroweak" force. Secondly, amongst the fundamental entities of the model were the charged W-particles which could be held to mediate charged-current processes *and* a neutral partner to these W's, which would lead to neutral-current processes. Thus, in its consequences for experiment, the Weinberg-Salam model differed from the conventional V–A theory of weak interactions precisely in that it required the existence of the weak neutral current.

This much was clear when Weinberg published his paper in 1967, but it is important to recognise that in 1967 Weinberg and his theoretical colleagues did not immediately begin to scream for neutral currents. To emphasise this, here is the citation record of Weinberg's paper from 1967 to 1973: 1967, 0; 1968, 0; 1969, 0; 1970, 1; 1971, 4; 1972, 64; 1973, 162. As one of Weinberg's Harvard colleagues remarked when Weinberg shared the 1979 Nobel Prize (with Salam and Sheldon Glashow) for this work: "rarely has so great an accomplishment been so widely ignored."[14] Far from immediately picking up the Weinberg-Salam model's distinctive prediction of neutral currents and screaming at the experimenters, particle theorists in the late 1960s simply accepted the reported non-existence of the phenomenon and ignored the model. However, as the citation record shows, this situation was transformed in the early 1970s and we can now proceed to see how this came about.

The Weinberg-Salam model was formulated in the language of a particular kind of quantum field theory known as a gauge theory. The first such theory had been formulated in 1954 by C. N. Yang and R. L. Mills, who were attempting to model a field theory of the strong interactions on the highly successful theory of the electromagnetic interactions—a theory known as quantum electrodynamics (or QED for short).

Gauge theories of both the weak and strong interactions enjoyed some popularity amongst particle theorists in the 1950s, but, for various reasons, in the 1960s gauge theories and quantum field theory in general were largely abandoned. The great revival in the fortunes of gauge theory began in 1971 when a Dutch graduate student, Gerard 't Hooft, published a proof that gauge theory was "renormalisable."

The significance of this was as follows. Quantum field theories are not exactly soluble—their predictions can only be calculated approximately. However, some theories are said to be renormalisable, which means that with the use of sophisticated mathematical techniques, sensible approximate calculations can be carried as far as the theorists wishes. The archetypal renormalisable field theory is QED, from which very precise—though still approximate—predictions can be extracted. This was shown in principle for QED in the late 1940s and subsequent concrete calculations exhibited a remarkable degree of agreement with experiment. Other theories, such as the V–A theory of the weak interactions, are agreed to be non-normalisable. In these theories, it seems to be impossible to make meaningful calculations beyond the first order of approximation.

In the hey-day of gauge theories—in the 1950s—it was hoped that they, like QED upon which they were modeled, could be shown to be renormalisable, but such a proof was not forthcoming. Neither, though, were they shown to be non-renormalisable. It remained a possibility that a sensible approximation scheme could be devised, but at this time no-one had found one. Some steps were made in this direction during the 1960s, but these concerned manifestly unrealistic formulations of gauge theory and were apparently only of purely theoretical and mathematical interest. 't Hooft's great achievement of 1971 was to show that a potentially realistic formulation of gauge theory—none other than the Weinberg–Salam model of electroweak interactions—was renormalisable.

Thus 't Hooft's work transformed theorists' perceptions of the Weinberg-Salam model. No longer was it simply a mathematical novelty: it was now an example of a potentially realistic renormalisable theory of the weak interaction, and, as such, it was amenable to all of the sophisticated mathematical techniques which had been developed in the context of QED. Theorists with the appropriate expertise wee quick to exploit this opportunity to transplant their techniques from QED to gauge theory, and the new field of theoretical practice which grew up accounts, in part, for the take-off of citations of Weinberg's paper following 't Hooft's work.

There was, however, a further dimension to the explosion of interest in the Weinberg-Salam model. I have described it as a potentially realistic model—in the sense that it described a conceivable state of the real world—but it did, of course, appear to be empirically false: neutral currents, the key attribute of the model, were still officially non-existent in the early 1970s. Thus a new theoretical industry developed, devoted to devising variants of the Weinberg-Salam model in which the predictions of neutral currents could be avoided. However, theorists concluded that the price to be paid for the evasion of neutral currents in a gauge model was the prediction of other hitherto unobserved phenomena—such as the existence of new, very massive leptons.

The Symbiosis of Theory and Experiment

In the early 1970s, then, a disjuncture had developed between theoretical and experimental practice in weak interaction physics. The growing band of gauge theorists working on electroweak unification, in particular, found themselves elaborating theories of natural phenomena which had no experimental counterparts. To take their arguments further, these theorists needed something new from their experimental colleagues, and they communicated this need in the most direct fashion. At CERN, gauge theorists in late 1971 arranged a presentation to the Gargamelle experimenters in which they stressed the importance of an active search for neutral currents, and thus succeeded in dislodging the interpretative practice of equating neutral-current type events with neutron background—in the minds of some of the experimenters, at least. At the same time in the United States, Weinberg himself convinced the NAL neutrino physicists of the need to search for neutral currents, and the HPW experiment was accordingly reconceptualised and redesigned to trigger on hadrons instead of on muons.

Thus, as a result of pressure from the theoretical community, the old interpretative practices of neutrino physics were tentatively discarded. It still remained to put something in their place but, as we have seen, the Gargamelle experimenters used Monte Carlo simulations of their neutron background to fill the gap and the HPW group used similar estimates to confront their missing-muon and punch-through problems. I have already stressed that the validity of these simulations and estimates was, in principle, arguable and we can now return to the question of why, despite this, they became accepted as a routine part of the interpretative practice of neutrino experiment in the 1970s.

The answer is simple: the various simulations and estimates implied the existence of the weak neutral current which was, in the early 1970s, a most socially-desirable phenomenon. To explain what I mean by this, let me consider the neutral current from the perspectives of the theoretical and experimental particle physics communities in turn.

The first point to note is that, as far as theorists were concerned, calculations of such quantities as the neutron background in the Gargamelle experiment were of no interest. The details of, say, the interactions between neutrons and nuclear matter were a "dead" area of particle theory—they engaged with no active stream of theoretical practice. As long as the inputs to the experimenters' Monte Carlos were "reasonable," theorists had no reason to question them—if, that is, they paid them any attention at all.

However, with regard to the weak neutral current the situation was quite different: this phenomenon engaged with the practice of the growing band of gauge theorists very directly and had two immediate consequences for it. Firstly, the neutral current was a phenomenon which gauge theorists could cite as *justification* for their practice—an argument that their work was sensible and should be taken seriously. Secondly, it was a phenomenon which gave them something new to do, the *subject matter* for further practice: they could, for example, compare the Gargamelle observations with expectations from existing electroweak models, devise new models, make predictions for further experiments, and so on. And it was, in fact, this stream of gauge-theoretic practice which set the scene for the great experimental discoveries of 1974—the "psi" particles—and for their interpretation in terms of "charm."

As far as the experimental particle physics community was concerned the view was much the same. The inputs to the Monte Carlos were a dead area for experimenters too and all that they would ask was that there be no manifest conflict with what little relevant data there were. On the other hand, the weak neutral current represented a whole new phenomenon which neutrino experimenters (and others) could explore using their existing techniques and developments thereof. In order to bring this phenomenon into being, bubble chamber physicists had only to take seriously the kind of neutron-background calculations which had already been performed—but not taken seriously—in the 1960s; and electronic experimenters had only to stop triggering on muons and to perform their own background estimates. In assenting to the reality of the neutral current the experimenters essentially got something for nothing. And again, the reality of the neutral current constituted both justification and subject matter for further experimental practice. Thus, for example, in early 1973 the Gargamelle experimenters made their existing evidence for the weak neutral current the basis for their (successful) request to the CERN management for beam time in which to take 2 million more pictures; and, in the following years, the investigation of the properties of the neutral current constituted one of the principal arguments for further generations of more sophisticated neutrino experiments.

So, both theorists and experimenters saw in the weak neutral current fruitful opportunities for future practice. And although it is implicit in what has been said above, I want to note explicitly here the *symbiotic* nature of the relation between experimental and theoretical practice which sustained and was sustained by the reality of the neutral current. The highly influential theorist Murray Gell-Mann pointed to this when in 1972—before the Gargamelle discovery—he noted that "the proposed [electroweak] models are a bonanza for experimentalists."[15] It was precisely the practice of gauge theorists like Gell-Mann which guaranteed that neutral currents would be seen as a significant topic for neutrino experimenters to explore.[16] And conversely, it was precisely the experimental reports on the neutral current which fed and legitimated the continuing practice of gauge theorists. As a real phenomenon, the weak neutral current was a bonanza for theorists and experimenters alike and the acceptance of novel interpretative practices was a small price to pay.

Discussion

In conclusion, let me summarise the history of the weak neutral current and the general form of my analysis.

The history of the neutral current can be divided into two periods of stability separated by a period of relative turmoil. The first stable period extended through the 1960s up to 1971. During this time theorists and experimenters were happy to agree that the neutral current did not exist. In 1971, 't Hooft showed that gauge field theories, including the unified electroweak gauge theory proposed in 1967 by Weinberg and Salam, were renormalisable. Immediately following 't Hooft's work a disjuncture developed, in which gauge theorists elaborated electroweak models which encompassed phenomena not known to the experimenter—such as the weak neutral current. Harmony between theory and experiment began to be restored in mid-1973 when experimenters, first at CERN and later at NAL, reported that the neutral current had manifested itself to them.

Compressed into a single paragraph, this sounds like the scientist's history of theoretical prediction followed by straightforward experimental verification—but I have tried to show that matters were by no means so straightforward. Firstly, I have tried to show that scientific experiment should not be equated with the passive and unproblematic observation of natural phenomena. Phenomena are grounded in experimental practices which appear unproblematic only as long as they are left unexamined. Crucial to the discovery of the weak neutral current—and crucial to the repair of the disjuncture between the experimental and theoretical particle physics communities—was a shift in the interpretative practice of neutrino experimenters. The interpretative practice of the 1960s, which supported the non-existence of the neutral current, was displaced by that of the 1970s, which made the neutral current manifest. I have tried to show that neither the practice of the 1960s nor that of the 1970s was in itself compelling of assent—each was open to counterargument. And I have therefore suggested that experimental practices and natural phenomena are inextricably bound together; assessment of one is ultimately an assessment of the other.[17]

Following on from this, I have tried to show that the assessment of natural phenomena is itself conditioned by the dynamical aspect of scientific practice: that is, by the continuing process of choice of experimenters to perform one experiment rather than another and of theorists to elaborate one theory rather than another. The central idea implicit in this aspect of the analysis has been that scientists assess phenomena in terms of their past experience and future goals; and that, within the dynamical system so constituted, natural phenomena are the medium which sustains, and is sustained by, a symbiosis of experimental and theoretical practice—a symbiosis wherein each realm of practice constitutes both justification and subject matter for the other. From this perspective, the two periods of stability in neutrino physics are straightforwardly understood: within each period, each generation of experiment fuelled the next generation of theorising and vice-versa. Thus, in the 1960s theoretical work within the V–A tradition and experimental work on neutrino interactions developed along parallel and mutually-reinforcing lines within a phenomenal world in which the neutral current had no part to play. Following the shifts in interpretative practice associated with the Gargamelle and HPW experiments a new symbiosis was established. Once more particle physicists had in hand the required tools—experimenters their neutrino detectors and interpretative practices; theorists their electroweak gauge theories—to proceed in a socially-constructive manner in a phenomenal world which now included the weak neutral current.

Less straightforward to understand is how such stable periods of symbiosis are disrupted: why, in particular, did a mismatch between theory and experiment develop in particle physics in the early 1970s? Here I have suggested that the "internal" dynamics of theoretical practice came to the fore. My argument has been that particle theorists saw in 't Hooft's 1971 demonstration of the renormalisability of gauge theory opportunities for constructive practice: all of the techniques which had been developed for handling renormalisable theories could be transplanted to this area, and indeed this is just what theorists with the appropriate expertise did. Significantly, in the present context, they did this with one eye on the possibility of symbiosis with their experimental colleagues, elaborating primarily those gauge theories which were physically realistic—the Weinberg-Salam model and variants of it. In the course of this theoretical work it became apparent that some new phenomenon was needed and as we have seen, neutrino experimenters modified their interpretative practices, produced the neutral current, and reestablished the symbiosis on a new footing.

Thus, as promised in the introduction to this account, the explanatory emphasis has been on what scientists *do* rather than upon the phenomena which they report. I have focussed upon two aspects of scientific practice: the interpretative aspect of experimental practice, whereby happenings in the laboratory are

transformed into reports about the natural world; and the dynamical aspect of both experimental and theoretical practice, relating to scientists' choices of which experiments to perform, which theories to elaborate and so on. My argument has been that, far from being distinct, these two aspects are bound up together at the level of natural phenomena. The relative acceptability of different experimental interpretative practices was conditioned by the expertise and objectives and experimenters and theorists.

Seen in this way, science no longer seems adequately described in terms of an adversarial relationship in which experiment tests theory. An image of experimenters and theorists as collaborators in the production, rather than the discovery, of a congenial phenomenal world seems more appropriate. This image of scientists as the producers of natural phenomena is, moreover, a stimulating one. It invites many questions concerning the nature and dynamics of scientific practice, the answers to some of which I have tried to sketch out here. I certainly would not claim to have given exhaustive answers to all of the questions which arise, but I hope that I have shown that they are interesting—and accessible to the historians proper methods. And this, I believe, is sufficient justification for not putting the phenomena first.

Notes

1. In using this term I do not mean to suggest that all scientists subscribe to such accounts, nor that their production is solely confined to scientists. I mean only to suggest that such accounts are routinely produced by members of the scientific community, for example in scientific textbooks and in popularisations addressed to non-expert audiences.
2. For an appropriate example of this style of historical account, see D. B. Cline, A. K. Mann and C. Rubbia, "The Detection of Neutral Weak Currents," *Scientific American*, 231 (December 1974), pp. 108–119.
3. Figure 3, for example, shows a photograph in which a neutrino is assumed to have entered from below travelling upwards. No track corresponds to

this neutrino, but the charged-particle tracks diverging from the lower vertex are ascribed to products of its interaction with an atomic nucleus within the liquid.

4. Readers of drafts of this paper have suggested that it shows that the Gargamelle experiment was "pretty shaky." This view is mistaken. The analysis of the neutron background problem in Gargamelle, for example, was far *more* detailed and thoroughgoing than the background analysis of routine experiments.

5. E. C. M. Young, "High Energy Neutrino Interactions," CERN Yellow Report, CERN 67-12 (April 1967), p. 41.

6. G. Myatt, "Background Problems in a Bubble Chamber Neutrino Experiment," *Neutrino Meeting*, CERN, Geneva, 13–14 January 1969, J. B. M. Pattison, C. A. Ramm and W. A. Venus (eds.), CERN Yellow Report CERN 69-28, pp. 145–158.

7. Ibid., p. 146.

8. Prior to the HPW experiment, five electronic neutrino experiments had been performed, two at Brookhaven (1961 and 1963); two at CERN (1963 and 1967); and one at the Argonne National Laboratory near Chicago (1965)....

9. This is in contrast with the bubble chambers, where any interaction results in tracks which appear on film, whether or not the experimenters are interested in such interactions.

10. P. Galison, "How the First Neutral Current Experiments Ended," *Reviews of Modern Physics*, 55 (1983) pp. 477–509.

11. This distrust of the HPW Monte Carlos was shared by physicists outside the collaboration....

12. Sciulli, "An Experimenter's History of Neutral Currents," *Progress in Particle and Nuclear Physics*, 2 (1979), pp. 41–87, at p. 46 (emphasis added).

13. J. J. Sakurai "Neutral Currents and Gauge Theories—Past, Present, and Future," *Current Trends in the Theory of Fields*, J. E. Lannutti and P. K. Williams (eds.) (New York: American Institute of Physics, 1978), pp. 38–80, at p. 45. Besides the 1960s Brookhaven and CERN neutrino experiments, Sakurai also mentioned a 1970 "beam dump" experiment performed at the Stanford Linear Accelerator center. Neutral-current type events were observed in this experiment but were again dismissed as presumably due to neutron background.

14. S. Coleman, "The 1979 Nobel Prize in Physics," Science, 206 (14 December 1979), pp. 1290–1292, at p. 1291. I have taken the citation count for Weinberg's paper from this article....

15. M. Gell-Mann, "General Status: Summary and Outlook," *Proceedings of the 16th International Conference on High Energy Physics*, NAL, 6–13 September 1972, J. D. Jackson and A. Roberts (eds.), (Batavia: NAL, 1972), Vol. 4, pp. 333–356 at p. 336.

16. As the neutrino experimenter quoted above put it (Sciulli, *op. cit.*, note 12, p. 45): By 1972 the theoretical community was entering a state of coherent excitation. As it became clear that these developments implied important opportunities for measurement, the excitement spread to the particle experimentalists.

17. I have focused upon the interpretative aspect of experimental practice because that was the most conspicuously arguable facet of the experiments in which the weak neutral current was discovered. I do not want to suggest, however, that other "instrumental" aspects of experimental practice are unproblematic. By "instrumental," I mean to refer to manipulative operations in the laboratory like setting up the apparatus, tuning it, making sure it "works" and so on. Such instrumental practices are surely bound up with both interpretative practices and the phenomena to which they give rise. As an example of such an instrumental practice, one can think of the episode in which the HPW group "improved" their apparatus, replacing the 4 foot iron shield with 13 inches of steel. At the time, this replacement was thought to be irrelevant to the phenomena at issue. It did, of course, serve to obliterate the neutral current signal, but one can well imagine that in a different context (e.g., if the Gargamelle group had not already published their discovery) this would simply have been taken to indicate that a genuine improvement had been made. As it was, the disappearance of the signal led the experimenters to reconsider their interpretative practice with regard to "punch through" and this eventually culminated in the reappearance of the signal. Thus, in this instance one can argue that instrumental practice, interpretative practice and natural phenomena had to be assessed together.

In general it seems reasonable to assume that natural phenomena float on a sea of interpretative and instrumental practices, all of which are in principle vulnerable to counterargument. To paraphrase Harry Collins, to decide whether a natural phenomenon exists one has simultaneously to decide what constitutes a "good" detector for that phenomenon, and the criteria of "goodness" are not defined in advance.

PART III

THE VALIDATION OF SCIENTIFIC KNOWLEDGE

Whether or not scientific knowledge provides us with true representations of the world, we have already noted, heavily depends on the nature of the empirical basis of scientific knowledge—the "facts" by means of which the theories of science are tested and judged acceptable or unacceptable—and the nature of the testing procedures themselves. In the previous section we investigated the empirical basis of scientific knowledge. In this section we shall investigate the validation procedures that make use of this basis.

Scientific theories are regularly proposed to explain the facts of observation. Indeed, that is a major goal of scientific theories. Yet before they can become accepted explanations, and thus part of scientific knowledge, scientific theories must prove their mettle. Until then they are merely hypotheses, and, as the history of science shows, even highly plausible hypotheses all too frequently turn out false. But how do scientific theories prove their mettle? What is the method by which they are tested and found acceptable or unacceptable in science?

It is commonplace that scientific theories are tested by the results of observation and experiment. Indeed, that is the hallmark of the empirical method, which is held to be a primary source of the success of science. But because scientific theories typically deal with unobservable entities and processes, such as genes and natural selection and electromagnetic fields, they cannot be directly tested by observation. Their method of observational testing is, instead, indirect. More specifically, what theories postulate about unobservable entities and processes has consequences for observable states of affairs; these consequences, in fact, constitute the empirical content of the theories. Hence scientific theories are tested by deducing from them consequences regarding observable states of affairs and then comparing these consequences with the results of observation and experiment.

Consider, for example, the transition from the phlogiston theory to the oxygen theory in the history of chemistry—the so-called "Chemical Revolution." When the oxygen theory was proposed by Lavoisier in the 1770s, the phlogiston theory was the generally accepted theory of combustion and calcination (slow combustion). According to the latter theory, combustibles and metals contained an "inflammable principle" called *phlogiston*, which they released on combustion and calcination, leaving ashy substances (elementary earths) as residues. The phlogiston theory thus implied that combustibles like wood and charcoal would lose weight on combustion. For if, as the phlogiston theory said, these substances were compounds of elementary earths and phlogiston, and if, as the theory said, combustion was a process in which phlogiston was given off, then it was deducible from the theory that these substances would lose weight whenever they underwent combustion. The phlogiston theory had other true observational consequences as well. For example, it implied that when metallic ores were heated with charcoal (as in smelting), they would turn into metals. The phlogiston would be transferred from the charcoal to the metallic elementary earths to produce metallic compounds, that is, metals.

But the phlogiston theory also had false observational consequences. For example, although it implied that metals, and combustibles such as sulfur and phosphorus, would lose weight on calcination and combustion, the fact was that they *gained* weight. And it was facts like these, anomalous for the phlogiston theory, that the oxygen theory was proposed to explain and *did* explain. Thus, if, as the oxygen theory said, metals and sulfur and phosphorus were elementary earths, and if, as that theory said, calcination and combustion were processes in which oxygen was absorbed from the air, then it was deducible from the theory that these substances would gain weight whenever they underwent calcination or combustion. The oxygen theory had many other true observational consequences. For example, the theory implied that combustion would not occur in a vacuum and that it would soon cease in an enclosed volume of air. The theory even implied that the combined weights of the *two* products of the combustion of substances like wood and charcoal (ashy residues and airs given off) would be greater than the weight of the original substances.

But what followed from these various true and false observational consequences of the phlogiston and oxygen theories? What judgments regarding the two theories could they support, and by what process of reasoning? Regarding such questions there has been, and still is, much disagreement in the philosophy of science. In fact, there are no fewer than six major approaches to such questions of theory testing currently in the forefront of discussion: justificationism; falsificationism; conventionalism; the methodology of scientific research programmes; Thomas Kuhn's sociological approach; and contextual empiricism. In what follows I shall briefly explain each of these approaches.

Justificationism

What followed from the various true and false observational consequences of the phlogiston and oxygen theories? Justificationists would say that the oxygen theory was shown to be very probably true by its observational consequences, whereas the phlogiston theory was shown to be definitely false by its observational consequences. Let me explain.

According to justificationism, since theories have an infinite number of observational consequences to be compared with the results of observation and experiment, theories can never be "verified"—that is, definitely shown to be true. They can, however, still be partially justified or "confirmed" to different degrees, showing that they are, to a greater or lesser degree, probably true. More specifically, each true consequence of a theory, regardless of whether it was taken into account when developing the theory or only discovered after the theory was already developed, is a positive instance of the theory adding to the degree of confirmation or degree of probability of the theory. And if a great many positive instances of the theory have been observed, while no negative instances have been observed—of course, the instances should be as diversified as possible—then the degree of confirmation or probability of the theory will be high. (Some justificationists hold that such degrees of confirmation will ultimately be capable of expression in quantitative terms and that a sufficiently developed inductive logic will tell scientists how to calculate them.) If, on the other hand, even a single negative instance is observed, then the theory will have been falsified.

Hence, justificationists would conclude that, since a great many positive instances of the oxygen theory *were* observed in the years after the proposal of that theory, while no negative instances were observed, the oxygen theory was shown to be highly probable. At the same time, the phlogiston theory was shown to be definitely false by its ever-accumulating negative instances. Small wonder that scientists abandoned the phlogiston theory in favor of the oxygen theory.

Rudolf Carnap, one of the most important advocates of justificationism, presents and defends that position in "The Confirmation of Laws and Theories."

Falsificationism

Falsificationists would agree that the phlogiston theory was shown to be definitely false at the time of the Chemical Revolution, but would claim that the oxygen theory was only shown to be *possibly* true—not, as the justificationists would say, very probably true. What is the difference? Falsificationists would explain that neither the truth nor the probable truth or "degree of confirmation" of a theory can be validly inferred from the truth of those of its observational consequences that scientists have examined. After all, such examined observational consequences, however numerous, represent a vanishingly small proportion of the infinite set of observational consequences of the theory. What's more, the entire examination has taken place in one tiny part of the universe during one tiny period of its duration, even though the theory being tested applies to the entire universe during the entire period of its duration. (Think of someone trying to infer the qualities of the Atlantic Ocean after having observed only a few drops of its water drawn during a one-minute interval from one spot on the beach at Coney Island!) The result is that the examined observational consequences of a theory provide very poor support for any claim about a theory's truth or even probable truth.

But if true observational consequences cannot furnish scientists with valid support for claiming that a theory is true or even probably true, *false* observational consequences *can* furnish scientists with valid support for claiming that a theory is *false*, since a true theory cannot have false consequences. Falsificationists conclude that scientific testing is a method of eliminating false theories by observation and experiment rather than a method of discovering true theories. And theories that are *not* eliminated in the testing process—that is to say, theories that are "corroborated"—are tentatively accepted because, unlike falsified theories, they *may* be true.

With regard to the Chemical Revolution, then, the falsificationist would say that the phlogiston theory was shown to be false, whereas the oxygen theory was shown to be possibly true. The falsificationist would hasten to add, however, that the oxygen theory was shown to be possibly true not by the facts that Lavoisier had taken into account when developing his new theory (though the justificationist would say that such facts had confirmatory value), but only by those facts that could have falsified the new theory once it was developed.

Karl Popper, currently the leading exponent of falsificationism, articulates and defends that position in "Science: Conjectures and Refutations."

Conventionalism

Conventionalists would disagree with both the justificationist and falsificationist accounts of the Chemical Revolution. Indeed, conventionalists would maintain that experimental results showed neither that the phlogiston theory was false nor that the oxygen theory was probably or even possibly true. Both theories could have accommodated all the experimental results. The oxygen theory was accepted and the phlogiston theory rejected because the oxygen theory was simpler, more coherent, more economical, and so on, than the phlogiston theory. And the same is true of any theory choice. Theories are not chosen on empirical grounds; given sufficient ingenuity, facts can be accommodated by any conceptual framework. Rather, theories are chosen by *convention,* on the basis of considerations like simplicity.

Conventionalists justify their stand by pointing out that theory testing is a more complicated process than justificationists and falsificationists allow. To test a theory, as justificationists and falsificationists have noted, consequences must be derived from it that can be compared with the results of observation and experiment. But, as these individuals have *not* noted, such consequences derive not from the hypothesis to be tested in isolation, but from that hypothesis in conjunction with a whole system of accepted theories. Thus, if the derived consequence is false, what deductively follows is not the falsity of the hypothesis under test but rather the falsity of a *conjunction* of theories one of which is the hypothesis at issue.

Consider, for example, one of the false consequences of the phlogiston theory, that metals will lose weight on calcination. According to justificationists and falsificationists, this consequence (as well as others) falsified the phlogiston theory. But the phlogiston theory alone does not entail this consequence. To derive it, a number of additional hypotheses were needed: that phlogiston has weight; that nothing having weight is added to metals as they calcinate; and that if something having weight is removed in a process while nothing having weight is added, then the result will weigh less than the original. Thus, what deductively followed from the observed weight increase of metals after calcination was not the falsity of the phlogiston theory, but the falsity of the *conjunction* of the phlogiston theory with these auxiliary hypotheses.

A number of options were then available. Scientists could have rejected the phlogiston theory, as Lavoisier did. Or scientists could have rejected one or more of the auxiliary hypotheses, as many phlogistonists did. For example, they could have hypothesized that phlogiston had negative weight (as phlogistonists had earlier done); that is, they could have rejected the first auxiliary hypothesis. Or they could have hypothesized that something having weight, such as Boyle's fire particles or Cavendish's precipitated water, was added to the metals as their phlogiston was released, which would have involved rejecting the second auxiliary hypothesis. Or they could have hypothesized, as de Morveau did in 1772, that if phlogiston is lighter than air, then removing it from a body immersed in air will cause that body to weigh more; that is, they could have rejected the third auxiliary hypothesis. So long as these or other kinds of revision succeeded in satisfying the requirements of experiment, they were all logically acceptable. And only considerations like simplicity could have decided among them. But, conventionalists assure us, the same is true in the case of any theory.

Pierre Duhem, a highly influential physicist, historian, and philosopher of science of the early part of this century, gives a forceful presentation of conventionalism in "Physical Theory and Experiment."

The Methodology of Scientific Research Programmes

Advocates of the methodology of scientific research programmes—Imre Lakatos and his followers—have amended the conventionalist account of theory testing in a number of ways. They grant conventionalists that a negative experimental result can never falsify a theory, but only a whole system of theories—that is, the conjunction of a theory under test and a set of auxiliary hypotheses. They grant conventionalists, therefore, that any theory can be saved from negative experimental results by suitable revisions of its auxiliary hypotheses. But they suggest that a standard is (and ought to be) imposed by scientists on the revisions by which a theory may be saved, a standard clearer and more rigorous than the conventionalists' simplicity, coherence, economy, or what have you. Indeed, if such a standard were not imposed, they emphasize, theory choice would be left to subjective taste or scientific fashion, leaving too much leeway for dogmatic adherence to a favorite theory.

But what standard do (and should) scientists impose on the revisions by which a theory may be saved? Lakatos and his followers suggest the following. Each revision made in a theory's auxiliary hypotheses to save that theory from a negative experimental result should render that theory and its auxiliary hypotheses capable of predicting all the facts they had previously predicted, together with the previously anomalous fact *and at least one new fact.* Then saving a theory with the help of auxiliary hypotheses that satisfy this standard will represent scientific progress, while saving a theory with the help of auxiliary hypotheses that do not satisfy this standard will represent scientific degeneration; and the degree of progress will be measured by the degree to which a theory and its auxiliary hypotheses lead to the discovery of new facts. But then, any scientific theory will be appraised together with its auxiliary hypotheses (as conventionalists said), and also together with its predecessors (as conventionalists did *not* say), so that we may see by what sort of change it was brought about. That is to say, the unit of appraisal will be a *series* of theory-systems, rather than a single theory-system (as with conventionalists) or a single theory (as with justificationists and falsificationists).

In the history of science, according to Lakatos, the series of theory-systems we have been discussing tend to be characterized by a remarkable continuity evolving from the "scientific research programmes" set out at their start. These scientific research programmes each consist of (1) a set of central theoretical assumptions (what we have been calling the "theory" and what Lakatos calls the "hard core" of the programme); (2) a directive that bids scientists to develop auxiliary hypotheses to save the central theoretical assumptions from negative experimental results (Lakatos calls this the "negative heuristic" of the programme); and (3) suggestions for developing such auxiliary hypotheses (Lakatos calls this the "positive heuristic" of the programme). If a research programme's development leads to scientific progress, it is successful, and if its development leads to scientific degeneration, it is unsuccessful—in which case its hard core of theoretical assumptions may have to be abandoned. In his "Falsification and the Methodology of Scientific Research Programmes," Lakatos emphasizes that the main problems of theory assessment cannot be satisfactorily explored except in this framework of scientific research programmes.

Regarding the Chemical Revolution, then, advocates of the methodology of scientific research programmes would grant conventionalists that the phlogiston and oxygen research programmes were both able to accommodate the main facts about combustion and calcination by 1785, though both programmes still faced some outstanding anomalies as well. But advocates of the methodology of scientific research programmes would quickly add that only the oxygen research programme accommodated these facts in a progressive way—that is, anticipated them in a coherent pattern of development. The phlogiston research programme, on the other hand, coped with these facts in a degenerating way—that is, in an incoherent manner *after* their discovery within the oxygen programme. The result was that, from 1785 on, the number of chemists who abandoned the phlogiston programme for the oxygen programme increased steadily, first in France, and then abroad.

Thomas Kuhn's Sociological Approach

But note that chemists did not abandon the phlogiston programme all at the same time: the scientific community's gradual shift of allegiance from the phlogiston programme to the oxygen programme, beginning in 1785, took at least seven years. What's more, not all chemists finally did abandon the phlogiston programme. For example, Henry Cavendish and Joseph Priestley, two of the greatest chemists of the period, were never reconciled to the oxygen theory. Facts like these, Thomas Kuhn would point out, dealing as they do with scientists well-versed in questions of scientific appraisal, are inexplicable from the point of view of the methodology of scientific research programmes. And they are inexplicable as well, Kuhn would add, from the points of view of justificationism, falsificationism, and conventionalism. For certainly, from these points of view, scientists should have found the oxygen theory well confirmed or well corroborated or simpler or progressive, and the phlogiston theory falsified or overly complex or degenerating, by some relatively definite time.

The problem, Kuhn would venture, is that the methodology of scientific research programmes, as well as justificationism, falsificationism, and conventionalism, make the question of theory assessment look simpler and more straightforward than it is. Indeed, as Kuhn points out in "Objectivity, Value Judgment, and Theory Choice," scientists use at least five criteria of theory assessment:

Accuracy: A theory's consequences should be in qualitative and quantitative agreement with the results of existing experiments and observations.

Consistency: A theory should be consistent with itself and with other currently accepted theories applicable to related aspects of nature.

Scope: A theory's consequences should extend far beyond the particular observations, laws, or subtheories it was initially designed to explain.

Simplicity: A theory should bring order to phenomena that in its absence would be individually isolated and, as a set, confused.

Fruitfulness: A theory should disclose new phenomena or previously unnoted relationships among phenomena already known.

But these criteria of theory assessment are individually imprecise—scientists may legitimately differ about their application to concrete cases—and, when applied together, the criteria repeatedly conflict with one another. As a consequence, scientists fully committed to the same criteria of theory assessment may nonetheless reach different conclusions when choosing between competing theories. The shared criteria of theory assessment, in short, function as values that influence theory choice rather than as rules that determine it, and they need to be fleshed out by individual idiosyncratic factors to explain the particular theoretical choices that particular scientists make. Finally, such criteria are not fixed once and for all except in a very rough sense: both their application and, more obviously, the relative weights attached to them have varied markedly with time and field of specialization, many of these variations associated with particular changes of theory.

Kuhn cautions, however, that such imprecision and conflict and incompleteness and variation in scientists' criteria for theory assessment do not justify the view that theory choice is a product of subjective taste or scientific fashion. For, he notes, objectivity is analyzable in terms of criteria like accuracy and consistency. If these criteria do not supply all the guidance that we have customarily expected of them, then it may be the nature rather than the limits of objectivity that is shown.

Contextual Empiricism

Ruth Hubbard would agree with Kuhn that criteria like accuracy and consistency cannot fully account for the theoretical choices scientists make. In "Have Only Men Evolved?," however, she disagrees with Kuhn's claim that science has been objective nonetheless.

Indeed, up till now we have been dealing with the question of the validation of scientific knowledge by focusing on theories like the phlogiston and oxygen theories of combustion. But, Hubbard points out, when we move from relatively impersonal theories like these from the physical sciences to theories from the natural and social sciences, the individual and social and political values and attitudes that scientists bring to science become a far more significant factor in theory invention and acceptance, and even in the observational data on which the theories are based. This is because such values and attitudes are now far more relevant to the subject matter of the theories.

Take the case of Darwin's theory of evolution as an example. As Hubbard would have it, it is far from clear that this theory scored especially well by Kuhn's standards of accuracy and consistency and the rest when it was first proposed. In fact, "given the looseness of many of his arguments—he credited himself with being an expert wriggler" (p. 230), Hubbard finds it "surprising" that Darwin's theory found such wide acceptance. What *was* crucial to its acceptance, she suggests, was the social outlook it expressed. The three main ideas of Darwin's theory, after all, were endless variation, natural selection from among the variants, and the resulting survival of the fittest. The intrinsic optimism of the theory, the picture of progressive development of species one from another, fit well with 19th century social doctrines of liberalism and laissez faire capitalism. More worrisome, Darwin's theory fit well with 19th century Victorian ideas of sex roles as well: its notion of natural selection via the mechanism of sex ("sexual selection") typecast males—including human males—as the active, mentally and physically superior sex relentlessly out to win the attention of passive females. And this androcentrism and sexism within Darwinism was another reason for the wide acceptance of the theory.

But if these Darwinian reflections of the social outlook of scientists were central to the reasons scientists accepted Darwinian evolutionary theory, then what grounds are there for believing that Darwinian theory—or, in fact, any other scientific theory for which comparable claims can be made—represents an objective account of the world?

> The mythology of science asserts that with many different scientists all asking their own questions and evaluating the answers independently, whatever personal bias creeps into their individual answers is cancelled out when the large picture is put together. This might conceivably be so if scientists were women and men from all sorts of different cultural and social backgrounds who came to science with very different ideologies and interests. But since, in fact, they have been predominantly university-trained white males from privileged social backgrounds, the bias has been narrow and the product often reveals more about the investigator than about the subject being researched. (p. 240)

The solution, suggests Hubbard, is to expose and analyse and consider alternatives to the values and attitudes that scientists have, consciously or not, introduced into their theories about the world.

We need to ask, however, what such exposure and analysis and consideration of alternatives can finally accomplish. If, as Hubbard suggests, there is no such thing as objective, value-free science, then exposure and analysis of the values in science, and even consideration of alternative values for science, can still not produce objective, value-free science. So what good can result? Helen Longino's views in "Can There Be a Feminist Science?" (p. 243) and in her book *Science as Social Knowledge: Values and Objectivity in Scientific Inquiry* (Princeton: Princeton University Press, 1990) can possibly provide an answer. Longino distinguishes between two kinds of values relevant to science, *constitutive values* and *contextual values*. Constitutive values—values like Kuhn's accuracy, consistency, and simplicity—are the source of the rules or norms (the requirement of repeatability of experiments, for example) governing scientific practice. Such values stem from the goals of science—for example, the goal to explain natural phenomena. Contextual values, on the other hand, are scientists' individual or group preferences regarding what ought to be, or what is best. These values stem from the social and cultural environment in which science is practiced. Longino argues that contextual values no less than constitutive values shape scientific research and its results. More specifically, contextual values can and do determine which questions are investigated and which ignored; can and do influence the selection of observational or experimental data and the way those data are expressed; can and do motivate the acceptance of global assumptions operating within an entire scientific field, or particular background assumptions facilitating inferences in specific areas of that field, or entire research programs within a field, and the like. In "Have Only Men Evolved?," Hubbard has given us examples of all these ways in which contextual values have shaped scientific research.

Scientific knowledge, then, is shaped by social ("contextual") values as well as cognitive ("constitutive") ones—a view of scientific knowledge that Longino calls *contextual empiricism*. But, Longino continues, it can be objective nonetheless. Indeed, Longino points out in *Science as Social Knowledge* that scientific objectivity in an important sense has to do with limiting the intrusion of individual subjective preferences into scientific knowledge, and hence, depends on the extent to which community criticism of individuals' scientific work, and responses to that criticism, are possible. More specifically, a science will be objective to the degree that the community which practices it satisfies a number of conditions. First, the members of the community must have recognized avenues—journals, conferences, and the like—for the criticism of evidence, methods, assumptions, and reasoning. Second, the members of the community must share standards—substantive principles as well as constitutive values and contextual values—that critics can invoke. Third, the community as a whole must be responsive to the criticism. That is, the beliefs of the scientific community as a whole and over time—as measured by such public phenomena as the content of textbooks, the distribution of grants and awards, and the flexibility of dominant world views—must change in response to the critical discussion taking place within it. Fourth, intellectual authority must be shared equally among qualified members. And fifth[*], alternative points of view that can serve as sources of criticism must be represented in the community, the more numerously the better. A science will be objective, then, to the degree that it satisfies the above conditions—to the degree that it permits what Longino calls "transformative criticism." Scientific objectivity for Longino thus demands just the kind of exposure and analysis and consideration of alternatives to science's contextual values that Hubbard has urged as the appropriate response to the androcentrism and sexism and other biases within Darwinism.

But in *Science as Social Knowledge* Longino has set out another important sense of scientific objectivity that is helpful for understanding Hubbard's claims. This second sense of scientific objectivity pertains not to the structure and functioning of scientific communities but to the *products* of those communities—the observation statements and theories and the like that those communities put forward as the results of their inquiries. In this sense a science is objective if its theories and other claims provide a true description of the world. It is in this sense that Hubbard has said that a science permeated with human values and organized by a system of categories made by human beings cannot be objective, cannot provide a true picture of a world that exists independently of humans. But this conclusion suggests a further response to the androcentrism and sexism and other biases within Darwinism and other scientific theories—a response beyond merely exposing and analyzing and considering alternatives to these values. If science is shaped by contextual values, and truth is not at issue, then why not simply allow one's feminist (or other) values to shape one's science instead of society's (sexist and androcentric) values? "Instead of remaining passive with respect to the data and what the data suggest, we can acknowledge our ability to affect the course of knowledge and fashion or favor research programs that are consistent with the values and commitments we express in the rest of our lives." (Longino, "Can There Be a Feminist Science?", p. 250) This would have the effect of transforming science from a sexist and androcentric enterprise and body of knowledge to a

---

[*]Longino cites only four conditions for objectivity in *Science as Social Knowledge* (see p. 76), but makes clear in her surrounding discussion that a fifth is also needed.

feminist one. In "Can There Be a Feminist Science?", Longino explores just this possibility as a way of choosing between rival research programs.

Summary

So, what is the method by which theories are tested and judged acceptable or unacceptable in science? In the foregoing I have sketched six major approaches to this question currently in the forefront of discussion: justificationism; falsificationism; conventionalism; the methodology of scientific research programmes; Thomas Kuhn's sociological approach; and contextual empiricism. As we have seen, these six approaches share certain features in common, though they also differ in crucial respects. Thus, they all allow that a scientific theory is tested by deducing from it consequences regarding observable states of affairs that are then compared with the results of observation and experiment, but they differ regarding what might follow from such a comparison. For justificationism and falsificationism, true observational consequences will warrant a judgment regarding the truth of a theory—either that it is probably true (for justificationism), or that it is possibly true (for falsificationism)—whereas false observational consequences will warrant a judgment that the theory is false. For conventionalism, the methodology of scientific research programmes, Kuhn's sociological approach, and contextual empiricism, on the other hand, neither true nor false observational consequences will warrant any judgment regarding the truth or falsity of the theory. According to these views scientists accept or reject a theory on the basis of its relative simplicity (for conventionalism), or its progressiveness (for the research programmes of the methodology of scientific research programmes), or its accuracy, consistency, scope, simplicity, and fruitfulness (for Kuhn's sociological approach), or any or all of these "constitutive values" as well as "contextual values" stemming from the social and cultural environment in which the theory evaluation occurs (for contextual empiricism). But nothing regarding the truth or falsity of the theory is held to follow from such features of it. Again, for justificationism, falsificationism, Kuhn's sociological approach, and contextual empiricism, the units of scientific knowledge and appraisal are theories, whereas for the other approaches these units are different—either systems of theories (for conventionalism), or research programmes (for the methodology of scientific research programmes).

The result of these differences, as we have seen, is that the accounts of scientific episodes suggested by the different approaches will be different: in such accounts scientists will be drawing different conclusions for different reasons at different times about different units of scientific knowledge and appraisal. This result, however, suggests a way to decide among the six approaches. As you study the selections that follow, aside from attending to the cogency of the arguments offered for each approach, see to what extent each approach makes sense of the history of science. Does it help us to understand why scientists said and did what they did? Does it help us, at least in some cases, to evaluate what scientists said and did—to distinguish good science from bad science and both from non-science? These are some of the questions you should have uppermost in your mind as you read through the selections that follow.

RUDOLF CARNAP

The Confirmation of
Laws and Theories

The observations we make in everyday life as well as the more systematic observations of science reveal certain repetitions or regularities in the world. Day always follows night; the seasons repeat themselves in the same order; fire always feels hot; objects fall when we drop them; and so on. The laws of science are nothing more than statements expressing these regularities as precisely as possible.

If a certain regularity is observed at all times and all places, without exception, then the regularity is expressed in the form of a "universal law." An example from daily life is "All ice is cold." This statement asserts that any piece of ice—at any place in the universe, at any time, past, present, or future—is (was, or will be) cold. Not all laws of science are universal. Instead of asserting that a regularity occurs in *all* cases, some laws assert that it occurs in only a

certain percentage of cases. If the percentage is specified or if in some other way a quantitative statement is made about the relation of one event to another, then the statement is called a "statistical law"—for example, "Ripe apples are usually red" or "Approximately half the children born each year are boys." Both types of law—universal and statistical—are needed in science. The universal laws are logically simpler, and for this reason we shall consider them first. In the early part of this discussion "laws" will usually mean universal laws.

Universal laws are expressed in the logical form of what is called in formal logic a "universal conditional statement." (. . . [W]e shall occasionally make use of symbolic logic, but only in a very elementary way.) For example, let us consider a law of the simplest possible type. It asserts that, whatever x may be, if x is

From Chapters 1, 2, 3, 23, and 24 of *Philosophical Foundations of Physics* by Rudolf Carnap, pp. 3–6, 19–22, 32–35, 225–235. Copyright © 1966 by Basic Books, Inc., publishers.

P, then *x* is also *Q*. This is written symbolically as follows:

$$(x) (Px \supset Qx)$$

The expression "(x)" on the left is called a "universal quantifier." It tells us that the statement refers to *all* cases of *x*, rather than to just a certain percentage of cases. "Px" says that *x* is *P*, and "Qx" says that *x* is *Q*. The symbol "$\supset$" is a connective. It links the term on its left to the term on its right. In English, it corresponds roughly to the assertion, "if . . . , then . . . ."

If "*x*" stands for any material body, then the law states that, for any material body *x*, if *x* has the property *P*, it also has the property *Q*. For instance, in physics we might say, "For every body *x*, if that body is heated, that body will expand." This is the law of thermal expansion in its simplest, nonquantitative form. In physics, of course, one tries to obtain quantitative laws and to qualify them so as to exclude exceptions; but, if we forget about such refinements, then this universal conditional statement is the basic logical form of all universal laws. Sometimes we may say that, not only does *Qx* hold whenever *Px* holds, but the reverse is also true; whenever *Qx* holds, *Px* holds also. Logicians call this a biconditional statement—a statement that is conditional in both directions. But of course this does not contradict the fact that in all universal laws we deal with universal conditionals, because a biconditional may be regarded as the conjunction of two conditionals.

Not all statements made by scientists have this logical form. A scientist may say, "Yesterday in Brazil, Professor Smith discovered a new species of butterfly." This is not the statement of a law. It speaks about a specified single time and place; it states that something happened at that time and place. Because statements such as this are about single facts, they are called "singular" statements. Of course, all our knowledge has its origin in singular statements—the particular observations of particular individu-

als. One of the big, perplexing questions in the philosophy of science is how we are able to go from such singular statements to the assertion of universal laws.

When statements by scientists are made in the ordinary word language, rather than in the more precise language of symbolic logic, we must be extremely careful not to confuse singular with universal statements. If a zoologist writes in a textbook, "The elephant is an excellent swimmer," he does not mean that a certain elephant, which he observed a year ago in a zoo, is an excellent swimmer. When he says "the elephant," he is using *the* in the Aristotelian sense; it refers to the entire class of elephants. All European languages have inherited from the Greek (and perhaps also from other languages) this manner of speaking in a singular way when actually a class or type is meant. The Greeks said, "Man is a rational animal." They meant, of course, all men, not a particular man. In a similar way, we say "the elephant" when we mean all elephants or "tuberculosis is characterized by the following symptoms . . ." when we mean not a singular case of tuberculosis, but all instances.

It is unfortunate that our language has this ambiguity, because it is a source of much misunderstanding. Scientists often refer to universal statements—or rather to what is expressed by such statements—as "facts." They forget that the word *fact* was originally applied (and we shall apply it exclusively in this sense) to singular, particular occurrences. If a scientist is asked about the law of thermal expansion, he may say, "Oh, thermal expansion. That is one of the familiar, basic facts of physics." In a similar way, he may speak of the fact that heat is generated by an electric current, the fact that magnetism is produced by electricity, and so on. These are sometimes considered familiar "facts" of physics. To avoid misunderstandings, we prefer not to call such statements "facts." Facts are particular events. "This morning in the laboratory, I sent an electric current through a wire coil with an iron body inside it, and I found that the iron body became magnetic." That is a fact unless, of course, I deceived myself in some way. However, if I was sober, if it was not too foggy in the room, and if no one has tinkered secretly with the apparatus to play a joke on me, then I may state as a factual observation that this morning that sequence of events occurred.

When we use the word *fact* we will mean it in the singular sense in order to distinguish it clearly from universal statements. Such universal statements will be called "laws" even when they are as elementary as the law of thermal expansion or, still more elementary, the statement "All ravens are black." I do not know whether this statement is true, but, assuming its truth, we will call such a statement a law of zoology. Zoologists may speak informally of such "facts" as "the raven is black" or "the octopus has eight arms," but, in our more precise terminology, statements of this sort will be called "laws."

Later we shall distinguish between two kinds of law—empirical and theoretical. Laws of the simple kind that I have just mentioned are sometimes called "empirical generalizations" or "empirical laws." They are simple because they speak of properties, like the color black or the magnetic properties of a piece of iron, that can be directly observed. The law of thermal expansion, for example, is a generalization based on many direct observations of bodies that expand when heated. In contrast, theoretical, nonobservable concepts, such as elementary particles and electromagnetic fields, must be dealt with by theoretical laws. We will discuss all this later. I mention it here because otherwise you might think that the examples I have given do not cover the kind of laws you have perhaps learned in theoretical physics.

To summarize, science begins with direct observations of single facts. Nothing else is observable. Certainly a regularity is not directly observable. It is only when many observations are compared with one another that regulari-

ties are discovered. These regularities are expressed by statements called "laws." . . .

Induction . . .

. . . Let us now ask how we arrive at such laws. On what basis are we justified in believing that a law holds? We know, of course, that all laws are based on the observation of certain regularities. They constitute indirect knowledge, as opposed to direct knowledge of facts. What justifies us in going from the direct observation of facts to a law that expresses certain regularities of nature? This is what in traditional terminology is called "the problem of induction."

Induction is often contrasted with deduction by saying that deduction goes from the general to the specific or singular, whereas induction goes the other way, from the singular to the general. This is a misleading oversimplification. In deduction, there are kinds of inferences other than those from the general to the specific; in induction there are also many kinds of inference. The traditional distinction is also misleading because it suggests that deduction and induction are simply two branches of a single kind of logic. John Stuart Mill's famous work, *A System of Logic*, contains a lengthy description of what he called "inductive logic" and states various canons of inductive procedure. Today we are more reluctant to use the term "inductive inference." If it is used at all, we must realize that it refers to a kind of inference that differs fundamentally from deduction.

In deductive logic, inference leads from a set of premises to a conclusion just as certain as the premises. If you have reason to believe the premises, you have equally valid reason to believe the conclusion that follows logically from the premises. If the premises are true, the conclusion cannot be false. With respect to induction, the situation is entirely different. The truth of an inductive conclusion is never certain. I do not mean only that the conclusion cannot be certain because it rests on premises that cannot be known with certainty. Even if the premises are assumed to be true and the inference is a valid inductive inference, the conclusion may be false. The most we can say is that, with respect to given premises, the conclusion has a certain degree of probability. Inductive logic tells us how to calculate the value of this probability.

We know that singular statements of fact, obtained by observation, are never absolutely certain because we may make errors in our observations; but, in respect to laws, there is still greater uncertainty. A law about the world states that, in any particular case, at any place and any time, if one thing is true, another thing is true. Clearly, this speaks about an infinity of possible instances. The actual instances may not be infinite, but there is an infinity of possible instances. A physiological law says that, if you stick a dagger into the heart of any human being, he will die. Since no exception to this law has ever been observed, it is accepted as universal. It is true, of course, that the number of instances so far observed of daggers being thrust into human hearts is finite. It is possible that some day humanity may cease to exist; in that case, the number of human beings, both past and future, is finite. But we do not know that humanity will cease to exist. Therefore, we must say that there is an infinity of possible instances, all of which are covered by the law. And, if there is an infinity of instances, no number of finite observations, however large, can make the "universal" law certain.

Of course, we may go on and make more and more observations, making them in as careful and scientific a manner as we can, until eventually we may say, "This law has been tested so many times that we can have complete confidence in its truth. It is a well-established, well-founded law." If we think about it, however, we see that even the best-founded laws of physics must rest on only a finite number of observations. It is always possible that tomorrow a counterinstance may be found. At no time is it possible to arrive at *complete* verifi-

cation of a law. In fact, we should not speak of "verification" at all—if by the word we mean a definitive establishment of truth—but only of confirmation.

Interestingly enough, although there is no way in which a law can be verified (in the strict sense), there is a simple way it can be falsified. One need find only a single counterinstance. The knowledge of a counterinstance may, in itself, be uncertain. You may have made an error of observation or have been deceived in some way. But, if we assume that the counterinstance is a fact, then the negation of the law follows immediately. If a law says that every object that is P is also Q and we find an object that is P and not Q, the law is refuted. A million positive instances are insufficient to verify the law; one counterinstance is sufficient to falsify it. The situation is strongly asymmetric. It is easy to refute a law; it is exceedingly difficult to find strong confirmation.

How do we find confirmation of a law? If we have observed a great many positive instances and no negative instance, we say that the confirmation is strong. How strong it is and whether the strength can be expressed numerically is still a controversial question in the philosophy of science. We will return to this in a moment. Here we are concerned only with making clear that our first task in seeking confirmation of a law is to test instances to determine whether they are positive or negative. This is done by using our logical schema to make predictions. A law states that (x) $(Px \supset Qx)$; hence, for a given object a, $Pa \supset Qa$. We try to find as many objects as we can (here symbolized by "a") that have the property P. We then observe whether they also fulfill the condition Q. If we find a negative instance, the matter is settled. Otherwise, each positive instance is additional evidence adding to the strength of our confirmation.

There are, of course, various methodological rules for efficient testing. For example, instances should be diversified as much as possible. If you are testing the law of thermal expansion, you should not limit your tests to solid substances. If you are testing the law that all metals are good conductors of electricity, you should not confine your tests to specimens of copper. You should test as many metals as possible under various conditions—hot, cold, and so on. We will not go into the many methodological rules for testing; we will only point out that in all cases the law is tested by making predictions and then seeing whether those predictions hold. In some cases, we find in nature the objects that we wish to test. In other cases, we have to produce them. In testing the law of thermal expansion, for example, we do not look for objects that are hot; we take certain objects and heat them. Producing conditions for testing has the great advantage that we can more easily follow the methodological rule of diversification; but whether we create the situations to be tested or find them ready-made in nature, the underlying schema is the same.

A moment ago I raised the question of whether the degree of confirmation of a law (or a singular statement that we are predicting by means of the law) can be expressed in quantitative form. Instead of saying that one law is "well founded" and that another law "rests on flimsy evidence," we might say that the first law has a 0.8 degree of confirmation, whereas the degree of confirmation for the second law is only 0.2. This question has long been debated. My own view is that such a procedure is legitimate and that what I have called "degree of confirmation" is identical with logical probability.

Such a statement does not mean much until we know what is meant by "logical probability." Why do I add the adjective "logical"? It is not customary practice; most books on probability do not make a distinction between various kinds of probability, one of which is called "logical." It is my belief, however, that there are two fundamentally different kinds of probability, and I distinguish between them by calling one "statistical probability" and the other "log-

ical probability." It is unfortunate that the same word, "probability," has been used in two such widely differing senses. Failing to make the distinction is a source of enormous confusion in books on the philosophy of science as well as in the discourse of scientists themselves. . . .

In my conception, logical probability is a logical relation somewhat similar to logical implication; indeed, I think probability may be regarded as a partial implication. If the evidence is so strong that the hypothesis follows logically from it—is logically implied by it—we have one extreme case in which the probability is 1. (Probability 1 also occurs in other cases, but this is one special case where it occurs.) Similarly, if the negation of a hypothesis is logically implied by the evidence, the logical probability of the hypothesis is 0. In between, there is a continuum of cases about which deductive logic tells us nothing beyond the negative assertion that neither the hypothesis nor its negation can be deduced from the evidence. On this continuum inductive logic must take over. But inductive logic is like deductive logic in being concerned solely with the statements involved, not with the facts of nature. By a logical analysis of a stated hypothesis h and stated evidence e, we conclude that h is not logically implied but is, so to speak, partially implied by e to the degree of so-and-so much.

At this point, we are justified, in my view, in assigning numerical value to the probability. If possible, we should like to construct a system of inductive logic of such a kind that for any pair of sentences, one asserting evidence e and the other stating a hypothesis h, we can assign a number giving the logical probability of h with respect to e. . . .

For this concept of probability, I also use the term "inductive probability," because I am convinced that this is the basic concept involved in all inductive reasoning and that the chief task of inductive reasoning is the evaluation of this probability. . . .

Statements giving values of statistical probability are not purely logical; they are factual statements in the language of science. When a medical man says that the probability is "very good" (or perhaps he uses a numerical value and says 0.7) that a patient will react positively to a certain injection, he is making a statement in medical science. When a physicist says that the probability of a certain radioactive phenomenon is so-and-so much, he is making a statement in physics. Statistical probability is a scientific, empirical concept. Statements about statistical probability are "synthetic" statements, statements that cannot be decided by logic but which rest on empirical investigations. On this point I agree fully with Mises, Reichenbach, and the statisticians. When we say, "With this particular die the statistical probability of throwing an ace is 0.157," we are stating a scientific hypothesis that can be tested only by a series of observations. It is an empirical statement because only an empirical investigation can confirm it.

As science develops, probability statements of this sort seem to become increasingly important, not only in the social science, but in modern physics as well. Statistical probability is involved not only in areas where it is necessary because of ignorance (as in the social sciences or when a physicist is calculating the path of a molecule in a liquid), but also as an essential factor in the basic principles of quantum theory. It is of the utmost importance for science to have a theory of statistical probability. Such theories have been developed by statisticians and, in a different way, by Mises and Reichenbach.

On the other hand, we also need the concept of logical probability. It is especially useful in metascientific statements, that is, statements about science. We say to a scientist, "You tell me that I can rely on this law in making a certain prediction. How well established is the law? How trustworthy is the prediction?" The scientist today may or may not be willing to answer a metascientific question of this kind in quantitative terms. But I believe that, once inductive logic is sufficiently developed, he could

reply, "This hypothesis is confirmed to degree 0.8 on the basis of the available evidence." A scientist who answers in this way is making a statement about a logical relation between the evidence and the hypothesis in question. The sort of probability he has in mind is logical probability, which I also call "degree of confirmation." His statement that the value of this probability is 0.8 is, in this context, not a synthetic (empirical) statement, but an analytic one. It is analytic because no empirical investigation is demanded. It expresses a logical relation between a sentence that states the evidence and a sentence that states the hypothesis. . . .

Theories and Nonobservables

One of the most important distinctions between two types of laws in science is the distinction between what may be called (there is no generally accepted terminology for them) empirical laws and theoretical laws. Empirical laws are laws that can be confirmed directly by empirical observations. The term "observable" is often used for any phenomenon that can be directly observed, so it can be said that empirical laws are laws about observables.

Here, a warning must be issued. Philosophers and scientists have quite different ways of using the terms "observable" and "nonobservable." To a philosopher, "observable" has a very narrow meaning. It applies to such properties as "blue," "hard," or "hot." These are properties directly perceived by the senses. To the physicist, the word has a much broader meaning. It includes any quantitative magnitude that can be measured in a relatively simple, direct way. A philosopher would not consider a temperature of, perhaps, 80 degrees centigrade, or a weight of 93½ pounds, an observable because there is no direct sensory perception of such magnitudes. To a physicist, both are observables because they can be measured in an extremely simple way. The object to be weighed is placed on a balance scale. The temperature is measured with a thermometer. The physicist would not say that the mass of a molecule, let alone the mass of an electron, is something observable, because here the procedures of measurement are much more complicated and indirect. But magnitudes that can be established by relatively simple procedures—length with a ruler, time with a clock, or frequency of light waves with a spectrometer—are called observables.

A philosopher might object that the intensity of an electric current is not really observed. Only a pointer position was observed. An ammeter was attached to the circuit and it was noted that the pointer pointed to a mark labeled 5.3. Certainly the current's intensity was not observed. It was *inferred* from what was observed.

The physicist would reply that this was true enough, but the inference was not very complicated. The procedure of measurement is so simple, so well established, that it could not be doubted that the ammeter would give an accurate measurement of current intensity. Therefore, it is included among what are called observables.

There is no question here of who is using the term "observable" in a right or proper way. There is a continuum which starts with direct sensory observations and proceeds to enormously complex, indirect methods of observation. Obviously no sharp line can be drawn across this continuum; it is a matter of degree. A philosopher is sure that the sound of his wife's voice, coming from across the room, is an observable. But suppose he listens to her on the telephone. Is her voice an observable or isn't it? A physicist would certainly say that when he looks at something through an ordinary microscope, he is observing it directly. Is this also the case when he looks into an electron microscope? Does he observe the path of a particle when he sees the track it makes in a bubble chamber? In general, the physicist speaks of observables in a very wide sense compared with the narrow sense of the philosopher, but, in both cases, the line separating observable from nonobservable is highly arbi-

trary. It is well to keep this in mind whenever these terms are encountered in a book by a philosopher or scientist. Individual authors will draw the line where it is most convenient, depending on their points of view, and there is no reason why they should not have this privilege.

Empirical laws, in my terminology, are laws containing terms either directly observable by the senses or measurable by relatively simple techniques. Sometimes such laws are called empirical generalizations, as a reminder that they have been obtained by generalizing results found by observations and measurements. They include not only simple qualitative laws (such as "All ravens are black") but also quantitative laws that arise from simple measurements. The laws relating pressure, volume, and temperature of gases are of this type. Ohm's law, connecting the electric potential difference, resistance, and intensity of current, is another familiar example. The scientist makes repeated measurements, finds certain regularities, and expresses them in a law. These are the empirical laws. . . . [T]hey are used for explaining observed facts and for predicting future observable events.

There is no commonly accepted term for the second kind of laws, which I call *theoretical laws*. Sometimes they are called abstract or hypothetical laws. "Hypothetical" is perhaps not suitable because it suggests that the distinction between the two types of laws is based on the degree to which the laws are confirmed. But an empirical law, if it is a tentative hypothesis, confirmed only to a low degree, would still be an empirical law although it might be said that it was rather hypothetical. A theoretical law is not to be distinguished from an empirical law by the fact that it is not well established, but by the fact that it contains terms of a different kind. The terms of a theoretical law do not refer to observables even when the physicist's wide meaning for what can be observed is adopted. They are laws about such entities as molecules, atoms, electrons, protons, electromagnetic fields, and others that cannot be measured in simple, direct ways.

If there is a static field of large dimensions, which does not vary from point to point, physicists call it an observable field because it can be measured with a simple apparatus. But if the field changes from point to point in very small distances, or varies very quickly in time, perhaps changing billions of times each second, then it cannot be directly measured by simple techniques. Physicists would not call such a field an observable. Sometimes a physicist will distinguish between observables and nonobservables in just this way. If the magnitude remains the same within large enough spatial distances, or large enough time intervals, so that an apparatus can be applied for a direct measurement of the magnitude, it is called a *macroevent*. If the magnitude changes within such extremely small intervals of space and time that it cannot be directly measured by simple apparatus, it is a *microevent*. (Earlier authors used the terms "microscopic" and "macroscopic," but today many authors have shortened these terms to "micro" and "macro.")

A microprocess is simply a process involving extremely small intervals of space and time. For example, the oscillation of an electromagnetic wave of visible light is a microprocess. No instrument can directly measure how its intensity varies. The distinction between macro- and microconcepts is sometimes taken to be parallel to observable and nonobservable. It is not exactly the same, but it is roughly so. Theoretical laws concern nonobservables, and very often these are microprocesses. If so, the laws are sometimes called microlaws. I use the term "theoretical laws" in a wider sense than this, to include all those laws that contain nonobservables, regardless of whether they are microconcepts or macroconcepts.

It is true, as shown earlier, that the concepts "observable" and "nonobservable" cannot be sharply defined because they lie on a continuum. In actual practice, however, the difference is usually great enough so there is not likely to be debate. All physicists would agree that the laws relating pressure, volume, and temperature of a gas, for example, are empirical laws. Here the amount of gas is large enough so that the magnitudes to be measured remain constant over a sufficiently large volume of space and period of time to permit direct, simple measurements which can then be generalized into laws. All physicists would agree that laws about the behavior of single molecules are theoretical. Such laws concern a microprocess about which generalizations cannot be based on simple, direct measurements.

Theoretical laws are, of course, more general than empirical laws. It is important to understand, however, that theoretical laws cannot be arrived at simply by taking the empirical laws, then generalizing a few steps further. How does a physicist arrive at an empirical law? He observes certain events in nature. He notices a certain regularity. He describes this regularity by making an inductive generalization. It might be supposed that he could now put together a group of empirical laws, observe some sort of pattern, make a wider inductive generalization, and arrive at a theoretical law. Such is not the case.

To make this clear, suppose it has been observed that a certain iron bar expands when heated. After the experiment has been repeated many times, always with the same result, the regularity is generalized by saying that this bar expands when heated. An empirical law has been stated, even though it has a narrow range and applies only to one particular iron bar. Now further tests are made of other iron objects with the ensuing discovery that every time an iron object is heated it expands. This permits a more general law to be formulated, namely that all bodies of iron expand when heated. In similar fashion, the still more general laws "All metals . . . ," then "All solid bodies . . ." are developed. These are all simple generalizations, each a bit more general than the previous one, but they are all empirical laws. Why? Because in each case the objects dealt with are observable (iron, copper, metal, solid bodies); in each case the increases in temperature and length are measurable by simple, direct techniques.

In contrast, a theoretical law relating to this process would refer to the behavior of molecules in the iron bar. In what way is the behavior of the molecules connected with the expansion of the bar when heated? You see at once that we are now speaking of nonobservables. We must introduce a theory—the atomic theory of matter—and we are quickly plunged into atomic laws involving concepts radically different from those we had before. It is true that these theoretical concepts differ from concepts of length and temperature only in the degree to which they are directly or indirectly observable, but the difference is so great that there is no debate about the radically different nature of the laws that must be formulated.

Theoretical laws are related to empirical laws in a way somewhat analogous to the way empirical laws are related to single facts. An empirical law helps to explain a fact that has been observed and to predict a fact not yet observed. In similar fashion, the theoretical law helps to explain empirical laws already formulated, and to permit the derivation of new empirical laws. Just as the single, separate facts fall into place in an orderly pattern when they are generalized in an empirical law, the single and separate empirical laws fit into the orderly pattern of a theoretical law. This raises one of the main problems in the methodology of science. How can the kind of knowledge that will justify the assertion of a theoretical law be obtained? An empirical law may be justified by making observations of single facts. But to justify a theoretical law, comparable observations cannot be made because the entities referred to in theoretical laws are nonobservables.

Before taking up this problem, some remarks made . . . earlier . . . about the use of the word "fact" should be repeated. It is important in the present context to be extremely careful in the use of this word because some authors, especially scientists, use "fact" or "empirical fact" for some propositions which I would call empirical laws. For example, many physicists will refer to the "fact" that the specific heat of copper is 0.090. I would call this a law because in its full formulation it is seen to be a universal conditional statement: "For any x, and any time t, if x is a solid body of copper, then the specific heat of x at t is 0.090." Some physicists may even speak of the law of thermal expansion, Ohm's law, and others, as facts. Of course, they can then say that theoretical laws help explain such facts. This sounds like my statement that empirical laws explain facts, but the word "fact" is being used here in two different ways. I restrict the word to particular, concrete facts that can be spatiotemporally specified, not thermal expansion in general, but *the* expansion of this iron bar observed this morning at ten o'clock when it was heated. It is important to bear in mind the restricted way in which I speak of facts. If the word "fact" is used in an ambiguous manner, the important difference between the ways in which empirical and theoretical laws serve for explanation will be entirely blurred.

How can theoretical laws be discovered? We cannot say, "Let's just collect more and more data, then generalize beyond the empirical laws until we reach theoretical ones." No theoretical law was ever found that way. We observe stones and trees and flowers, noting various regularities and describing them by empirical laws. But no matter how long or how carefully we observe such things, we never reach a point at which we observe a molecule. The term "molecule" never arises as a result of observations. For this reason, no amount of generalization from observations will ever produce a theory of molecular processes. Such a theory must arise in another way. It is stated not as a generalization of facts but as a hypothesis. The hypothesis is then tested in a manner analogous in certain ways to the testing of an empirical law. From the hypothesis, certain empirical laws are derived, and these empirical laws are tested in turn by observation of facts. Perhaps the empirical laws derived from the theory are already known and well confirmed. (Such laws may even have motivated the formulation of the theoretical law.) Regardless of whether the derived empirical laws are known and confirmed, or whether they are new laws confirmed by new observations, the confirmation of such derived laws provides indirect confirmation of the theoretical law.

The point to be made clear is this. A scientist does not start with one empirical law, perhaps Boyle's law for gases, and then seek a theory about molecules from which this law can be derived. The scientist tries to formulate a much more general theory from which a variety of empirical laws can be derived. The more such laws, the greater their variety and apparent lack of connection with one another, the stronger will be the theory that explains them. Some of these derived laws may have been known before, but the theory may also make it possible to derive new empirical laws which can be confirmed by new tests. If this is the case, it can be said that the theory made it possible to predict new empirical laws. The prediction is understood in a hypothetical way. If the theory holds, certain empirical laws will also hold. The predicted empirical law speaks about relations between observables, so it is now possible to make experiments to see if the empirical law holds. If the empirical law is confirmed, it provides indirect confirmation of the theory. Every confirmation of a law, empirical or theoretical, is, of course, only partial, never complete and absolute. But in the case of empirical laws, it is a more direct confirmation. The confirmation of a theoretical law is indirect, because it takes place only through the confirmation of empirical laws derived from the theory.

The supreme value of a new theory is its power to predict new empirical laws. It is true that it also has value in explaining known empirical laws, but this is a minor value. If a scientist proposes a new theoretical system, from which no new laws can be derived, then it is logically equivalent to the set of all known empirical laws. The theory may have a certain elegance, and it may simplify to some degree the

set of all known laws, although it is not likely that there would be an essential simplification. On the other hand, every new theory in physics that has led to a great leap forward has been a theory from which new empirical laws could be derived. If Einstein had done no more than propose his theory of relativity as an elegant new theory that would embrace certain known laws—perhaps also simplify them to a certain degree—then his theory would not have had such a revolutionary effect.

Of course it was quite otherwise. The theory of relativity led to new empirical laws which explained for the first time such phenomena as the movement of the perihelion of Mercury and the bending of light rays in the neighborhood of the sun. These predictions showed that relativity theory was more than just a new way of expressing the old laws. Indeed, it was a theory of great predictive power. The consequences that can be derived from Einstein's theory are far from being exhausted. These are consequences that could not have been derived from earlier theories. Usually a theory of such power does have an elegance, and a unifying effect on known laws. It is simpler than the total collection of known laws. But the great value of the theory lies in its power to suggest new laws that can be confirmed by empirical means.

Correspondence Rules

An important qualification must now be added. . . . The statement that empirical laws are derived from theoretical laws is an oversimplification. It is not possible to derive them directly because a theoretical law contains theoretical terms, whereas an empirical law contains only observable terms. This prevents any direct deduction of an empirical law from a theoretical one.

To understand this, imagine that we are back in the nineteenth century, preparing to state for the first time some theoretical laws about molecules in a gas. These laws are to describe the number of molecules per unit volume of the gas, the molecular velocities, and so forth. To simplify matters, we assume that all the molecules have the same velocity. (This was indeed the original assumption; later it was abandoned in favor of a certain probability distribution of velocities.) Further assumptions must be made about what happens when molecules collide. We do not know the exact shape of molecules, so let us suppose that they are tiny spheres. How do spheres collide? There are laws about colliding spheres, but they concern large bodies. Since we cannot directly observe molecules, we assume their collisions are analogous to those of large bodies; perhaps they behave like perfect billiard balls on a frictionless table. These are, of course, only assumptions; guesses suggested by analogies with known macrolaws.

But now we come up against a difficult problem. Our theoretical laws deal exclusively with the behavior of molecules, which cannot be seen. How, therefore, can we deduce from such laws a law about observable properties such as the pressure or temperature of a gas or properties of sound waves that pass through the gas? The theoretical laws contain only theoretical terms. What we seek are empirical laws containing observable terms. Obviously, such laws cannot be derived without having something else given in addition to the theoretical laws.

The something else that must be given is this: a set of rules connecting the theoretical terms with the observable terms. Scientists and philosophers of science have long recognized the need for such a set of rules, and their nature has been often discussed. An example of such a rule is "If there is an electromagnetic oscillation of a specified frequency, then there is a visible greenish-blue color of a certain hue." Here something observable is connected with a nonobservable microprocess.

Another example is "The temperature (measured by a thermometer and, therefore, an observable in the wider sense explained earlier)

of a gas is proportional to the mean kinetic energy of its molecules." This rule connects a nonobservable in molecular theory, the kinetic energy of molecules, with an observable, the temperature of the gas. If statements of this kind did not exist, there would be no way of deriving empirical laws about observables from theoretical laws about nonobservables.

Different writers have different names for these rules. I call them "correspondence rules." P. W. Bridgman calls them operational rules. Norman R. Campbell speaks of them as the "Dictionary."[1] Since the rules connect a term in one terminology with a term in another terminology, the use of the rules is analogous to the use of a French-English dictionary. What does the French word "cheval" mean? You look it up in the dictionary and find that it means "horse." It is not really that simple when a set of rules is used for connecting nonobservables with observables; nevertheless, there is an analogy here that makes Campbell's "Dictionary" a suggestive name for the set of rules.

There is a temptation at times to think that the set of rules provides a means for defining theoretical terms, whereas just the opposite is really true. A theoretical term can never be explicitly defined on the basis of observable terms, although sometimes an observable can be defined in theoretical terms. For example, "iron" can be defined as a substance consisting of small crystalline parts, each having a certain arrangement of atoms and each atom being a configuration of particles of a certain type. In theoretical terms then, it is possible to express what is meant by the observable term "iron," but the reverse is not true.

There is no answer to the question, "Exactly what is an electron?" . . . [T]his question . . . is the kind that philosophers are always asking scientists. They want the physicist to tell them just what he means by "electricity," "magnetism," "gravity," "a molecule." If the physicist explains them in theoretical terms, the philosopher may be disappointed. "That is not what I meant at all," he will say. "I want you to tell me, in ordinary language, what those terms mean." Sometimes the philosopher writes a book in which he talks about the great mysteries of nature. "No one," he writes, "has been able so far, and perhaps no one ever will be able, to give us a straightforward answer to the question, 'What is electricity?' And so electricity remains forever one of the great, unfathomable mysteries of the universe."

There is no special mystery here. There is only an improperly phrased question. Definitions that cannot, in the nature of the case, be given, should not be demanded. If a child does not know what an elephant is, we can tell him it is a huge animal with big ears and a long trunk. We can show him a picture of an elephant. It serves admirably to define an elephant in observable terms that a child can understand. By analogy, there is a temptation to believe that, when a scientist introduces theoretical terms, he should also be able to define them in familiar terms. But this is not possible. There is no way a physicist can show us a picture of electricity in the way he can show his child a picture of an elephant. Even the cell of an organism, although it cannot be seen with the unaided eye, can be represented by a picture because the cell can be seen when it is viewed through a microscope. But we do not possess a picture of the electron. We cannot say how it looks or how it feels, because it cannot be seen or touched. The best we can do is to say that it

is an extremely small body that behaves in a certain manner. This may seem to be analogous to our description of an elephant. We can describe an elephant as a large animal that behaves in a certain manner. Why not do the same with an electron?

The answer is that a physicist can describe the behavior of an electron only by stating theoretical laws, and these laws contain only theoretical terms. They describe the field produced by an electron, the reaction of an electron to a field, and so on. If an electron is in an electrostatic field, its velocity will accelerate in a certain way. Unfortunately, the electron's acceleration is an unobservable. It is not like the acceleration of a billiard ball, which can be studied by direct observation. There is no way that a theoretical concept can be defined in terms of observables. We must, therefore, resign ourselves to the fact that definitions of the kind that can be supplied for observable terms cannot be formulated for theoretical terms. . . .

Note

1. See Percy W. Bridgman, *The Logic of Modern Physics* (New York: Macmillan, 1927) and Norman R. Campbell, *Physics: The Elements* (Cambridge: Cambridge University Press, 1920). Rules of correspondence are discussed by Ernest Nagel, *The Structure of Science* (New York: Harcourt, Brace & World, 1961), pp. 97–105.

KARL POPPER

Science: Conjectures
and Refutations

There could be no fairer destiny for
any . . . theory than that it should point the
way to a more comprehensive theory in which
it lives on, as a limiting case.

ALBERT EINSTEIN

Mr. Turnbull had predicted evil consequences, . . .
and was now doing the best in his power to bring
about the verification of his own prophecies.

ANTHONY TROLLOPE

I

A lecture given at Peterhouse, Cambridge, in Summer 1953, as a part of a course on developments and trends in contemporary British philosophy, organized by the British Council; originally published under the title "Philosophy of Science: a Personal Report" in *British Philosophy in Mid-Century* Ed. C. A. Mace, 1957.

When I received the list of participants in this course and realized that I had been asked to speak to philosophical colleagues I thought, after some hesitation and consultation, that you would probably prefer me to speak about those problems which interest me most, and about those developments with which I am most intimately acquainted. I therefore decided to do what I have never done before: to give you a report on my own work in the philosophy of science since the autumn of 1919 when I first began to grapple with the problem *"When should a theory be ranked as scientific?"* or *"Is there a criterion for the scientific character or status of a theory?"*

The problem which troubled me at the time was neither "When is a theory true?" nor "When is a theory acceptable?" My problem was different. I *wished to distinguish between science and pseudo-science*, knowing very well that science often errs, and that pseudo-science may happen to stumble on the truth.

I knew, of course, the most widely accepted answer to my problem: that science is distinguished from pseudo-science—or from "metaphysics"—by its *empirical method,* which is essentially *inductive*, proceeding from observation or experiment. But this did not satisfy me. On the contrary, I often formulated my problem as one of distinguishing between a genuinely empirical method and a non-empirical or even a pseudo-empirical method—that is to say, a method which, although it appeals to observation and experiment, nevertheless does not come up to scientific standards. The latter method may be exemplified by astrology, with its stupendous mass of empirical evidence based on observation—on horoscopes and on biographies.

But as it was not the example of astrology which led me to my problem I should perhaps briefly describe the atmosphere in which my problem arose and the examples by which it was stimulated. After the collapse of the Austrian Empire there had been a revolution in Austria: The air was full of revolutionary slogans and ideas, and new and often wild theories. Among the theories which interested me Einstein's theory of relativity was no doubt by far the most important. Three others were Marx's theory of history, Freud's psychoanalysis, and Alfred Adler's so-called "individual psychology."

There was a lot of popular nonsense talked about these theories, and especially about rela-

tivity (as still happens even today), but I was fortunate in those who introduced me to the study of this theory. We all—the small circle of students to which I belonged—were thrilled with the result of Eddington's eclipse observations, which in 1919 brought the first important confirmation of Einstein's theory of gravitation. It was a great experience for us, one which had a lasting influence on my intellectual development.

The three other theories I have mentioned were also widely discussed among students at that time. I myself happened to come into personal contact with Alfred Adler, and even to cooperate with him in his social work among the children and young people in the working-class districts of Vienna where he had established social guidance clinics.

It was during the summer of 1919 that I began to feel more and more dissatisfied with these three theories—the Marxist theory of history, psychoanalysis, and individual psychology; and I began to feel dubious about their claims to scientific status. My problem perhaps first took the simple form, "What is wrong with Marxism, psychoanalysis, and individual psychology? Why are they so different from physical theories, from Newton's theory, and especially from the theory of relativity?"

To make this contrast clear I should explain that few of us at the time would have said that we believed in the *truth* of Einstein's theory of gravitation. This shows that it was not my doubting the *truth* of those other three theories which bothered me, but something else. Yet neither was it that I merely felt mathematical physics to be more *exact* than the sociological or psychological type of theory. Thus what worried me was neither the problem of truth, at that stage at least, nor the problem of exactness or measurability. It was rather that I felt that these other three theories, though posing as sciences, had in fact more in common with primitive myths than with science; that they resembled astrology rather than astronomy.

I found that those of my friends who were admirers of Marx, Freud, and Adler were impressed by a number of points common to these theories and especially by their apparent *explanatory power*. These theories appeared to be able to explain practically everything that happened within the fields to which they referred. The study of any of them seemed to have the effect of an intellectual conversion or revelation, opening your eyes to a new truth hidden from those not yet initiated. Once your eyes were thus opened you saw confirming instances everywhere: The world was full of *verifications* of the theory. Whatever happened always confirmed it. Thus its truth appeared manifest; and unbelievers were clearly people who did not want to see the manifest truth, who refused to see it, either because it was against their class interest, or because of their repressions which were still "unanalysed" and crying aloud for treatment.

The most characteristic element in this situation seemed to me the incessant stream of confirmations, of observations which "verified" the theories in question; and this point was constantly emphasized by their adherents. A Marxist could not open a newspaper without finding on every page confirming evidence for his interpretation of history, not only in the news, but also in its presentation—which revealed the class bias of the paper—and especially of course in what the paper did *not* say. The Freudian analysts emphasized that their theories were constantly verified by their "clinical observations." As for Adler, I was much impressed by a personal experience. Once, in 1919, I reported to him a case which to me did not seem particular Adlerian, but which he found no difficulty in analyzing in terms of his theory of inferiority feelings, although he had not even seen the child. Slightly shocked, I asked him how he could be so sure. "Because of my thousandfold experience," he replied; whereupon I could not help saying, "And with this new case, I suppose, your experience has become thousand-and-one-fold."

What I had in mind was that his previous observations may not have been much sounder than this new one; that each in its turn had been interpreted in the light of "previous experience," and at the same time counted as additional confirmation. What, I asked myself, did it confirm? No more than that a case could be interpreted in the light of the theory. But this meant very little, I reflected, since every conceivable case could be interpreted in the light of Adler's theory, or equally of Freud's. I may illustrate this by two very different examples of human behavior: that of a man who pushes a child into the water with the intention of drowning it, and that of a man who sacrifices his life in an attempt to save the child. Each of these two cases can be explained with equal ease in Freudian and in Adlerian terms. According to Freud the first man suffered from repression (say, of some component of his Oedipus complex), while the second man had achieved sublimation. According to Adler the first man suffered from feelings of inferiority (producing perhaps the need to prove to himself that he dared to commit some crime), and so did the second man (whose need was to prove to himself that he dared to rescue the child). I could not think of any human behavior which could not be interpreted in terms of either theory. It was precisely this fact—that they always fitted, that they were always confirmed—which in the eyes of their admirers constituted the strongest argument in favor of these theories. It began to dawn on me that this apparent strength was in fact their weakness.

With Einstein's theory the situation was strikingly different. Take one typical instance—Einstein's prediction, just then confirmed by the findings of Eddington's expedition. Einstein's gravitational theory had led to the result that light must be attracted by heavy bodies (such as the sun), precisely as material bodies were attracted. As a consequence it could be calculated that light from a distant fixed star whose apparent position was close to the sun would reach the earth from such a direction that the star would seem to be slightly shifted away from the sun; or, in other words, that stars close to the sun would look as if they had moved a little away from the sun, and from one another. This is a thing which cannot normally be observed since such stars are rendered invisible in daytime by the sun's overwhelming brightness; but during an eclipse it is possible to take photographs of them. If the same constellation is photographed at night one can measure the distances on the two photographs, and check the predicted effect.

Now the impressive thing about this case is the *risk* involved in a prediction of this kind. If observation shows that the predicted effect is definitely absent, then the theory is simply refuted. The theory is *incompatible with certain possible results of observation*—in fact with results which everybody before Einstein would have expected.[1] This is quite different from the situation I have previously described, when it turned out that the theories in question were compatible with the most divergent human behavior, so that it was practically impossible to describe any human behavior that might not be claimed to be a verification of these theories.

These considerations led me in the winter of 1919–20 to conclusions which I may now reformulate as follows.

1. It is easy to obtain confirmations, or verifications, for nearly every theory—if we look for confirmations.

2. Confirmations should count only if they are the result of *risky predictions*; that is to say, if, unenlightened by the theory in question, we should have expected an event which was incompatible with the theory—an event which would have refuted the theory.

3. Every 'good' scientific theory is a prohibition: It forbids certain things to happen. The more a theory forbids, the better it is.

4. A theory which is not refutable by any conceivable event is non-scientific. Irrefutability is not a virtue of a theory (as people often think) but a vice.

5. Every genuine *test* of a theory is an attempt to falsify it, or to refute it. Testability is falsifiability; but there are degrees of testability: Some theories are more testable, more exposed to refutation, than others; they take, as it were, greater risks.

6. Confirming evidence should not count *except when it is the result of a genuine test of the theory*; and this means that it can be presented as a serious but unsuccessful attempt to falsify the theory. (I now speak in such cases of "corroborating evidence.")

7. Some genuinely testable theories, when found to be false, are still upheld by their admirers—for example by introducing *ad hoc* some auxiliary assumption, or by reinterpreting the theory *ad hoc* in such a way that it escapes refutation. Such a procedure is always possible, but it rescues the theory from refutation only at the price of destroying, or at least lowering, its scientific status. (I later described such a rescuing operation as a *conventionalist twist* or a *conventionalist stratagem*.)

One can sum up all this by saying that *the criterion of the scientific status of a theory is its falsifiability, or refutability, or testability*.

II

I may perhaps exemplify this with the help of the various theories so far mentioned. Einstein's theory of gravitation clearly satisfied the criterion of falsifiability. Even if our measuring instruments at the time did not allow us to pronounce on the results of the tests with complete assurance, there was clearly a possibility of refuting the theory.

Astrology did not pass the test. Astrologers were greatly impressed, and misled, by what they believed to be confirming evidence—so much so that they were quite unimpressed by any unfavorable evidence. Moreover, by making their interpretations and prophecies sufficiently vague they were able to explain away anything that might have been a refutation of the theory had the theory and the prophecies been more precise. In order to escape falsification they destroyed the testability of their theory. It is a typical soothsayer's trick to predict things so vaguely that the predictions can hardly fail, that they become irrefutable.

The Marxist theory of history, in spite of the serious efforts of some of its founders and followers, ultimately adopted this soothsaying practice. In some of its earlier formulations (for example, in Marx's analysis of the character of the "coming social revolution") their predictions were testable, and in fact falsified.[2] Yet instead of accepting the refutations the followers of Marx reinterpreted both the theory and the evidence in order to make them agree. In this way they rescued the theory from refutation; but they did so at the price of adopting a device which made it irrefutable. They thus gave a "conventionalist twist" to the theory; and by this stratagem they destroyed its much advertised claim to scientific status.

The two psychoanalytic theories were in a different class. They were simply non-testable, irrefutable. There was no conceivable human behavior which could contradict them. This does not mean that Freud and Adler were not seeing certain things correctly: I personally do not doubt that much of what they say is of considerable importance and may well play its part one day in a psychological science which is testable. But it does mean that those "clinical observations" which analysts naively believe confirm their theory cannot do this any more than the daily confirmations which astrologers find in their practice.[3] And as for Freud's epic of the Ego, the Super-ego, and the Id, no substantially stronger claim to scientific status can be made for it than for Homer's collected stories from Olympus. These theories describe some facts, but in the manner of myths. They contain most interesting psychological suggestions, but not in a testable form.

At the same time I realized that such myths may be developed and become testable, that historically speaking all—or very nearly all—scientific theories originate from myths, and that a myth may contain important anticipations of scientific theories. Examples are Empedocles' theory of evolution by trial and error, or Parmenides' myth of the unchanging block universe in which nothing ever happens and which, if we add another dimension, becomes Einstein's block universe (in which, too, nothing ever happens, since everything is, four-dimensionally speaking, determined and laid down from the beginning). I thus felt that if a theory is found to be non-scientific, or "metaphysical" (as we might say), it is not thereby found to be unimportant, or insignificant, or "meaningless," or "nonsensical."[4] But it cannot claim to be backed by empirical evidence in the scientific sense—although it may easily be, in some genetic sense, the "result of observation."

(There were a great many other theories of this pre-scientific or pseudo-scientific character, some of them, unfortunately, as influential as the Marxist interpretation of history; for example, the racialist interpretation of history—another of those impressive and all-explanatory theories which act upon weak minds like revelations.)

Thus the problem which I tried to solve by proposing the criterion of falsifiability was neither a problem of meaningfulness or significance, nor a problem of truth or acceptability. It was the problem of drawing a line (as well as this can be done) between the statements, or systems of statements, of the empirical sciences, and all other statements—whether they are of a religious or of a metaphysical character, or simply pseudo-scientific. Years later—it must have been in 1928 or 1929—I called this first problem of mine the *problem of demarcation*. The criterion of falsifiability is a solution to this problem of demarcation, for it says that statements or systems of statements, in order to be ranked as scientific, must be capable of conflicting with possible, or conceivable, observations. . . .

IV

I have discussed the problem of demarcation in some detail because I believe that its solution is the key to most of the fundamental problems of the philosophy of science. . . . [B]ut only one of them—the *problem of induction*—can be discussed here at any length.

I had become interested in the problem of induction in 1923. Although this problem is very closely connected with the problem of demarcation, I did not fully appreciate the connection for about five years.

I approached the problem of induction through Hume. Hume, I felt, was perfectly right in pointing out that induction cannot be logically justified. He held that there can be no valid logical[5] arguments allowing us to establish *"that those instances, of which we have had no experience, resemble those, of which we have had experience."* Consequently, *"even after the observation of the frequent or constant conjunction of objects, we have no reason to draw any inference concerning any object beyond those of which we have had experience."* For "shou'd it be said that we have experience"[6]—experience teaching us that objects constantly conjoined with certain other objects continue to be so conjoined—then, Hume says, "I wou'd renew my question, *why from this experience we form any conclusion beyond those past instances, of which we have had experience."* In other words, an attempt to justify the practice of induction by an appeal to experience must lead to an *infinite regress.* As a result we can say that theories can never be inferred from observation statements, or rationally justified by them.

I found Hume's refutation of inductive inference clear and conclusive. But I felt completely dissatisfied with his psychological explanation of induction in terms of custom or habit. . . . that, like other habits, *our habit of believing in laws is the product of frequent repetition*—of the repeated observation that things of a certain kind are constantly conjoined with things of another kind. . . .

Hume, I felt, had never accepted the full force of his own logical analysis. Having refuted the logical idea of induction he was faced with the following problem: How do we actually obtain our knowledge, as a matter of psychological fact, if induction is a procedure which is logically invalid and rationally unjustifiable? There are two possible answers: (1) We obtain our knowledge by a non-inductive procedure. This answer would have allowed Hume to retain a form of rationalism. (2) We obtain our knowledge by repetition and induction, and therefore by a logically invalid and rationally unjustifiable procedure, so that all apparent knowledge is merely a kind of belief—belief based on habit. This answer would imply that even scientific knowledge is irrational, so that rationalism is absurd, and must be given up. (I shall not discuss here the age-old attempts, now again fashionable, to get out of the difficulty by asserting that though induction is of course logically invalid if we mean by *logic* the same as *deductive logic*, it is not irrational by its own standards, as may be seen from the fact that every reasonable man applies it *as a matter of fact*: It was Hume's great achievement to break this uncritical identification of the question of fact—*quid facti?*—and the question of justification or validity—*quid juris?* . . .

It seems that Hume never seriously considered the first alternative. Having cast out the logical theory of induction by repetition he struck a bargain with common sense, meekly allowing the reentry of induction by repetition, in the guise of a psychological theory. I proposed to turn the tables upon this theory of Hume's. Instead of explaining our propensity to expect regularities as the result of repetition, I proposed to explain repetition-for-us as the result of our propensity to expect regularities and to search for them.

Thus I was led by purely logical considerations to replace the psychological theory of induction by the following view. Without waiting, passively, for repetitions to impress or impose regularities upon us, we actively try to impose regularities upon the world. We try to discover similarities in it, and to interpret it in terms of laws invented by us. Without waiting for premises we jump to conclusions. These may have to be discarded later, should observations show that they are wrong.

This was a theory of trial and error—of *conjectures and refutations*. It made it possible to understand why our attempts to force interpretations upon the world were logically prior to the observation of similarities. Since there were logical reasons behind this procedure, I thought that it would apply in the field of science also; that scientific theories were not the digest of observations, but that they were inventions—conjectures boldly put forward for trial, to be eliminated if they clashed with observations; with observations which were rarely accidental but as a rule undertaken with the definite intention of testing a theory by obtaining, if possible, a decisive refutation.

V

The belief that science proceeds from observation to theory is still so widely and so firmly held that my denial of it is often met with incredulity. I have even been suspected of being insincere—of denying what nobody in his senses can doubt.

But in fact the belief that we can start with pure observations alone, without anything in the nature of a theory, is absurd; as may be illustrated by the story of the man who dedicated his life to natural science, wrote down everything he could observe, and bequeathed his priceless collection of observations to the Royal Society to be used as inductive evidence. This story should show us that though beetles may profitably be collected, observations may not.

Twenty-five years ago I tried to bring home the same point to a group of physics students in Vienna by beginning a lecture with the following instructions: "Take pencil and paper; carefully observe, and write down what you have observed!" They asked, of course, *what* I wanted them to observe. Clearly the instruction "Observe!" is absurd.[7] (It is not even idiomatic, unless the object of the transitive verb can be taken as understood.) Observation is always selective. It needs a chosen object, a definite task, an interest, a point of view, a problem. And its description presupposes a descriptive language, with property words; it presupposes similarity and classifications, which in its turn presupposes interests, points of view, and problems. "A hungry animal," writes Katz,[8] "divides the environment into edible and inedible things. An animal in flight sees roads to escape and hiding places. . . . Generally speaking, objects change . . . according to the needs of the animal." We may add that objects can be classified, and can become similar or dissimilar, *only* in this way—by being related to needs and interests. This rule applies not only to animals but also to scientists. For the animal a point of view is provided by its needs, the task of the moment, and its expectations; for the scientist by his theoretical interests, the special problem under investigation, his conjectures and anticipations, and the theories which he accepts as a kind of background: his frame of reference, his "horizon of expectations."

The problem "Which comes first, the hypothesis (*H*) or the observation (*O*)" is soluble, as is the problem "Which comes first, the hen (*H*) or the egg (*O*). The reply to the latter is "An earlier kind of egg"; to the former, "An earlier kind of hypothesis." It is quite true that any particular hypothesis we choose will have been preceded by observations—the observations, for example, which it is designed to explain. But these observations, in their turn, presupposed the adoption of a frame of reference, a frame of expectations, a frame of theories. If they were significant, if they created a need for explanation and thus gave rise to the invention of a hypothesis, it was because they could not be explained within the old theoretical framework, the old horizon of expectations. There is no danger here of an infinite regress. Going back to more and more primitive theories and myths we shall in the end find unconscious, *inborn* expectations. . . .

I may summarize some of my conclusions as follows:

1. Induction, i.e., inference based on many observations, is a myth. It is neither a psychological fact, nor a fact of ordinary life, nor one of scientific procedure.

2. The actual procedure of science is to operate with conjectures: to jump to conclusions—often after one single observation (as noticed, for example, by Hume and Born).

3. Repeated observations and experiments function in science as *tests* of our conjectures or hypothesis, i.e., as attempted refutations.

4. The mistaken belief in induction is fortified by the need for a criterion of demarcation which, it is traditionally but wrongly believed, only the inductive method can provide.

5. The conception of such an inductive method . . . implies a faulty demarcation.

6. None of this is altered in the least if we say that induction makes theories only probable rather than certain. . . .

IX

If, as I have suggested, the problem of induction is only an instance or facet of the problem of demarcation, then the solution to the problem of demarcation must provide us with a solution to the problem of induction. This is indeed the case, I believe, although it is perhaps not immediately obvious.

For a brief formulation of the problem of induction we can turn . . . to Born, who writes: ". . . no observation or experiment, however extended, can give more than a finite number of repetitions"; therefore, "the statement of a law—B depends on A—always transcends experience. Yet this kind of statement is made everywhere and all the time, and sometimes from scanty material."[9]

In other words, the logical problem of induction arises from (a) Hume's discovery (so well expressed by Born) that it is impossible to justify a law by observation or experiment, since it "transcends experience"; (b) the fact that science proposes and uses laws "everywhere and all the time." (Like Hume, Born is struck by the "scanty material," i.e., the few observed instances upon which the law may be based.) To this we have to add (c) *the principle of empiricism*, which asserts that in science only observation and experiment may decide upon the *acceptance or rejection* of scientific statements, including laws and theories.

These three principles, (a), (b), and (c), appear at first sight to clash; and this apparent clash constitutes the *logical problem of induction*.

Faced with this clash, Born gives up (c), the principle of empiricism (as Kant and many others, including Bertrand Russell, have done before him), in favor of what he calls a "metaphysical principle"; a metaphysical principle which he does not even attempt to formulate; which he vaguely describes as a "code or rule of craft"; and of which I have never seen any formulation which even looked promising and was not clearly untenable.

But in fact the principles (a) to (c) do not clash. We can see this the moment we realize that the acceptance by science of a law or of a theory is *tentative only*; which is to say that all laws and theories are conjectures, or tentative *hypotheses* (a position which I have sometimes called "hypotheticism"); and that we may reject a law or theory on the basis of new evidence, without necessarily discarding the old evidence which originally led us to accept it.[10]

The principle of empiricism (c) can be fully preserved, since the fate of a theory, its acceptance or rejection, is decided by observation and experiment—by the result of tests. So long as a theory stands up to the severest tests we can design, it is accepted; if it does not, it is rejected. But it is never inferred, in any sense, from the empirical evidence. There is neither a psychological nor a logical induction. *Only the falsity of the theory can be inferred from empirical evidence, and this inference is a purely deductive one.*

Hume showed that it is not possible to infer a theory from observation statements; but this does not affect the possibility of refuting a theory by observation statements. The full appreciation of this possibility makes the relation between theories and observations perfectly clear.

This solves the problem of the alleged clash between the principles (a), (b), and (c), and with it Hume's problem of induction.

X

Thus the problem of induction is solved. But nothing seems less wanted than a simple solution to an age-old philosophical problem. Wittgenstein and his school hold that genuine philosophical problems do not exist,[11] from which it clearly follows that they cannot be solved. Others among my contemporaries do believe that there are philosophical problems, and respect them, but they seem to respect them too much; they seem to believe that they are insoluble, if not taboo, and they are shocked and horrified by the claim that there is a simple, neat, and lucid, solution to any of them. If there is a solution it must be deep, they feel, or at least complicated.

However this may be, I am still waiting for a simple, neat, and lucid criticism of the solution which I published first in 1933 in my letter to the Editor of *Erkenntnis*, and later in *The Logic of Scientific Discovery*.

Of course, one can invent new problems of induction, different from the one I have formulated and solved. (Its formulation was half its solution.) But I have yet to see any reformulation of the problem whose solution cannot be easily obtained from my old solution. I am now going to discuss some of these reformulations.

One question which may be asked is this: How do we really jump from an observation statement to a theory?

Although this question appears to be psychological rather than philosophical, one can say something positive about it without invoking psychology. One can say first that the jump is not from an observation statement, but from a problem-situation, and that the theory must allow us *to explain* the observations which created the problem (that is, *to deduce* them from the theory strengthened by other accepted theories and by other observation statements, the so-called initial conditions). This leaves, of course, an immense number of possible theories, good and bad; and it thus appears that our question has not been answered.

But this makes it fairly clear that when we asked our question we had more in mind than "How do we jump from an observation statement to a theory?" The question we had in mind was, it now appears, "How do we jump from an observation statement to a *good* theory?" But to this the answer is: by jumping first to *any* theory and then testing it, to find whether it is good or not; i.e., by repeatedly applying the critical method, eliminating many bad theories, and inventing many new ones. Not everybody is able to do this; but there is no other way.

Other questions have sometimes been asked. The original problem of induction, it was said, is the problem of *justifying* induction, i.e., of justifying inductive inference. If you answer this problem by saying that what is called an "inductive inference" is always invalid and therefore clearly not justifiable, the following new problem must arise: How do you justify your method of trial and error? Reply: the method of trial and error is a *method of eliminating false theories* by observation statements; and the justification for this is the purely logical relationship of deducibility, which allows us to assert the falsity of universal statements if we accept the truth of singular ones.

Another question sometimes asked is this: Why is it reasonable to prefer non-falsified statements to falsified ones? To this question some involved answers have been produced, for example, pragmatic answers. But from a pragmatic point of view the question does not arise, since false theories often serve well enough: Most formulas used in engineering or navigation are known to be false, although they may be excellent approximations and easy to handle; and they are used with confidence by people who know them to be false.

The only correct answer is the straightforward one: because we search for truth (even though we can never be sure we have found it), and because the falsified theories are known or believed to be false, while the non-falsified theories may still be true. Besides, we do not prefer *every* non-falsified theory—only one which, in the light of criticism, appears to be better than its competitors, which solves our problems, which is well tested, and of which we think, or rather conjecture or hope (considering other provisionally accepted theories), that it will stand up to further tests.

It has also been said that the problem of induction is "Why is it *reasonable* to believe that the future will be like the past?" and that a satisfactory answer to this question should make it plain that such a belief is, in fact, reasonable. My reply is that it is reasonable to believe that the future will be very different from the past in many vitally important respects. Admittedly it is perfectly reasonable to *act* on the assumption that it will, in many respects, be like the past, and that well-tested laws will continue to hold (since we can have no better assumption to act upon); but it is also reasonable to believe that such a course of action will lead us at times into severe trouble, since some of the laws upon which we now heavily rely may easily prove unreliable. (Remember the midnight sun!) One might even say that to judge from past experience, and from our general scientific knowledge, the future will *not* be like the past, in perhaps most of the ways which those

have in mind who say that it will. Water will sometimes not quench thirst, and air will choke those who breathe it. An apparent way out is to say that the future will be like the past *in the sense that the laws of nature will not change*, but this is begging the question. We speak of a "law of nature" only if we think that we have before us a regularity which does not change; and if we find that it changes, then we shall not continue to call it a "law of nature." Of course our search for natural laws indicates that we hope to find them, and that we believe that there are natural laws, but our belief in any particular natural law cannot have a safer basis than our unsuccessful critical attempts to refute it.

I think that those who put the problem of induction in terms of the *reasonableness* of our beliefs are perfectly right if they are dissatisfied with a Humean, or post-Humean, skeptical despair of reason. We must indeed reject the view that a belief in science is as irrational as a belief in primitive magical practices—that both are a matter of accepting a "total ideology," a convention or a tradition based on faith. But we must be cautious if we formulate our problem, with Hume, as one of the reasonableness of our *beliefs*. We should split this problem into three—our old problem of demarcation, or of how to *distinguish* between science and primitive magic; the problem of the rationality of the scientific or critical *procedure*, and of the role of observation within it; and lastly the problem of the rationality of our *acceptance* of theories for scientific and for practical purposes. To all these three problems solutions have been offered here.

One should also be careful not to confuse the problem of the reasonableness of the scientific procedure and the (tentative) acceptance of the results of this procedure—i.e., the scientific theories—with the problem of the rationality or otherwise *of the belief that this procedure will succeed*. In practice, in practical scientific research, this belief is no doubt unavoidable and reasonable, there being no better alternative. But the belief is certainly unjustifiable in a theoretical sense, as I have argued . . . . More-over, if we could show, on general logical grounds, that the scientific quest is likely to succeed, one could not understand why anything like success has been so rare in the long history of human endeavors to know more about our world. . . .

Notes

1. This is a slight oversimplification, for about half of the Einstein effect may be derived from the classical theory, provided we assume a ballistic theory of light.
2. See, for example, my *Open Society and Its Enemies*, Ch. 15, Section iii, and notes 13–14.
3. "Clinical observations," like all other observations, are *interpretations in the light of theories* (see below, Sections iv ff.); and for this reason alone they are apt to seem to support those theories in the light of which they were interpreted. But real support can be obtained only from observations undertaken as tests (by "attempted refutations"); and for this purpose *criteria of refutation* have to be laid down beforehand: It must be agreed which observable situations, if actually observed, mean that the theory is refuted. But what kind of clinical responses would refute to the satisfaction of the analyst not merely a particular analytic diagnosis but psychoanalysis itself? And have such criteria ever been discussed or agreed upon by analysts? Is there not, on the contrary, a whole family of analytic concepts, such as "ambivalence" (I do not suggest that there is no such thing as ambivalence), which would make it difficult, if not impossible, to agree upon such criteria? Moreover, how much headway has been made in investigating the question of the extent to which the (conscious or unconscious) expectations and theories held by the analyst influence the "clinical responses" of the patient? (To say nothing about the conscious attempts to influence the patient by proposing interpretations to him, etc.) Years ago I introduced the term *Oedipus effect* to describe the influence of a theory or expectation or prediction *upon the event which it predicts* or describes: It will be remembered that the causal chain leading to Oedipus' parricide was started by the oracle's

prediction of this event. This is a characteristic and recurrent theme of such myths, but one which seems to have failed to attract the interest of the analysts, perhaps not accidentally. (The problem of confirmatory dreams suggested by the analyst is discussed by Freud, for example in *Gesammelte Schriften*, III, 1925, where he says on p. 314: "If anybody asserts that most of the dreams which can be utilized in an analysis . . . owe their origin to [the analyst's] suggestion, then no objection can be made from the point of view of analytic theory. Yet there is nothing in this fact," he surprisingly adds, "which would detract from the reliability of our results.")
4. The case of astrology, nowadays a typical pseudoscience, may illustrate this point. It was attacked, by Aristotelians and other rationalists, down to Newton's day, for the wrong reason—for its now accepted assertion that the planets had an "influence" upon terrestrial ("sublunar") events. In fact Newton's theory of gravity, and especially the lunar theory of the tides, was historically speaking an offspring of astrological lore. Newton, it seems, was most reluctant to adopt a theory which came from the same stable as for example, the theory that "influenza" epidemics are due to an astral "influence." And Galileo, no doubt for the same reason, actually rejected the lunar theory of the tides; and his misgivings about Kepler may easily be explained by his misgivings about astrology.
5. Hume does not say "logical" but "demonstrative," a terminology which, I think, is a little misleading. The following two quotations are from the *Treatise of Human Nature*, Book I, Part III, Sections vi and xii. (The italics are all Hume's.)
6. This and the next quotation are from *loc. cit.*, Section vi. See also Hume's *Enquiry Concerning Human Understanding*, Section IV, Part II, and his *Abstract*, edited by 1938 by J. M. Keynes and P. Sraffa, p. 15, and quoted in [my] *Logic of Scientific Discovery*, new appendix ★VII, text to note 6.
7. See Section 30 of *Logic of Scientific Discovery*.
8. D. Katz, *Animals and Men*, Ch. VI, footnote.
9. Max Born, *Natural Philosophy of Cause and Chance*, Oxford, 1949, p. 6.
10. I do not doubt that Born and many others would agree that theories are accepted only tentatively. But the widespread belief in induction shows that the far-reaching implications of this view are rarely seen.
11. Wittgenstein still held this belief in 1946. . . .

PIERRE DUHEM

Physical Theory
and Experiment

An Experiment in Physics Is Not Simply the Observation of a Phenomenon; It Is, Besides, the Theoretical Interpretation of This Phenomenon

. . . What exactly is an experiment in physics? This question will undoubtedly astonish more than one reader. Is there any need to raise it, and is not the answer self-evident? What more does "doing an experiment in physics" mean to anybody than producing a physical phenomenon under conditions such that it may be observed exactly and minutely by means of appropriate instruments?

Go into this laboratory; draw near this table crowded with so much apparatus: an electric battery, copper wire wrapped in silk, vessels filled with mercury, coils, a small iron bar carrying a mirror. An observer plunges the metallic stem of a rod, mounted with rubber, into small holes; the iron oscillates and, by means of the mirror tied to it, sends a beam of light over to a celluloid ruler, and the observer follows the movement of the light beam on it. There, no doubt, you have an experiment; by means of the vibration of this spot of light, this physicist minutely observes the oscillations of the piece of iron. Ask him now what he is doing. Is he going to answer, "I am studying the oscillations of the piece of iron carrying this mirror?" No, he will tell you that he is measuring the electrical resistance of a coil. If you are astonished and ask him what meaning these words have, and what relation they have to the phenomena he has perceived and that you have at the same time perceived, he will reply that your question would require some very long explanations, and he will recommend that you take a course in electricity.

It is indeed the case that the experiment you have seen done, like any experiment in physics, involves two parts. In the first place, it consists in the observation of certain facts; in order to make this observation it suffices for you to be attentive and alert enough with your senses. It is not necessary to know physics; the director

From Pierre Duhem, *The Aim and Structure of Physical Theory*, Trans. Philip P. Wiener. Copyright 1954; © 1982 renewed by Princeton University Press. Excerpts pp. 144–147, 183–190, 216–218. Reprinted by permission of Princeton University Press.

of the laboratory may be less skillful in this matter of observation than the assistant. In the second place, it consists in the interpretation of the observed facts; in order to make this interpretation it does not suffice to have an alert attention and practiced eye; it is necessary to know the accepted theories and to know how to apply them—in short, to be a physicist. Any man can, if he sees straight, follow the motions of a spot of light on a transparent ruler and see if it goes to the right or to the left or stops at such and such a point; for that he does not have to be a great cleric. But if he does not know electrodynamics, he will not be able to finish the experiment, he will not be able to measure the resistance of the coil.

Let us take another example. Regnault is studying the compressibility of gases; he takes a certain quantity of gas, encloses it in a glass tube, keeps the temperature constant, and measures the pressure the gas supports and the volume it occupies.

There you have, it will be said, the minute and exact observation of certain phenomena and certain facts. Certainly, in the hands and under the eyes of Regnault, in the hands and under the eyes of his assistants, concrete facts were produced; was the recording of these facts that Regnault reported his intended contribution to the advancement of physics? No. In a sighting device Regnault saw the image of a certain surface of mercury become level with a certain line; is that what he recorded in the report of his experiments? No, he recorded that the gas occupied a volume having such and such a value. An assistant raised and lowered the lens of a cathetometer until the image of another height of mercury became level with the hairline of the lens; he then observed the disposition of certain lines on the scale and on the vernier of the cathetometer; is that what we find in Regnault's memoir? No, we read there that the pressure supported by the gas had such and such a value. Another assistant saw the thermometer's liquid oscillate between two line-marks; is that what he reported? No, it was recorded that the temperature of the gas had varied between such and such degrees.

Now, what is the value of the volume occupied by the gas, what is the value of the pressure it supports, what is the degree of temperature to which it is brought? Are they three concrete objects? No, they are three abstract symbols which only physical theory connects to the facts really observed.

In order to form the first of these abstractions, the value of the volume of the enclosed gas, and to make it correspond with the observed fact, namely, the mercury becoming level with a certain line-mark, it was necessary to calibrate the tube, that is to say, to appeal not only to the abstract ideas of arithmetic and geometry and the abstract principles on which they rest, but also to the abstract idea of mass and to the hypotheses of general mechanics as well as of celestial mechanics which justify the use of the balance for the comparison of masses; it was necessary to know the specific weight of mercury at the temperature when the calibration was made, and for that its specific weight at 0° had to be known, which cannot be done without invoking the laws of hydrostatics; to know the law of the expansion of mercury, which is determined by means of an apparatus where a lens is used, certain laws of optics are assumed; so that the knowledge of a good many chapters of physics necessarily precedes the formation of that abstract idea, the volume occupied by a certain gas.

More complex by far and more intimately tied up with the most profound theories of physics is the genesis of that other abstract idea, the value of the pressure supported by the gas. In order to define and measure it, it has been necessary to use ideas of pressure and of force of cohesion that are so delicate and so difficult to acquire; it has been necessary to call for the help of Laplace's formula for the level of a barometer, a formula drawn from the laws of hydrostatics; it has been necessary to bring in the law of the compressibility of mercury whose determination is related to the most delicate and controversial questions of the theory of elasticity.

Thus, when Regnault did an experiment he had facts before his eyes and he observed phenomena, but what he transmitted to us of that experiment is not a recital of observed facts; what he gave us are abstract symbols which accepted theories permitted him to substitute for the concrete evidence he had gathered.

What Regnault did is what every experimental physicist necessarily does; that is why we can state the following principle . . . :

An experiment in physics is the precise observation of phenomena accompanied by an *interpretation* of these phenomena; this interpretation substitutes for the concrete data really gathered by observation abstract and symbolic representations which correspond to them by virtue of the theories admitted by the observer. . . .

An Experiment in Physics Can Never Condemn an Isolated Hypothesis but Only a Whole Theoretical Group

The physicist who carries out an experiment, or gives a report of one, implicitly recognizes the accuracy of a whole group of theories. Let us accept this principle and see what consequences we may deduce from it when we seek to estimate the role and logical import of a physical experiment.

In order to avoid any confusion we shall distinguish two sorts of experiments: experiments of *application*, which we shall first just mention, and experiments of *testing*, which will be our chief concern.

You are confronted with a problem in physics to be solved practically; in order to produce a certain effect you wish to make use of knowledge acquired by physicists; you wish to light an incandescent bulb; accepted theories indicate to you the means for solving the problem; but to make use of these means you have to secure certain information; you ought, I suppose, to determine the electromotive force of the battery of generators at your disposal; you measure this electromotive force: That is what I call an experiment of application. This experiment does not aim at discovering whether accepted theories are accurate or not; it merely intends to draw on these theories. In order to carry it out, you make use of instruments that these same theories legitimize; there is nothing to shock logic in this procedure.

But experiments of application are not the only ones the physicist has to perform; only with their aid can science aid practice, but it is not through them that science creates and develops itself; besides experiments of application, we have experiments of testing.

A physicist disputes a certain law; he calls into doubt a certain theoretical point. How will he justify these doubts? How will he demonstrate the inaccuracy of the law? From the proposition under indictment he will derive the prediction of an experimental fact; he will bring into existence the conditions under which this fact should be produced; if the predicted fact is not produced, the proposition which served as the basis of the prediction will be irremediably condemned.

F. E. Neumann assumed that in a ray of polarized light the vibration is parallel to the plane of polarization, and many physicists have doubted this proposition. How did O. Wiener undertake to transform this doubt into a certainty in order to condemn Neumann's proposition? He deduced from this proposition the following consequence: If we cause a light beam reflected at 45° from a plate of glass to interfere with the incident beam polarized perpendicularly to the plane of incidence, there ought to appear alternately dark and light interference bands parallel to the reflecting surface; he brought about the conditions under which these bands should have been produced and showed that the predicted phenomenon did not appear, from which he concluded that Neumann's proposition is false, viz., that in a polarized ray of light the vibration is not parallel to the plane of polarization.

Such a mode of demonstration seems as convincing and as irrefutable as the proof by reduction to absurdity customary among mathematicians; moreover, this demonstration is copied from the reduction to absurdity, experimental contradiction playing the same role in one as logical contradiction plays in the other.

Indeed, the demonstrative value of experimental method is far from being so rigorous or absolute: The conditions under which it functions are much more complicated than is supposed in what we have just said; the evaluation of results is much more delicate and subject to caution.

A physicist decides to demonstrate the inaccuracy of a proposition; in order to deduce from this proposition the prediction of a phenomenon and institute the experiment which is to show whether this phenomenon is or is not produced, in order to interpret the results of this experiment and establish that the predicted phenomenon is not produced, he does not confine himself to making use of the proposition in question; he makes use also of a whole group of theories accepted by him as beyond dispute. The prediction of the phenomenon, whose nonproduction is to cut off debate, does not derive from the proposition challenged if taken by itself, but from the proposition at issue joined to that whole group of theories; if the predicted phenomenon is not produced, not only is the proposition questioned at fault, but so is the whole theoretical scaffolding used by the physicist. The only thing the experiment teaches us is that among the propositions used to predict the phenomenon and to establish whether it would be produced, there is at least one error; but where this error lies is just what it does not tell us. The physicist may declare that this error is con-

tained in exactly the proposition he wishes to refute, but is he sure it is not in another proposition? If he is, he accepts implicitly the accuracy of all the other propositions he has used, and the validity of his conclusion is as great as the validity of his confidence.

Let us take as an example the experiment imagined by Zenker and carried out by O. Wiener. In order to predict the formation of bands in certain circumstances and to show that these did not appear, Wiener did not make use of merely the famous proposition of F. E. Neumann, the proposition which he wished to refute; he did not merely admit that in a polarized ray vibrations are parallel to the plane of polarization; but he used, besides this, propositions, laws, and hypotheses constituting the optics commonly accepted: He admitted that light consists in simple periodic vibrations, that these vibrations are normal to the light ray, that at each point the mean kinetic energy of the vibratory motion is a measure of the intensity of light, that the more or less complete attack of the gelatine coating on a photographic plate indicates the various degrees of this intensity. By joining these propositions, and many others that would take too long to enumerate, to Neumann's proposition, Wiener was able to formulate a forecast and establish that the experiment belied it. If he attributed this solely to Neumann's proposition, if it alone bears the responsibility for the error this negative result has put in evidence, then Wiener was taking all the other propositions he invoked as beyond doubt. But this assurance is not imposed as a matter of logical necessity; nothing stops us from taking Neumann's proposition as accurate and shifting the weight of the experimental contradiction to some other proposition of the commonly accepted optics; as H. Poincaré has shown, we can very easily rescue Neumann's hypothesis from the grip of Wiener's experiment on the condition that we abandon in exchange the hypothesis which takes the mean kinetic energy as the measure of the light intensity; we may, without being contradicted by the experiment, let the vibration be parallel to the plane of polarization, provided that we measure the light intensity by the mean potential energy of the medium deforming the vibratory motion.

These principles are so important that it will be useful to apply them to another example; again we choose an experiment regarded as one of the most decisive ones in optics.

We know that Neumann conceived the emission theory for optical phenomena. The emission theory supposes light to be formed of extremely thin projectiles, thrown out with very great speed by the sun and other sources of light; these projectiles penetrate all transparent bodies; on account of the various parts of the media through which they move, they undergo attractions and repulsions; when the distance separating the acting articles is very small these actions are very powerful, and they vanish when the masses between which they act are appreciably far from each other. These essential hypotheses joined to several others, which we pass over without mention, lead to the formulation of a complete theory of reflection and refraction of light; in particular, they imply the following proposition: The index of refraction of light passing from one medium into another is equal to the velocity of the light projectile within the medium it penetrates, divided by the velocity of the same projectile in the medium it leaves behind.

This is the proposition that Arago chose in order to show that the theory of emission is in contradiction with the facts. From this proposition a second follows: Light travels faster in water than in air. Now Arago had indicated an appropriate procedure for comparing the velocity of light in air with the velocity of light in water; the procedure, it is true, was inapplicable, but Foucault modified the experiment in such a way that it could be carried out; he found that the light was propagated less rapidly in water than in air. We may conclude from

this, with Foucault, that the system of emission is incompatible with the facts.

I say the *system* of emission and not the *hypothesis* of emission; in fact, what the experiment declares stained with error is the whole group of propositions accepted by Newton, and after him by Laplace and Biot, that is, the whole theory from which we deduce the relation between the index of refraction and the velocity of light in various media. But in condemning this system as a whole by declaring it stained with error, the experiment does not tell us where the error lies. Is it the fundamental hypothesis that light consists in projectiles thrown out with great speed by luminous bodies? Is it in some other assumption concerning the actions experienced by light corpuscles due to the media through which they move? We know nothing about that. It would be rash to believe, as Arago seems to have thought, that Foucault's experiment condemns once and for all the very hypothesis of emission, i.e., the assimilation of a ray of light to a swarm of projectiles. If physicists had attached some value to this task, they would undoubtedly have succeeded in founding on this assumption a system of optics that would agree with Foucault's experiment.

In sum, the physicist can never subject an isolated hypothesis to experimental test, but only a whole group of hypotheses; when the experiment is in disagreement with his predictions, what he learns is that at least one of the hypotheses constituting this group is unacceptable and ought to be modified; but the experiment does not designate which one should be changed.

We have gone a long way from the conception of the experimental method arbitrarily held by persons unfamiliar with its actual functioning. People generally think that each one of the hypotheses employed in physics can be taken in isolation, checked by experiment, and then, when many varied tests have established its validity, given a definitive place in the system of physics. In reality, this is not the case.

Physics is not a machine which lets itself be taken apart; we cannot try each piece in isolation and, in order to adjust it, wait until its solidity has been carefully checked. Physical science is a system that must be taken as a whole; it is an organism in which one part cannot be made to function except when the parts that are most remote from it are called into play, some more so than others, but all to some degree. If something goes wrong, if some discomfort is felt in the functioning of the organism, the physicist will have to ferret out through its effect on the entire system which organ needs to be remedied or modified without the possibility of isolating this organ and examining it apart. The watchmaker to whom you give a watch that has stopped separates all the wheelworks and examines them one by one until he finds the part that is defective or broken. The doctor to whom a patient appears cannot dissect him in order to establish his diagnosis; he has to guess the seat and cause of the ailment solely by inspecting disorders affecting the whole body. Now, the physicist concerned with remedying a limping theory resembles the doctor and not the watchmaker.

A "Crucial Experiment" Is Impossible in Physics

Let us press this point further, for we are touching on one of the essential features of experimental method, as it is employed in physics.

Reduction to absurdity seems to be merely a means of refutation, but it may become a method of demonstration: In order to demonstrate the truth of a proposition it suffices to corner anyone who would admit the contradictory of the given proposition into admitting an absurd consequence. We know to what extent the Greek geometers drew heavily on this mode of demonstration.

Those who assimilate experimental contradiction to reduction to absurdity imagine that in physics we may use a line of argument similar to the one Euclid employed so frequently in geometry. Do you wish to obtain from a group of phenomena a theoretically certain and indisputable explanation? Enumerate all the hypotheses that can be made to account for this group of phenomena; then, by experimental contradiction eliminate all except one; the latter will no longer be a hypothesis, but will become a certainty.

Suppose, for instance, we are confronted with only two hypotheses. Seek experimental conditions such that one of the hypotheses forecasts the production of one phenomena and the other the production of quite a different effect; bring these conditions into existence and observe what happens; depending on whether you observe the first or the second of the predicted phenomena, you will condemn the second or the first hypothesis; the hypothesis not condemned will be henceforth indisputable; debate will be cut off, and a new truth will be acquired by science. Such is the experimental test that the author of the *Novum Organum* called the *"fact of the cross,"* borrowing this expression from the crosses that at an intersection indicate the various roads.

We are confronted with two hypotheses concerning the nature of light; for Newton, Laplace, or Biot light consisted of projectiles hurled with extreme speed, but for Huygens, Young, or Fresnel light consisted of vibrations whose waves are propagated within an ether. These are the only two possible hypotheses as far as one can see: Either the motion is carried away by the body it excites and remains attached to it, or else it passes from one body to another. Let us pursue the first hypothesis; it declares that light travels more quickly in water than in air; but if we follow the second, it declares that light travels more quickly in air than in water. Let us set up Foucault's apparatus; we set into motion the turning mirror; we see two luminous spots formed before us, one colorless, the other greenish. If the greenish band is to the left of the colorless one, it means that light travels faster in water than in air, and that the hypothesis of vibrating waves is false. If, on the contrary, the greenish band is to the right of the colorless one, that means that light travels faster in air than in water, and that the hypothesis of emissions is condemned. We look through the magnifying glass used to examine the two luminous spots, and we notice that the greenish spot is to the right of the colorless one; the debate is over; light is not a body, but a vibratory wave motion propagated by the ether; the emission hypothesis has had its day; the wave hypothesis has been put beyond doubt, and the crucial experiment has made it a new article of the scientific credo.

What we have said in the foregoing paragraph shows how mistaken we should be to attribute to Foucault's experiment so simple a meaning and so decisive an importance; for it is not between two hypotheses, the emission and wave hypotheses, that Foucault's experiment judges trenchantly; it decides rather between two sets of theories, each of which has to be taken as a whole, i.e., between two entire systems, Newton's optics and Huygens' optics.

But let us admit for a moment that in each of these systems everything is compelled to be necessary by strict logic, except a single hypothesis; consequently, let us admit that the facts, in condemning one of the two systems, condemn once and for all the single doubtful assumption it contains. Does it follow that we can find in the "crucial experiment" an irrefutable procedure for transforming one of the two hypotheses before us into a demonstrated truth? Between two contradictory theorems of geometry there is no room for a third judgment; if one is false, the other is necessarily true. Do two hypotheses in physics ever constitute such a strict dilemma? Shall we ever dare to assert that no other hypothesis is imaginable? Light may be a swarm of projectiles, or it may be a vibratory motion whose waves are propagated in a medium; is it forbidden to be anything else at all? Arago undoubtedly thought so when he formulated this incisive alternative: Does light move more quickly in water than in

air? "Light is a body. If the contrary is the case, then light is a wave." But it would be difficult for us to take such a decisive stand; Maxwell, in fact, showed that we might just as well attribute light to a periodical electrical disturbance that is propagated within a dielectric medium.

Unlike the reduction to absurdity employed by geometers, experimental contradiction does not have the power to transform a physical hypothesis into an indisputable truth; in order to confer this power on it, it would be necessary to enumerate completely the various hypotheses which may cover a determinate group of phenomena; but the physicist is never sure he has exhausted all the imaginable assumptions. The truth of a physical theory is not decided by heads or tails. . . .

Good Sense Is the Judge of Hypotheses Which Ought to Be Abandoned

When certain consequences of a theory are struck by experimental contradiction, we learn that this theory should be modified but we are not told by the experiment what must be changed. It leaves to the physicist the task of finding out the weak spot that impairs the whole system. No absolute principle directs this inquiry, which different physicists may conduct in very different ways without having the right to accuse one another of illogicality. For instance, one may be obliged to safeguard certain fundamental hypotheses while he tries to reestablish harmony between the consequences of the theory and the facts by complicating the schematism in which these hypotheses are applied, by invoking various causes of error, and by multiplying corrections. The next physicist, disdainful of these complicated artificial procedures, may decide to change some one of the essential assumptions supporting the entire system. The first physicist does not have the right to condemn in advance the boldness of the second one, nor does the latter have the right to treat the timidity of the first physicist as absurd. The methods they follow are justifiable only by experiment, and if they both succeed in satisfying the requirements of experiment each is logically permitted to declare himself content with the work that he has accomplished.

That does not mean that we cannot very properly prefer the work of one of the two to that of the other. Pure logic is not the only rule for our judgments; certain opinions which do not fall under the hammer of the principle of contradiction are in any case perfectly unreasonable. These motives which do not proceed from logic and yet direct our choices, these "reasons which reason does not know" and which speak to the ample "mind of finesse" but not to the "geometric mind," constitute what is appropriately called good sense.

Now, it may be good sense that permits us to decide between two physicists. It may be that we do not approve of the haste with which the second one upsets the principles of a vast and harmoniously constructed theory whereas a modification of detail, a slight correction, would have sufficed to put these theories in accord with the facts. On the other hand, it may be that we may find it childish and unreasonable for the first physicist to maintain obstinately at any cost, at the price of continual repairs and many tangled-up stays, the worm-eaten columns of a building tottering in every part, when by razing these columns it would be possible to construct a simple, elegant, and solid system.

But these reasons of good sense do not impose themselves with the same implacable rigor that the prescriptions of logic do. There is something vague and uncertain about them; they do not reveal themselves at the same time with the same degree of clarity to all minds. Hence, the possibility of lengthy quarrels between the adherents of an old system and the partisans of a new doctrine, each camp claiming to have good sense on its side, each party finding the reasons of the adversary inadequate. The history of physics would furnish us with innumerable illustrations of these quarrels at all times and in all domains. Let us confine ourselves to the tenacity and ingenuity with which Biot by a continual bestowal of corrections and accessory hypotheses maintained the emissionist doctrine in optics, while Fresnel opposed this doctrine constantly with new experiments favoring the wave theory.

In any event this state of indecision does not last forever. The day arrives when good sense comes out so clearly in favor of one of the two sides that the other side gives up the struggle even though pure logic would not forbid its continuation. After Foucault's experiment had shown that light traveled faster in air than in water, Biot gave up supporting the emission hypothesis; strictly, pure logic would not have compelled him to give it up, for Foucault's experiment was *not* the crucial experiment that Arago thought he saw in it, but by resisting wave optics for a longer time Biot would have been lacking in good sense.

Since logic does not determine with strict precision the time when an inadequate hypothesis should give way to a more fruitful assumption, and since recognizing this moment belongs to good sense, physicists may hasten this judgment and increase the rapidity of scientific progress by trying consciously to make good sense within themselves more lucid and more vigilant. Now nothing contributes more to entangle good sense and to disturb its insight than passions and interests. Therefore, nothing will delay the decision which should determine a fortunate reform in a physical theory more than the vanity which makes a physicist too indulgent toward his own system and too severe toward the system of another. We are thus led to the conclusion so clearly expressed by Claude Bernard: The sound experimental criticism of a hypothesis is subordinated to certain moral conditions; in order to estimate correctly the agreement of a physical theory with the facts, it is not enough to be a good mathematician and skillful experimenter; one must also be an impartial and faithful judge.

IMRE LAKATOS

Falsification and the Methodology of Scientific Research Programmes

Methodological Falsificationism. The "Empirical Basis."

. . . There is an important demarcation between *"passivist"* and *"activist" theories of knowledge*. "Passivists" hold that true knowledge is Nature's imprint on a perfectly inert mind: Mental *activity* can only result in bias and distortion. The most influential passivist school is classical empiricism. "Activists" hold that we cannot read the book of Nature without mental activity, without interpreting it in the light of our expectations or theories.[1] Now *conservative "activists"* hold that we are born with our basic expectations; with them we turn the world into "our world" but must then live forever in the prison of our world. The idea that we live and die in the prison of our "conceptual frameworks" was developed primarily by Kant; pessimistic Kantians thought that the real world is forever unknowable because of this prison, while optimistic Kantians thought that God created our conceptual framework to fit the world. . . . But *revolutionary activists* believe that conceptual frameworks can be developed and also replaced by new, *better* ones; it is we who create our "prisons" and we can also, critically, demolish them. . . .

New steps from conservative to revolutionary activism were made by Whewell and then by Poincaré, Milhaud and Le Roy. . . . Poincaré, Milhaud and Le Roy . . . preferred to explain the continuing historical success of Newtonian mechanics by a *methodological decision* taken by scientists: After a considerable period of initial success scientists may *decide* not to allow the theory to be refuted. Once they have taken this decision, they solve (or dissolve) the apparent anomalies by auxiliary hypotheses or other "conventionalist stratagems."[2] This *conservative conventionalism* has, however, the disadvantage of making us unable to get out of our self-imposed prisons, once the first period of trial-and-error is over and the great decision taken. It cannot solve the problem of the elimination of those theories which have been triumphant for a long

From Sections 2 and 3 of "Falsification and the Methodology of Scientific Research Programmes" by Imre Lakatos, in *Criticism and the Growth of Knowledge*, Imre Lakatos and Alan Musgrave, Eds., pp. 104–108, 112, 114–125, 127–137, 154–155, 174–175, 189–195. Copyright © 1970 by Cambridge University Press. Reprinted by permission.

period. According to conservative convention-alism, experiments may have sufficient power to refute young theories, but not to refute old, es-tablished theories: *As science grows, the power of empirical evidence diminishes.*[3]

Poincaré's critics refused to accept his idea that, although the scientists build their concep-tual frameworks, there comes a time when these frameworks turn into prisons which can-not be demolished. This criticism gave rise to two rival schools of *revolutionary conventionalism*: Duhem's simplicism and Popper's methodolog-ical falsificationism.[4]

Duhem accepts the conventionalists' posi-tion that no physical theory ever crumbles merely under the weight of "refutations," but claims that it still may crumble under the weight of "continual repairs, and many tan-gled-up stays" when "the worm-eaten columns" cannot support "the tottering build-ing" any longer[5]; then the theory loses its orig-inal simplicity and has to be replaced. But falsification is then left to subjective taste or, at best, to scientific fashion, and leaves too much leeway for dogmatic adherence to a favorite theory. . . .

Popper set out to find a criterion which is both more objective and more hard-hitting. He could not accept the emasculation of empiri-cism, inherent even in Duhem's approach, and proposed a methodology which allows experi-ments to be powerful even in "mature" sci-ence. Popper's methodological falsificationism is both conventionalist and falsificationist, but he "differs from the [conservative] convention-alists in holding that the statements decided by agreement are *not* [spatio-temporally] universal but [spatio-temporally] singular."[6] . . .

The *conservative conventionalist* (or method-ological justificationist, if you wish) makes un-falsifiable by *fiat* some (spatio-temporally) universal theories, which are distinguished by their explanatory power, simplicity, or beauty. Our *revolutionary conventionalist* (or "method-ological falsificationist") makes unfalsifiable by

fiat some (spatio-temporally) singular state-ments which are distinguishable by the fact that there exists at the time a "relevant technique" such that "anyone who has learned it" will be able to *decide* that the statement is "acceptable."[7] Such a statement may be called an "observa-tional" or "basic" statement, but only in in-verted commas.[8] Indeed, the very selection of all such statements is a matter of a decision, which is not based on exclusively psychologi-cal considerations. This decision is then fol-lowed by a second kind of decision concerning the separation of the set of *accepted* basic state-ments from the rest.

. . . [T]he methodological falsificationist is not a justificationist, he has no illusions about "experimental proofs" and is fully aware of the fallibility of his decisions and the risks he is tak-ing.

The methodological falsificationist realizes that in the "experimental techniques" of the scientist fallible theories are involved,[9] "in the light of which" he interprets the facts. In spite of this he "applies" these theories, he regards them in the given context not as theories under test but as *unproblematic background knowl-edge*, "which we accept (tentatively) as unprob-lematic while we are testing the theory."[10] He may call these theories—and the statements whose truth-value he decides in their light— "observational," but this is only a manner of speech . . .[11] The methodological falsification-ist *uses our most successful theories as extensions of our senses*. . . . For instance, let us imagine that a big radio-star is discovered with a system of radio-star satellites orbiting it. We should like to test some gravitational theory on this plane-tary system—a matter of considerable interest. Now let us imagine that Jodrell Bank succeeds in providing a set of space-time co-ordinates of the planets which is inconsistent with the the-ory. We shall take these statements as potential falsifiers. Of course, these basic statements are not "observational" in the usual sense but only "'observational.'" They describe planets that neither the human eye nor optical instruments can reach. Their truth-value is arrived at by an "experimental technique." This "experimental technique" is based on the "application" of a well-corroborated theory of radio-optics. Calling these statements "observational" is no more than a manner of saying that, in the context of his problem, that is, in testing our gravitational theory, the methodological falsificationist uses radio-optics uncritically, as "background knowledge." *The need for decisions to demarcate the theory under test from unproblematic background knowledge is a characteristic feature of this brand of methodological falsificationism.* . . .

This consideration shows the conventional element in granting—in a given context—the (methodologically) "observational" status to theory. Similarly, there is a considerable conventional element in the decision concerning the actual truth-value of a basic statement which we take after we have decided which "observational theory" to apply. One single observation may be the stray result of some trivial error: In order to reduce such risks, methodological falsificationists prescribe some safety control. The simplest such control is to repeat the experiment (it is a matter of convention how many times). . . .

This is how the methodological falsificationist establishes his "empirical basis." (He uses quotation marks in order "to give ironical emphasis" to the term.[12]) This "basis" can be hardly called a "basis" by justificationist standards: There is nothing proven about it—it denotes "piles driven into a swamp."[13] Indeed, if this "empirical basis" clashes with a theory, the theory may be *called* "falsified," but it is not falsified in the sense that it is disproved. . . . If a theory is falsified, it is proven false; if it is "falsified," it may still be true. If we follow up this sort of "falsification" by the actual "elimination" of a theory, we may well end up by eliminating a true, and accepting a false, theory (a possibility which is thoroughly abhorrent to the old-fashioned justificationist). . . .

Methodological falsificationism represents a considerable advance beyond . . . conservative conventionalism. It recommends risky decisions. But the risks are daring to the point of recklessness and one wonders whether there is no way of lessening them.

Let us first have a closer look at the risks involved.

Decisions play a crucial role in this methodology—as in any brand of conventionalism. Decisions, however, may lead us disastrously astray. The methodological falsificationist is the first to admit this. But this, he argues, is the price which we have to pay for the possibility of progress. . . .

But is not the firm strategy of the brand of methodological falsificationism hitherto discussed *too firm?* Are not the decisions it advocates bound to be *too arbitrary?* . . .

If we look at the history of science, if we try to see how some of the most celebrated falsifications happened, we have to come to the conclusion that either some of them are plainly irrational or that they rest on rationality principles radically different from the ones we just discussed. . . .

Indeed, it is not difficult to see at least two crucial characteristics . . . [of] our methodological falsificationism which are clearly dissonant with the actual history of science: that (1) *a test is—or must be made—a two-cornered fight between theory and experiment so that in the final confrontation only these two face each other; and (2) the only interesting outcome of such confrontation is (conclusive) falsification: "[the only genuine] discoveries are refutations of scientific hypotheses."*[14] However, history of science suggests that (1') tests are—at least—three-cornered fights between rival theories and experiment and (2') some of the most interesting experiments result, *prima facie*, in confirmation rather than falsification.

But if—as seems to be the case—the history of science does not bear out our theory of scientific rationality, we have two alternatives. One alternative is to abandon efforts to give a rational explanation of the success of science. Scientific method (or "logic of discovery"), conceived as the discipline of rational appraisal of scientific theories—and of criteria of *progress*—vanishes. We, may, of course, still try to explain *changes* in "paradigms" in terms of social psychology. . . . This is Polanyi's and Kuhn's way.[15] The other alternative is to try at least to *reduce* the conventional element in falsificationism (we cannot possibly eliminate it) and replace the *naive* versions of methodological falsificationism—characterized by the theses (1) and (2) above—by a *sophisticated* version which would give a new *rationale* of falsification and thereby rescue methodology and the idea of scientific *progress*. This is Popper's way, and the one I intend to follow.

Sophisticated versus Naive Methodological Falsificationism. Progressive and Degenerating Problemshifts.

Sophisticated falsificationism differs from naive falsificationism both in its rules of *acceptance* (or "demarcation criterion") and its rules of *falsification* or elimination. For the naive falsificationist any theory which can be interpreted as experimentally falsifiable is "acceptable" or "scientific." For the sophisticated falsificationist a theory is "acceptable" or "scientific" only if it has corroborated excess empirical content over its predecessor (or rival), that is, only if it leads to the discovery of novel facts. This condition can be analysed into two clauses: that the new theory has excess empirical content ("*acceptability*"$_1$) and that some of this excess content is verified ("*acceptability*"$_2$). This first clause can be checked instantly . . . by *a priori* logical analysis; the second can be checked only empirically and this may take an indefinite time.

Again, for the naive falsificationist a theory is *falsified* by a ("fortified" . . .) "observational" statement which conflicts with it (or rather, which he decides to interpret as conflicting with it). The sophisticated falsificationist re-

gards a scientific theory T as falsified if and only if another theory T' has been proposed with the following characteristics: (1) T' has excess empirical content over T; that is, it predicts *novel* facts, that is, facts improbable in the light of, or even forbidden, by T;[16] (2) T' explains the previous success of T, that is, all the unrefuted content of T is contained (within the limits of observational error) in the content of T'; and (3) some of the excess content of T' is corroborated.[17]

In order to be able to appraise these definitions we need to understand their problem background and their consequences. First, we have to remember the conventionalists' methodological discovery that no experimental result can ever kill a theory: any theory can be saved from counterinstances either by some auxiliary hypothesis or by a suitable reinterpretation of its terms. Naive falsificationists solved this problem by relegating—in crucial contexts—the auxiliary hypotheses to the realm of unproblematic background knowledge, eliminating them from the deductive model of the test-situation and thereby *forcing* the chosen theory into logical isolation, in which it becomes a sitting target for the attack of test-experiments. But since this procedure did not offer a suitable guide for a rational reconstruction of the history of science, we may just as well completely rethink our approach. Why aim at falsification at any price? Why not rather impose certain standards on the theoretical adjustments by which one is allowed to save a theory? Indeed, some such standards have been well known for centuries, and we find them expressed in age-old wisecracks against *ad hoc* explanations, empty prevarications, face-saving, linguistic tricks.[18] We have already seen that Duhem adumbrated such standards in terms of "simplicity" and "good sense."[19] But *when* does lack of "simplicity" in the protective belt of theoretical adjustments reach the point at which the theory *must* be abandoned?[20] In what sense was Copernican theory, for instance, "simpler" than Ptolemaic?[21] The vague notion of Duhemian "simplicity" leaves, as the naive falsificationist correctly argued, the decision very much to taste and fashion.[22]

Can one improve on Duhem's approach? Popper did. His solution—a sophisticated version of methodological falsificationism—is more objective and more rigorous. Popper agrees with the conventionalists that theories and factual propositions can always be harmonized with the help of auxiliary hypotheses: He agrees that the problem is how to demarcate between scientific and pseudoscientific *adjustments*, between rational and irrational changes of theory. According to Popper, saving a theory with the help of auxiliary hypotheses which satisfy certain well-defined conditions represents scientific progress; but saving a theory with the help of auxiliary hypotheses which do not, represents degeneration. Popper calls such inadmissible auxiliary hypotheses *ad hoc* hypotheses, mere linguistic devices, "conventionalist stratagems."[23] But then any scientific theory has to be appraised together with its auxiliary hypotheses, initial conditions, etc., and, especially, together with its predecessors so that we may see by what sort of *change* it was brought about. Then, of course, what we appraise is a *series of theories* rather than isolated *theories*.

Now we can easily understand why we formulated the criteria of acceptance and rejection of sophisticated methodological falsificationism as we did.[24] But it may be worth while to reformulate them slightly, couching them explicitly in terms of *series of theories*.

Let us take a series of theories, T_1, T_2, T_3, . . . where each subsequent theory results from adding auxiliary clauses to (or from semantical reinterpretations of) the previous theory in order to accommodate some anomaly, each theory having at least as much content as the unrefuted content of its predecessor. Let us say that such a series of theories is *theoretically progressive* (or "constitutes a theoretically progressive problemshift") if each new theory has some ex-

cess empirical content over its predecessor; that is, if it predicts some novel, hitherto unexpected fact. Let us say that a theoretically progressive series of theories is also *empirically progressive* (or "constitutes an empirically progressive problemshift") if some of this excess empirical content is also corroborated, that is, if each new theory leads us to the actual discovery of some *new fact*.[25] Finally, let us call a problemshift *progressive* if it is both theoretically and empirically progressive, and *degenerating* if it is not.[26] We "*accept*" problemshifts as "scientific" only if they are at least theoretically progressive; if they are not, we "*reject*" them as "pseudoscientific." Progress is measured by the degree to which a problemshift is progressive, by the degree to which the series of theories leads us to the discovery of novel facts. We regard a theory in the series as "falsified" when it is superseded by a theory with higher corroborated content. . . .

This demarcation between progressive and degenerating problemshifts sheds new light on the appraisal of *scientific—or rather, progressive—explanations*. If we put forward a theory to resolve a contradiction between a previous theory and a counterexample in such a way that the new theory, instead of offering a content-increasing (scientific) *explanation*, only offers a content-decreasing (linguistic) *reinterpretation*, the contradiction is resolved in a merely semantical, unscientific way. *A given fact is explained scientifically only if a new fact is also explained with it.* . . .

Sophisticated falsificationism thus shifts the problem of how to appraise *theories* to the problem of how to appraise *series of theories*. Not an isolated *theory*, but only a series of theories can be said to be scientific or unscientific: to apply the term "scientific" to one *single* theory is a category mistake.[27]

The time-honoured empirical criterion for a satisfactory theory was agreement with the observed facts. Our empirical criterion for a series of theories is that it should produce new facts. *The idea of growth and the concept of empirical character are soldered into one.*

This revised form of methodological falsificationism has many new features. First, it denies that "in the case of a scientific theory, our decision depends upon the results of experiments. If these confirm the theory, we may accept it until we find a better one. If they contradict the theory, we reject it."[28] It denies that "what ultimately decides the fate of a theory is the result of a test, i.e., an agreement about basic statements."[29] Contrary to naive falsificationism, *no experiment, experimental report, observation statement or well-corroborated low-level falsifying hypothesis alone can lead to falsification. . . . There is no falsification before the emergence of a better theory.*[30] But then the distinctively negative character of naive falsificationism vanishes; criticism becomes more difficult, and also positive, constructive. But, of course, if falsification depends on the emergence of better theories, on the invention of theories which anticipate new facts, then falsification is *not* simply a relation between a theory and the empirical basis, but a multiple relation between competing theories, the original "empirical basis," and the empirical growth resulting from the competition. Falsification can thus be said to have a "*historical character.*"[31] Moreover, some of the theories which bring about falsification are frequently proposed *after* the "counterevidence." This may sound paradoxical for people indoctrinated with naive falsificationism. Indeed, this epistemological theory of the relation between theory and experiment differs sharply from the epistemological theory of naive falsificationism. The very term "counterevidence" has to be abandoned in the sense that no experimental result must be interpreted directly as "counterevidence." If we still want to retain this time-honoured term, we have to redefine it like this: "Counterevidence to T_1" is a corroborating instance to T_2, which is either inconsistent with or independent of T_1 (with the *proviso* that T_2 is a theory which satisfactorily explains the empirical success of T_1). This shows that "*crucial counterevidence*"—or "*crucial experiments*"—can be

recognized as such among the scores of anomalies only *with hindsight*, in the light of some superseding theory.[32]

Thus the crucial element in falsification is whether the *new theory* offers any novel, excess information compared with its predecessor and whether some of this excess information is corroborated. Justificationists valued "confirming" instances of a theory; naive falsificationists stressed "refuting" instances; for the [sophisticated] methodological falsificationists it is the—rather rare—corroborating instances of the *excess* information which are the crucial ones; these receive all the attention. We are no longer interested in the thousands of trivial verifying instances nor in the hundreds of readily available anomalies: The few crucial *excess-verifying instances* are decisive. This consideration rehabilitates—and reinterprets—the old proverb: *Exemplum docet, exempla obscurant.*

"Falsification" in the sense of naive falsificationism (corroborated counterevidence) is not a *sufficient* condition for eliminating a specific theory: In spite of hundreds of known anomalies we do not regard it as falsified (that is, eliminated) until we have a better one. Nor is "falsification" in the naive sense *necessary* for falsification in the sophisticated sense: A progressive problemshift does not have to be interspersed with "refutations." Science can grow without any "refutations" leading the way. Naive falsificationists suggest a linear growth of science, in the sense that theories are followed by powerful refutations which eliminate them; these refutations in turn are followed by new theories.[33] It is perfectly *possible* that theories be put forward "progressively" in such a rapid succession that the "refutation" of the nth appears only as the corroboration of the $n + I$th. The problem fever of science is raised by proliferation of rival theories rather than counterexamples or anomalies.

This shows that the slogan of *proliferation of theories* is much more important for sophisticated than for naive falsificationism. For the naive falsificationist science grows through repeated experimental overthrow of theories; new rival theories proposed before such "overthrows" may speed up growth but are not absolutely necessary . . . ; constant proliferation of theories is optional but not mandatory. For the sophisticated falsificationist proliferation of theories cannot wait until the accepted theories are "refuted" . . .[34] While naive falsificationism stresses "the urgency of replacing a *falsified* hypothesis by a better one,"[35] sophisticated falsificationism stresses the urgency of replacing *any* hypothesis by a better one. Falsification cannot "compel the theorist to search for a better theory,"[36] simply because falsification cannot precede the better theory. . . .

I should like to emphasize here a further distinctive feature of sophisticated methodological empiricism: the crucial role of excess corroboration. For the inductivist, learning about a new theory is learning how much confirming evidence supports it; about refuted theories one *learns* nothing (learning, after all, is to build up proven or probable *knowledge*). . . . For the sophisticated falsificationist, learning about a theory is primarily learning which new facts it anticipated; indeed, for the sort of Popperian empiricism I advocate, the only relevant evidence is the evidence anticipated by a theory, and *empiricalness (or scientific character) and theoretical progress are inseparably connected.* . . .

This idea is not entirely new. Leibnitz, for instance, in his famous letter to Conring in 1678, wrote: "It is the greatest commendation of an hypothesis (next to [proven] truth) if by its help predictions can be made even about phenomena or experiments not tried."[37] Leibnitz's view was widely accepted by scientists. But since all appraisal of a scientific theory was before Popper appraisal of its degree of justification, this position was regarded by some logicians as untenable. Mill, for instance, complains in 1843 in horror that "it seems to be thought that an hypothesis . . . is entitled to a more favourable reception, if besides accounting for all the facts previously known, it has led to the anticipation and prediction of others which experience afterwards verified."[38] Mill had a point; this appraisal was in conflict . . . with justificationism . . . : Why should an event *prove* more, if it was anticipated by theory than if it was known already before? As long as *proof* was the only criterion of the scientific character of a theory, Leibnitz's criterion could only be regarded as irrelevant.[39] Also, the *probability* of a theory given evidence cannot possibly be influenced, as Keynes pointed out, by *when* the evidence was produced; the probability of a theory given evidence can depend only on the theory and the evidence,[40] and not upon whether the evidence was produced before or after the theory.

In spite of this convincing justificationist criticism, the criterion survived among some of the best scientists, since it formulated their strong dislike of merely *ad hoc* explanations, which "though [they] truly express the facts [they set out to explain, are] not born out by any other phenomena."[41]

But it was only Popper who recognized that the *prima facie* inconsistency between the few odd, casual remarks against *ad hoc* hypotheses on the one hand and the huge edifice of justificationist philosophy of knowledge must be solved by demolishing justificationism and by introducing new, non-justificationist criteria for appraising scientific theories based on anti-adhocness.

Let us look at a few examples. Einstein's theory is not better than Newton's *because* Newton's theory was "refuted" but Einstein's was not: There are many known "anomalies" to Einsteinian theory. Einstein's theory is better than—that is, represents progress compared with—Newton's theory *anno 1916* (that is, Newton's laws of dynamics, law of gravitation, the known set of initial conditions, "minus" the list of known anomalies such as Mercury's perihelion) *because* it explained everything that Newton's theory had successfully explained, and it explained also to *some extent* some known anomalies and, in addition, forbade events like transmission of light along straight lines near large masses about which Newton's theory had said nothing but which had been permitted by other well-corroborated scientific theories of the day; moreover, *at least some* of the unexpected excess Einsteinian content was in fact *corroborated* (for instance, by the eclipse experiments). . . .

Let us finally consider how much conventionalism remains in sophisticated falsificationism. Certainly *less* than in naive falsificationism. We need *fewer* methodological decisions. . . . To show this we only have to realize that if a scientific theory, consisting of some "laws of nature," initial conditions, auxiliary theories . . . conflicts with some factual propositions we do not have to decide which —explicit or "hidden"—part to replace. We may try to replace *any* part and only when we have hit on an explanation of the anomaly with the help of some content-increasing change (or auxiliary hypothesis), and nature corroborates it, do we move on to eliminate the "refuted" complex. Thus sophisticated falsification is a slower but possibly safer process than naive falsification.

Let us take an example. Let us assume that the course of a planet differs from the one predicted. Some conclude that this refutes the dynamics and gravitational theory applied: The initial conditions and the *ceteris paribus* clause have been ingeniously corroborated. Others conclude that this refutes the initial conditions used n the calculations: Dynamics and gravitational theory have been superbly corroborated in the last two hundred years and all suggestions concerning further factors in play failed. Yet others conclude that this refutes the underlying [ceteris paribus] assumption that there were no other factors in play except for those which were taken into account: These people may possibly be motivated by the metaphysical principle that any explanation is only approximative because of the infinite complexity of the factors involved in determining any single event. Should we praise the first type as "*critical*," scold the second type as "*hack*," and con-

demn the third as "*apologetic*"? No. We do not need to draw any conclusions about such "refutation." We never reject a specific theory simply by *fiat*. If we have an inconsistency like the one mentioned, we do not have to decide which ingredients of the theory we regard as problematic and which ones as unproblematic: We regard all ingredients as problematic in the light of the conflicting accepted basic statement and try to replace all of them. If we succeed in replacing some ingredient in a "progressive" way (that is, the replacement has more corroborated empirical content than the original), we call it "falsified." . . .

We cannot avoid the decision which sort of propositions should be the "observational" ones and which the "theoretical" ones. We cannot avoid either the decision about the truth-value of some "observational propositions." These decisions are vital for the decision whether a problemshift is empirically progressive or degenerating. But the sophisticated falsificationist may at least mitigate the arbitrariness of this second decision by allowing for an *appeal procedure*.

Naive falsificationists do not lay down any such appeal procedure. They accept a basic statement if it is backed up by a well-corroborated falsifying hypothesis,[42] and let it overrule the theory under test—even though they are well aware of the risk.[43] But there is no reason why we should not regard a falsifying hypothesis—and the basic statement it supports—as being just as problematic as a falsified hypothesis. Now how exactly can we expose the problematicality of a basic statement? On what grounds can the protagonists of the "falsified" theory appeal and win?

Some people may say that we might go on testing the basic statement (or the falsifying hypothesis) "by their deductive consequences" until agreement is finally reached. In this testing we deduce—in the same deductive model—further consequences from the basic statement either with the help of the theory under test or some other theory which we regard as unproblematic. Although this procedure "has no natural end," we always come to a point when there is no further disagreement.[44]

But when the theoretician appeals against the verdict of the experimentalist, the appeal court does not normally cross-question the basic statement directly but rather questions the *interpretative theory* in the light of which its truth-value had been established.

One typical example of a series of successful appeals is the Proutians' fight against unfavourable experimental evidence from 1815 to 1911. For decades Prout's theory T ("that all atoms are compounds of hydrogen atoms and thus 'atomic weights' of all chemical elements must be expressible as whole numbers") and falsifying "observational" hypotheses, like Stas's "refutation" R ("the atomic weight of chlorine is 35.5") confronted each other. As we know, in the end T prevailed over R.

The first stage of any serious criticism of a scientific theory is to reconstruct, improve, its logical deductive articulation. Let us do this in the case of Prout's theory *vis à vis* Stas's refutation. First of all, we have to realize that in the formulation we just quoted, T and R were *not* inconsistent. (Physicists rarely articulate their theories sufficiently to be pinned down and caught by the critic.) In order to show them up as inconsistent we have to put them in the following form. T: "the atomic weight of all pure (homogeneous) chemical elements are multiples of the atomic weight of hydrogen," and R: "chlorine is a pure (homogeneous) chemical element and its atomic weight is 35.5." The last statement is in the form of a falsifying hypothesis which, if well corroborated, would allow us to use basic statements of the form B: "Chlorine X is a pure (homogeneous) chemical element and its atomic weight is 35.5"— where X is the proper name of a "piece" of chlorine determined, say, by its space-time coordinates.

But how well-corroborated is R? The first component of it says that R_1: "Chlorine X is a

pure chemical element." This was the verdict of the experimental chemist after a rigorous application of the "experimental techniques" of the day.

Let us have a closer look at the fine-structure of R_1. In fact R_1 stands for a conjunction of two longer statements, T_1 and T_2. The first statement, T_1, could be this: "If seventeen chemical purifying procedures $P_1, P_2 \ldots P_{17}$ are applied to a gas, what remains will be pure chlorine." T_2 is then: "X was subjected to the seventeen procedures $P_1, P_2 \ldots P_{17}$." The careful "experimenter" carefully applied all seventeen procedures: T_2 is to be accepted. But the conclusion that therefore what remained *must* be pure chlorine is a "hard fact" only in virtue of T_1. The experimentalist, while *testing T,* applied T_1. He *interpreted* what he saw in the light of T_1: The result was R_1. Yet in the mono-theoretical model of the explanatory theory under test this interpretative theory does not appear at all.

But what if T_1, the interpretative theory, is false? Why not "apply" T rather than T_1 and claim that atomic weights *must be* whole numbers? Then *this* will be a "hard fact" in the light of T, and T_1 will be overthrown. Perhaps additional new purifying procedures must be invented and applied.

The problem is then *not* when we should stick to a "*theory*" in the face of "*known facts*" and when the other way round. The problem is *not* what to do when "theories" clash with "facts." Such a "clash" is only suggested by the "*monotheoretical deductive model.*" Whether a proposition is a "*fact*" or a "*theory*" in the context of a test-situation depends on our methodological decision. "Empirical basis of a theory" is a monotheoretical notion, it is *relative* to some monotheoretical deductive structure. We may use it as first approximation; but in case of "appeal" by the theoretician, we must use a *pluralistic model.* In the pluralistic model the clash is not "between theories and facts" but between two high-level theories: between an *interpretative theory* to provide the facts and an *explanatory theory* to explain them; and the interpretative theory may be on quite as high a level as the explanatory theory. The clash is then not any more between a logically higher-level theory and a lower-level falsifying hypothesis. The problem should not be put in terms of whether a *"refutation"* is real or not. The problem is how to repair an *inconsistency* between the "explanatory theory" under test and the—explicit or hidden—"interpretative" theories; or, if you wish, *the problem is which theory to consider as the interpretative one which provides the "hard" facts and which the explanatory one which "tentatively" explains them.* In a mono-theoretical model we regard the higher-level theory as an *explanatory theory to be judged by the "facts"* delivered from outside (by the authoritative experimentalist): In the case of a clash we reject the explanation. In a pluralistic model we may decide, alternatively, to regard the higher-level theory as an *interpretative theory to judge the "facts"* delivered from outside: In case of a clash we may reject the "facts" as "monsters." In a pluralistic model of testing, several theories—more or less deductively organized—are soldered together.

This argument alone would be enough to show the correctness of the conclusion, which we drew from a different earlier argument, that experiments do not simply overthrow theories, that no theory forbids a state of affairs specifiable in advance. It is not that we propose a theory and Nature may shout NO; rather, we propose a maze of theories, and Nature may shout INCONSISTENT. . . .

The problem is then *shifted* from the old problem of replacing a theory refuted by "facts" to the new problem of how to resolve inconsistencies between closely associated theories. Which of the mutually inconsistent theories should be eliminated? The sophisticated falsificationist can answer that question easily: One has to try to replace first one, then the other, then possibly both, and opt for that new set-up which provides the biggest increase in corroborated content, which provides the most progressive problemshift.[45]

Thus we have established an appeal procedure in case the theoretician wishes to question the negative verdict of the experimentalist. The theoretician may demand that the experimentalist specify his "interpretative theory," and he may then replace it—to the experimentalist's annoyance—by a better one in the light of which his originally "refuted" theory may receive positive appraisal.[46]

But even this appeal procedure cannot do more than *postpone* the conventional decision. For the verdict of the appeal court is not infallible either. When we decide whether it is the replacement of the "interpretative" or of the "explanatory" theory that produces novel facts, we again must take a decision about the acceptance or rejection of basic statements. But then we have only *postponed*—and possibly *improved*—the decision, not avoided it. The difficulties concerning the empirical basis which confronted "naive" falsificationism cannot be avoided by "sophisticated" falsificationism either. Even if we regard a theory as "factual," that is, if our slow-moving and limited imagination cannot offer an alternative to it (as Feyerabend used to put it), we have to make, at least occasionally and temporarily, decisions about its truth-value. *Even then, experience still remains, in an important sense, the "impartial arbiter"*[47] *of scientific controversy.* We cannot get rid of the problem of the "empirical basis," if we want to learn from experience: but we can make our learning less dogmatic—but also less fast and less dramatic. By regarding some observational theories as problematic we may make our methodology more flexible: but we cannot articulate and include all "background knowledge" (or "background ignorance"?) into our critical deductive model. This process is bound to be piecemeal and some conventional line must be drawn at any given time.

This leads us to further problems. For one of the crucial features of sophisticated falsificationism is that it replaces the concept of *theory* as the basic concept of the logic of discovery by the concept of *series of theories*. *It is a succession of theories and not one given theory which is appraised as scientific or pseudo-scientific*. But the members of such series of theories are usually connected by a remarkable *continuity* which welds them into *research programmes*. This *continuity*—reminiscent of Kuhnian "normal science"—plays a vital role in the history of science; the main problems of the logic of discovery cannot be satisfactorily discussed except in the framework of a *methodology of research programmes*.

A Methodology of Scientific Research Programmes

I have discussed the problem of objective appraisal of scientific growth in terms of progressive and degenerating problemshifts in series of scientific theories. The most important such series in the growth of science are characterized by a certain *continuity* which connects their members. This continuity evolves from a genuine research programme adumbrated at the start. The programme consists of methodological rules: Some tell us what paths of research to avoid (*negative heuristic*), and others what paths to pursue (*positive heuristic*).

Even science as a whole can be regarded as a huge research programme with Popper's supreme heuristic rule: "Devise conjectures which have more empirical content than their predecessors." Such methodological rules may be formulated, as Popper pointed out, as metaphysical principles.[48] For instance, the *universal* anticonventionalist rule against exception-barring may be stated as the metaphysical principle: "Nature does not allow exceptions." This is why Watkins called such rules "influential metaphysics."[49]

But what I have primarily in mind is not science as a whole, but rather *particular* research programmes, such as the one known as "Cartesian metaphysics." Cartesian metaphysics, that is, the mechanistic theory of the universe—according to which the universe is a huge clockwork (and system of vortices) with push as the only cause of motion—functioned as a powerful heuristic principle. It discouraged work on scientific theories—like [the "essentialist" version of] Newton's theory of action at a distance—which were inconsistent with it (*negative heuristic*). On the other hand, it encouraged work on auxiliary hypotheses which might have saved it from apparent counterevidence—like Keplerian ellipses (positive heuristic).[50]

Negative Heuristic: The "Hard Core" of the Programme

All scientific research programmes may be characterized by their "*hard core*." The negative heuristic of the programme forbids us to direct the *modus tollens* at this "hard core." Instead, we must use our ingenuity to articulate or even invent "auxiliary hypotheses," which form a *protective belt* around this core, and we must redirect the *modus tollens* to *these*. It is this protective belt of auxiliary hypotheses which has to bear the brunt of tests and get adjusted and re-adjusted, or even completely replaced, to defend the thus-hardened core. A research programme is successful if all this leads to a progressive problemshift, unsuccessful if it leads to a degenerating problemshift.

The classical example of a successful research programme is Newton's gravitational theory, possibly the most successful research programme ever. When it was first produced, it was submerged in an ocean of "anomalies" (or, if you wish, "counterexamples"), and opposed by the observational theories supporting these anomalies. But Newtonians turned, with brilliant tenacity and ingenuity, one counter-instance after another into corroborating instances, primarily by overthrowing the original observational theories in the light of which this "contrary evidence" was established. In the process they themselves produced new counter-examples which they again resolved. They "turned each new difficulty into a new victory of their programme."[51]

In Newton's program the negative heuristic bids us to divert the *modus tollens* from Newton's three laws of dynamics and his law of gravitation. This "core" is "irrefutable" by the methodological decision of its protagonists: Anomalies must lead to changes only in the "protective" belt of auxiliary, "observational" hypotheses and initial conditions.[52]

... While "theoretical progress" (in the sense here described) may be verified immediately ... , "empirical progress" cannot, and in a research programme we may be frustrated by a long series of "refutations" before ingenious and lucky content-increasing auxiliary hypotheses turn a chain of defeats—*with hindsight*—into a resounding success story, either by revising some false "facts" or by adding novel auxiliary hypotheses. We may then say that we must require that each step of a research programme be consistently content-increasing: that each step constitute a *consistently progressive theoretical problemshift.* All we need in addition to this is that at least every now and then the increase in content should be seen to be retrospectively corroborated: The programme as a whole should also display an *intermittently progressive empirical shift.* We do not demand that each step produce *immediately* an *observed* new fact. Our term *intermittently* gives sufficient *rational* scope for dogmatic adherence to a programme in face of *prima facie* "refutations."

The idea of "negative heuristic" of a scientific research programme rationalizes classical conventionalism to a considerable extent. We may rationally decide not to allow "refutations" to transmit falsity to the hard core as long as the corroborated empirical content of the protective belt of auxiliary hypotheses increases. But our approach differs from Poincaré's justificationist conventionalism in the sense that, unlike Poincaré's, we maintain that if and when the programme ceases to anticipate novel facts, its hard core might have to be abandoned: that is, *our* hard core, unlike Poincaré's, may crumble under certain conditions.

In this sense we side with Duhem who thought that such a possibility must be allowed for;[53] but for Duhem the reason for such crumbling is purely *aesthetic,*[54] while for us it is mainly *logical and empirical.*

Positive Heuristic: The Construction of the "Protective Belt" and the Relative Autonomy of Theoretical Science

Research programmes, besides their negative heuristic, are also characterized by their positive heuristic.

Even the most rapidly and consistently progressive research programmes can digest their "counter-evidence" only piecemeal: Anomalies are never completely exhausted. But it should not be thought that yet unexplained anomalies—"puzzles" as Kuhn might call them—are taken in random order, and the protective belt built up in an eclectic fashion, without any preconceived order. The order is usually decided in the theoretician's cabinet, independently of the *known* anomalies. Few theoretical scientists engaged in a research programme pay undue attention to "refutations." They have a long-term research policy which anticipates these refutations. This research policy, or order of research, is set out—in more or less detail—in the *positive heuristic* of the research programme. The negative heuristic specifies the "hard core" of the programme which is "irrefutable" by the methodological decision of its protagonists; the positive heuristic consists of a partially articulated set of suggestions or hints on how to change, develop the "refutable variants" of the research programme, how to modify, sophisticate, the "refutable" protective belt.

The positive heuristic of the programme saves the scientist from becoming confused by the ocean of anomalies. The positive heuristic sets out a programme which lists a chain of ever more complicated *models* simulating reality: The scientist's attention is riveted on building his models following instructions which are laid down in the positive part of his programme. He ignores the *actual* counterexamples, the available "data."[55] Newton first worked out his programme for a planetary system with a fixed point-like sun and one single point-like planet. It was in this model that he derived his inverse square law for Kepler's ellipse. But this model was forbidden by Newton's own third law of dynamics; therefore, the model had to be replaced by one in which both sun and planet revolved round their common centre of gravity. This change was not motivated by any observation (the data did not suggest an "anomaly" here) but by a theoretical difficulty in developing the programme. Then he worked out the programme for more planets as if there were only heliocentric but no interplanetary forces. Then he worked out the case where the sun and planets were not mass-points but mass-*balls*. Again, for this change he did not *need* the observation of an anomaly; infinite density was forbidden by an (unarticulated) touchstone theory, therefore planets *had* to be extended. This change involved considerable mathematical difficulties, held up Newton's work—and delayed the publication of the *Principia* by more than a decade. Having solved this "puzzle," he started work on *spinning balls* and their wobbles. Then he admitted interplanetary forces and started work on *perturbations*. At this point he started to look more anxiously at the facts. Many of them were beautifully explained (qualitatively) by this model, many were not. It was then that he started to work on *bulging* planets, rather than round planets, etc.

Newton despised people who, like Hooke, stumbled on a first naive model but did not have the tenacity and ability to develop it into a research programme, and who thought that a first version, a mere aside, constituted a "discovery." He held up publication until his programme had achieved a remarkable progressive shift.[56]

Most, if not all, Newtonian "puzzles," leading to a series of new variants superseding each other, were foreseeable at the time of Newton's first naive model and no doubt Newton and his colleagues *did* foresee them: Newton must have been fully aware of the blatant falsity of his first variants.[57] Nothing shows the existence of a positive heuristic of a research programme clearer than this fact: This is why one speaks of "models" in research programmes. A "*model*" is a set of initial conditions (possibly together with some of the observational theories) which one knows is *bound* to be replaced during the further development of the programme, and one even knows, more or less, how. This shows once more how irrelevant "refutations" of any specific variant are in a research programme: Their existence is fully expected, the positive heuristic is there as the strategy both for predicting (producing) and digesting them. Indeed, if the positive heuristic is clearly spelt out, the difficulties of the programme are mathematical rather than empirical.[58] . . .

Our considerations show that the positive heuristic forges ahead with almost complete disregard of "refutations": It may seem that it is the "*verifications*"[59] rather than the refutations which provide the contact points with reality. Although one must point out that any "verification" of the $n + 1$th version of the programme is a refutation of the nth version, we cannot deny that *some* defeats of the subsequent versions are always foreseen: It is the "verifications" which keep the programme going, recalcitrant instances notwithstanding.

We may appraise research programmes, even after their "elimination," for their *heuristic power*. How many new facts did they produce, how great was "their capacity to explain their refutations in the course of their growth"?[60] . . .

Thus the methodology of scientific research programmes accounts for the *relative autonomy of theoretical science*: a historical fact whose rationality cannot be explained by the earlier falsificationists. Which problems scientists working in powerful research programmes rationally choose is determined by the positive heuristic of the programme rather than by psychologically worrying (or technologically urgent) anomalies. The anomalies are listed but shoved aside in the hope that they will turn, in due course, into corroborations of the programme. Only those scientists have to rivet their attention on anomalies who are either engaged in trial-and-error exercises . . . or who work in a degenerating phase of a research programme when the positive heuristic ran out of steam.

. . . The End of Instant Rationality

It would be wrong to assume that one must stay with a research programme until it has exhausted all its heuristic power, that one must not introduce a rival programme before everybody agrees that the point of degeneration has probably been reached. . . . *The history of science has been and should be a history of competing research programmes. . . .*

The idea of competing scientific research programmes leads us to the problem: *how are research programmes eliminated?* It has transpired from our previous considerations that a degenerating problemshift is no more a sufficient reason to eliminate a research programme than some old-fashioned "refutation" or a Kuhnian "crisis." *Can there be any objective* (as opposed to socio-psychological) *reason to reject a programme, that is, to eliminate its hard core and its programme for constructing protective belts?* Our answer, in outline, is that such an objective reason is provided by a rival research programme which explains the previous success of its rival and supersedes it by a further display of *heuristic power.*[61] . . .

In the light of this paper, the utopian idea of instant rationality becomes a hallmark of most brands of epistemology. Justificationists wanted scientific theories to be proved even before they were published; probabilists hoped a machine could flash up instantly the value (degree of confirmation) of a theory, given the evidence; naive falsificationists hoped that elimination at least was the instant result of the verdict of *experiment.*[62] I hope I have shown that *all these theories of instant rationality—and instant learning—fail.* . . . [R]ationality works much slower than most people tend to think, and, even then, fallibly. Minerva's owl flies at dusk. I also hope I have shown that the *continuity* in science, the *tenacity* of some theories, the rationality of a certain amount of dogmatism, can only be explained if we construe science as a battleground of research programmes rather than of isolated theories. One can understand very little of the growth of science when our paradigm of a chunk of scientific knowledge is an isolated theory like "All swans are white," standing aloof, without being embedded in a major research programme. . . .

Notes

1. This demarcation—and terminology—is due to Popper; cf. especially his [1934], Section 19 and his [1945], Chapter 23 and footnote 3 to Chapter 25.
2. Cf. especially Poincaré [1891] and [1902]; Milhaud [1896]; Le Roy [1899] and [1901]. It was one of the chief philosophical merits of conventionalists to direct the limelight to the fact that any theory can be saved by "conventionalist stratagems" from refutations. (The term *conventionalist stratagem* is Popper's; cf. the critical discussion of Poincaré's conventionalism in his [1934], especially Sections 19 and 20.)
3. Poincaré first elaborated his conventionalism only with regard to geometry (cf. his [1891]). Then Milhaud and Le Roy generalized Poincaré's idea to cover all branches of accepted physical theory. Poincaré's [1902] starts with a strong criticism of the Bergsonian Le Roy against whom he defends the empirical (falsifiable or "inductive") character of all physics *except for* geometry and mechanics. Duhem, in turn, criticized Poincaré: In his view there was a possibility of overthrowing even Newtonian mechanics.
4. The *loci classici* are Duhem's [1905] and Popper's [1934]. Duhem was not a *consistent* revolutionary conventionalist. Very much like Whewell, he thought that conceptual changes are only *preliminaries* to the final—if perhaps distant—"natural classification": "The more a theory is perfected, the more we apprehend that the logical order in which it arranges experimental laws is the reflection of an ontological order." In particular, he refused to see Newton's mechanics *actually* "crumbling" and characterized Einstein's relativity theory as the manifestation of a "frantic and hectic

race in pursuit of a novel idea" which "has turned physics into a real chaos where logic loses its way and commonsense runs away frightened" (Preface—of 1914—to the second edition of his [1905]).

5. Duhem [1905], Chapter VI, Section 10. [See above, p. 198—editor].

6. Popper [1934], Section 30. In this section I discuss the "*naive*" variant of Popper's methodological falsificationism. Thus, throughout the section "methodological falsificationism" stands for "naive methodological falsificationism"; for this "*naivety*," cf. *below*, pp. 201–202.

7. Popper [1934], Section 27.

8. Op cit. Section 28. For the non-basicness of these methodologically "basic" statements, cf. e.g. Popper [1934] *passim* and Popper [1959], p. 35, footnote ★2.

9. Cf. Popper [1934], end of Section 26 and also his [1968], pp. 291–2.

10. Cf. Popper [1963], p. 390.

11. Indeed, Popper carefully puts "observational" in quotes; cf. his [1934], Section 28.

12. Popper [1963], p. 387.

13. Popper [1934], Section 30; also cf. Section 29: "The Relativity of Basic Statements." [See above, pp. 81–84].

14. Agassi [1959]; he calls Popper's idea of science "scientia negativa" (Agassi [1968]).

15. Feyerabend, who contributed probably more than anybody else to the spread of Popper's ideas, seems now to have joined the enemy camp. Cf. his intriguing [1970].

16. I use *"prediction"* in a wide sense that includes *"postdiction."*

17. *For a detailed discussion of these acceptance and rejection rules and for references to Popper's work*, cf. my [1968a], pp. 375–90. . . .

18. Molière, for instance, ridiculed the doctors of his *Malade Imaginaire*, who offered the *virtus dormitiva* of opium as the answer to the question as to why opium produced sleep. One might even argue that Newton's famous dictum *hypotheses non fingo* was really directed against *ad hoc* explanations—like his own explanation of gravitational forces by an aether-model in order to meet Cartesian objections.

19. Cf. *above*, p. 200.

20. Incidentally, Duhem agreed with Bernard that experiments alone—without simplicity considerations—can decide the fate of theories in physiology. But in physics, he argued, they cannot ([1905] Chapter VI, Section I).

21. Koestler correctly points out that only Galileo created the myth that the Copernican theory was simple (Koestler [1959], p. 476); in fact, "the motion of the earth [had not] done much to simplify the old theories, for though the objectionable equants had disappeared, the system was still bristling with auxiliary circles" (Dreyer [1906], Chapter XIII).

22. Cf. *above*, p. 200.

23. Popper [1934], sections 19 and 20. . . .

24. Cf. *above*, p. 202.

25. If I already know P_1: "Swan A is white," P_ω: "All swans are white" represents no progress, because it may only lead to the discovery of such further similar facts as P_2: "Swan B is white." So-called "empirical generalizations" constitute no progress. A *new* fact must be improbable or even impossible in the light of previous knowledge. Cf. *above*, p. 202. . . .

26. The appropriateness of the term "problemshift" for a series of theories rather than of problems may be questioned. I chose it partly because I have not found a more appropriate alternative—"theoryshift" sounds dreadful—partly because theories are always problematical, they never solve all the problems they have set out to solve. Anyway, in the second half of the paper, the more natural term "research programme" will replace "problemshifts" in the most relevant contexts.

27. Popper's conflation of "theories" and "series of theories" prevented him from getting the basic ideas of sophisticated falsificationism across more successfully. His ambiguous usage led to such confusing formulations as "Marxism [as the core of a series of theories or of a research programme] is irrefutable" and, at the same time, "Marxism [as a particular conjunction of this core and some specified auxiliary hypotheses, initial conditions and a *ceteris paribus* clause] has been refuted." (Cf. Popper [1963].)

Of course, there is nothing wrong in saying that an isolated, single theory is "scientific" if it represents an advance on its predecessor, as long as one clearly realizes that in this formulation we appraise the theory as the outcome of—and in the context of—a certain historical development.

28. Popper [1945], Vol. II, p. 233. . . .

29. Popper [1934], Section 30.

30. "In most cases we have, before falsifying a hypothesis, another one up our sleeves" (Popper [1959], p. 87, footnote ★I). But, as our argument shows, we *must* have one. . . .

31. Cf. my [1968a], pp. 387 ff.

32. In the distorting mirror of naive falsificationism, new theories which replace old refuted ones are themselves born unrefuted. Therefore they do not believe that there is a relevant difference between

anomalies and crucial counterevidence. For them, anomaly is a dishonest euphemism for counterevidence. But in actual history new theories are born refuted: They inherit many anamolies of the old theory. Moreover, frequently it is *only* the new theory which dramatically predicts that fact which will function as crucial counterevidence against its predecessor, while the "old" anomalies may well stay on as "new" anomalies. . . .

33. Cf. Popper [1934], Section 85, p. 279 of the 1959 English translation.

34. Also cf. Feyerabend [1965], pp. 254–5.

35. Popper [1959], p. 87, footnote ★I.

36. Popper [1934], Section 30.

37. Cf. Leibnitz [1678]. The expression in brackets shows that Leibnitz regarded this criterion as second best and thought that the best theories are those which are proved. Thus Leibnitz's position —like Whewell's—is a far cry from fullfledged sophisticated falsificationism.

38. Mill [1843], vol. II, p. 23.

39. This was J. S. Mill's argument (*ibid*). He directed it against Whewell, who thought that "consilience of inductions" or successful prediction of improbable events *verifies* (that is, *proves*) a theory. (Whewell [1858], pp. 95–6.)

40. Keynes [1921], p. 305. But cf. my [1968a], p. 394.

41. This is Whewell's critical comment on an *ad hoc* auxiliary hypothesis in Newton's theory of light (Whewell [1858], Vol. II, p. 317.)

42. Popper [1934], Section 22.

43. Cf. e.g., Popper [1959], p. 107, footnote ★2.

44. This is argued in Popper [1934], Section 29.

45. For instance, in our earlier example (cf. *above*, p. 200 ff.) some may try to replace the gravitational theory with a new one and others may try to replace the radio-optics by a new one: We choose the way which offers the more spectacular growth, the more progressive problemshift.

46. A classical example of this pattern is Newton's relation to Flamsteed, the first Astronomer Royal. For instance, Newton visited Flamsteed on 1 September 1694, when working full time on his lunar theory; told him to reinterpret some of his data since they contradicted his own theory; and he explained to him exactly how to do it. Flamsteed obeyed Newton and wrote to him on 7 October: "Since you went home, I examined the observations I employed for determining the greatest equations of the earth's orbit, and considering the moon's places at the times. . . , I find that (*if, as you intimate, the earth inclines on that side the moon then is*) you may abate abt 20″ from it . . . ." Thus Newton constantly criticized and corrected Flamsteed's observational theories. Newton taught

Flamsteed, for instance, a better theory of the refractive power of the atmosphere; Flamsteed accepted this and corrected his original "data." One can understand the constant humiliation and slowly increasing fury of this great observer, having his data criticized and improved by a man who, on his own confession, made no observations himself: It was this feeling—I suspect—which led finally to a vicious personal controversy.

47. Popper [1945], Vol. II, Chapter 23, p. 218.

48. Popper [1934], Sections II and 70. I use "metaphysical" as a technical term of naive falsificationism: A contingent proposition is "metaphysical" if it has no "potential falsifiers."

49. Watkins [1958]. . . .

50. For this Cartesian research programme, cf. Popper [1958] and Watkins [1958], pp. 350–1.

51. Laplace [1796], Livre IV, Chapter ii.

52. The actual hard core of a programme does not actually emerge fully armed like Athene from the head of Zeus. It develops slowly, by a long, preliminary process of trial and error. In this paper this process is not discussed.

53. Cf. *above*, p. 200.

54. Ibid.

55. If a scientist (or mathematician) has a positive heuristic, he refuses to be drawn into observation. He will "lie down on his couch, shut his eyes and forget about the data." (Cf. my [1963–4], especially pp. 300 ff., where there is a detailed case study of such a programme.) Occasionally, of course, he will ask Nature a shrewd question: he will then be encouraged by Nature's *YES*, but not discouraged by its *NO*.

56. Reichenbach, following Cajori, gives a different explanation of what delayed Newton in the publication of his *Principia*: "To his disappointment he found that the observational results disagreed with his calculations. Rather than set any theory, however beautiful, before the facts, Newton put the manuscript of his theory into his drawer. Some twenty years later, after new measurements of the circumference of the earth had been made by a French expedition, Newton saw that the figures on which he had based his test were false and that the improved figures agreed with his theoretical calculation. It was only after this test that he published his law. . . . The story of Newton is one of the most striking illustrations of the method of modern science" (Reichenbach [1951], pp. 101–2). Feyerabend criticizes Reichenbach's account (Feyerabend) [1965], p. 229), but does not give an alternative *rationale*.

57. For a further discussion of Newton's research programme, cf. my [1970].

58. For this point cf. Truesdell [1960].
59. A "verification" is a corroboration of excess content in the expanding programme. But, of course, a "verification" does not *verify* a programme: It shows only its heuristic power.
60. Cf. my [1963–4], pp. 324–30. Unfortunately in 1963–4 I had not yet made a clear terminological distinction between theories and research programmes, and this impaired my exposition of a research programme in informal, quasi-empirical mathematics. There are fewer such shortcomings in my [1971].
61. I use "*heuristic power*" here as a technical term to characterize the power of a research programme to anticipate theoretically novel facts in its growth. I could of course use "*explanatory power*."
62. Of course, naive falsificationists may take some time to reach the "verdict of experiment": the experiment has to be repeated and critically considered. But once the discussion ends up in an agreement among the experts, and thus a "basic statement" becomes "accepted," and it has been decided which specific theory was hit by it, the naive falsificationist will have little patience with those who still "prevaricate."

References

Agassi [1959]: "How are Facts Discovered?" *Impulse*, 3, No. 10, pp. 2–4.

—— [1968]: "The Novelty of Popper's Philosophy of Science." *International Philosophical Quarterly*, 8, pp. 442–63.

Dreyer [1906]: *History of the Planetary Systems from Thales to Kepler*, 1906.

Duhem [1905]: *La Théorie Physique, Son Objet et Sa Structure*, 1905. English translation of the second (1914) edition: *The Aim and Structure of Physical Theory*, 1954.

Feyerabend [1965]: "Reply to Criticism," in Cohen and Wartofsky (*eds.*): *Boston Studies in the Philosophy of Science*, II, pp. 223–61.

—— [1970]: "Against Method," *Minnesota Studies for the Philosophy of Science*, 4, 1970.

Keynes [1921]: *A Treatise on Probability*, 1921.

Koestler [1959]: *The Sleepwalkers*, 1959.

Lakatos [1963–4]: "Proofs and Refutations," *The British Journal for the Philosophy of Science*, 14, pp. 1–25, 120–39, 221–43, 296–342.

—— [1968a]: "Changes in the Problem of Inductive Logic," in Lakatos (*ed.*): *The Problem of Inductive Logic*, 1968, pp. 315–417.

—— [1970]: *The Changing Logic of Scientific Discovery*, 1970.

—— [1971]: *Proofs and Refutations and Other Essays in the Philosophy of Mathematics*, 1971.

Laplace [1796]: *Exposition du Système du Monde*, 1796.

Leibniz [1678]: Letter to Conring, 19.3.1678.

Le Roy [1899]: "Science et Philosophie," *Revue de Métaphysique et de Morale*, 7, pp. 375–425, 503–62, 706–31.

Le Roy [1901]: "Un Positivisme Nouveau," *Revue de Métaphysique et de Morale*, 9, pp. 138–53.

Milhaud [1896]: "*La Science Rationnelle*," *Revue de Métaphysique et de Morale*, 4, pp. 280–302.

Mill [1843]: *A System of Logic, Ratiocinative and Inductive, Being a Connected View of the Principles of Evidence, and the Methods of Scientific Investigation*, 1843.

Poincaré [1891]: "Les géométries non euclidiennes," *Revue des Sciences Pures et Appliquées*, **2**, pp. 769–74.

—— [1902]: *La Science et l'Hypothèse*, 1902.

Popper [1934]: *Logik der Forschung*, 1935 (expanded English edition: Popper [1959]).

—— [1945]: *The Open Society and Its Enemies*, I–II, 1945.

—— [1958]: "Philosophy and Physics"; published in *Atti del XII Congresso Internazionale di Filosofia*, Vol. 2, 1960, pp. 363–74.

—— [1959]: *The Logic of Scientific Discovery*, 1959.

—— [1963]: *Conjectures and Refutations*, 1963.

—— [1968]: "Remarks on the Problems of Demarcation and Rationality," in Lakatos and Musgrave (*eds.*): *Problems in the Philosophy of Science*, 1968, pp. 88–102.

Reichenbach [1951]: *The Rise of Scientific Philosophy*, 1951.

Truesdell [1960]: "The Program toward Rediscovering the Rational Mechanics in the Age of Reason," *Archive of the History of Exact Sciences*, 1, pp. 3–36.

Watkins [1958]: "Influential and Confirmable Metaphysics," *Mind*, N.S. 67, pp. 344–65.

Whewell [1858]: *Novum Organon Renovatum*. Being the second part of the philosophy of the inductive sciences. Third edition, 1858.

THOMAS KUHN

Objectivity, Value Judgment, and Theory Choice

In the penultimate chapter of a controversial book first published fifteen years ago, I considered the ways scientists are brought to abandon one time-honored theory or paradigm in favor of another. Such decision problems, I wrote, "cannot be resolved by proof." To discuss their mechanism is, therefore, to talk "about techniques of persuasion, or about argument and counterargument in a situation in which there can be no proof." Under these circumstances, I continued, "lifelong resistance [to a new theory] . . . is not a violation of scientific standards. . . . Though the historian can always find men—Priestley, for instance—who were unreasonable to resist for as long as they did, he will not find a point at which resistance becomes illogical or unscientific."[1] Statements of that sort obviously raise the question of why, in the absence of binding criteria for scientific choice, both the number of solved scientific problems and the precision of individual problem solutions should increase so markedly with the passage of time. Confronting that issue, I sketched in my closing chapter a number of characteristics that scientists share by virtue of the training that licenses their membership in one or another community of specialists. In the absence of criteria able to dictate the choice of each individual, I argued, we do well to trust the collective judgment of scientists trained in this way. "What better criterion could there be," I asked rhetorically, "than the decision of the scientific group?"[2]

A number of philosophers have greeted remarks like these in a way that continues to surprise me. My views, it is said, make of theory choice "a matter for mob psychology."[3] Kuhn believes, I am told, that "the decision of a scientific group to adopt a new paradigm cannot be based on good reasons of any kind, factual

From *The Essential Tension: Selected Studies in Scientific Tradition and Change* by Thomas Kuhn (1977), pp. 320–339. © 1977 by the University of Chicago. Reprinted by permission of the author and University of Chicago Press.

or otherwise."[4] The debates surrounding such choices must, my critics claim, be for me "mere persuasive displays without deliberative substance."[5] Reports of this sort manifest total misunderstanding, and I have occasionally said as much in papers directed primarily to other ends. But those passing protestations have had negligible effect, and the misunderstandings continue to be important. I conclude that it is past time for me to describe, at greater length and with greater precision, what has been on my mind when I have uttered statements like the ones with which I just began. If I have been reluctant to do so in the past, that is largely because I have preferred to devote attention to areas in which my views diverge more sharply from those currently received than they do with respect to theory choice.

What, I ask to begin with, are the characteristics of a good scientific theory? Among a number of quite usual answers I select five, not because they are exhaustive, but because they are individually important and collectively sufficiently varied to indicate what is at stake. First, a theory should be accurate: Within its domain, that is, consequences deducible from a theory should be in demonstrated agreement with the results of existing experiments and observations. Second, a theory should be consistent, not only internally or with itself, but also with other currently accepted theories applicable to related aspects of nature. Third, it should have broad scope: In particular, a theory's consequences should extend far beyond the particular observations, laws, or subtheories it was initially designed to explain. Fourth, and closely related, it should be simple, bringing order to phenomena that in its absence would be individually isolated and, as a set, confused. Fifth—a somewhat less standard item, but one of special importance to actual scientific decisions—a theory should be fruitful of new research findings: It should, that is, disclose new phenomena or previously unnoted relationships among those already

known.[6] These five characteristics—accuracy, consistency, scope, simplicity, and fruitfulness—are all standard criteria for evaluating the adequacy of a theory. If they had not been, I would have devoted far more space to them in my book, for I agree entirely with the traditional view that they play a vital role when scientists must choose between an established theory and an upstart competitor. Together with others of much the same sort, they provide *the* shared basis for theory choice.

Nevertheless, two sorts of difficulties are regularly encountered by the men who must use these criteria in choosing, say, between Ptolemy's astronomical theory and Copernicus's, between the oxygen and phlogiston theories of combustion, or between Newtonian mechanics and the quantum theory. Individually the criteria are imprecise: Individuals may legitimately differ about their application to concrete cases. In addition, when deployed together, they repeatedly prove to conflict with one another; accuracy may, for example, dictate the choice of one theory, scope the choice of its competitor. Since these difficulties, especially the first, are also relatively familiar, I shall devote little time to their elaboration. Though my argument does demand that I illustrate them briefly, my views will begin to depart from those long current only after I have done so.

Begin with accuracy, which for present purposes I take to include not only quantitative agreement but qualitative as well. Ultimately it proves the most nearly decisive of all the criteria, partly because it is less equivocal than the others but especially because predictive and explanatory powers, which depend on it, are characteristics that scientists are particularly unwilling to give up. Unfortunately, however, theories cannot always be discriminated in terms of accuracy. Copernicus's system, for example, was not more accurate than Ptolemy's until drastically revised by Kepler more than sixty years after Copernicus's death. If Kepler or someone else had not found other reasons to choose heliocentric astronomy, those improvements in accuracy would never have been made, and Copernicus's work might have been forgotten. More typically, of course, accuracy does permit discriminations, but not the sort that lead regularly to unequivocal choice. The oxygen theory, for example, was universally acknowledged to account for observed weight relations in chemical reactions, something the phlogiston theory had previously scarcely attempted to do. But the phlogiston theory, unlike its rival, could account for the metals' being much more alike than the ores from which they were formed. One theory thus matched experience better in one area, the other in another. To choose between them on the basis of accuracy, a scientist would need to decide the area in which accuracy was more significant. About that matter chemists could and did differ without violating any of the criteria outlined above, or any others yet to be suggested.

However important it may be, therefore, accuracy by itself is seldom or never a sufficient criterion for theory choice. Other criteria must function as well, but they do not eliminate problems. To illustrate I select just two—consistency and simplicity—asking how they functioned in the choice between the heliocentric and geocentric systems. As astronomical theories both Ptolemy's and Copernicus's were internally consistent, but their relation to related theories in other fields was very different. The stationary central earth was an essential ingredient of received physical theory, a tight-knit body of doctrine that explained, among other things, how stones fall, how water pumps function, and why the clouds move slowly across the skies. Heliocentric astronomy, which required the earth's motion, was inconsistent with the existing scientific explanation of these and other terrestrial phenomena. The consistency criterion, by itself, therefore, spoke unequivocally for the geocentric tradition.

Simplicity, however, favored Copernicus, but only when evaluated in a quite special way.

If, on the one hand, the two systems were compared in terms of the actual computational labor required to predict the position of a planet at a particular time, then they proved substantially equivalent. Such computations were what astronomers did, and Copernicus's system offered them no labor-saving techniques; in that sense it was not simpler than Ptolemy's. If, on the other hand, one asked about the amount of mathematical apparatus required to explain, not the detailed quantitative motions of the planets, but merely their gross qualitative features—limited elongation, retrograde motion, and the like—then, as every schoolchild knows, Copernicus required only one circle per planet, Ptolemy two. In that sense the Copernican theory was the simpler, a fact vitally important to the choices made by both Kepler and Galileo and thus essential to the ultimate triumph of Copernicanism. But that sense of simplicity was not the only one available, nor even the one most natural to professional astronomers, men whose task was the actual computation of planetary position.

Because time is short and I have multiplied examples elsewhere, I shall here simply assert that these difficulties in applying standard criteria of choice are typical and that they arise no less forcefully in twentieth-century situations than in the earlier and better-known examples I have just sketched. When scientists must choose between competing theories, two men fully committed to the same list of criteria for choice may nevertheless reach different conclusions. Perhaps they interpret simplicity differently or have different convictions about the range of fields within which the consistency criterion must be met. Or perhaps they agree about these matters but differ about the relative weights to be accorded to these or to other criteria when several are deployed together. With respect to divergences of this sort, no set of choice criteria yet proposed is of any use. One can explain, as the historian characteristically does, why particular men made particular choices at particular times. But for that purpose one must go beyond the list of shared criteria to characteristics of the individuals who make the choice. One must, that is, deal with characteristics that vary from one scientist to another without thereby in the least jeopardizing their adherence to the canons that make science scientific. Though such canons do exist and should be discoverable (doubtless the criteria of choice with which I began are among them), they are not by themselves sufficient to determine the decisions of individual scientists. For that purpose the shared canons must be fleshed out in ways that differ from one individual to another.

Some of the differences I have in mind result from the individual's previous experience as a scientist. In what part of the field was he at work when confronted by the need to choose? How long had he worked there; how successful had he been; and how much of his work depended on concepts and techniques challenged by the new theory? Other factors relevant to choice lie outside the sciences. Kepler's early election of Copernicanism was due in part to his immersion in the Neoplatonic and Hermetic movements of his day; German Romanticism predisposed those it affected toward both recognition and acceptance of energy conservation; nineteenth-century British social thought had a similar influence on the availability and acceptability of Darwin's concept of the struggle for existence. Still other significant differences are functions of personality. Some scientists place more premium than others on originality and are correspondingly more willing to take risks; some scientists prefer comprehensive, unified theories to precise and detailed problem solutions of apparently narrower scope. Differentiating factors like these are described by my critics as subjective and are contrasted with the shared or objective criteria from which I began. Though I shall later question that use of terms, let me for the moment accept it. My point is, then, that every individual choice between competing theories depends on a mix-

ture of objective and subjective factors, or of shared and individual criteria. Since the latter have not ordinarily figured in the philosophy of science, my emphasis upon them has made my belief in the former hard for my critics to see.

What I have said so far is primarily simply descriptive of what goes on in the sciences at times of theory choice. As description, furthermore, it has not been challenged by my critics, who reject instead my claim that these facts of scientific life have philosophic import. Taking up that issue, I shall begin to isolate some, though I think not vast, differences of opinion. Let me begin by asking how philosophers of science can for so long have neglected the subjective elements which, they freely grant, enter regularly into the actual theory choices made by individual scientists? Why have these elements seemed to them an index only of human weakness, not at all of the nature of scientific knowledge?

One answer to that question is, of course, that few philosophers, if any, have claimed to possess either a complete or an entirely well-articulated list of criteria. For some time, therefore, they could reasonably expect that further research would eliminate residual imperfections and produce an algorithm able to dictate rational, unanimous choice. Pending that achievement, scientists would have no alternative but to supply subjectively what the best current list of objective criteria still lacked. That some of them might still do so even with a perfected list at hand would then be an index only of the inevitable imperfection of human nature.

That sort of answer may still prove to be correct, but I think no philosopher still expects that it will. The search for algorithmic decision procedures has continued for some time and produced both powerful and illuminating results. But those results all presuppose that individual criteria of choice can be unambiguously stated and also that, if more than one proves relevant, an appropriate weight function is at hand for their joint application. Unfortunately, where the choice at issue is between scientific theories, little progress has been made toward the first of these desiderata and none toward the second. Most philosophers of science would, therefore, I think, now regard the sort of algorithm which has traditionally been sought as a not quite attainable ideal. I entirely agree and shall henceforth take that much for granted.

Even an ideal, however, if it is to remain credible, requires some demonstrated relevance to the situations in which it is supposed to apply. Claiming that such demonstration requires no recourse to subjective factors, my critics seem to appeal, implicitly or explicitly, to the well-known distinction between the contexts of discovery and of justification.[7] They concede, that is, that the subjective factors I invoke play a significant role in the discovery or invention of new theories, but they also insist that that inevitably intuitive process lies outside of the bounds of philosophy of science and is irrelevant to the question of scientific objectivity. Objectivity enters science, they continue, through the processes by which theories are tested, justified, or judged. Those processes do not, or at least need not, involve subjective factors at all. They can be governed by a set of (objective) criteria shared by the entire group competent to judge.

I have already argued that that position does not fit observations of scientific life and shall now assume that that much has been conceded. What is now at issue is a different point: whether or not this invocation of the distinction between contexts of discovery and of justification provides even a plausible and useful idealization. I think it does not and can best make my point by suggesting first a likely source of its apparent cogency. I suspect that my critics have been misled by science pedagogy or what I have elsewhere called textbook science. In science teaching, theories are presented together with exemplary applications, and those applications may be viewed as evidence. But that is not their primary pedagogic function (science students are distressingly willing to receive the word from professors and texts). Doubtless *some* of them were *part* of the evidence at the time actual decisions were being made, but they represent only a fraction of the considerations relevant to the decision process. The context of pedagogy differs almost as much from the context of justification as it does from that of discovery.

Full documentation of that point would require longer argument than is appropriate here, but two aspects of the way in which philosophers ordinarily demonstrate the relevance of choice criteria are worth noting. Like the science textbooks on which they are often modelled, books and articles on the philosophy of science refer again and again to the famous crucial experiments: Foucault's pendulum, which demonstrates the motion of the earth; Cavendish's demonstration of gravitational attraction; or Fizeau's measurement of the relative speed of sound in water and air. These experiments are paradigms of good reason for scientific choice; they illustrate the most effective of all the sorts of argument which could be available to a scientist uncertain which of two theories to follow; they are vehicles for the transmission of criteria of choice. But they also have another characteristic in common. By the time they were performed no scientist still needed to be convinced of the validity of the theory their outcome is now used to demonstrate. Those decisions had long since been made on the basis of significantly more equivocal evidence. The exemplary crucial experiments to which philosophers again and again refer would have been historically relevant to theory choice only if they had yielded unexpected results. Their use as illustrations provides needed economy to science pedagogy, but they scarcely illuminate the character of the choices that scientists are called upon to make.

Standard philosophical illustrations of scientific choice have another troublesome characteristic. The only arguments discussed are, as I have previously indicated, the ones favorable to the theory that, in fact, ultimately triumphed. Oxygen, we read, could explain weight relations, phlogiston could not; but nothing is said about the phlogiston theory's power or about the oxygen theory's limitations. Comparisons of Ptolemy's theory with Copernicus's proceed in the same way. Perhaps these examples should not be given since they contrast a developed theory with one still in its infancy. But philosophers regularly use them nonetheless. If the only result of their doing so were to simplify the decision situation, one could not object. Even historians do not claim to deal with the full factual complexity of the situations they describe. But these simplifications emasculate by making choice totally unproblematic. They eliminate, that is, one essential element of the decision situations that scientists must resolve if their field is to move ahead. In those situations there are always at least some good reasons for each possible choice. Considerations relevant to the context of discovery are then relevant to justification as well; scientists who share the concerns and sensibilities of the individual who discovers a new theory are ipso facto likely to appear disproportionately frequently among that theory's first supporters. That is why it has been difficult to construct algorithms for theory choice, and also why such difficulties have seemed so thoroughly worth resolving. Choices that present problems are the ones philosophers of science need to understand. Philosophically interesting decision procedures must function where, in their absence, the decision might still be in doubt.

That much I have said before, if only briefly. Recently, however, I have recognized another, subtler source for the apparent plausibility of my critics' position. To present it, I shall briefly describe a hypothetical dialogue with one of them. Both of us agree that each scientist chooses between competing theories by deploying some Bayesian algorithm which permits him to compute a value for $p(T,E)$, i.e., for the probability of a theory T on the evidence E available both to him and to the other members of his professional group at a particular period of time. "Evidence," furthermore, we both interpret broadly to include such considerations as simplicity and fruitfulness. My critic asserts, however, that there is only one such value of p, that corresponding to objective choice, and he believes that all rational members of the group must arrive at it. I assert, on the other hand, for reasons previously given, that the factors he calls objective are insufficient to determine in full any algorithm at all. For the sake of the discussion I have conceded that each individual has an algorithm and that all their algorithms have much in common. Nevertheless, I continue to hold that the algorithms of individuals are all ultimately different by virtue of the subjective considerations with which each must complete the objective criteria before any computations can be done. If my hypothetical critic is liberal, he may now grant that these subjective differences do play a role in determining the hypothetical algorithm on which each individual relies during the early stages of the competition between rival theories. But he is also likely to claim that, as evidence increases with the passage of time, the algorithms of different individuals converge to the algorithm of objective choice with which his presentation began. For him the increasing unanimity of individual choices is evidence for their increasing objectivity and thus for the elimination of subjective elements from the decision process.

So much for the dialogue, which I have, of course, contrived to disclose the non sequitur underlying an apparently plausible position. What converges as the evidence changes over time need only be the values of p that individuals compute from their individual algorithms. Conceivably those algorithms themselves also become more alike with time, but the ultimate unanimity of theory choice provides no evidence whatsoever that they do so. If subjective factors are required to account for the decisions that initially divide the profession, they may still be present later when the profession agrees.

Though I shall not here argue the point, consideration of the occasions on which a scientific community divides suggests that they actually do so.

My argument has so far been directed to two points. It first provided evidence that the choices scientists make between competing theories depend not only on shared criteria—those my critics call objective—but also on idiosyncratic factors dependent on individual biography and personality. The latter are, in my critics' vocabulary, subjective, and the second part of my argument has attempted to bar some likely ways of denying their philosophic import. Let me now shift to a more positive approach, returning briefly to the list of shared criteria—accuracy, simplicity, and the like—with which I began. The considerable effectiveness of such criteria does not, I now wish to suggest, depend on their being sufficiently articulated to dictate the choice of each individual who subscribes to them. Indeed, if they were articulated to that extent, a behavior mechanism fundamental to scientific advance would cease to function. What the tradition sees as eliminable imperfections in its rules of choice I take to be in part responses to the essential nature of science.

As so often, I begin with the obvious. Criteria that influence decisions without specifying what those decisions must be are familiar in many aspects of human life. Ordinarily, however, they are called, not criteria or rules, but maxims, norms, or values. Consider maxims first. The individual who invokes them when choice is urgent usually finds them frustratingly vague and often also in conflict one with another. Contrast "He who hesitates is lost" with "Look before you leap," or compare "Many hands make light work" with "Too many cooks spoil the broth." Individually maxims dictate different choices, collectively none at all. Yet no one suggests that supplying children with contradictory tags like these is irrelevant to their education. Opposing maxims alter the nature of the decision to be made, highlight the essential issues it presents, and point to those remaining aspects of the decision for which each individual must take responsibility himself. Once invoked, maxims like these alter the nature of the decision process and can thus change its outcome.

Values and norms provide even clearer examples of effective guidance in the presence of conflict and equivocation. Improving the quality of life is a value, and a car in every garage once followed from it as a norm. But quality of life has other aspects, and the old norm has become problematic. Or again, freedom of speech is a value, but so is preservation of life and property. In application, the two often conflict, so that judicial soul-searching, which still continues, has been required to prohibit such behavior as inciting to riot or shouting fire in a crowded theater. Difficulties like these are an appropriate source for frustration, but they rarely result in charges that values have no function or in calls for their abandonment. That response is barred to most of us by an acute consciousness that there are societies with other values and that these value differences result in other ways of life, other decisions about what may and what may not be done.

I am suggesting, of course, that the criteria of choice with which I began function not as rules, which determine choice, but as values, which influence it. Two men deeply committed to the same values may nevertheless, in particular situations, make different choices as, in fact, they do. But that difference in outcome ought not to suggest that the values scientists share are less than critically important either to their decisions or to the development of the enterprise in which they participate. Values like accuracy, consistency, and scope may prove ambiguous in application, both individually and collectively; they may, that is, be an insufficient basis for a *shared* algorithm of choice. But they do specify a great deal: what each scientist must consider in reaching a decision, what he may or may not consider relevant, and what he can legitimately be required to report as the basis for the choice he has made. Change the list, for example by adding social utility as a criterion, and some particular choices will be different, more like those one expects from an engineer. Subtract accuracy of fit to nature from the list, and the enterprise that results may not resemble science at all, but perhaps philosophy instead. Different creative disciplines are characterized, among other things, by different sets of shared values. If philosophy and engineering lie too close to the sciences, think of literature or the plastic arts. Milton's failure to set *Paradise Lost* in a Copernican universe does not indicate that he agreed with Ptolemy but that he had things other than science to do.

Recognizing that criteria of choice can function as values when incomplete as rules has, I think, a number of striking advantages. First, as I have already argued at length, it accounts in detail for aspects of scientific behavior which the tradition has seen as anomalous or even irrational. More important, it allows the standard criteria to function fully in the earliest stages of theory choice, the period when they are most needed but when, on the traditional view, they function badly or not at all. Copernicus was responding to them during the years required to convert heliocentric astronomy from a global conceptual scheme to mathematical machinery for predicting planetary position. Such predictions were what astronomers valued; in their absence, Copernicus would scarcely have been heard, something which had happened to the idea of a moving earth before. That his own version convinced very few is less important than his acknowledgment of the basis on which judgments would have to be reached if heliocentricism were to survive. Though idiosyncrasy must be invoked to explain why Kepler and Galileo were early converts to Copernicus's system, the gaps filled by their efforts to perfect it were specified by shared values alone.

That point has a corollary which may be more important still. Most newly suggested theories do not survive. Usually the difficulties

that evoked them are accounted for by more traditional means. Even when this does not occur, much work, both theoretical and experimental, is ordinarily required before the new theory can display sufficient accuracy and scope to generate widespread conviction. In short, before the group accepts it, a new theory has been tested over time by the research of a number of men, some working within it, others within its traditional rival. Such a mode of development, however, *requires* a decision process which permits rational men to disagree, and such disagreement would be barred by the shared algorithm which philosophers have generally sought. If it were at hand, all conforming scientists would make the same decision at the same time. With standards for acceptance set too low, they would move from one attractive global viewpoint to another, never giving traditional theory an opportunity to supply equivalent attractions. With standards set higher, no one satisfying the criterion of rationality would be inclined to try out the new theory, to articulate it in ways which showed its fruitfulness or displayed its accuracy and scope. I doubt that science would survive the change. What from one viewpoint may seem the looseness and imperfection of choice criteria conceived as rules may, when the same criteria are seen as values, appear an indispensable means of spreading the risk which the introduction or support of novelty always entails.

Even those who have followed me this far will want to know how a value-based enterprise of the sort I have described can develop as a science does, repeatedly producing powerful new techniques for prediction and control. To that question, unfortunately, I have no answer at all, but that is only another way of saying that I make no claim to have solved the problem of induction. If science did progress by virtue of some shared and binding algorithm of choice, I would be equally at a loss to explain its success. The lacuna is one I feel acutely, but its presence does not differentiate my position from the tradition.

It is, after all, no accident that my list of the values guiding scientific choice is, as nearly as makes any difference, identical with the tradition's list of rules dictating choice. Given any concrete situation to which the philosopher's rules could be applied, my values would function like his rules, producing the same choice. Any justification of induction, any explanation of why the rules worked, would apply equally to my values. Now consider a situation in which choice by shared rules proves impossible, not because the rules are wrong but because they are, as rules, intrinsically incomplete. Individuals must then still choose and be guided by the rules (now values) when they do so. For that purpose, however, each must first flesh out the rules, and each will do so in a somewhat different way even though the decision dictated by the variously completed rules may proved unanimous. If I now assume, in addition, that the group is large enough so that individual differences distribute on some normal curve, then any argument that justifies the philosopher's choice by rule should be immediately adaptable to my choice by value. A group too small, or a distribution excessively skewed by external historical pressures, would, of course, prevent the argument's transfer.[8] But those are just the circumstances under which scientific progress is itself problematic. The transfer is not then to be expected.

I shall be glad if these references to a normal distribution of individual differences and to the problem of induction make my position appear very close to more traditional views. With respect to theory choice, I have never thought my departures large and have been correspondingly startled by such charges as "mob psychology," quoted at the start. It is worth noting, however, that the positions are not quite identical, and for that purpose an analogy may be helpful. Many properties of liquids and gases can be accounted for on the kinetic theory by supposing that all molecules travel at the same speed. Among such properties are the regularities known as Boyle's and Charles's laws. Other characteristics, most obviously evaporation, cannot be explained in so simple a way. To deal with them one must assume that molecular speeds differ, that they are distributed at random, governed by the laws of chance. What I have been suggesting here is that theory choice, too, can be explained only in part by a theory which attributes the same properties to all the scientists who must do the choosing. Essential aspects of the process generally known as verification will be understood only by recourse to the features with respect to which men may differ while still remaining scientists. The tradition takes it for granted that such features are vital to the process of discovery, which it at once and for that reason rules out of philosophical bounds. That they may have significant functions also in the philosophically central problem of justifying theory choice is what philosophers of science have to date categorically denied.

What remains to be said can be grouped in a somewhat miscellaneous epilogue. For the sake of clarity and to avoid writing a book, I have throughout this paper utilized some traditional concepts and locutions about the viability of which I have elsewhere expressed serious doubts. For those who know the work in which I have done so, I close by indicating three aspects of what I have said which would better represent my views if cast in other terms, simultaneously indicating the main directions in which such recasting should proceed. The areas I have in mind are: value invariance, subjectivity, and partial communication. If my views of scientific development are novel—a matter about which there is legitimate room for doubt—it is in areas such as these, rather than theory choice, that my main departures from tradition should be sought.

Throughout this paper I have implicitly assumed that, whatever their initial source, the criteria or values deployed in theory choice are fixed once and for all, unaffected by their participation in transitions from one theory to another. Roughly speaking, but only very roughly, I take that to be the case. If the list of relevant values is kept short (I have mentioned five, not all independent) and if their specification is left vague, then such values as accuracy, scope, and fruitfulness are permanent attributes of science. But little knowledge of history is required to suggest that both the application of these values and, more obviously, the relative weights attached to them have varied markedly with time and also with the field of application. Furthermore, many of these variations in value have been associated with particular changes in scientific theory. Though the experience of scientists provides no philosophical justification for the values they deploy (such justification would solve the problem of induction), those values are in part learned from that experience, and they evolve with it.

The whole subject needs more study (historians have usually taken scientific values, though not scientific methods, for granted), but a few remarks will illustrate the sort of variations I have in mind. Accuracy, as a value, has with time increasingly denoted quantitative or numerical agreement, sometimes at the expense of qualitative. Before early modern times, however, accuracy in that sense was a criterion only for astronomy, the science of the celestial region. Elsewhere it was neither expected nor sought. During the seventeenth century, however, the criterion of numerical agreement was extended to mechanics, during the late eighteenth and early nineteenth centuries to chemistry and such other subjects as electricity and heat, and in this century to many parts of biology. Or think of utility, an item of value not on my initial list. It too has figured significantly in scientific development, but far more strongly and steadily for chemists than for, say, mathematicians and physicists. Or consider scope. It is still an important scientific value, but important scientific advances have

repeatedly been achieved at its expense, and the weight attributed to it at times of choice has diminished correspondingly.

What may seem particularly troublesome about changes like these is, of course, that they ordinarily occur in the aftermath of a theory change. One of the objections to Lavoisier's new chemistry was the roadblocks with which it confronted the achievement of what had previously been one of chemistry's traditional goals: the explanation of qualities, such as color and texture, as well as of their changes. With the acceptance of Lavoisier's theory such explanations ceased for some time to be a value for chemists; the ability to explain qualitative variation was no longer a criterion relevant to the evaluation of chemical theory. Clearly, if such value changes had occurred as rapidly or been as complete as the theory changes to which they related, then theory choice would be value choice, and neither could provide justification for the other. But, historically, value change is ordinarily a belated and largely unconscious concomitant of theory choice, and the former's magnitude is regularly smaller than the latter's. For the functions I have here ascribed to values, such relative stability provides a sufficient basis. The existence of a feedback loop through which theory change affects the values which led to that change does not make the decision process circular in any damaging sense.

About a second respect in which my resort to tradition may be misleading, I must be far more tentative. It demands the skills of an ordinary language philosopher, which I do not possess. Still, no very acute ear for language is required to generate discomfort with the ways in which the terms "objectivity" and, more especially, "subjectivity" have functioned in this paper. Let me briefly suggest the respects in which I believe language has gone astray. "Subjective" is a term with several established uses: In one of these it is opposed to "objective," in another to "judgmental." When my critics describe the idiosyncratic features to which I appeal as subjective, they resort, erroneously I think, to the second of these senses. When they complain that I deprive science of objectivity, they conflate that second sense of subjective with the first.

A standard application of the term "subjective" is to matters of taste, and my critics appear to suppose that that is what I have made of theory choice. But they are missing a distinction standard since Kant when they do so. Like sensation reports, which are also subjective in the sense now at issue, matters of taste are undiscussable. Suppose that, leaving a movie theater with a friend after seeing a western, I exclaim: "How I liked that terrible potboiler!" My friend, if he disliked the film, may tell me I have low tastes, a matter about which, in these circumstances, I would readily agree. But, short of saying that I lied, he cannot disagree with my report that I liked the film or try to persuade me that what I said about my reaction was wrong. What is discussable in my remark is not my characterization of my internal state, my exemplification of taste, but rather my *judgment* that the film was a potboiler. Should my friend disagree on that point, we may argue most of the night, each comparing the film with good or great ones we have seen, each revealing, implicitly or explicitly, something about how he *judges* cinematic merit, about his aesthetic. Though one of us may, before retiring, have persuaded the other, he need not have done so to demonstrate that our difference is one of judgment, not taste.

Evaluations or choices of theory have, I think, exactly this character. Not that scientists never say merely, I like such and such a theory, or I do not. After 1926 Einstein said little more than that about his opposition to the quantum theory. But scientists may always be asked to explain their choices, to exhibit the basis for their judgments. Such judgments are eminently discussable, and the man who refuses to discuss his own cannot expect to be taken seriously. Though there are, very occa-

sionally, leaders of scientific taste, their existence tends to prove the rule. Einstein was one of the few, and his increasing isolation from the scientific community in later life shows how very limited a role taste alone can play in theory choice. Bohr, unlike Einstein, did discuss the bases for his judgment, and he carried the day. If my critics introduce the term "subjective" in a sense that opposes it to judgmental—thus suggesting that I make theory choice undiscussable, a matter of taste—they have seriously mistaken my position.

Turn now to the sense in which "subjectivity" is opposed to "objectivity," and note first that it raises issues quite separate from those just discussed. Whether my taste is low or refined, my report that I liked the film is objective unless I have lied. To my judgment that the film was a potboiler, however, the objective—subjective distinction does not apply at all, at least not obviously and directly. When my critics say I deprive theory choice of objectivity, they must, therefore, have recourse to some very different sense of subjective, presumably the one in which bias and personal likes or dislikes function instead of, or in the face of, the actual facts. But that sense of subjective does not fit the process I have been describing any better than the first. Where factors dependent on individual biography or personality must be introduced to make values applicable, no standards of factuality or actuality are being set aside. Conceivably my discussion of theory choice indicates some limitations of objectivity, but not by isolating elements properly called subjective. Nor am I even quite content with the notion that what I have been displaying are limitations. Objectivity ought to be analyzable in terms of criteria like accuracy and consistency. If these criteria do not supply all the guidance that we have customarily expected of them, then it may be the meaning rather than the limits of objectivity that my argument shows.

Turn, in conclusion, to a third respect, or set of respects, in which this paper needs to be recast. I have assumed throughout that the discussions surrounding theory choice are unproblematic, that the facts appealed to in such discussions are independent of theory, and that the discussions' outcome is appropriately called a choice. Elsewhere I have challenged all three of these assumptions, arguing that communication between proponents of different theories is inevitably partial, that what each takes to be facts depends in part on the theory he espouses, and that an individual's transfer of allegiance from theory to theory is often better described as conversion than as choice. Though all these theses are problematic as well as controversial, my commitment to them is undiminished. I shall not now defend them, but must at least attempt to indicate how what I have said here can be adjusted to conform with these more central aspects of my view of scientific development.

For that purpose I resort to an analogy I have developed in other places. Proponents of different theories are, I have claimed, like native speakers of different languages. Communication between them goes on by translation, and it raises all translation's familiar difficulties. That analogy is, of course, incomplete, for the vocabulary of the two theories may be identical, and most words function in the same ways in both. But some words in the basic as well as in the theoretical vocabularies of the two theories—words like "star" and "planet," "mixture" and "compound," or "force" and "matter"—do function differently. Those differences are unexpected and will be discovered and localized, if at all, only by repeated experience of communication breakdown. Without pursuing the matter further, I simply assert the existence of significant limits to what the proponents of different theories can communicate to one another. The same limits make it difficult or, more likely, impossible for an individual to hold both theories in mind together and compare them point by point with each other and with nature. That sort of comparison is, however, the process on which the

appropriateness of any word like "choice" depends.

Nevertheless, despite the incompleteness of their communication, proponents of different theories can exhibit to each other, not always easily, the concrete technical results achievable by those who practice within each theory. Little or no translation is required to apply at least some value criteria to those results. (Accuracy and fruitfulness are most immediately applicable, perhaps followed by scope. Consistency and simplicity are far more problematic.) However incomprehensible the new theory may be to the proponents of tradition, the exhibit of impressive concrete results will persuade at least a few of them that they must discover how such results are achieved. For that purpose they must learn to translate, perhaps by treating already published papers as a Rosetta stone or, often more effective, by visiting the innovator, talking with him, watching him and his students at work. Those exposures may not result in the adoption of the theory; some advocates of the tradition may return home and attempt to adjust the old theory to produce equivalent results. But others, if the new theory is to survive, will find that at some point in the language-learning process they have ceased to translate and begun instead to speak the language like a native. No process quite like choice has occurred, but they are practicing the new theory nonetheless. Furthermore, the factors that have led them to risk the conversion they have undergone are just the ones this paper has underscored in discussing a somewhat different process, one which, following the philosophical tradition, it has labeled theory choice.

Notes

1. *The Structure of Scientific Revolutions*, 2d ed. (Chicago, 1970), pp. 148, 151–52, 159. All the passages from which these fragments are taken appeared in the same form in the first edition, published in 1962.
2. Ibid., p. 170.

3. Imre Lakatos, "Falsification and the Methodology of Scientific Research Programs," in I. Lakatos and A. Musgrave, Eds., *Criticism and the Growth of Knowledge* (Cambridge, 1970), pp. 91–195. The quoted phrase, which appears on p. 178, is italicized in the original.

4. Dudley Shapere. "Meaning and Scientific Change," in R. G. Colodny, Ed., *Mind and Cosmos: Essays in Contemporary Science and Philosophy.* University of Pittsburgh Series in the Philosophy of Science, vol. 3 (Pittsburgh, 1966), pp. 41–85. The quotation will be found on p. 67.

5. Israel Scheffler, *Science and Subjectivity* (Indianapolis, 1967), p. 81.

6. The last criterion, fruitfulness, deserves more emphasis than it has yet received. A scientist choosing between two theories ordinarily knows that his decision will have a bearing on his subsequent research career. Of course he is especially attracted by a theory that promises the concrete successes for which scientists are ordinarily rewarded.

7. The least equivocal example of this position is probably the one developed in Scheffler, *Science and Subjectivity*, Chap. 4.

8. If the group is small, it is more likely that random fluctuations will result in its members' sharing an atypical set of values and therefore making choices different from those that would be made by a larger and more representative group. External environment—intellectual, ideological, or economic—must systematically affect the value system of much larger groups, and the consequences can include difficulties in introducing the scientific enterprise to societies with inimical values or perhaps even the end of that enterprise within societies where it had once flourished. In this area, however, great caution is required. Changes in the environment where science is practiced can also have fruitful effects on research. Historians often resort, for example, to differences between national environments to explain why particular innovations were initiated and at first disproportionately pursued in particular countries, e.g., Darwinism in Britain, energy conservation in Germany. At present we know substantially nothing about the minimum requisites of the social milieux within which a sciencelike enterprise might flourish.

RUTH HUBBARD

Have Only Men Evolved?

> . . . With the dawn of scientific investigation it might have
> been hoped that the prejudices resulting from lower conditions
> of human society would disappear, and that in their stead
> would be set forth not only facts, but deductions from facts,
> better suited to the dawn of an intellectual age. . . .
> The ability, however, to collect facts, and the power to general-
> ize and draw conclusions from them, avail little, when brought
> into direct opposition to deeply rooted prejudices.
>
> ELIZA BURT GAMBLE
> *The Evolution of Woman* (1894)

Science is made by people who live at a specific time in a specific place and whose thought
patterns reflect the truths that are accepted by
the wider society. Because scientific explanations have repeatedly run counter to the beliefs
held dear by some powerful segments of the society (organized religion, for example, has its
own explanations of how nature works), scientists are sometimes portrayed as lone heroes
swimming against the social stream. Charles
Darwin (1809–82) and his theories of evolution and human descent are frequently used to
illustrate this point. But Darwinism, on the
contrary, has wide areas of congruence with
the social and political ideology of nineteenth-
century Britain and with Victorian precepts of
morality, particularly as regards the relationships between the sexes. And the same Victorian notions still dominate contemporary
biological thinking about sex differences and
sex roles.

Science and the Social Construction of Reality

For humans, language plays a major role in
generating reality. Without words to objectify
and categorize our sensations and place them
in relation to one another, we cannot evolve a

tradition of what is real in the world. Our past experience is organized through language into our history within which we have set up new verbal categories that allow us to assimilate present and future experiences. If every time we had a sensation we gave it a new name, the names would have no meaning: lacking consistency, they could not arrange our experience into reality. For words to work, they have to be used consistently and in a sufficient variety of situations so that their volume—what they contain and exclude—becomes clear to all their users.

If I ask a young child, "Are you hungry?", she must learn through experience that "yes" can produce a piece of bread, a banana, an egg, or an entire meal; whereas "yes" in answer to "Do you want orange juice?" always produces a tart, orange liquid.

However, all acts of naming happen against a backdrop of what is socially accepted as real. The question is *who* has social sanction to define the larger reality into which one's everyday experiences must fit in order that one be reckoned sane and responsible. In the past, the Church had this right, but it is less looked to today as a generator of new definitions of reality, though it is allowed to stick by its old ones even when they conflict with currently accepted realities (as in the case of miracles). The State also defines some aspects of reality and can generate what George Orwell called Newspeak in order to interpret the world for its own political purposes. But, for the most part, at present science is the most respectable legitimator of new realities.

However, what is often ignored is that science does more than merely define reality; by setting up first the definitions—for example, three-dimensional (Euclidian) space—and then specific relationships within them—for example, parallel lines never meet—it automatically renders suspect the sense experiences that contradict the definitions. If we want to be respectable inhabitants of the Euclidian world,

every time we see railroad tracks meet in the distance we must "explain" how what we are seeing is consistent with the accepted definition of reality. Furthermore, through society's and our personal histories, we acquire an investment in our sense of reality that makes us eager to enlighten our children or uneducated "savages," who insist on believing that railroad tracks meet in the distance and part like curtains as they walk down them. (Here, too, we make an exception for the followers of some accepted religions, for we do not argue with equal vehemence against our fundamentalist neighbors, if they insist on believing literally that the Red Sea parted for the Israelites, or that Jesus walked on the Sea of Galilee.)

Every theory is a self-fulfilling prophecy that orders experience into the framework it provides. Therefore, it should be no surprise that almost any theory, however absurd it may seem to some, has its supporters. The mythology of science holds that scientific theories lead to the truth because they operate by consensus: they can be tested by different scientists, making their own hypotheses and designing independent experiments to test them. Thus, it is said that even if one or another scientist "misinterprets" his or her observations, the need for consensus will weed out fantasies and lead to reality. But things do not work that way. Scientists do not think and work independently. Their "own" hypotheses ordinarily are formulated within a context of theory, so that their interpretations by and large are sub-sets within the prevailing orthodoxy. Agreement therefore is built into the process and need tell us little or nothing about "truth" or "reality." Of course, scientists often disagree, but their quarrels usually are about details that do not contradict fundamental beliefs, whichever way they are resolved.[1] To overturn orthodoxy is no easier in science than in philosophy, religion, economics, or any of the other disciplines through which we try to comprehend the world and the society in which we live.

The very language that translates sense perceptions into scientific reality generates that reality by lumping certain perceptions together and sorting or highlighting others. But what we notice and how we describe it depends to a great extent on our histories, roles, and expectations as individuals and as members of our society. Therefore, as we move from the relatively impersonal observations in astronomy, physics and chemistry into biology and the social sciences, our science is increasingly affected by the ways in which our personal and social experience determine what we are able or willing to perceive as real about ourselves and the organisms around us. This is not to accuse scientists of being deluded or dishonest, but merely to point out that, like other people, they find it difficult to see the social biases that are built into the very fabric of what they deem real. That is why, by and large, only children notice that the emperor is naked. But only the rare child hangs on to that insight; most of them soon learn to see the beauty and elegance of his clothes.

In trying to construct a coherent, self-consistent picture of the world, scientists come up with questions and answers that depend on their perceptions of what has been, is, will be, and can be. There is no such thing as objective, value-free science. An era's science is part of its politics, economics and sociology: it is generated by them and in turn helps to generate them. Our personal and social histories mold what we perceive to be our biology and history as organisms, just as our biology plays its part in our social behavior and perceptions. As scientists, we learn to examine the ways in which our experimental methods can bias our answers, but we are not taught to be equally wary of the biases introduced by our implicit, unstated and often unconscious beliefs about the nature of reality. To become conscious of these is more difficult than anything else we do. But difficult as it may seem, we must try to do it if our picture of the world is to be more than

a reflection of various aspects of ourselves and of our social arrangements.[2]

Darwin's Evolutionary Theory

It is interesting that the idea that Darwin was swimming against the stream of accepted social dogma has prevailed, in spite of the fact that many historians have shown his thinking fitted squarely into the historical and social perspective of his time. Darwin so clearly and admittedly was drawing together strands that had been developing over long periods of time that the questions why he was the one to produce the synthesis and why it happened just then have clamored for answers. Therefore, the social origins of the Darwinian synthesis have been probed by numerous scientists and historians.

A belief that all living forms are related and that there also are deep connections between the living and non-living has existed through much of recorded human history. Through the animism of tribal cultures that endows everyone and everything with a common spirit; through more elaborate expressions of the unity of living forms in some Far Eastern and Native American belief systems; and through Aristotelian notions of connectedness runs the theme of one web of life that includes humans among its many strands. The Judaeo-Christian world view has been exceptional—and I would say flawed—in setting man (and I mean the male of the species) apart from the rest of nature by making him the namer and ruler of all life. The biblical myth of the creation gave rise to the separate and unchanging species which that second Adam, Linnaeus (1707–78), later named and classified. But even Linnaeus—though he began by accepting the belief that all existing species had been created by Jehovah during that one week long ago ("Nulla species nova")—had his doubts about their immutability by the time he had identified more than four thousand of them: some species appeared to be closely related, others seemed clearly transitional. Yet as Eiseley has pointed out, it is important to realize that:

> Until the scientific idea of 'species' acquired form and distinctness there could be no dogma of 'special' creation in the modern sense. This form and distinctness it did not possess until the naturalists of the seventeenth century began to substitute exactness of definition for the previous vague characterizations of the objects of nature.[3]

And he continues:

> . . . it was Linnaeus with his proclamation that species were absolutely fixed since the beginning who intensified the theological trend. . . . Science, in its desire for classification and order, . . . found itself satisfactorily allied with a Christian dogma whose refinements it had contributed to produce.

Did species exist before they were invented by scientists with their predilection for classification and naming? And did the new science, by concentrating on differences which could be used to tell things apart, devalue the similarities that tie them together? Certainly the Linnaean system succeeded in congealing into a relatively static form what had been a more fluid and graded world that allowed for change and hence for a measure of historicity.

The hundred years that separate Linnaeus from Darwin saw the development of historical geology by Lyell (1797–1875) and an incipient effort to fit the increasing number of fossils that were being uncovered into the earth's newly discovered history. By the time Darwin came along, it was clear to many people that the earth and its creatures had histories. There were fossil series of snails; some fossils were known to be very old, yet looked for all the world like present-day forms; others had no like descendants and had become extinct. Lamarck (1744–1829), who like Linnaeus began by believing in the fixity of species, by 1800 had formulated a theory of evolution that

involved a slow historical process, which he assumed to have taken a very, very long time.

Possibly one reason the theory of evolution arose in Western, rather than Eastern, science was that the descriptions of fossil and living forms showing so many close relationships made the orthodox biblical view of the special creation of each and every species untenable; and the question, how living forms merged into one another, pressed for an answer. The Eastern philosophies that accepted connectedness and relatedness as givens did not need to confront this question with the same urgency. In other words, where evidences of evolutionary change did not raise fundamental contradictions and questions, evolutionary theory did not need to be invented to reconcile and answer them. However one, and perhaps the most, important difference between Western evolutionary thinking and Eastern ideas of organismic unity lies in the materialistic and historical elements, which are the earmark of Western evolutionism as formulated by Darwin.

Though most of the elements of Darwinian evolutionary theory existed for at least a hundred years before Darwin, he knit them into a consistent theory that was in line with the mainstream thinking of his time. Irvine writes:

> The similar fortunes of liberalism and natural selection are significant. Darwin's matter was as English as his method. Terrestrial history turned out to be strangely like Victorian history writ large. Bertrand Russell and others have remarked that Darwin's theory was mainly 'an extension to the animal and vegetable world of laissez faire economics.' As a matter of fact, the economic conceptions of utility, pressure of population, marginal utility, barriers in restraint of trade, the division of labor, progress and adjustment by competition, and the spread of technological improvements can all be paralleled in *The Origin of Species*. But so, alas, can some of the doc-

trines of English political conservatism. In revealing the importance of time and the hereditary past, in emphasizing the persistence of vestigial structures, the minuteness of variations and the slowness of evolution, Darwin was adding Hooker and Burke to Bentham and Adam Smith. The constitution of the universe exhibited many of the virtues of the English constitution.[4]

One of the first to comment on this congruence was Karl Marx (1818–83) who wrote to Friedrich Engels (1820–95) in 1862, three years after the publication of *The Origin of Species*:

> It is remarkable how Darwin recognizes among beasts and plants his English society with its division of labour, competition, opening up of new markets, 'inventions,' and the Malthusian 'struggle for existence.' It is Hobbes's 'bellum omnium contra omnes,' [war of all against all] and one is reminded of Hegel's *Phenomenology*, where civil society is described as a 'spiritual animal kingdom,' while in Darwin the animal kingdom figures as civil society.[5]

A similar passage appears in a letter by Engels:

> The whole Darwinist teaching of the struggle for existence is simply a transference from society to living nature of Hobbes's doctrine of 'bellum omnium contra omnes' and of the bourgeois-economic doctrine of competition together with Malthus's theory of population. When this conjurer's trick has been performed . . . the same theories are transferred back again from organic nature into history and now it is claimed that their validity as eternal laws of human society has been proved.[5]

The very fact that essentially the same mechanism of evolution through natural selection was postulated independently and at about the same time by two English naturalists, Darwin and Alfred Russel Wallace (1823–1913), shows that the basic ideas were in the air—which is not to deny that it took genius to give them logical and convincing form.

Darwin's theory of *The Origin of Species by Means of Natural Selection*, published in 1859, accepted the fact of evolution and undertook to explain how it could have come about. He had amassed large quantities of data to show that historical change had taken place, both from the fossil record and from his observations as a naturalist on the Beagle. He pondered why some forms had become extinct and others had survived to generate new and different forms. The watchword of evolution seemed to be: be fruitful and modify, one that bore a striking resemblance to the ways of animal and plant breeders. Darwin corresponded with many breeders and himself began to breed pigeons. He was impressed by the way in which breeders, through careful selection, could use even minor variations to elicit major differences, and was searching for the analog in nature to the breeders' techniques of selecting favorable variants. A prepared mind therefore encountered Malthus's *Essay on the Principles of Population* (1798). In his *Autobiography*, Darwin writes:

> In October 1838, that is, fifteen months after I had begun my systematic enquiry, I happened to read for amusement Malthus on *Population*, and being well prepared to appreciate the struggle for existence which everywhere goes on from long-continued observation of the habits of animals and plants, it at once struck me that under these circumstances favourable variations would tend to be preserved and unfavourable ones to be destroyed. The result of this would be the formation of new species. Here, then, I had at last got a theory by which to work.[6]

Incidentally, Wallace also acknowledged being led to his theory by reading Malthus. Wrote Wallace:

> The most interesting coincidence in the matter, I think, is that I, *as well as Darwin,*

was led to the theory itself through Malthus. . . . It suddenly flashed upon me that all animals are necessarily thus kept down—'the struggle for existence'—while *variations*, on which I was always thinking, must necessarily often be *beneficial*, and would then cause those varieties to increase while the injurious variations diminished.[7] (Wallace's italics)

Both, therefore, saw in Malthus's struggle for existence the working of a natural law which effected what Herbert Spencer had called the "survival of the fittest."

The three principal ingredients of Darwin's theory of evolution are: endless variation, natural selection from among the variants, and the resulting survival of the fittest. Given the looseness of many of his arguments—he credited himself with being an expert wriggler—it is surprising that his explanation has found such wide acceptance. One reason probably lies in the fact that Darwin's theory was historical and materialistic, characteristics that are esteemed as virtues; another, perhaps in its intrinsic optimism—its notion of progressive development of species, one from another—which fit well into the meritocratic ideology encouraged by the early successes of British mercantilism, industrial capitalism and imperialism.

But not only did Darwin's interpretation of the history of life on earth fit in well with the social doctrines of nineteenth-century liberalism and individualism. It was used in turn to support them by rendering them aspects of natural law. Herbert Spencer is usually credited with having brought Darwinism into social theory. The body of ideas came to be known as social Darwinism and gained wide acceptance in Britain and the United States in the latter part of the nineteenth and on into the twentieth century. For example, John D. Rockefeller proclaimed in a Sunday school address:

The growth of a large business is merely the survival of the fittest. . . . The American Beauty rose can be produced in the splendor and fragrance which bring cheer to its beholder only by sacrificing the early buds which grow up around it. This is not an evil tendency in business. It is merely the working-out of a law of nature and a law of God.[8]

The circle was therefore complete: Darwin consciously borrowed from social theorists such as Malthus and Spencer some of the basic concepts of evolutionary theory. Spencer and others promptly used Darwinism to reinforce these very social theories and in the process bestowed upon them the force of natural law.[9]

Sexual Selection

It is essential to expand the foregoing analysis of the mutual influences of Darwinism and nineteenth-century social doctrine by looking critically at the Victorian picture Darwin painted of the relations between the sexes, and of the roles that males and females play in the evolution of animals and humans. For although the ethnocentric bias of Darwinism is widely acknowledged, its blatant sexism—or more correctly, androcentrism (male-centeredness)—is rarely mentioned, presumably because it has not been noticed by Darwin scholars, who have mostly been men. Already in the nineteenth century, indeed within Darwin's lifetime, feminists such as Antoinette Brown Blackwell and Eliza Burt Gamble called attention to the obvious male bias pervading his arguments.[10,11] But these women did not have Darwin's or Spencer's professional status or scientific experience; nor indeed could they, given their limited opportunities for education, travel and participation in the affairs of the world. Their books were hardly acknowledged or discussed by professionals, and they have been, till now, merely ignored and excluded from the record. However, it is important to expose Darwin's androcentrism, and not only for historical reasons, but because it remains an integral and unquestioned part of contemporary biological theories.

Early in *The Origin of Species*, Darwin defines sexual selection as one mechanism by which evolution operates. The Victorian and androcentric biases are obvious:

> This form of selection depends, not on a struggle for existence in relation to other organic beings or to external conditions, but on a struggle of individuals of one sex, generally males, for the possession of the other sex.[12]

And,

> Generally, the most vigorous males, those which are best fitted for their places in nature, will leave most progeny. But in many cases, victory depends not so much on general vigor, as on having special weapons confined to the male sex.

The Victorian picture of the active male and the passive female becomes even more explicit later in the same paragraph:

> The males of certain hymenopterous insects [bees, wasps, ants] have been frequently seen by that inimitable observer, M. Fabre, fighting for a particular female who sits by, an apparently unconcerned beholder of the struggle, and then retires with the conqueror.

Darwin's anthropomorphizing continues, as it develops that many male birds "perform strange antics before the females, which, standing by as spectators, at last choose the most attractive partner." However, he worries that whereas this might be a reasonable way to explain the behavior of peahens and female birds of paradise whose consorts anyone can admire, "it is doubtful whether [the tuft of hair on the breast of the wild turkey-cock] can be ornamental in the eyes of the female bird." Hence Darwin ends this brief discussion by saying that he "would not wish to attribute all sexual differences to this agency."

Some might argue in defense of Darwin that bees (or birds, or what have you) do act that way. But the very language Darwin uses to describe these behaviors disqualifies him as an "objective" observer. His animals are cast into roles from a Victorian script. And whereas no one can claim to have solved the important methodological question of how to disembarrass oneself of one's anthropocentric and cultural biases when observing animal behavior, surely one must begin by trying.

After the publication of *The Origin of Species*, Darwin continued to think about sexual selection, and in 1871, he published *The Descent of Man and Selection in Relation to Sex*, a book in which he describes in much more detail how sexual selection operates in the evolution of animals and humans.

In the aftermath of the outcry *The Descent* raised among fundamentalists, much has been made of the fact that Darwin threatened the special place Man was assigned by the Bible and treated him as though he was just another kind of animal. But he did nothing of the sort. The Darwinian synthesis did not end anthropocentrism or androcentrism in biology. On the contrary, Darwin made them part of biology by presenting as "facts of nature" interpretations of animal behavior that reflect the social and moral outlook of his time.

In a sense, anthropocentrism is implicit in the fact that we humans have named, catalogued, and categorized the world around us, including ourselves. Whether we stress our upright stance, our opposable thumbs, our brain, or our language, to ourselves we are creatures apart and very different from all others. But the scientific view of ourselves is also profoundly androcentric. *The Descent of Man* is quite literally *his* journey. Elaine Morgan rightly says:

> It's just as hard for man to break the habit of thinking of himself as central to the species as it was to break the habit of thinking of himself as central to the universe. He sees himself quite unconsciously as the main line of evolution, with a female satellite revolving around him as the moon

revolves around the earth. This not only causes him to overlook valuable clues to our ancestry, but sometimes leads him into making statements that are arrant and demonstrable nonsense. . . . Most of the books forget about [females] for most of the time. They drag her on stage rather suddenly for the obligatory chapter on Sex and Reproduction, and then say: 'All right, love, you can go now,' while they get on with the real meaty stuff about the Mighty Hunter with his lovely new weapons and his lovely new straight legs racing across the Pleistocene plains. Any modifications of her morphology are taken to be imitations of the Hunter's evolution, or else designed solely for his delectation.[13]

To expose the Victorian roots of post-Darwinian thinking about human evolution, we must start by looking at Darwin's ideas about sexual selection in *The Descent*, where he begins the chapter entitled "Principles of Sexual Selection" by setting the stage for the active, pursuing male:

With animals which have their sexes separated, the males necessarily differ from the females in their organs of reproduction; and these are the primary sexual characters. But the sexes differ in what Hunter has called secondary sexual characters, which are not directly connected with the act of reproduction; for instance, the male possesses certain organs of sense or locomotion, of which the female is quite destitute, or has them more highly-developed, in order that he may readily find or reach her; or again the male has special organs of prehension for holding her securely.[14]

Moreover, we soon learn:

In order that the males should seek efficiently, it would be necessary that they should be endowed with strong passions; and the acquirement of such passions would

naturally follow from the more eager leaving a larger number of offspring than the less eager.[15]

But Darwin is worried because among some animals, males and females do not appear to be all that different:

double process of selection has been carried on; that the males have selected the more attractive females, and the latter the more attractive males. . . . But from what we know of the habits of animals, this view is hardly probable, for the male is generally eager to pair with any female.[16]

Make no mistake, wherever you look among animals, eagerly promiscuous males are pursuing females, who peer from behind languidly drooping eyelids to discern the strongest and handsomest. Does it not sound like the wish-fulfillment dream of a proper Victorian gentleman?

This is not the place to discuss Darwin's long treatise in detail. Therefore, let this brief look at animals suffice as background for his section on Sexual Selection in Relation to Man. Again we can start on the first page: "Man is more courageous, pugnacious and energetic than woman, and has more inventive genius."[17] Among "savages," fierce, bold men are constantly battling each other for the possession of women and this has affected the secondary sexual characteristics of both. Darwin grants that there is some disagreement whether there are "inherent differences" between men and women, but suggests that by analogy with lower animals it is "at least probable." In fact, "Woman seems to differ from man in mental disposition, chiefly in her greater tenderness and less selfishness,"[18] for:

Man is the rival of other men; he delights in competition, and this leads to ambition which passes too easily into selfishness. These latter qualities seem to be his natural and unfortunate birthright.

This might make it seem as though women are better than men after all, but not so:

> The chief distinction in the intellectual powers of the two sexes is shown by man's attaining to a higher eminence, in whatever he takes up, than can women—whether requiring deep thought, reason, or imagination, or merely the use of the senses and hands. If two lists were made of the most eminent men and women in poetry, painting, sculpture, music (inclusive both of composition and performance), history, science, and philosophy, with half-a-dozen names under each subject, the two lists would not bear comparison. We may also infer . . . that if men are capable of a decided pre-eminence over women in many subjects, the average of mental power in man must be above that of woman. . . . [Men have had] to defend their females, as well as their young, from enemies of all kinds, and to hunt for their joint subsistence. But to avoid enemies or to attack them with success, to capture wild animals, and to fashion weapons, requires the aid of the higher mental faculties, namely, observation, reason, invention, or imagination. These various faculties will thus have been continually put to the test and selected during manhood.[19]

"Thus," the discussion ends, "man has ultimately become superior to woman" and it is a good thing that men pass on their characteristics to their daughters as well as to their sons, "otherwise it is probable that man would have become as superior in mental endowment to woman, as the peacock is in ornamental plumage to the peahen."

So here it is in a nutshell: men's mental and physical qualities were constantly improved through competition for women and hunting, while women's minds would have become vestigial if it were not for the fortunate circumstance that in each generation daughters inherit brains from their fathers.

Another example of Darwin's acceptance of the conventional mores of his time is his interpretation of the evolution of marriage and monogamy:

> . . . It seems probable that the habit of marriage, in any strict sense of the word, has been gradually developed; and that almost promiscuous or very loose intercourse was once very common throughout the world. Nevertheless, from the strength of the feeling of jealousy all through the animal kingdom, as well as from the analogy of lower animals . . . I cannot believe that absolutely promiscuous intercourse prevailed in times past. . . .[20]

Note the moralistic tone; and how does Darwin know that strong feelings of jealousy exist "all through the animal kingdom?" For comparison, it is interesting to look at Engels, who working largely from the same early anthropological sources as Darwin, had this to say:

> As our whole presentation has shown, the progress which manifests itself in these successive forms [from group marriage to pairing marriage to what he refers to as "monogamy supplemented by adultery and prostitution"] is connected with the peculiarity that women, but not men, are increasingly deprived of the sexual freedom of group marriage. In fact, for men group marriage actually still exists even to this day. What for the woman is a crime entailing grave legal and social consequences is considered honorable in a man or, at the worst, a slight moral blemish which he cheerfully bears. . . . Monogamy arose from the concentration of considerable wealth in the hands of a single individual—a man—and from the need to bequeath this wealth to the children of that man and of no other. For this purpose, the monogamy of the

woman was required, not that of the man, so this monogamy of the woman did not in any way interfere with open or concealed polygamy on the part of the man.[21]

Clearly, Engels did not accept the Victorian code of behavior as our natural biological heritage.

Sociobiology: A New Scientific Sexism

The theory of sexual selection went into a decline during the first half of this century, as efforts to verify some of Darwin's examples showed that many of the features he had thought were related to success in mating could not be legitimately regarded in that way. But it has lately regained its respectability, and contemporary discussions of reproductive fitness often cite examples of sexual selection.[22] Therefore, before we go on to discuss human evolution, it is helpful to look at contemporary views of sexual selection and sex roles among animals (and even plants).

Let us start with a lowly alga that one might think impossible to stereotype by sex. Wolfgang Wickler, an ethologist at the University of Munich, writes in his book on sexual behavior patterns (a topic which Konrad Lorenz tells us in the Introduction is crucial in deciding which sexual behaviors to consider healthy and which diseased):

> Even among very simple organisms such as algae, which have threadlike rows of cells one behind the other, one can observe that during copulation the cells of one thread act as males with regard to the cells of a second thread, but as females with regard to the cells of a third thread. The mark of male behavior is that the cell actively crawls or swims over to the other; the female cell remains passive.[23]

The circle is simple to construct: one starts with the Victorian stereotype of the active male and the passive female, then looks at animals, algae, bacteria, people, and calls all passive behavior feminine, active or goal-oriented behavior masculine. And it works! The Victorian stereotype is biologically determined: even algae behave that way.

But let us see what Wickler has to say about Rocky Mountain Bighorn sheep, in which the sexes cannot be distinguished on sight. He finds it "curious":

> that between the extremes of rams over eight years old and lambs less than a year old one finds every possible transition in age, but no other differences whatever; the bodily form, the structure of the horns, and the color of the coat are the same for both sexes.

Now note: ". . . the typical female behavior is absent from this pattern." Typical of what? Obviously not of Bighorn sheep. In fact we are told that "even the males often cannot recognize a female," indeed, "the females are only of interest to the males during rutting season." How does he know that the males do *not* recognize the females? Maybe these sheep are so weird that most of the time they relate to a female as though she were just another sheep, and whistle at her (my free translation of "taking an interest") only when it is a question of mating. But let us get at last to how the *females* behave. That is astonishing, for it turns out:

> that *both* sexes play two roles, either that of the male or that of the young male. Outside the rutting season the females behave like young males, during the rutting season like aggressive older males. (Wickler's italics)

In fact:

> There is a line of development leading from the lamb to the high ranking ram, and the female animals (♀) behave exactly as though they were in fact males (♂) whose development was retarded. . . . We can say

that the only fully developed mountain sheep are the powerful rams. . . .

At last the androcentric paradigm is out in the open: females are always measured against the standard of the male. Sometimes they are like young males, sometimes like older ones; but never do they reach what Wickler calls "the final stage of fully mature physical structure and behavior possible to this species." That, in his view, is reserved for the rams.

Wickler bases this discussion on observations by Valerius Geist, whose book, *Mountain Sheep*, contains many examples of how androcentric biases can color observations as well as interpretations and restrict the imagination to stereotypes. One of the most interesting is the following:

> Matched rams, usually strangers, begin to treat each other like females and clash until one acts like a female. This is the loser in the fight. The rams confront each other with displays, kick each other, threat jump, and clash till one turns and accepts the kicks, displays, and occasional mounts of the larger without aggressive displays. The loser is not chased away. The point of the fight is not to kill, maim, or even drive the rival off, but to treat him like a female.[24]

This description would be quite different if the interaction were interpreted as something other than a fight, say as a homosexual encounter, a game, or a ritual dance. The fact is that it contains none of the elements that we commonly associate with fighting. Yet because Geist casts it into the imagery of heterosexuality and aggression, it becomes perplexing.

There would be no reason to discuss these examples if their treatments of sex differences or of male/female behavior were exceptional. But they are in the mainstream of contemporary sociobiology, ethology, and evolutionary biology.

A book that has become a standard reference is George Williams's *Sex and Evolution*.[25] It abounds in blatantly biased statements that describe as "careful" and "enlightened" research reports that support the androcentric paradigm, and as questionable or erroneous those that contradict it. Masculinity and femininity are discussed with reference to the behavior of pipefish and seahorses; and cichlids and catfish are judged downright abnormal because both sexes guard the young. For present purposes it is sufficient to discuss a few points that are raised in the chapter entitled "Why are Males Masculine and Females Feminine and, Occasionally, Vice-Versa?"

The very title gives one pause, for if the words masculine and feminine do not mean of, or pertaining, respectively, to males and females, what *do* they mean—particularly in a scientific context? So let us read.

On the first page we find:

> Males of the more familiar higher animals take less of an interest in the young. In courtship they take a more active role, are less discriminating in choice of mates, more inclined toward promiscuity and polygamy, and more contentious among themselves.

We are back with Darwin. The data are flimsy as ever, but doesn't it sound like a description of the families on your block?

The important question is who are these "more familiar higher animals?" Is their behavior typical, or are we familiar with them because, for over a century, androcentric biologists have paid disproportionate attention to animals whose behavior resembles those human social traits that they would like to interpret as biologically determined and hence out of our control?

Williams's generalization quoted above gives rise to the paradox that becomes his chief theoretical problem:

> Why, if each individual is maximizing its own genetic survival should the female be less anxious to have her eggs fertilized than a male is to fertilize them, and why should

the young be of greater interest to one than to the other?

Let me translate this sentence for the benefit of those unfamiliar with current evolutionary theory. The first point is that an individual's *fitness* is measured by the number of her or his offspring that survive to reproductive age. The phrase, "the survival of the fittest," therefore signifies the fact that evolutionary history is the sum of the stories of those who leave the greatest numbers of descendants. What is meant by each individual "maximizing its own genetic survival" is that every one tries to leave as many viable offspring as possible. (Note the implication of conscious intent. Such intent is not exhibited by the increasing number of humans who intentionally *limit* the numbers of their offspring. Nor is one, of course, justified in ascribing it to other animals.)

One might therefore think that in animals in which each parent contributes half of each offspring's genes, females and males would exert themselves equally to maximize the number of offspring. However, we know that according to the patriarchal paradigm, males are active in courtship, whereas females wait passively. This is what Williams means by females being "less anxious" to procreate than males. And of course we also know that "normally" females have a disproportionate share in the care of their young.

So why these asymmetries? The explanation: "The *essential* difference between the sexes is that females produce large immobile gametes and males produce small mobile ones" (my italics). This is what determines their "different optimal strategies." So if you have wondered why men are promiscuous and women faithfully stay home and care for the babies, the reason is that males "can quickly replace wasted gametes and be ready for another mate," whereas females "can not so readily replace a mass of yolky eggs or find a substitute father for an expected litter." Therefore females must "show a much greater degree of caution" in the choice of a mate than males.

E. O. Wilson says that same thing somewhat differently:

> One gamete, the egg, is relatively very large and sessile; the other, the sperm, is small and motile. . . . The egg possesses the yolk required to launch the embryo into an advanced state of development. Because it represents a considerable energetic investment on the part of the mother the embryo is often sequestered and protected, and sometimes its care is extended into the postnatal period. *This is the reason why* parental care is *normally* provided by the female. . . .[26] (my italics)

Though these descriptions fit only some of the animal species that reproduce sexually, and are rapidly ceasing to fit human domestic arrangements in many portions of the globe,[27] they do fit the patriarchal model of the household. Clearly, androcentric biology is busy as ever trying to provide biological "reasons" for a particular set of human social arrangements.

The ethnocentrism of this individualistic, capitalistic model of evolutionary biology and sociobiology, with its emphasis on competition and "investments," is discussed by Sahlins in his monograph, *The Use and Abuse of Biology*.[5] He gives many examples from other cultures to show how these theories reflect a narrow bias that disqualifies them from masquerading as descriptions of universals in biology. But, like other male critics, Sahlins fails to notice the obvious androcentrism.

About thirty years ago, Ruth Herschberger wrote a delightfully funny book called *Adam's Rib*,[28] in which she spoofed the then current androcentric myths regarding sex differences. When it was reissued in 1970, the book was not out of date. In the chapter entitled "Society Writes Biology," she juxtaposes the then (and now) current patriarchal scenario of the dauntless voyage of the active, agile sperm toward the passively receptive, sessile egg to an improvised "matriarchal" account. In it the large, competent egg plays the central role and we feel only pity for the many millions of miniscule, fragile sperm most of which are too feeble to make it to fertilization.

This brings me to a question that always puzzles me when I read about the female's larger energetic investment in her egg than the male's in his sperm: there is an enormous disproportion in the *numbers* of eggs and sperms that participate in the act of fertilization. Does it really take more "energy" to generate the one or relatively few eggs than the large excess of sperms required to achieve fertilization? In humans the disproportion is enormous. In her life time, an average woman produces about four hundred eggs, of which in present-day Western countries, she will "invest" only in about 2.2.[29] Meanwhile the average man generates several billions of sperms to secure those same 2.2 investments!

Needless to say, I have no idea how much "energy" is involved in producing, equipping and ejaculating a sperm cell along with the other necessary components of the ejaculum that enable it to fertilize an egg, nor how much is involved in releasing an egg from the ovary, reabsorbing it in the oviduct if unfertilized (a partial dividend on the investment), or incubating 2.2 of them to birth. But neither do those who propound the existence and importance of women's disproportionate energetic investments. Furthermore, I attach no significance to these questions, since I do not believe that the details of our economic and social arrangements reflect our evolutionary history. I am only trying to show how feeble is the "evidence" that is being put forward to argue the evolutionary basis (hence *naturalness*) of woman's role as homemaker.

The recent resurrection of the theory of sexual selection and the ascription of asymmetry to the "parental investments" of males and females are probably not unrelated to the rebirth of the women's movement. We should remember that Darwin's theory of sexual selection was put forward in the midst of the first wave of feminism.[30] It seems that when women threaten to enter as equals into the world of af-

fairs, androcentric scientists rally to point out that our *natural* place is in the home.

The Evolution of Man

Darwin's sexual stereotypes are doing well also in the contemporary literature on human evolution. This is a field in which facts are few and specimens are separated often by hundreds of thousands of years, so that maximum leeway exists for investigator bias. Almost all the investigators have been men; it should therefore come as no surprise that what has emerged is the familiar picture of Man the Toolmaker. This extends so far that when skull fragments estimated to be 250,000 years old turned up among the stone tools in the gravel beds of the Thames at Swanscombe and paleontologists decided that they are probably those of a female, we read that "The Swanscombe woman, or her husband, was a maker of hand axes. . . ."[31] (Imagine the reverse: The Swanscombe man, or his wife, was a maker of axes. . . .) The implication is that if there were tools, the Swanscombe *woman* could not have made them. But we now know that even apes make tools. Why not women?

Actually, the idea that the making and use of tools were the main driving forces in evolution has been modified since paleontological finds and field observations have shown that apes both use and fashion tools. Now the emphasis is on the human use of tools as weapons for hunting. This brings us to the myth of Man the Hunter, who had to invent not only tools, but also the social organization that allowed him to hunt big animals. He also had to roam great distances and learn to cope with many and varied circumstances. We are told that this entire constellation of factors stimulated the astonishing and relatively rapid development of his brain that came to distinguish Man from his ape cousins. For example, Kenneth Oakley writes:

Men who made tools of the standard type . . . must have been capable of forming in their minds images of the ends to which they laboured. Human culture in all its diversity is the outcome of this capacity for conceptual thinking, but the leading factors in its development are tradition coupled with invention. The primitive hunter made an implement in a particular fashion largely because as a child he watched his father at work or because he copied the work of a hunter in a neighbouring tribe. The standard hand-axe was not conceived by any one individual *ab initio*, but was the result of exceptional individuals in successive generations not only copying but occasionally improving on the work of their predecessors. As a result of the cooperative hunting, migrations and rudimentary forms of barter, the traditions of different groups of primitive hunters sometimes became blended.[32]

It seems a remarkable feat of clairvoyance to see in such detail what happened some 250,000 years in pre-history, complete with the little boy and his little stone chipping set just like daddy's big one.

It is hard to know what reality lurks behind the reconstructions of Man Evolving. Since the time when we and the apes diverged some fifteen million years ago, the main features of human evolution that one can read from the paleontological finds are the upright stance, reduction in the size of the teeth, and increase in brain size. But finds are few and far between both in space and in time until we reach the Neanderthals some 70,000 to 40,000 years ago—a jaw or skull, teeth, pelvic bones, and often only fragments of them.[33] From such bits of evidence as these come the pictures and statues we have all seen of that line of increasingly straight and upright, and decreasingly hairy and ape-like men marching in single file behind *Homo sapiens*, carrying their clubs, stones, or axes; or that other one of a group of beetle-browed and bearded hunters bending

over the large slain animal they have brought into camp, while over on the side long-haired, broad-bottomed females nurse infants at their pendulous breasts.

Impelled, I suppose, by recent feminist critiques of the evolution of Man the Hunter, a few male anthropologists have begun to take note of Woman the Gatherer, and the stereotyping goes on as before. For example Howells, who acknowledges these criticisms as just, nonetheless assumes "the classic division of labor between the sexes" and states as fact that stone age men roamed great distances "on behalf of the whole economic group, while the women were restricted to within the radius of a fraction of a day's walk from camp." Needless to say, he does not *know* any of this.

One can equally well assume that the responsibilities of providing food and nurturing young were widely dispersed through the group that needed to cooperate and devise many and varied strategies for survival. Nor is it obvious why tasks needed to have been differentiated by sex. It makes sense that the gatherers would have known how to hunt the animals they came across; that the hunters gathered when there was nothing to catch, and that men and women did some of each, though both of them probably did a great deal more gathering than hunting. After all, the important thing was to get the day's food, not to define sex roles. Bearing and tending the young have not necessitated a sedentary way of life among nomadic peoples right to the present, and both gathering and hunting probably required movement over large areas in order to find sufficient food. Hewing close to home probably accompanied the transition to cultivation, which introduced the necessity to stay put for planting, though of course not longer than required to harvest. Without fertilizers and crop rotation, frequent moves were probably essential parts of early farming.

Being sedentary ourselves, we tend to assume that our foreparents heaved a great sigh of relief when they invented agriculture and could at last stop roaming. But there is no reason to believe this. Hunter/gatherers and other people who move with their food still exist. And what has been called the agricultural "revolution" probably took considerably longer than all of recorded history. During this time, presumably some people settled down while others remained nomadic, and some did some of each, depending on place and season.

We have developed a fantastically limited and stereotypic picture of ways of life that evolved over many tens of thousands of years, and no doubt varied in lots of ways that we do not even imagine. It is true that by historic times, which are virtually now in the scale of our evolutionary history, there were agricultural settlements, including a few towns that numbered hundreds and even thousands of inhabitants. By that time labor was to some extent divided by sex, though anthropologists have shown that right to the present, the division can be different in different places. There are economic and social reasons for the various delineations of sex roles. We presume too much when we try to read them in the scant record of our distant prehistoric past.

Nor are we going to learn them by observing our nearest living relatives among the apes and monkeys, as some biologists and anthropologists are trying to do. For one thing, different species of primates vary widely in the extent to which the sexes differ in both their anatomy and their social behavior, so that one can find examples of almost any kind of behavior one is looking for by picking the appropriate animal. For another, most scientists find it convenient to forget that present-day apes and monkeys have had as long an evolutionary history as we have had, since the time we and they went our separate ways many millions of years ago. There is no theoretical reason why their behavior should tell us more about our ancestry than our behavior tells us about theirs. It is only anthropocentrism that can lead someone to imagine

that "A possible preadaptation to human ranging for food is the behavior of the large apes, whose groups move more freely and widely compared to gibbons and monkeys, and whose social units are looser."[34] But just as in the androcentric paradigm men evolved while women cheered from the bleachers, so in the anthropocentric one, humans evolved while the apes watched from the trees. This view leaves out not only the fact that the apes have been evolving away from us for as long a time as we from them, but that certain aspects of their evolution may have been a response to our own. So, for example, the evolution of human habits may have put a serious crimp into the evolution of the great apes and forced them to stay in the trees or to hurry back into them.

The current literature on human evolution says very little about the role of language, and sometimes even associates the evolution of language with tool use and hunting—two purportedly "masculine" characteristics. But this is very unlikely because the evolution of language probably went with biological changes, such as occurred in the structure of the face, larynx, and brain, all slow processes. Tool use and hunting, on the other hand, are cultural characteristics that can evolve much more quickly. It is likely that the more elaborate use of tools, and the social arrangements that go with hunting and gathering, developed in part as a consequence of the expanded human repertory of capacities and needs that derive from our ability to communicate through language.

It is likely that the evolution of speech has been one of the most powerful forces directing our biological, cultural, and social evolution, and it is surprising that its significance has largely been ignored by biologists. But, of course, it does not fit into the androcentric paradigm. No one has ever claimed that women can not talk; so if men are the vanguard of evolution, humans must have evolved through the stereotypically male behaviors of competition, tool use, and hunting.

How to Learn Our History? Some Feminist Strategies

How *did* we evolve? Most people now believe that we became who we are by a historical process, but, clearly, we do not know its course, and must use more imagination than fact to reconstruct it. The mythology of science asserts that with many different scientists all asking their own questions and evaluating the answers independently, whatever personal bias creeps into their individual answers is cancelled out when the large picture is put together. This might conceivably be so if scientists were women and men from all sorts of different cultural and social backgrounds who came to science with very different ideologies and interests. But since, in fact, they have been predominantly university-trained white males from privileged social backgrounds, the bias has been narrow and the product often reveals more about the investigator than about the subject being researched.

Since women have not figured in the paradigm of evolution, we need to rethink our evolutionary history. There are various ways to do this:

(1) We can construct one or several estrocentric (female-centered) theories. This is Elaine Morgan's approach in her account of *The Descent of Woman* and Evelyn Reed's in *Woman's Evolution*.[35] Except as a way of parodying the male myths, I find it unsatisfactory because it locks the authors into many of the same unwarranted suppositions that underlie those very myths. For example, both accept the view that our behavior is biologically determined, that what we do is a result of what we were or did millions of years ago. This assumption is unwarranted given the enormous range of human adaptability and the rapid rate of human social and cultural evolution. Of course, there is a place for myth-making and I dream of a long poem that sings women's origins and tells how we felt and what we did; but I do not think that carefully constructed "sci-

entific" mirror images do much to counter the male myths. Present-day women do not know what prehistoric hunter/gatherer women were up to any more than a male paleontologist like Kenneth Oakley knows what the little toolmaker learned from his dad.

(2) Women can sift carefully the few available facts by paring away the mythology and getting as close to the raw data as possible. And we can try to see what, if any, picture emerges that could lead us to questions that perhaps have *not* been asked and that should, and could, be answered. One problem with this approach is that many of the data no longer exist. Every excavation removes the objects from their locale and all we have left is the researcher's descriptions of what they saw. Since we are concerned about unconscious biases, that is worrisome.

(3) Rather than invent our own myths, we can concentrate, as a beginning, on exposing and analyzing the male myths that hide our overwhelming ignorance, "for when a subject is highly controversial—and any question about sex is that—one cannot hope to tell the truth."[36] Women anthropologists have begun to do this. New books are being written, such as *The Female of the Species*[37] and *Toward an Anthropology of Women*,[38] books that expose the Victorian stereotype that runs through the literature of human evolution, and pull together relevant anthropological studies. More important, women who recognize an androcentric myth when they see one and who are able to think beyond it, must do the necessary work in the field, in the laboratories, and in the libraries, and come up with ways of seeing the facts and of interpreting them.[39]

None of this is easy, because women scientists tend to hail from the same socially privileged families and be educated in the same elite universities as our male colleagues. But since we are marginal to the mainstream, we may find it easier than they to watch ourselves push the bus in which we are riding.

As we rethink our history, our social roles, and our options, it is important that we be ever wary of the wide areas of congruence between what are obviously ethno- and androcentric assumptions and what we have been taught are the scientifically proven facts of our biology. Darwin was right when he wrote that "False facts are highly injurious to the progress of science, for they often endure long. . . ."[40] Androcentric science is full of "false facts" that have endured all too long and that serve the interests of those who interpret as women's biological heritage the sexual and social stereotypes we reject. To see our alternatives is essential if we are to acquire the space in which to explore who we are, where we have come from, and where we want to go.

Notes

I want to thank Gar Allen, Rita Arditti, Steve Gould and my colleagues in the editorial group that has prepared that book for their helpful criticisms of an earlier version of this manuscript.

1. For a discussion of this process, *see* Thomas S. Kuhn, *The Structure of Scientific Revolutions*, 2nd ed. (University of Chicago Press, 1970).
2. Berger and Luckmann have characterized this process as "trying to push a bus in which one is riding." [Peter Berger and Thomas Luckmann, *The Social Construction of Reality* (Garden City: Doubleday & Co., 1966), p. 12.] I would say that, worse yet, it is like trying to look out of the rear window to *watch* oneself push the bus in which one rides.
3. Loren Eiseley, *Darwin's Century* (Garden City: Doubleday & Co., Anchor Books Edition, 1961), p. 24.
4. William Irvine, *Apes, Angels, and Victorians* (New York: McGraw-Hill, 1972), p. 98.
5. Quoted in Marshall Sahlins, *The Use and Abuse of Biology* (Ann Arbor: University of Michigan Press, 1976), pp. 101–102.
6. Francis Darwin, ed., *The Autobiography of Charles Darwin* (New York: Dover Publications, 1958), pp. 42–43.
7. Ibid., pp. 200–201.
8. Richard Hofstadter, *Social Darwinism in American Thought* (Boston: Beacon Press, 1955), p. 45.
9. Though not himself a publicist for social Darwinism like Spencer, there can be no doubt that Darwin accepted its ideology. For example, near the end of *The Descent of Man* he writes: "There

should be open competition for all men; and the most able should not be prevented by laws or customs from succeeding best and rearing the largest number of offspring." Marvin Harris has argued that Darwinism, in fact, should be known as biological Spencerism, rather than Spencerism as social Darwinism. For a discussion of the issue, *pro* and *con*, *see* Marvin Harris, *The Rise of Anthropological Theory: A History of Theories of Culture* (New York: *Thomas Y. Crowell*, 1968), Ch. 5: Spencerism; and responses by Derek Freeman and others in *Current Anthropology* 15 (1974), 211–237.
10. Antoinette Brown Blackwell, *The Sexes Throughout Nature* (New York: G. P. Putnam's Sons, 1975; reprinted Westport, Conn.: Hyperion Press, 1978). Excerpts in which Blackwell argues against Darwin and Spencer have been reprinted in Alice S. Rossi, ed., *The Feminist Papers* (New York: Bantam Books, 1974), pp. 356–377.
11. Eliza Burt Gamble, *The Evolution of Woman: An Inquiry into the Dogma of Her Inferiority to Man* (New York: G. P. Putnam's Sons, 1894).
12. Charles Darwin, *The Origin of Species and the Descent of Man* (New York: Modern Library Edition), p. 69.
13. Elaine Morgan, *The Descent of Woman* (New York: Bantam Books, 1973), pp. 3–4.
14. Darwin, *Origin of Species . . .*, p. 567.
15. Ibid., p. 580.
16. Ibid., p. 582.
17. Ibid., p. 867.
18. Ibid., p. 873.
19. Ibid., p. 873–874.
20. Ibid., p. 895.
21. Frederick Engels, *The Origin of the Family, Private Property and the State*, E. B. Leacock, ed. (New York: International Publishers, 1972), p. 138.
22. One of the most explicit contemporary examples of this literature is E. O. Wilson's *Sociobiology: The New Synthesis* (Cambridge: Harvard University Press, 1975); *see* especially chapters 1, 14–16 and 27.
23. Wolfgang Wickler, *The Sexual Code: The Social Behavior of Animals and Men* (Garden City: Doubleday, Anchor Books, 1973), p. 23.
24. Valerius Geist, *Mountain Sheep* (Chicago: University of Chicago Press, 1971), p. 190.
25. George C. Williams, *Sex and Evolution* (Princeton: Princeton University Press, 1975).
26. Edward O. Wilson, *Sociobiology: The New Synthesis* (Cambridge: Harvard University Press, Belknap Press, 1975), pp. 316–317. Wilson and others claim that the growth of a mammalian fetus inside its mother's womb represents an energetic "investment" on her part, but it is not clear to me why

they believe that. Presumably the mother eats and metabolizes, and some of the food she eats goes into building the growing embryo. Why does that represent an investment of *her* energies? I can see that the embryo of an undernourished woman perhaps requires such an investment—in which case what one would have to do is see that the mother gets enough to eat. But what "energy" does a properly nourished woman "invest" in her embryo (or, indeed, in her egg)? It would seem that the notion of pregnancy as "investment" derives from the interpretation of pregnancy as a debilitating disease.

27. For example, at present in the United States, 24 percent of households are headed by women and 46 percent of women work outside the home. The fraction of women who work away from home while raising children is considerably larger in several European countries and in China.

28. Ruth Herschberger, *Adam's Rib* (1948; reprinted ed., New York: Harper and Row, 1970).

29. Furthermore, a woman's eggs are laid down while she is an embryo, hence at the expense of her mother's "metabolic investment." This raises the question whether grandmothers devote more time to grandchildren they have by their daughters than to those they have by their sons. I hope sociobiologists will look into this.

30. Nineteenth-century feminism is often dated from the publication in 1792 of Mary Wollstonecraft's (1759–1797) *A Vindication of the Rights of Woman*; it continued right through Darwin's century. Darwin was well into his work at the time of the Seneca Falls Declaration (1848), which begins with the interesting words: "When, in the course of human events, it becomes necessary for one portion of the family of man to assume among the people of the earth a position different from that which they have hitherto occupied, but one to which the *laws of nature and of nature's God* entitle them . . ." (my italics). And John Stuart Mill (1806–1873) published his essay on *The Subjection of Women* in 1869, ten years after Darwin's *Origin of Species* and two years before the *Descent of Man and Selection in Relation to Sex.*

31. William Howells, *Evolution of the Genus* Homo (Reading: Addison-Wesley Publishing Co., 1973), p. 88.

32. Kenneth P. Oakley, *Man the Toolmaker* (London: British Museum, 1972), p. 81.

33. There are also occasional more perfect skeletons, such as that of *Homo erectus* at Choukoutien, commonly known as Peking Man, who was in fact a woman.

34. Howells, p. 133.

35. Evelyn Reed, *Woman's Evolution* (New York: Pathfinder Press, 1975).

36. Virginia Woolf, *A Room of One's Own* (1945; reprinted ed., Penguin Books, 1970), p. 6.

37. M. Kay Martin and Barbara Voorhis, *The Female of the Species* (New York: Columbia University Press, 1975).

38. Rayna R. Reiter, ed., *Toward an Anthropology of Women* (New York: Monthly Review Press, 1975).

39. This is what Sarah Blaffer Hrdy and Nancy Tanner have done. *See* Sarah Blaffer Hrdy, *The Woman That Never Evolved* (Cambridge, MA: Harvard University Press, 1981); and Nancy Makepeace Tanner, *On Becoming Human* (Cambridge: Cambridge University Press, 1981).

40. Darwin, *Origin of Species* . . . , p. 909.

HELEN E. LONGINO

Can There Be a Feminist Science?

I

The question of this title conceals multiple ambiguities. Not only do the sciences consist of many distinct fields, but the term "science" can be used to refer to a method of inquiry, a historically changing collection of practices, a body of knowledge, a set of claims, a profession, a set of social groups, etc. And as the sciences are many, so are the scholarly disciplines that seek to understand them: philosophy, history, sociology, anthropology, psychology. Any answer from the perspective of some one of these disciplines will, then, of necessity, be partial. In this essay, I shall be asking about the possibility of theoretical natural science that is feminist and I shall ask from the perspective of a philosopher. Before beginning to develop my answer, however, I want to review some of the questions that could be meant, in order to arrive at the formulation I wish to address.

The question could be interpreted as factual, one to be answered by pointing to what feminists in the sciences are doing and saying: "Yes, and this is what it is." Such a response can be perceived as question-begging, however. Even such a friend of feminism as Stephen Gould dismisses the idea of a distinctively feminist or even female contribution to the sciences. In a generally positive review of Ruth Bleier's book, *Science and Gender*, Gould (1984) brushes aside her connection between women's attitudes and values and the interactionist science she calls for. Scientists (male, of course) are already proceeding with wholist and interactionist research programs. Why, he implied, should women or feminists have any particular, distinctive, contributions to make? There is not masculinist and feminist science, just good and bad science. The question of a feminist science cannot be settled by pointing, but involves a deeper, subtler investigation.

The deeper question can itself have several meanings. One set of meanings is sociological, the other conceptual. The sociological meaning proceeds as follows. We know what sorts of social conditions make misogynist science possible. The work of Margaret Rossiter (1982) on the history of women scientists in the United States and the work of Kathryn Addelson (1983) on the social structure of professional science detail the relations between a particular social structure for science and the kinds of science produced. What sorts of social conditions would make feminist science possible? This is an important question, one I am not equipped directly to investigate, although what I can investigate is, I believe, relevant to it. This is the second, conceptual, interpretation of the question: what sort of sense does it make to talk about a feminist science? Why is the question itself not an oxymoron, linking, as it does, values and ideological commitment with the idea of impersonal, objective, value-free, inquiry? This is the problem I wish to address in this essay.

The hope for a feminist theoretical natural science has concealed an ambiguity between content and practice. In the content sense the idea of a feminist science involves a number of assumptions and calls a number of visions to mind. Some theorists have written as though a feminist science is one the theories of which encode a particular world view, characterized by complexity, interaction and wholism. Such a science is said to be feminist because it is the expression and valorization of a female sensibility or cognitive temperament. Alternatively, it is claimed that women have certain traits (dispositions to attend to particulars, interactive rather than individualist and controlling social attitudes and behaviors) that enable them to understand the true character of natural processes (which are complex and interactive).[1] While proponents of this interactionist view see it as an improvement over most contemporary science, it has also been branded as soft—misdescribed as nonmathematical. Women in

the sciences who feel they are being asked to do not better science, but inferior science, have responded angrily to this characterization of feminist science, thinking that it is simply new clothing for the old idea that women can't do science. I think that the interactionist view can be defended against this response, although that requires rescuing it from some of its proponents as well. However, I also think that the characterization of feminist science as the expression of a distinctive female cognitive temperament has other drawbacks. It first conflates feminine with feminist. While it is important to reject the traditional derogation of the virtues assigned to women, it is also important to remember that women are *constructed* to occupy positions of social subordinates. We should not uncritically embrace the feminine.

This characterization of feminist science is also a version of recently propounded notions of a "women's standpoint" or a "feminist standpoint" and suffers from the same suspect universalization that these ideas suffer from. If there is one such standpoint, there are many: as Maria Lugones and Elizabeth Spelman spell out in their tellingly entitled article, "Have We Got a Theory for You!: Feminist Theory, Cultural Imperialism, and the Demand for 'The Woman's Voice,'" women are too diverse in our experiences to generate a single cognitive framework (Lugones and Spelman 1983). In addition, the sciences are themselves too diverse for me to think that they might be equally transformed by such a framework. To reject this concept of a feminist science, however, is not to disengage science from feminism. I want to suggest that we focus on science as practice rather than content, as process rather than product; hence, not on feminist science, but on doing science as a feminist.

The doing of science involves many practices: how one structures a laboratory (hierarchically or collectively), how one relates to other scientists (competitively or cooperatively), how and whether one engages in political struggles over affirmative action. It extends also to intellectual practices, to the activities of scientific inquiry, such as observation and reasoning. Can there be a feminist scientific inquiry? This possibility is seen to be problematic against the background of certain standard presuppositions about science. The claim that there could be a feminist science in the sense of an intellectual practice is either nonsense because oxymoronic as suggested above or the claim is interpreted to mean that established science (science as done and dominated by men) is wrong about the world. Feminist science in this latter interpretation is presented as correcting the errors of masculine, standard science and as revealing the truth that is hidden by masculine "bad" science, as taking the sex out of science.

Both of these interpretations involve the rejection of one approach as incorrect and the embracing of the other as the way to a truer understanding of the natural world. Both trade one absolutism for another. Each is a side of the same coin, and that coin, I think, is the idea of value-free science. This is the idea that scientific methodology guarantees the independence of scientific inquiry from values or value-related considerations. A science or a scientific research program informed by values is *ipso facto* "bad science." "Good science" is inquiry protected by methodology from values and ideology. This same idea underlies Gould's response to Bleier, so it bears closer scrutiny. In the pages that follow, I shall examine the idea of value-free science and then apply the result of that examination to the idea of feminist scientific inquiry.

II

I distinguish two kinds of values relevant to the sciences. Constitutive values, internal to the sciences, are the source of the rules determining what constitutes acceptable scientific practice or scientific method. The personal, social and cultural values, those group or individual preferences about what ought to be, I call con-

textual values, to indicate that they belong to the social and cultural context in which science is done (Longino 1983c). The traditional interpretation of the value-freedom of modern natural science amounts to a claim that its constitutive and contextual features are clearly distinct from and independent of one another, that contextual values play no role in the inner workings of scientific inquiry, in reasoning and observation. I shall argue that this construal of the distinction cannot be maintained.

There are several ways to develop such an argument. One scholar is fond of inviting her audience to visit any science library and peruse the titles on the shelves. Observe how subservient to social and cultural interests are the inquiries represented by the book titles alone! Her listeners would soon abandon their ideas about the value-neutrality of the sciences, she suggests. This exercise may indeed show the influence of external, contextual considerations on what research gets done/supported (i.e., on problem selection). It does not show that such considerations affect reasoning or hypothesis acceptance. The latter would require detailed investigation of particular cases or a general conceptual argument. The conceptual argument involves developing some version of what is known in philosophy of science as the underdetermination thesis, i.e., the thesis that a theory is always underdetermined by the evidence adduced in its support, with the consequence that different or incompatible theories are supported by or at least compatible with the same body of evidence. I shall sketch a version of the argument that appeals to features of scientific inference.

One of the rocks on which the logical positivist program foundered was the distinction between theoretical and observational language. Theoretical statements contain, as fundamental descriptive terms, terms that do not occur in the description of data. Thus, hypotheses in particle physics contain terms like "electron," "pion," "muon," "electron spin," etc. The evidence for a hypothesis such as "A pion decays sequentially into a muon, then a positron" is obviously not direct observations of pions, muons and positrons, but consists largely in photographs taken in large and complex experimental apparati: accelerators, cloud chambers, bubble chambers. The photographs show all sorts of squiggly lines and spirals. Evidence for the hypotheses of particle physics is presented as statements that describe these photographs. Eventually, of course, particle physicists point to a spot on a photograph and say things like "Here a neutrino hits a neutron." Such an assertion, however, is an interpretive achievement that involves collapsing theoretical and observational moments. A skeptic would have to be supplied a complicated argument linking the elements of the photograph to traces left by particles themselves. What counts as theory and what as data in a pragmatic sense change over time, as some ideas and experimental procedures come to be securely embedded in a particular framework and others take their place on the horizons. As the history of physics shows, however, secure embeddedness is no guarantee against overthrow.

Logical positivists and their successors hoped to model scientific inference formally. Evidence of hypotheses, data, were to be represented as logical consequences of hypotheses. When we try to map this logical structure onto the sciences, however, we find that hypotheses are, for the most part, not just generalizations of data statements. The links between data and theory, therefore, cannot be adequately represented as formal or syntactic, but are established by means of assumptions that make or imply substantive claims about the field over which one theorizes. Theories are confirmed via the confirmation of their constituent hypotheses, so the confirmation of hypotheses and theories is relative to the assumptions relied upon in asserting the evidential connection. Confirmation of such assumptions, which are often unarticulated, is itself subject to similar relativization. And it is these assumptions that can

be the vehicle for the involvement of considerations motivated primarily by contextual values (Longino 1979, 1983a).

The point of this extremely telescoped argument is that one can't give an a priori specification of confirmation that effectively eliminates the role of value-laden assumptions in legitimate scientific inquiry without eliminating auxiliary hypotheses (assumptions) altogether. This is not to say that all scientific reasoning involves value-related assumptions. Sometimes auxiliary assumptions will be supported by mundane inductive reasoning. But sometimes they will not be. In any given case, they may be metaphysical in character; they may be untestable with present investigative techniques; they may be rooted in contextual, value-related considerations. If, however, there is no a priori way to eliminate such assumptions from evidential reasoning generally, and, hence, no way to rule out value-laden assumptions, then there is no formal basis for arguing that an inference mediated by contextual values is thereby bad science.

A comparable point is made by some historians investigating the origins of modern science. James Jacob (1977) and Margaret Jacob (1976) have, in a series of articles and books, argued that the adoption of conceptions of matter by 17th century scientists like Robert Boyle was inextricably intertwined with political considerations. Conceptions of matter provided the foundation on which physical theories were developed and Boyle's science, regardless of his reasons for it, has been fruitful in ways that far exceed his imaginings. If the presence of contextual influences were grounds for disallowing a line of inquiry, then early modern science would not have gotten off the ground.

The conclusion of this line of argument is that constitutive values conceived as epistemological (i.e., truth-seeking) are not adequate to screen out the influence of contextual values in the very structuring of scientific knowledge. Now the ways in which contextual values do, if they do, influence this structuring and interact, if they do, with constitutive values has to be determined separately for different theories and fields of science. But this argument, if it's sound, tells us that this sort of inquiry is perfectly respectable and involves no shady assumptions or unargued intuitively based rejections of positivism. It also opens the possibility that one can make explicit value commitments and still do "good" science. The conceptual argument doesn't show that all science is value-laden (as opposed to metaphysics-laden)—that must be established on a case-by-case basis, using the tools not just of logic and philosophy but of history and sociology as well. It does show that not all science is value-free and, more importantly, that it is not necessarily in the nature of science to be value-free. If we reject that idea we're in a better position to talk about the possibilities of feminist science.

III

In earlier articles (Longino 1981, 1983b; Longino and Doell 1983), I've used similar considerations to argue that scientific objectivity has to be reconceived as a function of the communal structure of scientific inquiry rather than as a property of individual scientists. I've then used these notions about scientific methodology to show that science displaying masculine bias is not *ipso facto* improper or "bad" science; that the fabric of science can neither rule out the expression of bias nor legitimate it. So I've argued that both the expression of masculine bias in the sciences and feminist criticism of research exhibiting that bias are—shall we say—business as usual; that scientific inquiry should be expected to display the deep metaphysical and normative commitments of the culture in which it flourishes; and finally that criticism of the deep assumptions that guide scientific reasoning about data is a proper part of science.

The argument I've just offered about the idea of a value-free science is similar in spirit to those earlier arguments. I think it makes it possible to see these questions from a slightly different angle.

There is a tradition of viewing scientific inquiry as somehow inexorable. This involves supposing that the phenomena of the natural world are fixed in determinate relations with each other, that these relations can be known and formulated in a consistent and unified way. This is not the old "unified science" idea of the logical positivists, with its privileging of physics. In its "unexplicated" or "pre-analytic" state, it is simply the idea that there is one consistent, integrated or coherent, true theoretical treatment of all natural phenomena. (The indeterminacy principle of quantum physics is restricted to our understanding of the behavior of certain particles that themselves underlie the fixities of the natural world. Stochastic theories reveal fixities, but fixities among ensembles rather than fixed relations among individual objects or events.) The scientific inquirer's job is to discover those fixed relations. Just as the task of Plato's philosophers was to discover the fixed relations among forms and the task of Galileo's scientists was to discover the laws written in the language of the grand book of nature, geometry, so the scientist's task in this tradition remains the discovery of fixed relations however conceived. These ideas are part of the realist tradition in the philosophy of science.

It's no longer possible, in a century that has seen the splintering of the scientific disciplines, to give such a unified description of the objects of inquiry. But the belief that the job is to discover fixed relations of some sort, and that the application of observation, experiment and reason leads ineluctably to unifiable, if not unified, knowledge of an independent reality, is still with us. It is evidenced most clearly in two features of scientific rhetoric: the use of the passive voice as in "it is concluded that . . ." or "it has been discovered that . . ." and the attribution of agency to the data, as in "the data suggest. . . ." Such language has been criticized for the abdication of responsibility it indicates. Even more, the scientific inquirer, and we with her, become passive observers, victims of the truth. The idea of a value-free science is integral to this view of scientific inquiry. And if we reject that idea we can also reject our roles as passive onlookers, helpless to affect the course of knowledge.

Let me develop this point somewhat more concretely and autobiographically. Biologist Ruth Doell and I have been examining studies in three areas of research on the influence of sex hormones on human behavior and cognitive performance: research on the influence of pre-natal, *in utero*, exposure to higher or lower than normal levels of androgens and estrogens on so-called "gender-role" behavior in children, influence of androgens (pre- and post-natal) on homosexuality in women, and influence of lower than normal (for men) levels of androgen at puberty on spatial abilities (Doell and Longino 1988).

The studies we looked at are vulnerable to criticism of their data and their observation methodologies. They also show clear evidence of androcentric bias—in the assumption that there are just two sexes and two genders (us and them), in the designation of appropriate and inappropriate behaviors for male and female children, in the caricature of lesbianism, in the assumption of male mathematical superiority. We did not find, however, that these assumptions mediated the inferences from data to theory that we found objectionable. These sexist assumptions did affect the way the data were described. What mediated the inferences from the alleged data (i.e., what functioned as auxiliary hypotheses or what provided auxiliary hypotheses) was what we called the linear model—the assumption that there is a direct one-way causal relationship between pre- or post-natal hormone levels and later behavior or cognitive performance. To put it crudely, fetal gonadal hormones organize the brain at critical periods of development. The organism is thereby disposed to respond in a range of ways to a range of environmental stimuli. The assumption of unidirectional programming is supposedly supported by the finding of such a relationship in other mammals; in particular, by experiments demonstrating the dependence of sexual behaviors—mounting and lordosis—on peri-natal hormone exposure and the finding of effects of sex hormones on the development of rodent brains. To bring it to bear on humans is to ignore, among other things, some important differences between human brains and those of other species. It also implies a willingness to regard humans in a particular way—to see us as produced by factors over which we have no control. Not only are we, as scientists, victims of the truth, but we are the prisoners of our physiology.[2] In the name of extending an explanatory model, human capacities for self-knowledge, self-reflection, self-determination are eliminated from any role in human action (at least in the behaviors studied).

Doell and I have therefore argued for the replacement of that linear model of the role of the brain in behavior by one of much greater complexity that includes physiological, environmental, historical and psychological elements. Such a model allows not only for the interaction of physiological and environmental factors but also for the interaction of these with a continuously self-modifying, self-representational (and self-organizing) central processing system. In contemporary neurobiology, the closest model is that being developed in the group selectionist approach to higher brain function of Gerald Edelman and other researchers (Edelman and Mountcastle 1978). We argue that a model of at least that degree of complexity is necessary to account for the human behaviors studies in the sex hormones and behavior research and that if gonadal hormones function at all at these levels, they will probably be found at most to facilitate or inhibit neural processing in general. The strategy we take in our argument is to show that the degree of intentionality involved in the behaviors in question is greater than is presupposed by the hormonal influence researchers and to argue that this degree of intentionality implicates the higher brain processes.

To this point Ruth Doell and I agree. I want to go further and describe what we've done from the perspective of the above philosophical discussion of scientific methodology.

Abandoning my polemical mood for a more reflective one, I want to say that, in the end, commitment to one or another model is strongly influenced by values or other contextual features. The models themselves determine the relevance and interpretation of data. The linear or complex models are not in turn independently or conclusively supported by data. I doubt for instance that value-free inquiry will reveal the efficacy or inefficacy of intentional states or of physiological factors like hormone exposure in human action. I think instead that a research program in neuroscience that assumes the linear model and sex-gender dualism will show the influence of hormone exposure on gender-role behavior. And I think that a research program in neuroscience and psychology that proceeds on the assumption that humans do possess the capacities for self-consciousness, self-reflection, and self-determination, and then asks how the structure of the human brain and nervous system enables the expression of these capacities, will reveal the efficacy of intentional states (understood as very complex sorts of brain states).

While this latter assumption does not itself contain normative terms, I think that the decision to adopt it is motivated by value-laden considerations—by the desire to understand ourselves and others as self-determining (at least some of the time), that is, as capable of acting on the basis of concepts or representations of ourselves and the world in which we act. (Such representations are not necessarily correct, they are surely mediated by our cultures; all we wish to claim is that they are efficacious.) I think further that this desire on Ruth Doell's and my part is, in several ways, an aspect of our feminism. Our preference for a neurobiological model that allows for agency, for the efficacy of intentionality, is partly a validation of our (and everyone's) subjective ex-

perience of thought, deliberation and choice. One of the tenets of feminist research is the valorization of subjective experience, and so our preference in this regard conforms to feminist research patterns. There is, however, a more direct way in which our feminism is expressed in this preference. Feminism is many things to many people, but it is at its core in part about the expansion of human potentiality. When feminists talk of breaking out and do break out of socially prescribed sex-roles, when feminists criticize the institutions of domination, we are thereby insisting on the capacity of humans—male and female—to act on perceptions of self and society and to act to bring about changes in self and society on the basis of those perceptions. (Not overnight and not by a mere act of will. The point is that we act.) And so our criticism of theories of the hormonal influence or determination of so-called gender-role behavior is not just a rejection of the sexist bias in the description of the phenomena—the behavior of the children studied, the sexual lives of lesbians, etc.—but of the limitations on human capacity imposed by the analytic model underlying such research.[3]

While the argument strategy we adopt against the linear model rests on a certain understanding of intention, the values motivating our adoption of that understanding remain hidden in that polemical context. Our political commitments, however, presuppose a certain understanding of human action, so that when faced with a conflict between these commitments and a particular model of brain-behavior relationships we allow the political commitments to guide the choice.

The relevance of my argument about value-free science should be becoming clear. Feminists—in and out of science—often condemn masculine bias in the sciences from the vantage point of commitment to a value-free science. Androcentric bias, once identified, can then be seen as a violation of the rules, as "bad" science. Feminist science, by contrast, can eliminate that bias and produce better, good, more true, or gender-free science. From that perspective the process I've just described is anathema. But if scientific methods generated by constitutive values cannot guarantee independence from contextual values, then that approach to sexist science won't work. We cannot restrict ourselves simply to the elimination of bias, but must expand our scope to include the detection of limiting and interpretive frameworks and the finding or construction of more appropriate frameworks. We need not, indeed should not, wait for such a framework to emerge from the data. In waiting, if my argument is correct, we run the danger of working unconsciously with assumptions still laden with values from the context we seek to change. Instead of remaining passive with respect to the data and what the data suggest, we can acknowledge our ability to affect the course of knowledge and fashion or favor research programs that are consistent with the values and commitments we express in the rest of our lives. From this perspective, the idea of a value-free science is not just empty, but pernicious.

Accepting the relevance to our practice as scientists of our political commitments does not imply simple and crude impositions of those ideas onto the corner of the natural world under study. If we recognize, however, that knowledge is shaped by the assumptions, values and interests of a culture and that, within limits, one can choose one's culture, then it's clear that as scientists/theorists we have a choice. We can continue to do establishment science, comfortably wrapped in the myths of scientific rhetoric, or we can alter our intellectual allegiances. While remaining committed to an abstract goal of understanding, we can choose to whom, socially and politically, we are accountable in our pursuit of that goal. In particular we can choose between being accountable to the traditional establishment or to our political comrades.

Such accountability does not demand a radical break with the science one has learned and practiced. The development of a "new" science involves a more dialectical evolution and

more continuity with established science than the familiar language of scientific revolutions implies.

In focusing on accountability and choice, this conception of feminist science differs from those that proceed from the assumption of a congruence between certain models of natural processes and women's inherent modes of understanding.[4] I am arguing instead for the deliberate and active choice of an interpretive model and for the legitimacy of basing that choice on political considerations in this case. Obviously model choice is also constrained by (what we know of) reality, that is, by the data. But reality (what we know of it) is, I have already argued, inadequate to uniquely determine model choice. The feminist theorists mentioned above have focused on the relation between the content of a theory and female values or experiences, in particular on the perceived congruence between interactionist, wholist visions of nature and a form of understanding and set of values widely attributed to women. In contrast, I am suggesting that a feminist scientific practice admits political considerations as relevant constraints on reasoning, which, through their influence on reasoning and interpretation, shape content. In this specific case, those considerations in combination with the phenomena support an explanatory model that is highly interactionist, highly complex. This argument is so far, however, neutral on the issue of whether an interactionist and complex account of natural processes will always be the preferred one. If it is preferred, however, this will be because of explicitly political considerations and not because interactionism is the expression of "women's nature."

The integration of a political commitment with scientific work will be expressed differently in different fields. In some, such as the complex of research programs having a bearing on the understanding of human behavior, certain moves, such as the one described above, seem quite obvious. In others it may not be clear how to express an alternate set of values in inquiry, or what values would be appropriate. The first step, however, is to abandon the idea that scrutiny of the data yields a seamless web of knowledge. The second is to think through a particular field and try to understand just what its unstated and fundamental assumptions are and how they influence the course of inquiry. Knowing something of the history of a field is necessary to this process, as is continued conversation with other feminists.

The feminist interventions I imagine will be local (i.e., specific to a particular area of research); they may not be exclusive (i.e., different feminist perspectives may be represented in theorizing); and they will be in some way continuous with existing scientific work. The accretion of such interventions, of science done by feminists as feminists, and by members of other disenfranchised groups, has the potential, nevertheless, ultimately to transform the character of scientific discourse.

Doing science differently requires more than just the will to do so and it would be disingenuous to pretend that our philosophies of science are the only barrier. Scientific inquiry takes place in a social, political and economic context that imposes a variety of institutional obstacles to innovation, let alone to the intellectual working out of oppositional and political commitments. The nature of university career ladders means that one's work must be recognized as meeting certain standards of quality in order that one be able to continue it. If those standards are intimately bound up with values and assumptions one rejects, incomprehension rather than conversion is likely. Success requires that we present our work in a way that satisfies those standards and it is easier to do work that looks just like work known to satisfy them than to strike out in a new direction. Another push to conformity comes from the structure of support for science. Many of the scientific ideas argued to be consistent with a feminist politics have a distinctively nonproduction orientation.[5] In the example discussed above, thinking of the brain as hormonally pro-grammed makes intervention and control more likely than does thinking of it as a self-organizing, complexly interactive system. The doing of science, however, requires financial support and those who provide that support are increasingly industry and the military. As might be expected they support research projects likely to meet their needs, projects that promise even greater possibilities for intervention in and manipulation of natural processes. Our sciences are being harnessed to the making of money and the waging of war. The possibility of alternate understandings of the natural world is irrelevant to a culture driven by those interests. To do feminist science we must change the social and political context in which science is done.

So: can there be a feminist science? If this means: is it in principle possible to do science as a feminist?, the answer must be: yes. If this means: can we in practice do science as feminists?, the answer must be: not until we change present conditions.

Notes

1. This seems to be suggested in Bleier (1984), Rose (1983) and in Sandra Harding's (1980) early work.
2. For a striking expression of this point of view see Witelson (1985).
3. Ideological commitments other than feminist ones may lead to the same assumptions and the variety of feminisms means that feminist commitments can lead to different and incompatible assumptions.
4. Cf. note 1, above.
5. This is not to say that interactionist ideas may not be applied in productive contexts, but that, unlike linear causal models, they are several steps away from the manipulation of natural processes immediately suggested by the latter. See Keller (1985), especially Chapter 10.

References

Addelson, Kathryn Pine. 1983. "The Man of Professional Wisdom." In *Discovering Reality*, ed. Sandra Harding and Merrill Hintikka. Dordrecht: Reidel.

Bleier, Ruth. 1984. *Science and Gender*. Elmsford, NY: Pergamon.

Doell, Ruth and Helen E. Longino. "Sex Hormones and Human Behavior: A Critique of the Linear Model." *Journal of Homosexuality* 15, 3/4: pp. 55–78.

Edelman, Gerald and Vernon Mountcastle. 1978. *The Mindful Brain.* Cambridge, MA: MIT Press.

Gould, Stephen J. 1984. Review of Ruth Bleier, *Science and Gender. New York Times Book Review,* VVI, 7 (August 12): 1.

Harding, Sandra. 1980. "The Norms of Inquiry and Masculine Experience." In *PSA 1980,* Vol. 2, ed. Peter Asquith and Ronald Giere. East Lansing, MI: Philosophy of Science Association.

Jacob, James R. 1977. *Robert Boyle and English Revolution, A Study in Social and Intellectual Change.* New York: Franklin.

Jacob, Margaret C. 1976. *The Newtonians and the English Revolution, 1689–1720.* Ithaca, NY: Cornell University Press.

Keller, Evelyn Fox. 1985. *Reflections on Gender and Science.* New Haven, CT: Yale University Press.Longino, Helen. 1979. "Evidence and Hypothesis." *Philosophy of Science* 46 (1): pp. 35–56.

———. 1981. "Scientific Objectivity and Feminist Theorizing." *Liberal Education* 67 (3): pp. 33–41.

———. 1983a. "The Idea of a Value-free Science." Paper presented to the Pacific Division of the American Philosophical Association, March 25, Berkeley, CA.

———. 1983b. "Scientific Objectivity and Logics of Science." *Inquiry* 26 (1): pp. 85–106.

———. 1983c. "Beyond 'Bad Science.'" *Science, Technology and Human Values* 8(1): pp. 7–17.

Longino, Helen and Ruth Doell. 1983. "Body, Bias and Behavior." *Signs* 9(2): pp. 206–227.

Lugones, Maria and Elizabeth Spelman. 1983. "Have We Got a Theory for You! Feminist Theory, Cultural Imperialism and the Demand for 'The Woman's Voice.'" *Hypatia 1,* published as a special issue of *Women's Studies International Forum* 6 (6): pp. 573–581.

Rose, Hilary. 1983. "Hand, Brain, and Heart: A Feminist Epistemology for the Natural Sciences." *Signs* 9 (1): pp. 73–90.

Rossiter, Margaret, 1982. *Women Scientists in America: Struggles and Strategies to 1940.* Baltimore, MD: Johns Hopkins University Press.

Witelson, Sandra. 1985. "An Exchange on Gender." *New York Review of Books* (October 24).

PART IV

THE HISTORICAL DEVELOPMENT OF SCIENTIFIC KNOWLEDGE

Our main concern throughout this book is with the question whether scientific knowledge provides us with true representations of the world (the scientific realist position), or only with representations that are useful for various purposes, such as, for prediction and control of the environment (the scientific anti-realist position). In the previous two sections we witnessed some of the controversy that has surrounded this question—both on the observational level (the empirical basis of scientific knowledge) and on the theoretical level (the validation of scientific theories). There is, however, another vantage point from which we can pursue this question before we reflect on our conclusions in Part V, and that is a thoroughly historical one. Indeed, whatever the philosophical controversy that has surrounded our question, if history discloses a marked stability in the claims of science, then that will count in favor of scientific realism, and if history discloses a marked instability, then that will count in favor of anti-realism. Let me explain.

Perusing almost any science text gives one the impression that, by and large, science has developed in a cumulative way. More specifically, the impression is that, after, perhaps, an initial period of groping toward the right questions and the right methods, the history of a scientific field consists of a series of individual

253

discoveries and inventions, namely, the ones reported in the field's texts; that, one by one, in a process like the addition of bricks to a building, scientists—working with the same methods, aims, and problems as their modern counterparts, and observing the same world—have added another fact, concept, law, or theory to the modern body of technical knowledge. Consider, for example, elementary physics texts. What you are likely to find described and applied in them are Galileo's laws dealing with the motion of objects (falling stones, pendula, balls on inclined planes) near the surface of the earth, Kepler's laws dealing with the motion of the planets around the sun, Newton's more general laws of motion and law of universal gravitation dealing with the motion and causes of motion of any terrestrial and celestial object whatever, Einstein's still more general theory of relativity dealing with the motion and causes of motion of atomic and nuclear particles as well as all terrestrial and celestial objects, and so on. These laws and theories are represented in such physics texts as permanent additions to scientific knowledge, obtained by using sound scientific procedures. And they are represented as progressively revealing the truth about the world.

This cumulative model of scientific development implicit in much science textbook writing—that a scientific field typically develops by adding new knowledge to the knowledge already accumulated—is central to Carl Hempel's widely influential account of explanation and prediction as the fundamental goals of scientific research, and it is central as well to the related conception of science as progressing toward a unified system of knowledge. But this cumulative model of scientific development has also drawn much criticism during more than three decades of intensive discussion on scientific change. Two alternative views have played a prominent role in that discussion: the evolutionary model of scientific development, associated with Karl Popper, and the revolutionary model of scientific development, associated with Thomas Kuhn. In addition, a promising gradualist model of scientific development has more recently been proposed by Larry Laudan. I shall discuss each of these models in turn.

The Cumulative Model of Scientific Development

According to Carl Hempel and his many followers, the fundamental goals of scientific research are to predict (and, whenever possible, control) the events that occur in the world, and to explain them. And both of these goals are fulfilled in the same way—by discovering laws under which the events can be subsumed, laws that show that the events are to be expected. But what is it to subsume events under laws?

In logic an argument is a set of statements, one or more of which—the premises—are given in justification of the remaining statement—the conclusion. The aim of an argument, of course, is to provide strong grounds for believing the conclusion. This aim is generally fulfilled under two conditions: (1) There is a special logical relation, called *validity*, between the premises and conclusion of the argument, such that if the premises are true, the conclusion either has to be true or is very probably true; and (2) The premises of the argument *are* true. Arguments fulfilling these two conditions are called *sound* arguments.

Consider, for example, the following two arguments:

1. All the coins in Bank A are shiny pennies.
   Sonya has shaken a coin out of Bank A.
   _____
   The coin Sonya has shaken out of Bank A is a shiny penny.

2. 90% of the coins in Bank B are shiny pennies.
   Sonya has shaken a coin out of Bank B.
   _____
   The coin Sonya has shaken out of Bank B is a shiny penny.

In the first argument the logical relation of validity holding between the premises and the conclusion is such that, if the premises are true, then the conclusion *has* to be true. Arguments of this kind, in which the premises, if true, logically guarantee the truth of the conclusion, or at least purport to do so, are called *deductive* arguments. Given the logical relation of validity holding between the premises and conclusion of the first argument, and assuming that the premises *are* true, we have the strongest possible grounds for believing the conclusion. In the second argument, the logical relation of validity holding between the premises and the conclusion is such that, if the premises are true, then the conclusion is *very probably* true. Arguments of this kind, in which the premises, if true, show that the conclusion is very probably true, or at least purport to do so, are called *inductive* arguments. Given the logical relation of validity holding between the premises and conclusion of the second argument, and assuming that the premises *are* true, we have strong, but not conclusive, grounds for believing the conclusion.

According to Hempel's "covering law model" of scientific explanation sketched out in "Explanation in Science," scientific explanations are deductive or inductive arguments. These arguments are composed of (1) a conclusion, called the *explanandum*, describing the phenomenon to be explained, and (2) a set of premises, called the *explanans*, describing the facts and (universal or statistical) laws provided to account for the explanandum. As with other arguments, the aim of scientific explanations is to provide strong grounds for believing the explanandum—more precisely, to provide strong grounds for believing that the phenomenon described in the explanandum was to be expected. And as with other arguments, this aim is generally fulfilled under two conditions: (1) There is a logical relation of validity holding between the explanans and explanandum of the explanation, such that if the explanans is true, the explanandum either has to be true or is very probably true; and (2) The explanans *is* true.

For Hempel, then, the ultimate goal of science is to explain and predict events, that is to say, to (deductively or inductively) subsume events under empirical laws.

But science raises the question "Why?" also with respect to the uniformities expressed by such laws, and often answers it in basically the same manner, namely, by subsuming the uniformities under more inclusive laws, and eventually under comprehensive theories. For example, the question, "Why do Galileo's and Kepler's laws hold?" is answered by showing that these laws are but special consequences of the Newtonian laws of motion and of gravitation; and these, in turn, may be explained by subsumption under the more comprehensive general theory of relativity. (pp. 262–263)

As a result a scientific field typically develops in a cumulative way, by adding new knowledge to the knowledge already accumulated—indeed, by adding new knowledge that systematizes the knowledge already accumulated, but also moves beyond it. The new knowledge at each stage is thus not only an addition to, but also a unifier of, what went before.

In "Unity of Science as a Working Hypothesis," Paul Oppenheim and Hilary Putnam suggest what the end result of this explanatory project is likely to be—a state of "unitary science" in which not only individual fields have developed in a cumulative yet progressively more systematized way, but all of science as well. To describe this state of science more clearly, let us envision science divided into six levels of theories dealing with the following six levels of objects: (6) social groups; (5) multicellular living things; (4) cells; (3) molecules; (2) atoms; and (1) elementary particles. And let us speak of the "reduction" of the theories of one level to the theories of the next lower level when the lower-level theories can explain all the observational data explained by the higher-level theories. In this case the number of theories really needed for explanation of such data would be reduced to those on the lower level. And similarly, the objects really needed for explanation of such data would correspondingly be reduced to those on the lower level. Leaving out questions of convenience, we could then simply omit the higher-level theories and objects from science as superfluous for explanatory purposes. In these terms the state of unitary science would be a state of science in which the theories of each level would be reduced to theories of the next lower level, the theories of the lowest level being those to which all the theories of science would finally be reduced in a cumulative way. These theories of the lowest level would thus be the theories which could explain all observational data, and the objects of the lowest level they dealt with would thus be the only objects needed to explain all observational data. These theories of the lowest level would thus be the final and complete result of the scientific enterprise.

So much for the state of unitary science. Has science actually been moving toward this state? Oppenheim and Putnam argue that it has. The evidence they present includes examples of a variety of successful reductions of theories between all successive pairs of the six levels cited above, as well as such indirect evidence as successes at synthesizing things of each level out of things of the next lower level, and evidence to the effect that each level is, in evolution, prior to the one above it. But Oppenheim and Putnam's ultimate point is not so much that science *has been* moving toward a state of unitary science as that, for a variety of reasons (methodological and pragmatic, as well as empirical), we ought to *accept as a working hypothesis* that science *can* achieve this state, and structure scientific research accordingly.

The Evolutionary Model of Scientific Development

According to the cumulative model of scientific development, as we have seen, laws like those formulated by Galileo, Kepler, Newton, and Einstein are permanent additions to scientific knowledge, progressively revealing the truth about the world. But only the slightest investigation will demonstrate that this account is inaccurate. After all, Galileo's and Kepler's laws are incompatible with Newtonian mechanics; for example, according to Galileo's laws the acceleration due to gravity of an object near the surface of the earth is constant, whereas according to Newtonian mechanics that acceleration varies with the height of the object from the surface of the earth. And Newtonian mechanics is, likewise, incompatible with Einstein's theory; according to Newtonian mechanics, for example, the mass of an object is a constant property, whereas according to Einsteinian theory the mass of an object varies with its velocity. Newtonian mechanics *corrects* Galileo's and Kepler's laws: They are a good approximation to the more accurate laws deducible from it. Newtonian mechanics does not add to or generalize or explain Galileo's and Kepler's laws. And similarly, Einstein's theory corrects Newtonian mechanics. How can we capture this prevalent kind of situation in a model of scientific development?

According to the evolutionary model proposed by Karl Popper, science is a means used by human beings to adapt to their environment. Such adaptation starts with the dominant scientific theories of a field (an inherited structure), which are then exposed to an environment of experimental tests. In response to negative results of such tests (challenges from the environment), new tentative theories (variations of the inherited structure) are produced by methods that are at least partly random. The new tentative theories must, of course, lead to at least some results that conflict with those of the original theories—must, therefore, be incompatible with the original theories—or they could not hope to deal with the negative experimental results faced by the original theories. A natural selection from the new tentative theories then follows, allowing only the more well-adapted theories to survive and be transmitted in turn.

Thus, according to the evolutionary model of scientific development, the new theories in a field are *replacements of*, rather than additions to, older theories in the field. In this sense the development of the field is not cumulative. But in another sense, we are told, that development *is* cumulative, for the new theories in a field typically yield results at least as good as those of their predecessors in all those areas in which the predecessors were successful, while yielding different and better results in other areas as well. Thus, the new theories typically preserve the successes of their predecessors while adding to them, allowing a closer adaptation to nature. Indeed, according to the evolutionary model, this preservation of old successes and addition of new successes is the mark of scientific progress, allowing rational assessment of scientific change.

In "The Rationality of Scientific Revolutions," Karl Popper sets out the evolutionary model of scientific development.

The Revolutionary Model of Scientific Development

According to the revolutionary model of scientific development associated with Thomas Kuhn, the kind of cumulative scientific development described in the evolutionary model never really occurs. After all, we are told, the new theories that replace older theories give scientists new ways of thinking about the world, new ways of describing the world, including observable objects and events, even new ways of seeing the world. Indeed, in a sense, the new theories give scientists new worlds to investigate—a Newtonian world in which objects naturally move in straight lines rather than a Galilean world in which they naturally move in circles, or an Einsteinian world in which the shape, size, mass, and other properties of objects vary with one's frame of reference rather than a Newtonian world in which such properties are intrinsic to their objects. Such new theories, moreover, give scientists new methods of investigating these new worlds—for example, rules of inference that allow the postulation of unobservable objects rather than rules of inference that preclude the postulation of such objects. Such new theories also give scientists new goals to pursue when investigating these new worlds, such as the goal of explaining phenomena in terms of entities and processes that are better understood than what is to be explained, or that can be represented by mechanical models, or that are picturable, or the like.

The conclusion, according to the revolutionary model, is that when theories change, the world of scientists, their methods, and their goals, and thus, the successes these allow, change as well. The historical development of a scientific field is thus a succession of scientific revolutions, a succession, that is, of radical shifts of theory and associated fact, methods, and goals, with (unlike the cumulative model) no progress toward one complete set of truths about the world, and (unlike the evolutionary model) no progress toward ever more successful accounts of the world. Progress nonetheless occurs. It occurs between scientific revolutions, as each new theory is developed and extended to new areas of application. And it occurs across scientific revolutions as well. At least the scientific community most intimately involved with a revolutionary change of theory would represent that change as progress, and, we are told, as practitioners of the relevant specialty they are the ones best fitted by training and experience to judge.

In "The Function of Dogma in Scientific Research" and "The Nature and Necessity of Scientific Revolutions," Thomas Kuhn gives his now-classic defense of the revolutionary model of scientific development.

The Gradualist Model of Scientific Development

The gradualist model of scientific development espoused by Larry Laudan presents yet another account of scientific change. According to this account, new theories have given scientists new worlds to investigate, but, as a matter of historical fact, they have not always given scientists new methods of investigating these new worlds, or new goals to pursue when investigating them. Indeed, we are told, scientific theories, methods, and goals have tended to function as independent elements in the history of science. Sometimes the theories of a scientific field have changed, sometimes its methods, and sometimes its goals. Occasionally two of these elements have changed simultaneously. But rarely have all three changed at once. To be sure, the great transitions in the history of science—for example, from an Aristotelian to a Newtonian worldview, or from nineteenth-century mechanistic psychology to psychoanalysis—that did involve changes of all three kinds of elements, have appeared to us as abrupt Kuhnian revolutionary changes because our characterizations of these changes have compressed or telescoped a number of gradual changes (one element at a time) into one abrupt change.

The historical development of a scientific field, according to the gradualist model, is thus a succession of separate changes of theory, methods, and goals— that is, a more gradual version of the kind of development described in the revolutionary model. Like the revolutionary model (and unlike the cumulative model) the gradualist model allows no progress toward one complete set of truths about the world, and like the revolutionary model (and unlike the evolutionary model) it allows no progress toward ever more successful accounts of the world. But unlike the revolutionary model it allows progress of another sort. Thus, if a scientific community's methods fail to justify their theories, or if their methods fail to promote their goals, or if their goals prove to be utopian, the scientific community will have compelling reasons for replacing one element or another of their worldview with an element that does the job better. And, once made, that replacement will represent progress. In short, the gradualist model, unlike the revolutionary model, allows the sort of progress that occurs when a change of one component of a scientific field (for example, its methods) occurs, and is rationally justified, given the character of its other components (its theories and goals).

In "Dissecting the Holist Picture of Scientific Change," Larry Laudan argues for the gradualist model of scientific development.

Summary

We have now considered four models of scientific development—the cumulative model, the evolutionary model, the revolutionary model, and the gradualist model. Each offers us a different account of scientific progress and a correspondingly different account of the typical historical development of scientific fields. Thus, according to the cumulative model, a scientific field progresses when it gains new empirical laws to explain its facts, or new theories to explain its empirical laws or other theories, and the typical historical development of a scientific field is a succession of such additions. According to the evolutionary model, a scientific field progresses when it replaces current theories with new, more successful theories, and the typical historical development of a scientific field is a succession of such replacements. According to the revolutionary model, a scientific field progresses when it replaces current theories and associated facts, methods, and goals with new theories and associated facts, methods, and goals, and the typical historical development of a scientific field is a succession of such radical replacements. And finally, according to the gradualist model, a scientific field progresses when it justifiably replaces current theories or methods or goals with new theories or methods or goals, and the typical historical development of a scientific field is a succession of such limited replacements.

How do you choose among these alternative models of scientific development? Obviously a careful reading of each of the selections that follow will be helpful, particularly if you pay close attention to the reasons given by each author for his position, and the examples offered in support or illustration. You might then consider how closely each model fits selected noncontroversial examples of scientific progress. These might be cases the authors themselves take up, or cases already familiar to you or in which you have an interest. Furthermore, how closely does each model fit other cases in other scientific fields? Bear in mind that a model that fits one scientific field fairly well, at least for some part of its history, may not fit other scientific fields nearly as well (not every scientific field may develop in the same way), so that we may need different models of scientific development for different scientific fields. And bear in mind that some hybrid of the different models, or some model of your own creation, might be better yet.

CARL G. HEMPEL

Explanation in Science

Introduction

Among the diverse factors that have encouraged and sustained scientific inquiry through its long history are two pervasive human concerns which provide, I think, the basic motivation for all scientific research. One of these is man's persistent desire to improve his strategic position in the world by means of dependable methods for predicting and, whenever possible, controlling the events that occur in it. The extent to which science has been able to satisfy this urge is reflected impressively in the vast and steadily widening range of its technological applications. But besides this practical concern, there is a second basic motivation for the scientific quest, namely, man's insatiable intellectual curiosity, his deep concern to *know* the world he lives in, and to *explain*, and thus to *understand*, the unending flow of phenomena it presents to him.

In times past questions as to the *what* and the *why* of the empirical world were often answered by myths; and to some extent, this is so even in our time. But gradually, the myths are displaced by the concepts, hypotheses, and theories developed in the various branches of empirical science, including the natural sciences, psychology, and sociological as well as historical inquiry. What is the general character of the understanding attainable by these means, and what is its potential scope? In this paper I will try to shed some light on these questions by examining what seem to me the two basic types of explanation offered by the natural sciences. . . .

Two Basic Types of Scientific Explanation

Deductive-Nomological Explanation

In his book, *How We Think*,[1] John Dewey describes an observation he made one day when, washing dishes, he took some glass tumblers out of the hot soap suds and put them upside

From "Explanation in Science and in History," by Carl G. Hempel, pp. 9–16, in *Frontiers of Science and Philosophy*, Robert G. Colodny, Ed., © 1962 by The University of Pittsburgh Press. Reprinted by permission of The University of Pittsburgh Press.

down on a plate: he noticed that soap bubbles emerged from under the tumblers' rims, grew for a while, came to a standstill, and finally receded inside the tumblers. Why did this happen? The explanation Dewey outlines comes to this: In transferring a tumbler to the plate, cool air is caught in it; this air is gradually warmed by the glass, which initially has the temperature of the hot suds. The warming of the air is accompanied by an increase in its pressure, which in turn produces an expansion of the soap film between the plate and the rim. Gradually, the glass cools off, and so does the air inside, with the result that the soap bubbles recede.

This explanatory account may be regarded as an argument to the effect that the event to be explained (let me call it the explanandum-event) was to be expected by reason of certain explanatory facts. These may be divided into two groups: (i) particular facts and (ii) uniformities expressed by general laws. The first group includes facts such as these: the tumblers had been immersed, for some time, in soap suds of a temperature considerably higher than that of the surrounding air; they were put, upside down, on a plate on which a puddle of soapy water had formed, providing a connecting soap film, etc. The second group of items presupposed in the argument includes the gas laws and various other laws that have not been explicitly suggested concerning the exchange of heat between bodies of different temperature, the elastic behavior of soap bubbles, etc. If we imagine these various presuppositions explicitly spelled out, the idea suggests itself of construing the explanation as a deductive argument of this form:

$$(D) \qquad \frac{\begin{array}{c} C_1, C_2 \ldots, C_k \\ L_1, L_2 \ldots, L_r \end{array}}{E}$$

Here, $C_1, C_2 \ldots, C_k$ are statements describing the particular facts invoked; $L_1, L_2 \ldots, L_r$ are general laws: jointly, these statements will be said to form the explanans. The conclusion E is a statement describing the explanandum-event; let me call it the explanandum-statement, and let me use the word "explanandum" to refer either to E or to the event described by it.

The kind of explanation thus characterized I will call *deductive-nomological explanation*; for it amounts to a deductive subsumption of the explanandum under principles which have the character of general laws: it answers the question "*Why* did the explanandum event occur?" by showing that the event resulted from the particular circumstances specified in $C_1, C_2, \ldots, C_k$ in accordance with the laws $L_1, L_2 \ldots, L_r$. This conception of explanation, as exhibited in schema (D), has therefore been referred to as the covering law model, or as the deductive model, of explanation.[2]

A good many scientific explanations can be regarded as deductive-nomological in character. Consider, for example, the explanation of mirror-images, of rainbows, or of the appearance that a spoon handle is bent at the point where it emerges from a glass of water: in all these cases, the explanandum is deductively subsumed under the laws of reflection and refraction. Similarly, certain aspects of free fall and of planetary motion can be accounted for by deductive subsumption under Galileo's or Kepler's laws.

In the illustrations given so far the explanatory laws had, by and large, the character of empirical generalizations connecting different observable aspects of the phenomena under scrutiny: angle of incidence with angle of reflection or refraction, distance covered with falling time, etc. But science raises the question "Why?" also with respect to the uniformities expressed by such laws, and often answers it in basically the same manner, namely, by subsuming the uniformities under more inclusive laws, and eventually under comprehensive theories. For example, the question, "Why do Galileo's and Kepler's laws hold?" is answered by showing that these laws are but special consequences of the Newtonian laws of motion and of gravitation; and these, in turn, may be explained by subsumption under the more comprehensive general theory of relativity. Such subsumption under broader laws or theories usually increases both the breadth and the depth of our scientific understanding. There is an increase in breadth, or scope, because the new explanatory principles cover a broader range of phenomena; for example, Newton's principles govern free fall on the earth and on other celestial bodies, as well as the motions of planets, comets, and artificial satellites, the movements of pendulums, tidal changes, and various other phenomena. And the increase thus effected in the depth of our understanding is strikingly reflected in the fact that, in the light of more advanced explanatory principles, the original empirical laws are usually seen to hold only approximately, or within certain limits. For example, Newton's theory implies that the factor g in Galileo's law, $s = \frac{1}{2}gt^2$, is not strictly a constant for free fall near the surface of the earth; and that, since every planet undergoes gravitational attraction not only from the sun, but also from the other planets, the planetary orbits are not strictly ellipses, as stated in Kepler's laws.

One further point deserves brief mention here. An explanation of a particular event is often conceived as specifying its *cause*, or causes. Thus, the account outlined in our first illustration might be held to explain the growth and the recession of the soap bubbles by showing that the phenomenon was *caused* by a rise and a subsequent drop of the temperature of the air trapped in the tumblers. Clearly, however, these temperature changes provide the requisite explanation only in conjunction with certain other conditions, such as the presence of a soap film, practically constant pressure of the air surrounding the glasses, etc. Accordingly, in the context of explanation, a cause must be allowed to consist in a more or less complex set of particular circumstances; these might be described by a set of sentences: C_1, C_2, . . . , C_k. And, as suggested by the principle "Same cause, same effect," the assertion that

those circumstances jointly caused a given event described, let us say, by a sentence E— implies that whenever and wherever circumstances of the kind in question occur, an event of the kind to be explained comes about. Hence, the given causal explanation implicitly claims that there are general laws—such as L_1, L_2 . . . , L_r in schema (D)—by virtue of which the occurrence of the causal antecedents mentioned in C_1, C_2, . . . , C_k is a sufficient condition for the occurrence of the event to be explained. Thus, the relation between causal factors and effect is reflected in schema (D): causal explanation is deductive-nomological in character. (However, the customary formulations of causal and other explanations often do not explicitly specify all the relevant laws and particular facts: to this point, we will return later.)

The converse does not hold: there are deductive-nomological explanations which would not normally be counted as causal. For one thing, the subsumption of laws, such as Galileo's or Kepler's laws, under more comprehensive principles is clearly not causal in character: we speak of causes only in reference to *particular* facts or events, and not in reference to *universal facts* as expressed by general laws. But not even all deductive-nomological explanations of particular facts or events will qualify as causal; for in a causal explanation some of the explanatory circumstances will temporally precede the effect to be explained: and there are explanations of type (D) which lack this characteristic. For example, the pressure which a gas of specified mass possesses at a given time might be explained by reference to its temperature and its volume at the same time, in conjunction with the gas law which connects simultaneous values of the three parameters.[3]

In conclusion, let me stress once more the important role of laws in deductive-nomological explanation: the laws connect the explanandum event with the particular conditions cited in the explanans, and this is what confers upon the latter the status of explanatory (and, in some cases, causal) factors in regard to the phenomenon to be explained.

Probabilistic Explanation

In deductive-nomological explanation as schematized in (D), the laws and theoretical principles involved are of *strictly universal form*: they assert that in *all* cases in which certain specified conditions are realized an occurrence of such and such a kind will result; the law that any metal, when heated under constant pressure, will increase in volume, is a typical example; Galileo's, Kepler's, Newton's, Boyle's, and Snell's laws, and many others, are of the same character.

Now let me turn next to a second basic type of scientific explanation. This kind of explanation, too, is nomological, i.e., it accounts for a given phenomenon by reference to general laws or theoretical principles; but some or all of these are of *probabilistic-statistical form*, i.e., they are, generally speaking, assertions to the effect that if certain specified conditions are realized, then an occurrence of such and such a kind will come about with such and such a statistical probability.

For example, the subsiding of a violent attack of hay fever in a given case might well be attributed to, and thus explained by reference to, the administration of 8 milligrams of chlor-trimeton. But if we wish to connect this antecedent event with the explanandum, and thus to establish its explanatory significance for the latter, we cannot invoke a universal law to the effect that the administration of 8 milligrams of that antihistamine will invariably terminate a hay fever attack: this simply is not so. What can be asserted is only a generalization to the effect that administration of the drug will be followed by relief with high statistical probability, i.e., roughly speaking, with a high relative frequency in the long run. The resulting explanans will thus be of the following type:

> John Doe had a hay fever attack and took 8 milligrams of chlor-trimeton.

The probability for subsidence of a hay fever attack upon administration of 8 milligrams of chlor-trimeton is high.

Clearly, this explanans does not deductively imply the explanandum, "John Doe's hay fever attack subsided"; the truth of the explanans makes the truth of the explanandum not certain (as it does in a deductive-nomological explanation) but only more or less likely or, perhaps, "practically" certain.

Reduced to its simplest essentials, a probabilistic explanation thus takes the following form:

$$Fi$$
(P) $\underline{p(O,F) \text{ is very high}}$ makes very likely
$$Oi$$

The explanandum, expressed by the statement "Oi," consists in the fact that in the particular instance under consideration, here called i (e.g., John Doe's allergic attack), an outcome of kind O (subsidence) occurred. This is explained by means of two explanans-statements. The first of these, "Fi," corresponds to $C_1, C_2, \ldots, C_k$ in (D); it states that in case i, the factors F (which may be more or less complex) were realized. The second expresses a law of probabilistic form, to the effect that the statistical probability for outcome O to occur in cases where F is realized is very high (close to 1). The double line separating explanandum from explanans is to indicate that, in contrast to the case of deductive-nomological explanation, the explanans does not logically imply the explanandum, but only confers a high likelihood upon it. The concept of likelihood here referred to must be clearly distinguished from that of statistical probability, symbolized by "p" in our schema. A statistical probability is, roughly speaking, the long run relative frequency with which an occurrence of a given kind (say, F) is accompanied by an "outcome" of a specified kind (say, O). Our likelihood, on the other hand, is a relation (capable of gradations) not between kinds of occurrences, but between statements. The likelihood referred to in (P) may be characterized as the strength of the inductive support, or the degree of rational credibility, which the explanans confers upon the explanandum; or, in Carnap's terminology, as the *logical,* or *inductive,* (in contrast to statistical) *probability* which the explanandum possesses relative to the explanans.

Thus, probabilistic explanation, just like explanation in the manner of schema (D), is nomological in that it presupposes general laws; but because these laws are of statistical rather than of strictly universal form, the resulting explanatory arguments are inductive rather than deductive in character. An inductive argument of this kind *explains* a given phenomenon by showing that, in view of certain particular events and certain statistical laws, its occurrence was to be expected with high logical, or inductive, probability.

By reason of its inductive character, probabilistic explanation differs from its deductive-nomological counterpart in several other important respects; for example, its explanans may confer upon the explanandum a more or less high degree of inductive support; in this sense, probabilistic explanation admits of degrees, whereas deductive-nomological explanation appears as an either-or affair: a given set of universal laws and particular statements either does or does not imply a given explanandum statement. A fuller examination of these differences, however, would lead us far afield and is not required for the purposes of this paper.[4]

One final point: the distinction here suggested between deductive-nomological and probabilistic explanation might be questioned on the ground that, after all, the universal laws invoked in a deductive explanation can have been established only on the basis of a finite body of evidence, which surely affords no exhaustive verification, but only more or less strong probability for it; and that, therefore, all scientific laws have to be regarded as probabilistic. This argument, however confounds a logical issue with an epistemological one: it fails to distinguish properly between the *claim* made by a given law-statement and the *degree of confirmation,* or *probability,* which it possesses on the available evidence. It is quite true that statements expressing laws of either kind can be only incompletely confirmed by any given finite set—however large—of data about particular facts; but law-statements of the two different types make claims of different kinds, which are reflected in their logical forms: roughly, a universal law-statement of the simplest kind asserts that *all* elements of an indefinitely large reference class (e.g., copper objects) have a certain characteristic (e.g., that of being good conductors of electricity); while statistical law-statements assert that in the long run, a specified proportion of the members of the reference class have some specified property. And our distinction of two types of law and, concomitantly, of two types of scientific explanation, is based on this difference in claim as reflected in the difference of form.

The great scientific importance of probabilistic explanation is eloquently attested to by the extensive and highly successful explanatory use that has been made of fundamental laws of statistical form in genetics, statistical mechanics, and quantum theory.

Elliptic and Partial Explanations: Explanation Sketches

As I mentioned earlier, the conception of deductive-nomological explanation reflected in our schema (D) is often referred to as the covering law model, or the deductive model, of explanation: similarly, the conception underlying schema (P) might be called the probabilistic or the inductive-statistical, model of explanation. The term "model" can serve as a useful reminder that the two types of explanation as characterized above constitute ideal types or theoretical idealizations and are not intended to reflect the manner in which working scientists actually formulate their explanatory accounts. Rather, they are meant to provide explications, or rational reconstructions, or theoretical models, of certain modes of scientific explanation.

In this respect our models might be compared to the concept of mathematical proof (within a given theory) as construed in metamathematics. This concept, too, may be regarded as a theoretical model: it is not intended to provide a descriptive account of how proofs are formulated in the writings of mathematicians: most of these actual formulations fall short of rigorous and, as it were, ideal, metamathematical standards. But the theoretical model has certain other functions: it exhibits the rationale of mathematical proofs by revealing the logical connections underlying the successive steps; it provides standards for a critical appraisal of any proposed proof constructed within the mathematical system to which the model refers; and it affords a basis for a precise and far-reaching theory of proof, provability, decidability, and related concepts. I think the two models of explanation can fulfill the same functions, if only on a much more modest scale. For example, the arguments presented in constructing the models give an indication of the sense in which the models exhibit the rationale and the logical structure of the explanations they are intended to represent. . . .

Notes

1. See John Dewey, *How We Think* (Boston, New York, Chicago, 1910), chapter 6.
2. For a fuller presentation of the model and for further references, see, for example, C. G. Hempel and P. Oppenhiem, "Studies in the Logic of Explanation," *Philosophy of Science* 15 (1948), pp. 135–75 (Sections 1–7 of this article, which contain all the fundamentals of the presentation, are reprinted in H. Feigl and M. Brodbeck, eds., *Readings in the Philosophy of Science* (New York, 1953)—The suggestive term "covering-law model" is W. Dray's; cf. his *Laws and Explanation in History* (Oxford 1957), chapter 1. . . .)
3. The relevance of the covering-law model to causal explanation is examined more fully in section 4 of C. G. Hempel, "Deductive-Nomological *vs.* Statistical Explanation," in H. Feigl, et al., eds., *Minnesota Studies in the Philosophy of Science*, vol 3 (Minneapolis: University of Minnesota Press, 1962).
4. The concept of probabilistic explanation, and some of the peculiar logical and methodological problems engendered by it, are examined in some detail in Part II of the essay cited in note 3.

PAUL OPPENHEIM AND HILARY PUTNAM

Unity of Science as a Working Hypothesis

Introduction

The expression "Unity of Science" is often encountered, but its precise content is difficult to specify in a satisfactory manner. It is the aim of this paper to formulate a precise concept of Unity of Science and to examine to what extent that unity can be attained.

A concern with Unity of Science hardly needs justification. We are guided especially by the conviction that Science of Science, i.e., the meta-scientific study of major aspects of science, is the natural means for counterbalancing specialization by promoting the integration of scientific knowledge. The desirability of this goal is widely recognized—for example, many universities have programs with this end in view—but it is often pursued by means different from the one just mentioned, and the conception of the Unity of Science might be especially suited as an organizing principle for an enterprise of this kind.

As a preliminary, we will distinguish, in order of increasing strength, three broad concepts of Unity of Science:

First, Unity of Science in the weakest sense is attained to the extent to which all the terms of science[1] are reduced to the terms of some one discipline (e.g., physics, or psychology). This concept of *Unity of Language* (10) may be replaced by a number of sub-concepts depending on the manner in which one specifies the notion of "reduction" involved. Certain authors, for example, construe reduction as the *definition* of the terms of science by means of those in the selected basic discipline. . . .

Second, Unity of Science in a stronger sense (because it implies Unity of Language, whereas the reverse is not the case) is represented by *Unity of Laws* (10). It is attained to the extent to which the laws of science become reduced to the laws of some one discipline. If the ideal of such an all-comprehensive explanatory system were realized, one could call it *Unitary*

From "Concepts, Theories, and the Mind-body Problem," in *Minnesota Studies in the Philosophy of Science*, Vol. II, Herbert Feigl, Michael Scriven, and Grover Maxwell, Eds., pp. 3–36. Copyright © 1958 by University of Minnesota Press. Reprinted by permission.

Science (15, 16, 17, 70). The exact meaning of "Unity of Laws" depends, again, on the concept of "reduction" employed.

Third, Unity of Science in the strongest sense is realized if the laws of science are not only reduced to the laws of some one discipline, but the laws of that discipline are in some intuitive sense "unified" or "connected." It is difficult to see how this last requirement can be made precise, and it will not be imposed here. . . .

In the present paper, the term "Unity of Science" will be used in two senses to refer, first, to an ideal *state* of science, and, second, to a pervasive *trend* within science, seeking the attainment of that ideal.

In the first sense, "Unity of Science" means the state of unitary science. It involves the two constituents mentioned above: unity of vocabulary, or "Unity of Language," and unity of explanatory principles, or "Unity of Laws." That Unity of Science, in this sense, can be fully realized constitutes an over-arching meta-scientific hypothesis which enables one to see a unity in scientific activities that might otherwise appear disconnected or unrelated, and which encourages the construction of a unified body of knowledge.

In the second sense, Unity of Science exists as a trend within scientific inquiry, whether or not unitary science is ever attained, and notwithstanding the simultaneous existence (and, of course, legitimacy) of other, even *incompatible*, trends. . . .

Unity of Science and Micro-reduction

In this paper we shall employ a concept of reduction introduced by Kemeny and Oppenheim in their paper on the subject (41), to which the reader is referred for a more detailed exposition. The principal requirements may be summarized as follows: Given two theories T_1

and T_2, T_2 is said to be *reduced* to T_1 if and only if:

1. The vocabulary of T_2 contains terms not in the vocabulary of T_1.

2. Any observational data explainable by T_2 are explainable by T_1.

3. T_1 is at least as well systematized as T_2. (T_1 is normally more complicated than T_2; but this is allowable, because the reducing theory normally explains more than the reduced theory. However, the "ratio" so to speak, of simplicity to explanatory power should be at least as great in the case of the reducing theory as in the case of the reduced theory.)[2]

Kemeny and Oppenheim also define the reduction of a branch of science B_2 by another branch B_1 (e.g., the reduction of chemistry to physics). Their procedure is as follows: Take the accepted theories of B_2 at a given time t as T_2. Then B_2 *is reduced to B_1 at time t* if and only if there is some theory T_1 in B_1 at t such that T_1 reduces T_2 (41). Analogously, if *some* of the theories of B_2 are reduced by some T_1 belonging to branch B_1 at t, we shall speak of a *partial reduction* of B_2 to B_1 at t. This approach presupposes (1) the familiar assumption that some division of the total vocabulary of both branches into theoretical and observational terms is given, and (2) that the two branches have the same observational vocabulary.

The essential feature of a *micro*-reduction is that the branch B_1 deals with parts of the objects dealt with by B_2. We must suppose that corresponding to each branch we have a specified universe of discourse U_{Bi};[3] and that we have a part–whole relation, PT (66; 67, especially p. 91). Under the following conditions we shall say that the reduction of B_2 to B_1[4] is a *micro-reduction:* B_2 is reduced to B_1; and the objects in the universe of discourse of B_2 are wholes which possess a decomposition (66; 67, especially p. 91) into proper parts, all of which belong to the universe of discourse of B_1. For example, let us suppose B_2 is a branch of science which has multicellular living things as its universe of discourse. Let B_1 be a branch with cells as its universe of discourse. Then the things in the universe of discourse of B_2 can be decomposed into proper parts belonging to the universe of discourse of B_1. If, in addition, it is the case that B_1 reduces B_2 at the time t, we shall say that B_1 *micro-reduces* B_2 *at time t.*

We shall also say that a branch B_1 is a *potential micro-reducer* of a branch B_2 if the objects in the universe of discourse of B_2 are wholes which possess a decomposition into proper parts, all of which belong to the universe of discourse of B_1. The definition is the same as the definition of "micro-reduces" except for the omission of the clause "B_2 is reduced to B_1."

Any microreduction constitutes a step in the direction of *Unity of Language* in science. For, if B_1 reduces B_2, it explains everything that B_2 does (and normally, more besides). Then, even if we cannot define B_1 analogues for some of the theoretical terms of B_2, we can *use B_1 in place of B_2.* Thus any reduction, in the sense explained, permits a "reduction" of the total vocabulary of science by making it possible to dispense with some terms. Not every reduction moves in the direction of Unity of Science; for instance reductions *within* a branch lead to a simplification of the vocabulary of science, but they do not necessarily lead in the direction of Unity of Science as we have characterized it (although they may at times fit into that trend). However, *micro*-reductions, and even partial micro-reductions, insofar as they permit us to replace some of the terms of one branch of science by terms of another, *do* move in this direction.

Likewise, the micro-reduction of B_2 to B_1 moves in the direction of *Unity of Laws*; for it "reduces" the total number of scientific laws by making it possible, in principle, to dispense with the laws of B_2 and explain the relevant observations by using B_1.

The relations "micro-reduces" and "potential micro-reducer" have very simple properties: (1) they are transitive (this follows from the transitivity of the relations "reduces" and "Pt"); (2) they are irreflexive (no branch can micro-reduce itself); (3) they are asymmetric (if B_1 micro-reduces B_2, B_2 never micro-reduces B_1). . . .

The just-mentioned . . . property of the relation "micro-reduces"—its transitivity—is of great importance for the program of Unity of Science. It means that micro-reductions have a *cumulative* character. That is, if a branch B_3 is micro-reduced to B_2, and B_2 is in turn micro-reduced to B_1, then B_3 is automatically micro-reduced to B_1. This simple fact is sometimes overlooked in objections to the theoretical possibility of attaining unitary science by means of micro-reduction. Thus it has been contended that one manifestly cannot explain human behavior by reference to the laws of atomic physics. It would indeed be fantastic to suppose that the simplest regularity in the field of psychology could be explained directly— i.e., "skipping" intervening branches of science[5]—by employing subatomic theories. But one may believe in the attainability of unitary science without thereby committing oneself to this absurdity. It is not absurd to suppose that psychological laws may eventually be explained in terms of the behavior of individual neurons in the brain; that the behavior of individual cells—including neurons—may eventually be explained in terms of their biochemical constitution; and that the behavior of molecules—including the macro-molecules that make up living cells—may eventually be explained in terms of atomic physics. If this is achieved, then psychological laws will have, *in principle*, been reduced to laws of atomic physics, although it would nevertheless be hopelessly impractical to try to derive the behavior of a single human being directly from his constitution in terms of elementary particles.

Unitary science certainly does not exist today. But will it ever be attained? It is useful to divide this question into two subquestions: (1) If unitary science can be attained at all, *how* can it be attained? (2) *Can* it be attained at all?

First of all, there are various abstractly possible ways in which unitary science might be attained. However, it seems very doubtful, to say the least, that a branch B_2 could be reduced to a branch B_1, if the things in the universe of discourse of B_2 are not themselves in the universe of discourse of B_1 and also do not possess a decomposition into parts in the universe of discourse of B_1. ("They don't speak about the same things.")

It does not follow that B_1 must be a potential *micro*-reducer of B_2, i.e., that all reductions are micro-reductions.

There are many cases in which the reducing theory and the reduced theory belong to the same branch, or to branches with the same universe of discourse. When we come, however, to branches with different universes—say, physics and psychology—it seems clear that the possibility of reduction depends on the existence of a structural connection between the universes via the "Pt" relation. Thus one cannot plausibly suppose—for the present at least—that the behavior of inorganic matter is explainable by reference to psychological laws; for inorganic materials do not consist of living parts. One supposes that psychology may be reducible to physics, but not that physics may be reducible to psychology!

Thus, the only method of attaining unitary science that appears to be seriously available at present is micro-reduction.

To turn now to our second question, *can* unitary science be attained? We certainly do not wish to maintain that it has been *established* that this is the case. But it does not follow, as some philosophers seem to think, that a tentative acceptance of the hypothesis that unitary science can be attained is therefore a mere "act of faith." We believe that this hypothesis is *credible*;[6] and we shall attempt to support this in the latter part

of this paper, by providing empirical, methodological, and pragmatic reasons in its support. We therefore think the assumption that unitary science can be attained through cumulative micro-reduction recommends itself *as a working hypothesis*.[7] That is, we believe that it is in accord with the standards of reasonable scientific judgment to tentatively accept this hypothesis and to work on the assumption that further progress can be made in this direction, without claiming that its truth has been established, or denying that success may finally elude us.

Reductive Levels

As a basis for our further discussion, we wish to consider now the possibility of ordering branches in such a way as to indicate the major potential micro-reductions standing between the present situation and the state of unitary science. The most natural way to do this is by their universes of discourse. We offer, therefore, a system of *reductive levels* so chosen that a branch with the things of a given level as its universe of discourse will always be a potential micro-reducer of any branch with things of the next higher level (if there is one) as its universe of discourse.

Certain conditions of adequacy follow immediately from our aim. Thus:

1. There must be several levels.

2. The number of levels must be finite.

3. There must be a unique lowest level (i.e., a unique "beginner" under the relation "potential micro-reducer"); this means that success at transforming all the *potential* micro-reductions connecting these branches into *actual* micro-reductions must, *ipso facto*, mean reduction to a single branch.

4. Any thing of any level except the lowest must possess a decomposition into things belonging to the next lower level. In this sense each level will be as it were a "common denominator" for the level immediately above it.

5. Nothing on any level should have a part on any higher level.

6. The levels must be selected in a way which is "natural"[8] and justifiable from the standpoint of present-day empirical science. In particular, the step from any one of our reductive levels to the next lower level must correspond to what is, scientifically speaking, a crucial step in the trend toward overall physicalistic reduction.

The accompanying list gives the levels we shall employ;[9] the reader may verify that the six conditions we have listed are all satisfied.

6	Social groups
5	(Multicellular) living things
4	Cells
3	Molecules
2	Atoms
1	Elementary particles

Any whole which possesses a decomposition into parts, all of which are on a given level, will be counted as also belonging to that level. Thus each level includes all higher levels. Thus each level includes all higher levels. However, the highest level to which a thing belongs will be considered the "proper" level of that thing. . . .

We maintain that each of our levels is *necessary* in the sense that it would be utopian to suppose that one might reduce all of the major theories or a whole branch concerned with any one of our six levels to a theory concerned with a lower level, *skipping* entirely the *immediately* lower level; and we maintain that our levels are *sufficient* in the sense that it would *not* be utopian to suppose that a major theory on any one of our levels *might* be directly reduced to the next lower level. (Although this is *not* to deny that it may be convenient, in special cases, to introduce intervening steps.) . . .

The Credibility of Our Working Hypothesis

. . . Among the factors on which the degree of credibility of *any* empirical hypothesis depends are (40, p. 307) the *simplicity* of the hypothesis,

the *variety* of the evidence, its *reliability*, and, last but not least, the *factual support* afforded by the evidence. We proceed to discuss each of these factors.

As for the *simplicity* of the hypothesis that unitary science can be attained, it suffices to consider the traditional alternatives mentioned by those who oppose it. "Hypotheses" such as Psychism and Neo-Vitalism assert that the various objects studied by contemporary science have special parts or attributes, unknown to present-day science, in addition to those indicated in our system of reductive levels. For example, men are said to have not only cells as parts; there is also an immaterial "psyche"; living things are animated by "entelechies" or "vital forces"; social groups are moved by "group minds." But, in none of these cases are we provided *at present* with postulates or coordinating definitions which would permit the derivation of testable predictions. Hence, the claims made for the hypothetical entities just mentioned lack any clear scientific meaning; and as a consequence, the question of supporting evidence cannot even be raised.

On the other hand, if the effort at micro-reduction should seem to fail, we cannot preclude the introduction of theories postulating presently unknown relevant parts or presently unknown relevant attributes for some or all of the objects studied by science. Such theories are perfectly admissible, provided they have genuine explanatory value. For example, Dalton's chemical theory of molecules might not be reducible to the best available theory of atoms at a given time if the latter theory ignores the existence of the electrical properties of atoms. Thus the hypothesis of micro-reducibility,[10] as the meaning is specified at a particular time, may be false because of the insufficiency of the theoretical apparatus of the reducing branch.

Of course, a new working hypothesis of micro-reducibility, obtained by enlarging the list of attributes associated with the lowest level, might then be correct. However, if there are presently unknown attributes of a more radical kind (e.g., attributes which are relevant for explaining the behavior of living, but not of non-living things), then no such simple "repair" would seem possible. In this sense, Unity of Science is an alternative to the view that it will eventually be necessary to *bifurcate* the conceptual system of science, by the postulation of new entities or new attributes unrelated to those needed for the study of inanimate phenomena.

The requirement that there be *variety* of evidence assumes a simple form in our present case. If all the past successes referred to a single pair of levels, then this would be poor evidence indeed that theories concerning each level can be reduced by theories concerning a lower level. For example, if all the past successes were on the atomic level, we should hardly regard as justified the inference that laws concerning social groups can be explained by reference to the "individual psychology" of the members of those groups. Thus, the first requirement is that one should be able to provide examples of successful micro-reductions between several pairs of levels, preferably between all pairs.

Second, within a given level what is required is, preferably, examples of different kinds, rather than a repetition of essentially the same example many times. In short, one wants good evidence that *all* the phenomena of the given level can be micro-reduced.

We shall present below a survey of the past successes in each level. This survey is, of course, only a sketch; the successful micro-reductions and projected micro-reductions in biochemistry alone would fill a large book. But even from this sketch it will be apparent, we believe, how great the variety of these successful micro-reductions is in both the respects discussed.

Moreover, we shall, of course, present only evidence from authorities regarded as *reliable* in the particular area from which the theory or experiment involved is drawn.

The important factor *factual support* is discussed only briefly now, because we shall devote to it many of the following pages and would otherwise interrupt our presentation.

The first question raised in connection with any hypothesis is, of course, what *factual* support it possesses; that is, what confirmatory or disconfirmatory evidence is available. The evidence supporting a hypothesis is conveniently subdivided into that providing *direct* and that providing *indirect* factual support. By the direct factual support for a hypothesis we mean, roughly,[11] the proportion of confirmatory as opposed to disconfirmatory instances. By the indirect factual support, we mean the inductive support obtained from other well-confirmed hypotheses that lend credibility to the given hypothesis. . . .

As our hypothesis is that theories of each reductive level can be micro-reduced by theories of the next lower level, a "confirming instance" is simply any successful micro-reduction between any two of our levels. The *direct* factual support for our hypothesis is thus provided by the *past successes* at reducing laws about the things on each level by means of laws referring to the parts on lower (usually, the next lower) levels. In the sequel, we shall survey the past successes with respect to each pair of levels.

As *indirect* factual support, we shall cite evidence supporting the hypothesis that each reductive level is, in evolution and ontogenesis (in a wide sense presently to be specified) prior to the one above it. The hypothesis of *evolution* means here that (for n = 1 . . . 5) there was a time when there were things of level n, but no things of any higher level. This hypothesis is highly speculative on levels 1 and 2; fortunately the micro-reducibility of the molecular to the atomic level and of the atomic level to the elementary particle level is relatively well established on other grounds.

Similarly, the hypothesis of ontogenesis is that, in certain cases, for any *particular* object on level n, there was a time when it did not exist, but when some of its parts on the next lower level existed; and that it developed or was causally produced out of these parts.

The reason for our regarding evolution and ontogenesis as providing indirect factual support for the Unity of Science hypothesis may be formulated as follows:

Let us, as is customary in science, assume causal determination as a guiding principle, i.e., let us assume that things that appear later in time can be accounted for in terms of things and processes at earlier times. Then, if we find that there was a time when a certain whole did not exist, and that things on a lower level came together to form that whole, it is very natural to suppose that the characteristics of the whole can be causally explained by reference to these earlier events and parts; and that the theory of these characteristics can be micro-reduced by a theory involving only characteristics of the parts.

For the same reason, we may cite as further indirect factual support for the hypothesis of empirical Unity of Science the various successes at *synthesizing* things of each level out of things on the next lower level. Synthesis strongly increases the evidence that the characteristics of the whole in question are causally determined by the characteristics, including spatio-temporal arrangement, of its parts by showing that the object is produced, under controlled laboratory conditions, whenever parts with those characteristics are arranged in that way.

The consideration just outlined seems to us to constitute an argument against the view that, as objects of a given level combine to form wholes belonging to a higher level, there appear certain new phenomena which are "emergent" (31, p. 151; 67, p. 93) in the sense of being forever irreducible to laws governing the phenomena on the level of the parts. What our argument opposes is not, of course, the obviously true statement that there are many phenomena which are not reducible by currently available theories pertaining to lower levels; our working hypothesis rejects merely the claim of absolute irreducibility, unless such a claim is supported by a theory which has a sufficiently high degree of credibility; thus far we are not aware of any such theory. It is not sufficient, for example, simply to advance the claim that certain phenomena considered to be specifically human, such as the use of verbal language, in an abstract and generalized way, can never be explained on the basis of neurophysiological theories, or to make the claim that this conceptual capacity distinguishes man in principle and not only in degree from nonhuman animals.

Let us mention in passing certain *pragmatic* and *methodological* points of view which speak in favor of our working hypothesis:

1. It is of *practical* value because it provides a good synopsis of scientific activity and of the relations among the several scientific disciplines.

2. It is, as has often been remarked, *fruitful* in the sense of stimulating many different kinds of scientific research. By way of contrast, belief in the *irreducibility* of various phenomena has yet to yield a single accepted scientific theory.

3. It corresponds *methodologically* to what might be called the "Democritean tendency" in science; that is, the pervasive methodological tendency[12] to try, insofar as is possible, to explain apparently dissimilar phenomena in terms of qualitatively identical parts and their spatio-temporal relations.

Past Successes at Each Level

By comparison with what we shall find on lower levels, the micro-reduction of level 6 to lower ones has not yet advanced very far, especially in regard to human societies. This may have at least two reasons: First of all, the body of well established theoretical knowledge on level 6 is still rather rudimentary, so that there is not much to be micro-reduced. Second, while various precise theories concerning certain special types of phenomena on level 5 have been developed, it seems as if a good deal of further theoretical knowledge concerning other areas on the same level will be needed before reductive success on a larger scale can be expected.[13] However, in the case of certain very primitive groups of organisms, astonishing successes have been achieved. For instance, the differentiation into social castes among certain kinds of insects has been tentatively explained in terms of the secretion of so-called social hormones (3).

Many writers[14] believe that there are some laws common to all forms of animal association, including that of humans. Of greater potential relevance to such laws are experiments dealing with "pecking order" among domestic fowl (25). In particular, experiments showing that the social structure can be influenced by the amount of male hormone in individual birds suggest possible parallels farther up the evolutionary scale.

With respect to the problems of human social organization, as will be seen presently, two things are striking: (1) The most developed body of theory is undoubtedly in the field of *economics*, and this is at present entirely micro-reductionistic in character; (2) The main approaches to *social* theory are *all* likewise of this character. (The technical term *micro-reduction* is not, of course, employed by writers in these fields. However, many writers have discussed "the Principle of Methodological Individualism";[15] and this is nothing more than the special form our working hypothesis takes in application to human social groups.)

In economics, if very weak assumptions are satisfied, it is possible to represent the way in which an individual orders his choices by means of an individual preference function. In terms of these functions, the economist attempts to explain group phenomena, such as

the market, to account for collective consumer behavior, to solve the problems of welfare economics, etc. As theories for which a micro-reductionistic derivation is accepted in economics we could cite all the standard macro-theories, e.g., the theories of the business cycle, theories of currency fluctuation (Gresham's law to the effect that bad money drives out good is a familiar example), the principle of marginal utility, the law of demand, laws connecting change in interest rate with changes in inventory, plans, equipment, etc. The relevant point is while the economist is no longer dependent on the oversimplified assumption of "economic man," the explanation of economic phenomena is still in terms of the preferences, choices, and actions available to *individuals*.

In the realm of *sociology*, one can hardly speak of any major theory as "accepted." But it is of interest to survey some of the major theoretical approaches from the standpoint of micro-reduction.

On the one hand, there is the *economic determinism* represented by Marx and Veblen. In the case of Marx the assumptions of classical economics are openly made: Individuals are supposed—at least on the average, and in the long run—to act in accordance with their material interests. From this assumption, together with a theory of the business cycle which, for all its undoubted originality, Marx based on the classical laws of the market, Marx derives his major laws and predictions. Thus Marxist sociology is micro-reductionistic in the same sense as classical economics and shares the same basic weakness (the assumption of "economic man").

Veblen, although stressing class interests and class divisions as did Marx, introduces some non-economic factors to his sociology. His account is ultimately in terms of individual psychology; his hypothesis of "conspicuous consumption" is a brilliant—and characteristic—example.

Max Weber produced a sociology strongly antithetical to Marx's. Yet each of his explana-

275

tions of group phenomena is ultimately in terms of individual psychology, e.g., in his discussion of political parties, he argues that people *enjoy* working under a "charismatic" leader, etc.

Indeed the psychological (and hence micro-reductionistic) character of the major sociologies (including those of Mannheim, Simmel, etc., as well as the ones mentioned above [47, 75, 82, 91] is often recognized. Thus one may safely say that while there is no one accepted sociological theory, all of these theoretical approaches represent attempted micro-reductions.

Since Schleiden and Schwann (1838/9), it is known that all living things consist of cells. Consequently, explaining the laws valid on level 5 by those on the cell level means micro-reducing all phenomena of plants and animals to level 4.

As instances of past successes in connection with level 5 we have chosen to cite, in preference to other types of example, micro-reductions and projected micro-reductions dealing with *central nervous systems* as wholes and nerve cells as parts. Our selection of these examples has not been determined by anthropocentrism. First of all, substantially similar problems arise in the case of multicellular animals, as nearly all of them possess a nervous system; and, second, the question of micro-reducing those aspects of behavior that are controlled by the central nervous system in man and the higher animals is easily the most significative (74, p. 1) one at this level, and therefore most worth discussing.

Very great activity is, in fact, apparent in the direction of micro-reducing the phenomena of the central nervous system. Much of this activity is very recent; and most of it falls under two main headings: *neurology*, and the *logical design of nerve nets*. (Once again, the technical term *microreduction* is not actually employed by workers in these fields. Instead, one finds widespread and lasting discussion concerning the advantages of "molecular" versus "molar"[16] explanations and concerning "reductionism."[17]

Theories constructed by neurologists are the product of highly detailed experimental work in neuroanatomy, neurochemistry, and neurophysiology, including the study of electric activity of the nervous system, e.g., electroencephalography.[18]

As a result of these efforts, it has proved possibly to advance more or less hypothetical explanations on the cellular level for such phenomena as association, memory, motivation, emotional disturbance, and some of the phenomena connected with learning, intelligence, and perception. For example, a theory of the brain has been advanced by Hebb (28) which accounts for all of the above-mentioned phenomena. A classical psychological law, the Weber-Fechner law (insofar as it seems to apply), has likewise been micro-reduced, as a result of the work of Hoagland (32).

We turn now to *the logical design* of nerve nets: The logician Turing[19] proposed (and solved) the problem of giving a characterization of *computing machines* in the widest sense—mechanisms for solving problems by effective series of logical operations. This naturally suggests the idea of seeing whether a "Turing machine" could consist of the elements used in neurological theories of the brain; that is, whether it could consist of a network of neurons. Such a nerve network could then serve as a hypothetical model for the brain.

Such a network was first constructed by McCulloch and Pitts.[20] The basic element is the neuron, which, at any instant, is either *firing* or *not firing* (quiescent). On account of the "all or none" character of the activity of this basic element, the *nerve net* designed by McCulloch and Pitts constitutes, as it were, a digital computer. The various relations of propositional logic can be represented by instituting suitable connections between neurons; and in this way the hypothetical net can be "programmed" to solve any problem that will yield to a predetermined sequence of logical or mathematical operations. McCulloch and Pitts employ approximately 10^4 elements in their net; in this respect they are well below the upper limit set by neurological investigation, since the number of neurons in the brain is estimated to be of the order of magnitude of 10^{10}. In other respects, their model was, however, unrealistic: No allowance is made for time delay, or for random error, both of which are important features of all biological processes.

Nerve nets incorporating both of these features have been designed by von Neumann. Von Neumann's model employs bundles of nerves rather than single nerves to form a network; this permits the simultaneous performance of each operation as many as 20,000 times as a check against error. This technique of constructing a computer is impractical at the level of present-day technology, von Neumann admits, "but quite practical for a perfectly conceivable, more advanced technology, and for the natural relay-organs (neurons). I.e., it merely calls for micro-componentry, which is not at all unnatural as a concept on this level" (85, p. 87). Still further advances in the direction of adapting these models to neurological data are anticipated. In terms of such nerve nets it is possible to give hypothetical micro-reductions for *memory, exact thinking, distinguishing similarity or dissimilarity of stimulus patterns, abstracting* of "essential" components of a stimulus pattern, *recognition of shape* regardless of form *and of chord* regardless of pitch (phenomena of great importance in Gestalt psychology [5, pp. 128, 129, 152]), *purposeful behavior* as controlled by negative feedback, *adaptive behavior*, and *mental disorders*.

It is the task of the neurophysiologist to test these models by investigating the existence of such nets, scanning units, reverberating networks, and pathways of feedback, and to provide physiological evidence of their functioning. Promising studies have been made in this respect.

As past successes in connection with level 4 (i.e., as cases in which phenomena involving whole cells[21] have been explained by theories concerning the molecular level) we shall cite

micro-reductions dealing with three phenomena that have a fundamental character for all of biological science: the *decoding, duplication*, and *mutation* of the genetic information that is ultimately responsible for the development and maintenance of order in the cell. Our objective will be to show that at least one well-worked-out micro-reducing theory has been advanced for each phenomenon.[22] (The special form taken by our working hypothesis on this level is "methodological mechanism.")

Biologists have long had good evidence indicating that the genetic information in the cell's nucleus—acting as an "inherited message"—exerts its control over cell biochemistry through the production of specific protein catalysts (enzymes) that mediate particular steps (reactions) in the chemical order that is the cell's life. The problem of "*decoding*" the control information in the nucleus thus reduces to how the specific molecules that comprise it serve to specify the construction of specific protein catalysts. The problem of *duplication* (one aspect of the overall problem of inheritance) reduces to how the molecules of genetic material can be copied—like so many "blueprints." And the problem of *mutation* (elementary steps in the evolution of new inheritable messages) reduces to how "new" forms of the genetic molecules can arise.

In the last twenty years evidence has accumulated implicating *desoxyribose nucleic acid* (DNA) as the principal "message-carrying" molecule and constituting the genetic material of the chromosomes. Crick and Watson's[23] brilliant analysis of DNA structure leads to powerful micro-reducing theories that explain the decoding and duplication of DNA. It is known that the giant molecules that make up the nucleic acids have, like proteins (42, 58, 59), the structure of a backbone with side groups attached. But, whereas the proteins are polypeptides, or chains of amino-acid residues (slightly over 20 kinds of amino acids are known), the nucleic acids have a phosphate-sugar back-bone, and there are only 4 kinds of side groups, all of which are nitrogen bases (purines and pyrimidines). Crick and Watson's model contains a pair of DNA chains wound around a common axis in the form of two interlocking helices. The two helices are held together (forming a helical "ladder") by hydrogen bonds between pairs of the nitrogen bases, one belonging to each helix. Although 4 bases occur as side groups, only 2 of 16 conceivable pairings are possible, for steric reasons. These 2 pairs of bases recur along the length of the DNA molecule and thus invite a picturesque analogy with the dots and dashes of the Morse code. They can be arranged in any sequence: There is enough DNA in a single cell of the human body to encode in this way 1000 large textbooks. The model can be said to imply that the genetic "language" of the inherited control message is a "language of surfaces": The information in DNA structure is decoded as a sequence of amino acids in the proteins which are synthesized under ultimate DNA control. The surface structure of the DNA helix, dictated by the sequence of base pairs, specifies like a template[24] the sequence of amino acids laid down end to end in the fabrication of polypeptides.

Watson and Crick's model immediately suggests how the DNA might produce an exact copy of itself—for transmission as an inherited message to the succeeding generation of cells. The DNA molecule, as noted above, consists of two interwoven helices, each of which is the complement of the other. Thus each chain may act as a mold on which a complementary chain can be synthesized. The two chains of a DNA molecule need only unwind and separate. Each begins to build a new complement onto itself, as loose units, floating in the cell, attach themselves to the bases in the single DNA chain. When the process is completed, there are two pairs of chains where before there was only one![25]

Mutation of the genetic information has been explained in a molecular (micro-reduction) theory advanced some years ago by Del-brück.[26] Delbrück's theory was conceived long before the newer knowledge of DNA was available; but it is a very general model in no way vitiated by Crick and Watson's model of the particular molecule constituting the genetic material. Delbrück, like many others, assumed that the gene is a single large "nucleo-protein" molecule. (This term is used for macromolecules, such as viruses and the hypothetical "genes," which consist of protein and nucleic acid. Some recent theories even assume that an entire chromosome is a single such molecule.) According to Delbrück's theory, different quantum levels within the atoms of the molecule correspond to different hereditary characteristics. A mutation is simply a quantum jump of a rare type (i.e., one with a high activation energy). The observed variation of the spontaneous mutation rate with temperature is in good quantitative agreement with the theory.

Such hypotheses and models as those of Crick and Watson, and of Delbrück, are at present far from sufficient for a complete micro-reduction of the major biological generalizations, e.g., evolution and general genetic theory (including the problem of the control of development). But they constitute an encouraging start toward this ultimate goal and, to this extent, an indirect support for our working hypothesis.

Only in the twentieth century has it been possible to micro-reduce to the atomic and in some cases directly to the subatomic level most of the *macro-physical* aspects of matter (e.g., the high fluidity of water, the elasticity of rubber, and the hardness of diamond) as well as the *chemical* phenomena of the elements, i.e., those changes of the peripheral electrons which leave the nucleus unaffected. In particular, electronic theories explain, e.g., the laws governing valence, the various types of bonds, and the "resonance" of molecules between several equivalent electronic structures. A complete explanation of these phenomena and those of the Periodic Table is possible only with the help of Pauling's exclusion principle, which states in one form that no two electrons of the same atom can be alike in all of 4 "quantum numbers." While some molecular laws are not yet micro-reduced, there is every hope that further successes will be obtained in these respects. Thus Pauling (55, 56) writes:

> There are still problems to be solved, and some of them are great problems—an example is the problem of the detailed nature of catalytic activity. We can feel sure, however, that this problem will in the course of time be solved in terms of quantum theory as it now exists: There seems little reason to believe that some fundamental new principle remains to be discovered in order that catalysis be explained (56).

Micro-reduction of level 2 to level 1 has been mentioned in the preceding section because many molecular phenomena are at present (skipping the atomic level) explained with reference to laws of elementary particles.[27] Bohr's basic (and now somewhat outdated) model of the atom as a kind of "solar system" of elementary particles is today part of everyone's conceptual apparatus, while the mathematical development of theory in its present form is formidable indeed! Thus we shall not attempt to give any details of this success. But the high rate of progress in this field certainly gives reason to hope that the unsolved problems, especially as to the forces that hold the nucleus together, will likewise be explained in terms of an elementary particle theory.

Evolution, Ontogenesis, and Synthesis

As pointed out on pp. 272–273, *evolution* provides *indirect* factual support for the working hypothesis that unitary science is attainable. Evolution (in the present sense) is an overall phenomenon involving all levels, from 1 through 6; the mechanisms of chance variation and "selection" operate throughout in ways characteristic for the evolutionary level in-

volved.[28] Time scales have, indeed, been worked out by various scientists showing the times when the first things of each level first appeared.[29] (These times are, of course, the less hypothetical, the higher the level involved.) But even if the hypothesis of evolution should fail to hold in the case of certain levels, it is important to note that whenever it *does* hold —whenever it *can* be shown that things of a given level existed before things of the next higher level came into existence—some degree of indirect support is provided to the particular special case of our working hypothesis that concerns those two levels.

The hypothesis of "evolution" is most speculative insofar as it concerns levels 1 to 3. Various cosmological hypotheses are at present undergoing lively discussion.[30] According to one of these, strongly urged by Gamow (20, 21, 22), the first nuclei did not form out of elementary particles until five to thirty minutes after the start of the universe's expansion; molecules may not have been able to exist until considerably later. Most present-day cosmologists still subscribe to such evolutionary views of the universe, i.e., there was a "zero point" from which the evolution of matter began, with diminishing density through expansion. However, H. Bondi, T. Gold, and F. Hoyle have advanced a conflicting idea, the "steady state" theory, according to which there is no "zero point" from which the evolution of matter began, but matter is continuously created, so that its density remains constant in spite of expansion. There seems to be hope that these rival hypotheses will be submitted to specific empirical tests in the near future. But, fortunately, we do not have to depend on hypotheses that are still so highly controversial: As we have seen, the micro-reducibility of molecular and atomic phenomena is today not open to serious doubt.

Less speculative are theories concerning the origin of life (transition from level 3 to level 4). Calvin (9; Fox, 18) points out that four mechanisms have been discovered which lead to the formation of amino acids and other organic materials in a mixture of gases duplicating the composition of the primitive terrestrial atmosphere.[31] These have, in fact, been tested experimentally with positive results. Many biologists today accept with Oparin (53) the view that the evolution of life as such was not a single chance event but a long process possibly requiring as many as two billion years, until precellular living organisms first appeared.

According to such views, "chemical evolution" gradually leads in an appropriate environment to evolution in the familiar Darwinian sense. In such a process, it hardly has meaning to speak of a point at which "life appeared." To this day controversies exist concerning the "dividing line" between living and non-living things. In particular, viruses are classified by some biologists as *living*, because they exhibit *self-duplication* and *mutability*; but most biologists refuse to apply the term to them, because viruses exhibit these characteristic phenomena of life only due to activities of a living cell with which they are in contact. But, wherever one draws the line,[32] non-living molecules preceded primordial living substance, and the latter evolved gradually into highly organized living units, the unicellular ancestors of all living things. The "first complex molecules endowed with the faculty of reproducing their own kind" must have been synthesized—and with them the beginning of evolution in the Darwinian sense—a few billion years ago, Goldschmidt (23, p. 84) asserts: "All the facts of biology, geology, paleontology, biochemistry, and radiology not only agree with this statement but actually prove it."

Evolution at the next two levels (from level 4 to level 5, and from 5 to 6) is not speculative at all, but forms part of the broad line of Darwinian evolution, so well marked out by the various kinds of evidence referred to in the statement just quoted. The line of development is again a continuous one;[33] and it is to some extent arbitrary (as in the case of "living" versus "non-living") to give a "point" at which

true multicellulars first appeared, or at which an animal is "social" rather than "solitary." But in spite of this arbitrariness, it is safe to say that:

a. Multicellulars evolved from what were originally competing single cells; the "selection" by the environment was in this case determined by the superior survival value of the cooperative structure.[34]

b. Social animals evolved from solitary ones for similar reasons; and, indeed, there were millions of years during which there were *only* solitary animals on earth and not yet their organizations into social structures.[35]

To illustrate *ontogenesis*, we must show that particular things of a particular level have arisen out of particular things of the next lower level. For example, it is a consequence of most contemporary cosmological theories—whether of the evolutionary or of the "steady state" type—that each existent atom must have originally been formed by a union of elementary particles. (Of course an atom of an element may subsequently undergo "transmutation.") However, such theories are extremely speculative. On the other hand, the chemical union of atoms to form molecules is commonplace in nature.

Coming to the higher levels of the reductive hierarchy, we have unfortunately a hiatus at the level of cells. Individual cells do *not*, as far as our observations go, ever develop out of individual molecules; on the contrary, "cells come only from cells," as Virchow stated about one hundred years ago. However, a characteristic example of ontogenesis of things of one level out of things of the next lower level is afforded by the development of multicellular organisms through the process of mitosis and cell division. All the hereditary characteristics of the organism are specified in the "genetic information" carried in the chromosomes of each individual cell, and are transmitted to the resultant organism through cell division and mitosis.

A more startling example of ontogenesis at this level is provided by the *slime molds* studied by Bonner (3). These are isolated amoebae; but, at a certain stage, they "clump" together chemotactically and form a simple multicellular organism, a sausage-like "slug"! This "slug" crawls with comparative rapidity and good coordination. It even has senses of a sort, for it is attracted by light.

As to the level of social groups, we have some ontogenetic data, however slight; for children, according to the well-known studies of Piaget (62, 63) (and other authorities on child behavior), acquire the capacity to cooperate with one another, to be concerned with each other's welfare, and to form groups in which they treat one another as peers, only after a number of years (not before seven years of age, in Piaget's studies). Here one has in a rudimentary form what we are looking for: the ontogenetic development of progressively more social behavior (level 6) by what begin as relatively "egocentric" and unsocialized individuals (level 5).

Synthesis affords factual support for micro-reduction much as ontogenesis does; however, the evidence is better because synthesis usually takes place under *controlled* conditions. Thus it enables one to show that one can obtain an object of the kind under investigation *invariably* by instituting the appropriate causal relations among the parts that go to make it up. For this reason, we may say that success in synthesizing is as strong evidence as one can have for the possibility of micro-reduction, short of actually finding the micro-reducing theory.

To begin on the lowest level of the reductive hierarchy, that one can obtain an atom by bringing together the appropriate elementary particles is a basic consequence of elementary nuclear physics. A common example from the operation of atomic piles is the synthesis of deuterium. This proceeds as one bombards protons (in, e.g., hydrogen gas) with neutrons.

The synthesis of a molecule by chemically uniting atoms is an elementary laboratory demonstration. One familiar example is the union of oxygen and hydrogen gas. Under the influence of an electric spark one obtains the appearance of H_2O molecules.

The next level is that of life. "On the border-line" are the viruses. Thus success at synthesizing a virus out of non-living macro-molecules would count as a first step to the synthesis of cells (which at present seems to be an achievement for the far distant future).

While success at synthesizing a virus out of atoms is not yet in sight, synthesis out of *non-living* highly complex macro-molecules has been accomplished. At the University of California Virus Laboratory (19), protein obtained from viruses has been mixed with nucleic acid to obtain active virus. The protein does not behave like a virus—it is completely non-infectious. However, the reconstituted virus has the same structure as "natural" virus and will produce the tobacco mosaic disease when applied to plants. Also new "artificial" viruses have been produced by combining the nucleic acid from one kind of virus with the protein from a different kind. Impressive results in synthesizing proteins have been accomplished; e.g., R. B. Woodward and C. H. Schramm (95; see also Nogushi and Hayakawa, 52; and Oparin, 53) have synthesized "protein analogues"— giant polymers containing at least 10,000 amino-acid residues.

At the next level, no one has of course synthesized a whole multicellular organism out of individual cells; but here too there is an impressive partial success to report. Recent experiments have provided detailed descriptions of the manner in which cells organize themselves into whole multicellular tissues. These studies show that even isolated whole cells, when brought together in random groups, could effectuate the characteristic construction of such tissues.[36] Similar phenomena are well known in the case of sponges and fresh-water polyps.

Lastly, the "synthesis" of a new social group by bringing together previously separated individuals is extremely familiar, e.g., the organization of new clubs, trade unions, professional associations, etc. One has even the deliberate formation of whole new societies, e.g., the formation of the Oneida community of utopians in the nineteenth century, or of the state of Israel by Zionists in the twentieth.

There have been experimental studies in this field; among them, the pioneer work of Kurt Lewin and his school is especially well known.[37]

Concluding Remarks

The possibility that all science may one day be reduced to micro-physics (in the sense in which chemistry seems today to be reduced to it), and the presence of a unifying trend toward micro-reduction running through much of scientific activity, have often been noticed both by specialists in the various sciences and by meta-scientists. But these opinions have, in general, been expressed in a more or less vague manner without very deep-going justification. It has been our aim, first, to provide precise definitions for the crucial concepts involved, and, second, to reply to the frequently made accusations that belief in the attainability of unitary science is "a mere act of faith." We hope to have shown that, on the contrary, a tentative acceptance of this belief, an acceptance of it as a working hypothesis, is *justified*, and that the hypothesis is *credible*, partly on methodological grounds (e.g., the simplicity of the hypothesis, as opposed to the bifurcation that rival suppositions create in the conceptual system of science), and partly because there is really a large mass of direct and indirect evidence in its favor. . . .

Notes

AUTHORS' NOTE: We wish to express our thanks to C. G. Hempel for constructive criticism. The responsibility for any shortcomings is, however, exclusively ours.

1. Science, in the wider sense, may be understood as including the formal disciplines, mathematics, and logic, as well as the empirical ones. In this paper, we shall be concerned with science only in the sense of empirical disciplines, including the socio-humanistic ones.

2. By a *theory* (in the widest sense) we mean any hypothesis, generalization, or law (whether deterministic or statistical), or any conjunction of these; likewise by *phenomena* (in the widest sense) we shall mean either particular occurrences or theoretically formulated general patterns. Throughout this paper, *explanation* (*explainable*, etc.) is used as defined in Hempel and Oppenheim (31) [see previous selection].

3. If we are willing to adopt a "Taxonomic System" for classifying all the things dealt with by science, then the various classes and subclasses in such a system could represent the possible "universes of discourse." In this case, the U_{Bi} of any branch would be associated with the extension of a taxonomic term in the sense of Oppenheim (54).

4. Henceforth, we shall as a rule omit the clause "at time t."

5. Of course, in some cases, such "skipping" does occur in the process of micro-reduction, as shall be illustrated later on.

6. As to degree of *credibility*, see Kemeny and Oppenheim (40, especially p. 307).

7. The "acceptance, as an overall fundamental working hypothesis, of the reduction theory, with physical science as most general, to which all others are reducible; with biological science less general; and with social science least general of all" has been emphasized by Hockett (33, especially p. 571).

8. As to *natural*, see Hempel (29, p. 52), and Hempel and Oppenheim (30, pp. 107, 110).

9. Many well known hierarchical orders of the same kind (including some compatible with ours) can be found in modern writings. It suffices to give the following quotation from an article by L. von Bertalanffy (83, p. 164): "Reality, in the modern conception, appears as a tremendous hierarchical order of organized entities, leading, in a superposition of many levels, from physical and chemical to biological and sociological systems. Unity of Science is granted, not by an utopian reduction of all sciences to physics and chemistry, but by the structural uniformities of the different levels of reality." As to the last sentence, we refer on pp. 269–270 to the problem noted. Von Bertalanffy has done pioneer work in developing a General System Theory that, in spite of some differences of emphasis, is an interesting contribution to our problem.

10. The statement that B_2 is *micro-reducible* to B_1 means

(according to the analysis we adopt here) that some true theory belonging to B_1—i.e., some true theory with the appropriate vocabulary and universe of discourse, whether accepted or not, and whether it is ever even written down or not—micro-reduces every true theory of B_2. This seems to be what people have in mind when they assert that a given B_2 may not be reduced to a given B_1 at a certain time, but may nonetheless be reducible (micro-reducible) to it.

11. See Kemeny and Oppenheim (40, p. 307); also for "related concepts," like Carnap's "degree of confirmation" see Carnap (11).

12. Though we cannot accept Sir Arthur Eddington's idealistic implications, we quote from his *Philosophy of Physical Science* (14, p. 125): "I conclude therefore that our engrained form of thought is such that we shall not rest satisfied until we are able to represent all physical phenomena as an interplay of a fast number of structural units intrinsically alike. All the diversity of phenomena will be then seen to correspond to different forms of relatedness of these units or, as we should usually say, different configurations."

13. M. Scriven has set forth some suggestive considerations on this subject in his essay, "A Possible Distinction between Traditional Scientific Disciplines and the Study of Human Behavior" (69).

14. See, e.g., Kartman (38), with many quotations, references, and notes, some of them micro-reductionistic.

15. This term has been introduced by F. A. Hayek (27). See also Watkins (86, especially pp. 729–732) and Watkins (87). We owe valuable information in economics to W. J. Baumol, Princeton University.

16. This distinction, first made by C. D. Broad (6, p. 616), adopted by E. C. Tolman (79), C. L. Hull (35), and others, is still in use, in spite of objections against this terminology.

17. This is the form our working hypothesis takes on this level in this field. See in this connection the often quoted paper by K. MacCorquodale and P. E. Meehl, "On a Distinction between Hypothetical Constructs and Intervening Variable" (45), and some of the discussions in the "Symposium on the Probability Approach in Psychology" (65), as well as references therein, to H. Feigl, W. Koehler, D. Krech, and C. C. Pratt.

18. As to *neuroanatomy*, see, e.g., W. Penfield (61); as to *neurochemistry*, see, e.g., Rosenblueth (68, especially Chapter 26 for acetylcholine and the summaries on pp. 134–135, 274–275; as to *The Electric Activity of the Nervous System*, see the book of this title by Brazier (5). See this last book also for

neuroanatomy, neurophysiology, neurochemistry. See Brazier (5, pp. 128, 129, 152) for micro-reduction of *Gestalt phenomena* mentioned below.

19. Turing (80, 81). For an excellent popular presentation, see Kemeny (39).

20. See the often quoted paper by McCulloch and Pitts (46), and later publications by these authors, as well as other papers in this field in the same *Bulletin of Mathematical Biophysics*, e.g., by N. Rashevsky. See also Platt (64) for a "complementary approach that might be called amplifier theory." For more up to date details, see Shannon and McCarthy's (71) *Automata Studies*, including von Neumann's model, discussed by him (71, pp. 43–98).

21. Throughout this paper, *cell* is used in a wide sense, i.e., "unicellular" organism or single cell in a multicellular organism.

22. For more details and much of the following, see Simpson, Pittendrigh and Tiffany (76), Goldschmidt (24), and Horowitz (34). For valuable suggestions we are indebted to C. S. Pittendrigh, who also coined the terms "message carrying molecule" and "languages of surface" used in our text.

23. See in reference to the following discussion Watson and Crick (88), also (89), and (90), and Crick (12).

24. Pauling and Delbrück (60). A micro-reducing theory has been proposed for these activities using the "lock-key" model. See Pauling, Campbell and Pressmann (57), and Burnet (8).

25. For a mechanical model, see von Neumann (84) and Jacobson (36).

26. See Timoféeff-Ressovsky (78, especially pp. 108–138). It should, however, be noted that since Delbrück's theory was put forward, his model has proved inadequate for explaining genetic facts concerning mutation. And it is reproduced here only as a historical case of a micro-reducing theory that, in its day, served valuable functions.

27. We think that, throughout this paper, our usage of thing language also on this level is admissible in spite of well-known difficulties and refer, e.g., to Born (4) and Johnson (37).

28. See, e.g., Broad (6, especially p. 93), as to "a general tendency of one order to combine with each other under suitable conditions to form complexes of the next order." See also Blum (1 and 2, especially p. 608); Needham (51, especially pp. 184–185); and Dodd (13).

29. This wording takes care of *regression*, a reversal of trend, illustrated, e.g., by parasitism.

30. For a clear survey of cosmological hypotheses see the twelve articles published in the issue of

Scientific American cited under Gamow (22).

31. Perhaps the most sensational method is an experiment suggested by H. C. Urey and made by S. L. Miller (48, 49), according to which amino acids are formed when an electric discharge passes through a mixture of methane, hydrogen, ammonia, and water.

32. "Actually life has many attributes, almost any one of which we can reproduce in a nonliving system. It is only when they all appear to a greater or lesser degree in the same system simultaneously that we call it living" (Calvin, 9, p. 252). Thus the dividing line between "living" and "nonliving" is obtained by transforming an underlying "multidimensional concept of order" (see Hempel and Oppenheim, 30, pp. 65–77), in a more or less arbitrary way, into a dichotomy. See also Stanley (ii, especially pp. 15 and 16 of the reprint of this article).

33. See note 32 above.

34. For details, see Lindsey (43, especially pp. 136–139, 152–153, 342–344). See also Burkholder (7).

35. See, e.g., the publications (92, 93, 94) by Wheeler. See also Haskins (26, especially pp. 30–36). Since we are considering evolution on level 6 as a whole, we can refrain from discussing the great difference between, on the one hand, chance mutations, natural selection, and "instinctive" choices and, on the other hand, the specific faculty of man of consciously and willfully directing social evolution in time stretches of specifically small orders of magnitude (see Zilsel, 96).

36. See Moscana (50) and his references, especially to work by the same author and by Paul Weiss.

37. See Lippitt (44). For recent experiments, see Sherif and Sherif (73, Chapters 6 and 9), and Sherif (72).

References

1. Blum, H. F. *Time's Arrow and Evolution.* Princeton: Princeton Univ. Press, 1951.
2. Blum, H. F. "Perspectives in Evolution," *American Scientist*, 43:595–610 (1955).
3. Bonner, J. T. *Morphogenesis.* Princeton: Princeton Univ. Press, 1952.
4. Born, M. "The Interpretation of Quantum Mechanics," *British Journal for the Philosophy of Science*, 3:95–109 (1953).
5. Bazier, M. A. B. *The Electric Activity of the Nervous System.* London: Sir Isaac Pitman & Sons, Ltd., 1951.
6. Broad, C. D. *The Mind and Its Place in Nature.*

New York: Harcourt, Brace, 1925.
7. Burkholder, P. R. "Cooperation and Conflict among Primitive Organisms," *American Scientist*, 40:601–631 (1952).
8. Burnet, M. "How Antibodies Are Made," *Scientific American*, 191:74–78 (November 1954).
9. Calvin, M. "Chemical Evolution and the Origin of Life," *American Scientist*, 44:248–263 (1956).
10. Carnap, R. *Logical Foundations of the Unity of Science, International Encyclopedia of Unified Science.* Vol. I, pp. 42–62. Chicago: Univ. of Chicago Press, 1938.
11. Carnap, R. *Logical Foundations of Probability.* Chicago: Univ. of Chicago Press, 1950.
12. Crick, F. H. C. "The Structure of Hereditary Material," *Scientific American*, 191:54–61 (October 1954).
13. Dodd, S. C. "A Mass-Time Triangle," *Philosophy of Science*, 11:233–244 (1944).
14. Eddington, Sir Arthur. *The Philosophy of Physical Science.* Cambridge: Cambridge University Press, 1949.
15. Feigl, H. "Logical Empiricsm," in D. D. Runes (ed.), *Twentieth Century Philosophy*, pp. 371–416. New York: Philosophical Library, 1943. Reprinted in H. Feigl and W. Sellars (eds.), *Readings in Philosophical Analysis.* New York: Appleton-Century-Crofts, 1949.
16. Feigl, H. "Unity of Science and Unitary Science," in H. Feigl and M. Brodbeck (eds.), *Readings in the Philosophy of Science*, pp. 382–384. New York: Appleton-Century-Crofts, 1953.
17. Feigl, H. "Functionalism, Psychological Theory and the Uniting Sciences: Some Discussion Remarks," *Psychological Review*, 62:232–235 (1955).
18. Fox, S. W. "The Evolution of Protein Molecules and Thermal Synthesis of Biochemical Substances," *American Scientist*, 44:347–359 (1956).
19. Fraenkel-Conrat, H. "Rebuilding a Virus," *Scientific American*, 194:42–47 (June 1956).
20. Gamow, G. "The Origin and Evolution of the Universe," *American Scientist*, 39:393–406 (1951).
21. Gamow, G. *The Creation of the Universe.* New York: Viking Press, 1952.
22. Gamow, G. "The Evolutionary Universe," *Scientific American*, 195:136–154 (September 1956).
23. Goldschmidt, R. B. "Evolution, as Viewed by One Geneticist," *American Scientist*, 40:84–98 (1952).
24. Goldschmidt, R. B. *Theoretical Genetics.* Berkeley and Los Angeles: Univ. of California Press, 1955.
25. Guhl, A. M. "The Social Order of Chickens," *Scientific American*, 194:42–46 (February 1956).
26. Haskins, C. P. *Of Societies and Man.* New York: Norton & Co., 1951.

27. Hayek, F. A. *Individualism and the Economic Order.* Chicago: Univ. of Chicago Press, 1948.

28. Hebb, D. O. *The Organization of Behavior.* New York: Wiley, 1949.

29. Hempel, C. G. *Fundamentals of Concept Formation in the Imperical Sciences,* Vol. II, No. 7 of *International Encyclopedia of Unified Science.* Chicago: Univ. of Chicago Press, 1952.

30. Hempel, C. G., and P. Oppenheim. *Der Typusbegriff im Lichte der neuen Logik; wissen-schaftstheoretische Untersuchengen zur Konstitutionsforschung und Psychologie.* Leiden: A. W. Sythoff, 1936.

31. Hempel, C. G., and P. Oppenheim. "Studies in the Logic of Explanation," *Philosophy of Science,* 15:135–175 (1948).

32. Hoagland, H. "The Weber-Fechner Law and the All-or-None Theory," *Journal of General Psychology,* 3:351–373 (1930).

33. Hockett, C. H. "Biophysics, Linguistics, and the Unity of Science," *American Scientist,* 36:558–572 (1948).

34. Horowitz, N. H. "The Gene," *Scientific American,* 195:78–90 (October 1956).

35. Hull, C. L. *Principles of Animal Behavior.* New York: D. Appleton-Century, Inc., 1943.

36. Jacobson, H. "Information, Reproduction, and the Origin of Life," *American Scientist,* 43:119–127 (1955).

37. Johnson, M. "The Meaning of Time and Space in Philosophies of Science," *American Scientist,* 39:412–431 (1951).

38. Kartman, L. "Metaphorical Appeals in Biological Thought," *American Scientist,* 44:296–301 (1956).

39. Kemeny, J. G. "Man Viewed as a Machine," *Scientific American,* 192:58–66 (April 1955).

40. Kemeny, J. G., and P. Oppenheim. "Degree of Factual Support," *Philosophy of Science,* 19:307–324 (1952).

41. Kemeny, J. G., and P. Oppenheim. "On Reduction," *Philosophical Studies,* 7:6–19 (1956).

42. Linderstrom-Lang, K. U. "How Is a Protein Made?" *American Scientist,* 41:100–106 (1953).

43. Lindsey, A. W. *Organic Evolution.* St. Louis: C. V. Mosby Company, 1952.

44. Lippitt, R. "Field Theory and Experiment in Social Psychology," *American Journal of Sociology,* 45:26–79 (1939).

45. MacCorquodale, K., and P. E. Meehl. "On a Distinction Between Hypothetical Constructs and Intervening Variables," *Psychological Review,* 55:95–105 (1948).

46. McCulloch, W. S., and W. Pitts. "A Logical Calculus of the Ideas Immanent in Nervous Activity," *Bulletin of Mathematical Biophysics,* 5:115–133 (1943).

47. Mannheim, K. *Ideology and Utopia.* New York: Harcourt, Brace, 1936.

48. Miller, S. L. "A Production of Amino Acids Under Possible Primitive Earth Conditions," *Science,* 117:528–529 (1953).

49. Miller, S. L. "Production of Some Organic Compounds Under Possible Primitive Earth Conditions," *Journal of the American Chemical Society,* 77:2351–2361 (1955).

50. Moscana, A. "Development of Heterotypic Combinations of Dissociated Embryonic Chick Cells," *Proceedings of the Society for Experimental Biology and Medicine,* 92:410–416 (1956).

51. Needham, J. *Time.* New York: Macmillan, 1943.

52. Nogushi, J., and T. Hayakawa. Letter to the Editor, *Journal of the American Chemical Society,* 76:2846–2848 (1954).

53. Oparin, A. I. *The Origin of Life.* New York: Macmillan, 1938 (Dover Publications, Inc. edition, 1953).

54. Oppenheim, P. "Dimensions of Knowledge," *Revue Internationale de Philosophie,* Fascicule 40, Section 7 (1957).

55. Pauling, L. "Chemical Achievement and Hope for the Future," *American Scientist,* 36:51–58 (1948).

56. Pauling, L. "Quantum Theory and Chemistry," *Science,* 113:92–94 (1951).

57. Pauling, L., D. H. Campbell, and D. Pressmann. "The Nature of Forces between Antigen and Antibody and of the Precipitation Reaction," *Physical Review,* 63:203–219 (1943).

58. Pauling, L., and R. B. Corey. "Two Hydrogen-Bonded Spiral Configurations of the Polypeptide Chain," *Journal of the American Chemical Society,* 72:5349 (1950).

59. Pauling, L., and R. B. Corey, "Atomic Coordination and Structure Factors for Two Helical Configurations," *Proceedings of the National Academy of Science* (U.S.), 37:235 (1951).

60. Pauling, L., and M. Delbrück. "The Nature of Intermolecular Forces Operative in Biological Processes," *Science,* 92:585–586 (1940).

61. Penfield, W. "The Cerebral Cortex and the Mind of Man," in P. Laslett (ed.), *The Physical Basis of Mind,* pp. 56–64. Oxford: Blackwell, 1950.

62. Piaget, J. *The Moral Judgment of the Child.* London: Kegan Paul, Trench, Trubner and Company, Ltd., 1932.

63. Piaget, J. *The Language and Thought of the Child.* London: Kegan Paul, Trench, Trubner and Company; New York: Harcourt, Brace, 1926.

64. Platt, J. R. "Amplification Aspects of Biological Response and Mental Activity," *American Scientist,* 44:180–197 (1956).

65. Probability Approach in Psychology (Symposium), *Psychological Review,* 62:193–242 (1955).

66. Rescher, N. "Axioms of the Part Relation," *Philosophical Studies*, 6:8–11 (1955).

67. Rescher, N. and P. Oppenheim. "Logical Analysis of Gestalt Concepts," *British Journal for the Philosophy of Science*, 6:89–106 (1955).

68. Rosenblueth, A. *The Transmission of Nerve Impulses at Neuroeffector Junctions and Peripheral Synapses.* New York: Technological Press of MIT and Wiley, 1950.

69. Scriven, M. "A Possible Distinction between Traditional Scientific Disciplines and the Study of Human Behavior," in H. Feigl and M. Scriven (eds.), Vol. I, *Minnesota Studies in the Philosophy of Science*, pp. 330–339. Minneapolis: Univ. of Minnesota Press, 1956.

70. Sellars, W. "A Semantical Solution of the Mind-Body Problem," *Methodos*, 5:45–84 (1953).

71. Shannon, C. E., and J. McCarthy (eds.), *Automata Studies.* Princeton: Princeton Univ. Press, 1956.

72. Sherif, M. "Experiments in Group Conflict," *Scientific American*, 195:54–58 (November 1956).

73. Sherif, M., and C. W. Sherif. *An Outline of Social Psychology.* New York: Harper, 1956.

74. Sherrington, C. *The Integrative Action of the Nervous System.* New Haven: Yale Univ. Press, 1948.

75. Simmel, G. *Sociologie.* Leipzig: Juncker und Humblot, 1908.

76. Simpson, G. G., C. S. Pittendrigh, and C. H. Tiffany. *Life.* New York: Harcourt, Brace, 1957.

77. Stanley, W. M. "The Structure of Viruses," reprinted from publication No. 14 of the *American Association for the Advancement of Science, The Cell and Protoplasm*, pp. 120–135 (reprint consulted) (1940).

78. Timoféeff-Ressovsky, N. W. *Experimentelle Mutationsforschung in der Vererbungslehre.* Dresden und Leipzig: Verlag von Theoder Steinkopff, 1937.

79. Tolman, E. C. *Purposive Behavior in Animals and Men.* New York: The Century Company, 1932.

80. Turing, A. M. "On Computable Numbers, With an Application to the Entscheidungsproblem," *Proceedings of the London Mathematical Society*, Ser. 2, 42:230–265 (1936).

81. Turing, A. M. "A Correction," *Proceedings of the London Mathematical Society*, Ser. 2, 43:544–546 (1937).

82. Veblen, T. *The Theory of the Leisure Class.* London: Macmillan, 1899.

83. Von Bertalanffy, L. "An Outline of General System Theory," *The British Journal for the Philosophy of Science*, 1:134–165 (1950).

84. Von Neumann, J. "The General and Logical Theory of Automata," in L. A. Jeffress (ed.), *Cerebral Mechanisms in Behavior; The Hixon Symposium*, pp. 20–41. New York: John Wiley and Sons, Inc., 1951.

85. Von Neumann, J. "Probabilistic Logics and the Synthesis of Reliable Organisms from Unreliable Components," in C. E. Shannon and J. McCarthy (eds.), *Automata Studies.* Princeton: Princeton Univ. Press, 1956.

86. Watkins, J. W. N. "Ideal Types and Historical Explanation," in H. Feigl and M. Brodbeck (eds.), *Readings in the Philosophy of Science*, pp. 723–743. New York: Appleton-Century-Crofts, 1953.

87. Watkins, J. W. N. "A Reply," *Philosophy of Science*, 22:58–62 (1955).

88. Watson, J. D., and F. H. C. Crick. "The Structure of DNA," *Cold Spring Harbor Symposium on Quantitative Biology*, 18:123–131 (1953).

89. Watson, J. D., and F. H. C. Crick. "Molecular Structure of Nucleic Acids—A Structure for Desoxyribosenucleic Acid," *Nature*, 171:737–738 (1953).

90. Watson, J. D., and F. H. C. Crick. "Genetical Implications of the Structure of Desoxyribosenucleic Acid," *Nature*, 171:964–967 (1953).

91. Weber, M. *The Theory of Social and Economic Organization*, translated by A. M. Henderson and T. Persons. New York: Oxford Univ. Press, 1947.

92. Wheeler, W. M. *Social Life Among the Insects.* New York: Harcourt, Brace, 1923.

93. Wheeler, W. M. *Emergent Evolution and the Development of Societies.* New York: Norton & Co., 1928.

94. Wheeler, W. M. "Animal Societies," *Scientific Monthly*, 39:289–301 (1934).

95. Woodward, R. B., and C. H. Schramm. Letter to the Editor, *Journal of the American Chemical Society*, 69:1551 (1947).

96. Zilsel, E. "History and Biological Evolution," *Philosohy of Science*, 7:121–128 (1940).

KARL POPPER

The Rationality of Scientific Revolutions

The title of this series of Spencer lectures, *Progress and Obstacles to Progress in the Sciences*, was chosen by the organizers of the series. The title seems to me to imply that progress in science is a good thing, and that an obstacle to progress is a bad thing, a position held by almost everybody, until quite recently. Perhaps I should make clear at once that I accept this position, although with some slight and fairly obvious reservations to which I shall briefly allude later. Of course, obstacles which are due to the inherent difficulty of the problems tackled are welcome challenges. (Indeed, many scientists were greatly disappointed when it turned out that the problem of tapping nuclear energy was comparatively trivial, involving no new revolutionary change of theory.) But stagnation in science would be a curse. Still, I agree with Professor Bodmer's suggestion that scientific advance is only a *mixed* blessing[1] Let us face it:

Blessings *are* mixed, with some exceedingly rare exceptions.

My talk will be divided into two parts. The first part (Sections I–VIII) is devoted to progress in science, and the second part (Sections IX–XIV) to some of the social obstacles to progress.

Remembering Herbert Spencer, I shall discuss progress in science largely *from an evolutionary point of view*—more precisely, from the point of view of the theory of natural selection. Only the end of the first part (that is, Section VIII), will be spent in discussing the progress of science *from a logical point of view*, and in proposing *two rational criteria* of progress in science, which will be needed in the second part of my talk.

In the second part I shall discuss a few obstacles to progress in science, more especially ideological obstacles; and I shall end (Sections

From *Problems of Scientific Revolution: Progress and Obstacles to Progress in the Sciences*, The Herbert Spencer Lectures 1973, Rom Harré, Ed. (1975), pp. 72–101. © 1975, 1981 by Sir Karl Popper and reprinted by permission of the author.

XI–XIV) by discussing the distinction be-tween, on the one hand, *scientific revolutions*, which are subject to rational criteria of progress, and on the other hand, *ideological revolutions*, which are only rarely rationally defensible. It appeared to me that this distinction was sufficiently interesting to call my lecture "The Rationality of Scientific Revolutions." The emphasis here must be, of course, on the word "scientific."

I

I now turn to progress in science. I will be looking at progress in science from a biological or evolutionary point of view. I am far from suggesting that this is the most important point of view for examining progress in science. But the biological approach offers a convenient way of introducing the two leading ideas of the first half of my talk. They are the ideas of *instruction* and of *selection*.

From a biological or evolutionary point of view, science, or progress in science, may be regarded as a means used by the human species to adapt itself to the environment: to invade new environmental niches, and even to invent new environmental niches.[2] This leads to the following problem.

We can distinguish between three levels of adaptation: genetic adaptation; adaptive behavioral learning; and scientific discovery, which is a special case of adaptive behavioral learning. My main problem in this part of my talk will be to enquire into the similarities and dissimilarities between the strategies of progress or adaptation on the *scientific* level and on those two other levels: the *genetic* level and the *behavioral* level. And I will compare the three levels of adaptation by investigating the role played on each level by *instruction* and by *selection*.

II

In order not to lead you blindfolded to the result of this comparison I will anticipate at once my main thesis. It is a thesis asserting the *fundamental similarity of the three levels*, as follows.

On all three levels—genetic adaptation, adaptive behavior, and scientific discovery—the mechanism of adaptation is fundamentally the same.

This can be explained in some detail.

Adaptation starts from an inherited *structure* which is basic for all three levels: *the gene structure of the organism*. To it corresponds, *on the* behavioral level, *the innate repertoire* of the types of behavior which are available to the organism, and on the scientific level, *the dominant scientific conjectures or theories*. These *structures* are always transmitted by *instruction*, on all three levels: by the replication of the coded genetic instruction on the genetic and the behavioral levels, and by social tradition and imitation on the behavioral and the scientific levels. On all three levels, the *instruction* comes from *within the structure*. If mutations or variations or errors occur, then these are new instructions, which also arise *from within the structure*, rather than *from without*, from the environment.

These inherited structures are exposed to certain pressures, or challenges, or problems: to selection pressures; to environmental challenges; to theoretical problems. In response, variations of the genetically or traditionally inherited *instructions* are produced[3] *by* methods which are at least partly *random*. On the genetic level, these are mutations and recombinations[4] of the coded instruction; on the behavioral level, they are tentative variations and recombinations within the repertoire; on the scientific level, they are new and revolutionary tentative theories. On all three levels we get new tentative trial instructions, or, briefly, tentative trials.

It is important that these tentative trials are changes that originate *within* the individual structure in a more or less random fashion—on all three levels. The view that they are *not* due to instruction from without, from the environment, is supported (if only weakly) by the fact that very similar organisms may sometimes respond in very different ways to the same new environmental challenge.

The next stage is that of *selection* from the available mutations and variations: those of the new tentative trials which are badly adapted are eliminated. *This is the stage of the elimination of error.* Only the more or less well adapted trial instructions survive and are inherited in their turn. Thus we may speak of *adaptation by "the method of trial and error"* or better, by "the method of trial and the elimination of error." The elimination of error, or of badly adapted trial instructions, is also called *natural selection*: it is a kind of "negative feedback." It operates on all three levels.

It is to be noted that in general *no equilibrium state of adaptation* is reached by any one application of the method of trial and the elimination of error, or by natural selection. First, because no perfect or optimal trial solutions to the problem are likely to be offered; secondly—and this is more important—because the emergence of new structures, or of new instructions, involves a change in the environmental situation. New elements of the environment may become relevant; and in consequence, new pressures, new challenges, new problems may arise, as a result of the structural changes which have arisen from within the organism.

On the genetic level the change may be a mutation of a gene, with a consequent change of an enzyme. Now the network of enzymes forms the more intimate environment of the gene structure. Accordingly, there will be a change in this intimate environment; and with it, new relationships between the organism and the more remote environment may arise; and further, new selection pressures.

The same happens on the behavioral level, for the adoption of a new kind of behavior can be equated in most cases with the adoption of a new ecological niche. As a consequence, new selection pressures will arise, and new genetic changes.

On the scientific level, the tentative adoption of a new conjecture or theory may solve one or two problems, but it invariably opens up many *new* problems; for a new revolutionary theory functions exactly like a new and powerful sense organ. If the progress is significant then the new problems will differ from the old problems: The new problems will be on a radically different level of depth. This happened, for example, in relativity; it happened in quantum mechanics; and it happens right now, most dramatically, in molecular biology. In each of these cases, new horizons of unexpected problems were opened up by the new theory.

This, I suggest, is the way in which science progresses. And our progress can best be gauged by comparing our old problems with our new ones. If the progress that has been made is great, then the new problems will be of a character undreamt of before. There will be deeper problems, and, besides, there will be more of them. The further we progress in knowledge, the more clearly we can discern the vastness of our ignorance.[5]

I will now sum up my thesis.

On all three levels which I am considering—the genetic, the behavioral, and the scientific levels—we are operating with inherited structures which are passed on by instruction, either through the genetic code or through tradition. On all the three levels, new structures and new instructions arise by trial changes from *within the structure*: by tentative trials which are subject to natural selection or the elimination of error.

III

So far I have stressed the *similarities* in the working of the adaptive mechanism on the three levels. This raises an obvious problem: What about the *differences*?

The main difference between the genetic and the behavioral level is this. Mutations on the genetic level are not only random but completely "blind," in two senses.[6] First, they are in no way goal directed. Secondly, the survival of a mutation cannot influence the further mutations, not even the frequencies or probabilities of their occurrence; though admittedly, the *survival* of a mutation may sometimes determine what kind of mutations may possibly *survive* in future cases. On the behavioral level, trials are also more or less random, but they are no longer completely "blind" in either of the two senses mentioned. First, they are goal directed; and secondly, animals may learn from the outcome of a trial: They may learn to avoid the type of trial behavior which has led to a failure. (They may even avoid it in cases in which it could have succeeded.) Similarly, they may also learn from success; and successful behavior may be repeated, even in cases in which it is not adequate. However, a certain degree of "blindness" is inherent in all trials.[7]

Behavioral adaptation is usually an intensely active process: The animal—especially the young animal at play—and even the plant, are actively investigating the environment.[8]

This activity, which is largely genetically programmed, seems to me to mark an important difference between the genetic level and the behavioral level. I may here refer to the experience which the Gestalt psychologists call "insight;" an experience that accompanies many behavioral discoveries.[9] However, it must not be overlooked that even a discovery accompanied by "insight" may be *mistaken*: Every trial, even one with "insight," is of the nature of a conjecture or a hypothesis. Köhler's apes, it will be remembered, sometimes hit with "insight" on what turns out to be a mistaken attempt to solve their problem; and even great mathematicians are sometimes misled by intuition. Thus animals and men have to try out their hypotheses; they have to use the method of trial and of error elimination.

On the other hand I agree with Köhler and Thorpe[10] that the trials of problem-solving animals are in general not completely blind. Only in extreme cases, when the problem which confronts the animal does not yield to the making of hypotheses, will the animal resort to

more or less blind and random attempts in order to get out of a disconcerting situation. Yet even in these attempts, goal-directedness is usually discernible, in sharp contrast to the blind randomness of genetic mutations and recombinations.

Another difference between genetic change and adaptive behavioral change is that the former *always* establishes a rigid and almost invariable genetic structure. The latter, admittedly, leads *sometimes* also to a fairly rigid behavior pattern which is dogmatically adhered to; radically so in the case of "imprinting" (Konrad Lorenz); but in other cases it leads to a flexible pattern which allows for differentiation or modification—for example, it may lead to exploratory behavior, or to what Pavlov called the "freedom reflex."[11]

On the scientific level, discoveries are revolutionary and creative. Indeed, a certain creativity may be attributed to all levels, even to the genetic level: New trials, leading to new environments and thus to new selection pressures, create new and revolutionary results on all levels, even though there are strong conservative tendencies built into the various mechanisms of instruction.

Genetic adaptation can of course operate only within the time span of a few generations—at the very least, say, one or two generations. In organisms which replicate very quickly this may be a short time span, and there may be simply no room for behavioral adaptation. More slowly reproducing organisms are compelled to invent behavioral adaptation in order to adjust themselves to quick environmental changes. They thus need a behavioral repertoire, with types of behavior of greater or lesser latitude or range. The repertoire, and the latitude of the available types of behavior can be assumed to be genetically programmed; and since, as indicated, a new type of behavior may be said to involve the choice of a new environmental niche, new types of behavior may indeed be genetically creative, for they may in their turn determine new selection pressures and thereby indirectly decide upon the future evolution of the genetic structure.[12]

On the level of scientific discovery two new aspects emerge. The most important one is that scientific theories can be formulated linguistically, and that they can even be published. Thus they become objects outside ourselves: objects open to investigation. As a consequence, they are now open to *criticism*. Thus we can get rid of a badly fitting theory before the adoption of the theory makes us unfit to survive: By criticizing our theories we can let our theories die in our stead. This is of course immensely important.

The other aspect is also connected with language. It is one of the novelties of human language that it encourages story telling, and thus *creative imagination*. Scientific discovery is akin to explanatory story telling, to myth making and to poetic imagination. The growth of imagination enhances of course the need for some control, such as, in science, inter-personal criticism—the friendly hostile cooperation of scientists which is partly based on competition and partly on the common aim to get nearer to the truth. This, and the role played by instruction and tradition, seems to me to exhaust the main sociological elements inherently involved in the progress of science; though more could be said of course about the social obstacles to progress, or the social dangers inherent in progress.

IV

I have suggested that progress in science, or scientific discovery, depends on *instruction* and *selection*: on a conservative or traditional or historical element, and on a revolutionary use of trial and the elimination of error by criticism, which includes severe empirical examinations or tests; that is, attempts to probe into the possible weaknesses of theories, attempts to refute them.

Of course, the individual scientist may wish to establish his theory rather than to refute it. But from the point of view of progress in science, this wish can easily mislead him. Moreover, if he does not himself examine his favorite theory critically, others will do so for him. The only results which will be regarded by them as supporting the theory will be the failures of interesting attempts to refute it; failures to find counter-examples where such counter-examples would be most expected, in the light of the best of the competing theories. Thus it need not create a great obstacle to science if the individual scientist is biased in favor of a pet theory. Yet I think that Claude Bernard was very wise when he wrote: "Those who have an excessive faith in their ideas are not well fitted to make discoveries.[13]

All this is part of the critical approach to science, as opposed to the inductivist approach; or of the Darwinian or eliminationist or selectionist approach, as opposed to the Lamarckian approach, which operates with the idea of *instruction from without*, or from the environment, while the critical or selectionist approach only allows *instruction from within*—from within the structure itself.

In fact, I contend that *there is no such thing as instruction from without the structure*, or the passive reception of a flow of information which impresses itself on our sense organs. All observations are theory impregnated: There is no pure, disinterested, theory-free observation. (To see this, we may try, using a little imagination, to compare human observation with that of an ant or a spider.)

Francis Bacon was rightly worried about the fact that our theories may prejudice our observations. This led him to advise scientists that they should avoid prejudice by purifying their minds of all theories. Similar recipes are still given.[14] But to attain objectivity we cannot rely on the empty mind: Objectivity rests on criticism, on critical discussion, and on the critical examination of experiments.[15] And we must recognize, particularly, that our very sense organs incorporate what amount to prejudices. I have stressed before (in Section II) that theories are like sense organs. Now I wish to stress that our sense organs are like theories. They *incorporate* adaptive theories (as has been shown in the case of rabbits and cats). And these theories are the result of natural selection. . . .

VIII

So far I have considered progress in science mainly from a biological point of view; however, it seems to me that the following two logical points are crucial.

First, in order that a new theory should constitute a discovery or a step forward it should conflict with its predecessor; that is to say, it should lead to at least some conflicting results. But this means, from a logical point of view, that it should contradict[16] its predecessor: It should overthrow it.

In this sense, progress in science—or at least striking progress—is always revolutionary.

My second point is that progress in science, although revolutionary rather than merely cumulative, is in a certain sense always conservative: A new theory, however revolutionary, must always be able to explain fully the success of its predecessor. In all those cases in which its predecessor was successful, it must yield results at least as good as those of its predecessor and, if possible, better results. Thus in these cases the predecessor theory must appear as a good approximation to the new theory, while there should be, preferably, other cases where the new theory yields different and better results than the old theory.

The important point about the two logical criteria which I have stated is that they allow us to decide of any new theory, even before it has been tested, whether it will be better than the old one, provided it stands up to tests. But this means that, in the field of science, we have something like a criterion for judging the quality of a theory as compared with its predecessor, and therefore a criterion of progress. And so it means that progress in science can be assessed rationally. This possibility explains why, in science, only progressive theories are re-

garded as interesting; and it thereby explains why, as a matter of historical fact, the history of science is, by and large, a history of progress. (Science seems to be the only field of human endeavor of which this can be said.)

As I have suggested before, scientific progress is revolutionary. Indeed, its motto could be that of Karl Marx: "Revolution in permanence." However, scientific revolutions are rational in the sense that, in principle, it is rationally decidable whether or not a new theory is better than its predecessor. Of course, this does not mean that we cannot blunder. There are many ways in which we can make mistakes. . . .

It should be obvious that the objectivity and the rationality of progress in science is not due to the personal objectivity and rationality of the scientist.[17] Great science and great scientists, like great poets, are often inspired by non-rational intuitions. So are great mathematicians. As Poincaré and Hadamard have pointed out,[18] a mathematical proof may be discovered by unconscious trials, guided by an inspiration of a decidedly aesthetic character, rather than by rational thought. This is true, and important. But obviously, it does not make the result, the mathematical proof, irrational. In any case, a proposed proof must be able to stand up to critical discussion, to its examination by competing mathematicians. And this may well induce the mathematical inventor to check, rationally, the results which he reached unconsciously or intuitively. Similarly, Kepler's beautiful Pythagorean dreams of the harmony of the world system did not invalidate the objectivity, the testability, the rationality of his three laws, nor the rationality of the problem which these laws posed for an explanatory theory.

With this, I conclude my two logical remarks on the progress of science; and I now move on to the second part of my lecture, and with it to remarks which may be described as partly sociological, and which bear on *obstacles* to progress in science.

IX

I think that the main obstacles to progress in science are of a social nature and that they may be divided into two groups: economic obstacles and ideological obstacles.

On the economic side poverty may, trivially, be an obstacle (although great theoretical and experimental discoveries have been made in spite of poverty). In recent years, however, it has become fairly clear that affluence may also be an obstacle: Too many dollars may chase too few ideas. Admittedly, even under such adverse circumstances progress *can* be achieved. But the spirit of science is in danger. Big Science may destroy great science, and the publication explosion may kill ideas: Ideas, which are only too rare, may become submerged in the flood. The danger is very real, and it is hardly necessary to enlarge upon it, but I may perhaps quote Eugene Wigner, one of the early heroes of quantum mechanics, who sadly remarks, "The spirit of science has changed."[19]

This is indeed a sad chapter. But since it is all too obvious I shall not say more about the economic obstacles to progress in science; instead, I will turn to discuss some of the ideological obstacles.

X

The most widely recognized of the ideological obstacles is ideological or religious intolerance, usually combined with dogmatism and lack of imagination. Historical examples are so well known that I need not dwell upon them. Yet it should be noted that even suppression may lead to progress. The martyrdom of Giordano Bruno and the trial of Galileo may have done more in the end for the progress of science than the Inquisition could do against it.

The strange case of Aristarchus and the original heliocentric theory opens perhaps a different problem. Because of his heliocentric theory Aristarchus was accused of impiety by Cleanthes, a Stoic. But this hardly explains the obliteration of the theory. Nor can it be said

that the theory was too bold. We know that Aristarchus's theory was supported, a century after it was first expounded, by at least one highly respected astronomer (Seleucus).[20] And yet, for some obscure reason, only a few brief reports of the theory have survived. Here is a glaring case of the only too frequent failure to keep alternative ideas alive.

Whatever the details of the explanation, the failure was probably due to dogmatism and intolerance. But new ideas should be regarded as precious, and should be carefully nursed, especially if they seem to be a bit wild. I do not suggest that we should be eager to accept new ideas *just* for the sake of their newness. But we should be anxious not to suppress a new idea even if it does not appear to us to be very good.

There are many examples of neglected ideas, such as the idea of evolution before Darwin, or Mendel's theory. A great deal can be learned about obstacles to progress from the history of these neglected ideas. An interesting case is that of the Viennese physicist Arthur Haas who in 1910 partly anticipated Niels Bohr. Haas published a theory of the hydrogen spectrum based on a quantization of J. J. Thomson's atom model: Rutherford's model did not yet exist. Haas appears to have been the first to introduce Planck's quantum of action into atomic theory with a view to deriving the spectral constants. In spite of his use of Thomson's atom model, Haas almost succeeded in his derivation; and as Max Jammer explains in detail, it seems quite possible that the theory of Haas (which was taken seriously by Sommerfeld) indirectly influenced Niels Bohr.[21] In Vienna, however, the theory was rejected out of hand; it was ridiculed and decried as a silly joke by Ernst Lecher (whose early experiments had impressed Heinrich Hertz[22]), one of the professors of physics at the University of Vienna, whose somewhat pedestrian and not very inspiring lectures I attended some eight or nine years later.

A far more surprising case, also described by Jammer,[23] is the rejection in 1913 of Einstein's photon theory, first published in 1905, for which he was to receive the Nobel prize in 1921. This rejection of the photon theory formed a passage within a petition recommending Einstein for membership of the Prussian Academy of Science. The document, which was signed by Max Planck, Walther Nernst, and two other famous physicists, was most laudatory and asked that a slip of Einstein's (such as they obviously believed his photon theory to be) should not be held against him. This confident manner of rejecting a theory which, in the same year, passed a severe experimental test undertaken by Millikan, has no doubt a humorous side; yet it should be regarded as a glorious incident in the history of science, showing that even a somewhat dogmatic rejection by the greatest living experts can go hand in hand with a most liberal-minded appreciation: These men did not dream of suppressing what they believed was mistaken. Indeed, the wording of the apology for Einstein's slip is most interesting and enlightening. The relevant passage of the petition says of Einstein: "That he may sometimes have gone too far in his speculations, as for example in his hypothesis of light quanta, should not weigh too heavily against him. For nobody can introduce, even into the most exact of the natural sciences, ideas which are really new, without sometimes taking a risk."[24] This is well said, but it is an understatement. One has always to take the risk of being mistaken and also the less important risk of being misunderstood or misjudged.

However, this example shows, drastically, that even great scientists sometimes fail to reach that self-critical attitude which would prevent them from feeling very sure of themselves while gravely misjudging things.

Yet a limited amount of dogmatism is necessary for progress: Without a serious struggle for survival in which the old theories are tenaciously defended, none of the competing theories can show their mettle, that is, their explanatory power and their truth content. In-

tolerant dogmatism, however, is one of the main obstacles to science. Indeed, we should not only keep alternative theories alive by discussing them, but we should systematically look for new alternatives; and we should be worried whenever there are no alternatives—whenever a dominant theory becomes too exclusive. The danger to progress in science is much increased if the theory in question obtains something like a monopoly.

XI

But there is even a greater danger: A theory, even a scientific theory, may become an intellectual fashion, a substitute for religion, an entrenched ideology. And with this I come to the main point of this second part of my lecture—the part that deals with obstacles to progress in science, to the distinction between scientific revolutions and ideological revolutions.

For in addition to the always important problem of dogmatism and the closely connected problem of ideological intolerance, there is a different and, I think, a more interesting problem. I mean the problem which arises from certain links between science and ideology, links which do exist but which have led some people to conflate science and ideology and to muddle the distinction between scientific and ideological revolutions.

I think that this is quite a serious problem at a time when intellectuals, including scientists, are prone to fall for ideologies and intellectual fashions. This may well be due to the decline of religion, to the unsatisfied and unconscious religious needs of our fatherless society.[25] During my lifetime I have witnessed, quite apart from the various totalitarian movements, a considerable number of intellectually highbrow and avowedly nonreligious movements with aspects whose religious character is unmistakable once your eyes are open to it.[26] The best of these many movements was that which was inspired by the father figure of Einstein. It was the best, because of Einstein's always modest and highly self-critical attitude and his humanity and tolerance. Nevertheless, I shall later have a few words to say about what seem to me the less satisfactory aspects of the Einsteinian ideological revolution.

I am not an essentialist, and I shall not discuss here the essence or nature of "ideologies." I will merely state very generally and vaguely that I am going to use the term "ideology" for *any non-scientific* theory or creed or view of the world which proves attractive, and which interests people, including scientists. (Thus there may be very helpful and also very destructive ideologies from, say, a humanitarian or a rationalist point of view.[27]) I need not say more about ideologies in order to justify the sharp distinction which I am going to make between science[28] and "ideology," and further, between *scientific revolutions* and *ideological revolutions*. But I will elucidate this distinction with the help of a number of examples.

These examples will show, I hope, that it is important to distinguish between a scientific revolution in the sense of a rational overthrow of an established scientific theory by a new one and all processes of "social entrenchment" or perhaps "social acceptance" of ideologies, including even those ideologies which incorporate some scientific results.

XII

As my first example I choose the Copernican and Darwinian revolutions, because in these two cases a scientific revolution gave rise to an ideological revolution. Even if we neglect here the ideology of "Social Darwinism,"[29] we can distinguish a scientific and an ideological component in both these revolutions.

The Copernican and Darwinian revolutions were *ideological* insofar as they both changed man's view of his place in the Universe. They clearly were *scientific* insofar as each of them overthrew a dominant scientific theory: a dominant astronomical theory and a dominant biological theory.

It appears that the ideological impact of the Copernican and also of the Darwinian theory was so great because each of them clashed with a religious dogma. This was highly significant for the intellectual history of our civilization, and it had repercussions on the history of science (for example, because it led to a tension between religion and science). And yet, the historical and sociological fact that the theories of both Copernicus and Darwin clashed with religion is completely irrelevant for the rational evaluation of the scientific theories proposed by them. Logically it has nothing whatsoever to do with the *scientific* revolution started by each of the two theories.

It is therefore important to distinguish between scientific and ideological revolutions particularly in those cases in which the ideological revolutions interact with revolutions in science.

The example, more especially, of the Copernican ideological revolution may show that even an ideological revolution might well be described as "rational." However, while we have a logical criterion of progress in science—and thus of rationality—we do not seem to have anything like general criteria of progress or of rationality outside science (although this should not be taken to mean that outside science there are no such things as standards of rationality). Even a highbrow intellectual ideology which bases itself on accepted scientific results may be irrational, as is shown by the many movements of modernism in art (and in science), and also of archaism in art, movements which in my opinion are intellectually insipid since they appeal to values which have nothing to do with art (or science). Indeed, many movements of this kind are just fashions which should not be taken too seriously.[30]

Proceeding with my task of elucidating the distinction between scientific and ideological revolutions, I will now give several examples of major scientific revolutions which did not lead to any ideological revolution.

The revolution of Faraday and Maxwell was, from a scientific point of view, just as great as that of Copernicus, and possibly greater: It dethroned Newton's central dogma—the dogma of central forces. Yet it did *not* lead to an ideological revolution, though it inspired a whole generation of physicists.

J. J. Thomson's discovery (and theory) of the electron was also a major revolution. To overthrow the age-old theory of the indivisibility of the atom constituted a scientific revolution easily comparable to Copernicus's achievement: When Thomson announced it, physicists thought he was pulling their legs. But it did not create an ideological revolution. And yet, it overthrew both of the two rival theories which for 2400 years had been fighting for dominance in the theory of matter—the theory of indivisible atoms, and that of the continuity of matter. To assess the revolutionary significance of this breakthrough it will be sufficient to remind you that it introduced structure as well as electricity into the atom, and thus into the constitution of matter. Also, the quantum mechanics of 1925 and 1926, of Heisenberg and of Born, of de Broglie, of Schrödinger and of Dirac, was essentially a quantization of the theory of the Thomson electron. And yet Thomson's scientific revolution did not lead to a new ideology.

Another striking example is Rutherford's overthrow in 1911 of the model of the atom proposed by J. J. Thomson in 1903. Rutherford had accepted Thomson's theory that the positive charge must be distributed over the whole space occupied by the atom. This may be seen from his reaction to the famous experiment of Geiger and Marsden. They found that when they shot alpha particles at a very thin sheet of gold foil, a few of the alpha particles—about one in twenty thousand—were reflected by the foil rather than merely deflected. Rutherford was incredulous. As he said later,

"It was quite the most incredible event that has ever happened to me in my life. It was almost as incredible as if you fired a fifteen-inch shell at a piece of tissue paper and it came back and hit you."[31] This remark of Rutherford's shows the utterly revolutionary character of the discovery. Rutherford realized that the experiment refuted Thomson's model of the atom, and he replaced it by his nuclear model of the atom. This was the beginning of nuclear science. Rutherford's model became widely known, even among non-physicists. But it did not trigger off an ideological revolution.

One of the most fundamental scientific revolutions in the history of the theory of matter has never even been recognized as such. I mean the refutation of the electromagnetic theory of matter which had become dominant after Thomson's discovery of the electron. Quantum mechanics arose as part of this theory, and it was essentially this theory whose "completeness" was defended by Bohr against Einstein in 1935, and again in 1949. Yet in 1934 Yukawa had outlined a new quantum-theoretical approach to nuclear forces which resulted in the overthrow of the electromagnetic theory of matter after forty years of unquestioned dominance.[32]

There are many other major scientific revolutions which failed to trigger off any ideological revolution; for example, Mendel's revolution (which later saved Darwinism from extinction). Others are X-rays, radioactivity, the discovery of isotopes, and the discovery of superconductivity. To all these, there was no corresponding ideological revolution. Nor do I see as yet an ideological revolution resulting from the breakthrough of Crick and Watson.

XIII

Of great interest is the case of the so-called Einsteinian revolution—I mean Einstein's scientific revolution, which among intellectuals had an ideological influence comparable to that of the Copernican or Darwinian revolutions.

Of Einstein's many revolutionary discoveries in physics, there are two which are relevant here.

The first is special relativity, which overthrows Newtonian kinematics, replacing Galileo invariance by Lorentz invariance.[33] Of course, this revolution satisfies our criteria of rationality: The old theories are explained as approximately valid for velocities which are small compared with the velocity of light. . . .

General relativity was in my opinion one of the greatest scientific revolutions ever, because it clashed with the greatest and best tested theory ever—Newton's theory of gravity and of the solar system. It contains, as it should, Newton's theory as an approximation; yet it contradicts it in several points. It yields different results for elliptic orbits of appreciable eccentricity; and it entails the astonishing result that any physical particle (photons included) which approaches the center of a gravitational field with a velocity exceeding six-tenths of the velocity of light is not accelerated by the gravitational field, as in Newton's theory, but decelerated: that is, not attracted by a heavy body, but repelled.[34]

This most surprising and exciting result has stood up to tests. . . . Nevertheless, Einstein never believed that his theory was true. He shocked Cornelius Lanczos in 1922 by saying that his theory was merely a passing stage; he called it "ephemeral."[35] And he said to Leopold Infeld[36] that the left-hand side of his field equation[37] (the curvature tensor) was as solid as a rock, while the right-hand side (the momentum–energy tensor) was as weak as straw. . . .

However, the ideological elements of the Einsteinian revolution influenced scientists, and thereby the history of science; and this influence was not all to the good.

First of all, the myth that Einstein had reached his result by an essential use of epistemological and especially operationalist methods had in my opinion a devastating effect upon science. (It is irrelevant whether you get your results—especially good results—by dreaming them, or by drinking black coffee, or even from a mistaken epistemology.)[38] Secondly, it led to the belief that quantum mechanics, the second great revolutionary theory of the century, must outdo the Einsteinian revolution, especially with respect to its epistemological depth. It seems to me that this belief affected some of the great founders of quantum mechanics,[39] and also some of the great founders of molecular biology.[40] It led to the dominance of a subjectivist interpretation of quantum mechanics; an interpretation which I have been combating for almost forty years. I cannot here describe the situation, but while I am aware of the dazzling achievement of quantum mechanics (which must not blind us to the fact that it is seriously incomplete[41]) I suggest that the orthodox interpretation of quantum mechanics is not part of physics, but an ideology. In fact, it is part of a modernistic ideology; and it has become a scientific fashion which is a serious obstacle to the progress of science.

XIV

I hope that I have made clear the distinction between a scientific revolution and the ideological revolution which may sometimes be linked with it. The ideological revolution may serve rationality or it may undermine it. But it is often nothing but an intellectual fashion. Even if it is linked to a scientific revolution it may be of a highly irrational character, and it may consciously break with tradition.

But a scientific revolution, however radical, cannot really break with tradition, since it must preserve the success of its predecessors. This is why scientific revolutions are rational. By this I do not mean, of course, that the great scientists who make the revolution are, or ought to be, wholly rational beings. On the contrary: Although I have been arguing here for the rationality of scientific revolutions, my guess is that should individual scientists ever become "objective and rational" in the sense of "impartial and detached," then we should indeed find the revolutionary progress of science barred by an impenetrable obstacle.

Notes

I wish to thank Troels Eggers Hansen, The Rev. Michael Sharratt, Dr. Herbert Spengler, and Dr. Martin Wenham for critical comments on this lecture.

1. See, in the present series of Herbert Spencer Lectures, the concluding remark of the contribution by Professor W. F. Bodmer. My own misgivings concerning scientific advance and stagnation arise mainly from the changed spirit of science, and from the unchecked growth of Big Science which endangers great science. (See Section IX of this lecture.) Biology seems to have escaped this danger so far, but not, of course, the closely related dangers of large-scale application.

2. The formation of membrane proteins, of the first viruses, and of cells, may perhaps have been among the earliest inventions of new environmental niches, though it is possible that other environmental niches (perhaps networks of enzymes invented by otherwise naked genes) may have been invented even earlier.

3. It is an open problem whether one can speak in these terms ("in response") about the genetic level . . . Yet if there were no variations, there could not be adaptation or evolution; and so we can say that the occurrence of mutations is either partly controlled by a need for them, or functions as if it was.

4. When in this lecture I speak, for brevity's sake, of *mutation*, the possibility of recombination is of course always tacitly included.

5. The realization of our ignorance has become pinpointed as a result, for example, of the astonishing revolution brought about by molecular biology.

6. For the use of the term *blind* (especially in the second sense) see D. T. Campbell, "Methodological Suggestions from a Comparative Psychology of Knowledge Processes," *Inquiry* 2, 152–82 (1959); "*Blind Variation and Selective Retention in Creative Thought as in Other Knowledge Processes*," *Psychol. Rev.* 67, 380–400 (1960); and "Evolutionary Epistemology," in *The Philosophy of Karl Popper*, The Library of Living Philosophers (ed. P. A. Schilpp), pp. 413–63, The Open Court Publishing Co., La Salle, Illinois (1974).

7. While the "blindness" of trials is relative to what we have found out in the past, randomness is relative to a set of elements (forming the "sample space"). On the genetic level these "elements" are the four nucleotide bases; on the behavioral level they are the constituents of the organism's repertoire of behavior. These constituents may assume different weights with respect to different needs or goals, and the weights may change through experience (lowering the degree of "blindness").

8. On the importance of active participation, see R. Held and A. Hein, "Movement-produced Stimulation in the Development of Visually Guided Behavior," *J. Comp. Physiol. Psychol.* 56 872–6 (1963); cf. J. C. Eccles *Facing Reality*, pp. 66–7. The activity is, at least partly, one of producing hypotheses: see J. Krechevsky, "'Hypothesis' versus 'Chance' in the Pre-solution Period in Sensory Discrimination-learning," *Univ. Calif. Publ. Psychol.* 6, 27–44 (1932) (reprinted in *Animal Problem Solving* [ed. A. J. Riopelle], pp. 183–97, Penguin Books, Hardmondsworth [1967].

9. I may perhaps mention here some of the differences between my views and the views of the Gestalt school. (Of course, I accept the fact of Gestalt perception; I am only dubious about what may be called Gestalt philosophy.)

   I conjecture that the unity, or the articulation, of perception is more closely dependent on the motor control systems and the efferent neural systems of the brain than on afferent systems, that it is closely dependent on the behavioral repertoire of the organism. I conjecture that a spider or a mouse will never have insight (as had Köhler's ape) into the possible unity of the two sticks which can be joined together, because handling sticks of that size does not belong to their behavioral repertoire. All this may be interpreted as a kind of generalization of the James-Lange theory of emotions (1884; see William James, *The Principles of Psychology*, Vol. II, pp. 449 ff. [1809] Macmillan and Co., London), extending the theory from our emotions to our perceptions (especially to Gestalt perceptions), which thus would not be "given" to us (as in Gestalt theory) but rather "made" by us, by decoding (comparatively "given") clues. The fact that the clues may mislead (optical illusions in man; dummy illusions in animals, etc.) can be explained by the biological need to impose our behavioral interpretations upon highly simplified clues. The conjecture that our decoding of what the senses tell us depends on our behavioral repertoire may explain part of the gulf that lies between animals and man, for through the evolution of the human language our repertoire has become unlimited.

10. See W. H. Thorpe, *Learning and Instinct in Animals*, pp. 99 ff. Methuen, London (1956); 1963 edn, pp. 100–47; W. Köhler, *The Mentality of Apes* (1925); Penguin Books edn, (1957), pp. 166 ff.

11. See I. P. Pavlov, *Conditioned Reflexes*, esp. pp. 11–12, Oxford University Press (1927). In view of what he calls "exploratory behavior" and the closely related "freedom behavior"—both obviously genetically based—and of the significance of these for scientific activity, it seems to me that the behavior of behaviorists who aim to supersede the value of freedom by what they call "positive reinforcement" may be a symptom of an unconscious hostility to science. Incidentally, what B. F. Skinner (cf. his *Beyond Freedom and Dignity* (1972) Cape, London) calls "the literature of freedom" did not arise as a result of negative reinforcement, as he suggests. It arose, rather, with Aeschylus and Pindar, as a result of the victories of Marathon and Salamis.

12. Thus exploratory behavior and problem-solving create new conditions for the evolution of genetic systems, conditions which deeply affect the natural selection of these systems. One can say that once a certain latitude of behavior has been attained—as it has been attained even by unicellular organisms (see especially the classic work of H. S. Jennings, *The Behavior of the Lower Organisms*, Columbia University Press, New York [1906]—the initiative of the organism in selecting its ecology or habitat takes the lead, and natural selection within the new habitat follows the lead. In this way, Darwinism can simulate Lamarckism, and even Bergson's "creative evolution." This has been recognized by strict Darwinists. For a brilliant presentation and summary of the history, see Sir Alister Hardy, *The Living Stream*, Collins, London (1965), especially Lectures VI, VII, and VIII, where many references to earlier literature will be found, from James Hutton (who died in 1797) onwards (see pp. 178 ff.). See also Ernst Mayr, *Animal Species and Evolution*, The Belknap Press, Cambridge, Mass., and Oxford University Press, London (1963), pp. 604 ff. And 611; Erwin Schrödinger, *Mind and Matter*, Cambridge University Press (1958), Ch. 2; F. W. Braestrup, "The Evolutionary Significance of Learning," in *Vidensk. Meddr dansk naturh. Foren.* 134, 89–102 (1971) (with a bibliography); and also my first Herbert Spencer Lecture (1961) now in my *Objective Knowledge*, Clarendon Press, Oxford (1972, 1973).

13. Quoted by Jacques Hadamard, *The Psychology of Invention in the Mathematical Field*, Princeton University Press (1945), and Dover edition (1954), p. 48.

14. Behavioral psychologists who study "experimenter bias" have found that some albino rats perform decidedly better than others if the experimenter is led to believe (wrongly) that the former belong to a strain selected for high intelligence: see, "The Effect of Experimenter Bias on the Performance of the Albino Rat," *Behav. Sci.* 8, 183–9 (1963). The lesson drawn by the authors of this paper is that experiments should be made by "research assistants who do not know what outcome is desired" (p. 188). Like Bacon, these authors pin their hopes on the empty mind, forgetting that the expectations of the director of research may communicate themselves, without explicit disclosure, to his research assistants, just as they seem to have communicated themselves from each research assistant to his rats.

15. Compare my *Logic of Scientific Discovery*, Section 8, and my *Objective Knowledge*.

16. Thus Einstein's theory *contradicts* Newton's theory (although it contains Newton's theory as an approximation): In contradistinction to Newton's theory, Einstein's theory shows, for example, that in strong gravitational fields there cannot be a Keplerian elliptic orbit with appreciable eccentricity but without corresponding precession of the perihelion (as observed of Mercury).

17. Cf. my criticism of the so-called "sociology of knowledge" in Ch. 23 of my *Open Society*, and pp. 155 f. of my *Poverty of Historicism*.

18. Cf. Jacques Hadamard, *The Psychology of Invention in the Mathematical Field* (see note 13 above).

19. A conversation with Eugene Wigner, *Science* 181, 527–33 (1973); see p. 533.

20. For Aristarchus and Seleucus see Sir Thomas Heath, *Aristarchus of Samos*, Clarendon Press, Oxford (1966).

21. See Max Jammer, *The Conceptual Development of Quantum Mechanics*, pp. 40–2; McGraw-Hill, New York (1966).

22. See Heinrich Hertz, *Electric Waves*, Macmillan and Co., London (1894); Dover edn, New York (1962), pp. 12, 187 f., 273.

23. See Jammer, op. cit., pp. 43 f., and Théo Kahan, "Un document historique de l'académie des sciences de Berlin sur l'activité scientific d'Albert Einstein" (1913), *Archs. Ind. Hist. Sci.* 15, 337–42 (1962); see esp. p. 340.

24. Compare Jammer's slightly different translation, loc. cit.

25. Our Western societies do not, but their structure, satisfy the need for a father figure. I discussed the problems that arise from this fact briefly in my

(unpublished) William James Lectures in Harvard (1950). My late friend, the psychoanalyst Paul Federn, showed me shortly afterwards an earlier paper of his devoted to this problem.

26. An obvious example is the role of prophet played, in various movements, by Sigmund Freud, Arnold Schönberg, Karl Kraus, Ludwig Witgenstein, and Herbert Marcuse.

27. There are many kinds of "ideologies" in the wide and (deliberately) vague sense of the term I used in the text, and therefore many aspects to the distinction between science and ideology. Two may be mentioned here. One is that scientific theories can be distinguished or "demarcated" (see note 28) from non-scientific theories which, nevertheless, may strongly influence scientists and even inspire their work. (This influence, of course, may be good or bad or mixed.) A very different aspect is that of entrenchment: A scientific theory may function as an ideology if it becomes socially entrenched. This is why, when speaking of the distinction between scientific revolutions and ideological revolutions, I include among ideological revolutions changes in non-scientific ideas which may inspire the work of scientists and also changes in the social entrenchment of what may otherwise be a scientific theory. (I owe the formulation of the points in this note to Jeremy Shearmur who has also contributed to other points dealt with in this lecture.)

28. In order not to repeat myself too often, I did not mention in this lecture my suggestion for a criterion of the empirical character of a theory (falsifiability or refutability as the criterion of demarcation between empirical theories and non-empirical theories). Since in English "science" means "empirical science," and since the matter is sufficiently fully discussed in my books, I have written things like the following (for example, in *Conjectures and Refutations*, p. 39): " . . . in order to be ranked as scientific, [statements] must be capable of conflicting with possible, or conceivable, observations." Some people seized upon this like a shot (as early as 1932, I think). "What about your own gospel?" is the typical move. (I found this objection again in a book published in 1973.) My answer to the objection, however, was published in 1934 (see my *Logic of Scientific Discovery*, Ch 2, Section 10 and elsewhere). I may restate my answer: My gospel is not "scientific," that is, it does not belong to empirical science, but it is, rather, a (normative) *proposal*. My gospel (and also my answer) is, incidentally, criticizable, though not just by observation, and it has been criticized.

29. For a criticism of Social Darwinism see my *Open Society*, Ch. 10, note 71.

30. Further to my use of the vague term "ideology" (which includes all kinds of theories, beliefs, and attitudes, including some that may influence scientists) it should be clear that I intend to cover by this term not only historicist fashions like "modernism," but also serious, and rationally discussable, metaphysical and ethical ideas. I may perhaps refer to Jim Erikson, a former student of mine in Christchurch, New Zealand, who once said in a discussion: "We do not suggest that science invented intellectual honesty, but we do suggest that intellectual honesty invented science." A very similar idea is to be found in Ch. ix ("The Kingdom and the Darkness") of Jacques Monod's book *Chance and Necessity*, Knopf, New York (1971). See also my *Open Society*, Vol. ii, Ch. 24 ("The Revolt against Reason"). We might say, of course, that an ideology which has learned from the critical approach of the sciences is likely to be more rational than one which clashes with science.

31. Lord Rutherford, "The Development of the Theory of Atomic Structure," in J. Needham and W. Pagel (eds), *Background of Modern Science*, pp. 61–74, Cambridge University Press (1938); the quotation is from p. 68.

32. See my "Quantum Mechanics without 'the Observer'," in *Quantum Theory and Reality* (ed. Mario Bunge), esp. pp. 8–9, Springer-Verlag, New York (1967).

The fundamental idea (that the inertial mass of the electron is in part explicable as the inertia of the moving electromagnetic field) that led to the electromagnetic theory of matter is due to J. J. Thomson, "On the Electric and Magnetic Effects Produced by the Motion of Electrified Bodies," *Phil. Mag.* (5th Ser.) 11, 229–49 (1881), and to O. Heaviside, "On the Electromagnetic Effects due to the Motion of Electrification through a Dialectric," *Phil. Mag.* (5th Ser.) 27, 324–39 (1889). It was developed by W. Kaufmann ("Die magnetische und elektrische Ablenkbarkeit der Bequerelstrahlen und die scheinbare Masse der Elektronen," *Gött. Nachr.* 143–55 [1901], "Ueber die elektromagnetische Masse des Elektrons," 291–6 [1902], "Ueber die 'Elektromagnetische Masse' der Elektronen," 90–103 [1903]) and M. Abraham ("Dynamik des Elektrons," *Gött. Nachr.* 20–41 [1902], "Prinzipien der Dynamik des Elektrons," *Annin Phys.* [4th Ser.], 10, 105–7 [1903]) into the thesis that the mass of the electron is a purely electromagnetic effect. (See W. Kaufmann, "Die elektromagnetische Masse des Elektrons," *Phys. Z.* 4, 54–7 [1902–3] and M. Abraham,

"Prinzipien der Dynamik des Elektrons," *Phys. Z.* 4, pp. 57–63 [1902–3] and M. Abraham, *Theorie der Elektrizität*, Vol. ii, pp. 136–249, Leipzig [1905].) The idea was strongly supported by H. A. Lorentz, "Elektromagnetische verschijnselen in een stelsel dat zich met willekeurige snelheid, kleiner dan die van het licht, beweegt," *Versl. Gewone Vergad. wis- en natuurk. Afd. K. Akad. Wet. Amst.* 12, second part, 986–1009 (1903–4), and by Einstein's special relativity, leading to results deviating from those of Kaufmann and Abraham. The electromagnetic theory of matter had a great ideological influence on scientists because of the fascinating possibility of *explaining matter*. It was shaken and modified by Rutherford's discovery of the nucleus (and the proton) and by Chadwick's discovery of the neutron, which may help to explain why its final overthrow by the theory of nuclear forces was hardly taken notice of.

33. The revolutionary power of special relativity lies in a new point of view which allows the derivation and interpretation of the Lorentz transformations from two simple first principles. The greatness of this revolution can be best gauged by reading Abraham's book (Vol. ii, referred to in note 32 above). This book, which is slightly earlier than Poincaré's and Einstein's papers on relativity, contains a full discussion of the problem situation, of Lorentz's theory of the Michelson experiment, and even of Lorentz's local time. Abraham comes, for example on pp. 143 f. and 370 f., quite close to Einsteinian ideas. It even seems as if Max Abraham was better informed about the problem situation than was Einstein. Yet there is no realization of the revolutionary potentialities of the problem situation; quite the contrary. For Abraham writes in his Preface, dated March 1905: "The theory of electricity now

appears to have entered a state of quieter development." This shows how hopeless it is even for a great scientist like Abraham to foresee the future development of his science.

34. More precisely, a body falling from infinity with a velocity $v > c/3^{1/2}$ toward the center of a gravitational field will be constantly decelerated in approaching this center.

35. See C. Lanczos, op. cit., p. 196.

36. See Leopold Infeld, *Quest*, p. 90. Victor Gollancz, London (1941).

37. See A. Einstein, "Die Feldgleichungen der Gravitation," *Sber. Akad. Wiss. Berlin*, Part 2, 844–7 (1915); "Die Grundlage der Allgemeinen Relativitätstheorie," *Annin Phys.*, (4th Ser.) 49, 769–822 (1916).

38. I believe that §2 of Einstein's famous paper, "Die Grundlage der allgemeinen Relativitätstheorie" (see Note 37 above; English translation, "The Foundation of the General Theory of Relativity," *The Principle of Relativity*, pp. 111–64 uses most questionable epistemological arguments *against* Newton's absolute space and *for* a very important theory.

39. Especially Heisenberg and Bohr.

40. Apparently it affected Max Delbrück; see *Perspectives in American History*, Vol. 2, Harvard University Press (1968), "Emigré Physicists and the Biological Revolution," by Donald Fleming, pp. 152–89, especially Sections iv and v. (I owe this reference to Professor Mogens Blegvad.)

41. It is clear that a physical theory which does not explain such constants as the electric elementary quantum (or the fine structure constant) is incomplete, to say nothing of the mass spectra of the elementary particles. See my paper, "Quantum Mechanics without 'the Observer'," referred to in note 32 above.

THOMAS S. KUHN

The Function of Dogma in Scientific Research[1]

At some point in his or her career every member of this Symposium has, I feel sure, been exposed to the image of the scientist as the uncommitted searcher after truth. He is the explorer of nature—the man who rejects prejudice at the threshold of his laboratory, who collects and examines the bare and objective facts, and whose allegiance is to such facts and to them alone. These are the characteristics which make the testimony of scientists so valuable when advertising proprietary products in the United States. Even for an international audience, they should require no further elaboration. To be scientific is, among other things, to be objective and open-minded.

Probably none of us believes that in practice the real-life scientist quite succeeds in fulfilling this ideal. Personal acquaintance, the novels of Sir Charles Snow, or a cursory reading of the history of science provides too much counter-evidence. Though the scientific enterprise may be open-minded, whatever this application of that phrase may mean, the individual scientist is very often not. Whether his work is predominantly theoretical or experimental, he usually seems to know, before his research project is even well under way, all but the most intimate details of the result which that project will achieve. If the result is quickly forthcoming, well and good. If not, he will struggle with his apparatus and with his equations until, if at all possible, they yield results which conform to the sort of pattern which he has foreseen from the start. Nor is it only through his own research that the scientist displays his firm convictions about the phenomena which nature can yield and about the ways in which these may be fitted to theory. Often the same convictions show even more clearly in his response to the work produced by others. From Galileo's reception of Kepler's research to Nägeli's reception of Mendel's, from Dalton's rejection of Gay Lussac's results to Kelvin's rejection of Maxwell's, unexpected novelties of fact and

Reprinted from *Scientific Change*, Alistair C. Crombie, Ed. (1963), pp. 347–369. © 1963 by Heinemann Educational Books, Ltd. Reprinted by permission of Basic Books, Inc., publishers.

theory have characteristically been resisted and have often been rejected by many of the most creative members of the professional scientific community. The historian, at least, scarcely needs Planck to remind him that "A new scientific truth is not usually presented in a way that convinces its opponents . . . ; rather they gradually die off, and a rising generation is familiarized with the truth from the start."[2]

Familiar facts like these—and they could easily be multiplied—do not seem to bespeak an enterprise whose practitioners are notably open-minded. Can they all be reconciled with our usual image of productive scientific research? If such a reconciliation has not seemed to present fundamental problems in the past, that is probably because resistance and preconception have usually been viewed as extraneous to science. They are, we have often been told, no more than the product of inevitable *human* limitations; a proper scientific method has no place for them; and that method is powerful enough so that no mere human idiosyncrasy can impede its success for very long. On this view, examples of a scientific *parti pris* are reduced to the status of anecdotes, and it is that evaluation of their significance that this essay aims to challenge. Verisimilitude, alone, suggests that such a challenge is required. Preconception and resistance seem the rule rather than the exception in mature scientific development. Furthermore, under normal circumstances they characterize the very best and most creative research as well as the more routine. Nor can there be much question where they come from. Rather than being characteristics of the aberrant individual, they are community characteristics with deep roots in the procedures through which scientists are trained for work in their profession. Strongly held convictions that are prior to research often seem to be a precondition for success in the sciences.

Obviously I am already ahead of my story, but in getting there I have perhaps indicated its principal theme. Though preconception and resistance to innovation could very easily choke off scientific progress, their omnipresence is nonetheless symptomatic of characteristics upon which the continuing vitality of research depends. Those characteristics I shall collectively call the dogmatism of mature science, and in the pages to come I shall try to make the following points about them. Scientific education inculcates what the scientific community had previously with difficulty gained—a deep commitment to a particular way of viewing the world and of practicing science in it. That commitment can be, and from time to time is, replaced by another, but it cannot be merely given up. And, while it continues to characterize the community of professional practitioners, it proves in two respects fundamental to productive research. By defining for the individual scientist both the problems available for pursuit and the nature of acceptable solutions to them, the commitment is actually constitutive of research. Normally the scientist is a puzzle-solver like the chess player, and the commitment induced by education is what provides him with the rules of the game being played in his time. In its absence he would not be a physicist, chemist, or whatever he has been trained to be.

In addition, commitment has a second and largely incompatible research role. Its very strength and the unanimity with which the professional group subscribes to it provides the individual scientist with an immensely sensitive detector of the trouble spots from which significant innovations of fact and theory are almost inevitably educed. In the sciences most discoveries of unexpected fact and all fundamental innovations of theory are responses to a prior breakdown in the rules of the previously established game. Therefore, though a quasi-dogmatic commitment is, on the one hand, a source of resistance and controversy, it is also instrumental in making the sciences the most consistently revolutionary of all human activities. One need make neither resistance nor dogma a virtue to recognize that no mature science could exist without them. Before examining further the nature and effects of scientific dogma, consider the pattern of education through which it is transmitted from one generation of practitioners to the next. Scientists are not, of course, the only professional community that acquires from education a set of standards, tools, and techniques which they later deploy in their own creative work. Yet even a cursory inspection of scientific pedagogy suggests that it is far more likely to induce professional rigidity than education in other fields, excepting, perhaps, systematic theology. Admittedly the following epitome is biased toward the American pattern, which I know best. The contrasts at which it aims must, however, be visible, if muted, in European and British education as well.

Perhaps the most striking feature of scientific education is that, to an extent quite unknown in other creative fields, it is conducted through textbooks, works written especially for students. Until he is ready, or very nearly ready, to begin his own dissertation, the student of chemistry, physics, astronomy, geology, or biology is seldom either asked to attempt trial research projects or exposed to the immediate products of research done by others—to, that is, the professional communications that scientists write for their peers. Collections of "source readings" play a negligible role in *scientific* education. Nor is the science student encouraged to read the historical classics of his field—works in which he might encounter other ways of regarding the questions discussed in his text, but in which he would also meet problems, concepts and standards of solution that his future profession had long since discarded and replaced.[3] Whitehead somewhere caught this quite special feature of the sciences when he wrote, "A science that hesitates to forget its founders is lost."

An almost exclusive reliance on textbooks is not all that distinguishes scientific education. Students in other fields are, after all, also exposed to such books, though seldom beyond the second year of college and even in those early years not exclusively. But in the sciences different textbooks display different subject matters rather than, as in the humanities and many social sciences, exemplifying different approaches to a single problem field. Even books that compete for adoption in a single science course differ mainly in level and pedagogic detail, not in substance or conceptual structure. One can scarcely imagine a physicist's or chemist's saying that he had been forced to begin the education of his third-year class almost from first principles because its previous exposure to the field had been through books that consistently violated his conception of the discipline. Remarks of that sort are not by any means unprecedented in several of the social sciences. Apparently scientists agree about what it is that every student of the field must know. That is why, in the design of a pre-professional curriculum, they can use textbooks instead of eclectic samples of research.

Nor is the characteristic technique of textbook presentation altogether the same in the sciences as elsewhere. Except in the occasional introductions that students seldom read, science texts make little attempt to describe the *sorts* of problems that the professional may be asked to solve or to discuss the *variety* of techniques that experience has made available for their solution. Instead, these books exhibit, from the very start, concrete problem-solutions that the profession has come to accept as paradigms, and they then ask the student, either with a pencil and paper or in the laboratory, to solve for himself problems closely modelled in method and substance upon those through which the text has led him. Only in elementary language instruction or in training a musical instrumentalist is so large or essential a use made of "finger exercises." And those are just the fields in which the object of instruction is to produce with maximum rapidity strong "mental sets" or *Einstellungen*. In the sciences, I suggest, the effect of these techniques is much the same. Though scientific development is particularly productive of consequential novelties, scientific education remains a relatively dogmatic initiation into a pre-established problem-solving tradition that the student is neither invited nor equipped to evaluate.

The pattern of systematic textbook education just described existed in no place and in no science (except perhaps elementary mathematics) until the early nineteenth century. But before that date a number of the more developed sciences clearly displayed the special characteristics indicated above, and in a few cases had done so for a very long time. Where there were no textbooks there had often been universally received paradigms for the practice of individual sciences. These were scientific achievements reported in books that all the practitioners of a given field knew intimately and admired, achievements upon which they modelled their own research and which provided them with a measure of their own accomplishment. Aristotle's *Physica*, Ptolemy's *Almagest*, Newton's *Principia* and *Opticks*, Franklin's *Electricity*, Lavoisier's *Chemistry*, and Lyell's *Geology*—these works and many others all served for a time implicitly to define the legitimate problems and methods of a research field for succeeding generations of practitioners. In their day each of these books, together with others modelled closely upon them, did for its field much of what textbooks now do for these same fields and for others besides.

All of the works named above are, of course, classics of science. As such their role may be thought to resemble that of the main classics in other creative fields, for example the works of a Shakespeare, a Rembrandt, or an Adam Smith. But by calling these works, or the achievements which lie behind them, paradigms rather than classics, I mean to suggest that there is something else special about them, something which sets them apart both from some other classics of science and from all the classics of other creative fields.

Part of this "something else" is what I shall call the exclusiveness of paradigms. At any time the practitioners of a given specialty may rec-

ognize numerous classics, some of them—like the works of Ptolemy and Copernicus or Newton and Descartes—quite incompatible one with the other. But that same group, if it has a paradigm at all, can have only one. Unlike the community of artists—which can draw simultaneous inspiration from the works of, say, Rembrandt *and* Cézanne and which therefore studies both—the community of astronomers had no alternative to choosing *between* the competing models of scientific activity supplied by Copernicus and Ptolemy. Furthermore, having made their choice, astronomers could thereafter neglect the work which they had rejected. Since the sixteenth century there have been only two full editions of the *Almagest*, both produced in the nineteenth century and directed exclusively to scholars. In the mature sciences there is no apparent function for the equivalent of an art museum or a library of classics. Scientists know when books, and even journals, are out of date. Though they do not then destroy them, they do, as any historian of science can testify, transfer them from the active departmental library to desuetude in the general university depository. Up-to-date works have taken their place, and they are all that the further progress of science requires.

This characteristic of paradigms is closely related to another, and one that has a particular relevance to my selection of the term. In receiving a paradigm the scientific community commits itself, consciously or not, to the view that the fundamental problems there resolved have, in fact, been solved once and for all. That is what Lagrange meant when he said of Newton: "There is but one universe, and it can happen to but one man in the world's history to be the interpreter of its laws."[4] The example of either Aristotle or Einstein proves Lagrange wrong, but that does not make the fact of his commitment less consequential to scientific development. Believing that what Newton had done need not be done again, Lagrange was not tempted to fundamental reinterpretations of nature. Instead, he could take up where the men who shared his Newtonian paradigm had left off, striving both for neater formulations of that paradigm and for an articulation that would bring it into closer and closer agreement with observations of nature. That sort of work is undertaken only by those who feel that the model they have chose is entirely secure. There is nothing quite like it in the arts, and the parallels in the social sciences are at best partial. Paradigms determine a developmental pattern for the mature sciences that is unlike the one familiar in other fields.

That difference could be illustrated by comparing the development of a paradigm-based science with that of, say, philosophy or literature. But the same effect can be achieved more economically by contrasting the early developmental pattern of almost any science with the pattern characteristic of the same field in its maturity. I cannot here avoid putting the point too starkly, but what I have in mind is this. Excepting in those fields which, like biochemistry, originated in the combination of existing specialties, paradigms are a relatively late acquisition in the course of scientific development. During its early years a science proceeds without them, or at least without any so unequivocal and so binding as those named illustratively above. Physical optics before Newton or the study of heat before Black and Lavoisier exemplifies the pre-paradigm developmental pattern that I shall immediately examine in the history of electricity. While it continues, until, that is, a first paradigm is reached, the development of a science resembles that of the arts and of most social sciences more closely than it resembles the pattern which astronomy, say, had already acquired in antiquity and which all the natural sciences make familiar today.

To catch the difference between pre- and post-paradigm scientific development, consider a single example. In the early eighteenth century, as in the seventeenth and earlier, there were almost as many views about the nature of electricity as there were important electrical experimenters, men like Hauksbee, Gray, De-

saguliers, Du Fay, Nollet, Watson, and Franklin. All their numerous concepts of electricity had something in common—they were partially derived from experiment and observation and partially from one or another version of the mechanico-corpuscular philosophy that guided all scientific research of the day. Yet these common elements gave their work no more than a family resemblance. We are forced to recognize the existence of several competing schools and sub-schools, each deriving strength from its relation to a particular version (Cartesian or Newtonian) of the corpuscular metaphysics, and each emphasizing the particular cluster of electrical phenomena which its own theory could do most to explain. Other observations were dealt with by *ad hoc* elaborations or remained as outstanding problems for further research.[5]

One early group of electricians followed seventeenth-century practice, and thus took attraction and frictional generation as the fundamental electrical phenomena. They tended to treat repulsion as a secondary effect (in the seventeenth century it had been attributed to some sort of mechanical rebounding) and also to postpone for as long as possible both discussion and systematic research on Gray's newly discovered effect, electrical conduction. Another closely related group regarded repulsion as the fundamental effect, while still another took attraction and repulsion together to be equally elementary manifestations of electricity. Each of these groups modified its theory and research accordingly, but they then had as much difficulty as the first in accounting for any but the simplest conduction effects. Those effects provided the starting point for still a third group, one which tended to speak of electricity as a "fluid" that ran through conductors rather than as an "effluvium" that emanated from non-conductors. This group, in its turn, had difficulty reconciling its theory with a number of attractive and repulsive effects.[6]

At various times all these schools made significant contributions to the body of concepts, phenomena, and techniques from which Franklin drew the first paradigm for electrical science. Any definition of the scientist that excludes the members of these schools will exclude their modern successors as well. Yet anyone surveying the development of electricity before Franklin may well conclude that, though the field's practitioners were scientists, the immediate result of their activity was something less than science. Because the body of belief he could take for granted was very small, each electrical experimenter felt forced to begin by building his field anew from its foundations. In doing so his choice of supporting observation and experiment was relatively free, for the set of standard methods and phenomena that every electrician must employ and explain was extraordinarily small. As a result, throughout the first half of the century, electrical investigations tended to circle back over the same ground again and again. New effects were repeatedly discovered, but many of them were rapidly lost again. Among those lost were many effects due to what we should now describe as inductive charging and also Du Fay's famous discovery of the two sorts of electrification. Franklin and Kinnersley were surprised when, some fifteen years later, the latter discovered that a charged ball which was repelled by rubbed glass would be attracted by rubbed sealing-wax or amber.[7] In the absence of a well-articulated and widely received theory (a desideratum which no science possesses from its very beginning and which few if any of the social sciences have achieved today), the situation could hardly have been otherwise. During the first half of the eighteenth century there was no way for electricians to distinguish consistently between electrical and non-electrical effects, between laboratory accidents and essential novelties, or between striking demonstration and experiments which revealed the essential nature of electricity.

This is the state of affairs which Franklin changed.[8] His theory explained so many—though not all—of the electrical effects recog-

nized by the various earlier schools that within a generation all electricians had been converted to some view very like it. Though it did not resolve quite all disagreements, Franklin's theory was electricity's first paradigm, and its existence gives a new tone and flavor to the electrical researches of the last decades of the eighteenth century. The end of inter-school debate ended the constant reiteration of fundamentals; confidence that they were on the right track encouraged electricians to undertake more precise, esoteric, and consuming sorts of work. Freed from concern with any and all electrical phenomena, the newly united group could pursue selected phenomena in far more detail, designing much special equipment for the task and employing it more stubbornly and systematically than electricians had ever done before. In the hands of a Cavendish, a Coulomb, or a Volta the collection of electrical facts and the articulation of electrical theory were, for the first time, highly directed activities. As a result the efficiency and effectiveness of electrical research increased immensely, providing evidence for a societal version of Francis Bacon's acute methodological dictum: "Truth emerges more readily from error than from confusion."

Obviously I exaggerate both the speed and the completeness with which the transition to a paradigm occurs. But that does not make the phenomenon itself less real. The maturation of electricity as a science is not coextensive with the entire development of the field. Writers on electricity during the first four decades of the eighteenth century possessed far more information about electrical phenomena than had their sixteenth- and seventeenth-century predecessors. During the half-century after 1745 very few new sorts of electrical phenomena were added to their lists. Nevertheless, in important respects the electrical writings of the last two decades of the century seemed further removed from those of Gray, Du Fay, and even Franklin than are the writings of these early eighteenth-century electricians from those of their predecessors a hundred years before. Some time between 1740 and 1780 electricians, as a group, gained what astronomers had achieved in antiquity, students of motion in the Middle Ages, of physical optics in the late seventeenth century, and of historical geology in the early nineteenth. They had, that is, achieved a paradigm, possession of which enabled them to take the foundation of their field for granted and to push on to more concrete and recondite problems.[9] Except with the advantage of hindsight, it is hard to find another criterion that so clearly proclaims a field of science.

These remarks should begin to clarify what I take a paradigm to be. It is, in the first place, a fundamental scientific achievement and one which includes both a theory and some exemplary applications to the results of experiment and observation. More important, it is an open-ended achievement, one which leaves all sorts of research still to be done. And, finally, it is an accepted achievement in the sense that it is received by a group whose members no longer try to rival it or to create alternates for it. Instead, they attempt to extend and exploit it in a variety of ways to which I shall shortly turn. That discussion of the work that paradigms leave to be done will make both their role and the reasons for their special efficacy clearer still. But first there is one rather different point to be made about them. Though the reception of a paradigm seems historically prerequisite to the most effective sorts of scientific research, the paradigms which enhance research effectiveness need not be and usually are not permanent. On the contrary, the developmental pattern of mature science is usually from paradigm to paradigm. It differs from the pattern characteristic of the early or pre-paradigm period not by the total elimination of debate over fundamentals, but by the drastic restriction of such debate to occasional periods of paradigm change.

Ptolemy's *Almagest* was not, for example, any less a paradigm because the research tradi-

tion that descended from it had ultimately to be replaced by an incompatible one derived from the work of Copernicus and Kepler. Nor was Newton's *Opticks* less a paradigm for eighteenth-century students of light because it was later replaced by the ether-wave theory of Young and Fresnel, a paradigm which in its turn gave way to the electromagnetic displacement theory that descends from Maxwell. Undoubtedly the research work that any given paradigm permits results in lasting contributions to the body of scientific knowledge and technique, but paradigms themselves are very often swept aside and replaced by others that are quite incompatible with them. We can have no recourse to notions like the "truth" or "validity" of paradigms in our attempt to understand the special efficacy of the research which their reception permits.

On the contrary, the historian can often recognize that in declaring an older paradigm out of date or in rejecting the approach of some one of the pre-paradigm schools a scientific community has rejected the embryo of an important scientific perception to which it would later be forced to return. But it is very far from clear that the profession delayed scientific development by doing so. Would quantum mechanics have been born sooner if nineteenth-century scientists had been more willing to admit that Newton's corpuscular view of light might still have something significant to teach them about nature? I think not, although in the arts, the humanities, and many social sciences that less doctrinaire view is very often adopted toward classic achievements of the past. Or would astronomy and dynamics have advanced more rapidly if scientists had recognized that Ptolemy and Copernicus had chosen equally legitimate means to describe the earth's position? That view was, in fact, suggested during the seventeenth century. But in the interim it was firmly rejected together with Ptolemaic astronomy, emerging again only in the very late nineteenth century when, for the first time, it had concrete relevance to unsolved problems generated by the continuing practice of non-relativistic physics. One could argue, as indeed by implication I shall, that close eighteenth- and nineteenth-century attention either to the work of Ptolemy or to the relativistic views of Descartes, Huygens, and Leibniz would have delayed rather than accelerated the revolution in physics with which the twentieth century began. Advance from paradigm to paradigm rather than through the continuing competition between recognized classics may be a functional as well as a factual characteristic of mature scientific development.

Much that has been said so far is intended to indicate that—except during occasional extraordinary periods to be discussed in the last section of this paper—the practitioners of a mature scientific specialty are deeply committed to some one paradigm-based way of regarding and investigating nature. Their paradigm tells them about the sorts of entities with which the universe is populated and about the way the members of that population behave; in addition, it informs them of the questions that may legitimately be asked about nature and of the techniques that can properly be used in the search for answers to them. In fact, a paradigm tells scientists so much that the questions it leaves for research seldom have great intrinsic interest to those outside the profession. Though educated men as a group may be fascinated to hear about the spectrum of fundamental particles or about the processes of molecular replication, their interest is usually quickly exhausted by an account of the beliefs that already underlie research on these problems. The outcome of the individual research project is indifferent to them, and their interest is unlikely to awaken again until, as with parity nonconservation, research unexpectedly leads to paradigm-change and to a consequent alteration in the beliefs which guide research. That, no doubt, is why both historians and popularizers have devoted so much of their attention to the revolutionary episodes which result in change of paradigm and have so largely neglected the sort of work that even the greatest scientists necessarily do most of the time.

My point will become clearer if I now ask what it is that the existence of a paradigm leaves for the scientific community to do. The answer—as obvious as the related existence of resistance to innovation and as often brushed under the carpet—is that scientists, given a paradigm, strive with all their might and skill to bring it into closer and closer agreement with nature. Much of their effort, particularly in the early stages of a paradigm's development, is directed to articulating the paradigm, rendering it more precise in areas where the original formulation has inevitably been vague. For example, knowing that electricity was a fluid whose individual particles act upon one another at a distance, electricians after Franklin could attempt to determine the quantitative law of force between particles of electricity. Others could seek the mutual interdependence of spark length, electroscope deflection, quantity of electricity, and conductor-configuration. These were the sorts of problems upon which Coulomb, Cavendish, and Volta worked in the last decades of the eighteenth century, and they have many parallels in the development of every other mature science. Contemporary attempts to determine the quantum mechanical forces governing the interactions of nucleons fall precisely in this same category, paradigm-articulation.

That sort of problem is not the only challenge which a paradigm sets for the community that embraces it. There are always many areas in which a paradigm is assumed to work but to which it has not, in fact, yet been applied. Matching the paradigm to nature in these areas often engages much of the best scientific talent in any generation. The eighteenth-century attempts to develop a Newtonian theory of vibrating strings provide one significant example, and the current work on a quantum mechanical theory of solids provides another. In addition, there is always much fascinating work to be done in improving the match between a paradigm and nature in an area where at least limited agreement has already been demonstrated. Theoretical work on problems like these is illustrated by eighteenth-century research on the perturbations that cause planets to deviate from their Keplerian orbits as well as by the elaborate twentieth-century theory of the spectra of complex atoms and molecules. And accompanying all these problems and still others besides is a recurring series of instrumental hurdles. Special apparatus had to be invented and built to permit Coulomb's determination of the electrical force law. New sorts of telescopes were required for the observations that, when completed, demanded an improved Newtonian perturbation theory. The design and construction of more flexible and more powerful accelerators is a continuing desideratum in the attempt to articulate more powerful theories of nuclear forces. These are the sorts of work on which almost all scientists spend almost all of their time.[10]

Probably this epitome of normal scientific research requires no elaboration in this place, but there are two points that must now be made about it. First, all of the problems mentioned above were paradigm-dependent, often in several ways. Some—for example, the derivation of perturbation terms in Newtonian planetary theory—could not even have been stated in the absence of an appropriate paradigm. With the transition from Newtonian to relativity theory a few of them became different problems and not all of these have yet been solved. Other problems—for example, the attempt to determine a law of electric forces—could be and were at least vaguely stated before the emergence of the paradigm with which they were ultimately solved. But in that older form they proved intractable. The men who described electrical attractions and repulsions in terms of effluvia attempted to measure the resulting forces by placing a charged disc at a measured distance beneath one pan of a balance. Under those circumstances no consistent or interpretable results were obtained. The prerequisite for success proved to be a paradigm that reduced electrical action to a gravity-like action between point particles at a distance. After Franklin electricians thought of electrical action in those terms; both Coulomb and Cavendish designed their apparatus accordingly. Finally, in both these cases and in all the others as well a commitment to the paradigm was needed simply to provide adequate motivation. Who would design and build elaborate special-purpose apparatus, or who would spend months trying to solve a particular differential equation, without a quite firm guarantee that his effort, if successful, would yield the anticipated fruit?

This reference to the anticipated outcome of a research project points to the second striking characteristic of what I am now calling normal, or paradigm-based, research. The scientist engaged in it does not at all fit the prevalent image of the scientist as explorer or as inventor of brand new theories which permit striking and unexpected predictions. On the contrary, in all the problems discussed above everything but the detail of the outcome was known in advance. No scientist who accepted Franklin's paradigm could doubt that there was a law of attraction between small particles of electricity, and they could reasonably suppose that it would take a simple algebraic form. Some of them had even guessed that it would prove to be an inverse square law. Nor did Newtonian astronomers and physicists doubt that Newton's laws of motion and of gravitation could ultimately be made to yield the observed motions of the moon and planets even though, for over a century, the complexity of the requisite mathematics prevented good agreements being uniformly obtained. In all these problems, as in most others that scientists undertake, the challenge is not to uncover the unknown but to obtain the known. Their fascination lies not in what success may be expected to disclose but in the difficulty of obtaining success at all. Rather than resembling exploration, normal research seems like the effort to assemble a Chinese cube whose finished outline is known from the start.

Those are the characteristics of normal research that I had in mind when, at the start of this essay, I described the man engaged in it as a puzzle-solver, like the chess player. The paradigm he has acquired through prior training provides him with the rules of the game, describes the pieces with which it must be played, and indicates the nature of the required outcome. His task is to manipulate those pieces within the rules in such a way that the required outcome is produced. If he fails, as most scientists do in at least their first attacks upon any given problem, that failure speaks only to his lack of skill. It cannot call into question the rules that his paradigm has supplied, for without those rules there would have been no puzzle with which to wrestle in the first place. No wonder, then, that the problems (or puzzles) which the practitioner of a mature science normally undertakes presuppose a deep commitment to a paradigm. And how fortunate it is that that commitment is not lightly given up. Experience shows that, in almost all cases, the reiterated efforts, either of the individual or of the professional group, do at last succeed in producing within the paradigm a solution to even the most stubborn problems. That is one of the ways in which science advances. Under those circumstances can we be surprised that scientists resist paradigm-change? What they are defending is, after all, neither more nor less than the basis of their professional way of life.

By now one principal advantage of what I began by calling scientific dogmatism should be apparent. As a glance at any Baconian natural history or a survey of the pre-paradigm development of any science will show, nature is vastly too complex to be explored even approximately at random. Something must tell the scientist where to look and what to look for, and that something, though it may not last beyond his generation, is the paradigm with which his education as a scientist has supplied

him. Given that paradigm and the requisite confidence in it, the scientist largely ceases to be an explorer at all, or at least to be an explorer of the unknown. Instead, he struggles to articulate and concretize the known, designing much special-purpose apparatus and many special-purpose adaptations of theory for that task. From those puzzles of design and adaptation he gets his pleasure. Unless he is extraordinarily lucky, it is upon his success with them that his reputation will depend. Inevitably the enterprise which engages him is characterized, at any one time, by drastically restricted vision. But within the region upon which vision is focused the continuing attempt to match paradigms to nature results in a knowledge and understanding of esoteric detail that could not have been achieved in any other way. From Copernicus and the problem of precession to Einstein and the photo-electric effect, the progress of science has again and again depended upon just such esoterica. One great virtue of commitment to paradigms is that it frees scientists to engage themselves with tiny puzzles.

Nevertheless, this image of scientific research as puzzle-solving or paradigm-matching must be, at the very least, thoroughly incomplete. Though the scientist may not be an explorer, scientists do again and again discover new and unexpected sorts of phenomena. Or again, though the scientist does not normally strive to invent new sorts of basic theories, such theories have repeatedly emerged from the continuing practice of research. But neither of these types of innovation would arise if the enterprise I have been calling normal science were always successful. In fact, the man engaged in puzzle-solving very often resists substantive novelty, and he does so for good reason. To him it is a change in the rules of the game and any change of rules is intrinsically subversive. That subversive element is, of course, most apparent in major theoretical innovations like those associated with the names of Copernicus, Lavoisier, or Einstein. But the discovery of an unanticipated phenomenon can have the same destructive effects, although usually on a smaller group and for a far shorter time. Once he had performed his first follow-up experiments, Roentgen's glowing screen demonstrated that previously standard cathode ray equipment was behaving in ways for which no one had made allowance. There was an unanticipated variable to be controlled; earlier researches, already on their way to becoming paradigms, would require re-evaluation; old puzzles would have to be solved again under a somewhat different set of rules. Even so readily assimilable a discovery as that of X rays can violate a paradigm that has previously guided research. It follows that, if the normal puzzle-solving activity were altogether successful, the development of science could lead to no fundamental innovations at all.

But of course normal science is not always successful, and in recognizing that fact we encounter what I take to be the second great advantage of paradigm-based research. Unlike many of the early electricians, the practitioner of a mature science knows with considerable precision what sort of result he should gain from his research. As a consequence he is in a particularly favorable position to recognize when a research problem has gone astray. Perhaps, like Galvani or Roentgen, he encounters an effect that he knows ought not to occur. Or perhaps, like Copernicus, Planck, or Einstein, he concludes that the reiterated failures of his predecessors in matching a paradigm to nature is presumptive evidence of the need to change the rules under which a match is to be sought. Or perhaps, like Franklin or Lavoisier, he decides after repeated attempts that no existing theory can be articulated to account for some newly discovered effect. In all of these ways and in others besides the practice of normal puzzle-solving science can and inevitably does lead to the isolation and recognition of anomaly. That recognition proves, I think, prerequisite for almost all discoveries of new sorts of phenomena and for all fundamental innovations in

scientific theory. After a first paradigm has been achieved, a breakdown in the rules of the pre-established game is the usual prelude to significant scientific innovation.

Examine the case of discoveries first. Many of them, like Coulomb's law or a new element to fill an empty spot in the periodic table, present no problem. They were not "new sorts of phenomena" but discoveries anticipated through a paradigm and achieved by expert puzzle-solvers: That sort of discovery is a natural product of what I have been calling normal science. But not all discoveries are of that sort: Many could not have been anticipated by any extrapolation from the known; in a sense they had to be made "by accident." On the other hand the accident through which they emerged could not ordinarily have occurred to a man just looking around. In the mature sciences discovery demands much special equipment, both conceptual and instrumental, and that special equipment has invariably been developed and deployed for the pursuit of the puzzles of normal research. Discovery results when that equipment fails to function as it should. Furthermore, since some sort of at least temporary failure occurs during almost every research project, discovery results only when the failure is particularly stubborn or striking and only when it seems to raise questions about accepted beliefs and procedures. Established paradigms are thus often doubly prerequisite to discoveries. Without them the project that goes astray would not have been undertaken. And even when the project has gone astray, as most do for a while, the paradigm can help to determine whether the failure is worth pursuing. The usual and proper response to a failure in puzzle-solving is to blame one's talents or one's tools and to turn next to another problem. If he is not to waste time, the scientist must be able to discriminate essential anomaly from mere failure.

That pattern—discovery through an anomaly that calls established techniques and beliefs in doubt—has been repeated again and again in the course of scientific development. New-ton discovered the composition of white light when he was unable to reconcile measured dis-persion with that predicted by Snell's recently discovered law of refraction.[11] The electric bat-tery was discovered when existing detectors of static charges failed to behave as Franklin's par-adigm said they should.[12] The planet Neptune was discovered through an effort to account for recognized anomalies in the orbit of Uranus.[13] The element chlorine and the compound car-bon monoxide emerged during attempts to reconcile Lavoisier's new chemistry with labo-ratory observations.[14] The so-called noble gases were the products of a long series of investiga-tions initiated by a small but persistent anom-aly in the measured density of atmospheric nitrogen.[15] The electron was posited to explain some anomalous properties of electrical con-duction through gases, and its spin was sug-gested to account for other sorts of anomalies observed in atomic spectra.[16] Both the neutron and the neutrino provide other examples, and the list could be extended almost indefinitely.[17] In the mature sciences unexpected novelties are discovered principally after something has gone wrong.

If, however, anomaly is significant in prepar-ing the way for new discoveries, it plays a still larger role in the invention of new theories. Contrary to a prevalent, though by no means universal, belief, new theories are not invented to account for observations that have not pre-viously been ordered by theory at all. Rather, at almost all times in the development of any advanced science, all the facts whose relevance is admitted seem either to fit existing theory well or to be in the process of conforming. Making them conform better provides many of the standard problems of normal science. And almost always committed scientists suc-ceed in solving them. But they do not always succeed, and, when they fail repeatedly and in increasing numbers, then their sector of the scientific community encounters what I am elsewhere calling "crisis." Recognizing that

something is fundamentally wrong with the theory upon which their work is based, scien-tists will attempt more fundamental articula-tions of theory than those which were admissible before. (Characteristically, at times of crisis, one encounters numerous different versions of the paradigm theory.[18]) Simultane-ously they will often begin more nearly ran-dom experimentation within the area of difficulty, hoping to discover some effect that will suggest a way to set the situation right. Only under circumstances like these, I suggest, is a fundamental innovation in scientific theory both invented and accepted.

The state of Ptolemaic astronomy was, for example, a recognized scandal before Coperni-cus proposed a basic change in astronomical theory, and the preface in which Copernicus described his reasons for innovation provides a classic description of the crisis state.[19] Galileo's contributions to the study of motion took their point of departure from recognized difficulties with medieval theory, and Newton reconciled Galileo's mechanics with Copernicanism.[20] Lavoisier's new chemistry was a product of the anomalies created jointly by the proliferation of new gases and the first systematic studies of weight relations.[21] The wave theory of light was developed amid growing concern about anomalies in the relation of diffraction and po-larization effects to Newton's corpuscular the-ory.[22] Thermodynamics, which later came to seem a superstructure for existing sciences, was established only at the price of rejecting the previously paradigmatic caloric theory.[23] Quantum mechanics was born from a variety of difficulties surrounding black-body radia-tion, specific heat, and the photo-electric ef-fect.[24] Again the list could be extended, but the point should already be clear. New theories arise from work conducted under old ones, and they do so only when something is observed to have gone wrong. Their prelude is widely recognized anomaly, and that recognition can come only to a group that knows very well what it would mean to have things go right.

Because limitations of space and time force me to stop at this point, my case for dogmatism must remain schematic. I shall not here even attempt to deal with the fine structure that scientific development exhibits at all times. But there is another more positive qualification of my thesis, and it requires one closing comment. Though successful research demands a deep commitment to the status quo, innovation remains at the heart of the enterprise. Scientists are *trained* to operate as puzzle-solvers from established rules, but they are also *taught* to regard themselves as explorer and inventors who know no rules except those dictated by nature itself. The result is an acquired tension, partly within the individual and partly within the community, between professional skills on the one hand and professional ideology on the other. Almost certainly that tension and the ability to sustain it are important to science's success. Insofar as I have dealt exclusively with the dependence of research upon tradition, my discussion is inevitably one-sided. On this whole subject there is a great deal more to be said.

But to be one-sided is not necessarily to be wrong, and it may be an essential preliminary to a more penetrating examination of the requisites for successful scientific life. Almost no one, perhaps no one at all, needs to be told that the vitality of science depends on the continuation of occasional tradition-shattering innovations. But the apparently contrary dependence of research upon a deep commitment to established tools and beliefs receives the very minimum of attention. I urge that it be given more. Until that is done, some of the most striking characteristics of scientific education and development will remain extraordinarily difficult to understand.

Notes

1. The ideas developed in this paper have been abstracted, in a drastically condensed form, from the first third of my monograph, *The Structure of Scientific Revolutions*, published during 1962 by the University of Chicago Press. Some of them were also partially developed in an earlier essay, "The Essential Tension: Tradition and Innovation in Scientific Research," which appeared in Calvin W. Taylor (ed.), *The Third (1959) University of Utah Research Conference on the Identification of Creative Scientific Talent* (Salt Lake City 1959).

   On this whole subject see also I. B. Cohen, "Orthodoxy and Scientific Progress," *Proceedings of the American Philosophical Society*, XCVI (1952) pp. 505–12, and Bernard Barber, "Resistance by Scientists to Scientific Discovery," *Science*, CXXXIV (1961) pp. 596–602. I am indebted to Mr. Barber for an advance copy of that helpful paper. Above all, those concerned with the importance of quasi-dogmatic commitments as a requisite for productive scientific research should see the works of Michael Polanyi, particularly his *Personal Knowledge* (Chicago, 1958) and *The Logic of Liberty* (London, 1951). The discussion which follows this paper will indicate that Mr. Polanyi and I differ somewhat about what scientists are committed to, but that should not disguise the very great extent of our agreement about the issues discussed explicitly below.

2. *Wissenschaftliche Selbstbiographie* (Leipzig, 1948) 22, my translation.

3. The individual sciences display some variation in these respects. Students in the newer and also in the less theoretical sciences—e.g., parts of biology, geology, and medical science—are more likely to encounter both contemporary and historical source materials than those in, say, astronomy, mathematics, or physics.

4. Quoted in this form by S. F. Mason, *Main Currents of Scientific Thought* (New York, 1956) 254. The original, which is identical inspirit but not in words, seems to derie from Delambre's contemporary éloge, *Memoires de . . . l'Institut . . . , année 1812*, 2nd part (Paris, 1816) p. xlvi.

5. Much documentation for this account of electrical development can be retrieved from Duane Roller and Duane H. D. Roller, *The Development of the Concept of Electric Charge: Electricity form the Greeks to Coulomb* (Harvard Case Histories in Experimental Science, VIII, Cambridge, Mass., 1954) and from I. B. Cohen, *Franklin and Newton: An Inquiry into Speculative Newtonian Experimental Science and Franklin's Work in Electricity as an Example Thereof* (Philadelphia, 1956). For analytic detail I am, however, very much indebted to a still unpublished paper by my student, John L. Heilbron, who has also assisted in the preparation of the three notes that follow.

6. This division into schools is still somewhat too simplistic. After 1720 the basic division is between the French school (Du Fay, Nollet, etc.) who base their theories on attraction—repulsion effects and the English school (Desaguliers, Watson, etc.) who concentrate on conduction effects. Each group had immense difficulty in explaining the phenomena that the other took to be basic. (See, for example, Needham's report of Lemonier's investigations, in *Philosophical Transactions*, XLIV, 1746, p. 247). Within each of these groups, and particularly the English, one can trace further subdivision depending upon whether attraction or repulsion is considered the more fundamental electrical effect.

7. Du Fay's discovery that there are two sorts of electricity and that these are mutually attractive but self-repulsive is reported and documented in great experimental detail in the fourth of his famous memoirs on electricity: "de l'Attraction & Répulsion des Corps Electriques," *Memoires de . . . l'Académie . . . de l'année 1733* (Paris, 1735) pp. 457–76. These memoirs were well known and widely cited, but Desaguliers seems to be the only electrician who, for almost two decades, even mentions that some charged bodies will attract each other (*Philosophical Transactions . . .* , XLII, 1741–2, pp. 140–3). For Franklin's and Kinnersley's "surprise" see I. B. Cohen (ed.), *Benjamin Franklin's Experiments: A New Edition of Franklin's Experiments and Observations on Electricity* (Cambridge, Mass., 1941) pp. 250–5. Note also that, though Kinnersley had *produced* the effect, neither he nor Franklin seems ever to have *recognized* that two resinously charged bodies would repel each other, a phenomenon directly contrary to Franklin's theory.

8. The change is not, of course, due to Franklin alone nor did it occur overnight. Other electricians, most notably William Watson, anticipated parts of Franklin's theory. More important, it was only after essential modifications, due principally to Aepinus, that Franklin's theory gained the general currency requisite for a paradigm. And even then there continued to be two formulations of the theory: the Franklin—Aepinus one-fluid form and a two-fluid form due principally to Symmer. Electricians soon reached the conclusion that no electrical test could possibly discriminate between the two theories. Until the discovery of the battery, when the choice between a one-fluid and two-fluid theory began to make an occasional difference in the design and analysis of experiments, the two were equivalent.

9. Note that this first electrical paradigm was fully effective only until 1800, when the discovery of the battery and the multiplication of electrochemical effects initiated a revolution in electrical theory. Until a new paradigm emerged from that revolution, the literature of electricity, particularly in England, reverted in many respects to the tone characteristic of the first half of the eighteenth century.

10. The discussion in this paragraph and the next is considerably elaborated in my paper, "The Function of Measurement in Modern Physical Science," *Isis*, LII (1961) pp. 161–93.

11. See my "Newton's Optical Papers" in I. B. Cohen (ed.), *Isaac Newton's Papers & Letters on Natural Philosophy* (Cambridge Mass., 1958) pp. 27–45.

12. Luigi Galvani, *Commentary on the Effects of Electricity on Muscular Motion*, trans. By M. G. Foley with notes and an introduction by I. B. Cohen (Norwalk, Conn., 1954) pp. 27–9.

13. Angus Armitage, *A Century of Astronomy* (London, 1950) pp. 111–15.

14. For chlorine see Ernst von Meyer, *A History of Chemistry from the Earliest Times to the Present Day*, trans. G. M'Gowan (London, 1891) pp. 224–7. For carbon monoxide see Hermann Kopp. *Geschichte der Chemie* (Braunschweig, 1845) III, pp. 294–6.

15. William Ramsay, *The Gases of the Atmosphere: the History of their Discovery* (London, 1896) Chs. 4 and 5.

16. J. J. Thomson, *Recollections and Reflections* (New York, 1937) 325–71; T. W. Chalmers, *Historic Researches: Chapters in the History of Physical and Chemical Discovery* (London, 1949) 187–217; and F. K. Richtmeyer, E. H. Kennard and T. Lauritsen, *Introduction to Modern Physics* (5th ed., New York, 1955) p. 212.

17. Ibid, pp. 466–470; and Rogers D. Rusk, *Introduction to Atomic and Nuclear Physics* (New York, 1958) pp. 328–30.

18. One classic example, for which see the reference cited below in the next note, is the proliferation of geocentric astronomical systems in the years before Copernicus's heliocentric reform. Another, for which see J. R. Partington and D. McKie, "Historical Studies of the Phlogiston Theory," *Annals of Science* II (1937) 361–404, III (1938) pp. 1–58, 337–71, and IV (1939) pp. 113–49, is the multiplicity of "phlogiston theories" produced in response to the general recognition that weight is always gained on combustion and the experimental discovery of many new gases after 1760.

The same proliferation of versions of accepted theories occurred in mechanics and electromagnetism in the two decades preceding Einstein's special relativity theory. (E. T. Whittaker, *History of the Theories of Aether and Electricity*, 2nd ed., 2 vols., London 1951–53, I, Ch. 12, and II, Ch. 2. I concur in the widespread judgment that this is a very biased account of the genesis of relativity theory, but it contains just the detail necessary to make the point here at issue.)

19. T. S. Kuhn, *The Copernican Revolution: Planetary Astronomy in the Development of Western Thought* (Cambridge, Mass., 1957) pp. 133–40.

20. For Galileo see Alexandre Koyré, *Études Galiléennes* (3 vols., Paris, 1939); for Newton see Kuhn, op. cit. pp. 228–60 and 289–91.

21. For the proliferation of gases see Partington, *A Short History of Chemistry* (2nd ed., London, 1948) Ch. 6; for the role of weight relations see Henry Guerlac, "The Origin of Lavoisier's Work on Combustion," *Archives Internationales d'histoire des sciences*, XII (1959) pp. 113–35.

22. Whittaker, *Aether and Electricity*, II, 94–109; William Whewell, *History of the Inductive Sciences* (revised ed., 3 vols., London, 1847) II, pp. 213–71; and Kuhn, "Function of Measurement," p. 181 n.

23. For a general account of the beginnings of thermodynamics (including much relevant bibliography) see my "Energy Conservation as an Example of Simultaneous Discovery" in Marshall Clagett (ed.), *Critical Problems in the History of Science* (Madison, Wisc., 1959) pp. 321–56. For the special problems presented to caloric theorists by energy conservation see the Carnot papers, there cited in n. 2, and also S. P. Thomson, *The Life of William Thomson, Baron Kelvin of Largs* (2 vols., London, 1910) Ch. 6.

24. Richtmeyer et al., *Modern Physics*, pp. 89–94, 124–32, and 409–14; Gerald Holton, *Introduction to Concepts and Theories in Physical Science* (Cambridge, Mass., 1953) pp. 528–45.

THOMAS KUHN

The Nature and Necessity of Scientific Revolutions

. . . What are scientific revolutions, and what is their function in scientific development? . . . [S]cientific revolutions are here taken to be those non-cumulative developmental episodes in which an older paradigm is replaced in whole or in part by an incompatible new one. There is more to be said, however, and an essential part of it can be introduced by asking one further question. Why should a change of paradigm be called a revolution? In the face of the vast and essential differences between political and scientific development, what parallelism can justify the metaphor that finds revolutions in both?

One aspect of the parallelism must already be apparent. Political revolutions are inaugurated by a growing sense, often restricted to a segment of the political community, that existing institutions have ceased adequately to meet the problems posed by an environment that they have in part created. In much the same way, scientific revolutions are inaugurated by a growing sense, again often restricted to a narrow subdivision of the scientific community, that an existing paradigm has ceased to function adequately in the exploration of an aspect of nature to which that paradigm itself had previously led the way. In both political and scientific development the sense of malfunction that can lead to crisis is prerequisite to revolution. Furthermore, though it admittedly strains the metaphor, that parallelism holds not only for the major paradigm changes, like those attributable to Copernicus and Lavoisier, but also for the far smaller ones associated with the assimilation of a new sort of phenomenon, like oxygen or X rays. Scientific revolutions . . . need seem revolutionary only to those whose paradigms are affected by them. To outsiders they may, like the Balkan revolutions of the early twentieth century, seem normal parts of the developmental process. Astronomers, for example, could accept X rays as a mere addition to knowledge, for their paradigms were unaffected by the existence of the new radiation. But for men like Kelvin, Crookes, and Roentgen, whose research dealt with radiation theory or with cathode ray tubes, the emergence of X rays necessarily violated one paradigm as it created another. That is why these rays could be discovered only through something's first going wrong with normal research.

This genetic aspect of the parallel between political and scientific development should no longer be open to doubt. The parallel has, however, a second and more profound aspect upon which the significance of the first depends. Political revolutions aim to change political institutions in ways that those institutions themselves prohibit. Their success therefore necessitates the partial relinquishment of one set of institutions in favor of another, and in the interim, society is not fully governed by institutions at all. Initially it is crisis alone that attenuates the role of political institutions as we have already seen it attenuate the role of paradigms. In increasing numbers individuals become increasingly estranged from political life and behave more and more eccentrically within it. Then, as the crisis deepens, many of these individuals commit themselves to some concrete proposal for the reconstruction of society in a new institutional framework. At that point the society is divided into competing camps or parties, one seeking to defend the old institutional constellation, the others seeking to institute some new one. And, once that polarization has occurred, *political recourse fails*. Because they differ about the institutional matrix within which political change is to be achieved and evaluated, because they acknowledge no supra-institutional framework for the adjudication of revolutionary difference, the parties to a revolutionary conflict must finally resort to the techniques of mass persuasion, often including force. Though revolutions have had a

vital role in the evolution of political institutions, that role depends upon their being partially extrapolitical or extrainstitutional events.

The remainder of this essay aims to demonstrate that the historical study of paradigm change reveals very similar characteristics in the evolution of the sciences. Like the choice between competing political institutions, that between competing paradigms proves to be a choice between incompatible modes of community life. Because it has that character, the choice is not and cannot be determined merely by the evaluative procedures characteristic of normal science, for these depend in part upon a particular paradigm, and that paradigm is at issue. When paradigms enter, as they must, into a debate about paradigm choice, their role is necessarily circular. Each group uses its own paradigm to argue in that paradigm's defense.

The resulting circularity does not, of course, make the arguments wrong or even ineffectual. The man who premises a paradigm when arguing in its defense can nonetheless provide a clear exhibit of what scientific practice will be like for those who adopt the new view of nature. That exhibit can be immensely persuasive, often compellingly so. Yet, whatever its force, the status of the circular argument is only that of persuasion. It cannot be made logically or even probabilistically compelling for those who refuse to step into the circle. The premises and values shared by the two parties to a debate over paradigms are not sufficiently extensive for that. As in political revolutions, so in paradigm choice—there is no standard higher than the assent of the relevant community. To discover how scientific revolutions are effected, we shall therefore have to examine not only the impact of nature and of logic, but also the techniques of persuasive argumentation effective within the quite special groups that constitute the community of scientists.

To discover why this issue of paradigm choice can never be unequivocally settled by logic and experiment alone, we must shortly examine the nature of the differences that separate the proponents of a traditional paradigm from their revolutionary successors. . . . We have, however, already noted numerous examples of such differences, and no one will doubt that history can supply many others. What is more likely to be doubted than their existence—and what must therefore be considered first—is that such examples provide essential information about the nature of science. Granting that paradigm rejection has been a historic fact, does it illuminate more than human credulity and confusion? Are there intrinsic reasons why the assimilation of either a new sort of phenomenon or a new scientific theory must demand the rejection of an older paradigm?

First notice that if there are such reasons, they do not derive from the logical structure of scientific knowledge. In principle, a new phenomenon might emerge without reflecting destructively upon any part of past scientific practice. Though discovering life on the moon would today be destructive of existing paradigms (these tell us things about the moon that seem incompatible with life's existence there), discovering life in some less well-known part of the galaxy would not. By the same token, a new theory does not have to conflict with any of its predecessors. It might deal exclusively with phenomena not previously known, as the quantum theory deals (but, significantly, not exclusively) with subatomic phenomena unknown before the twentieth century. Or again, the new theory might be simply a higher level theory than those known before, one that linked together a whole group of lower level theories without substantially changing any. Today, the theory of energy conservation provides just such links between dynamics, chemistry, electricity, optics, thermal theory, and so on. Still other compatible relationships between old and new theories can be conceived. Any and all of them might be exemplified by the historical process through which science has developed. If they were, scientific development would be genuinely cumulative. New sorts of phenomena would simply disclose order in an aspect of nature where none had been seen before. In the evolution of science new knowledge would replace ignorance rather than replace knowledge of another and incompatible sort.

Of course, science (or some other enterprise, perhaps less effective) might have developed in that fully cumulative manner. Many people have believed that it did so, and most still seem to suppose that cumulation is at least the ideal that historical development would display if only it had not so often been distorted by human idiosyncrasy. There are important reasons for that belief. . . . Nevertheless, despite the immense plausibility of that ideal image, there is increasing reason to wonder whether it can possibly be an image of *science*. After the pre-paradigm period the assimilation of all new theories and of almost all new sorts of phenomena has in fact demanded the destruction of a prior paradigm and a consequent conflict between competing schools of scientific thought. Cumulative acquisition of unanticipated novelties proves to be an almost non-existent exception to the rule of scientific development. The man who takes historic fact seriously must suspect that science does not tend toward the ideal that our image of its cumulativeness has suggested. Perhaps it is another sort of enterprise.

If, however, resistant facts can carry us that far, then a second look at the ground we have already covered may suggest that cumulative acquisition of novelty is not only rare in fact but improbable in principle. Normal research, which *is* cumulative, owes its success to the ability of scientists regularly to select problems that can be solved with conceptual and instrumental techniques close to those already in existence. (That is why an excessive concern with useful problems, regardless of their relation to existing knowledge and technique, can so easily inhibit scientific development.) The man who is striving to solve a problem defined by existing knowledge and technique is not, however, just looking around. He knows what he wants to achieve, and he designs his instruments and directs his thoughts accordingly. Unanticipated novelty, the new discovery, can emerge only to the extent that his anticipations about nature and his instruments prove wrong. Often the importance of the resulting discovery will itself be proportional to the extent and stubbornness of the anomaly that foreshadowed it. Obviously, then, there must be a conflict between the paradigm that discloses anomaly and the one that later renders the anomaly lawlike. . . .

The same argument applies even more clearly to the invention of new theories. There are, in principle, only three types of phenomena about which a new theory might be developed. The first consists of phenomena already well explained by existing paradigms, and these seldom provide either motive or point of departure for theory construction. When they do . . . the theories that result are seldom accepted, because nature provides no ground for discrimination. A second class of phenomena consists of those whose nature is indicated by existing paradigms but whose details can be understood only through further theory articulation. These are the phenomena to which scientists direct their research much of the time, but that research aims at the articulation of existing paradigms rather than at the invention of new ones. Only when these attempts at articulation fail do scientists encounter the third type of phenomena, the recognized anomalies whose characteristic feature is their stubborn refusal to be assimilated to existing paradigms. This type alone gives rise to new theories. Paradigms provide all phenomena except anomalies with a theory-determined place in the scientist's field of vision.

But if new theories are called forth to resolve anomalies in the relation of an existing theory to nature, then the successful new theory must somewhere permit predictions that are different from those derived from its predecessor. That difference could not occur if the two were logically compatible. In the process of being assimilated, the second must displace the first. Even a theory like energy conservation, which today seems a logical superstructure that relates to nature only through independently established theories, did not develop historically without paradigm destruction. Instead, it emerged from a crisis in which an essential ingredient was the incompatibility between Newtonian dynamics and some recently formulated consequences of the caloric theory of heat. Only after the caloric theory had been rejected could energy conservation become part of science.[1] And only after it had been part of science for some time could it come to seem a theory of a logically higher type, one not in conflict with its predecessors. It is hard to see how new theories could arise without these destructive changes in beliefs about nature. Though logical inclusiveness remains a permissible view of the relation between successive scientific theories, it is a historical implausibility.

A century ago it would, I think, have been possible to let the case for the necessity of revolutions rest at this point. But today, unfortunately, that cannot be done because the view of the subject developed above cannot be maintained if the most prevalent contemporary interpretation of the nature and function of scientific theory is accepted. That interpretation, closely associated with early logical positivism and not categorically rejected by its successors, would restrict the range and meaning of an accepted theory so that it would not possibly conflict with any later theory that made predictions about some of the same natural phenomena. The best-known and the strongest case for this restricted conception of a scientific theory emerges in discussions of the relation between contemporary Einsteinian dynamics and the older dynamical equations that descend from Newton's *Principia*. From the viewpoint of this essay these two theories are fundamentally incompatible in the sense illustrated by the relation of Copernican to Ptolemaic astronomy: Einstein's theory can be accepted only with the recognition that Newton's was wrong. Today this remains a minority view.[2] We must therefore examine the most prevalent objections to it.

The gist of these objections can be developed as follows. Relativistic dynamics cannot have shown Newtonian dynamics to be wrong, for Newtonian dynamics is still used with great success by most engineers and, in selected applications, by many physicists. Furthermore, the propriety of this use of the older theory can be proved from the very theory that has, in other applications, replaced it. Einstein's theory can be used to show that predictions from Newton's equations will be as good as our measuring instruments in all applications that satisfy a small number of restrictive conditions. For example, if Newtonian theory is to provide a good approximate solution, the relative velocities of the bodies considered must be small compared with the velocity of light. Subject to this condition and a few others, Newtonian theory seems to be derivable from Einsteinian, of which it is therefore a special case.

But, the objection continues, no theory can possibly conflict with one of its special cases. If Einsteinian science seems to make Newtonian dynamics wrong, that is only because some Newtonians were so incautious as to claim that Newtonian theory yielded entirely precise results or that it was valid at very high relative velocities. Since they could not have had any evidence for such claims, they betrayed the standards of science when they made them. In so far as Newtonian theory was ever a truly scientific theory supported by valid evidence, it still is. Only extravagant claims for the theory—claims that were never properly parts of science—can have been shown by Einstein to be wrong. Purged of these merely human extravagances, Newtonian theory has never been challenged and cannot be.

Some variant of this argument is quite sufficient to make any theory ever used by a signif-

icant group of competent scientists immune to attack. The much-maligned phlogiston theory, for example, gave order to a large number of physical and chemical phenomena. It explained why bodies burned—they were rich in phlogiston—and why metals had so many more properties in common than did their ores. The metals were all compounded from different elementary earths combined with phlogiston, and the latter, common to all metals, produced common properties. In addition, the phlogiston theory accounted for a number of reactions in which acids were formed by the combustion of substances like carbon and sulphur. Also, it explained the decrease of volume when combustion occurs in a confined volume of air—the phlogiston released by combustion "spoils" the elasticity of the air that absorbed it, just as fire "spoils" the elasticity of a steel spring.[3] If these were the only phenomena that the phlogiston theorists had claimed for their theory, that theory could never have been challenged. A similar argument will suffice for any theory that has ever been successfully applied to any range of phenomena at all.

But to save theories in this way, their range of application must be restricted to those phenomena and to that precision of observation with which the experimental evidence in hand already deals.[4] Carried just a step further (and the step can scarcely be avoided once the first is taken), such a limitation prohibits the scientist from claiming to speak "scientifically" about any phenomenon not already observed. Even in its present form the restriction forbids the scientist to rely upon a theory in his own research whenever that research enters an area or seeks a degree of precision for which past practice with the theory offers no precedent. These prohibitions are logically unexceptionable. But the result of accepting them would be the end of the research through which science may develop further.

By now that point too is virtually a tautology. Without commitment to a paradigm there could be no normal science. Furthermore, that commitment must extend to areas and to degrees of precision for which there is no full precedent. If it did not, the paradigm could provide no puzzles that had not already been solved. Besides, it is not only normal science that depends upon commitment to a paradigm. If existing theory binds the scientist only with respect to existing applications, then there can be no surprises, anomalies, or crises. But these are just the signposts that point the way to extraordinary science. If positivistic restrictions on the range of a theory's legitimate applicability are taken literally, the mechanism that tells the scientific community what problems may lead to fundamental change must cease to function. And when that occurs, the community will inevitably return to something much like its pre-paradigm state, a condition in which all members practice science but in which their gross product scarcely resembles science at all. Is it really any wonder that the price of significant scientific advance is a commitment that runs the risk of being wrong?

More important, there is a revealing logical lacuna in the positivist's argument, one that will reintroduce us immediately to the nature of revolutionary change. Can Newtonian dynamics really be *derived* from relativistic dynamics? What would such a derivation look like? Imagine a set of statements, E_1, E_2, . . . , E_n, which together embody the laws of relativity theory. These statements contain variables and parameters representing spatial position, time, rest mass, etc. From them, together with the apparatus of logic and mathematics, is deducible a whole set of further statements, including some that can be checked by observation. To prove the adequacy of Newtonian dynamics as a special case, we must add to the E_i's additional statements like $(v/c)^2 < 1$, restricting the range of the parameters and variables. This enlarged set of statements is then manipulated to yield a new set, N_1, N_2, . . . , N_m, which is identical in form with Newton's laws of motion, the law of gravity, and so on. Apparently Newtonian dynamics has been de-

rived from Einsteinian, subject to a few limiting conditions.

Yet the derivation is spurious, at least to this point. Though the N_i's are a special case of the laws of relativistic mechanics, they are not Newton's Laws. Or at least they are not unless those laws are reinterpreted in a way that would have been impossible until after Einstein's work. The variables and parameters that in the Einsteinian E_i's represented spatial position, time, mass, etc., still occur in the N_i's; and they there still represent Einsteinian space, time, and mass. But the physical referents of these Einsteinian concepts are by no means identical with those of the Newtonian concepts that bear the same name. (Newtonian mass is conserved; Einsteinian is convertible with energy. Only at low relative velocities may the two be measured in the same way, and even then they must not be conceived to be the same.) Unless we change the definitions of the variables in the N_i's, the statements we have derived are not Newtonian. If we do change them, we cannot properly be said to have *derived* Newton's Laws, at least not in any sense of "derive" now generally recognized. Our argument has, of course, explained why Newton's Laws ever seemed to work. In doing so it has justified, say, an automobile driver in acting as though he lived in a Newtonian universe. An argument of the same type is used to justify teaching earth-centered astronomy to surveyors. But the argument has still not done what it purported to do. It has not, that is, shown Newton's Laws to be a limiting case of Einstein's. For in the passage to the limit it is not only the forms of the laws that have changed. Simultaneously we have had to alter the fundamental structural elements of which the universe to which they apply is composed.

This need to change the meaning of established and familiar concepts is central to the revolutionary impact of Einstein's theory. Though subtler than the changes from geocentrism to heliocentrism, from phlogiston to oxygen, or from corpuscles to waves, the resulting conceptual transformation is no less decisively destructive of a previously established paradigm. We may even come to see it as a prototype for revolutionary reorientations in the sciences. Just because it did not involve the introduction of additional objects or concepts, the transition from Newtonian to Einsteinian mechanics illustrates with particular clarity the scientific revolution as a displacement of the conceptual network through which scientists view the world.

These remarks should suffice to show what might, in another philosophical climate, have been taken for granted. At least for scientists, most of the apparent differences between a discarded scientific theory and its successor are real. Though an out-of-date theory can always be viewed as a special case of its up-to-date successor, it must be transformed for the purpose. And the transformation is one that can be undertaken only with the advantages of hindsight, the explicit guidance of the more recent theory. Furthermore, even if that transformation were a legitimate device to employ in interpreting the older theory, the result of its application would be a theory so restricted that it could only restate what was already known. Because of its economy, that restatement would have utility, but it could not suffice for the guidance of research.

Let us, therefore, now take it for granted that the differences between successive paradigms are both necessary and irreconcilable. Can we then say more explicitly what sorts of differences these are? The most apparent type has already been illustrated repeatedly. Successive paradigms tell us different things about the population of the universe and about that population's behavior. They differ, that is, about such questions as the existence of subatomic particles, the materiality of light, and the conservation of heat or of energy. These are the substantive differences between successive paradigms, and they require no further illustration. But paradigms differ in more than substance, for they are directed not only to nature but also

back upon the science that produced them. They are the source of the methods, problem-field, and standards of solution accepted by any mature scientific community at any given time. As a result, the reception of a new paradigm often necessitates a redefinition of the corresponding science. Some old problems may be relegated to another science or declared entirely "unscientific." Others that were previously non-existent or trivial may, with a new paradigm, become the very archetypes of significant scientific achievement. And as the problems change, so, often, does the standard that distinguishes a real scientific solution from a mere metaphysical speculation, word game, or mathematical play. The normal-scientific tradition that emerges from a scientific revolution is not only incompatible but often actually incommensurable with that which has gone before.

The impact of Newton's work upon the normal seventeenth-century tradition of scientific practice provides a striking example of these subtler effects of paradigm shift. Before Newton was born the "new science" of the century had at last succeeded in rejecting Aristotelian and scholastic explanations expressed in terms of the essences of material bodies. To say that a stone fell because its "nature" drove it toward the center of the universe had been made to look a mere tautological wordplay, something it had not previously been. Henceforth the entire flux of sensory appearances, including color, taste, and even weight, was to be explained in terms of the size, shape, position, and motion of the elementary corpuscles of base matter. The attribution of other qualities to the elementary atoms was a resort to the occult and therefore out of bounds for science. Molière caught the new spirit precisely when he ridiculed the doctor who explained opium's efficacy as a soporific by attributing to it a dormitive potency. During the last half of the seventeenth century many scientists preferred to say that the round shape of the opium particles enabled them to soothe the nerves about which they moved.[5]

In an earlier period explanations in terms of occult qualities had been an integral part of productive scientific work. Nevertheless, the seventeenth century's new commitment to mechanico-corpuscular explanation proved immensely fruitful for a number of sciences, ridding them of problems that had defied generally accepted solution and suggesting others to replace them. In dynamics, for example, Newton's three laws of motion are less a product of novel experiments than of the attempt to reinterpret well-known observations in terms of the motions and interactions of primary neutral corpuscles. Consider just one concrete illustration. Since neutral corpuscles could act on each other only by contact, the mechanico-corpuscular view of nature directed scientific attention to a brand-new subject of study, the alteration of particulate motions by collisions. Descartes announced the problem and provided its first putative solution. Huyghens, Wren, and Wallis carried it still further, partly by experimenting with colliding pendulum bobs, but mostly by applying previously well-known characteristics of motion to the new problem. And Newton embedded their results in his laws of motion. The equal "action" and "reaction" of the third law are the changes in quantity of motion experienced by the two parties to a collision. The same change of motion supplies the definition of dynamical force implicit in the second law. In this case, as in many others during the seventeenth century, the corpuscular paradigm bred both a new problem and a large part of that problem's solution.[6]

Yet, though much of Newton's work was directed to problems and embodied standards derived from the mechanico-corpuscular world view, the effect of the paradigm that resulted from his work was a further and partially destructive change in the problems and standards legitimate for science. Gravity, interpreted as an innate attraction between every pair of particles of matter, was an occult quality in the same sense as the scholastics' "tendency to fall" had been. Therefore, while the standards of corpuscularism remained in effect, the search for a mechanical explanation of gravity was one of the most challenging problems for those who accepted the *Principia* as paradigm. Newton devoted much attention to it and so did many of his eighteenth-century successors. The only apparent option was to reject Newton's theory for its failure to explain gravity, and that alternative, too, was widely adopted. Yet neither of these views ultimately triumphed. Unable either to practice science without the *Principia* or to make that work conform to the corpuscular standards of the seventeenth century, scientists gradually accepted the view that gravity was indeed innate. By the mid-eighteenth century that interpretation had been almost universally accepted, and the result was a genuine reversion (which is not the same as a retrogression) to a scholastic standard. Innate attractions and repulsions joined size, shape, position, and motion as physically irreducible primary properties of matter.[7]

The resulting change in the standards and problem-field of physical science was once again consequential. By the 1740s, for example, electricians could speak of the attractive "virtue" of the electrical fluid without thereby inviting the ridicule that had greeted Molière's doctor a century before. As they did so, electrical phenomena increasingly displayed an order different from the one they had shown when viewed as the effects of a mechanical effluvium that could act only by contact. In particular, when electrical action-at-a-distance became a subject for study in its own right, the phenomenon we now call charging by induction could be recognized as one of its effects. Previously, when seen at all, it had been attributed to the direct action of electrical "atmospheres" or to the leakages inevitable in any electrical laboratory. The new view of inductive effects was, in turn, the key to Franklin's analysis of the Leyden jar and thus to the emergence of a new and Newtonian paradigm for electricity. Nor were dynamics and electricity the only scientific fields affected by the legit-imization of the search for forces innate to matter. The large body of eighteenth-century literature on chemical affinities and replacement series also derives from this supramechanical aspect of Newtonianism. Chemists who believed in these differential attractions between the various chemical species set up previously unimagined experiments and searched for new sorts of reactions. Without the data and the chemical concepts developed in that process, the later work of Lavoisier and, more particularly, of Dalton would be incomprehensible.[8] Changes in the standards governing permissible problems, concepts, and explanations can transform a science. . . .

Other examples of these nonsubstantive differences between successive paradigms can be retrieved from the history of any science in almost any period of its development. For the moment let us be content with just two other and far briefer illustrations. Before the chemical revolution, one of the acknowledged tasks of chemistry was to account for the qualities of chemical substances and for the changes these qualities underwent during chemical reactions. With the aid of a small number of elementary "principles"—of which phlogiston was one—the chemist was to explain why some substances are acidic, others metalline, combustible, and so forth. Some success in this direction had been achieved. We have already noted that phlogiston explained why the metals were so much alike, and we could have developed a similar argument for the acids. Lavoisier's reform, however, ultimately did away with chemical "principles," and thus ended by depriving chemistry of some actual and much potential explanatory power. To compensate for this loss, a change in standards was required. During much of the nineteenth-century failure to explain the qualities of compounds was no indictment of a chemical theory.[9]

Or again, Clerk Maxwell shared with other nineteenth-century proponents of the wave theory of light the conviction that light waves must be propagated through a material ether. Designing a mechanical medium to support such waves was a standard problem for many of his ablest contemporaries. His own theory, however, the electromagnetic theory of light, gave no account at all of a medium able to support light waves, and it clearly made such an account harder to provide than it had seemed before. Initially, Maxwell's theory was widely rejected for those reasons. But, like Newton's theory, Maxwell's proved difficult to dispense with, and as it achieved the status of a paradigm, the community's attitude toward it changed. In the early decades of the twentieth century Maxwell's insistence upon the existence of a mechanical ether looked more and more like lip service, which it emphatically had not been, and the attempts to design such an ethereal medium were abandoned. Scientists no longer thought it unscientific to speak of an electrical "displacement" without specifying what was being displaced. The result, again, was a new set of problems and standards, one which, in the event, had much to do with the emergence of relativity theory.[10]

These characteristic shifts in the scientific community's conception of its legitimate problems and standards would have less significance to this essay's thesis if one could suppose that they always occurred from some methodologically lower to some higher type. In that case their effects, too, would seem cumulative. No wonder that some historians have argued that the history of science records a continuing increase in the maturity and refinement of man's conception of the nature of science.[11] Yet the case for cumulative development of science's problems and standards is even harder to make than the case of cumulation of theories. The attempt to explain gravity, though fruitfully abandoned by most eighteenth-century scientists, was not directed to an intrinsically illegitimate problem; the objections to innate forces were neither inherently unscientific nor metaphysical in some pejorative sense. There are no external standards to permit a judgment of that sort. What occurred was neither a decline nor a raising of standards, but simply a change demanded by the adoption of a new paradigm. Furthermore, that change has since been reversed and could be again. In the twentieth century Einstein succeeded in explaining gravitational attractions, and that explanation has returned science to a set of canons and problems that are, in this particular respect, more like those of Newton's predecessors than of his successors. Or again, the development of quantum mechanics has reversed the methodological prohibition that originated in the chemical revolution. Chemists now attempt, and with great success, to explain the color, state of aggregation, and other qualities of the substances used and produced in their laboratories. A similar reversal may even be underway in electromagnetic theory. Space, in contemporary physics, is not the inert and homogenous substratum employed in both Newton's and Maxwell's theories; some of its new properties are not unlike those once attributed to the ether; we may someday come to know what an electric displacement is.

By shifting emphasis from the cognitive to the normative functions of paradigms, the preceding examples enlarge our understanding of the ways in which paradigms give form to the scientific life. Previously, we had principally examined the paradigm's role as a vehicle for scientific theory. In that role it functions by telling the scientist about the entities that nature does and does not contain and about the ways in which those entities behave. That information provides a map whose details are elucidated by mature scientific research. And since nature is too complex and varied to be explored at random, that map is as essential as observation and experiment to science's continuing development. Through the theories they embody, paradigms prove to be constitutive of the research activity. They are also, however, constitutive of science in other respects, and that is now the point. In particular, our most recent examples show that paradigms provide scientists not only with a map but also with some of the directions essential for map-making. In learning a paradigm the scientist acquires theory, methods, and

standards together, usually in an inextricable mixture. Therefore, when paradigms change, there are usually significant shifts in the criteria determining the legitimacy both of problems and of proposed solutions.

That observation returns us to the point from which this section began, for it provides our first explicit indication of why the choice between competing paradigms regularly raises questions that cannot be resolved by the criteria of normal science. To the extent, as significant as it is incomplete, that two scientific schools disagree about what is a problem and what a solution, they will inevitably talk through each other when debating the relative merits of their respective paradigms. In the partially circular arguments that regularly result, each paradigm will be shown to satisfy more or less the criteria that it dictates for itself and to fall short of a few of those dictated by its opponent. There are other reasons, too, for the incompleteness of logical contact that consistently characterizes paradigm debates. For example, since no paradigm ever solves all the problems it defines and since no two paradigms leave all the same problems unsolved, paradigm debates always involve the question: Which problems is it more significant to have solved? Like the issue of competing standards, that question of values can be answered only in terms of criteria that lie outside of normal science altogether, and it is that recourse to external criteria that most obviously makes paradigm debates revolutionary . . . .

Notes

1. Silvanus P. Thompson, *Life of William Thomson Baron Kelvin of Largs* (London, 1910), I, pp. 266–81.
2. See, for example, the remarks by P. P. Wiener in *Philosophy of Science*, XXV (1958), pp. 298.
3. James B. Conant, *Overthrow of the Phlogiston Theory* (Cambridge, 1950), pp. 13–16; and J. R. Partington, *A Short History of Chemistry* (2d ed.; London, 1951), pp. 85–88. The fullest and most sympathetic account of the phlogiston theory's achievements is by H. Metzger, *Newton, Stahl, Boerhaave et al doctrine chimique* (Paris, 1930), Part II.

4. Compare the conclusions reached through a very different sort of analysis by R. B. Braithwaite, *Scientific Explanation* (Cambridge, 1953). pp. 50–87, esp. p. 76.

5. For corpuscularism in general, see Marie Boas, "The Establishment of the Mechanical Philosophy," *Osiris*, X (1952), 412–541. For the effect of particle-shape on taste, see ibid., p. 483.

6. R. Dugas, *La mécanique au XVIIe siècle* (Neuchatel, 1954), pp. 177–85, 284–98, 345–56.

7. I. B. Cohen, *Franklin and Newton: An Inquiry into Speculative Newtonian Experimental Science and Franklin's Work in Electricity as an Example Thereof* (Philadelphia, 1956), Chaps. vi–vii.

8. For electricity, see ibid., Chaps. viii–ix. For chemistry, see Metzger, op. cit., Part I.

9. E. Meyerson, *Identity and Reality* (New York, 1930), Chap. x.

10. E. T. Whittaker, *A History of the Theories of Aether and Electricity*, II (London, 1953), pp. 28–30.

11. For a brilliant and entirely up-to-date attempt to fit scientific development into this Procrustean bed, see C. C. Gillispie, *The Edge of Objectivity: An Essay in the History of Scientific Ideas* (Princeton, 1960).

LARRY LAUDAN

Dissecting the Holist Picture of Scientific Change

It is now more than twenty years since the appearance of Thomas Kuhn's *The Structure of Scientific Revolutions*. For many of us entering the field two decades ago, that book made a powerful difference. Not because we fully understood it; still less because we became converts to it. It mattered, rather, because it posed in a particularly vivid form some direct challenges to the empiricism we were learning from the likes of Hempel, Nagel, Popper, and Carnap.

Philosophers of science of that era had no doubts about whom and what the book was attacking. If Kuhn was right, all the then-reigning methodological orthodoxies were simply wrong. It was a good deal less clear what Kuhn's positive message amounted to, and not entirely because many of Kuhn's philosophical readers were too shocked to read him carefully. Was he saying that theories were really and always incommensurable so that rival scientists invariably misunderstood one another, or did

he mean it when he said that the problem-solving abilities of rival theories could be objectively compared? Did he really believe that accepting a new theory was a "conversion experience," subject only to the Gestalt-like exigencies of the religious life? In the first wave of reaction to Kuhn's bombshell, answers to such questions were not easy to find.

Since 1962 most of Kuhn's philosophical writings have been devoted to clearing up some of the ambiguities and confusions generated by the language of the first edition of *The Structure of Scientific Revolutions*. By and large, Kuhn's message has been an ameliorative and conciliatory one, to such an extent that some passages in his later writings make him sound like a closet positivist. More than one commentator has accused the later Kuhn of taking back much of what made his message interesting and provocative in the first place.[1]

But that is not entirely fair, for if many of Kuhn's clarifications have indeed taken the

Reprinted from Chapter 4 of *Science and Values* by Larry Laudan (1984), pp. 67–102, 141–144. Reprinted by permission of University of California Press.

sting out of what we once thought Kuhn's position was, there are several issues about which the later Kuhn is both clear *and* controversial. Significantly, several of those are central to the themes of this essay . . . .

Kuhn, then, will be my immediate target, but I would be less than candid if I did not quickly add that the views I discuss here have spread considerably beyond the Kuhnian corpus. To some degree, almost all of us who wrote about scientific change in the 1970s (present company included) fell prey to some of the confusions I describe. In trying to characterize the mechanisms of theory change, we have tended to lapse into sloppy language for describing change. However, because Kuhn's is the best-known account of scientific change, and because Kuhn most overtly makes several of the mistakes I want to discuss, this chapter focuses chiefly on his views. Similar criticisms can be raised with varying degrees of severity against authors as diverse as Foucault, Lakatos, Toulmin, Holton, and Laudan.

Kuhn on the Units of Scientific Change

It is notorious that the key Kuhnian concept of a paradigm is multiply ambiguous. Among its most central meanings are the following three: First and foremost, a paradigm offers a conceptual framework for classifying and explaining natural objects. That is, it specifies in a generic way the sorts of entities that are thought to populate a certain domain of experience and it sketches out how those entities generally interact. In short, every paradigm will make certain claims about what populates the world. Such ontological claims mark that paradigm off from others, since each paradigm is thought to postulate entities and modes of interaction which differentiate it from other paradigms. Second, a paradigm will specify the appropriate methods, techniques, and tools of inquiry for studying the objects in the relevant domain of application. Just as different para-

digms have different ontologies, so they involve substantially different methodologies. (Consider, for instance, the very different methods of research and theory evaluation associated with behaviorism and cognitive psychology respectively.) These methodological commitments are persistent ones, and they characterize the paradigm throughout its history. Finally, the proponents of different paradigms will, according to Kuhn, espouse different sets of cognitive goals or ideals. Although the partisans of two paradigms may (and usually do) share some aims in common, Kuhn insists that the goals are not fully overlapping between followers of rival paradigms. Indeed, to accept a paradigm is, for Kuhn, to subscribe to a complex of cognitive values which the proponents of no other paradigm accept fully.

Paradigm change, on this account, clearly represents a break of great magnitude. To trade in one paradigm for another is to involve oneself in changes at each of . . . three levels . . . : We give up one ontology for another, one methodology for another, and one set of cognitive goals for another. Moreover, according to Kuhn, this change is *simultaneous* rather than *sequential.* . . .

. . . Kuhn portrays paradigm changes in ways that make them seem to be abrupt and global ruptures in the life of a scientific community. So great is this supposed transition that several of Kuhn's critics have charged that, despite Kuhn's proclaimed intentions to the contrary, his analysis inevitably turns scientific change into a nonrational or irrational process. In part, but only in part, it is Kuhn's infelicitous terminology that produces this impression. Notoriously, he speaks of the acceptance of a new paradigm as a "conversion experience,"[2] conjuring up a picture of the scientific revolutionary as a born-again Christian, long on zeal and short on argument. At other times he likens paradigm change to an "irreversible Gestalt-shift."[3] Less metaphorically, he claims that there is never a point at which it is "unreasonable" to hold onto an old paradigm rather than to accept a new one.[4] Such language does not encourage one to imagine that paradigm change is exactly the result of a careful and deliberate weighing-up of the respective strengths of rival contenders. But impressions based on some of Kuhn's more lurid language can probably be rectified by cleaning up some of the vocabulary of *The Structure of Scientific Revolutions*, a task on which Kuhn has been embarked more or less since the book first appeared.[5] No changes of terminology, however, will alter the fact that some central features of Kuhn's model of science raise serious roadblocks to a rational analysis of scientific change. The bulk of this chapter is devoted to examining some of those impediments. Before we turn to that examination, however, I want to stress early on that my complaint with Kuhn is not merely that he has failed to give any normatively robust or rational account of theory change, serious as that failing is. As I show below, he has failed even at the descriptive or narrative task of offering an accurate story about the manner in which large-scale changes of scientific allegiance occur.

But there is yet a more fundamental respect in which Kuhn's approach presents obstacles to an understanding of the dynamics of theory change. Specifically, by insisting that individual paradigms have an integral and static character—that changes take place only between, rather than within, paradigms—Kuhn has missed the single feature of science which promises to mediate and rationalize the transition from one world view or paradigm to another. Kuhn's various writings on this subject leave the reader in no doubt that he thinks the parts of a paradigm go together as an inseparable package. As he puts it in *The Structure of Scientific Revolutions*, "In learning a paradigm the scientist acquires theory, methods, and standards together, usually in an *inextricable* mix."[6] This theme of the inextricable and inseparable ingredients of a paradigm is a persistent one in Kuhn's work. One key aim of this chapter is to show how drastically we need to alter Kuhn's

views about how tightly the pieces of a paradigm's puzzle fit together before we can expect to understand how paradigmlike change occurs.

Loosening Up the Fit

Without too heavy an element of caricature, we can describe world-view models such as Kuhn's along the following lines: One group or faction in the scientific community accepts a particular "big picture." That requires acquiescence in a certain ontology of nature, acceptance of a specific set of rules about how to investigate nature, and adherence to a set of cognitive values about the teleology of natural inquiry (i.e., about the goals that science seeks). On this analysis, large-scale scientific change involves the replacement of one such world view by another, a process that entails the simultaneous repudiation of the key elements of the old picture and the adoption of corresponding (but of course different) elements of the new. In short, scientific change looks something like Figure 1.

When scientific change is construed so globally, it is no small challenge to see how it could be other than a conversion experience. If different scientists not only espouse different theories but also subscribe to different standards of appraisal and ground those standards in different and conflicting systems of cognitive goals, then it is difficult indeed to imagine that scientific change could be other than a whimsical change of style or taste. There could apparently never be compelling grounds for saying that one paradigm is better than another, for one has to ask: Better relative to which

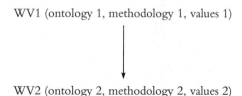

WV1 (ontology 1, methodology 1, values 1)

WV2 (ontology 2, methodology 2, values 2)

Figure 1 Kuhn's picture of theory change

standards and whose goals? To make matters worse—much worse—Kuhn often suggested that each paradigm is more or less automatically guaranteed to satisfy its own standards and to fail the standards of rival paradigms, thus producing a kind of self-reinforcing solipsism in science. As he once put it, "To the extent, as significant as it is incomplete, that two scientific schools disagree about what is a problem and what is a solution, they will inevitably talk through each other when debating the merits of their respective paradigms. In the partially circular arguments that regularly result, *each* paradigm will be shown to satisfy more or less the criteria that it dictates for itself and to fall short of those dictated by its opponent."[7] Anyone who writes prose of this sort must think that scientific decision-making is fundamentally capricious. Or at least so many of us thought in the mid- and late 1960s, as philosophers began to digest Kuhn's ideas. In fact, if one looks at several discussions of Kuhn's work dating from that period, one sees this theme repeatedly. Paradigm change, it was said, could not possibly be a reasoned or rational process. Kuhn, we thought, has made science into an irrational "monster."

Kuhn's text added fuel to the fire by seeming to endorse such a construal of his own work. In a notorious discussion of the shift from the chemistry of Priestley to that of Lavoisier and Dalton, for instance, Kuhn asserted that it was perfectly reasonable for Priestley to hold onto phlogiston theory, just as it was fully rational for most of his contemporaries to be converting to the oxygen theory of Lavoisier. According to Kuhn, Priestley's continued adherence to phlogiston was reasonable because—given Priestley's cognitive aims and the methods he regarded as appropriate—his own theory continued to look good. Priestley lost the battle with Lavoisier, not because Priestley's paradigm was objectively inferior to its rivals, but rather because most of the chemists of the day came to share Lavoisier's and Dalton's views about what was important and how it should be investigated.

The clear implication of such passages in Kuhn's writings is that interparadigmatic debate is necessarily inconclusive and thus can never be brought to rational closure. When closure does occur, it must therefore be imposed on the situation by such external factors as the demise of some of the participants or the manipulation of the levers of power and reward within the institutional structure of the scientific community. Philosophers of science, almost without exception, have found such implications troubling, for they directly confute what philosophers have been at pains for two millennia to establish: to wit, that scientific disputes, and more generally all disagreements about matters of fact, are in principle open to rational clarification and resolution. It is on the strength of passages such as those I have mentioned that Kuhn has been charged with relativism, subjectivism, irrationalism, and a host of other sins high on the philosopher's hit list.

There is some justice in these criticisms of Kuhn's work, for . . . Kuhn has failed over the past twenty years to elaborate any coherent account of consensus formation, that is, of the manner in which scientists could ever agree to support one world view rather than another. But that flaw, serious though it is, can probably be remedied. . . . [W]e solve the problem of consensus once we realize that *the various components of a world view are individually negotiable and individually replaceable in a piecemeal fashion* (that is, in such a manner that replacement of one element need not require wholesale repudiation of all the other components). Kuhn himself grants, of course, that some components of a world view can be revised; that is what "paradigm articulation" is all about. But for Kuhn, as for such other world view theorists as Lakatos and Foucault, the central commitments of a world view, its "hard core" (to use Lakatos's marvelous phrase), are not revisable—short of rejecting the entire world view. The core ontology of a world view or paradigm, along with its methodology and axiology, comes on a take-it-or-leave-it basis. Where these levels of commitment are concerned, Kuhn (along with such critics of his as Lakatos) is an uncompromising holist. Consider, for instance, his remark: "Just because it is a transition between incommensurables, the transition between competing paradigms cannot be made a step at a time . . . like the Gestalt-switch, it must occur all at once or not at all."[8] Kuhn could hardly be less ambiguous on this point.

But paradigms or research programs need not be so rigidly conceived, and typically they are not so conceived by scientists; nor, if we reflect on it a moment, should they be so conceived. . . . [T]here are complex justificatory interconnections among a scientist's ontology, his methodology, and his axiology. If a scientist's methodology fails to justify his ontology; if his methodology fails to promote his cognitive aims; if his cognitive aims prove to be utopian—in all these cases the scientists will have compelling reasons for replacing one component or other of his world view with an element that does the job better. Yet he need not modify everything else.

To be more precise, the choice confronting a scientist whose world view is under strain in this manner need be nothing like as stark as the choice sketched in Figure 1 (where it is a matter of sticking with what he knows best unchanged or throwing that over for something completely different), but rather a choice where the modification of one core element— while retaining the others—may bring a decided improvement. Schematically, the choice may be one between

$$O^1 \ \& \ M^1 \ \& \ A^1 \tag{1}$$

and

$$O^2 \ \& \ M^1 \ \& \ A^1 \tag{2}$$

Or, between (1) and

$$O^1 \ \& \ M^2 \ \& \ A^1 \tag{3}$$

Or, to exhaust the simple cases, it may be between (1) and

$$O^1 \ \& \ M^1 \ \& \ A^2 \tag{4}$$

. . . [C]hoices like those between (1) and (2), or between (1) and (3), are subject to strong normative constraints. And . . . choices of the sort represented between (1) and (4) are also, under certain circumstances, equally amenable to rational analysis.

In all these examples there is enough common ground between the rivals to engender hope of finding an "Archimedean standpoint" which can rationally mediate the choice. When such commonality exists, there is no reason to regard the choice as just a matter of taste or whim; nor is there any reason to say of such choices, as Kuhn does (recall his characterization of the Priestley–Lavoisier exchange), that there can be no compelling grounds for one preference over another. Provided theory change occurs one level at a time, there is ample scope for regarding it as a thoroughly reasoned process.

But the crucial question is whether change actually does occur in this manner. If one thinks quickly of the great transitions in the history of science, they *seem* to preclude such a stepwise analysis. The shift from (say) an Aristotelian to a Newtonian world view clearly involved changes on all three levels. So, too, did the emergence of psychoanalysis from nineteenth-century mechanistic psychology. But before we accept this wholesale picture of scientific change too quickly, we should ask whether it might not acquire what plausibility it enjoys only because our characterizations of such historical revolutions make us compress or telescope a number of gradual changes (one level at a time, as it were) into what, at our distance in time, can easily appear as an abrupt and monumental shift.

By way of laying out the core features of a more gradualist (and, I argue, historically more faithful) picture of scientific change, I will sketch a highly idealized version of theory change. Once it is in front of us, I will show in detail how it makes sense of some real cases of scientific change. Eventually, we will want a model that can show how one might move from an initial state of disagreement between rival traditions or paradigms to consensus about which one is better. But, for purposes of exposition, I want to begin with a rather simpler situation, namely, one in which consensus in favor of one world view or tradition gives way eventually to consensus in favor of another, without scientists ever being faced with a choice as stark as that between two well-developed, and totally divergent, rival paradigms. My "tall tale," represented schematically in Figure 2, might go like this: At any given time, there will be at least one set of values, methods, and theories which one can identify as operating in any field or subfield of science. Let us call this collective C_1, and its components T_1, M_1, and A_1. These components typically stand in . . . complex justificatory relationships to one another . . . ; that is, A_1 will justify M_1 and harmonize with T_1; M_1 will justify T_1 and exhibit the realizability of A_1; and T_1 will constrain M_1 and exemplify A_1. Let us suppose that someone then proposes a new theory, T_2, to replace T_1. The rules M_1 will be consulted and they may well indicate grounds for preferring T_2 to T_1. Suppose that they do, and that we thereby replace T_1 with T_2. As time goes by, certain scientists may develop reservations about M_1 and propose a new and arguably superior methodology, M_2. Now a choice must be made between M_1 and M_2. As we have seen, that requires determining whether M_1 or M_2 offers more promise of realizing our aims. Since that determination will typically be an empirical matter, both A_1 and the then-prevailing theory, T_2, will have to be consulted to ascertain whether M_1 or M_2 is optimal for securing A_1. Suppose that, in comparing the relative efficacy of achieving the shared values, A_1, cogent arguments can be made to show that M_2 is superior to M_1. Under the circumstances, assuming scientists behave rationally, M_2 will replace M_1. This means that as new theories, T_3, T_4, . . . , T_n, emerge later, they will be assessed by rules M_2 rather than M_1. Suppose, still further along in this fairy tale, we imagine a challenge to the basic values themselves. Someone may, for instance, point to new evidence suggesting that some element

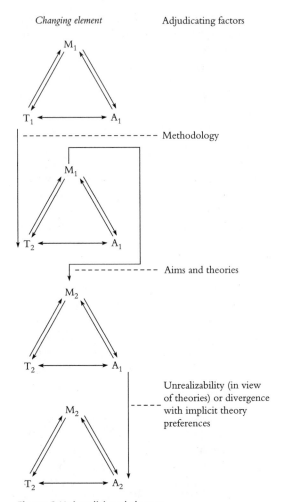

Figure 2 Unitraditional change

or other of A_1 is unrealizable. Someone else may point out that virtually none of the theories accepted by the scientific community as instances of good science exemplify the values expressed in A_1. (Or, it may be shown that A_1 is an inconsistent set in that its component aspirations are fundamentally at odds with one another.) Under such circumstances, scientists may rationally decide to abandon A_1 and to take up an alternative, consistent set of values, A_2, should it be available . . .

Now that we have this hypothetical sequence before us, let us imagine a historian called Tom, who decides many years later to study this episode. He will doubtless be struck by the fact that a group of scientists who once accepted values A_1, rules M_1, and theory T_1 came over the course of, say, a decade or two to abandon the whole lot and to accept a new complex, C_2, consisting of A_2, M_2, and T_2. Tom will probably note, and rightly too, that the partisans of C_2 have precious little in common with the devotees of C_1. Surely, Tom may well surmise, here was a scientific revolution if ever there was one, for there was dramatic change at every level. If Tom decides to call the view that scientists eventually came to hold "Paradigm 2," and the view from which they began "Paradigm 1," then he will be able to document the existence of a massive paradigm shift between what (at our remoteness in time) appear to be conceptually distant and virtually incommensurable paradigms.

The point, of course, is that a sequence of belief changes which, described at the microlevel, appears to be a perfectly reasonable and rational sequence of events may appear, when represented in broad brushstrokes that drastically compress the temporal dimension, as a fundamental and unintelligible change of world view. This kind of tunnel vision, in which a sequence of gradual shifts is telescoped into one abrupt and mighty transformation, is a folly which every historian is taught to avoid. Yet knowing that one should avoid it and actually doing so are two different things. Once we recognize this fallacy for what it is, we should probably hesitate to accept too quickly the models of the holists and big-picture builders. For, if our fairy story has anything of the truth about it (that is, if change is, or more weakly even if it could be, more piecemeal than the holistic accounts imply), there may yet be room for incorporating changes of methods and of cognitive values into a rational account of scientific activity. My object in the rest of this chapter is to offer some reasons to believe that the fairy tale is a good deal closer to the mark than its holistic rivals.

But before I present the evidence needed for demythologizing my story, we have to add a new twist to it. As I pointed out above, this story concerns what I call a "unitraditional paradigm shift." It reveals how it might be possible for scientists, originally advocates of one tradition or paradigm, to come around eventually to accept what appears to be a very different view of the world, not to say a very different view of what science is. I call such a change unitraditional because it is not prompted or provoked by the availability of a well-articulated rival world view. If you like, the unitraditional picture explains how one could get paradigm change by developments entirely internal to the dynamic of a particular paradigm. More interesting, and more challenging, is the problem of multitraditional paradigm shifts, that is, basic changes of world view which arise from competition between rival paradigms. To deal with such cases, we need to complicate our fairy story a bit.

Here, we need to imagine two of our complexes already well developed, and radically divergent (i.e., with different ontologies, different methodologies, and different axiologies). If we ask under what circumstances it would be reasonable for the partisans of C_1 to abandon it and accept C_2, some answers come immediately to mind. Suppose, for instance, it can be shown that the central theories of C_1 look worse than the theories of C_2, even by the standards of C_1. . . . Kuhn denies that this is possible, since he says that the theories associated with a particular paradigm will always look better by its standards than will the theories of rival paradigms. . . . But as we have already seen, there is no way of guaranteeing in advance that the methods and standards of C_1 will always give the epistemic nod to theories associated with C_1, since it is always possible (and has sometimes happened) that rival paradigms to C_1 will develop theories that do a better job of satisfying the methodological demands of C_1 than do the theories developed within C_1 itself. Alternatively, suppose someone shows that there is a set of methods M_2 which is more nearly optimal than M_1 for achieving the aims of C_1, and that those methods give the epistemic nod to the theories of C_2 rather than those of C_1. Or, suppose that someone shows that the goals of C_1 are deeply at odds with the attributes of some of the major theories of science—theories that the partisans of C_1 themselves endorse—and that, by contrast, the cognitive values of C_2 are typified by those same theories. Again, new evidence might emerge that indicates the nonrealizability of some of the central cognitive aims of C_1 and the achievability of the aims of C_2. In all these circumstances (and several obvious ones which I shall not enumerate), the only reasonable thing for a scientist to do would be to give up C_1 and to embrace C_2.

. . . [W]e see that the transition from one paradigm or world view to another can itself be a step-wise process, requiring none of the wholesale shifts in allegiance at every level required by Kuhn's analysis. The advocates of C_1 might, for instance, decide initially to accept many of the substantive theories of C_2, while still retaining for a time the methodology and axiology of C_1. At a later stage they might be led by a different chain of arguments and evidence to accept the methodology of C_2 while retaining C_1's axiology. Finally, they might eventually come to share the values of C_2. As William Whewell showed more than a century ago, precisely some such series of shifts occurred in the gradual capitulation of Cartesian physicists to the natural philosophy of Newton.[9]

In effect, I am claiming the solution of the problem of consensus formation in the multi-paradigm situation to be nothing more than a special or degenerate instance of unitraditional change. It follows that, if we can show that the unitraditional fairy tale has something going for it, then we will solve both forms of the consensus-formation problem simultaneously. The core question is whether the gradualist myth, which I have just sketched out, is better

supported by the historical record than the holistic picture associated with Kuhn.

One striking way of formulating the contrast between the piecemeal and the holistic models, and thus designing a test to choose between them, is to ask a fairly straightforward question about the historical record: Is it true that the major historical shifts in the methodological rules of science and in the cognitive values of scientists have invariably been contemporaneous with one another *and* with shifts in substantive theories and ontologies? The holistic account is clearly committed to an affirmative answer to the question. Indeed, it is a straightforward corollary of Kuhn's analysis that changes in rules or values, when they occur, will occur only when a scientific revolution takes place, that is, only when there is a concomitant shift in theories, methods, and values. A change in values without an associated change in basic ontology is not a permissible variation countenanced in the Kuhnian scheme.[10] Nor is a change in methods possible for Kuhn without a paradigm change. Kuhn's analysis flatly denies that the values and norms of a "mature" science can shift in the absence of a revolution. Yet there are plenty of examples one may cite to justify the assertion made here that changes at the three levels do not always go together. I shall mention two such examples.

Consider, first, a well-known shift at the level of methodological rules. From the time of Bacon until the early nineteenth century most scientists subscribed to variants of the rules of inductive inference associated with Bacon, Hume, and Newton. The methods of agreement, difference, and concomitant variations were a standard part of the repertoire of most working scientists for two hundred years. These rules, at least as then understood, foreclosed the postulation of any theoretical or hypothetical entities, since observable bodies were the only sort of objects and properties to which one could apply traditional inductive methods. More generally . . . , thinkers of the

Enlightenment believed it important to develop rules of inquiry which would exclude unobservable entities and bring to heel the tendency of scientists to indulge their *l'espirit de système*. Newton's famous third rule of reasoning in philosophy, the notorious "hypotheses non fingo," was but a particularly succinct and influential formulation of this trenchant empiricism.

It is now common knowledge that by the late nineteenth century this methodological orientation had largely vanished from the writings of major scientists and methodologists. Whewell, Peirce, Helmholtz, Mach, Darwin, Hertz, and a host of other luminaries had, by the 1860s and 1870s, come to believe that it was quite legitimate for science to postulate unobservable entities, and that most of the traditional rules of inductive reasoning had been superseded by the logic of hypothetico-deduction. Elsewhere I have described this shift in detail.[11] What is important for our purposes is both that it occurred and when it occurred. That it took place would be denied, I think, by no one who studies the record; determining precisely when it occurred is more problematic, although probably no scholar would quarrel with the claim that it comes in the period from 1800 to 1860. And a dating as fuzzy as that is sufficient to make out my argument.

For here we have a shift in the history of the explicit methodology of the scientific community as significant as one can imagine—from methods of enumerative and eliminative induction to the method of hypothesis—occurring across the spectrum of the theoretical sciences, from celestial mechanics to chemistry and biology. . . . Yet where is the larger and more global scientific revolution of which this methodological shift was the concomitant? There were of course revolutions, and important ones, in this period. Yet this change in methodology cannot be specifically linked to any of the familiar revolutions of the period. The method of hypothesis did not become the orthodoxy in science of the late nineteenth

century because it rode on the coattails of any specific change in ontology or scientific values. So far as I can see, this methodological revolution was independent of any particular program of research in any one of the sciences, which is not to say that it did not reflect some very general tendencies appearing across the board in scientific research. The holist model, which would have us believe that changes in methodological orientation are invariably linked to changes in values and ontology, is patently mistaken here. Nor, if one reflects on the nature of methodological discussion, should we have expected otherwise. . . . [M]ethodological rules can reasonably be criticized and altered if one discovers that they fail optimally to promote our cognitive aims. If our aims shift, as they would in a Kuhnian paradigm shift, we would of course expect a reappraisal of our methods of inquiry in light of their suitability for promoting the new goals. But, even when our goals shift not at all, we sometimes discover arguments and evidence which indicate that the methods we have been using all along are not really suitable for our purposes. Such readjustments of methodological orientation, in the absence of a paradigm shift . . . pose a serious anomaly for Kuhn's analysis.

What about changes in aims, as opposed to rules? Is it not perhaps more plausible to imagine, with Kuhn, that changes of cognitive values are always part of broader shifts of paradigm or world views? Here again, the historical record speaks out convincingly against this account. Consider, very briefly, one example: the abandonment of "infallible knowledge" as an epistemic aim for science. As before, my historical account will have to be "potted" for purposes of brevity; but there is ample serious scholarship to back up the claims I shall be making.[12]

That scholarship has established quite convincingly that, during the course of the nineteenth century, the view of science is aiming at certainty gave way among most scientists to a more modest program of producing theories that were plausible, probable, or well tested. As Peirce and Dewey have argued, this shift represents one of the great watersheds in the history of scientific philosophy: the abandonment of the quest for certainty. More or less from the time of Aristotle onward, scientists had sought theories that were demonstrable and apodictically certain. Although empiricists and rationalists disagreed about precisely how to certify knowledge as certain and incorrigible, all agreed that science was aiming exclusively at the production of such knowledge. This same view of science largely prevailed at the beginning of the nineteenth century. But by the end of that century this demonstrative and infallibilist ideal was well and truly dead. Scientists of almost every persuasion were insistent that science could, at most, aspire to the status of highly probable knowledge. Certainty, incorrigibility, and indefeasibility ceased to figure among the central aims of most twentieth-century scientists.

The full story surrounding the replacement of the quest for certainty by a thoroughgoing fallibilism is long and complicated; I have attempted to sketch out parts of that story elsewhere.[13] What matters for our purposes here is not so much the details of this epistemic revolution, but the fact that this profound transformation was not specifically associated with the emergence of any new scientific paradigms or research programs. The question of timing is crucial, for it is important to see that this deep shift in axiological sensibilities was independent of any specific change in scientific world view or paradigm. No new scientific tradition or paradigm in the nineteenth century was associated with a specifically fallibilist axiology. Quite the reverse, fallibilism came to be associated with virtually every major program of scientific research by the mid- to late nineteenth century. Atomists and antiatomists, wave theorists and particle theorists, Darwinians and Lamarckians, uniformitarians and catastrophists—all subscribed to the new consensus about the corrigibility and indemonstrability of scientific theories. A similar story could be told about other cognitive values which have gone the way of all flesh. The abandonment of intelligibility, of the requirement of picturable or mechanically constructible models of natural processes, of the insistence on "complete" descriptions of nature—all reveal a similar pattern. The abandonment of each of these cognitive ideals was largely independent of shifts in basic theories about nature.

Once again, the holistic approach leads to expectations that are confounded by the historical record. Changes in values and changes in substantive ontologies or methodologies show no neat isomorphism. Change certainly occurs at all levels, and sometimes changes are concurrent, but there is no striking covariance between the timing of changes at one level and the timing of those at any other. I conclude from such examples that scientific change is substantially more piecemeal than the holistic model would suggest. Value changes do not always accompany, nor are they always accompanied by, changes in scientific paradigm. Shifts in methodological rules may, but need not, be associated with shifts in either values or ontologies. The three levels, although unquestionably interrelated, do not come as an inseparable package on a take-it-or-leave-it basis.

This result is of absolutely decisive importance for understanding the processes of scientific change. Because these changes are not always concomitant, we are often in a position to hold one or two of the three levels fixed while we decide whether to make modifications at the disputed level. The existence of these (temporarily) fixed and thus shared points of perspective provides a crucial form of triangulation. Since theories, methodologies, and axiologies stand together in a kind of justificatory triad, we can use those doctrines about which there is agreement to resolve the remaining areas where we disagree. The uncontested levels will not always resolve the controversy, for underdetermination is an ever present possibility. But the fact that the levels of agreement are sometimes insufficient to terminate the controversy provides no comfort for

Kuhn's subjectivist thesis that those levels of agreement are never sufficient to resolve the debate. As logicians say, we need to be very careful about our quanitifiers here. Some writers have not always exercised the care they should. Kuhn, for instance, confusedly slides from (*a*) the correct claim that the shared values of scientists are, in certain situations, incapable of yielding unambiguously a preference between two rival theories to (*b*) the surely mistaken claim that the shared values of scientists are never sufficient to warrant a preference between rival paradigms. Manifestly in some instances, the shared rules and standards of methodology are unavailing. But neither Kuhn nor anyone else has established that the rules, evaluative criteria, and values to which scientists subscribe are generally so ambiguous in application that virtually any theory or paradigm can be shown to satisfy them. And we must constantly bear in mind the point that, even when theories are underdetermined by a set of rules or standards, many theories will typically be ruled out by the relevant rules; and if one party to a scientific debate happens to be pushing for a theory that can be shown to violate those rules, then the rules will eliminate that theory from contention.

What has led holistic theorists to misdescribe so badly the relations among these various sorts of changes? As one who was himself once an advocate of such an account, I can explain specifically what led me into thinking that change on the various levels was virtually simultaneous. If one focuses, as most philosophers of science have, on the processes of justification in science, one begins to see systemic linkages among what I earlier called factual, methodological, and axiological ideas. One notices further that beliefs at all three levels shift through time. Under the circumstances it is quite natural to conjecture that these various changes may be interconnected. Specifically, one can imagine that the changes might well be simultaneous, or at least closely dependent on one another. The suggestion is further borne out—at least to a first approximation—

by an analysis of some familiar scientific episodes. It is clear, for instance, that the scientific revolution of the seventeenth century brought with it changes in theories, ontologies, rules, and values. Equally, the twentieth-century revolution in relativity theory and quantum mechanics brought in its wake a shift in both methodological and axiological orientations among theoretical physicists. But as I have already suggested, these changes came seriatim, not simultaneously. More to the point, it is my impression that the overwhelming majority of theory transitions in the history of science (including shifts as profound as that from creationist biology to evolution, from energeticist to atomistic views on the nature of matter, from catastrophism to uniformitarianism in geology, from particle to wave theories of light) have not taken place by means of Gestalt-like shifts at all levels concurrently. Often, change occurs on a single level only (e.g., the Darwinian revolution or the triumph of atomism, where it was chiefly theory or ontology that changed); sometimes it occurs on two levels simultaneously; rarely do we find an abrupt and wholesale shift of doctrines at all three levels.

This fact about scientific change has a range of important implications for our understanding of scientific debate and scientific controversy. Leaving aside the atypical case of simultaneous shifts at all three levels . . . , it means that most instances of scientific change—including most of the events we call scientific revolutions—occur amid a significant degree of consensus at a variety of levels among the contending parties. Scientists may, for instance, disagree about specific theories yet agree about the appropriate rules for theory appraisal. They may even disagree about both theories and rules but accept the same cognitive values. Alternatively, they may accept the same theories and rules yet disagree about the cognitive values they espouse. In all these cases there is no reason to speak (with Kuhn) of "incommensurable choices" or "conversion experiences," or (with Foucault) about abrupt "ruptures of thought," for there is in each instance the possibility of bringing the disagreement to rational closure. Of course, it may happen in specific cases that the mechanisms of rational adjudication are of no avail, for the parties may be contending about matters that are underdetermined by the beliefs and standards the contending parties share in common. But, even here, we can still say that there are rational rules governing the game being played, and that the moves being made (i.e., the beliefs being debated and the arguments being arrayed for and against them) are in full compliance with the rules of the game.

Above all, we must bear in mind that it has never been established that such instances of holistic change constitute more than a tiny fraction of scientific disagreements. Because such cases are arguably so atypical, it follows that sociologists and philosophers of science who predicate their theories of scientific change and cognition on the presumed ubiquity of irresolvable standoffs between monolithic world views (of the sort that Kuhn describes in *Structure of Scientific Revolutions*) run the clear risk of failing to recognize the complex ways in which rival theories typically share important background assumptions in common. To put it differently, global claims about the immunity of interparadigmatic disputes to rational adjudication (and such claims are central in the work of both Kuhn and Lakatos) depend for their plausibility on systematically ignoring the piecemeal character of most forms of scientific change and on a gross exaggeration of the impotence of rational considerations to bring such disagreements to closure. Beyond that, I have argued that, even if interparadigmatic clashes had the character Kuhn says they do (namely, of involving little or no overlap at any of the three levels), it still would not follow that there are no rational grounds for a critical and comparative assessment of the rival paradigms. In sum, no adequate support has been provided for the claim that clashes between rival scientific camps can never, or rarely ever, be resolved in an objective fashion. The

problem of consensus formation, which I earlier suggested was the great Kuhnian enigma, . . . can be resolved, but only if we realize that science has adjudicatory mechanisms whose existence has gone unnoticed by Kuhn and the other holists.

Notes

1. Alan Musgrave spoke for many of Kuhn's readers when he noted, apropos of the second edition of *The Structure of Scientific Revolutions*, that in "his recent writings, then, Kuhn disowns most of the challenging ideas ascribed to him by his critics . . . the new, more real Kuhn who emerges . . . [is] but a pale reflection of the old, revolutionary Kuhn" (Musgrave, 1980, p. 51).
2. Kuhn, 1962.
3. Ibid.
4. Ibid., p. 159.
5. As Kuhn himself remarks, he has been attempting "to eliminate misunderstandings for which my own past rhetoric is doubtless partially responsible" (1970, pp. 259–260).
6. Kuhn, 1962, p. 108; my italics. [p. 274 above]
7. Ibid., pp. 108–109. [p. 275 above]
8. Ibid., p. 149.
9. See Whewell's remarkably insightful essay of 1851, where he remarks, apropos the transition from one global theory to another: "the change . . . is effected by a transformation, or series of transformations, of the earlier hypothesis, by means of which it is brought nearer and nearer to the second [i.e., later]" (1851, p. 139).
10. Some amplification of this point is required. Kuhn evidently believes that there are some values that transcend specific paradigms. He mentions such examples as the demand for accuracy, consistency, and simplicity. The fortunes of these values are not linked to specific paradigms. Thus, if they were to change, such change would presumably be independent of shifts in paradigms. In Kuhn's view, however, these values have persisted unchanged since the seventeenth century. Or, rather, scientists have invoked these values persistently since that time; strictly speaking, on Kuhn's analysis, these values are changing constantly, since each scientist interprets them slightly differently.
11. See Laudan, 1981.
12. For an extensive bibliography on this issue, see Laudan, 1968.
13. See Laudan, 1981.

PART V

REALISM VERSUS ANTI-REALISM: THE ONTOLOGICAL IMPORT OF SCIENTIFIC KNOWLEDGE

D o the theories of science give a literally true account of the way the world is? Do the entities and processes they postulate really exist? Consider one such theory, Copernican astronomy. When it was proposed in the middle of the sixteenth century, a small group of astronomers thought that its central hypothesis—that the earth moves while the sun and stars do not, the actual motions of the earth explaining the merely apparent motions of the sun and stars—was literally true. This hypothesis was, after all, supported by a wide variety of observational evidence, and it did, after all, lead to the discovery of new facts. What's more, Copernican astronomy explained facts that its predecessor, Ptolemaic astronomy, merely postulated (for example, that the five visible planets, but not the sun or moon, show retrograde motion), and it provided determinate values of quantities that Ptolemaic astronomy had not (for example, the distances of the planets). Most astronomers, however, while granting that Copernicus's theory was an improvement over Ptolemy's in both observational accuracy and theoretical adequacy, still emphasized that Copernicus's theory conflicted with other accepted knowledge (for example, Holy Scripture and Aristotelian physics), and was, at any rate, only one of the systems that could be constructed to account for the observational data. They concluded that Copernicus's theory was merely a calculating device, useful for deriving important astronomical information, but not to be taken as literally true. Who was right?

This kind of question seemed settled in Part III. There we considered six major approaches to theory testing currently in the forefront of discussion: justificationism; falsificationism; conventionalism; the methodology of scientific research programmes; Thomas Kuhn's sociological approach; and contextual empiricism. All six approaches allowed that a scientific theory is tested by deducing from it consequences regarding observable states of affairs that are then compared with the results of observation and experiment. But the approaches differed regarding what might follow from such a comparison. For justificationism and falsificationism, true observational consequences warranted a judgment regarding the *truth* of a theory—either that it is probably true (for justificationism), or that it is possibly true (for falsificationism)—whereas false observational consequences warranted a judgment that the theory is false. For conventionalism, the methodology of scientific research programmes, Kuhn's sociological approach, and contextual empiricism, on the other hand, neither true nor false observational consequences warranted *any* judgment regarding the truth or falsity of the theory. Instead, these approaches suggested that a scientific theory is accepted or rejected on the basis of considerations other than its truth (or possible truth or probable truth) or falsity, such as its relative simplicity (for conventionalism) or its progressiveness (for the research programmes of the methodology of scientific research programmes) or its accuracy, consistency, scope, simplicity, and fruitfulness (for Kuhn's sociological approach), or any or all of these "constitutive values" as well as "contextual values" stemming from the social and cultural environment in which the theory evaluation occurs (for contextual empiricism). And nothing regarding the truth or falsity of the theory was held to follow from such features of it.

In short, by the end of Part III, if you had accepted justificationism or falsificationism, you would have said that the theories of science do (or probably do, or possibly do) give a literally true account of the way the world is. On the other hand, if you had accepted conventionalism, the methodology of scientific research programmes, Kuhn's sociological approach, or contextual empiricism, you would have had *no* grounds to say that the theories of science give a literally true account of the way the world is—you would have had no grounds to say this, that is, unless you had an independent argument to the effect that simplicity or progressiveness or the like is a mark of truth.

Of course all this assumed that the observational reports against which the consequences of a theory were compared in the process of testing it were *true*. And thus, all this was complicated by the sceptical challenges to that assumption posed in Part II. There we found that two conditions would ensure the truth of observational reports:

1. The observational reports included in the empirical basis must express only what is directly observed. They must not go beyond what is directly observed, or else they will say more than can be justified by the observations they report.

2. What is directly observed must correspond to what is there in the world, as measured by what other people also observe. It must contain nothing that is personal or subjective or idiosyncratic.

But we also found that philosophers and others denied that these conditions were met by scientists' observational reports. Thus, regarding condition 1, Popper argued that scientists' observation reports, being statements, inherently go beyond what is included in direct observation and, in any case, can be justified only by other statements, not by direct observation. Shapin added that scientists' observation reports are accepted not because they express what has been directly observed, but because of the way the reports are expressed, the instrumentation that has been used in coming to assert them, and the like. And Pickering added that scientists' observation reports reflect the interpretative practices in effect at the time of the reports, and change with changes in those practices even when the content of observation stays the same. Regarding condition 2, Hanson argued that what is directly observed depends upon an observer's theories and knowledge and training, and changes with changes in these. In consequence, what is directly observed will vary from observer to observer, depending on the observer's theories and knowledge and training. And Oakley suggested that an observer's gender and political outlook (and perhaps also class and race and ethnicity) can affect the observer's research goals and methods, and thereby, the observer's observational data as well. In consequence, one scientist's observational data need not correspond to other scientists' observational data. The upshot of these challenges was that, unless you could answer them, or bypass them and devise an argument independent of conditions 1 and 2 for the claim that scientists' observational reports are true, you were left with no grounds for saying that they are, and hence, no grounds for saying that the theories tested with their help are true (or probably true, or possibly true).

In Part IV, we investigated the historical development of scientific knowledge. In particular, we considered four models of scientific development—the cumulative model, the evolutionary model, the revolutionary model, and the gradualist model. Each of these models offered us a different account of scientific progress and a correspondingly different account of the typical historical development of scientific fields. Thus, according to the cumulative model, a scientific field progresses when it gains new empirical laws to explain its facts, or new theories to explain its empirical laws or other theories, and the typical historical development of a scientific field is a succession of such additions. According to the evolutionary model, a scientific field progresses when it replaces current theories with new, more successful theories, and the typical historical development of a scientific field is a succession of such replacements. According to the revolutionary model, a scientific field progresses when it replaces current theories and associated facts, methods, and goals with new theories and associated facts, methods, and goals, and the typical historical development of a scientific field is a succession of such radical replacements. And finally, according to the gradualist model, a scientific field progresses when it justifiably replaces its current theories or methods or goals with new theories or methods or goals, and the typical historical development of a scientific field is a succession of such limited replacements.

In short, by the end of Part IV, if you had accepted the evolutionary, revolutionary, or gradualist models of scientific development you would have said that scientific theories are regularly replaced—are regularly *falsified*, in the language of justificationism and falsificationism. In other words, you would have said that *all* scientific theories have been falsified, save for the current ones. And you would have said that the current theories will likewise be falsified in the future. By the end of Part IV, then, only if you had accepted the cumulative model of scientific development could you still have said that the theories of science give a literally true account of the way the world is.

What, then, is the answer—the view that the theories of science give a literally true account of the world, including the (postulated) "theoretical" world of entities and processes beyond what we can observe (a scientific realist★ answer), or the view that the theories of science are mere calculating devices, useful fictions, convenient methods of representation, or the like, helpful only for predicting and organizing truths about the observable world (a scientific anti-realist answer)? Without a doubt the majority of scientists and philosophers of science today lean toward scientific realism, and many arguments have been offered in its support. Thus, for example, in "The Ontological Status of Theoretical Entities," Grover Maxwell draws attention to the tenuous nature of the observational-theoretical distinction itself. Consider the so-called "theoretical entities" postulated by a successful scientific theory, which are considered suspect simply because we cannot observe them. What exactly, asks Maxwell, is the nature of their problematic "theoretical" status? Is it that they are entities we cannot observe except with, say, a high-power microscope? Except with a low-power microscope? Except with eyeglasses? Is it that they are entities we cannot observe *at all* with *any* presently available instrument of observation, given our present sensory capacities? Is it that they are entities we cannot observe at all with any *possible* instrument of observation and any *possible* sensory capacities we might attain? But do we know of *anything* that fits this last description? Maxwell concludes that our drawing of the observational-theoretical distinction at any particular place "is an accident and a function of our physiological makeup, our current state of knowledge, and the instruments we happen to have available and, therefore, that it has no ontological significance [i.e., significance in terms of what actually exists] whatever." But with the collapse of the observational-theoretical distinction, of course, goes the collapse of anti-realism itself: the theoretical world, and the statements that describe it, then have no status different from the observable world and the statements that describe it.

★We might call this *scientific realism on the theoretical level* to distinguish it from the scientific realism on the observational level that we explored in Part II.

Maxwell's line of defense is not the only argument for scientific realism. In "Arguments Concerning Scientific Realism," Bas van Fraassen surveys other main arguments in addition to Maxwell's—for example, that only realism allows the explanation of regularities in observable phenomena, and that this is a foremost objective of science; that only realism can explain the usefulness of scientific theories, and make sense of the distinction between correct scientific theories and merely useful, but false, ones; and that only realism can explain the ongoing success of mature scientific fields. Van Fraassen concludes, however, that all these arguments are flawed. In their place he recommends a version of anti-realism he calls *constructive empiricism*: "Science aims to give us theories which are empirically adequate"—that is, which always make true predictions about the observable things and events in the world; "and acceptance of a theory involves as belief only that it is empirically adequate." (p. 358)

For his part, Ernan McMullin in "A Case for Scientific Realism" surveys all the current arguments for *anti-realism*: from science (for example, that the most successful theories of science—quantum mechanics, elementary-particle theory, and classical mechanics before them—require anti-realistic interpretations); from the history of science (for example, that most of the best scientific theories of the past have now been discarded, and that the history of successful scientific theories traces the development not of a single, ever more accurate and detailed picture of the world, but of markedly dissimilar and discontinuous pictures); from philosophy (for example, that scientific realism makes use of obscure notions, such as "truth" as some sort of "correspondence" with an inaccessable "external world"). McMullin concludes that all *these* arguments are flawed as well, and argues, instead, for his own version of realism: "that the long-term success of a scientific theory gives reason to believe that something like the entities and structure postulated by the theory actually exists."

Is McMullin's position, then, the one we are left with after all the surveys and critiques of arguments on both sides of the realism/anti-realism controversy? Arthur Fine does not think so. In "The Natural Ontological Attitude" he suggests that arguments like McMullin's that explain the success of science in terms of the empirical hypothesis of scientific realism simply beg the question. After all, Fine argues, if inferring the truth of a scientific theory from some of the observable facts explained by the theory is thought to be suspect and in need of further justification—as it is by many on both sides of the realism/anti-realism controversy—then how is inferring the truth of scientific realism from some of the observable—historical—facts of ongoing scientific success that are explained by realism any less suspect and in need of further justification? But this question naturally leads to another. If scientific realism *is* an empirical hypothesis—to the effect that scientific theories are true and the entities they postulate are real—then isn't the realism/anti-realism question simply a *scientific* question, on a par with other scientific questions? And if so, what can *philosophers* offer here?

Fine makes clear what philosophers *have* offered. Both realists and anti-realists, he points out, take for granted the methods and the results of science—the theories, observable facts, modes of inference, and the rest, accepted and used by the scientific establishment. This taken for granted body of knowledge and practice is, in fact, the "core" of their respective positions. What distinguishes realists from anti-realists, then, is what they add onto this core—their *interpretations* of it. Those anti-realists called *instrumentalists*, for example, add on their interpretation of accepted scientific theories as tools or *instruments* for prediction and control of the environment. Realists, on the other hand, add on their interpretation of accepted scientific theories as true descriptions of the world—that is, as statements that "correspond to" the world. Fine, however, suggests a third option—the core position itself, and all by itself. This third option he calls the *natural ontological attitude* toward science, the attitude that eschews both realist and anti-realist interpretations. Such an attitude, Fine argues, allows science to speak for itself—to provide its own local interpretations of its own results, rather than be interpreted by either realism or anti-realism in a global way. If we take this attitude, Fine suggests, then the global interpretations of realism and anti-realism will appear as idle overlays to science: not necessary, not warranted, and, in the end, probably not even intelligible.

Evelyn Fox Keller, Michael Gardner, and Ian Hacking all seem to exemplify, though in different ways, Fine's natural ontological attitude. In "Critical Silences in Scientific Discourse: Problems of Form and Re-Form" Keller provides a further understanding of the limitations of realism and anti-realism as global interpretations of science, and thereby supports Fine's rejection of them. In "Realism and Instrumentalism in Pre-Newtonian Astronomy" and in "Experimentation and Scientific Realism," on the other hand, Michael Gardner and Ian Hacking seem to be doing exactly what Fine recommends: letting science—theoretical science for Gardner and experimental science for Hacking—speak for itself. In so doing, they both conclude that the usual way of conceiving the realism/anti-realism question must be changed.

Consider Keller first. Scientific knowledge, according to her, is composed of representations of the world that exert an impact on the world, and this impact, like all forces, has both magnitude and direction. As Keller would have it, the applications of scientific theories are already implicit in the very framing of the questions within the research programs leading to those theories, and such applications form the (conscious or unconscious) motivation for the research. The program of modern genetics, for example, in a sense "already has, written into its very structure, a blueprint for eugenics" and "nuclear weapons are prebuilt into the program of nuclear physics." This means that we as a society have to attend to the directionality of scientific knowledge. Other representations of the world involving other impacts are possible, and the current ones, as instanced by the above and other cases, are simply unacceptable: our survival, and much else, are put into question by them. But realism and anti-realism as global interpretations of science obscure all this. After all, scientific knowledge is portrayed by realism as simply a mirror image or snapshot of reality, detached from its social origins and effects on the world (the responsibility for which is borne entirely by "technology," perhaps with the help of "politics"). Scientific knowledge, for realism, is "pure knowledge," with the conflation of "abstract," "conceptual," "theoretical," "autonomous," "innocent," "blameless," "unblemished," and "virtuous," that that concept involves. And anti-realism, although it denies that scientific knowledge is pure in this way, a mirror image of reality, detached from applications, although, in fact, it focuses *entirely* on the applications of scientific knowledge, still never talks about *specifics*. To be sure, anti-realism claims that scientific knowledge is *only useful*, not true, but never says what scientific knowledge is useful *for*—how it generates jobs and doable problems and emotionally and aesthetically satisfying explanations; how it wins allies and students and grants; how it produces technological goods, and so forth. But it is the specifics that we need to consider if we want to redirect science in more acceptable ways. We need to spell out in detail how science *works*. In short, both realism and anti-realism as global interpretations of science foreclose questions we need to pursue in order to understand and intelligently deal with science.

Gardner rejects realism and anti-realism as global interpretations of science for different reasons. He has pointed out in earlier work that the realism/anti-realism question, as usually conceived, is the question whether scientific theories are correctly interpreted realistically—that is, as literally true—or instrumentalistically—that is, as merely convenient devices for summarizing, systematizing, and deducing observable facts. This question, Gardner has suggested, requires a single answer applicable to all theories. But a question such as this, about the proper interpretation of scientific theories, should be settled through an examination of particular scientific theories rather than in general terms, given the possibility that the question might have different answers for different theories. Indeed, a common pattern in the history of science is that a theory is first put forward or accepted merely as an idealization or calculational device and only later comes to be regarded as literally true. Gardner has thus suggested a successor question to the realism/anti-realism question: Under what conditions is it reasonable to accept a theory on a realistic interpretation (as literally true) rather than on an instrumentalist interpretation (as not literally true but convenient for summarizing, systematizing, and deducing, a given body of information)? In "Realism and Instrumentalism in Pre-Newtonian Astronomy," which is part of a program aimed at answering this question, Gardner examines the debate over the status of Copernican astronomy in the sixteenth century. He finds that Copernican astronomy was accepted on a realistic interpretation or on an instrumentalist interpretation depending on whether the theory was thought to satisfy or fail to satisfy conditions like the following: (1) the theory satisfies the laws of physics; (2) the theory is consistent with other putative knowledge (for example, the Scriptures); (3) the theory is consistent with all observational data; (4) the theory contains only determinate quantities; (5) the theory is able to predict novel facts; (6) the theory has a central hypothesis supported by a large variety of evidence; (7) the theory is within the realm of possible human knowledge; (8) the theory explains facts that competing theories merely postulate; and (9) the theory agrees with some of the nonobservational claims of some previous theories purporting to explain the same observations. If, as is plausible, these conditions, which are operative in the case of Copernican astronomy, are also found to be operative in a variety of other cases in which the realism/instrumentalism issue has arisen, we might then accept them as good reasons for adopting a theory on a realistic interpretation. The justification for such an answer to our new version of the realism/anti-realism question would, of course, be that the answer agrees with the judgments of most good scientists of the past and present on most of the relevant occasions.

Hacking's suggested revision of the realism/anti-realism question takes a different form from Gardner's. Focusing on experimental science rather than theoretical science, Hacking suggests, in essence, that we ask: Under what conditions is it reasonable to accept the entities postulated by a theory (and this includes processes, states, fields, and the like) as real existents rather than as mere hypothetical entities? Like Gardner's revised version of the realism/anti-realism question, this version allows us to form different judgments about the entities postulated by different theories and by the same theory at different stages of development. But unlike Gardner's version, this version of the realism/anti-realism question focuses on the reality of the entities postulated by a theory rather than on the truth of the theory. And this is as it should be, according to Hacking, given that a false theory as well as a true one might postulate real entities, and that different, and even incompatible, theories have frequently postulated the same entities (think of all the different theories that have postulated electrons or atoms). Finally, based on the widespread and, he thinks, reasonable practices of experimental scientists, Hacking offers the following answer to his revised version of the realism/anti-realism question: When scientists' understanding of the causal properties of postulated entities allows them to use such entities as tools to investigate other aspects of nature, then it is reasonable to accept such entities as real existents. Note that accepting such entities as real existents does not commit scientists to accepting as true any particular theory in which the entities are postulated.

Are we now in a position to answer the realism/anti-realism question? We have considered three versions of this question:

1. Do the theories of science give a literally true account of the way the world is, or are they mere calculating devices, useful fictions, convenient methods of representation, or the like, helpful only for predicting and organizing truths about the observable world? Alternatively, does science *aim* to give us theories of the one kind, or does it aim to give us theories of the other?

2. Under what conditions is it reasonable to accept a theory on a realistic interpretation (as literally true) rather than on an instrumentalist interpretation (as not literally true, but convenient for summarizing, systematizing, and deducing a given body of information)?

3. Under what conditions is it reasonable to accept the entities postulated by a theory, or something like those entities—and this includes processes, states, fields, and the like—as real existents rather than as mere hypothetical entities?

We have also considered some of the factors that motivate particular answers to the realism/anti-realism question in one or another of its versions:

a. The empirical basis of scientific knowledge: Can the sceptical challenges to its truth be overcome?

b. The validation of scientific knowledge: Is it correctly described by justificationism, falsificationism, conventionalism, the methodology of scientific research programmes, Thomas Kuhn's sociological approach, or contextual empiricism?

c. The historical development of scientific knowledge: Is it correctly described by the cumulative model, the evolutionary model, the revolutionary model, or the gradualist model?

d. The need to explain various features of science (such as the usefulness of its theories or its ongoing success) and the need to explain various features of the world (such as regularities in observable phenomena)

e. The past and present practices of theoretical scientists in cases in which the realism/anti-realism issue has arisen

f. The present (and past?) practices of experimental scientists in cases in which the realism/anti-realism issue arises

The extreme difficulty of the realism/anti-realism question should now be apparent. Not only is the form of the question controversial, and the factors that need to be considered complex, but also these factors may very well conflict with one another. Thus, for example, your view of scientific validation may conflict with the past and present practices of theoretical scientists in cases in which the realism/anti-realism issue has arisen. In our consideration of scientific validation, after all, no provision was made for different modes of theory acceptance, such as accepting a theory as literally true vs. accepting it as useful but not literally true. Again, as we have seen, your view of scientific validation may conflict with your view of scientific development—justificationism, for example, leading you to say that theories with much positive evidence and no negative evidence in their behalf are probably true, whereas the evolutionary model of scientific development leads you to say that such theories will be shown to be false. Such conflicts must, of course, be resolved before an answer to the realism/anti-realism question can be had, and in resolving them you may need to revise or refine one or more of factors a–f and even one of questions 1–3. But take heart: In making these revisions or refinements you will be putting the final touches on your own unified and comprehensive philosophy of science.

GROVER MAXWELL

The Ontological Status
of Theoretical Entities

That anyone today should seriously contend that the entities referred to by scientific theories are only convenient fictions, or that talk about such entities is translatable without remainder into talk about sense contents or everyday physical objects, or that such talk should be regarded as belonging to a mere calculating device and, thus, without cognitive content—such contentions strike me as so incongruous with the scientific and rational attitude and practice that I feel this paper *should* turn out to be a demolition of straw men. But the instrumentalist views of outstanding physicists such as Bohr and Heisenberg are too well known to be cited, and in a recent book of great competence, Professor Ernest Nagel concludes that "the opposition between [the realist and the instrumentalist] views [of theories] is a conflict over preferred modes of speech" and "the question as to which of them is the

'correct position' has only terminological interest."[1] The phoenix, it seems, will not be laid to rest.

The literature on the subject is, of course, voluminous, and a comprehensive treatment of the problem is far beyond the scope of one essay. I shall limit myself to a small number of constructive arguments (for a radically realistic interpretation of theories) and to a critical examination of some of the more crucial assumptions (sometimes tacit, sometimes explicit) that seem to have generated most of the problems in this area.[2]

The Problem

Although this essay is not comprehensive, it aspires to be fairly self-contained. Let me, therefore, give a pseudohistorical introduction to the problem with a piece of science fiction (or fictional science).

In the days before the advent of microscopes, there lived a Pasteur-like scientist whom, following the usual custom, I shall call Jones. Reflecting on the fact that certain diseases seemed to be transmitted from one person to another by means of bodily contact or by contact with articles handled previously by an afflicted person, Jones began to speculate about the mechanism of the transmission. As a "heuristic crutch," he recalled that there is an obvious *observable* mechanism for transmission of certain afflictions (such as body lice), and he postulated that all, or most, infectious diseases were spread in a similar manner but that in most cases the corresponding "bugs" were too small to be seen and, possibly, that some of them lived inside the bodies of their hosts. Jones proceeded to develop his theory and to examine its testable consequences. Some of these seemed to be of great importance for preventing the spread of disease.

After years of struggle with incredulous recalcitrance, Jones managed to get some of his preventative measures adopted. Contact with or proximity to diseased persons was avoided when possible, and articles which they handled were "disinfected" (a word coined by Jones) either by means of high temperatures or by treating them with certain toxic preparations which Jones termed "disinfectants." The results were spectacular: within ten years the death rate had declined 40 percent. Jones and his theory received their well-deserved recognition.

However, the "crobes" (the theoretical term coined by Jones to refer to the disease-producing organisms) aroused considerable anxiety among many of the philosophers and philosophically inclined scientists of the day. The expression of this anxiety usually began something like this: "In order to account for the facts, Jones must assume that his crobes are too small to be seen. Thus the very postulates of his theory preclude their being observed; they are *unobservable in principle*." (Recall that no one had envisaged such a thing as a microscope.) This common prefatory remark was

then followed by a number of different "analyses" and "interpretations" of Jones' theory. According to one of these, the tiny organisms were merely convenient fictions—*façons de parler*—extremely useful as heuristic devices for facilitating (in the "context of discovery") the thinking of scientists but not to be taken seriously in the sphere of cognitive knowledge (in the "context of justification"). A closely related view was that Jones' theory was merely an instrument, useful for organizing observation statements and (thus) for producing desired results, and that, therefore, it made no more sense to ask what was the nature of the entities to which it referred than it did to ask what was the nature of the entities to which a hammer or any other tool referred.[3] "Yes," a philosopher might have said, "Jones' theoretical expressions are just meaningless sounds or marks on paper which, when correlated with observation sentences by appropriate syntactical rules, enable us to predict successfully and otherwise organize data in a convenient fashion." These philosophers called themselves "instrumentalists." . . .

Now virtually all who held any of the views so far noted granted, even insisted, that theories played a useful and legitimate role in the scientific enterprise. Their concern was the elimination of "pseudo problems" which might arise, say, when one began wondering about the "reality of supraempirical entities," etc. However, there was also a school of thought, founded by a psychologist named Pelter, which differed in an interesting manner from such positions as these. Its members held that while Jones' crobes might very well exist and enjoy "full-blown reality," they should not be the concern of medical research at all. They insisted that if Jones had employed the correct methodology, he would have discovered, even sooner and with much less effort, all of the observation laws relating to disease contraction, transmission, etc. without introducing superfluous links (the crobes) into the causal chain.

Now, lest any reader find himself waxing impatient, let me hasten to emphasize that this crude parody is not intended to convince anyone, or even to cast serious doubt upon sophisticated varieties of any of the reductionistic positions caricatured (some of them not too severely, I would contend) above. I am well aware that there are theoretical entities and theoretical entities, some of whose conceptual and theoretical statuses differ in important respects from Jones' crobes. (I shall discuss some of these later.) Allow me, then, to bring the Jonesean prelude to our examination of observability to a hasty conclusion.

Now Jones had the good fortune to live to see the invention of the compound microscope. His crobes were "observed" in great detail, and it became possible to identify the specific kind of *microbe* (for so they began to be called) which was responsible for each different disease. Some philosophers freely admitted error and were converted to realist positions concerning theories. . . . Others contrived means of modifying their views much less drastically. One group maintained that Jones' crobes actually never had been unobservable in principle, for, they said, the theory did not imply the impossibility of finding a means (e.g., the microscope) of observing them. A more radical contention was that the crobes were not observed at all; it was argued that what was seen by means of the microscope was just a shadow or an image rather than a corporeal organism.

The Observational-Theoretical Dichotomy

Let us turn from these fictional philosophical positions and consider some of the actual ones to which they roughly correspond. Taking the last one first, it is interesting to note the following passage from Bergmann: "But it is only fair to point out that if this . . . methodological and terminological analysis [for the thesis that there are no atoms] . . . is strictly adhered to, even stars and microscopic objects are not physical things in a literal sense, but merely by courtesy of language and pictorial imagination. This might seem awkward. But when I look through a microscope, all I see is a patch of color which creeps through the field like a shadow over a wall. And a shadow, though real, is certainly not a physical thing."[4]

I should like to point out that it is also the case that if this analysis is strictly adhered to, we cannot observe physical things through opera glasses, or even through ordinary spectacles, and one begins to wonder about the status of what we see through an ordinary windowpane. And what about distortions due to temperature gradients—however small and, thus, always present—in the ambient air? It really *does* "seem awkward" to say that when people who wear glasses describe what they see they are talking about shadows, while those who employ unaided vision talk about physical things—or that when we look through a window-pane, we can only *infer* that it is raining, while if we raise the window, we may "observe directly" that it is. The point I am making is that there is, in principle, a continuous series beginning with looking through a vacuum and containing these as members: looking through a windowpane, looking through glasses, looking through binoculars, looking through a low-power microscope, looking through a high-power microscope, etc., in the order given. The important consequence is that, so far, we are left without criteria which would enable us to draw a nonarbitrary line between "observation" and "theory." Certainly, we will often find it convenient to draw such a to-some-extent-arbitrary line; but its position will vary widely from context to context. (For example, if we are determining the resolving characteristics of a certain microscope, we would certainly draw the line beyond ordinary spectacles, probably beyond simple magnifying glasses, and possibly beyond another microscope with a lower power of resolution.) But what ontological ice does a mere methodologically convenient observational-theoretical dichotomy cut?

Does an entity attain physical thinghood and/or "real existence" in one context only to lose it in another? Or, we may ask, recalling the continuity from observable to unobservable, is what is seen through spectacles a "little bit less real" or does it "exist to a slightly less extent" than what is observed by unaided vision?

However, it might be argued that things seen through spectacles and binoculars look like ordinary physical objects, while those seen through microscopes and telescopes look like shadows and patches of light. I can only reply that this does not seem to me to be the case, particularly when looking at the moon, or even Saturn, through a telescope or when looking at a small, though "directly observable," physical object through a low-power microscope. Thus, again, a continuity appears.

"But," it might be objected, "theory tells us that what we see by means of a microscope is a real image, which is certainly distinct from the object on the stage." Now first of all, it should be remarked that it seems odd that one who is espousing an austere empiricism which requires a sharp observational-language/theoretical-language distinction (and one in which the former language has a privileged status) should need a theory in order to tell him what is observable. But, letting this pass, what is to prevent us from saying that we still observe the object on the stage, even though a "real image" may be involved? . . . (Compare the traditional puzzles: Do I see one physical object or two when I punch my eyeball? Does one object split into two? Or do I see one object and one image? Etc.)

Another argument for the continuous transition from the observable to the unobservable (theoretical) may be adduced from theoretical considerations themselves. For example, contemporary valency theory tells us that there is a virtually continuous transition from very small molecules (such as those of hydrogen) through "medium-sized" ones (such as those of the fatty acids, polypeptides, proteins, and viruses) to extremely large ones (such as crystals of the salts, diamonds, and lumps of polymeric plastic). The molecules in the last-mentioned group are macro, "directly observable" physical objects but are, nevertheless, genuine, single molecules; on the other hand, those in the first mentioned group have the same perplexing properties as subatomic particles (de Broglie waves, Heisenberg indeterminacy, etc.). Are we to say that a large protein molecule (e.g., a virus) which can be "seen" only with an electron microscope is a little less real or exists to somewhat less an extent than does a molecule of a polymer which can be seen with an optical microscope? And does a hydrogen molecule partake of only an infinitesimal portion of existence or reality? Although there certainly *is* a continuous transition from observability to unobservability, any talk of such a continuity from full-blown existence to nonexistence is, clearly, nonsense.

Let us now consider the next to last modified position which was adopted by our fictional philosophers. According to them, it is only those entities which are *in principle* impossible to observe that present special problems. What kind of impossibility is meant here? Without going into a detailed discussion of the various types of impossibility, about which there is abundant literature with which the reader is no doubt familiar, I shall assume what usually seems to be granted by most philosophers who talk of entities which are unobservable in principle—i.e., that the theory(s) itself (coupled with a physiological theory of perception, I would add) entails that such entities are unobservable.

We should immediately note that if this analysis of the notion of unobservability (and, hence, of observability) is accepted, then its use as a means of delimiting the observation language seems to be precluded for those philosophers who regard theoretical expressions as elements of a calculating device—as meaningless strings of symbols. For suppose they wished to determine whether or not 'electron' was a theoretical term. First, they must see whether the theory entails the sentence 'Electrons are unobservable.' So far, so good, for their calculating devices are said to be able to select genuine sentences, provided they contain no theoretical terms. But what about the selected "sentence" itself? Suppose that 'electron' is an observation term. It follows that the expression is a genuine sentence and asserts that electrons are unobservable. But this entails that 'electron' is *not* an observation term. Thus if 'electron' is an observation term, then it is *not* an observation term. Therefore it is not an observation term. But then it follows that 'Electrons are unobservable' is not a genuine sentence and does not assert that electrons are unobservable, since it is a meaningless string of marks and does not assert anything whatever. Of course, it could be stipulated that when a theory "selects" a meaningless expression of the form 'Xs are unobservable,' then 'X' is to be taken as a theoretical term. But this seems rather arbitrary.

But, assuming that well-formed theoretical expressions are genuine sentences, what shall we say about unobservability in principle? I shall begin by putting my head on the block and argue that the present-day status of, say, electrons is in many ways similar to that of Jones' crobes before microscopes were invented. I am well aware of the numerous theoretical arguments for the impossibility of observing electrons. But suppose new entities are discovered which interact with electrons in such a mild manner that if an electron is, say, in an eigenstate of position, then, in certain circumstances, the interaction does not disturb it. Suppose also that a drug is discovered which vastly alters the human perceptual apparatus—perhaps even activates latent capacities so that a new sense modality emerges. Finally, suppose that in our altered state we are able to perceive (not necessarily visually) by means of these new entities in a manner roughly analogous to that by which we now see by means of photons. To make this a little more plausible, suppose that the energy eigenstates of the electrons in some

of the compounds present in the relevant perceptual organ are such that even the weak interaction with the new entities alters them and also that the cross sections, relative to the new entities, of the electrons and other particles of the gases of the air are so small that the chance of any interaction here is negligible. Then we might be able to "observe directly" the position and possibly the approximate diameter and other properties of some electrons. It would follow, of course, that quantum theory would have to be altered in some respects, since the new entities do not conform to all its principles. But however improbable this may be, it does not, I maintain, involve any logical or conceptual absurdity. Furthermore, the modification necessary for the inclusion of the new entities would not necessarily change the meaning of the term 'electron.'

Consider a somewhat less fantastic example, and one which does not involve any change in physical theory. Suppose a human mutant is born who is able to "observe" ultraviolet radiation, or even X rays, in the same way we "observe" visible light.

Now I think that it is extremely improbable that we will ever observe electrons directly (i.e., that it will ever be reasonable to assert that we have so observed them). But this is neither here nor there; it is not the purpose of this essay to predict the future development of scientific theories, and, hence, it is not its business to decide what actually is observable or what will become observable (in the more or less intuitive sense of 'observable' with which we are now working). After all, we are operating, here, under the assumption that it is theory, and thus science itself, which tells us what is or is not, in this sense, observable (the 'in principle' seems to have become superfluous). And this is the heart of the matter; for it follows that, at least for this sense of 'observable,' there are no a priori or philosophical criteria for separating the observable from the unobservable. By trying to show that we can talk about the *possibility* of observing electrons without committing logical or conceptual blunders, I have been trying to support the thesis that any (non-logical) term is a *possible* candidate for an observation term.

There is another line which may be taken in regard to delimitation of the observation language. According to it, the proper term with which to work is not 'obser*vable*' but, rather 'obser*ved*.' There immediately comes to mind the tradition beginning with Locke and Hume (No idea without a preceding impression!), running through Logical Atomism and the Principle of Acquaintance, and ending (perhaps) in contemporary positivism. . . .

Now, according to this view, all descriptive terms of the observation language must refer to that which has been observed. How is this to be interpreted? Not too narrowly, presumably, otherwise each language user would have a different observation language. The name of my Aunt Mamie of California, whom I have never seen, would not be in my observation language, nor would 'snow' be an observation term for many Floridians. One could, of course, set off the observation language by means of this awkward restriction, but then, obviously, not being the referent of an observation term would have no bearing on the ontological status of Aunt Mamie or that of snow.

Perhaps it is intended that the referents of observation terms must be members of a *kind* some of whose members have been observed or instances of a *property* some of whose instances have been observed. But there are familiar difficulties here. For example, given any entity, we can always find a kind whose only member is the entity in question; and surely expressions such as 'men over 14 feet tall' should be counted as observational even though no instances of the "property" of being a man over 14 feet tall have been observed. . . .

. . . Although I have contended that the line between the observable and the unobservable is diffuse, that it shifts from one scientific problem to another, and that it is constantly being pushed toward the "unobservable" end of the spectrum as we develop better means of observation—better instruments it would, nevertheless, be fatuous to minimize the importance of the observation base, for it is absolutely necessary as a confirmation base for statements which do refer to entities which are unobservable at a given time. But we should take as its basis and its unit not the "observational term" but, rather, the quickly decidable sentence. (I am indebted to Feyerabend, *loc. cit.*, for this terminology.) A quickly decidable sentence (in the technical sense employed here) may be defined as a singular, nonanalytic sentence such that a reliable, reasonably sophisticated language user can very quickly decide[5] whether to assert it or deny it when he is reporting on an occurrent situation. 'Observation term' may now be defined as a 'descriptive (nonlogical) term which may occur in a quickly decidable sentence,' and 'observation sentence' as a 'sentence whose only descriptive terms are observation terms.' . . .

It is interesting and important to note that . . . we can, with due effort and reflection, train ourselves to "observe directly" what were once theoretical entities. . . . Those which most readily come to mind involve the use of instruments as aids to observation. Indeed, using our painfully acquired theoretical knowledge of the world, we come to see that we "directly observe" many kinds of so-called theoretical things. After listening to a dull speech while sitting on a hard bench, we begin to become poignantly aware of the presence of a considerably strong gravitational field, and as Professor Feyerabend is fond of pointing out, if we were carrying a heavy suitcase in a changing gravitational field, we could observe the changes of the $G_{\mu\nu}$ of the metric tensor.

I conclude that our drawing of the observational-theoretical line at any given point is an accident and a function of our physiological makeup, our current state of knowledge, and the instruments we happen to have available and, therefore, that it has no ontological significance whatever.

Notes

1. E. Nagel, *The Structure of Science* (New York: Harcourt, Brace, and World, 1961), Ch. 6.

2. For the genesis and part of the content of some of the ideas expressed herein, I am indebted to a number of sources; some of the more influential are H. Feigl, "Existential Hypotheses," *Philosophy of Science*, 17:35–62 (1950); P. K. Feyerabend, "An Attempt at a Realistic Interpretation of Experience," *Proceedings of the Aristotelian Society*, 58:144–170 (1958); N. R. Hanson, *Patterns of Discovery* (Cambridge: Cambridge University Press, 1958); E. Nagel, *loc. cit.*; Karl Popper, *The Logic of Scientific Discovery* (London: Hutchinson, 1959); M. Scriven, "Definitions, Explanations, and Theories," in *Minnesota Studies in the Philosophy of Science*, Vol. II, H. Feigl, M. Scriven, and G. Maxwell, eds. (Minneapolis: University of Minnesota Press, 1958); Wilfrid Sellars, "Empiricism and the Philosophy of Mind," in *Minnesota Studies in the Philosophy of Science*, Vol. I, H. Feigl and M. Scriven, eds. (Minneapolis: University of Minnesota Press, 1956), and "The Language of Theories," in *Current Issues in the Philosophy of Science*, H. Feigl and G. Maxwell, eds. (New York: Holt, Rinehart, and Winston, 1961).

3. I have borrowed the hammer analogy from E. Nagel, "Science and [Feigl's] Semantic Realism," *Philosophy of Science*, 17:174–181 (1950), but it should be pointed out that Professor Nagel makes it clear that he does not necessarily subscribe to the view which he is explaining.

4. G. Bergmann, "Outline of an Empiricist Philosophy of Physics," *American Journal of Physics*, 11:248–258; 335–342 (1943), reprinted in *Readings in the Philosophy of Science*, H. Feigl and M. Brodbeck, eds. (New York: Appleton-Century-Crofts, 1953), pp. 262–287.

5. We may say "noninferentially" decide, provided this is interpreted liberally enough to avoid starting the entire controversy about observability all over again.

BAS VAN FRAASSEN

Arguments Concerning Scientific Realism

The rigor of science requires that we distinguish well the undraped figure of nature itself from the bay-colored vesture with which we clothe it at our pleasure.

—HEINRICH HERTZ,
quoted by Ludwig Boltzmann, letter to *Nature*, 28 February 1895

In our century, the first dominant philosophy of science was developed as part of logical positivism. Even today, such an expression as "the received view of theories" refers to the views developed by the logical positivists, although their heyday preceded the Second World War.

. . . I shall examine and criticize the main arguments that have been offered for scientific realism. These arguments occurred frequently as part of a critique of logical positivism. But it is surely fair to discuss them in isolation, for even if scientific realism is most easily under-

stood as a reaction against positivism, it should be able to stand alone. The alternative view which I advocate—for lack of a traditional name I shall call it *constructive empiricism*—is equally at odds with positivist doctrine.

Scientific Realism and Constructive Empiricism

In philosophy of science, the term "scientific realism" denotes a precise position on the question of how a scientific theory is to be understood, and what scientific activity really is. I shall attempt to define this position, and to canvass its possible alternatives. Then I shall indicate, roughly and briefly, the specific alternative which I shall advocate. . . .

Statement of Scientific Realism

What exactly is scientific realism? A naïve statement of the position would be this: The

Reprinted from *The Scientific Image* by Bas C. van Fraassen, Chapter 2, pp. 6–25, 31–34, 37–40, 216–219, Copyright © 1982 by Bas C. van Fraassen, Reprinted by permission of Oxford University Press.

picture which science gives us of the world is a true one, faithful in its details, and the entities postulated in science really exist—the advances of science are discoveries, not inventions. That statement is too naïve; it attributes to the scientific realist the belief that today's theories are correct. It would mean that the philosophical position of an earlier scientific realist such as C. S. Peirce had been refuted by empirical findings. I do not suppose that scientific realists wish to be committed, as such, even to the claim that science will arrive in due time at theories true in all respects—for the growth of science might be an endless self-correction; or worse, Armageddon might occur too soon.

But the naïve statement has the right flavor. It answers two main questions: It characterizes a scientific theory as a story about what there really is, and scientific activity as an enterprise of discovery, as opposed to invention. The two questions of what a scientific theory is, and what a scientific theory does, must be answered by any philosophy of science. The task we have at this point is to find a statement of scientific realism that shares these features with the naïve statement, but does not saddle the realists with unacceptably strong consequences. It is especially important to make the statement as weak as possible if we wish to argue against it, so as not to charge at windmills.

As clues I shall cite some passage, most of which will also be examined below in the contexts of the authors' arguments. A statement of Wilfrid Sellars is this:

> to have good reason for holding a theory is *ipso facto* to have good reason for holding that the entities postulated by the theory exist.[1]

This addresses a question of epistemology, but also throws some indirect light on what it is, in Sellars's opinion, to hold a theory. Brian Ellis, who calls himself a scientific entity realist rather than a scientific realist, appears to agree with that statement of Sellars, but gives the following formulation of a stronger view:

I understand scientific realism to be the view that the theoretical statements of science are, or purport to be, true generalized descriptions of reality.[2]

This formulation has two advantages: It focuses on the understanding of the theories without reference to reasons for belief, and it avoids the suggestion that to be a realist you must believe current scientific theories to be true. But it gains the latter advantage by use of the word *purport*, which may generate its own puzzles.

Hilary Putnam gives a formulation which he says he learned from Michael Dummett:

> A realist (with respect to a given theory or discourse) holds that (1) the sentences of that theory are true or false; and (2) that what makes them true or false is something external—that is to say, it is not (in general) our sense data, actual or potential, or the structure of our minds, or our language, etc.[3]

He follows this soon afterwards with a further formulation which he credits to Richard Boyd:

> That terms in mature scientific theories typically refer (this formulation is due to Richard Boyd), that the theories accepted in a mature science are typically approximately true, that the same term can refer to the same thing even when it occurs in different theories—these statements are viewed by the scientific realist . . . as part of any adequate scientific description of science and its relations to its objects.[4]

None of these were intended as definitions. But they show I think that truth must play an important role in the formulation of the basic realist position. They also show that the formulation must incorporate an answer to the question what it is to *accept* or *hold* a theory. I shall now propose such a formulation, which seems to me to make sense of the above remarks, and also renders intelligible the reasoning by realists which I shall examine below—without burdening them with more than the minimum required for this.

Science aims to give us, in its theories, a literally true story of what the world is like; and acceptance of a scientific theory involves the belief that it is true. This is the correct statement of scientific realism.

Let me defend this formulation by showing that it is quite minimal, and can be agreed to by anyone who considers himself a scientific realist. The naïve statement said that science tells a true story; the correct statement says only that it is the aim of science to do so. The aim of science is of course not to be identified with individual scientists' motives. The aim of the game of chess is to checkmate your opponent; but the motive for playing may be fame, gold, and glory. What the aim is determines what counts as success in the enterprise as such; and this aim may be pursued for any number of reasons. Also, in calling something *the* aim, I do not deny that there are other subsidiary aims which may or may not be means to that end: Everyone will readily agree that simplicity, informativeness, predictive power, explanation are (also) virtues. Perhaps my formulation can even be accepted by any philosopher who considers the most important aim of science to be something which only *requires* the finding of true theories—given that I wish to give the weakest formulation of the doctrine that is generally acceptable.

I have added "literally" to rule out as realist such positions as imply that science is true if "properly understood" but literally false or meaningless. For that would be consistent with conventionalism, logical positivism, and instrumentalism. I will say more about this below.

The second part of the statement touches on epistemology. But it only equates acceptance of a theory with belief in its truth.[5] It does not imply that anyone is ever rationally warranted in forming such a belief. We have to make room for the epistemological position, today the subject of considerable debate, that a rational person never assigns personal probability 1 to any proposition except a tautology. It would, I think, be rare for a scientific realist to take this stand in epistemology, but it is certainly possible.[6]

To understand qualified acceptance we must first understand acceptance *tout court*. If acceptance of a theory involves the belief that it is true, then tentative acceptance involves the tentative adoption of the belief that it is true. If belief comes in degrees, so does acceptance, and we may then speak of a degree of acceptance involving a certain degree of belief that the theory is true. This must of course be distinguished from belief that the theory is approximately true, which seems to mean belief that some member of a class centering on the mentioned theory is (exactly) true. In this way the proposed formulation of realism can be used regardless of one's epistemological persuasion.

Alternatives to Realism

Scientific realism is the position that scientific theory construction aims to give us a literally true story of what the world is like, and that acceptance of a scientific theory involves the belief that it is true. Accordingly, anti-realism is a position according to which the aim of science can well be served without giving such a literally true story, and acceptance of a theory may properly involve something less (or other) than belief that it is true.

What does a scientist do then, according to these different positions? According to the realist, when someone proposes a theory, he is asserting it to be true. But according to the anti-realist, the proposer does not assert the theory; *he displays it* and claims certain virtues for it. These virtues may fall short of truth: empirical adequacy, perhaps; comprehensiveness, acceptability for various purposes. This will have to be spelled out, for the details here are not determined by the denial of realism. For now we must concentrate on the key notions that allow the generic division.

The idea of a literally true account has two aspects: The language is to be literally construed; and so construed, the account is true.

This divides the anti-realists into two sorts. The first sort holds that science is or aims to be true, properly (but not literally) construed. The second holds that the language of science should be literally construed, but its theories need not be true to be good. The anti-realism I shall advocate belongs to the second sort.

It is not so easy to say what is meant by a literal construal. The idea comes perhaps from theology, where fundamentalists construe the Bible literally, and liberals have a variety of allegorical, metaphorical, and analogical interpretations, which "demythologize." The problem of explicating "literal construal" belongs to the philosophy of language. . . .

The decision to rule out all but literal construals of the language of science rules out those forms of anti-realism known as *positivism* and *instrumentalism*. First, on a literal construal, the apparent statements of science really are statements, *capable of* being true or false. Secondly, although a literal construal can elaborate, it cannot change logical relationships. (It is possible to elaborate, for instance, by identifying what the terms designate. The "reduction" of the language of phenomenological thermodynamics to that of statistical mechanics is like that: Bodies of gas are identified as aggregates of molecules, temperature as mean kinetic energy, and so on.) . . . Most specifically, if a theory says that something exists, then a literal construal may elaborate on what that something is, but will not remove the implication of existence. . . .

Constructive Empiricism

To insist on a literal construal of the language of science is to rule out the construal of a theory as a metaphor or simile, or as intelligible only after it is "demythologized" or subjected to some other sort of "translation" that does not preserve logical form. If the theory's statements include "There are electrons," then the theory says that there are electrons. If in addition they include "Electrons are not planets," then the theory says, in part, that there are entities other than planets.

But this does not settle very much. It is often not at all obvious whether a theoretical term refers to a concrete entity or a mathematical entity. Perhaps one tenable interpretation of classical physics is that there are no concrete entities which are forces—that "there are forces such that . . ." can always be understood as a mathematical statement asserting the existence of certain functions. That is debatable.

Not every philosophical position concerning science which insists on a literal construal of the language of science is a realist position. For this insistence relates not at all to our epistemic attitudes toward theories, nor to the aim we pursue in constructing theories, but only to the correct understanding of *what a theory says*. (The fundamentalist theist, the agnostic, and the atheist presumably agree with each other [though not with liberal theologians] in their understanding of the statement that God, or gods, or angels exist.) After deciding that the language of science must be literally understood, we can still say that there is no need to believe good theories to be true, nor to believe *ipso facto* that the entities they postulate are real.

Science aims to give us theories which are empirically adequate; and acceptance of a theory involves as belief only that it is empirically adequate. This is the statement of the anti-realist position I advocate; I shall call it *constructive empiricism*.

This formulation is subject to the same qualifying remarks as that of scientific realism on pp. 355–357 above. In addition it requires an explication of "empirically adequate." For now, I shall leave that with the preliminary explication that a theory is empirically adequate exactly if what it says about the observable things and events in this world is true—exactly if it "saves the phenomena." A little more precisely: Such a theory has at least one model that all the actual phenomena fit inside. I must emphasize that this refers to *all* the phenomena; these are not exhausted by those actually observed, nor even by those observed at some time, whether past, present, or future. . . .

The distinction I have drawn between realism and anti-realism, insofar as it pertains to acceptance, concerns only how much belief is involved therein. Acceptance of theories (whether full, tentative, to a degree, etc.) is a phenomenon of scientific activity which clearly involves more than belief. One main reason for this is that we are never confronted with a complete theory. So if a scientist accepts a theory, he thereby involves himself in a certain sort of research programme. That programme could well be different from the one acceptance of another theory would have given him, even if those two (very incomplete) theories are equivalent to each other with respect to everything that is observable—insofar as they go.

Thus acceptance involves not only belief but a certain commitment. Even for those of us who are not working scientists, the acceptance involves a commitment to confront any future phenomena by means of the conceptual resources of this theory. It determines the terms in which we shall seek explanations. If the acceptance is at all strong, it is exhibited in the person's assumption of the rule of explainer, in his willingness to answer questions *ex cathedra*. Even if you do not accept a theory, you can engage in discourse in a context in which language use is guided by that theory—but acceptance produces such contexts. There are similarities in all of this to ideological commitment. A commitment is of course not true or false: The confidence exhibited is that it will be *vindicated*.

This is a preliminary sketch of the *pragmatic* dimension of theory acceptance. Unlike the epistemic dimension, it does not figure overtly in the disagreement between realist and anti-realist. But because the amount of belief involved in acceptance is typically less according to anti-realists, they will tend to make more of the pragmatic aspects. It is as well to note here the important difference. Belief that a theory is true, or that it is empirically adequate, does not imply, and is not implied by, belief that full acceptance of the theory will be vindicated. To see this, you need only consider here a person who has quite definite beliefs about the future

of the human race, or about the scientific community and the influences thereon and practical limitations we have. It might well be, for instance, that a theory which is empirically adequate will not combine easily with some other theories which we have accepted in fact, or that Armageddon will occur before we succeed. Whether belief that a theory is true, or that it is empirically adequate, can be equated with belief that acceptance of it would, under ideal research conditions, be vindicated in the long run, is another question. It seems to me an irrelevant question within philosophy of science, because an affirmative answer would not obliterate the distinction we have already established by the preceding remarks. (The question may also assume that counterfactual statements are objectively true or false, which I would deny.)

Although it seems to me that realists and anti-realists need not disagree about the pragmatic aspects of theory acceptance, I have mentioned it here because I think that typically they do. We shall find ourselves returning time and again, for example, to requests for explanation to which realists typically attach an objective validity which anti-realists cannot grant.

The Theory/Observation "Dichotomy"

For good reasons, logical positivism dominated the philosophy of science for thirty years. In 1960, the first volume of *Minnesota Studies in the Philosophy of Science* published Rudolf Carnap's "The Methodological Status of Theoretical Concepts," which is, in many ways, the culmination of the positivist programme. It interprets science by relating it to an observation language (a postulated part of natural language which is devoid of theoretical terms). Two years later this article was followed in the same series by Grover Maxwell's "The Ontological Status of Theoretical Entities," in title and theme a direct counter to Carnap's. This is the *locus classicus* for the new realists' contention that the theory/observation distinction cannot be drawn.

I shall examine some of Maxwell's points directly, but first a general remark about the issue. Such expressions as "theoretical entity" and "observable–theoretical dichotomy" are, on the face of it, examples of category mistakes. Terms or concepts are theoretical (introduced or adapted for the purposes of theory construction); entities are observable or unobservable. This may seem a little point, but it separates the discussion into two issues. Can we divide our language into a theoretical and non-theoretical part? On the other hand, can we classify objects and events into observable and unobservable ones?

Maxwell answers both questions in the negative, while not distinguishing them too carefully. On the first, where he can draw on well-known supportive essays by Wilfrid Sellars and Paul Feyerabend, I am in total agreement. All our language is thoroughly theory-infected. If we could cleanse our language of theory-laden terms, beginning with the recently introduced ones like "VHF receiver," continuing through "mass" and "impulse" to "element" and so on into the prehistory of language formation, we would end up with nothing useful. The way we talk, and scientists talk, is guided by the pictures provided by previously accepted theories. This is true also, as Duhem already emphasized, of experimental reports. . . .

But does this mean that we must be scientific realists? We surely have more tolerance of ambiguity than that. The fact that we let our language be guided by a given picture, at some point, does not show how much we believe about that picture. When we speak of the sun coming up in the morning and setting at night, we are guided by a picture now explicitly disavowed. When Milton wrote *Paradise Lost* he deliberately let the old geocentric astronomy guide his poem, although various remarks in passing clearly reveal his interest in the new astronomical discoveries and speculations of his time. These are extreme examples, but show that no immediate conclusions can be drawn from the theory-ladenness of our language.

However, Maxwell's main arguments are directed against the observable—unobservable distinction. Let us first be clear on what this distinction was supposed to be. The term "observable" classifies putative entities (entities which may or may not exist). A flying horse is observable—that is why we are so sure that there aren't any—and the number seventeen is not. There is supposed to be a correlate classification of human acts: An unaided act of perception, for instance, is an observation. A calculation of the mass of a particle from the deflection of its trajectory in a known force field, is not an observation of that mass.

It is also important here not to confuse *observing* (an entity, such as a thing, event, or process) and *observing that* (something or other is the case). Suppose one of the Stone Age people recently found in the Philippines is shown a tennis ball or a car crash. From his behavior, we see that he has noticed them; for example, he picks up the ball and throws it. But he has not seen *that* it is a tennis ball, or *that* some event is a car crash, for he does not even have those concepts. He cannot get that information through perception; he would first have to learn a great deal. To say that he does not see the same things and events as we do, however, is just silly; it is a pun which trades on the ambiguity between seeing and seeing that. (The truth-conditions for our statement "*x* observes *that A*" must be such that what concepts *x* has, presumably related to the language *x* speaks if he is human, enter as a variable into the correct truth definition, in some way. To say that *x* observed the tennis ball, therefore, does not imply at all that *x* observed that it was a tennis ball; that would require some conceptual awareness of the game of tennis.)

The arguments Maxwell gives about observability are of two sorts: one directed against the possibility of drawing such distinctions, the other against the importance that could attach to distinctions that can be drawn.

The first argument is from the continuum of cases that lie between direct observation and inference:

> there is, in principle, a continuous series beginning with looking through a vacuum and containing these as members: looking through a windowpane, looking through glasses, looking through binoculars, looking through a low-power microscope, looking through a high-power microscope, etc., in the order given. The important consequence is that, so far, we are left without criteria which would enable us to draw a non-arbitrary line between "observation" and "theory".[7]

This continuous series of supposed acts of observation does not correspond directly to a continuum in what is supposed observable. For if something can be seen through a window, it can also be seen with the window raised. Similarly, the moons of Jupiter can be seen through a telescope; but they can also be seen without a telescope if you are close enough. That something is observable does not automatically imply that the conditions are right for observing it now. The principle is:

> X is observable if there are circumstances which are such that, if X is present to us under those circumstances, then we observe it.

This is not meant as a definition, but only as a rough guide to the avoidance of fallacies.

We may still be able to find a continuum in what is supposed detectable: Perhaps some things can only be detected with the aid of an optical microscope, at least; perhaps some require an electron microscope, and so on. Maxwell's problem is: Where shall we draw the line between what is observable and what is only detectable in some more roundabout way?

Granted that we cannot answer this question without arbitrariness, what follows? That "observable" is a *vague predicate*. There are many puzzles about vague predicates, and many sophisms designed to show that, in the presence of vagueness, no distinction can be drawn at all. In Sextus Empiricus, we find the argument that incest is not immoral, for touching your mother's big toe with your little finger is not immoral, and all the rest differs only by degree. But predicates in natural language are almost all vague, and there is no problem in their use; only in formulating the logic that governs them.[8] A vague predicate is usable provided it has clear cases and clear counter-cases. Seeing with the unaided eye is a clear case of observation. Is Maxwell then perhaps challenging us to present a clear counter-case? Perhaps so, for he says "I have been trying to support the thesis that any (non-logical) term is a *possible* candidate for an observation term."

A look through a telescope at the moons of Jupiter seems to me a clear case of observation, since astronauts will no doubt be able to see them as well from close up. But the purported observation of micro-particles in a cloud chamber seems to me a clearly different case—if our theory about what happens there is right. The theory says that if a charged particle traverses a chamber filled with saturated vapor, some atoms in the neighborhood of its path are ionized. If this vapor is decompressed, and hence becomes supersaturated, it condenses in droplets on the ions, thus marking the path of the particle. The resulting silver-grey line is similar (physically as well as in appearance) to the vapor trail left in the sky when a jet passes. Suppose I point to such a trail and say: "Look, there is a jet!"; might you not say: "I see the vapor trail, but where is the jet?" Then I would answer: "Look just a bit ahead of the trail . . . there! Do you see it?" Now, in the case of the cloud chamber this response is not possible. So while the particle is detected by means of the cloud chamber, and the detection is based on observation, it is clearly not a case of the particle's being observed.

As second argument, Maxwell directs our attention to the "can" in "what is observable is what can be observed." An object might of course be temporarily unobservable—in a rather different sense: It cannot be observed in the circumstances in which it actually is at the moment, but could be observed if the circumstances were more favorable. In just the same way, I might be temporarily invulnerable or invisible. So we should concentrate on "observable" *tout court*, or on (as he prefers to say) "unobservable in principle." This Maxwell explains as meaning that the relevant scientific theory *entails* that the entities cannot be observed in any circumstances. But this never happens, he says, because the different circumstances could be ones in which we have different sense organs—electron-microscope eyes, for instance.

This strikes me as a trick, a change in the subject of discussion. I have a mortar and pestle made of copper and weighing about a kilo. Should I call it breakable because a giant could break it? Should I call the Empire State Building portable? Is there no distinction between a portable and a console record player? The human organism is, from the point of view of physics, a certain kind of measuring apparatus. As such it has certain inherent limitations—which will be described in detail in the final physics and biology. It is these limitations to which the "able" in "observable" refers—our limitations, *qua* human beings.

As I mentioned, however, Maxwell's article also contains a different sort of argument: Even if there is a feasible observable/unobservable distinction, this distinction has no importance. The point at issue for the realist is, after all, the reality of the entities postulated in science. Suppose that these entities could be classified into observable and others; what relevance should that have to the question of their existence?

Logically, none. For the term "observable" classifies putative entities and has logically nothing to do with existence. But Maxwell must have more in mind when he says: "I conclude that the drawing of the observational–theoretical line at any given point is an accident and a function of our physiological make-up, . . . and, therefore, that it has no ontological significance whatever."[9] No ontological significance if the question is only whether "observable" and "exists" imply each other—for they do not; but significance for the question of scientific realism?

Recall I defined scientific realism in terms of the aim of science and epistemic attitudes. The question is what aim scientific activity has, and how much we shall believe when we accept a scientific theory. What is the proper form of acceptance: belief that the theory, as a whole, is true; or something else? To this question, what is observable by us seems eminently relevant. Indeed, we may attempt an answer at this point: To accept a theory is (for us) to believe that it is empirically adequate—that what the theory says *about what is observable* (by us) is true.

It will be objected at once that, on this proposal, what the anti-realist decides to believe about the world will depend in part on what he believes to be his, or rather the epistemic community's, accessible range of evidence. At present, we count the human race as the epistemic community to which we belong; but this race may mutate, or that community may be increased by adding other animals (terrestrial or extra-terrestrial) through relevant ideological or moral decisions ("to count them as persons"). Hence the anti-realist would, on my proposal, have to accept conditions of the form

> If the epistemic community changes in fashion Y, then my beliefs about the world will change in manner Z.

To see this as an objection to anti-realism is to voice the requirement that our epistemic policies should give the same results independent of our beliefs about the range of evidence accessible to us. That requirement seems to me in no way rationally compelling; it could be honored, I should think, only through a thoroughgoing scepticism or through a commitment to wholesale leaps of faith. But we cannot settle the major questions of epistemology *en passant* in philosophy of science; so I shall just conclude that it is, on the face of it, not irrational to commit oneself only to a search for theories that are empirically adequate, ones whose models fit the observable phenomena, while recognizing that what counts as an observable phenomenon is a function of what the epistemic community is (that *observable* is *observable-to-us*).

The notion of empirical adequacy in this answer will have to be spelled out very carefully if it is not to bite the dust among hackneyed objections. . . . But the point stands: Even if observability has nothing to do with existence (is, indeed, too anthropocentric for that), it may still have much to do with the proper epistemic attitude to science. . . .

Limits of the Demand for Explanation

In this section and the next. . . , I shall examine arguments for realism that point to explanatory power as a criterion for theory choice. That this is indeed a criterion I do not deny. But these arguments for realism succeed only if the demand for explanation is supreme—if the task of science is unfinished, *ipso facto*, as long as any pervasive regularity is left unexplained. I shall object to this line of argument, as found in the writings of Smart, Reichenbach, Salmon, and Sellars, by arguing that such an unlimited demand for explanation leads to a demand for hidden variables, which runs contrary to at least one major school of thought in twentieth-century physics. I do not think that even these philosophers themselves wish to saddle realism with logical links to such

consequences; but realist yearnings were born among the mistaken ideals of traditional metaphysics.

In his book *Between Science and Philosophy*, Smart gives two main arguments for realism. One is that only realism can respect the important distinction between *correct* and *merely useful* theories. He calls "instrumentalist" any view that locates the importance of theories in their use, which requires only empirical adequacy and not truth. But how can the instrumentalist explain the usefulness of his theories?

> Consider a man (in the sixteenth century) who is a realist about the Copernican hypothesis but instrumentalist about the Ptolemaic one. He can explain the instrumental usefulness of the Ptolemaic system of epicycles because he can prove that the Ptolemaic system can produce almost the same predictions about the apparent motions of the planets as does the Copernican hypothesis. Hence the assumption of the realist truth of the Copernican hypothesis explains the instrumental usefulness of the Ptolemaic one. Such an explanation of the instrumental usefulness of certain theories would not be possible if *all* theories were regarded as merely instrumental.[10]

What exactly is meant by "such an explanation" in the last sentence? If no theory is assumed to be true, then no theory has its usefulness explained as following from the truth of another one—granted. But would we have less of an explanation of the usefulness of the Ptolemaic hypothesis if we began instead with the premise that the Copernican gives implicitly a very accurate description of the motions of the planets as observed from earth? This would not assume the truth of Copernicus's heliocentric hypothesis, but would still entail that Ptolemy's simpler description was also a close approximation of those motions.

However, Smart would no doubt retort that such a response pushes the question only one step back: What explains the accuracy of predictions based on Copernicus's theory? If I say, the empirical adequacy of that theory, I have merely given a verbal explanation. For of course Smart does not mean to limit his question to actual and possible predictions—it really concerns all actual and possible predictions and retrodictions. To put it quite concretely: What explains the fact that all observable planetary phenomena fit Copernicus's theory (if they do)? From the medieval debates, we recall the nominalist response that the basic regularities are merely brute regularities and have no explanation. So here the anti-realist must similarly say: That the observable phenomena exhibit these regularities, because of which they fit the theory, is merely a brute fact, and may or may not have an explanation in terms of unobservable facts "behind the phenomena"—it really does not matter to the goodness of the theory, nor to our understanding of the world.

Smart's main line of argument is addressed to exactly this point. In the same chapter he argues as follows. Suppose that we have a theory T which postulates micro-structure directly, and macro-structure indirectly. The statistical and approximate laws about macroscopic phenomena are only partially spelled out perhaps, and in any case derive from the precise (deterministic or statistical) laws about the basic entities. We now consider theory T', which is part of T, and says only what T says about the macroscopic phenomena. (How T' should be characterized I shall leave open, for that does not affect the argument here.) Then he continues:

> I would suggest that the realist could (say) . . . that the success of T' is explained by the fact that the original theory T is true of the things that it is ostensibly about; in other words by the fact that there really are electrons or whatever is postulated by the theory T. If there were no such things, and if T were not true in a realist way, would not the success of T' be quite inexplicable? One would have to suppose that there were

innumerable lucky accidents about the behavior mentioned in the observational vocabulary, so that they behaved miraculously *as if* they were brought about by the nonexistent things ostensibly talked about in the theoretical vocabulary.[11]

In other passages, Smart speaks similarly of "cosmic coincidences." The regularities in the observable phenomena must be explained in terms of deeper structure, for otherwise we are left with a belief in lucky accidents and coincidences on a cosmic scale.

I submit that if the demand for explanation implicit in these passages were precisely formulated, it would at once lead to absurdity. For if the mere fact of postulating regularities, without explanation, makes T' a poor theory, T will do no better. If, on the other hand, there is some precise limitation on what sorts of regularities can be postulated as basic, the context of the argument provides no reason to think that T' must automatically fare worse than T.

In any case, it seems to me that it is illegitimate to equate being a lucky accident, or a coincidence, with having no explanation. It was by coincidence that I met my friend in the market—but I can explain why I was there, and he can explain why he came, so together we can explain how this meeting happened. We call it a coincidence, not because the occurrence was inexplicable, but because we did not severally go to the market in order to meet.[12] There cannot be a requirement upon science to provide a theoretical elimination of coincidences, or accidental correlations in general, for that does not even make sense. There is nothing here to motivate the demand for explanation, only a restatement in persuasive terms. . . .

Limits to Explanation: A Thought Experiment

Wilfrid Sellars was one of the leaders of the return to realism in philosophy of science and has, in his writings of the past three decades, developed a systematic and coherent scientific realism. I have discussed a number of his views and arguments elsewhere; but will here concentrate on some aspects that are closely related to the arguments of Smart, Reichenbach, and Salmon just examined.[13] Let me begin by setting the state in the way Sellars does.

There is a certain oversimplified picture of science, the "levels picture," which pervades positivist writings and which Sellars successfully demolished.[14] In that picture, singular observable facts ("this crow is black") are scientifically explained by general observable regularities ("all crows are black"), which in turn are explained by highly theoretical hypotheses not restricted in what they say to the observable. The three levels are commonly called those of *fact*, of *empirical law*, and of *theory*. But, as Sellars points out, theories do not explain, or even entail such empirical laws—they only show why observable things obey these so-called laws to the extent they do.[15] Indeed, perhaps we have no such empirical laws at all: All crows are black—except albinos: water boils at 100°C—provided atmospheric pressure is normal; falling body accelerates—provided it is not intercepted, or attached to an aeroplane by a static line; and so forth. On the level of the observable we are liable to find only putative laws heavily subject to unwritten *ceteris paribus* qualifications.

This is, so far, only a methodological point. We do not really expect theories to "save" our common everyday generalizations, for we ourselves have no confidence in their strict universality. But a theory which says that the micro-structure of things is subject to *some* exact, universal regularities must imply the same for those things themselves. This, at least, is my reaction to the points so far. Sellars, however, sees an inherent inferiority in the description of the observable alone, an incompleteness which requires (*sub specie* the aims of science) an introduction of an unobservable reality behind the phenomena. This is brought out by an interesting "thought-experiment."

Imagine that at some early stage of chemistry it had been found that different samples of gold dissolve in *aqua regia* at different rates, although "as far as can be observationally determined, the specimens and circumstances are identical."[16] Imagine further that the response of chemistry to this problem was to postulate two distinct microstructures for the different samples of gold. Observationally unpredictable variation in the rate of dissolution is explained by saying that the samples are mixtures (not compounds) of these two (observationally identical) substances, each of which has a fixed rate of dissolution.

In this case we have explanation through laws which have no observational counterparts that can play the same role. Indeed, no explanation seems possible unless we agree to find our physical variables outside the observable. But science aims to explain, must try to explain, and so must require a belief in this unobservable micro-structure. So Sellars contends.

There are at least three questions before us. Did this postulation of micro-structure really have no new consequences for the observable phenomena? Is there really such a demand upon science that it must explain—even if the means of explanation bring no gain in empirical predictions? And thirdly, could a *different* rationale exist for the use of a micro-structure picture in the development of a scientific theory in a case like this?

First, it seems to me that these hypothetical chemists did postulate new observable regularities as well. Suppose the two substances are A and B, with dissolving rates x and $x + y$ and that every gold sample is a mixture of these substances. Then it follows that every gold sample dissolves at a rate no lower than x and no higher than $x + y$; *and* that between these two any value may be found—to within the limits of accuracy of gold mixing. None of this is implied by the data that different samples of gold have dissolved at various rates between x and $x + y$. So Sellars's first contention is false.

We may assume, for the sake of Sellars's example, that there is still no way of predicting dissolving rates any further. Is there then a categorical demand upon science to explain this variation which does not depend on other observable factors? . . . [A] precise version of such a demand (Reichenbach's principle of the common cause) could result automatically in a demand for hidden variables, providing a "classical" underpinning for indeterministic theories. Sellars recognized very well that a demand for hidden variables would run counter to the main opinions current in quantum physics. Accordingly he mentions ". . . the familiar point that the irreducibly and lawfully statistical ensembles of quantum-mechanical theory are mathematically inconsistent with the assumption of hidden variables."[17] Thus, he restricts the demand for explanation, in effect, to just those cases where it is *consistent* to add hidden variables to the theory. And consistency is surely a logical stopping point.

This restriction unfortunately does not prevent the disaster. For while there are a number of proofs that hidden variables cannot be supplied so as to turn quantum mechanics into a classical sort of deterministic theory, those proofs are based on requirements much stronger than consistency. To give an example, one such assumption is that two distinct physical variables cannot have the same statistical distributions in measurement on all possible states.[18] Thus it is assumed that, if we cannot point to some possible difference in empirical predictions, then there is no real difference at all. If such requirements were lifted, and consistency alone were the criterion, hidden variables could indeed be introduced. I think we must conclude that science, in contrast to scientific realism, does not place an overriding value on explanation in the absence of any gain for empirical results.

Thirdly, then, let us consider how an antirealist could make sense of those hypothetical chemists' procedure. After pointing to the new empirical implications which I mentioned two paragraphs ago, he would point to method-ological reasons. By imagining a certain sort of micro-structure for gold and other metals, say, we might arrive at a theory governing many observationally disparate substances; and this might then have implications for new, wider empirical regularities when such substances interact. This would only be a hope, of course; no hypothesis is guaranteed to be fruitful—but the point is that the true demand on science is not for explanation *as such*, but for imaginative pictures which have a hope of suggesting new statements of observable regularities and of correcting old ones. . . .

. . . The Ultimate Argument

. . . In ["What Is Mathematical Truth," Putnam] directs himself to scientific realism . . . and formulates it in terms borrowed, he says, from Richard Boyd. The new formulation comes in the course of a new argument for scientific realism, which I shall call the Ultimate Argument:

> the positive argument for realism is that it is the only philosophy that doesn't make the success of science a miracle. That terms in mature scientific theories typically refer (this formulation is due to Richard Boyd), that the theories accepted in a mature science are typically approximately true, that the same term can refer to the same thing even when it occurs in different theories— these statements are viewed by the scientific realist not as necessary truths but as part of the only scientific explanation of the success of science, and hence as part of any adequate scientific description of science and its relations to its objects.[19]

Science, apparently, is required to explain its own success. There is this regularity in the world, that scientific predictions are regularly fulfilled; and this regularity, too, needs an explanation. Once *that* is supplied we may perhaps hope to have reached the *terminus de jure*?

The explanation provided is a very traditional one—*adequatio ad rem*, the "adequacy" of the theory to its objects, a kind of mirroring of the structure of things by the structure of ideas—Aquinas would have felt quite at home with it.

Well, let us accept for now this demand for a scientific explanation of the success of science. Let us also resist construing it as merely a restatement of Smart's "cosmic coincidence" argument, and view it instead as the question why we have successful scientific theories at all. Will this realist explanation with the Scholastic look be a scientifically acceptable answer? I would like to point out that science is a biological phenomenon, an activity by one kind of organism which facilitates its interaction with the environment. And this makes me think that a very different kind of scientific explanation is required.

I can best make the point by contrasting two accounts of the mouse who runs from its enemy, the cat. St. Augustine already remarked on this phenomenon, and provided an intensional explanation: The mouse *perceives that* the cat is its enemy, hence the mouse runs. What is postulated here is the "adequacy" of the mouse's thought to the order of nature: The relation of enmity is correctly reflected in his mind. But the Darwinist says: Do not ask why the *mouse* runs from its enemy. Species which did not cope with their natural enemies no longer exist. That is why there are only ones who do.

In just the same way, I claim that the success of current scientific theories is no miracle. It is not even surprising to the scientific (Darwinist) mind. For any scientific theory is born into a life of fierce competition, a jungle red in tooth and claw. Only the successful theories survive—the ones which *in fact* latched on to actual regularities in nature.[20]

Notes

1. *Science, Perception and Reality* (New York: Humanities Press, 1962); cf. the footnote on p. 97. See also my review of his *Studies in Philosophy and Its History*, in *Annals of Science*, January 1977.
2. Brian Ellis, *Rational Belief Systems* (Oxford: Blackwell, 1979), p. 28.
3. Hilary Putnam, *Mathematics, Matter and Method*

(Cambridge: Cambridge University Press, 1975), Vol. 1, pp. 69f.
4. Putnam, op. cit., p. 73, n. 29. The argument is reportedly developed at greater length in Boyd's forthcoming book *Realism and Scientific Epistemology* (Cambridge University Press).
5. Hartry Field has suggested that "acceptance of a scientific theory involves the belief that it is true" be replaced by "any reason to think that any part of a theory is not, or might not be, true, is reason not to accept it." The drawback of this alternative is that it leaves open what epistemic attitude acceptance of a theory does involve. This question must also be answered, and as long as we are talking about full acceptance—as opposed to tentative or partial or otherwise qualified acceptance—I cannot see how a realist could do other than equate that attitude with full belief. (That theories believed to be false are used for practical problems, for example, classical mechanics for orbiting satellites, is of course a commonplace.) For if the aim is truth, and acceptance requires belief that the aim is served . . . I should also mention the statement of realism at the beginning of Richard Boyd, "Realism, Underdetermination, and a Causal Theory of Evidence," *Noûs*, 7 (1973), 1–12. Except for some doubts about his use of the terms *explanation* and *causal relation* I intend my statement of realism to be entirely in accordance with his. Finally, see C. A. Hooker, "Systematic Realism," *Synthese*, 26 (1974), 409–97; esp. pp. 409 and 426.
6. More typical of realism, it seems to me, is the sort of epistemology found in Clark Glymour's book, *Theory and Evidence* (Princeton: Princeton University Press, 1980), except of course that there it is fully and carefully developed in one specific fashion. (See esp. his chapter "Why I Am Not a Bayesian" for the present issue.) . . .
7. G. Maxwell, "The Ontological Status of Theoretical Entities." *Minnesota Studies in Philosophy of Science*, III (1962), p. 7. [See this volume, p. 350]
8. There is a great deal of recent work on the logic of vague predicates; especially important, to my mind, is that of Kit Fine ("Vagueness, Truth, and Logic," *Synthese*, 30 (1975), 265–300) and Hans Kamp. The latter is currently working on a new theory of vagueness that does justice to the "vagueness of vagueness" and the context-dependence of standards of applicability for predicates.
9. Op. cit., p. 15. . . . [See this volume, p. 353]
10. J. J. C. Smart, *Between Science and Philosophy* (New York Random House, 1968), p. 151.
11. Ibid., pp. 150f.
12. This point is clearly made by Aristotle, *Physics*, II, Chs. 4–6 (see esp. 196^a 1–20; 196^b 20–197^a 12).

13. See my "Wilfrid Sellars on Scientific Realism," *Dialogue*, 14 (1975), 606–16; W. Sellars, "Is Scientific Realism Tenable?", pp. 307–34 in F. Suppe and P. Asquith (eds.), *PSA 1976* (East Lansing, Mich.: Philosophy of Science Association, 1977), vol. II, pp. 307–34; and my "On the Radical Incompleteness of the Manifest Image," ibid., pp. 335–43; and see n. 1 above.

14. W. Sellars, "The Language of Theories," in his *Science, Perception, and Reality* (London: Routledge and Kegan Paul, 1963).

15. Op. cit., p. 121.

16. Ibid., p. 11.

17. Ibid., p. 123.

18. See my "Semantic Analysis of Quantum Logic," in C. A. Hooker (ed.), *Contemporary Research in the Foundations and Philosophy of Quantum Theory* (Dordrecht: Reidel, 1973), Part III, Sects. 5 and 6.

19. See n. 4 above.

20. Of course, we can ask specifically why the *mouse* is one of the surviving species, how *it* survives, and answer this, on the basis of whatever scientific theory we accept, in terms of its brain and environment. The analogous question for theories would be why, say, Balmer's formula for the line spectrum of hydrogen survives as a successful hypothesis. In that case too we explain, on the basis of the physics we accept row, why the spacing of those lines satisfies the formula. Both the question and the answer are very different from the global question of the success of science, and the global answer of realism. The realist may now make the *further* objection that the anti-realist cannot answer the question about the mouse specifically, nor the one about Balmer's formula, in this fashion, since the answer is in part an assertion that the scientific theory, used as basis of the explanation, is true. This is a quite different argument, which I . . . take up in Ch. 4, Sect. 4, and Ch. 5 [of *The Scientific Image*]. . . .

ERNAN MCMULLIN

A Case for
Scientific Realism

When Galileo argued that the familiar patterns of light and shade on the face of the full moon could best be accounted for by supposing the moon to possess mountains and seas like those of earth, he was employing a joint mode of inference and explanation that was by no means new to natural science but which since then has come to be recognized as central to scientific explanation. In a retroduction, the scientist proposes a model whose properties allow it to account for the phenomena singled out for explanation. Appraisal of the model is a complex affair, involving criteria such as a coherence and fertility, as well as adequacy in accounting for the data. The theoretical constructs employed in the model may be of a kind already familiar (such as "mountain" and "sea" in Galileo's moon model) or they may be created by the scientist specifically for the case at hand (such as "galaxy," "gene," or "molecule").

Does a successful retroduction permit an inference to the existence of the entities postulated in the model? The instincts of the working scientist are to respond with a strong affirmative. Galaxies, genes, and molecules exist (he would say) in the straightforward sense in which the mountains and seas of the earth exist. The immense and continuing success of the retroductions employing these constructs is (in the scientist's eyes) a sufficient testimony to this. Scientists are likely to treat with incredulity the suggestion that constructs such as these are no more than convenient ways of organizing the data obtained from sophisticated instruments, or that their enduring success ought not lead us to believe that the world actually contains entities corresponding to them. The near-invincible belief of scientists is that we come to discover more and more of the entities of which the world is composed through the constructs around which scientific theory is built.[1]

But how reliable *is* this belief? And how is it to be formulated? This is the issue of scientific realism that has once again come to be vigorously debated among philosophers, after a period of relative neglect. The "Kuhnian revolution" in the philosophy of science has had two quite opposite effects in this regard. On the one hand, the new emphasis on the *practice* of science as the proper basis for the philosophy of science led to a more sensitive appreciation of the role played by theoretical constructs in guiding and defining the work of science. The restrictive empiricism of the logical positivists had earlier shown itself in their repeated attempts to "reduce" theoretical terms to the safer language of observation. The abandonment of this program was due not so much to the failure of the reduction techniques as to a growing realization that theoretical terms have a distinctive and indispensable part to play in science.[2] It was only a step from this realization to an acknowledgment that these terms carry with them an ontology, though admittedly an incomplete and tentative one. For a time, it seemed as though realism was coming into its own again.

But there were also new influences in the opposite direction. The focus of attention in the philosophy of science was now on scientific change rather than on the traditional topic of justification, and so the instability of scientific concepts became a problem with which the realist had to wrestle. For the first time, philosophers of language were joining the fray, and puzzles about truth and reference began to build into another challenge for realism. And so antirealism has reemerged, this time, however, much more sophisticated than it was in its earlier positivist dress.

When I say "antirealism," I make it sound like a single coherent position. But of course, antirealism is at least as far from a single coherent position as realism itself is. Though my concern is to construct a case for realism, it will be helpful first to survey the sources and varieties of antirealism. I will comment on these as I go, noting ambiguities and occasional misunderstandings. This will help to clarify the sort of scientific realism that in the end can be defended.

Sources of Antirealism: Science

Classical Mechanics

It is important to recall that scientists themselves have often been dubious about some of their own theoretical constructs, not because of some general antirealist sentiment, but because of some special features of the particular constructs themselves. Such constructs may seem like extra baggage—additional interpretations imposed on the theories themselves—much as the crystalline spheres seemed to many of the astronomers of the period between Ptolemy and Copernicus. Or it may be very difficult to characterize them in a consistent way, a problem that frequently bedeviled the proponents of ethers and fluids in nineteenth-century mechanics.

The most striking example of this sort of hesitation is surely that of Newton in regard to his primary explanatory construct, *attraction*. Despite the success of the mechanics of the *Principia*, Newton was never comfortable with the implications of the notion of attraction and the more general notion of force. Part of his uneasiness stemmed from his theology; he could not conceive that matter might of itself be active and thus in some sense independent of God's directing power. The apparent implication of action at a distance also distressed him. But then, how were these forces to be understood ontologically? *Where* are they, in what do they reside, and does the postulating of an inverse-square law of force between sun and planet say anything more than that each tends to move in a certain way in the proximity of the other?

The Cartesians, Leibniz, and later Berkeley, charged that the new mechanics did not really *explain* motion, since its central notion, *force*, could not be given an acceptable interpretation. Newton was sensitive to this charge and, in the decades following the publication of *Principia*, kept trying to find an ontology that might satisfy his critics.[3] He tried "active principles" that would somehow operate outside bodies. He even tried to reintroduce an ether with an extraordinary combination of properties—this despite his convincing refutation of mechanical ethers in *Principia*.[4] None of these ideas, however, were satisfactory. There were either problems of coherence and fit (the ether) or of specification (the active principles). After Newton's death, the predictive successes of his mechanics gradually stilled the doubts about the explanatory credentials of its central concept. But these doubts did not entirely vanish; Mach's *Science of Mechanics* (1881) would give them enduring form.

What are the implications of this often-told story for the realist thesis? It might seem that the failure of the attempts to interpret the concept of force in terms of previously familiar causal categories was a failure for realism also, and that the gradual laying aside in mechanics of questions about the underlying ontology was, in effect, an endorsement of antirealism. This would be so, however, only if one were to suppose the realist to be committed to theories that permit interpretation in familiar categories or, at the very least, in categories that are immediately interpretable. Naïve realism of *this* sort is, indeed, easily undermined. But this is not the view that scientific realists ordinarily defend, as will be seen.

How should Newton's attempts at "interpretation" be regarded, after the fact? Were they an improper intrusion of "metaphysics," the sort of thing that science today would bar? The term "underlying ontology" that I have used might mislead here. A scientist *can* properly attempt to specify the mechanisms that underlie his equations. Newton's ether *might* have worked out; it was a potentially testable hypothesis, prompted by analogies with the basic explanatory paradigm of an earlier mechanical

tradition. The metaphor of "active principle" proved a fruitful one; it was the ancestor of the notion of field, which would much later show its worth.[5] . . .

Scientists have never thought themselves disqualified from pursuing one of a number of physical models that, for the moment, appear empirically equivalent. As metaphors, these models may give rise to quite different lines of inquiry, leading eventually to their empirical separation. Or it may be that one of the alternative models appears undesirable on other grounds than immediate empirical adequacy (as action at a distance did to Newton). If prolonged efforts to separate the models empirically are unsuccessful, or if it comes to be shown that the models are in principle empirically equivalent, scientists will, of course, turn to other matters. But this is not a rejection of realism. It is, rather, an admission that no decision can be made in this case as to what the theory, on a realist reading, commits us to. . . .

Quantum Mechanics

In the debates between realists and antirealists, one claim that antirealists constantly make is that quantum mechanics has decided matters in their favor. In particular, the outcome of the famous controversy involving Bohr and Einstein, leading to the defeat (in most physicists' eyes) of Einstein, is taken to be a defeat for realism also. Once again, I want to show that this inference cannot be directed against the realist position proper.

Was the Copenhagen interpretation of quantum mechanics antirealist in its thrust?[6] Did Bohr's "complementary principle" imply that the theoretical entities of the new mechanics do not license any sort of existence claims about the structures of the world? It would seem not, for Bohr argues that the world is much more complex than classical physics supposed, and that the debate as to whether the basic entities of optics and mechanics are waves or particles cannot be resolved because its terms are inadequate. Bohr believes that the wave picture and the particle picture are *both* applicable, that *both* are needed, each in its own proper context. He is not holding that from his interpretation of quantum mechanics nothing can be inferred about the entities of which the world is composed; quite the reverse. He is arguing that what can be inferred is entirely at odds with what the classical world view would have led one to expect.

Of course, Einstein was a realist in regard to science. But he was also much more than a realist. He maintained a quite specific view about the nature of the world and about its relationship to observation; namely, that dynamic variables have unique real values at all times, that measurement reveals (or should reveal) these values as they exist prior to the measurement, and that there is a deterministic relationship between successive sets of these values. It was this further specification of realism that Bohr disputed.[7]

What we have discovered as a result of this controversy is, in the first instance, something about the kind of world we live in.[8] The dynamical variables associated with its macro- and microconstituents are measurement-dependent in an unexpected way. (E. Wigner tried to show more specifically that they are *observer*-dependent, in the sense of being affected by the consciousness of the observer, but few have followed him in this direction.) Does the fact that quantum systems are partially indeterminate in this way affect the realist thesis? Not as far as I can see. . . . It *does* mean, of course, that the quantum formalism is incomplete by the standards of classical mechanics and that a quantum system lacks some kinds of ontological determinacy that classical systems possessed.

This was what Einstein objected to. This was why he sought an "underlying reality" (specifiable ultimately in terms of "hidden parameters" or the like) which would restore determinism of the classical sort. But to search for a completeness of the classical sort was no more "realist" than to maintain (as Bohr did) that the

old completeness could never be regained. Recall that realism has to do with the existence-implications of the theoretical entities of successful theories. Einstein's ideal of physics would have the world entirely determinate against the mapping of variables of a broadly Newtonian type; Bohr's would not. The implications for the realist of Bohr's science are, it is true, more difficult to grasp. But why should we have expected the ontology of the microworld to be like that of the macroworld? Newton's third rule of philosophizing (which decreed that the macroworld should resemble the microworld in all essential details) was never more than a pious hope.

Elementary-Particle Physics

And this dissimilarity of the macrolevel and microlevel is even plainer when one turns from dynamic variables to the entities which these variables characterize. In the plate tectonic model that has had such striking success in recent geology, the continents are postulated to be carried on large plates of rocky material which underlie the continents as well as the oceans and which move very slowly relative to one another. There is no problem as to what an existence-claim means in this case. But problems do arise when we consider such microentities as electrons. For one thing, these are not particles strictly speaking, though custom dies hard and the label "elementary-particle physics" is still widely used. Electrons do not obey classical (Boltzman) statistics, as the familiar enduring individuals of our middle-sized world do.

The use of namelike terms, such as "electron," and the apparent causal simplicity of oil-drop or cloud-track experiments, could easily mislead one into supposing that electrons are very small localized individual entities with the standard mechanical properties of mass and momentum. Yet a bound electron might more accurately be thought of as a state of the system in which it is bound than as a separate discriminable entity. It is only because the charge it carries (which is a measure of the proton coupling to the electron) happens to be small that the free electron can be represented as a independent entity. When the coupling strength is greater, as it is between such nuclear entities as protons and neutrons, the matter becomes even more problematic. According to relativistic quantum theory, the forces between these entities are produced by the exchange of mesons. What is meant by "particle" in this instance reduces to the expression of a force characteristic of a particular field, a far cry from the hard massy points of classical mechanics. And the situation is still more complicated if one turns to the quark hypothesis in quantum field theory. Though quarks are supposed to "constitute" such entities as protons, they cannot be regarded as "constituents" in the ordinary physical sense; that is, they cannot be dissociated nor can they exist in the free state.

The moral is not that elementary-particle physics makes no sort of realist claim, but that the claim it makes must be construed with caution. The denizens of the microworld with their "strangeness" and "charm" can hardly be said to be imaginable in the ordinary sense. At that level, we have lost many of the familiar bearings (such as individuality, sharp location, and measurement-independent properties) that allow us to anchor the reference of existence-claims in such macrotheories as geology or astrophysics. But imaginability must not be made the test for ontology. The realist claim is that the scientist is discovering the structures of the world; it is not required in addition that these structures be imaginable in the categories of the macroworld. . . .

Sources of Antirealism: History of Science

The most obvious source of antirealism in recent decades is the new concern for the history of science on the part of philosophers of sci-

ence. Thomas Kuhn's emphasis on the discontinuity that, according to him, characterizes the "revolutionary" transitions in the history of science also led him to a rejection of realism: "I can see [in the systems of Aristotle, Newton and Einstein] no coherent direction of ontological development."[9] Kuhn is willing to attribute a cumulative character to the low-level empirical laws of science. But he denies any cumulative character to theory: theories come and go, and many leave little of themselves behind.

Among the critics of realism, Larry Laudan is perhaps the one who sets most store in considerations drawn from the history of science. He displays an impressive list of once-respected theories that now have been discarded, and guesses that "for every highly successful theory in the past of science which we now believe to be a genuinely referring theory, one could find half a dozen once successful theories which we now regard as substantially non-referring."[10]

To meet this challenge adequately, it would be necessary to look closely at Laudan's list of discarded theories, and that would require an essay in its own right. But a few remarks are in order. The sort of theory on which the realist grounds his argument is one in which an increasingly finer specification of internal structure has been obtained over a long period, in which the theoretical entities function *essentially* in the argument and are not simply intuitive postulations of an "underlying reality," and in which the original metaphor has proved continuously fertile and capable of increasingly further extension. (More on this will follow.)

This excludes most of Laudan's examples right away. The crystalline spheres of ancient astronomy, the universal Deluge of catastrophist geology, theories of spontaneous generation—none of these would qualify. That is not to say that the entities or events they postulated were not firmly believed in by their proponents. But realism is not a blanket approval for all the entities postulated by long-supported theories of the past. Ethers and fluids are a special category, and one which Laudan stresses. I would argue that these were often, though not always, interpretive additions, that is, attempts to specify what "underlay" the equations of the scientist in a way which the equations (as we now see) did not really sanction. The optical ether, for example, in whose existence Maxwell had such confidence, was no more than a carrier for variations in the electromagnetic potentials. It seemed obvious that a vehicle of some sort *was* necessary; undulations cannot occur (as it was often pointed out) unless there is something to undulate! Yet nothing could be inferred about the carrier itself; it was an "I-know-not-what," precisely the sort of unknowable "underlying reality" that the antirealist so rightly distrusts.

The theory of circular inertia and the effluvial theory of static electricity were first approximations, crude it is true, but effective in that the metaphors they suggested gradually were winnowed through, and something of the original was retained. Phlogiston left its anti-self, oxygen, behind. The view that the continents were static, which preceded the plate-tectonic model of contemporary geology, was not a theory; it was simply an assumption, one that is correct to a fairly high approximation. The early theories of the nucleus, which assumed it to be homogeneous, were simply idealizations; it was not known whether the nucleus was homogeneous or not, but a decision on that could be put off until first the notion of the nuclear atom itself could be fully explored. These are all examples given by Laudan. Clearly, they need more scrutiny than I have given them. But equally clearly, Laudan's examples may not be taken without further examination to count on the antirealist side. The value of this sort of reminder, however, is that it warns the realist that the ontological claim he makes is at best tentative, for surprising reversals *have* happened in the history of science. But the nonreversals (and a long list is easy to

construct here also) still require some form of (philosophic) explanation, or so I shall argue.

Sources of Antirealism: Philosophy

According to the classic ideal of science as demonstration which dominated Western thought from Aristotle down to Descartes, hypothesis can be no more than a temporary device in science. Of course, one can find an abundance of retroductive reasoning in Aristotle's science as in Descartes', a tentative working back from observed effect to unobserved cause. But there was an elaborate attempt to ensure that *real* science, *scientia propter quid*, would not contain theoretical constructs of a hypothetical kind. And there was a tendency to treat these latter constructs as fictions, in particular the constructs of mathematical astronomy. Duhem has left us a chronicle of the antirealism with which the medieval philosophers regarded the epicycles and eccentrics of the Ptolemaic astronomer.

Empiricism

As the bar to hypothesis gradually came to be dropped in the seventeenth century, another source of opposition to theoretical constructs began to appear. The new empiricism was distrustful of unobserved entities, particularly those that were unobservable in principle. One finds this sort of skepticism already foreshadowed in some well-known chapters of Locke's *Essay Concerning Human Understanding*. Locke concluded there (Book IV) that a "science of bodies" may well be forever out of reach because there is no way to reason securely from the observed secondary qualities of things to the primary qualities of the minute parts on which those secondary qualities are supposed to depend. Hume went much further and restricted science to the patterning of sense impressions. He simply rejects the notion of cause according to which one could try to infer from these impressions to the unobserved entities causing them.

Kant tried to counter this challenge to the realistic understanding of Newtonian physics. He argued that entities such as the "magnetic matter pervading all bodies" need not be perceivable by the unaided senses in order to qualify as real.[11] He established a notion of cause sufficiently large to warrant causal inference from sense-knowledge to such unobservables as the "magnetic matter." . . .

Despite Kant's efforts, the skeptical empiricism of Hume has continued to find admirers. The logical positivists were attracted by it but were sufficiently impressed by the central role of theoretical constructs in science not to be quite so emphatic in their rejection of the reality of unobservable theoretical entities. The issue itself tended to be pushed aside and to be treated by them as undecidable; E. Nagel's *The Structure of Science* gives classical expression to this view. This sort of agnosticism alternated with a more definitely skeptical view in logical positivist writings. If one takes empiricism as a starting point, it is tempting to push it (as Hume did) to yield the demand not just that every claim about the world must ultimately rest on sense experience but that every admissible entity must be directly certifiable by sense experience.

This is the position taken by Bas van Fraassen. His antirealism is restricted to those theoretical entities that are in principle unobservable. He has no objection to allowing the reality of such theoretical entities as stars (interpreted as large glowing masses of gas) because these are, in his view, observable in principle since we could approach them by spaceship, for example. It is part of what he calls the "empirical adequacy" of a stellar theory that it should predict what we would observe should we come to a star. This criterion, which he makes the single aim of science, is sufficiently broad, therefore, to allow reality-claims for any theoretical entity that, though at present unobserved, is at least in principle directly observable by us.

One immediate difficulty with this position is, of course, the distinction drawn between the observable and the unobservable. Since entities on one side of the line are ontologically respectable and those on the other are not, it is altogether crucial that there be some way not only to draw the distinction but also to confer on it the significance that van Fraassen attributes to it. In one of the classic papers in defense of scientific realism, Grover Maxwell argued in 1962 that there is a continuum in the spectrum of observation from ordinary unaided seeing down to the operation of a high-power microscope.[12] Van Fraassen concedes that the distinction is not a sharp one, that "observe" is a vague predicate, but insists that it is sufficient if the ends of the spectrum be clearly distinct, that is, that there be at least some clear cases of supposed interaction with theoretical entities which would not count as "observing."[13] He takes the operation of a cloud chamber, with its ionized tracks allegedly indicating the presence of charged entities such as electrons, to be a case where "observe" clearly ought not to be used. One must not say, on noting such a track: I observed an electron.

To lay as much weight as this on the contingencies of the human sense organs is obviously problematic, as van Fraassen recognizes. There are organisms with sense-organs very different from ours that can perceive phenomena such as ultraviolet light or the direction of optical polarization. Why could there not, in principle, be organisms much smaller than we, able to perceive microentities that for us are theoretical and able also to communicate with us? Is not the notion "observable in principle" hopelessly vague in the face of this sort of objection? How can it be used to draw a usable distinction between theoretical entities that do have ontological status and those that do not? Van Fraassen's response is cautious:

It is, on the face of it, not irrational to commit oneself only to a search for theories that are empirically adequate, ones whose models fit the observable phenomena, while recognizing that what counts as an observable phenomenon is a function of what the epistemic community is (that *observable* is *observable-to-us*).[14]

So "observable" means here "observable in principle by us with the sense organs we presently have." But once again, why would "unobservable" in this sense be allowed the implications for epistemology and ontology that van Fraassen wants to attach to it?[15] The question is not whether the aim of science ought to be broadened to include the search for unobservable but real entities, though something could be said in favor of such a proposal. It is sufficient for the purposes of the realist to ask whether theories that are in van Fraassen's sense empirically adequate can also be shown under certain circumstances to have likely ontological implications.

Van Fraassen allows that the moons of Jupiter can be observed through a telescope; this counts as observation proper "since astronauts will no doubt be able to see them as well from close up."[16] But one cannot be said to "observe" by means of a high-power microscope (he alleges) because no such direct alternative is available to us in this case. What matters here is not so much the way the instrument works, the precise physical or theoretical principles involved. It is whether there is also, in principle, a direct unmediated alternative mode of observation available to us. The entity need not be observable *in practice*. The iron core that geologists tell us lies at the center of the earth is certainly not observable in practice; it is a theoretical entity since its existence is known only through a successful theory, but it may nonetheless be regarded as real, van Fraassen would say, because *in principle* we could go down there and check it out.

The quality of the evidence for this geological entity might, however, seem no better than that available for the chromosome viewed by

microscope. Van Fraassen rests his case on an analysis of the aims of science, in an abstract sense of the term "aim," on the "epistemic attitude" (as he calls it) proper to science as an activity. And he thinks that reality-claims in the case of the chromosomes, but not the iron core, lie outside the permissible aims of science. Is there any way to make this distinction more plausible?

Reference

Some theoretical entities (such as the iron core or the star) are of a kind that is relatively familiar from other contexts. We do not need a theory to tell us that iron exists or how it may be distinguished. But electrons are what quantum theory says they are, and our only warrant for knowing that they exist is the success of that theory. So there is a special class of theoretical entities whose *entire* warrant lies in the theory built around them. They correspond more or less to the unobservables of van Fraassen.

What makes them vulnerable is that the theory postulating them may itself change or even be dropped. This is where the problems of meaning change and of theory replacement so much discussed in recent philosophy of science become relevant. The antirealist might object to a reality-claim for electrons or genes not so much because they are unobservable but because the reference of the term "electron" may shift as theory changes. . . .

One way for a realist to evade objections of this kind is to focus on the manner in which theoretical entities can be causally connected with our measurement apparatus. An electron may be defined as the entity that is causally responsible for, among other things, certain kinds of cloud tracks. A small number of parameters, such as mass and charge, can be associated with it. Such an entity will be said to exist, that is, not to be an artifact of the apparatus, if a number of convergent sorts of causal lines lead to it. There would still have to be a theory of some sort to enable the causal tracking to be carried out. But the reason to affirm the entity's existence lies not in the success of the theory in which it plays an explanatory role, but in the operation of traceable causal lines. Ian Hacking urges that this defense of realism, which relies on experiential interactions, avoids the problems of . . . [theory change].[17]

Truth as Correspondence

The most energetic criticisms of realism, of late, have been coming from those who see it as the embodiment of an old-fashioned, and now (in their view) thoroughly discredited, attachment to the notion of truth as some sort of "correspondence" with an "external world." These criticisms take quite different forms, and it is impossible to do them justice in a short space. The rejected doctrine is one that would hold that even in the ideal limit, the best scientific theory, one that has all the proper methodological virtues, could be false. This embodies what the critics have come to call the "God's eye view," the view that there may be more to the world than our language and our sciences can, even in principle, express. They concede that the doctrine has been a persuasive one ("it is impossible to find a philosopher before Kant who was *not* a . . . realist");[18] its denial seems, indeed, shockingly anthropomorphic. But they are in agreement that no philosophic sense can be made of the central metaphor of correspondence: "To single out a correspondence between two domains, one needs some independent access to both domains."[19] And, of course, an independent "access to the noumenal objects" is impossible.

The two main protagonists of this view are, perhaps, Rorty and Putnam. Rorty is the more emphatic of the two. He defends a form of pragmatism that discounts the traditional preoccupations of the philosopher with such Platonic notions as truth and goodness. . . . The pragmatist

> drops the notion of truth as correspondence with reality altogether, and says that modern science does not enable us to cope

because it corresponds, it just plain enables us to cope. His argument for the view is that several hundred years of effort have failed to make interesting sense of the notion of "correspondence," either of thoughts to things or of words to things.[20]

. . . Readers will have to decide for themselves whether my argument below does "make interesting sense" or not.

Varieties of Antirealism

It may be worthwhile at this point, looking back at the territory we have traversed, to draw two rough distinctions between types of antirealism. *General antirealism* denies ontological status to theoretical entities of science generally, while *limited antirealism* denies it only to certain classes of theoretical entities, such as those that are said to be unobservable in principle. Thus, the arguments of Laudan, based as they are on a supposedly general review of the history of scientific theories, would lead him to a *general* form of antirealism, one that would exclude existence status to *any* theoretical entity whose existence is warranted only by the success of the theory in which it occurs. In contrast, van Fraassen is claiming, as I have shown, only a *limited* form of antirealism.

Second, we might distinguish between *strong antirealism* which denies any kind of ontological status to all (or part) of the theoretical entities of science, and *weak antirealism* which allows theoretical entities existence of an everyday "chairs and goldfish" kind,[21] but insists that there is some further sense of "really really there," which realists purportedly have in mind, that is to be rejected. Classical instrumentalism would be of the former kind (strong antirealists), whereas many of the more recent critics of scientific realism appear to fall in the latter category (weak antirealists). These (weak antirealist) critics are often, as I have shown, hard to place. They reject any attempt to justify scientific realism as involving dubious metaphysics, but appear to accept a weak (realist) claim of the "everyday" kind without any form of supporting argument.[22] Their rhetoric is antirealist in tone, but their position often seems compatible with the most basic claim of scientific realism, namely that there is reason to believe that the theoretical terms of successful theories refer. This gives the weak antirealists' position a puzzling sort of undeclared status where they appear to have the best of both worlds. I am inclined to think that their effort to have it both ways must in the end fail.

The Convergences of Structural Explanation

The basic claim made by scientific realism, once again, is that the long-term success of a scientific theory gives reason to believe that something like the entities and structure postulated by the theory actually exists. There are four important qualifications built into this: (1) the theory must be successful over a significant period of time; (2) the explanatory success of the theory gives some reason, though not a conclusive warrant, to believe it; (3) what is believed is that the theoretical structures are *something like* the structure of the real world; (4) no claim is made for a special, more basic, privileged, form of existence for the postulated entities.[23] These qualifications: "significant period," "some reason," "something like," sound very vague, of course, and vagueness is a challenge to the philosopher. Can they not be made more precise? I am not sure that they can; efforts to strengthen the thesis of scientific realism have, as I have shown, left it open to easy refutation.

The case for scientific realism can be made in a variety of ways. Maxwell, Salmon, Newton-Smith, Boyd, Putnam, and others have argued it in well-known essays. I am not going to comment on their arguments here since my aim is to outline what I think to be the best case for scientific realism. My argument will, of course, bear many resemblances to theirs.

What may be the most distinctive feature of my argument is my stress on structural types of explanation, and on the role played by the criterion of fertility in such explanations.

Stage one of the argument will be directed especially against general antirealism. I want to argue that in many parts of natural science there has been, over the last two centuries, a progressive discovery of *structure*. Scientists construct theories which explain the observed features of the physical world by postulating models of the hidden structure of the entities being studied. This structure is taken to account causally for the observable phenomena, and the theoretical model provides an approximation of the phenomena from which the explanatory power of the model derives. This is the standard account of structural explanation, the type of explanation that first began to show its promise in the eighteenth and early nineteenth centuries in such sciences as geology and chemistry.[24]

I want to consider some of the areas where the growth in our knowledge of structure has been relatively steady. Let me begin with geology, a good place for a realist to begin. The visible strata and their fossil contents came to be interpreted as the evidence for an immense stretch of time past in which various processes such as sedimentation and volcanic activity occurred. There was a lively debate about the mechanisms of mountain building and the like, but gradually a more secure knowledge of the past aeons built up. The Carboniferous period succeeded the Devonian and was, in turn, succeeded by the Permian. The length of the periods, the climatic changes, and the dominant life forms were gradually established with increasing accuracy. It should be stressed that a geological period, such as the Devonian, is a theoretical entity. Further, it is, in principle, inaccessible to our direct observation. Yet our theories have allowed us to set up certain temporal boundaries, in this case (the Devonian period) roughly 400 to 350 million years ago, when the dominant life form on earth was fish and a number of important developments in the vertebrate line occurred.

The long-vanished species of the Devonian are theoretical entities about which we have come to know more and more in a relatively steady way. Of course, there have been controversies, particularly over the sudden extinction of life forms such as occurred at the end of the Cretaceous period and over the precise evolutionary relationships among given species. But the very considerable theory changes that have occurred since Hutton's day do not alter the fact that the growth in our knowledge of the sorts of life forms that inhabited the earth aeons ago has been pretty cumulative. The realist would say that the success of this synthesis of geological, physical, and biological theories gives us good reason to believe that species of these kinds did exist at the times and in the conditions proposed. Most antirealists (I suspect) would agree. But if they do, they must concede that this mode of retroductive argument can warrant, at least in some circumstances, a realist implication.

Geologists have also come to know (in the scientists' sense of the term "know") a good deal about the interior of the earth. There is a discontinuity between the material of the crust and the much denser mantle, the "Moho" as it is called after its Yugoslavian discoverer, about 5 kilometers under the ocean bed and much deeper, around 30 or 40 kilometers, under the continents. There is a further discontinuity between the solid mantle and the molten core at a depth of 2,900 kilometers. All this is inferred from the characteristics of seismic waves at the surface. Does this structural model of the earth simply serve as a device to enable the scientist to predict the seismic findings more accurately, or does it enable an additional ontological claim to be made about the actual hidden structures of earth? The realist would argue that the explanatory power of the geologist's hypothesis, its steadily improving accuracy, gives good ground to suppose that something can be inferred about real structures that lie far beneath us.

An elegant example of a quite different sort would come from cell biology. Here, the techniques of microscopy have interwoven with the theories of genetics to produce an ever more detailed picture of what goes on inside the cell. The chromosome first appeared under a microscope; only gradually was the gene, the theoretical unit of hereditary transmission, linked to it. Later the gene came to be associated with a particular locus on the chromosome. The unraveling by Crick and Watson of the biochemical structure of the chromosome made it possible to define the structure of the gene in a relatively simple way and has allowed at least the beginnings of an understanding of how the gene operates to direct the growth of the organism. In his book, *The Matter of Life*, Michael Simon has traced this story in some detail, and has argued that its progressive character can best be understood in terms of a realist philosophy of science.[25]

One further example of this sort of progression can be found in chemistry. The complex molecules of both inorganic and organic chemistry have been more accurately charted over the past century. The atomic constituents and the spatial relations among them can be specified on the basis both of measurement, using X-ray diffraction patterns, for example, and on the basis of a theory that specifies where each kind of atom *ought* to fit. Indeed, this knowledge has enabled a computer program to be designed that can "invent" molecules, can suggest that certain configurations would yield a new type of complex molecule and can even predict what some of the molecule's properties are likely to be.

To give a realist construal to the molecular models of the chemist is not to imply that the nature of the constituent atoms and of the bonding between them is exhaustively known. It is only to suppose that the elements and spatial relationships of the model disclose, in a partial and tentative way, real structures within complex molecules. These structures are coming to be more exactly charted, using a variety of techniques both experimental and theoretical. The coherence of the outcome of these widely different techniques, and the reliability of the chemist's intuitions as he decides which atom must fit a particular spot in the lattice, are most easily understood in terms of the realist thesis.

These examples may serve to make two points. The first is that the discontinuous replacement account of the history of theories favored by antirealists is seen to be one-sided. If one focuses on global explanatory theories, particularly in mechanics, it can come to seem that theoretical entities are modified beyond recognition as theories change. Dirac's electron has little in common with the original Thomson electron; Einstein's concept of time is a long way from Newton's, and so on. These conventional examples of conceptual change could themselves be scrutinized to see whether they will bear the weight the antirealist gives them. But it may be more effective to turn from explanatory elements such as electrons to explanatory structures such as those of the organic chemist, and note, as a historical fact, the high degree of continuity in the relevant history.

Second, one could note the sort of confidence that scientists have in structural explanations of this sort. It is not merely a confidence in the empirical adequacy of the predictions these models enable them to make. It is a confidence in the model itself as an analysis of complex real structure. Look at any textbook of polymer chemistry to verify this. Of course, the chemists could be wrong to build this sort of realist expectation into their work, but the arguments of philosophers are not likely to convince them of it.

A third consequence one might draw from the history of the structural sciences is that there is a single form of retroductive inference involved throughout. As C. S. Peirce stressed in his discussion of retroduction, it is the degree of success of the retroductive hypothesis that warrants the degree of its acceptance as truth. The point is a simple one, and indeed is already implicit in Aristotle's *Posterior Analytics.* Aristotle indicates that what certifies as *demonstrative* a piece of reasoning about the relation between the nearness of planets and the fact that they do not twinkle, is the degree to which the reasoning *explains.* This connection between the explanatory and the epistemic character of scientific reasoning is constantly stressed in Renaissance and early modern discussions of hypothetical reasoning.[26]

What the history of recent science has taught us is not that retroductive inference yields a plausible knowledge of causes. We already knew this on *logical* grounds. What we have learned is that retroductive inference *works* in the world we have and with the senses we have for investigating that world. This is a contingent fact, as far as I can see. This is why realism as I have defined it is in part an empirical thesis. There could well be a universe in which observable regularities would *not* be explainable in terms of hidden structures, that is, a world in which retroduction would not work. Indeed, until the eighteenth century, there was no strong empirical case to be made against that being *our* universe. Scientific realism is not a logical doctrine about the implications of successful retroductive inference. Nor is it a metaphysical claim about how any world *must* be. It has both logical and metaphysical components. It is a quite limited claim that purports to explain why certain ways of proceeding in science have worked out as well as they (contingently) have.

That they have worked out well in such structural sciences as geology, astrophysics, and molecular biology, is apparent. And the presumption in these sciences is that the model-structures provide an increasingly accurate insight into the real structures that are causally responsible for the phenomena being explained. This may be thought to give a reliable presumption in favor of the realist implications of retroductive inference in natural science generally. But one has to be wary here. Much depends on the sort of theoretical entity one is dealing with; I have already noted, for instance, some of the perplexities posed by quantum-mechanical entities. Much depends too on how *well* the theoretical entity has served to explain: How important a part of the theory has it been? Has it been a sort of optional extra feature like the solid spheres of Ptolemaic astronomy? Or has it guided research in the way the Bohr model of the hydrogen atom did? What kind of fertility has the theoretical entity shown?

Fertility and Metaphor

Kuhn lists five values that scientists look for when evaluating a scientific theory: predictive accuracy, consistency, breadth of scope, simplicity, fertility.[27] It is the last of these that bears most directly on the problem of realism. Fertility is usually equated with the ability to make novel predictions. A good theory is expected to predict novel phenomena, that is, phenomena that were not part of the set to be explained. The further in kind these novel phenomena are from the original set, and thus the more unexpected they are, the better the model is said to be. The display of this sort of fertility reduces the likelihood of the theory's being an ad hoc one, one invented just for the original occasion but with no further scope to it.

There has been much debate about the significance of this notion of ad hoc. Clearly, it will appeal to the realist and will seem arbitrary to the antirealist. The realist takes an ad hoc hypothesis not to be a genuine theory, that is, not to give any insight into real structure and therefore to have no ground for further extension. The fact that it accounts for the original data is accidental and testifies to the ingenuity of the inventor rather than to any deeper fit. When the theory is first proposed, it is often difficult to tell whether or not it is ad hoc on the basis of the other criteria of theory appraisal. This is why fertility is so important a criterion from the realist standpoint.

The antirealist will insist that the novel facts predicted by the theory simply increase its scope and thus make it more acceptable. They will say that there is no significance to the time order in which predictions are made; if they are successful, they count as evidence whether or not they pertain to the data originally to be explained. . . . Yet scientists seem to set a lot of store in the notion of ad hoc. Are scientific institutions sufficiently captured by a translation into antirealist language? Is an ad hoc hypothesis one that just happens not to be further generalizable, or is it one that does not give sufficient insight into real structure to permit any further extension?

Rather than debate this already much-debated issue further, let me turn to a second aspect of fertility which is less often noted but which may be more significant for our problem.[28] The first aspect of fertility, novelty, had to do with what could logically be inferred from the theory, its logical resources, one might put it. But a good model has more resources than these. If an anomaly is encountered or if the theory is unable to predict one way or the other in a domain where it seems it *should* be able to do so, the model itself may serve to suggest possible modifications or extensions. These are *suggested*, not implied. Therefore, a creative move on the part of the scientist is required.

In this case, the model functions somewhat as a metaphor does in language. The poet uses a metaphor not just as decoration but as a means of expressing a complex thought. A good metaphor has its own sort of precision, as any poet will tell you. It can lead the mind in ways that literal language cannot. The poet who is developing a metaphor is led by suggestion, not by implication; the reader of the poem queries the metaphor and searches among its many resonances for the ones that seem best to bear insight. The simplistic "man is a wolf" examples of metaphor have misled philosophers into supposing that what is going on in metaphor is a comparison between two already partly understood things. The only challenge then would be to decide in what respects the analogy holds. In the more complex metaphors of modern poetry, something much more interesting is happening. The metaphor is helping to illuminate something that is not well understood in advance, perhaps, some aspect of human life that we find genuinely puzzling or frightening or mysterious. The manner in which such metaphors work is by tentative suggestion. The minds of poet and reader alike are actively engaged in creating. Obviously, much more would need be said about this, but it would lead me too far afield at this point.[29]

The good model has something of this metaphoric power.[30] Let me recall another one here, from geology once again. It had long been known that the west coast of Africa and the east coast of South America show striking similarities in terms of strata and their fossil contents. In 1915, Alfred Wegener put forward a hypothesis to explain these and other similarities, such as those between the major systems of folds in Europe and North America. The continental drift notion that he developed in *The Origins of Continents and Oceans* was not at first accepted, although it admittedly did explain a great deal. There were too many anomalies: How could the continents cut through the ocean floor, for example, since the material of the ocean floor is considerably harder than that of the continents? In the 1960s, new evidence of seafloor spreading led H. Hess and others to a modification of the original model. The moving elements are not the continents but rather vast plates on which the continents as well as the seafloor are carried. And so the continental drift hypothesis developed into the plate tectonic model.

The story has been developed so ably from the methodological standpoint by Rachel Laudan[31] and Henry Frankel[32] that I can be very brief, and simply refer you to their writings. The original theoretical entity, a floating continent, did not logically entail the plates of the new model. But in the context of anomalies and new evidence, it did *suggest* them. And these plates in turn suggested new modifications. What happens when the plates pull apart are seafloor rifts, with quite specific properties. The upwelling lava will have magnetic directional properties that will depend on its orientation relative to the earth's magnetic field at the time. This allows the lava to be dated, and the gradual pulling apart of the plates to be charted. It was the discovery of such dated strips paralleling the midocean rifts that proved decisive in swinging geologists over to the new model in the mid-1960s. What happens when the plates collide? One is carried down under (subduction); the other may be upthrust to form a mountain ridge. One can see here how the original metaphor is gradually extended and made more specific. . . .

. . . What provides the continuity is the underlying metaphor of moving continents that had been in contact a long time ago and had very gradually developed over the course of time. One feature of the original theory, that the continents are the units, is eventually dropped; other features, such as what happens when the floating plates collide, are thought through and made specific in ways that allow a whole mass of new data to fall into place.

How does all this bear on the argument for realism? The answer should be obvious. This kind of fertility is a persistent feature of structural explanations in the natural sciences over the last three centuries and especially during the last century. How can it best be understood? It appears to be a contingent feature of the history of science. There seems to be no a priori reason why it *had* to work out that way, as I have already shown. What best explains it is the supposition that the model approximates sufficiently well the structures of the world that are causally responsible for the phenomena to be explained to make it profitable for the scientist to take the model's metaphoric extensions seriously. It is because there is something like a floating plate under our feet that it is proper to ask: What happens when plates collide, and what mechanisms would suffice to keep them in motion? These questions do not arise from the original theory if it is taken as no more than a formalism able to give a reasonably accurate predictive account of the data then at hand. If the continental drift hypothesis had no implications for what is really going on beneath us, for the hidden structures responsible for the phenomena of the earth's surface, then the subsequent history of that hypothesis would be unintelligible. The antirealist cannot, it seems to me, make sense of such sequences, which are pretty numerous in the recent history of all the natural sciences, basic mechanics, as always, constituting a special case.

One further point is worth stressing in regard to our geological story. Some theoretical features of the model, such as the midocean rifts, could be checked directly and their existence observationally shown. Here, as so often in science, theoretical entities previously unobserved, or in some cases even thought to be unobservable, are in fact observed and the expectations of theory are borne out, to no one's surprise. The separation between observable and unobservable postulated by many antirealists in regard to ontological status does not seem to stand up. . . .

Epilogue

Finally, I return to the weighty issues of reference and truth which are so dear to the heart of the philosopher. Clearly, my views on metaphor would lead me to reject the premise on which so much of the recent debate on realism has been based. Van Fraassen puts it thus:

> Science aims to give us, in its theories, a literally true story of what the world is like; and acceptance of a scientific theory involves the belief that it is true. This is the correct statement of scientific realism.[33]

I do not think that acceptance of a scientific theory involves the belief that it is true. Science aims at fruitful metaphor and at ever more de-

tailed structure. To suppose that a theory is literally true would imply, among other things, that no further anomaly could, in principle, arise from any quarter in regard to it. At best, it is hard to see this as anything more than an idealized "horizon-claim," which would be quite misleading if applied to the actual work of the scientist. The point is that the resources of metaphor are essential to the work of science and that the construction and retention of metaphor must be seen as part of the aim of science.

Scientists in general accept the quantum theory of radiation. Do they believe it to be true? Scientists are very uncomfortable at this use of the word "true," because it suggests that the theory is definitive in its formulation. As has often been pointed out, the notion of *acceptance* is very complex, indeed ambiguous. It is basically a pragmatic notion: one accepts an explanation as the best one available; one accepts a theory as a good basis for further research, and so forth. In no case would it be correct to say that acceptance of a theory entails belief in its truth.

The realist would not use the term "true" to describe a good theory. He would suppose that the structures of the theory give some insight into the structures of the world. But he could not, in general, say how good the insight is. He has no independent access to the world, as the antirealist constantly reminds him. His assurance that there is a fit, however rough, between the structures of the theory and the structures of the world comes not from a comparison between them but from the sort of argument I sketched above, which concludes that only this sort of reasoning would explain certain contingent features of the history of recent science. The term "approximate truth," which has sometimes been used in this debate, is risky because it immediately invites questions such as: *how* approximate?, and how is the degree of approximation to be measured? If I am right in my presentation of realism, these questions are unanswerable because they are inappropriate.

The language of theoretical explanation is of a quite special sort. It is open-ended and ever capable of further development. It is metaphoric in the sense in which the poetry of the symbolists is metaphoric, not because it uses explicit analogy or because it is imprecise, but because it has resources of suggestion that are the most immediate testimony of its ontological worth. Thus, the M. Dummett-Putnam claim that a realist is committed to holding with respect to any given theory, that the sentences of the theory are either true or false,[34] quite misses the mark where scientific realism is concerned. Indeed, I am tempted to say (though this would be a bit too strong) that if they are literally true or false, they are not of much use as the basis for a research program.

Ought the realist be apologetic, as his pragmatist critic thinks he should be, about such vague-sounding formulations as these: that a good model gives an insight into real structure and that the long-term success of a theory, in most cases, gives reason to believe that something like the theoretical entities of that theory actually exist? I do not think so. The temptation to try for a sharper formulation must be resisted by the realist, since it would almost certainly compromise the sources from which his case derives its basic strength. And the antirealist must beware of the opposite temptation to suppose that whatever cannot be said in a semantically definitive way is not worth saying.

Notes

The first version of this essay was delivered as an invited paper at the Western Division meeting of the American Philosophical Association in April 1981. I am indebted to Larry Laudan for his incisive commentary on that occasion, and to the numerous discussions we have had on this topic.

1. It was the confidence that, as a student of physics, I had developed in this belief that led me, in my first published paper in philosophy, to formulate a defense of scientific realism against the instrumentalism prevalent at the time among philosophers of science. (See "Realism in Modern Cosmology," *Proceedings American Catholic Philosophical Association*

29 [1955]: 137–150.) Much has changed in philosophy of science since that time; a different sort of defense is (as we shall see) now called for.
2. This is the theme of C. G. Hempel's classic essay, "The Theoretician's Dilemma," *Minnesota Studies in the Philosophy of Science* 3 (1958): 37–98.
3. For the details of this story, see E. McMullin, *Newton on Matter and Activity* (Notre Dame: University of Notre Dame Press, 1978), especially chap. 4: "How Is Matter Moved?"
4. In a recent critique of "metaphysical realism," Hilary Putnam has Newton defending the view that particles act at a distance across empty space. *Reason, Truth and History* (Cambridge: Cambridge University Press, 1981), p. 73. Though the *Principia* has often been made to yield that claim, this view is, in fact, the one alternative that Newton at all times steadfastly rejected.
5. Newton's other suggestion, briefly explored in the 1690s, that forces might be nothing other than the manifestations of God's direct involvement in the governance of the universe, *could*, however, be properly described as "metaphysical'; this is not, of course, to say that it was illegitimate.
6. As Fine argues in "The Natural Ontological Attitude," this volume [pp. 386–396].
7. Richard Healey calls it "naïve realism"; "naïve" not in a deprecatory sense, but as connoting the "natural attitude." See "Quantum Realism: Naïveté Is No Excuse," *Synthese* 42 (1979): pp. 121–144.
8. Especially owing to the developments in recent years of the original quantum formalism, associated not only with physicists (Bell, Kochen, Specker, Wigner) but also with philosophers of science (Cartwright, Fine, Gibbins, Glymour, Putnam, Redhead, Shimony, van Fraassen, and others).
9. T. Kuhn, *The Structure of Scientific Revolutions*, 2d ed. (Chicago: University of Chicago Press, 1970), p. 206.
10. See, in particular, L. Laudan, "A Confutation of Convergent Realism," in *Scientific Realism* ed. J. Leplin. The quotation is from p. 232.
11. E. Kant, *Critique of Pure Reason*, A226/B273.
12. G. Maxwell, "The Ontological Status of Theoretical Entities," *Minnesota Studies in Philosophy of Science* 3 (1962): pp. 3–27, [Reprinted in this volume, p. 348–354].
13. Van Fraassen, *The Scientific Image*, p. 16, [see this volume, p. 360]
14. Ibid., p. 19,. [see this volume, p. 363]
15. Van Fraassen complicates the picture further by also allowing the sense of "observable" to depend on the theory being tested. "To find the limits of

what is observable in the world described by theory T, we must inquire into T itself, and the theories used as auxiliaries in the testing and application of T." Ibid., p. 57.

16. Ibid., p.16, [see this volume, p. 360].
17. See I. Hacking, "Experimentation and Scientific Realism," this volume [pp. 428–440]. It is not clear to me whether one comes up with the same list of entities using Hacking's way as one does with the more usual form of argument relying on explanatory efficacy.
18. Putnam, *Reason, Truth and History*, p. 57.
19. Ibid., 74.
20. R. Rorty, *Conseuqences of Pragmatism* (Minneapolis: University of Minnesota Press, 1982), xvii.
21. This is what Horwich calls "epistemological realism." P. Horwich, The Three Forms of Realism," *Synthese* 51 [1982] p. 181. I am not as convinced as he is that this position is "opposed only by the rare skeptic."
22. Fine's essay in this volume appears to fall into this category. The first section of it is devoted to a critique of all the arguments normally brought in support of scientific realism; the second section argues that instrumentalism had a much more salutary influence than realism did on the growth of modern science. But the final section proposes, as the consequence of a "natural ontological attitude," that "there really are molecules and atoms" and rejects the instrumentalist assertion that they are just fictions. But some argument is needed for this, beyond calling this attitude "natural." And to say that the realist adds to this acceptable "core position" an unacceptable "foot-stamping shout of 'Really,'" an "emphasis that all this is really so," leaves me puzzled as to what this difference is supposed to amount to.
23. The issues as to whether these entities *ought* to be attributed privileged status (as materialism and various forms of reductionism maintain) will not be discussed here.
24. I traced the history and main features of this form of explanation in "Structural Explanation," *American Philosophical Quarterly* 15 (1978): pp. 139–147.
25. M. Simon, *The Matter of Life* (New Haven: Yale University Press, 1971).

26. See the discussion of this in E. McMullin, "The Conception of Science in Galileo's Work," *New Perspectives on Galileo*, ed. R. Butts and J. Pitt (Dordrecht: Reidel, 1978), pp. 209–257.
27. T. Kuhn, *The Essential Tension* (Chicago: University of Chicago Press, 1977), pp. 321–322. [see this volume, pp. 213] See also E. McMullin, "Values in Science," PSA Presidential Address 1982, in *PSA 1982*, vol. 2.
28. For a fuller discussion of the criterion of fertility, see E. McMullin, "The Fertility of Theory and the Unit for Appraisal in Science," *Boston Studies in the Philosophy of Science*, ed. R. S. Cohen et al., 39 (1976): pp. 395–432.
29. See, for instance, P. Wheelwright, *Metaphor and Reality* (Bloomington: Indiana University Press, 1962), esp. chap. 4, "Two Ways of Metaphor"; and E. McMullin, "The Motive for Metaphor," *Proceedings American Catholic Philosophical Association* 55 (1982): pp. 27–39.
30. I have elsewhere developed one instance of this in some detail, the Bohr model of the H-atom as it guided research from 1911 to 1926. See E. McMullin, "What Do Physical Models Tell Us?" in *Logic, Methodology and Philosophy of Science*, Proceedings Third International Congress, ed. B. van Rootselaar (Amsterdam, 1968), 3: pp. 389–396.
31. See, for example, R. Laudan, "The Recent Revolution in Geology and Kuhn's Theory of Scientific Change," in *Paradigms and Revolutions*, ed. G. Gutting (Notre Dame: University of Notre Dame Press, 1980), pp. 284–296; R. Laudan, "The Method of Multiple Working Hypotheses and the Development of Plate-Tectonic Theory," in press.
32. H. Frankel, "The Reception and Acceptance of Continental Drift Theory as a Rational Episode in the History of Science," in *The Reception of Unconventional Science*, ed. S. Mauskopf (Boulder: Westview Press, 1978), pp. 51–89; H. Frankel, "The Career of Continental Drift Theory," *Studies in the History and Philosophy of Science* 10 (1979): pp. 21–66.
33. Van Fraassen, *The Scientific Image*, p. 8.
34. H. Putnam, "What Is Mathematical Truth?", *Mathematics, Matter and Method* (Cambridge: Cambridge University Press), pp. 69–70.

ARTHUR FINE

The Natural
Ontological Attitude

Let us fix our attention out of ourselves as much as possible; let us chace our imagination to the heavens, or to the utmost limits of the universe; we never really advance a step beyond ourselves, nor can conceive any kind of existence, but those perceptions, which have appear'd in that narrow compass. This is the universe of the imagination, nor have we any idea but what is there produced.

—HUME, *TREATISE*
Book 1, Part II, Section VI

Realism is dead. Its death was announced by the neopositivists who realized that they could accept all the results of science, including all the members of the scientific zoo, and still declare that the questions raised by the existence claims of realism were mere pseudoquestions. Its death was hastened by the debates over the interpretation of quantum theory, where Bohr's nonrealist philosophy was seen to win out over Einstein's passionate realism. Its death was certified, finally, as the last two generations of physical scientists turned their backs on realism and have managed, nevertheless, to do science successfully without it. To be sure, some recent philosophical literature, and some of the best of it represented by contributors to this book, has appeared to pump up the ghostly shell and to give it new life. But I think these efforts will eventually be seen and understood as the first stage in the process of mourning, the stage of denial. This volume contains some further expressions of this denial. But I think we shall pass through this first stage and into that of acceptance, for realism is well and truly dead, and we have work to get on with, in identifying a suitable successor. To aid that work I want to do three things in this essay.

First, I want to show that the arguments in favor of realism are not sound, and that they provide no rational support for belief in realism. Then, I want to recount the essential role of nonrealist attitudes for the development of science in this century, and thereby (I hope) to loosen the grip of the idea that only realism provides a progressive philosophy of science. Finally, I want to sketch out what seems to me a viable nonrealist position, one that is slowly gathering support and that seems a decent philosophy for postrealist times.[1]

Arguments for Realism

Recent philosophical argument in support of realism tries to move from the success of the scientific enterprise to the necessity for a realist account of its practice. As I see it, the arguments here fall on two distinct levels. On the ground level, as it were, one attends to particular successes; such as novel, confirmed predictions, striking unifications of disparate-seeming phenomena (or fields), successful piggybacking from one theoretical model to another, and the like. Then, we are challenged to account for such success, and told that the best and, it is slyly suggested, perhaps, the *only* way of doing so is on a realist basis. . . . But there is a second level of realist argument, the methodological level, that derives from Popper's attack on instrumentalism as inadequate to account for the details of his own, falsificationist methodology. Arguments on this methodological level have been skillfully developed by Richard Boyd,[2] and by one of the earlier Hilary Putnams.[3] These arguments focus on the methods embedded in scientific practice, methods teased out in ways that seem to me accurate and perceptive about ongoing science. We are then challenged to account for why these methods lead to scientific success and told that the best, and (again) perhaps, the only truly adequate way of explaining the matter is on the basis of realism.

. . . I want to point out a deep and, I think, insurmountable problem with this entire strategy of defending realism, as I have laid it out above. . . .

Those suspicious of realism, from A. Osiander to H. Poincaré and P. Duhem to the "constructive empiricism" of Van Fraassen,[4] have been worried about the significance of the explanatory apparatus in scientific investigations. While they appreciate the systematization and coherence brought about by scientific explanation, they question whether acceptable explanations need to be true and, hence, whether the entities mentioned in explanatory principles need to exist.[5] Suppose they are right. Suppose, that is, that the usual explanation-inferring devices in scientific practice do not lead to principles that are reliably true (or nearly so), nor to entities whose existence (or near-existence) is reliable. In that case, the usual abductive methods that lead us to good explanations (even to "the best explanation") cannot be counted on to yield results even approximately true. But the strategy that leads to realism, as I have indicated, is just such an ordinary sort of abductive inference. Hence, if the nonrealist were correct in his doubts, then such an inference to realism as the best explanation (or the like), while possible, would be of no significance—. . . . It seems, then, that . . . to argue for realism one must employ methods more stringent than those in ordinary scientific practice. In particular, one must not beg the question as to the significance of explanatory hypotheses by assuming that they carry truth as well as explanatory efficacy.

There is a second way of seeing the same result. Notice that the issue over realism is precisely the issue as to whether we should believe in the reality of those individuals, properties, relations, processes, and so forth, used in well-supported explanatory hypotheses. Now what *is* the hypothesis of realism, as it arises as an explanation of scientific practice? It is just the hypothesis that our accepted scientific theories are approximately true, where "being approximately true" is taken to denote an extratheoretical relation between theories and the world. Thus, to address doubts over the reality of relations posited by explanatory hypotheses, the realist proceeds to introduce a further explanatory hypothesis (realism), itself positing such a relation (approximate truth). Surely anyone serious about the issue of realism, and with an open mind about it, would have to behave inconsistently if he were to accept the realist move as satisfactory.

Thus, both at the ground level and at the level of methodology, no support accrues to realism by showing that realism is a good hypothesis for explaining scientific practice. If we are open-minded about realism to begin with, then such a demonstration (even if successful) merely begs the question that we have left open ("need we take good explanatory hypotheses as true?"). Thus, . . . we must employ patterns of argument more stringent than the usual abductive ones. What might they be? Well, the obvious candidates are patterns of induction leading to empirical generalizations. But, to frame empirical generalizations, we must first have some observable connections between observables. For realism, this must connect theories with the world by way of approximate truth. But no such connections are observable and, hence, suitable as the basis for an inductive inference. I do not want to labor the points at issue here. They amount to the well-known idea that realism commits one to an unverifiable correspondence with the world. So far as I am aware, no recent defender of realism has tried to make a case based on a . . . strategy of using suitably stringent grounds and, given the problems over correspondence, it is probably just as well.

The strategy of arguments to realism as a good explanatory hypothesis, then, *cannot* (logically speaking) be effective for an open-minded nonbeliever. . . .

. . . In the next two sections, I will try to show that this situation is just as well, for realism has not always been a progressive factor in the development of science and, anyway, there is a position other than realism that is more attractive.

Realism and Progress

If we examine the two twentieth-century giants among physical theories, relativity and the quantum theory, we find a living refutation of the realist's claim that only his view of science explains its progress, and we find some curious twists and contrasts over realism as well. The theories of relativity are almost singlehandedly the work of Albert Einstein. Einstein's early positivism and his methodological debt to Mach (and Hume) leap right out of the pages of the 1905 paper on special relativity.[6] The same positivist strain is evident in the 1916 general relativity paper as well, where Einstein (in Section 3 of that paper) tries to justify his requirement of general covariance by means of a suspicious-looking verificationist argument which, he says, "takes away from space and time the last remnants of physical objectivity."[7] A study of his tortured path to general relativity (see here the brilliant work of John Earman, following on earlier hints by Banesh Hoffmann)[8] shows the repeated use of this Machist line, always used to deny that some concept has a real referent. Whatever other, competing strains there were in Einstein's philosophical orientation (and there certainly were others), it would be hard to deny the importance of this instrumentalist/positivist attitude in liberating Einstein from various realist commitments. Indeed, on another occasion, I would argue in detail that without the "freedom from reality" provided by his early reverence for Mach, a central tumbler necessary to unlock the secret of special relativity would never have fallen into place.[9] A few years after his work on general relativity, however, roughly around 1920, Einstein underwent a philosophical conversion, turning away from his positivist youth (he was forty-one in 1920) and becoming deeply committed to realism.[10] His subsequent battle with the quantum theory, for example, was fought much more over the issue of realism than it was over the issue of causality or determinism (as it is usually portrayed). In particular, following his conversion, Einstein wanted to claim genuine reality for the central theoretical entities of the general theory, the four-dimensional space-time manifold and associated sensor fields. This is a serious business for if we grant his claim, then not only do space and time cease to be real but so do virtually all of the usual dynamical quantities.[11] Thus motion, as we understand it, itself ceases to be real. The current generation of philosophers of space and time (led by Howard Stein and John Earman) have followed Einstein's lead here. But, interestingly, not only do these ideas boggle the mind of the average man in the street (like you and me), they boggle most contemporary scientific minds as well.[12] That is, I believe the majority opinion among working, knowledgeable scientists is that general relativity provides a magnificent organizing tool for treating certain gravitational problems in astrophysics and cosmology. But few, I believe, give credence to the kind of realist existence and nonexistence claims that I have been mentioning. For relativistic physics, then, it appears that a nonrealist attitude was important in its development, that the founder nevertheless espoused a realist attitude to the finished product, but that most who actually use it think of the theory as a powerful instrument, rather than as expressing a "big truth."

With quantum theory, this sequence gets a twist. Heisenberg's seminal paper of 1925 is prefaced by the following abstract, announcing, in effect, his philosophical stance: "In this paper an attempt will be made to obtain bases for a quantum-theoretical mechanics based exclusively on relations between quantities observable in principle."[13] In the body of the paper, Heisenberg not only rejects any reference to unobservables; he also moves away from the very idea that one should try to form any picture of a reality underlying his mechanics. To be sure, E. Schrödinger, the second father of quantum theory, seems originally to

have had a vague picture of an underlying wavelike reality for his own equation. But he was quick to see the difficulties here and, just as quickly, although reluctantly, abandoned the attempt to interpolate any reference to reality.[14] These instrumentalist moves, away from a realist construal of the emerging quantum theory, were given particular force by Bohr's so-called "philosophy of complementarity"; and this nonrealist position was consolidated at the time of the famous Solvay conference, in October of 1927, and is firmly in place today. Such quantum nonrealism is part of what every graduate physicist learns and practices. It is the conceptual backdrop to all the brilliant successes in atomic, nuclear, and particle physics over the past fifty years. Physicists have learned to think about their theory in a highly nonrealist way, and doing just that has brought about the most marvelous predictive success in the history of science.

The war between Einstein, the realist, and Bohr, the nonrealist, over the interpretation of quantum theory was not, I believe, just a sideshow in physics, nor an idle intellectual exercise. It was an important endeavor undertaken by Bohr on behalf of the enterprise of physics as a progressive science. For Bohr believed (and this fear was shared by Heisenberg, A. Sommerfield, W. Pauli, and M. Born—and all the major players) that Einstein's realism, if taken seriously, would block the consolidation and articulation of the new physics and, thereby, stop the progress of science. They were afraid, in particular, that Einstein's realism would lead the next generation of the brightest and best students into scientific dead ends. Alfred Landé, for example, as a graduate student, was interested in spending some time in Berlin to sound out Einstein's ideas. His supervisor was Sommerfield, and recalling this period, Landé, writes

> The more pragmatic Sommerfeld . . . warned his students, one of them this writer, not to spend too much time on the hopeless task of "explaining" the quantum

but rather to accept it as fundamental and help work out its consequences.[15]

The task of "explaining" the quantum, of course, is the realist program for identifying a reality underlying the formulas of the theory and thereby explaining the predicative success of the formulas as approximately true descriptions of this reality. It is this program that I have criticized in the first part of this paper, and this same program that the builders of quantum theory saw as a scientific dead end. Einstein knew perfectly well that the issue was joined right here. In the summer of 1935, he wrote to Schrödinger,

> The real problem is that physics is a kind of metaphysics; physics describes "reality". But we do not know what "reality" is. We know it only through physical description. . . . But the Talmudic philosopher sniffs at "reality", as at a frightening creature of the naïve mind.[16]

By avoiding the bogey of an underlying reality, the "Talmudic" originators of quantum theory seem to have set subsequent generations on precisely the right path. Those inspired by realist ambitions have produced no predictively successful physics. Neither Einstein's conception of a unified field nor the ideas of the de Broglie group about pilot waves, nor the Bohm-inspired interest in hidden variables has made for scientific progress. . . .

One can hardly doubt the importance of a nonrealist attitude for the development and practically infinite success of the quantum theory. Historical counterfactuals are always tricky, but the sterility of actual realist programs in this area at least suggests that Bohr and company were right in believing that the road to scientific progress here would have been blocked by realism. The founders of quantum theory never turned on the nonrealist attitude that served them so well. Perhaps that is because the central underlying theoretical device of quantum theory, the densities of

a complex-valued and infinite-dimensional wave function, are even harder to take seriously than is the four-dimensional manifold of relativity. But now, there comes a most curious twist. For just as the practitioners of relativity, I have suggested, ignore the *realist* interpretation in favor of a more pragmatic attitude toward the space-time structure, the quantum physicists would appear to make a similar reversal and to forget their nonrealist history and allegiance when it comes time to talk about new discoveries.

Thus, anyone in the business will tell you about the exciting period, in the fall of 1974, when the particle group at Brookhaven, led by Samuel Ting, discovered the J particle, just as a Stanford team at the Stanford Linear Accelerator Center (SLAC), under Burton Richter, independently found a new particle they called "ψ". These turned out to be one and the same, the so-called ψ/J particle (Mass 3,098 MeV, Spin 1, Resonance 67 KeV, Strangeness 0). To explain this new entity, the theoreticians were led to introduce a new kind of quark, the so-called charmed quark. The ψ/J particle is then thought to be made up out of a charmed quark and an anticharmed quark, with their respective spins aligned. But if this is correct, then there ought to be other such pairs anti-aligned, or with variable spin alignments, and these ought to make up quite new observable particles. Such predictions from the charmed-quark model have turned out to be confirmed in various experiments.

In this example, I have been intentionally a bit more descriptive in order to convey the realist feel to the way scientists speak in this area. For I want to ask whether this is a return to realism or whether, instead, it can somehow be reconciled with a fundamentally nonrealist attitude[17] I believe that the nonrealist option is correct, but I will not defend that answer here, however, because its defense involves the articulation of a compelling and viable form of nonrealism; and that is the task of the third (and final) section of this paper.

Nonrealism

Even if the realist happens to be a talented philosopher, I do not believe that, in his heart, he relies for his realism on the rather sophisticated form of abductive argument that I have examined and rejected in the first section of this paper, and which the history of twentieth-century physics shows to be fallacious. Rather, if his heart is like mine (and I *do* believe in a common nature), then I suggest that a more simple and homely sort of argument is what grips him. It is this, and I will put it in the first person. I certainly trust the evidence of my senses, on the whole, with regard to the existence and features of everyday objects. And I have similar confidence in the system of "check, double-check, triple-check" of scientific investigation, as well as the other safeguards built into the institutions of science. So, if the scientists tell me that there really are molecules, and atoms, and ψ/J particles and, who knows, maybe even quarks, then so be it. I trust them and, thus, must accept that there really such things, with their attendant properties and relations. Moreover, if the instrumentalist (or some other member of the species "non-realistica") comes along to say that these entities, and their attendants, are just fictions (or the like), then I see no more reason to believe him than to believe that *he is* a fiction, made up (somehow) to do a job on me; which I do not believe. It seems, then, that I had better be a realist. One can summarize this homely and compelling line as follows: it is possible to accept the evidence of one's senses and to accept, *in the same way*, the confirmed results of science only for a realist; hence, I should be one (and so should you!).

What is it to accept the evidence of one's senses and, *in the same way*, to accept confirmed scientific theories? It is to take them into one's life as true, with all that implies concerning adjusting one's behavior, practical and theoretical, to accommodate these truths. Now, of course, there are truths, and truths. Some are more central to us and our lives, some less so. I might be mistaken about anything, but were I mistaken about where I am right now, that might affect me more than would my perhaps mistaken belief in charmed quarks. Thus, it is compatible with the homely line of argument that some of the scientific beliefs that I hold are less central than some, for example, perceptual beliefs. Of course, were I deeply in the charmed-quark business, giving up that belief might be more difficult than giving up some at the perceptual level. (Thus we get the phenomenon of "seeing what you believe," as is well known to all thoughtful people.) When the homely line asks us, then, to accept the scientific results "in the same way" in which we accept the evidence of our senses, I take it that we are to accept them both as true. I take it that we are being asked not to distinguish between kinds of truth or modes of existence or the like, but only among truths themselves, in terms of centrality, degrees of belief, or such.

Let us suppose this understood. Now, do you think that Bohr, the archenemy of realism, could toe the homely line? Could Bohr, fighting for the sake of science (against Einstein's realism) have felt compelled either to give up the results of science, or else to assign to its "truths" some category different from the truths of everyday life? It seems unlikely. And thus, unless we uncharitably think Bohr inconsistent on this basic issue, we might well come to question whether there is any necessary connection moving us from accepting the results of science as true to being a realist.[18]

Let me use the term "antirealist" to refer to any of the many different specific enemies of realism: the idealist, the instrumentalist, the phenomenalist, the empiricist (constructive or not), the conventionalist, the constructivist, the pragmatist, and so forth. Then, it seems to me that both the realist and the antirealist must toe what I have been calling "the homely line." That is, they must both accept the certified results of science as on par with more homely and familiarly supported claims. That is not to say that one party (or the other) cannot distinguish more from less well-confirmed claims at home or in science; nor that one cannot single out some particular mode of inference (such as inference to the best explanation) and worry over its reliability, both at home and away. It is just that one must maintain parity. Let us say, then, that both realist and antirealist accept the results of scientific investigations as "true," on par with more homely truths. (I realize that some antirealists would rather use a different word, but no matter.) And call this acceptance of scientific truths the "core position."[19] What distinguishes realists from antirealists, then, is what they add onto this core position.

The antirealist may add onto the core position a particular analysis of the concept of truth, as in the pragmatic and instrumentalist and conventionalist conceptions of truth. Or the antirealist may add on a special analysis of concepts, as in idealism, constructivism, phenomenalism, and in some varieties of empiricism. These addenda will then issue in a special meaning, say, for existence statements. Or the antirealist may add on certain methodological strictures, pointing a wary finger at some particular inferential tool, or constructing his own account for some particular aspects of science (e.g., explanations or laws). Typically, the antirealist will make several such additions to the core.

What then of the realist, what does he add to his core acceptance of the results of science as really true? My colleague, Charles Chastain, suggested what I think is the most graphic way of stating the answer—namely, that what the realist adds on is a desk-thumping, foot-stamping shout of "Really!" So, when the realist and antirealist agree, say, that there really are electrons and that they really carry a unit negative charge and really do have a small mass (of about 9.1×10^{-28} grams), what the realist wants to add is the emphasis that all this is really so. "There really are electrons, really!" This typical realist emphasis serves both a negative and a positive function. Negatively, it is meant to deny the additions that the antirealist would

make to that core acceptance which both parties share. The realist wants to deny, for example, the phenomenalistic reduction of concepts or the pragmatic conception of truth. The realist thinks that these addenda take away from the substantiality of the accepted claims to truth or existence. "No," says he, "they *really* exist, and not in just your diminished antirealist sense." Positively, the realist wants to explain the robust sense in which *he* takes these claims to truth or existence, namely, as claims about reality—what is really, really the case. The full-blown version of this involves the conception of truth as correspondence with the world, and the surrogate use of approximate truth as near-correspondence. We have already seen how these ideas of correspondence and approximate truth are supposed to explain what *makes* the truth *true* whereas, in fact, they function as mere trappings, that is, as superficial decorations that may well attract our attention but do not compel rational belief. Like the extra "really," they are an arresting foot-thump and, logically speaking, of no more force.

It seems to me that when we contrast the realist and the antirealist in terms of what they each want to add to the core position, a third alternative emerges—and an attractive one at that. It is the core position itself, *and all by itself*. If I am correct in thinking that, at heart, the grip of realism only extends to the homely connection of everyday truths with scientific truths, and that good sense dictates our acceptance of the one on the same basis as our acceptance of the other, then the homely line makes the core position, all by itself, a compelling one, one that we ought to take to heart. Let us try to do so, and to see whether it constitutes a philosophy, and an attitude toward science, that we can live by.

The core position is neither realist nor antirealist; it mediates between the two. It would be nice to have a name for this position, but it would be a shame to appropriate another "ism" on its behalf, for then it would appear to be just one of the many contenders for ontological allegiance. I think it is not just one of that crowd but rather, as the homely line behind it suggests, it is for commonsense epistemology—the natural ontological attitude. Thus, let me introduce the acronym *NOA* (pronounced as in "Noah"), for *natural ontological attitude*, and, henceforth, refer to the core position under that designation.

To begin showing how NOA makes for an adequate philosophical stance toward science, let us see what it has to say about ontology. When NOA counsels us to accept the results of science as true, I take it that we are to treat truth in the usual referential way, so that a sentence (or statement) is true just in case the entities referred to stand in the referred-to relations. Thus, NOA . . . commits us, via truth, to the existence of the individuals, properties, relations, processes, and so forth referred to by the scientific statements that we accept as true. Our belief in their existence will be just as strong (or weak) as our belief in the truth of the bit of science involved, and degrees of belief here, presumably, will be tutored by ordinary relations of confirmation and evidential support, subject to the usual scientific canons. In taking this referential stance, NOA is not committed to the progressivism that seems inherent in realism. For the realist, as an article of faith, sees scientific success, over the long run, as bringing us closer to the truth. His whole explanatory enterprise, using approximate truth, forces his hand in this way. But, a "noaer" (pronounced as "knower") is not so committed. As a scientist, say, within the context of the tradition in which he works, the noaer, of course, will believe in the existence of those entities to which his theories refer. But should the tradition change, say in the manner of the conceptual revolutions that Kuhn dubs "paradigm shifts," then nothing in NOA dictates that the change be assimilated as being progressive, that is, as a change where we learn more accurately about *the same things*. NOA is perfectly consistent with the Kuhnian alternative, which construes such changes as wholesale changes of reference. Unlike the realist, adherents to NOA are free to examine the facts in cases of paradigm shift, and

to see whether or not a convincing case for stability of reference across paradigms can be made without superimposing on these facts a realist-progressivist superstructure. . . .

So far I have managed to avoid what, for the realist, is the essential point, for what of the "external world"? How can I talk of reference and of existence claims unless I am talking about referring to things right out there in the world? And here, of course, the realist, again, wants to stamp his feet. I think the problem that makes the realist want to stamp his feet, shouting "Really!" (and invoking the external world) has to do with the stance the realist tries to take vis-à-vis the game of science. The realist, as it were, tries to stand outside the arena watching the ongoing game and then tries to judge (from this external point of view) what the point is. It is, he says, *about* some area external to the game. The realist, I think, is fooling himself. For he cannot (really!) stand outside the arena, nor can he survey some area off the playing field and mark it out as what the game is about.

Let me try to address these two points. How are we to arrive at the judgment that, in addition to, say, having a rather small mass, electrons are objects "out there in the external world"? Certainly, we can stand off from the electron game and survey its claims, methods, predictive success, and so forth. But what stance could we take that would enable us to judge what the theory of electrons is *about*, other than agreeing that it is about electrons? It is not like matching a blueprint to a house being built, or a map route to a country road. For we are *in* the world, both physically and conceptually. That is, *we* are among the objects of science, and the concepts and procedures that we use to make judgments of subject matter and correct application are themselves part of that same scientific world. Epistemologically, the situation is very much like the situation with regard to the justification of induction. For the problem of the external world (so-called) is how to satisfy the realist's demand that we justify the existence claims sanctioned by science (and, therefore, by NOA) as claims to the existence of entities "out there." In the case of induction, it is clear that only an inductive justification will do, and it is equally clear that no inductive justification will do at all. So too with the external world, for only ordinary scientific inferences to existence will do, and yet none of them satisfies the demand for showing that the existent is really "out there." I think we ought to follow Hume's prescription on induction, with regard to the external world. There is no possibility for justifying the kind of externality that realism requires, yet it may well be that, in fact, we cannot help yearning for just such a comforting grip on reality. I shall return to this theme at the close of the paper.

If I am right, then the realist is chasing a phantom, and we cannot actually do more, with regard to existence claims, than follow scientific practice, just as NOA suggests. . . .

Indeed, perhaps the greatest virtue of NOA is to call attention to just how minimal an adequate philosophy of science can be. (In this respect, NOA might be compared to the minimalist movement in art.) For example, NOA helps us to see that realism differs from various antirealisms in this way: realism adds an outer direction to NOA, that is, the external world and the correspondence relation of approximate truth; antirealisms (typically) add an inner direction, that is, human-oriented reductions of truth, or concepts, or explanations (as in my opening citation from Hume). NOA suggests that the legitimate features of these additions are already contained in the presumed equal status of everyday truths with scientific ones, and in our accepting them both as *truths*. No other additions are legitimate, and none are required.

It will be apparent by now that a distinctive feature of NOA, one that separates it from similar views currently in the air, is NOA's stubborn refusal to amplify the concept of truth, by providing a theory or analysis (or even a metaphorical picture). Rather, NOA recognizes in "truth" a concept already in use and

agrees to abide by the standard rules of usage. . . . Thus NOA respects the customary "grammar" of "truth" (and its cognates). Likewise, NOA respects the customary epistemology, which grounds judgments of truth in perceptual judgments and various confirmation relations. As with the use of other concepts, disagreements are bound to arise over what is true (for instance, as to whether inference to the best explanation is always truth-conferring). NOA pretends to no resources for settling these disputes, for NOA takes to heart the great lesson of twentieth-century analytic and Continental philosophy, namely, that there *are* no general methodological or philosophical resources for deciding such things. The mistake common to realism and all the antirealisms alike is their commitment to the existence of such nonexistent resources. If pressed to answer the question of what, then, does it *mean* to say that something is true (or to what does the truth of so-and-so commit one), NOA will reply by pointing out the logical relations engendered by the specific claim and by focusing, then, on the concrete historical circumstances that ground that particular judgment of truth. For, after all, there *is* nothing more to say.

Because of its parsimony, I think the minimalist stance represented by NOA marks a revolutionary approach to understanding science. It is, I would suggest, as profound in its own way as was the revolution in our conception of morality, when we came to see that founding morality on God and His Order was *also* neither legitimate nor necessary. Just as the typical theological moralist of the eighteenth century would feel bereft to read, say, the pages of *Ethics*, so I think the realist must feel similarly when NOA removes that "correspondence to the external world" for which he so longs. I too have regret for that lost paradise, and too often slip into the realist fantasy. I use my understanding of twentieth-century physics to help me firm up my convictions about NOA, and I recall some words of Mach, which I offer as a comfort and as a closing. With reference to realism, Mach writes

> It has arisen in the process of immeasurable time without the intentional assistance of man. It is a product of nature, and preserved by nature. Everything that philosophy has accomplished . . . is, as compared with it, but an insignificant and ephemeral product of art. The fact is, every thinker, every philosopher, the moment he is forced to abandon his one-sided intellectual occupation . . . , immediately returns [to realism].
>
> Nor is it the purpose of these "introductory remarks" to discredit the standpoint [of realism]. The task which we have set ourselves is simply to show why and for what purpose we hold that standpoint during most of our lives, and why and for what purpose we are . . . obliged to abandon it.

These lines are taken from Mach's *The Analysis of Sensations* (Sec. 14). I recommend that book as effective realism-therapy, a therapy that works best (as Mach suggests) when accompanied by historicophysical investigations (real versions of the breakneck history of my second section, "Realism and Progress"). For a better philosophy, however, I recommend NOA.

Notes

1. In the final section, I call this postrealism "NOA." Among recent views that relate to NOA, I would include Hilary Putnam's "internal realism," Richard Rorty's "epistemological behaviorism," the "semantic realism" espoused by Paul Horwich, parts of the "Mother Nature" story told by William Lycan, and the defense of common sense worked out by Joseph Pitt (as a way of reconciling W. Sellars's manifest and scientific images). For references, see Hilary Putnam, *Meaning and the Moral Sciences* (London: Routledge and Kegan Paul, 1978); Richard Rorty, *Philosophy and the Mirror of Nature* (Princeton: Princeton University Press, 1979); Paul Horwich, "Three Forms of Realism," *Synthese* 51 (1982): pp. 181–201; William G. Lycan, "Epistemic Value" (preprint,

1982); and Joseph C. Pitt, *Pictures, Images and Conceptual Change* (Dordrecht: D. Reidel, 1981). The reader will note that some of the above consider their views a species of realism, whereas others consider their views antirealist. As explained below, NOA marks the divide; hence its "postrealism."

2. Richard N. Boyd, "Scientific Realism and Naturalistic Epistemology," in *PSA* (1980), vol. 2, ed. P. D. Asquith and R. N. Giere (E. Lansing: Philosophy of Science Association, 1981), pp. 613–662. See also, Boyd's article in [*Scientific Realism*, ed. J. Leplin], and further references there.

3 . Hilary Putnam, "The Meaning of 'Meaning,'" in *Language, Mind and Knowledge*, ed. K. Gunderson (Minneapolis: University of Minnesota Press, 1975), pp. 131–193. See also his article in [*Scientific Realism*, ed. J. Leplin].

4. Bas C. van Fraassen, *The Scientific Image* (Oxford: The Clarendon Press, 1980). See especially pp. 97–101 for a discussion of the truth of explanatory theories. To see that the recent discussion of realism is joined right here, one should contrast van Fraassen with W. H. Newton-Smith, *The Rationality of Science* (London: Routledge and Kegan Paul, 1981), esp. chap. 8.

5. Nancy Cartwright's *How The Laws of Physics Lie* (Oxford: Oxford University Press, 1983) includes some marvelous essays on these issues.

6. See Gerald Holdon, "Mach, Einstein, and the Search for Reality," in his *Thematic Origins of Scientific Thought* (Cambridge: Harvard University Press, 1973), 219–259. I have tried to work out the precise role of this positivist methodology in my "The Young Einstein and the Old Einstein," in *Essays in Memory of Imré Lakatos*, ed. R. S. Cohen et al. (Dordrecht: D. Reidel, 1976), pp. 145–159.

7. A. Einstein et al., *The Principle of Relativity*, trans. W. Perrett and G. B. Jeffrey (New York: Dover, 1952), p. 117.

8. John Earman et al., "Lost in the Tensors," *Studies in History and Philosophy of Science* 9 (1978): pp. 251–278. The tortuous path detailed by Earman is sketched by B. Hoffmann, *Albert Einstein, Creator and Rebel* (New York: New American Library, 1972), pp. 116–128. A nontechnical and illuminating account is given by John Stachel, "The Genesis of General Relativity," in *Einstein Symposium Berlin*, ed. H. Nelkowski et al. (Berlin: Springer-Verlag, 1980).

9. I have in mind the role played by the analysis of simultaneity in Einstein's path to special relativity.

Despite the important study by Arthur Miller, *Albert Einstein's Special Theory of Relativity* (Reading: Addison-Wesley, 1981), and an imaginative pioneering work by John Earman (and collaborators), the details of which I have been forbidden to disclose, I think the role of positivist analysis in the 1905 paper has yet to be properly understood. My ideas here were sparked by Earman's playful reconstructions. So I cannot expose my ideas until John is ready to expose his.

10. Peter Barker, "Einstein's Later Philosophy of Science," in *After Einstein*, ed. P. Barker and C. G. Shugart (Memphis: Memphis State University Press, 1981), pp. 133–146, is a nice telling of this story.

11. Roger Jones in "Realism About What?" (in draft) explains very nicely some of the difficulties here.

12. I think the ordinary, deflationist attitude of working scientists is much like that of Steven Weinberg, *Gravitation and Cosmology: Principles and Applications of the General Theory of Relativity* (New York: Wiley, 1972).

13. See B. L. van der Waerden, *Sources of Quantum Mechanics* (New York: Dover, 1967), p. 261.

14. See Linda Wessels, "Schrödinger's Route to Wave Mechanics," *Studies in History and Philosophy of Science* 10 (1979): pp. 311–350.

15. A. Landé, "Albert Einstein and the Quantum Riddle," *American Journal of Physics* 42 (1974): 460.

16. Letter to Schrödinger, June 19, 1935. See my "Einstein's Critique of Quantum Theory: The Roots and Significance of EPR," in *After Einstein* (see n. 10), pp. 147–158, for a fuller discussion of the contents of this letter.

17. The nonrealism that I attribute to students and practitioners of the quantum theory requires more discussion and distinguishing of cases and kinds

than I have room for here. It is certainly not the all-or-nothing affair I make it appear in the text. I hope to carry out some of the required discussion in a talk for the American Philosophical Association meetings, Pacific Division, March 1983, entitled "Is Scientific Realism Compatible with Quantum Physics?" My thanks to Paul Teller and James Cushing, each of whom saw the need for more discussion here.

18. I should be a little more careful about the historical Bohr than I am in the text. For Bohr himself would seem to have wanted to truncate the homely line somewhere between the domain of chairs and tables and atoms, whose existence he plainly accepted, and that of electrons, where he seems to have thought the question of existence (and of realism, more generally) was no longer well defined. An illuminating and provocative discussion of Bohr's attitude toward realism is given by Paul Teller, "The Projection Postulate and Bohr's Interpretation of Quantum Mechanics," pp. 201–223 n. 3. Thanks, again, to Paul for helping to keep me honest.

19. In this context, for example, van Fraassen's "constructive empiricism" would prefer the concept of empirical adequacy, reserving "truth" for an (unspecified) literal interpretation and believing in that truth only among observables. It is clear, nevertheless, that constructive empiricism follows the homely line and accepts the core position. Indeed, this seems to be its primary motivating rationale. If we reread constructive empiricism in our terminology, then, we would say that it accepts the core position but adds to it a construal of truth as empirical adequacy. Thus, it is antirealist, just as suggested in the next paragraph below.

EVELYN FOX KELLER

Critical Silences in Scientific Discourse: Problems of Form and Re-Form

Part I: Introduction (The Question I Would Like to Ask)

I begin with a few philosophical platitudes about the nature of scientific knowledge upon which I *think* we can agree, but which, in any case, will serve to define my own point of departure. First,

- Scientific theories neither mirror nor correspond to reality.

- Like all theories, they are models, in Geertz's (1973) terms, both models of and models for, but especially, they are models *for*; scientific theories represent in order to intervene, if only in search of confirmation. And the world in which they aim to intervene is, first and foremost, the world of material (that is, physical) reality. For this reason, I prefer to call them tools. From the first experiment to the latest technology,

they facilitate our actions in and on that world, enabling us not to mirror, but to bump against, to perturb, to transform that material reality. In this sense, scientific theories are tools for changing the world.

- Such theories, or stories, are invented, crafted, or constructed by human subjects, interacting both with other human subjects and with nonhuman subjects/objects.

- But even granted that they are constructed, and even abandoning the hope for a one-to-one correspondence with the real, the effectiveness of these tools in changing the world has something to do with the relation between theory and reality. To the extent that scientific theories do in fact "work"—that is, lead to action on things and people that, in extreme cases (for example, nuclear weaponry), appear to be independent of any belief system—they

Presented at the Institute for Advanced Study, Princeton, N. J., on February 4, 1988. I am indebted to the National Endowment for the Humanities for supporting this work. Reprinted by permission.

must be said to possess a kind of "adequacy" in relation to a world that is not itself constituted symbolically—a world we might designate as "residual reality."

■ I take this world of "residual reality" to be vastly larger than any possible representation we might construct. Accordingly, different perspectives, different languages will lead to theories that not only attach to the real in different ways (that is, carve the world at different joints), but they will attach to different parts of the real—and perhaps even differently to the same parts.

So far so good. All these differences seem to reveal a space indicating the operation of choice in the construction of scientific knowledge. Yet, the moment we attempt to juxtapose the representational plasticity of scientific theories with their instrumental efficacy, this space seems to disappear before our eyes, leaving in its place an aura of inevitability.

From critical theory, to hermeneutics, to pragmatism, the standard response to so-called relativist arguments has been that the scientific stories are different from other stories for the simple reason that they "work." If there is a single overriding point I want to make in this essay, it is to identify a chronic ellipsis in these responses: As routinely as the effectiveness of science is invoked, equally routine is the failure to go on to say what it is that science works *at*, to note that "working" is a necessary but not sufficient constraint. Science gives us models/representations that permit us to manipulate parts of the world in particular ways. In a way, Charles Taylor says it all: The inescapable difference between theoretical and atheoretical cultures, he says, lies in the technological success of modern scientific culture, and to bring his point home, he cites the nineteenth-century British ditty, "Whatever happens, We have got The Gatling gun, And they have not" (in Hollis and Lukes 1982:104). What I am saying is that it is not sufficient to grant that scientific ways of knowing have instrumental value, or

that they proceed out of instrumental interests: Neither instruments themselves, nor the values, interests or efficacy associated with them are devoid of aim. To be sure, instrumental knowledge has force in the world, but force, as we learned in freshman physics, is a vector. It has not only magnitude, but directionality as well. And if we grant directionality to the force of scientific knowledge, then the obvious question arises: In what other directions might science work? Toward what other aims? Furthermore, by what criteria are we to measure science's instrumental success? Surely, not simply by the magnitude of its impact on the world—not if we also ask what, if anything, guarantees that the particular ways in which our best science "works" are humanly adaptive? And finally, if they are not, how might we re-vision the scientific project—as it were, to make it "work" better?

Such questions may seem obvious enough, but we know that past attempts to deal with them have been notoriously unsuccessful. Most recently, and arguably with some more success than their predecessors, feminist critics of science have suggested that the particular directions that the forms of scientific knowledge have taken since the seventeenth century are grounded in (or at least supported by) a historically explicit identification of scientific values with the values our particular cultural tradition takes to be masculine, and a collateral and equally explicit exclusion of those values which have been labeled "feminine." In contrast to other attempts, such as, for example, Marcuse's (1964) earlier vision of an "erotic science," feminist analyses of science have given us some strategies for identifying both the dynamics and consequences of such a "genderization of science." In particular, we have grounded our critique by looking to the history of science for traces of alternative visions and practices present within our own Western traditions, even within the domain of modern science. These traditions prove rich in such variability, and their history does indeed provide evidence for at least a loose conjunction between criteria of selection and prevailing gender ideologies.

It is apparent that we ourselves have tended to fall into the old (and notably counterproductive) polarity between understanding and manipulation, concentrating our critical attention on alternative meanings of the former, and disdaining the latter. It is as if, entrapped by the bifurcation between representing and intervening, we have come to agree with the critical theorists that it is control and prediction in themselves that must be the culprit. (See, for example, *The Race to the Double Helix*, BBC film 1987, in which Rosalind Franklin is quoted as saying, "I just want to look, not touch."[1])

Coincidentally, feminist critics of science have been almost totally silent on the subject of physics—historically (at least until current developments in molecular biology), the most powerful agent of change to come out of the entire corpus of scientific knowledge. True, sociologists of science have balked at the conventional privileging of physics, at accepting the hierarchical organization of knowledge that places physics at the apex of knowledge, and they have had good (and obvious) reasons for doing so.[2] Yet, however extensive its social and rhetorical inflation, the status that physics enjoys today cannot be separated from its newly proven prowess in not only moving the world, but making it shake at its very roots.

In short, feminist theory has helped us to revision science as a discourse, but not as an agent of change. And it is this latter question that I want to press on now. Since it is demonstrably possible to envision different kinds of representations, we need now to ask what different possibilities of change might be entailed by these different kinds of representation? For this, we need to understand the enmeshing of representing and intervening, how particular representations are already committed to particular kinds of interventions. Is there, for instance, a sense in which we might say that the program of modern genetics already has, written into its

very structure, a blueprint for eugenics? Or that nuclear weapons are prebuilt into the program for nuclear physics? And if so, what kinds of theories of the natural world would enable us to act on the world differently?

In other words, I start by repudiating the view of an undirected search for knowledge, leading inexorably to the science of genetics, out of which suddenly and unexpectedly emerges the wherewithal for a fully fledged and perhaps even unstoppable eugenics program. I want to ask instead, how might the very framing of the questions of genetics already commit us to the possibility of eugenics? At the same time, however, I take it as self-evident that no simple account can be given of the conjunction between knowledge, power, and desire. The story of DNA does not map on to the eugenics script in any straightforward way, any more than the story of nuclear physics could be made to simply map on to the bomb—if only because the array of motivations and consequences attaching to both these stories is vastly more complex. Nonetheless, there is reason to suspect that somewhere in the project of genetics there is already contained not only the possibility but the expectation of eugenics, just as the anticipation of explosive power is somewhere contained in the project of nuclear physics. But none of us, it seems, is able to say much about where, and how.[3] The difficulty we encounter is not in documenting either potential or anticipation of these consequences— that part is easy. Rather, it is in showing the influence of such ambitions on the structure and form of the biological and physical theories that realize them. *That* question appears to be foreclosed every which way we turn. And since I'm convinced that the question not only makes sense, but also has a kind of urgency, I'm led to ask: What is the nature of the impasse that obstructs its pursuit? In other words, although I take it that there *are* (at least some) real objects in the world, the barriers that prevent us from asking manifestly sensible questions are not among them. These are constructed alongside, and perhaps even as part and parcel of, the process that yields our scientific representation of the real.

So this essay is not about re-visioning or re-forming science, but about the obstacles such an effort encounters, especially in relation to physics. I want to take you on a tour of the ways in which these questions appear to get foreclosed if you happen to have been working in physics, biology, or the history, philosophy, or sociology of science over the last couple of decades. In other words, if you happen to be me.

At the end, I will offer some suggestions of what I think we need to get beyond these obstacles—namely, a better and fuller understanding of *how science works*. Perhaps such an understanding might itself prove to be a tool for change, especially, for re-visions and re-form.

Part II: Some Obstacles in the Way

Physics: The Ideology of "Pure" Science

I start as a scientist. I was drawn into physics by an image of the discipline as the most rarified, purely mental—and pristine—endeavor of which human beings were capable. In theoretical physics I saw the promise of touching the world at its innermost being, a touching made possible by the power of pure thought. Physics appeared to me as a vision of exquisite power, but it was not the power of a Francis Bacon, it was more like the power imaged by Einstein— the power of connections, of being "sympathetically in touch with" reality, the power to feel rather than to move the world.

I of course did not invent this picture; I learned it from the community into which I was being inducted. However idiosyncratic my own personal embellishment, my romance with physics was part of a collective romance: It was the romance of pure science, communicated to me in its basic form and content by my teachers. I learned that, at its best, science was pure in all the senses listed by my thesaurus: It was pure in the sense of autonomous,

virtuous, absolute, and elitist, in the sense of abstract, conceptual, and theoretical; in the sense of immaculate, unblemished, and virginal—perhaps above all, in the sense of innocent and blameless. Its antithesis—decorum prevents the purists among us from calling it "impure"—is called (instead) "applied science," or often, more simply, technology or engineering. In other words, this complex and multifunctional vision of a pure, autonomous science carries with it, or perhaps I should say, is premised on, the certitude of a clear demarcation between pure and applied, between science and technology. Pure scientists might claim responsibility for the ultimate power to make the world move (although the purest of the pure would likely disclaim interest even in such potential movement), but with this demarcation, all responsibility for *what* changes are effected, for the choice of direction in which the world is moved, is disowned—that responsibility is located squarely in the lap of applied science, technology, or even better, in politics.

The notion that science might, or ought to, be "pure" was of course hardly new to scientists of my own generation.[4] It was preceded by a tradition begun long before World War II, and it continues—at least in its essential form— as an article of fundamental faith for most scientists today, perhaps especially for theoretical physicists. One might say that it is an ideal that finds its ultimately graphic representation here in the location, design, and organization of the Institute for Advanced Study. Yet, its invocation at that particular time in history (late 1950s and early 1960s) must be seen as at least ironic. World War II had triggered a transformation in American science, especially in physics, that left the demarcation between pure and applied science, between science and technology, increasingly difficult to locate in any space outside the hearts and minds of pure scientists. The exigencies of war precipitated a convergence between pure and applied, between basic and mission-oriented research— and more generally between academic science, industry, and the military—that culminated in, but did not end with, Hiroshima and Nagasaki. Some would even argue that it began there. Between 1938 and 1945, the military investment in R&D increased by an absolute factor of 50, and a relative factor of 3 (that is, from 30 percent to more than 90 percent of the total research budget). After the end of World War II, military expenditure in R&D remained roughly constant (with only a slight slump in the immediate postwar years), and by the late 1950s, actually came to exceed its wartime high, even when calculated in constant dollars.[5] The funds for what alternatively gets called basic, pure, or fundamental research increased hand-in-hand with the funds for applied (or mission-oriented) research. The rationale for this increase in support for basic research was straightforward. As Alan Waterman explained his own program in the Office of Naval Research (this was 1950):

> [Since] it is assumed that something like the present degree of emergency will persist for an unforeseeable period of years . . . it is believed equally important to secure "defense in depth" . . . on the research and development front by providing stable, continuous support to basic research (from Forman 1987, p. 159).

In other words, even while insisting that the value of basic research was not to be tied to its utility, scientists supported the general conviction that had been driven home by the atom bomb; namely, that "our national security rests on superior science." Their double message was clear and open: On the one hand, basic research was, in both the form of its questions and the content of its answers. Entirely autonomous of any uses to which it might be put; at the same time, however, it was necessary to the maintenance of an adequate military defense.[6]

Early on, the irony of this not so much new as newly fraught cleavage between purity and danger in the character of scientific knowledge had found eloquent graphic representation in a popular image—an image first presented on the cover of *Time* magazine in 1946, but persisting as a kind of cultural symbol ever since. This is the juxtaposition of the face of Albert Einstein, the equation, $E = mc^2$, and the ominous mushroom cloud—an association, as it happened, that served both scientists and the public remarkably well. The sad, gentle face that was known throughout the world as an exemplar of pacifism stands here for the pure scientist; $E = mc^2$ for Einstein's notoriously abstract and obscure theory of relativity, the theory that was popularly said to be comprehensible to only twelve people in the world; and the mushroom cloud, well, we know what that stands for.[7] In conjoining these three images, the deeply ambiguous and profoundly troubling relation between science and the military acquires a message of tragic inexorability. If Einstein's pure and abstruse researches into the mysteries of space, time, and matter could result in a weapon as literally earth shattering as the atomic bomb, belief in choice and responsibility is radically confounded. Surely no one could hold Einstein himself, the pure scientist, to blame. No one would want to claim that Einstein, or anyone else, for that matter, could have forseen the monstrous cloud in the elegant symmetries of Lorentz invariance. And furthermore (with that sleight of hand that has become so familiar), even if one could, surely no one is suggesting that the acquisition of such pure knowledge could, or should, be curtailed?

There is indeed tragedy in this vision of science, but there is no tragic flaw—nor, finally, is there any responsibility.[8] Scientists work to increase our fund of knowledge of the natural world as they must, for sooner or later, knowledge will out. Knowledge, as a distinguished physicist recently explained to me, can be thought of as an expanding sphere of light in a background of darkness. Its only directionality is outward; it just grows, without direction, and without aim.

It is noteworthy, however, that this use of Einstein to imply a relation between science and weapons beyond (at least our) control bespeaks more mystery than history: As anyone who was connected with the actual developments knows, neither Einstein nor the theory of relativity had very much to do with the development of the atom bomb. There *was* a chain of events linking basic (or pure) physics to the bomb, but it proceeded less through the theory of relativity than through research in nuclear physics. This other history (more familiar to scientists than to the general public) can be traced back to Rutherford and Soddy's 1903 calculations of the energy released by radioactive decay. Forty years before the Manhattan Project, and two years before Einstein published his special theory of relativity, Rutherford remarked "that, could a proper detonator be found, it was just conceivable that a wave of atomic disintegration might be started through matter, which would indeed make this old world vanish in smoke"—his biographer called it a "playful suggestion," and Soddy, though he took it more seriously, consoled himself with the faith that "We may trust Nature to guard her secret" (Rhodes 1986:44). From that point on, the possibility of an atomic bomb was never far from the consciousness of nuclear physicists.[9] If one particular scientist were to be singled out in the chain reaction that led from Rutherford to Oppenheimer, it ought perhaps be Leo Szilard (the man who thought the possibility of building an atomic bomb so likely that he patented his recipe for it in 1934), not Einstein. Einstein, after all, was only the signator of the letter that first alerted FDR of the possibility (and necessity) of making such a weapon; Szilard was its primary author.[10] Beginning with that letter, and persisting throughout the postwar years, it could be said that Einstein's principal role was that of icon, and there is reason to believe that he knew it. An apocryphal story floating around the Institute tells us that one day, asked by a stranger on the train what he did, Einstein replied, "I'm an artist's model."

Like all successful myths, the myths surrounding Einstein's office persist (in both popular and scientific imagination, sometimes even alongside an awareness of their mythical character) because they work. In particular, they work *to* sustain belief in the a priori aimlessness and essential purity of scientific knowledge, even in the face of the unprecedented dangers that knowledge has enabled. Einstein's image effectively effaces all those others who cannot be said to be entirely innocent, precisely because they did anticipate the ominous cloud, and nonetheless worked actively toward it—either believing such an eventuality unlikely, or believing it all too likely. And the displacement is effective, at least in part, *because* of the congruence between the plasticity of Einstein's image and the (now necessary) ambiguity in the meaning of the term "pure": at once genuine, plain, blameless, innocent, virtuous, unblemished, abstract, conceptual, and theoretical. Thus bolstered, our confidence in the purity of scientific knowledge—even, or especially, at that historic moment which finds science at its most impure—works, in turn, to foreclose the questions we would otherwise ask about the aims of science, about the ways in which both the form and content of scientific knowledge have been shaped by the motivations driving it (either from below, in the consciousness or unconscious of individual scientists, or from above, in the programs of the sponsoring agencies). Most crucially, such confidence prevents us from thinking about the possibility of redirecting science, of doing it differently. For how can one redirect a venture that has no direction?

History, Philosophy, and Sociology of Science: The Focus on Truth OR Consequences, But Never Both

On these absolutely vital questions, working scientists are predictably silent. More oddly though, the analytic disciplines that grew around the natural sciences after World War II have been equally silent. Throughout this critical transformation in both the scale and character of scientific research, well into the 1960s, prevailing conventions in the history, philosophy, and sociology of science worked collectively and separately in ways that tacitly supported the inviolability of the scientific preserve. Historians of science, by concentrating their attention on the internal or strictly cognitive development of science; philosophers of science, first, by their embrace of logical positivism, and even after attention shifted to the debate between rationality and realism, through an unspoken agreement to privilege questions of truth over questions of consequences; and sociologists of science, by their focus on the professionalization of scientists, and on scientific knowledge "as simply another commodity" (Dennis 1987:510). In these various ways, all of the disciplines devoted to analysis of the growth of scientific knowledge tacitly cooperated in demarcating the internal dynamics of science from its social and political influences. What inquiry was conducted into the changing character of American science was largely confined to the subject of external (that is, political or social) changes in the relation of society (or government) *to* science. And by definitions then current, this version of the problem both ensured its exclusion from the history and philosophy of science and helped delimit sociological inquiry to the "so-called external relations of science." The net result was to effectively foreclose inquiry into the formative influence of social and political factors on the development of scientific knowledge itself, and, in that evasion, to permit the dual rationale of science—as an intrinsic good *and* as an activity to be supported because of its utilitarian outcomes—to remain intact. In 1962, when A. Hunter Dupree's own research into the growing interdependence of science and government led him to write, "In the near future lies the possibility that social relations may be the key to the internal development of science as well" (1962, 135:1119–21), his suggestion fell on uncomprehending ears.

It may be worth distinguishing at this point between the kinds of questions that *couldn't* be asked from those that might have been asked but for the most part simply weren't, or if

asked, weren't pursued. Even granting a view of scientific knowledge based on the model of discovery—of taming, or illuminating, the great unknown—there remains the question of what kinds of things we choose to know, in what directions we aim our great searchlight of scientific inquiry. In this view, it may not be seen as mattering in the long run, but it will surely be acknowledged that, in the short run, the profile of scientific research (even of basic research) depends on funding priorities. The more resources invested in one line of research, say laser physics, the more rapidly we accumulate knowledge about how to build a laser. These are obvious points; they grant that the particular content, even if not the form, of our knowledge may well depend on where we invest our energies. Such a picture does indeed disturb the isotropic, expanding sphere of light conception of the growth of scientific knowledge, but only slightly. It posits time as the great leveler. Ian Hacking calls this the "menu view" of knowledge:

> We cannot afford (or eat) all three of the entrees; meat, fish, and vegetarian. So we settle on one, but our choice does not affect the menu. Choosing meat today has no consequences for fish tomorrow, unless the restauranteur did not purchase enough fish, guessing we would go for meat again. But that defect can be cured in one more day, and the menu is restored (1987:238).

Hacking suggests that this view "deflects us from the menu itself"; by focusing on the *content*, it deflects us from thinking about the *forms* of scientific knowledge, about "what is held to be thinkable, or possible, at some moment in time" (p. 243).[11] But a prior point also needs to be noted: Obvious as such questions are, the disciplinary structures that were in place until the early or mid-1960s labeled them as concerns of ethics and policy, not as properly belonging to the history, philosophy, or even (for the most part) the sociology of science. They stood as self-evident observations that could perhaps serve as starting points for policy or protest, but not for investigation into *how* the profile, even the short-run profile, of scientific knowledge is affected.[12] And without such an investigation, we have no way of knowing whether content and form can in fact be so easily separated—whether what is known is so readily separable from what is knowable, or for that matter, from what we *want* to know, and, of course, want to do. The truth is, we never really asked. Our confidence in scientific realism was so strong that it preempted even those questions that were ostensibly within its own sway, but that, if pursued, might have led us beyond naïve faith.

In the past twenty-five years, however, all that seems to have changed. A revolution has taken place in the history and sociology of science, and, on a smaller scale, even in the philosophy of science. With the exception of natural scientists themselves, few people in the academy still believe in the inexorability, inevitability, or even purity of scientific truth—in the expanding sphere of light picture of scientific knowledge. Historians of science have demonstrated that the very ideal of pure science is itself a historical construction, maintained by normative conventions of scientific discourse (see for example, Markus 1987). In the new history and sociology of science, Robert Young's rallying cry of the mid-1970s ("Science *is* social relations") has become a methodological principle. When field studies of actual laboratory practices began to appear, it quickly became fashionable (in some quarters at least) to conclude "that nothing extraordinary and nothing 'scientific' was happening inside the sacred walls of these temples" (Latour 1983:141), that "the very distinction between 'social' and 'technical' is produced through scientists' own interpretive practices" (Knorr-Cetina and Mulkay 1983:13). From our present vantage point, Dupree looks to have been remarkably prescient.

Yet, in spite of the enormous increase in our sophistication about how science works, there remains one crucial respect in which we are as

helpless today as we were in the early sixties: As soon as we try to think about how science might be different, we are met by the same impasse as before, though perhaps from the opposite side.

Social studies of science describe a science that is if not exactly out of control, for all practical purposes, beyond the possibility of control. It is as if, in disdaining the instrumentalist agenda of the natural sciences, the aspiration of prediction and control, sociologists of science have opted for a different (pretechnological) model of science for themselves: naturalist rather than empirical, descriptive rather than predictive; once again, representing, not intervening. But with a crucial difference. The confidence the early naturalists shared in full—that the basic order of things is good—is gone. Now, however, we may be finding sustenance in another illusion: the move that turns Bacon on his head and asserts, not knowledge is power, but power is knowledge—that the real locus of politics is in the force of representations; that doing is in the knowing.

Though the new sociology of science may in fact have grown out of an explicitly political agenda that can be traced back to Hessen and Bernal, by the late seventies and early eighties, earlier ambitions to reclaim science "for the people" seemed to have largely vanished. Much as in contemporary philosophical discourse, critical focus has come to revolve around claims to truth in science, leaving its consequences, once again, out of bounds. With the shift from naïve realism to relativism, as even Latour acknowledges, "The terms have changed, the belief in the 'scientificity' of science has disappeared, but the same respect for the boundaries of scientific activity is manifested by both schools of thought" (Latour 1983:142). Accordingly, all questions about how that activity might be redirected have remained unaskable. With the shift of disciplinary structures that permitted the embrace of science as social relations, somehow, even the simple questions about the influence of funding on the shape of scientific knowledge that, as realists, we might have asked but didn't, became (or remained) virtually invisible. Until the last couple of years, even such relatively straightforward questions as these have managed almost entirely to elude the attention of historians and sociologists of science.[13] It would appear that, when we were naïve realists, faithful to the ideals of pure science, we were either too timid or didn't know how to ask; and as relativists, disabused of both "purity" and "scientificity," we somehow lost interest.[14]

Signs of Change

Still, even if neither realism nor relativism provided us with the interest, courage, or conceptual handle with which to approach such questions, I want to suggest that the tension made conspicuous by their opposition may now enable (perhaps even demand) a beginning. In part, I draw confidence from the upsurge (I'll resist the temptation to say explosion) of research activity we have begun to see just in the last two or three years, centering on the impact of World War II on American science. To name just a few: Bromberg, Forman, Heilbron, Schweber, Kevles, Pickering, Roe Smith, Reingold, Seidel . . . are all now hard at work documenting the impact that military funding has had on the growth of post–World War II American science (especially physics)—a necessary precursor to (indeed, that makes it possible to ask) the kinds of questions that Hacking, or I, want to ask. In fact, it is from Forman's comprehensive review of the development of the physics "behind quantum electronics"—stimulated most immediately by the striking parallels between funding patterns of the 1950s and those of the 1980s—that I have drawn many of the quotes and figures cited here. Forman's introductory and concluding remarks are at once compelling and poignant:

> The picture drawn here may be surprising to those of us who have viewed science

with much the same ideological commitments as those most devoted to its pursuit. We, like them, saw the enormous expansion of basic physical research after World War II as a good in itself, a praise-worthy diversion of temporal resources to transcendental goals. We, like them, have been pleased to suppose that science was here using society to its own ends (1987:150).

In the end, Forman recognizes in this supposition what he calls "scientists' own false consciousness,"

> which succeeded so well in what it was intended to do, to mislead others even as it blinded themselves. On the one hand they focused so narrowly on immediate cognitive goals of their work as to miss its instrumental significance . . . to their military patrons. On the other hand they pretended a fundamental character to their work that it scarcely had, and/or compartmentalized, as scientifically irrelevant, the very large technical component that bought them their quota of scientific freedom. . . . Though they have maintained the illusion of autonomy with pertinacity, the physicists had lost control of their discipline (1987:228).

It is Forman's actual investigation that leads him to this conclusion, but the mere fact that he, along with so many of his colleagues, has now taken up this work is striking in itself. Surely (as I've already indicated) that fact has something to do with the current escalation in political pressures on scientific communities. But it also has a great deal to do with the extent to which the earlier, and crucially inhibiting, confidence in the purity and autonomy of science (that even Forman shared) has now been eroded by the intellectual pressures growing out of developments in the social studies of science. It is in just this sense that I take the confrontation between realism and relativism as having generated a place to start.

But to continue the analysis, to now try to understand the impact of our military aspirations on the *forms* (as well as the content) of scientific knowledge, is of course harder. If nothing else, the last twenty-five years in the history, philosophy, and sociology of science have taught us the inadequacy of any simple view of a direct, or witting, relation between military aims and the forms of knowledge. As Hacking writes,

> There is no monolithic military conspiracy . . . to determine the kinds of possibilities in terms of which we shall describe and interact with the cosmos. But our ways of worldmaking . . . are increasingly funded by one overall motivation. If content is what we can see, and form is what we cannot, but which determines the possibilities of what we can see, we have a new cause to worry about weapons research. It is not just the weapons . . . that are being funded, but the world of mind and technique in which those weapons are devised. The forms of that world can come back to haunt us even when the weapons themselves are gone. For we are creating forms of knowledge which—spinoffs or not—have a homing device. More weapons, for example (1987:259–60).

Part III: Conclusion

To sum up and recapitulate, I suggested at the beginning that what we need for the task of re-visioning science is a better understanding of *how science works*. Scientific theories impinge on the real, but they do so selectively, not neutrally, effecting some kinds of change rather than others. And to make sense of how science works, we need to account for the process by which such selectivity operates. In other words, we need to enlarge our understanding of the meaning of the verb "to work" to include action on human as well as nonhuman subjects. In my remaining few minutes, let me try, very

schematically, to sketch out a way of doing this.

If scientific theories are produced by particular groups of people, interacting among themselves, with nonscientists, and with nonhuman subjects (Latour would call all these participants "actors"), then the effectiveness of the resulting theories must be judged in terms of all these interactions that generate them. These interactions, internal and external together, produce an interlocking system of needs and desires demanding at least partial satisfaction by any theory or research program that is said to "work." Intentionality might be said to be located in the production of this system of needs, consequentiality in its satisfaction.

A certain amount (perhaps even much) of the work that a successful theory or research program must do can be described in strictly human (psychosocial, political, and economic) terms. It must be able to generate jobs and doable problems; it must offer explanations that provide aesthetic and emotional satisfaction; it must work rhetorically to recruit students, "win allies," get grants from the National Science Foundation. In short, it must have the power to persuade a number of different constituencies—the funding agencies, the scientists themselves, the public at large, the potential recruits—where even within each of these constituencies, interests are multiple, overlapping, and shifting. For example, a student might be drawn into physics by promises of beauty, elegance, simplicity, certainty, the sheer erotics of knowing, a good job, and/or epistemological, social, or technological prowess. The relative weight of these different appeals will of course vary with time, circumstance, and individual idiosyncrasy. In the 1960s, for example, an educational film was made for high-school students that began with Jerrold Zacharias banging his fist, proclaiming, "Physics is about power!" For emphasis, a mushroom cloud fills the screen. To seventeen-year-olds, the promise of such prowess necessarily appeals more to personal than political desires: It promises to make one big, strong, and "manly"—as an individual rather than as a nation. Fortuitously, perhaps, the same rhetoric could also be used for legislators; then, as now, there was enough of a convergence of interests in this promissory note to appeal both to a pool of potential recruits and to funding agencies. But the promises held out—to future physicists as well as to legislators—must be made good. For a research program to work, it must satisfy the desires that motivate it, at least well enough to keep it going. In the short run, a stable network of interests might be well enough satisfied without the need to invoke any particular interactions between science and the nonhuman world: Jobs, satisfying explanations, doable problems might all be generated by the human work of a research program. But over the long run, even these promises demand satisfaction in terms of direct interactions with (or intervention in) the world of nonhuman subjects. By scientists' own internal ethic, explanations must provide at least some predictive success to remain satisfying; and by the social and political ethic justifying their support, this predictive success must enable the production of at least some of the technological "goods" the public thinks it is paying for.

The truly remarkable thing about physics, and now, molecular biology as well, is that it has been able to realize so many of these needs and desires, that it has produced a body of theory that matches the world well enough to satisfy this network of overlapping interests, that has given us stories good enough (or true enough) to enable us to change the world in ways that we seem to want. That success I think is testimony, above all, to the resourcefulness of physicists. Out of their interactions with each other, with the public at large, with their own heritage, and with a judiciously culled set of facets of the inanimate world, they have succeeded in producing tools that appear to dissolve nature's resistance to our own needs.

But in marveling over their extraordinary success, we need also to consider the almost equally remarkable particularity (perhaps even singularity) of our needs, of the facets of the natural world we designate for experimental and theoretical inquiry (that is, what it is we seek to know about), and of the social arrangements that facilitate the convergence of these needs and facets. All of these, separately and convergently, are products of a particular historical moment. Consider, for example, the availability of jobs down the road at Jet Propulsion Laboratories for the Cal Tech students who, for kicks, spend their Saturday nights building spectacular explosive devices; or the consonance between the explanatory preferences of particular groups of scientists and the psychosocial and political norms of these same groups; or the dependence of technical or mathematical feasibility on available resources. With so much contingency in view, we might now be able to ask how this same resourcefulness might be employed toward the fulfillment of other desires, satisfying a convergence of human interests that would be yielded by different social arrangements.

To be sure, the possibilities of alternative nodes of convergence between the technical and the social are severely limited. As Gyorgy Markus writes, "If history teaches us anything, it is . . . that among the great many imaginable and perhaps desirable things at any historical moment, only very few have any chance of a practical-social realizability" (1987:46). But embedding the directionality of scientific work in its variable psychosocial and political context on the one side, and in the invariant capaciousness of its epistemic potential on the other, brings the possibility of alternative directions within at least imaginative reach. Given our remarkable ingenuity, skill, and imagination, I have no doubt that, with sufficient interest, we could develop representations of natural phenomena adequate to the task of changing the world in different ways—perhaps, as some have hoped, giving us solar energy, rather than nuclear power; ecological rather than pathogenic medicine; better rearing rather than better breeding of our offspring. We have proven that we are smart enough to learn what we need to know to get much of what we want; perhaps it's time we thought more about what we want. It is of course true, and I have not forgotten, that our interests are neither unitary nor consensual, nor are they themselves free of the network of interactions that make science "work": Wanting, knowing, and doing are *all* mutually implicated. Nevertheless, there may still be *something* that grounds this entire process, a point on which the convergence of our interests might be said to be obligatory—and that is on the matter of survival. After all, for whom or for what can a science that provides tools powerful enough to destroy even their own makers be said to work?

Notes

1. Indeed, feminist criticism itself provides us with ways of thinking about other meanings of control that may be extremely useful for undermining this simplistic dichotomy. A metaphor that I find particularly useful comes from parenting: No one would suggest that a loving parent ought to be content to simply "look," disavowing all attempts to shape and control. At the same time, attempts at forms of control that are too rigid or too intrusive are also understood to be counterproductive, if not actually destructive. I suggest that the work of "mothering," performed either by mothers or fathers (see, for example, Ruddick 1989), provides a promising metaphor for thinking about alternative relations between scientific knowledge and effective action.
2. For example, physics is not an obviously applicable model even for the biological sciences, much less for the human sciences. An adequate account of its historical preeminence—of why the explanations of the universe that physics offers have seemed so extraordinarily satisfying—would surely require attention to the social and rhetorical dynamics that have helped to sustain it.
3. The beginnings of such an account is attempted in Keller (1990), reprinted in Kay (1992).
4. See, for example, Robert Proctor (1991) for a fuller discussion of the history of the idea of "pure science."
5. The figures cited here are taken from Forman (1987).

6. For an example of how this duality was argued in practice, consider Columbia University's proposal to the Office of Naval Research for support of an "Ultra-high energy machine." It read: "The whole field of nuclear physics and nuclear energy is based on a rather scanty theoretical foundation. . . . One must be prepared for the most extraordinary surprises such as came about through the discovery of nuclear fission. No real security can exist until this whole field of nuclear and high energy phenomena are understood as well as electromagnetic phenomena" (quoted in Forman 1987, n. 132, p. 222).
7. See also A. T. Friedman and C. C. Donley (1985) for discussion of this juxtaposition.
8. With this logic, responsibility is shifted ever outward, from the pure scientist responsible only for "knowledge," to the engineers who make the weapons, and finally, to the politicians who choose to use them. As Richard Rhodes (author of the widely acclaimed new history of the atomic bomb) has written:
   Science is sometimes blamed for the nuclear dilemma. Such blame confuses the messenger with the message. Otto Hahn and Fritz Strassmann did not invent nuclear fission; they discovered it. It was there all along waiting for us, the turn of the screw. If the bomb seems brutal and scientists criminal for assisting at its birth, consider: would anything less absolute have convinced institutions capable of perpetrating the First and Second World Wars . . . to cease and desist? (1986:784)
9. Soddy inspired the term "atomic bomb." He wrote: "If it could be tapped and controlled what an agent it would be in shaping the world's destiny! The man who put his hand on the lever by which a parsimonious nature regulates so jealously the output of this store of energy would possess a weapon by which he could destroy the earth if he chose" (from Rhodes, 1986 p. 44). Although neither Rutherford nor Soddy thought such an eventuality likely (Rutherford later called it "moonshine," and Soddy consoled himself with trust in nature ["We may trust Nature to guard her secret"]), H. G. Wells apparently thought Nature rather less trustworthy. In 1914 he published his vision of global atomic war (*The World Set Free*), set in the year 1956. Nineteen years later, stimulated by his reading of Wells, Szilard contrived his scheme for a chain reaction.
10. The influence of his letter has itself been popularly overestimated. At least equally important was the train of events set into motion by the calculations of Peierls and Frisch, and the memo they and

Oliphant sent to the Tizard Committee in early 1940 (see Rhodes 1986).

11. As well, I would add, as what counts as knowledge. For both Hacking's notion of "forms" of scientific knowledge and my own, the important point is their inherent directionality.

12. We cannot look to scientists themselves for an answer to this question because for the most part they do not, perhaps even cannot, know. I recall, for example, my own work as a newly vintaged theoretical physicist on a problem I saw as being of purely theoretical interest (Keller 1965). Only many years later—and only by reading historical accounts such as Forman's (1987)—did I learn, to my utter astonishment, that the problem had not only arisen from the needs of laser physics, but also that its solution might possibly even have contributed to the subsequent development of laser weapons.

13. Paul Forman may be speaking for his entire generation when he describes his own response to Hunter Dupree's call of twenty-five years ago as "fascinated but fearful," a fascination itself "rigidly clamped between attraction and repugnance." MacKenzie, however, goes considerably further, suggesting "a form of intellectual treachery" (1986:363).

14. Suggesting, perhaps, that neither the history, philosophy, nor sociology of science are any more immune to socio-political interests than are the natural sciences themselves.

References

Dennis, M. A. "Accounting for Research: New Histories of Corporate Laboratories and the Social History of American Science." *Social Studies of Science* 17:479–518, 1987.

Dupree, A. H. "Government and Science in an Age of Scientific Revolution," *Science* 135:1119–21, 1962.

Forman, P. "Behind Quantum Electronics: National Security as a Basis for Physical Research in the United States, 1940–1960," 1987.

Friedman, A. T. and C. C. Donley. *Einstein as Myth and Muse*. Cambridge: Cambridge Univ. Press, 1985.

Geertz, C. *The Interpretation of Cultures*. Basic Books, 1973.

Hacking, I. "Weapons Research and the Form of Scientific Knowledge." *Canadian Journal of Philosophy*, Supp. Vol. 12:237–60, 1987.

Hollis, M. and S. Lukes. *Rationality and Relativism*. Cambridge, MA: MIT Press, 1982.

Kay, L. *The Molecular Vision of Life*. Cambridge: Cambridge Univ. Press, 1992.

Keller, E. F. "Physics and the Emergence of Molecular Biology." *J. Hist. Biol.* 23(3): 389–409, 1990.

Keller, E. F. "Statistics of the Thermal Radiation Field." *Physical Review* 139, 1B, B202, 1965.

Knorr-Cetina, K. and M. Mulkay, eds. *Science Observed: Perspectives on the Social Study of Science*. London and Los Angeles: Sage, 1983.

Latour, B. "Give Me a Laboratory and I Will Raise the World." In *Science Observed: Perspectives on the Social Study of Science*, ed. K. Knorr-Cetina and M. Mulkay, pp. 141–87. London and Los Angeles: Sage, 1983.

MacKenzie, D. "Science and Technology Studies and the Question of the Military." *Social Studies of Science* 16:361–71, 1986.

Marcuse, H. *One-Dimensional Man*. Boston: Beacon Press, 1964.

Markus, G. "Why Is There No Hermeneutics of the Natural Sciences?" *Science in Context* 1(1): 5–51, 1987.

Proctor, R. *Value Free Science? Purity and Power in Modern Knowledge*. Cambridge: Harvard Univ. Press, 1991.

Rhodes, R. *The Making of the Atomic Bomb*. New York: Simon and Schuster, 1986.

Ruddick, S. *Maternal Thinking*. Boston: Beacon Press, 1989.

MICHAEL R. GARDNER

Realism and Instrumentalism in Pre-Newtonian Astronomy

Introduction

There is supposed to be a problem in the philosophy of science called "realism versus instrumentalism." In the version with which I am concerned, this supposed problem is whether scientific theories in general are put forward as true, or whether they are put forward as untrue, but nonetheless convenient devices for the prediction (and retrodiction) of observable phenomena.

I have argued elsewhere (1979) that this problem is misconceived. Whether a theory is put forward as true or merely as a device depends on various aspects of the theory's structure and content, and on the nature of the evidence for it. I illustrated this thesis with a discussion of the nineteenth-century debates about the atomic theory. I argued that the atomic theory was initially regarded by most of the scientific community as a set of false statements useful for the deduction and systematization of the various laws regarding chemical combination, thermal phenomena, etc.; and that a gradual transition occurred in which the atomic theory came to be regarded as a literally true picture of matter. I claimed, moreover, that the historical evidence shows that this transition occurred because of increases in the theory's proven predictive power; because of new determinations of hitherto indeterminate magnitudes through the use of measurement results and well-tested hypotheses; and because of changes in some scientists' beliefs about what concepts may appear in fundamental explanations. I posed it as a problem in that paper whether the same or similar factors might be operative in other cases in the history of science; and I suggested that it might be possible, on the basis of an examination of several cases

From Sections 1, 8, 9, 10, and 11 of "Realism and Instrumentalism in Pre-Newtonian Astronomy" by Michael Gardner, in *Testing Scientific Theories*, John Earman, Ed., *Minnesota Studies in the Philosophy of Science*, Vol. X © 1983 Minneapolis: University of Minnesota, pp. 201–202, 237–265. Used by permission.

in which the issue of realistic vs. instrumental acceptance of a theory has been debated, to put forward a (normative) theory of when it is reasonable to accept a theory as literally true and when as only a convenient device.

For simplicity I shall usually speak of the acceptance-status of a theory as a whole. But sometimes it will be helpful to discuss individual hypotheses within a theory, when some are to be taken literally and others as conceptual devices.

In the present paper I would like to discuss a closely analogous case—the transition, during the Copernican revolution, in the prevailing view of the proper purpose and correlative mode of acceptance of a theory of the planetary motions. I shall briefly discuss the evidence—well known to historians—that from approximately the time of Ptolemy until Copernicus, most astronomers held that the purpose of planetary theory is to permit the calculations of the angles at which the planets appear from the earth at given times, and not to describe the planets' true orbits in physical space. For a few decades after Copernicus's death, except among a handful of astronomers, his own theory was accepted (if at all) as only the most recent and most accurate in a long series of untrue prediction-devices. But eventually the Copernican theory came to be accepted as the literal truth, or at least close to it. That this transition occurred is well known; why it occurred has not been satisfactorily explained, as I shall try to show. I shall then try to fill in this gap in the historical and philosophical literature. In the concluding section I shall also discuss the relevance of this case to theses, other than the one just defined, which go by the name "realism." . . .

The Instrumentalist Reception of Copernicanism

In the half-century or so after the publication of *De Revolutionibus*, Copernicus's theory was widely perceived as an improvement upon Ptolemy's in regard to observational accuracy and theoretical adequacy, and yet was almost universally regarded as untrue or at best highly uncertain (Kuhn 1957, pp. 185–188; Westman 1972a, pp. 234–236). A concise expression of instrumental acceptance occurs in an astronomical textbook of 1594 by Thomas Blundeville: "Copernicus . . . affirmeth that the earth turneth about and that the sun standeth still in the midst of the heavens, by help of which false supposition he hath made truer demonstrations of the motions and revolutions of the celestial spheres, than ever were made before" (quoted in Johnson 1937, p. 207).

Crucial in promoting this point of view, especially in the leading German universities, was a group of astronomers led by Phillipp Melanchthon (1497–1560) of the University of Wittenberg. Generally speaking, their opinion was that Copernicus's theory was credible primarily just in regard to its determinations of observed angles; that it was preferable to Ptolemy's in that it eschewed the abhorrent equant[1]; but that the new devices needed to be transformed into a geostatic frame of reference, since the earth does not really move (Westman 1975a, pp. 166–167). For example, Melanchthon praised parts of Copernicus's theory in 1549 for being "so beautifully put together" and used some of his data, but held that the theory must be rejected on a realistic interpretation because it conflicts with Scripture and with the Aristotelian doctrine of motion (Westman 1975a, p. 173). Similarly, Melanchthon's distinguished disciple Erasmus Reinhold was plainly more impressed by the fact that "we are liberated from an equant by the assumption of this [Copernican] theory" (as Rheticus had put it in Rosen 1959, p. 135) than by the theory's revolutionary cosmology. On the title page of his own copy of *De Revolutionibus*, Reinhold wrote out Copernicus's principle of uniform motion in red letters. And in his annotations he consistently singled out for summary and comment Copernicus's accomplishments in eliminating the equant, because of which (he said) "the science of the celestial motions was almost in ruins; the studies and works of this author have restored it." Thus Reinhold saw Copernicus entirely as the reactionary thinker he in some respects was, returning astronomy to its true foundations on uniform circular motions. In contrast, the paucity of Reinhold's annotations on the cosmological arguments of Book I indicates little interest, and in an unpublished commentary on Copernicus's work he maintained a neutral stance on the question of whether the earth really moves. But there was no doubt in his mind that Copernicus's geometric constructions provided a superior basis for computing planetary positions, and the many users of Reinhold's *Prutenic Tables* (1551) found out he was right, whatever their own cosmological views (Westman 1975a, pp. 174–178).

An especially influential advocate of instrumental acceptance in our sense—i.e., with an explicit denial of truth—of the Copernican theory was Caspar Peucer, Melanchthon's successor as rector at Wittenberg. Like his predecessor and mentor, Peucer used Copernican values for various parameters, but denied the theory's truth on Scriptural and Aristotelian physical grounds in his popular textbook of 1553. He also suggested in 1568 that if certain parts of Copernicus's theory were reformulated in a geostatic frame, "then I believe that the same [effects] would be achieved without having to change the ancient hypotheses" (quoted in Westman 1975a, pp. 178–181).

We have already seen one reason why the Wittenberg school refused to grant realistic acceptance to the Copernican theory: namely, that on a realistic interpretation the theory conflicts with Aristotelian physics and with Holy Scripture. (. . . [A] parallel argument from Aristotelian physics had often been given against a realistically interpreted Ptolemaic theory.) But let us consider whether something else was involved as well. Westman makes some intriguing suggestions about this:

. . . what the Wittenberg interpretation *ignored* was as important as that which it either asserted or denied. In the writings both public and private of nearly every author of the generation which first received the work of Copernicus, the new analysis of the relative *linear* distances of the planets is simply passed over in silence. . . . questions about the Copernican ordering of the planets were not seen as important topics of investigation. In annotated copies of *De Revolutionibus* which are datable from the period *circa* 1543–1570, passages in Book I extolling the newly discovered harmony of the planets and the eulogy to the sun, with its Hermetic (magical) implications, were usually passed over in silence (Westman 1975a, pp. 167, 181). . . .

Although Westman deserves our thanks for pointing this out, he makes no effort to explain why a lack of interest in Copernicus's planetary harmony and distances was associated with a witholding of realistic acceptance. Can we get any deeper? Consider first the question of distances, deferring that of harmony. In another paper (1979) I argued that a principle P operative in the nineteenth-century debates about the reality of atoms was that *it is an objection to the acceptance of a theory on a realistic interpretation that it contains or implies the existence of indeterminate quantities.* . . . [T]his principle played at least some role in astronomy: Ptolemy's theory had indeterminate planetary distances and tended to be refused realistic acceptance. One might well wonder, however, how this principle could explain refusal to accept the literal truth of Copernicus's theory, since he did make the planetary distances determinate. The answer appeals to a variant of P called P': *Persons who either reject or ignore a theory's determinations of magnitudes from measurements via its hypotheses will tend to refuse it realistic acceptance.* P', though not precisely a corollary of P, is plausible given P: Someone who rejects a theory's magnitude-determinations is likely to do so because he regards the hypotheses used as not well tested and hence regards the magnitudes as indeterminate; and someone who ignores the determinations is unaware of someone who ignores the determinations is unaware of some of the support for realistic acceptance. Principle P' certainly fits the behavior as described by Westman of the first-generation response to Copernicus, especially among the Wittenberg group.

It also fits Johannes Praetorius (1537–1616), who studied astronomy at Wittenberg and later taught there and elsewhere. He expressed his instrumental acceptance of the Copernican theory as follows in a manuscript begun in 1592:

> Now, just as everyone approves the calculations of Copernicus (which are available to all through Erasmus Reinhold under the title *Prutenic Tables*), so everyone clearly abhors his hypotheses on account of the multiple motion of the earth. . . . we follow Ptolemy, in part, and Copernicus, in part. That is, if one retains the suppositions of Ptolemy, one achieves the same goal that Copernicus attained with his new constructions (Westman 1975b, p. 293).

Like others associated with Wittenberg, Praetorius was most impressed by the improvements in observational accuracy over Ptolemy and even over Copernicus himself, that were achieved by Reinhold on Copernican assumptions, and by Copernicus's elimination of the "absurd" equant. But unlike the first generation at his school, he paid careful attention to Copernicus's determinations of the planetary distances and to his evocations of the planetary system's "harmony" or "symmetry" (i.e., unified overall structure) that the new theory makes evident. Thus in lectures written in 1594 he listed Copernicus's values for the planetary distances and remarked about them: "this symmetry of all the orbs appears to fit together with the greatest consonance so that nothing can be inserted between them and no space remains to be filled. Thus, the distance from the convex orb of Venus to the concave orb of Mars takes up 730 earth semidiameters, in which space the great orb contains the moon and earth and moving epicycles"[2] (quotations etc. in Westman 1975b, pp. 298–299).

Another point emerges from this quotation: Praetorius evidently followed the tradition of thinking of the planets as moving on solid spheres. This assumption created difficulties for him when he attempted to transform Copernicus's system into a geostatic one. For he found that using Copernicus's distances, "there would occur a great confusion of orbs (especially with Mars). . . . because it would then occupy not only the Sun's orb but also the great part of Venus'. . . ." Since intersections of the spheres are impossible, he argued, Copernicus's distances "simply cannot be allowed." He therefore roughly doubled the distance to Saturn, on the ground that there will still be plenty of distance to the stars, and claimed that with that done, "nothing prohibits us . . . from making Mars' orb greater so that it will not invade the territory of the Sun." (Westman 1975b, p. 298) Plainly, on Praetorius's version of the Copernican theory, the planetary distances are indeterminate: they are set through entirely theoretical considerations regarding the relative sizes of the spheres, instead of being computed from observational data via well-tested hypotheses. Because he rejected Copernicus's determinations of the distances, it is in accord with principle P' that he rejected Copernicus's theory on a realistic interpretation. And since the distances are indeterminate (even though specified) on his own theory, it is in accordance with our principle P that he granted instrumental acceptance to his own astronomical theory, since he refused realistic acceptance to any:

. . . the astronomer is free to devise or imagine circles, epicycles and similar devices although they might not exist in nature. . . . The astronomer who endeavors to discuss the truth of the positions of these or those bodies acts as a Physicist and not as an astronomer—and, in my opinion, he arrives at nothing with certainty (Westman 1975b, p. 303).

This quotation reveals that Praetorius was influenced by two additional factors . . . counting against realistic acceptance of an astronomical theory. One is that *the theory is independent of physics*: that it is either outside the domain of physics, or if literally interpreted is inconsistent with the true principles of physics. (. . . Ptolemy, who seems sometimes to have been thinking of parts of his theory as mere devices, held to the first kind of independence; and . . . Proclus used the second as an argument against realistic acceptance of a Ptolemaic theory.) The second factor influencing Praetorius was the argument, also found in Proclus and others, that no realistically interpreted astronomical theory can be known to be true.

Another argument . . . found in the pre-Copernican period (e.g., in Proclus) against realistic acceptance of any planetary theory was that alternative systems of orbits may be compatible with the appearances; and that no particular system, therefore, can be asserted as literally true. A strengthened version of principle *P*—no theory *T* containing indeterminate quantities should receive realistic acceptance—is closely related to Proclus's principle, since various settings of the indeterminate parameters in *T* would in some cases produce various alternative theories equally compatible with the data. But although the notion that indeterminate quantities count against realistic acceptance continued to play a role in post-Copernican astronomy, Proclus's principle came under attack and seems not to have played much (if any) role in the thinking of instrumentally Copernican astronomers. For

example, the influential Jesuit astronomer Christopher Clavius wrote in 1581 that it is not enough merely to speculate that there *may* be some other method than ours of accounting for the celestial appearances. For the argument to have any force, our opponents must actually produce the alternative. And if it turns out to be a "more convenient way [specifically, of dealing with the appearances] . . . we shall be content and will give them very hearty thanks." But failing such a showing, we are justified in believing that the best theory we actually have (Ptolemy's, he thought) is "highly probable"; for the use of Proclus's principle would destroy not just realistically interpreted astronomy, but all of natural philosophy: "If they cannot show us some better way, they certainly ought to accept this way, inferred as it is from so wide a variety of phenomena; unless in fact they wish to destroy . . . Natural Philosophy. . . . For as often as anyone inferred a certain cause from its observable effects, I might say to him precisely what they say to us—that forsooth it may be possible to explain those effects by some cause as yet unknown to us" (Blake 1960, pp. 31–37). Although this gets us ahead of and even beyond our story, eventually a principle very much like Clavius's appeared as Newton's fourth rule of reasoning in philosophy:

> *In experimental philosophy we are to look upon propositions inferred by general induction from phenomena as accurately or very nearly true, notwithstanding any contrary hypotheses that may be imagined, till such time as other phenomena occur by which they may either be made more accurate, or liable to exceptions.*
> This rule we must follow, that the argument of induction may not be evaded by hypotheses (Newton 1934, p. 400).

Newton's rule is a stronger critical tool than Clavius's, since even if the alternative "hypothesis" is actually produced (but, by definition of "hypothesis," not by deduction from phenomena), Newton refused it consideration, whereas

Clavius might even have preferred it if it proved to be more convenient, or better in accord with physics and Scripture.

Clavius thought that although Copernicus's theory was approximately as accurate as Ptolemy's, it was false because it conflicted with physics and Scripture. So he accorded the Copernican theory instrumental acceptance, and the Ptolemaic theory realistic acceptance as an approximation. In addition to consistency with physics and Scripture, he used one other consideration in favor of realistic acceptance which, I have argued elsewhere (1979), was also operative in the nineteenth-century atomic debates. It is progressiveness—i.e., the power of a theory to inform us of "novel" facts, of facts the theory's inventor did not know at the time of the invention. (See my 1982 paper on this definition of "novel.") Thus Clavius argued in favor of a realistic acceptance of Ptolemy's theory:

> But by the assumption of Eccentric[3] and Epicyclic spheres not only are all the appearances already known accounted for, but also future phenomena are predicted, the time of which is altogether unknown: thus, if I am in doubt whether, for example, the full moon will be eclipsed in September, 1583, I shall be assured by calculation from the motions of the Eccentric and Epicyclic spheres, that the eclipse will occur, so that I shall doubt no further. . . . it is incredible that we force the heavens (but we seem to force them, if the Eccentrics and Epicycles are figments, as our adversaries will have it) to obey the figments of our minds and to move as we will or in accordance with our principles (Blake 1960, p. 34).

Here we have as clear an example as could be desired of an explicit distinction being made between realistic and instrumental acceptance, and of progressiveness being used to decide between them.

The instrumentally Copernican astronomers discussed so far—i.e., astronomers who pre-ferred Copernican angle-determinations but thought the theory needed a geostatic transformation—either ignored or rejected Copernicus's determinations of the planets' distances. But this is not true of the most famous of their group, Tycho Brahe. Like the members of the Wittenberg circle, with whom he had extensive contact, Tycho wrote in 1574 that although Copernicus "considered the course of the heavenly bodies more accurately than anyone else before him" and deserved further credit for eliminating the "absurd" equant, still "he holds certain [theses] contrary to physical principles, for example, . . . that the earth . . . move(s) around the Sun. . . ." He therefore invented his own system, which was essentially Copernicus's subjected to a transformation that left the earth stationary, the sun in orbit around it, and the other planets on moving orbits centered at the sun. Having become convinced that there are no solid spheres carrying the planets, since the comets he had observed would have to penetrate them, he did not share Praetorius's motivation of altering the Copernican distances, and therefore retained them (Westman 1975b, pp. 305–313, 329; see Kuhn 1957, pp. 201–204).

Now the case of Tycho may seem to be anomalous from the standpoint of principles P and P': For Tycho accorded Copernicus's theory only instrumental acceptance, and yet neither ignored nor rejected Copernicus's determinations of the planetary distances. He would have conceded that these quantities were determinate, since he knew they could be computed from observations and certain of Copernicus's hypotheses on the *relative* positions of the planets, hypotheses that Tycho accepted and regarded as well tested. But this objection to P ignores its implicit ceteris paribus clause: P requires only that the determinateness of a theory's quantities should count in favor of realistic acceptance, and that indeterminateness should count against; there may nonetheless be countervailing considerations. Tycho's reasoning is entirely in accord with this notion. In one of his own copies of *De Revolutionibus*, Tycho underlined the passage . . . in which Copernicus stated that his theory links together the planetary distances, and commented on the passage: "The reason for the revival and establishment of the Earth's motion." And next to the passage . . . in which Copernicus spoke of the "symmetry of the universe" made evident by explaining so many varied phenomena in terms of the earth's motion, Tycho wrote: "The testimonies of the planets, in particular, agree precisely with the Earth's motion and thereupon the hypotheses assumed by Copernicus are strengthened" (Westman 1975b, p. 317). Despite these favorable remarks, Tycho rejected the Copernican theory on the sorts of grounds with which we are now familiar: that it conflicts with Scripture, physical theory, and certain observational data—specifically, Tycho's failure to detect the annual stellar parallax[4] entailed by the earth's motion, and the relatively large apparent sizes of the stars given the great distances entailed by the undetectability of parallax (Dreyer 1953, pp. 360–361). Although these considerations prevailed in his mind, it is still plain from the marginal notes just quoted that in accordance with principle *P* he counted it in favor of realistic acceptance of the hypothesis of the earth's motion that it made the planetary distances determinate and also (a point not yet discussed in this context) that *it satisfies Copernicus's principle of variety of evidence.* . . .

That variety of evidence (metaphorically, "symmetry" or "harmony") counted in favor of realistic acceptance is also indicated by Westman's remark that in the period of instrumental acceptance of Copernicus's theory his remarks on harmony tended to be ignored.

We can sum up our discussion of the instrumental acceptance of the Copernican theory by listing the factors that, in the immediately post-Copernican period, were counted in favor of, or whose absence was counted against, acceptance on a realistic interpretation:

On such an interpretation, the theory

1. satisfies the laws of physics,
2. is consistent with other putative knowledge (e.g., the Scriptures),
3. is consistent with all observational data,
4. contains only determinate quantities,
5. is able to predict novel facts,
6. has a central hypothesis supported by a large variety of evidence,
7. is within the realm of possible human knowledge.

Failing any of (1)–(3), a theory (if we assume it is still a convenient prediction-device in a certain domain) will tend to be accorded instrumental acceptance (with denial of truth). Supposed failure of (4)–(7) leads only to scepticism regarding truth.

We can now turn to those who accepted the Copernican theory on a realistic interpretation. If the foregoing is correct and complete, we should not find anything new.

Realistic Acceptance of Copernicanism

. . . [T]he first person to accept the Copernican theory as literally true was Copernicus himself. . . . [H]e argued explicitly that his theory satisfies the laws of physics, makes the planetary distances determinate, and has a central hypothesis supported by a wide variety of evidence. He also mentioned no observational data inconsistent with his theory, and implied in his prefatory letter to the Pope that Scripture conflicts with his theory only if "wrongly twisted." Since these considerations were all "in the air" in Copernicus's period as counting in favor of realistic acceptance, I think it is plausible to regard them as his reasons, although he did not make this more obvious by citing them in the context of an explicit distinction between realistic vs. instrumental acceptance.

The second astronomer to give realistic acceptance to Copernicanism was undoubtedly Georg Joachim Rheticus. He left Wittenberg to live and study with Copernicus (from 1539 to 1541), during which time he became familiar with the still unpublished Copernican theory. In 1540 he published *Narratio Prima*, the first printed account of the new theory of "my teacher," as he called Copernicus. In this work he nowhere indicated that he thought the theory to be just a convenient device. Moreover, he claimed (falsely) for unspecified reasons that at least some aspects of the Copernican theory could not be subjected to the sort of geostatic transformation (permitting instrumental acceptance) favored by others associated with Wittenberg: "I do not see how the explanation of precession[5] is to be transferred to the sphere of stars" (Rosen 1959, pp. 4–5, 10, 164). Finally, in two copies of *De Revolutionibus* he crossed out Osiander's preface with red pencil or crayon (Gingerich 1973c, p. 514). So it is obvious enough that his acceptance was realistic.

But why? First, he thought the theory is consistent with the most important relevant law of physics—uniform circularity of celestial motion—and all observational data:

> . . . you see that here in the case of the moon we are liberated from an equant by the assumption of this theory, which, moreover, corresponds to experience and all the observations. My teacher dispenses with equants for the other planets as well . . . (Rosen 1959, p. 135).
> . . . my teacher decided that he must assume such hypotheses as would contain causes capable of confirming the truth of the observations of previous centuries, and such as would themselves cause, we may hope, all future astronomical predictions of the phenomena to be found true (Rosen 1959, pp. 142–143).

It is somewhat puzzling that Copernicus's repudiation of the equant was a basis for both realistic and instrumental acceptance. The explanation is perhaps that his principle of uniformity can be thought of as an aesthetic virtue of a calculation-device—it is "pleasing to the mind" (Copernicus, in Rosen 1959, p. 57)—or as a physical principle (Copernicus 1976, Book I, chapter 4).

In the last quotation from Rheticus, he invoked the criterion of progressiveness (5), since he implied that the predictions were not known to be correct on some other ground (such as simple induction). He also contrasted the Copernican and Ptolemaic hypotheses in regard to the determinateness of planetary distances:

> . . . what dispute, what strife there has been until now over the position of the spheres of Venus and Mercury, and their relation to the sun. . . . Is there anyone who does not see that it is very difficult and even impossible ever to settle this question while the common hypotheses are accepted? For what would prevent anyone from locating even Saturn below the sun, provided that at the same time he preserved the mutual proportions of the spheres and epicycle, since in these same hypotheses there has not yet been established the common measure of the spheres of the planets. . . .
> However, in the hypotheses of my teacher, . . . (t)heir common measure is the great circle which carries the earth . . . (Rosen 1959, pp. 146–147).

It will be noted that Rheticus ignored the nesting-shell hypothesis[6] and took the Ptolemaic distances as entirely unspecified. Finally, Rheticus argued that Copernicus's central hypothesis that the earth moves was supported by a wide variety of evidence—specifically, the apparent motions of the five visible planets. "For all these phenomena appear to be linked most nobly together, as by golden chain; and each of the planets, by its position and order and every inequality of its motion, bears witness that the earth moves . . ." (Rosen 1959, p. 165). God arranged the universe thus "lest any of the motions attributed to the earth should seem to be supported by insufficient evidence" (Rosen 1959, p. 161). Rheticus, then, appealed to criteria (1), (3), (4), (5), and (6) for realistic acceptance—criteria, I have argued, that were widely accepted in his period. . . .

We find realistic acceptance and reasoning similar to that of Copernicus and Rheticus in another early Copernican, Michael Mästlin (1550–1631), whose support was crucial because of the pro-Copernican influence Mästlin exerted on his student Kepler. In his annotations of a copy of De Revolutionibus, which are consistently approving of Copernicus, he complained that Osiander's preface had made the mistake of "shattering [astronomy's] foundations" and suffered from "much weakness in his meaning and reasoning." This indicates that his acceptance was realistic. Commenting on Copernicus's attempts in Book I of De Revolutionibus to answer Ptolemy's physical arguments against the earth's motion, he wrote: "He resolves the objections which Ptolemy raises in the Almagest, Book I, chapter 7." So he evidently thought the Copernican theory satisfied the laws of physics. Finally, referring to Copernicus's arguments from determinateness of distances and variety of evidence, he wrote: "Certainly this is the great argument, viz. that all the phenomena as well as the order and magnitude of the orbs are bound together in the motion of the earth. . . . moved by this argument I approve of the opinions and hypotheses of Copernicus" (Quoted in Westman 1975b, pp. 329–334). Mästlin's realistic acceptance, then, was based at least on criteria (1), (4), and (6).

Kepler

The trend toward realistic acceptance of a heliostatic theory culminated in the work of Kepler. As Duhem wrote, "the most resolute and illustrious representative [of the realistic tradition of Copernicus and Rheticus] is, unquestionably, Kepler" (1960, p. 100). Kepler was quite explicit in making the distinction between realistic and instrumental acceptance of astronomical theories in general and of Copernicus's in particular, and explicit in saying where he stood on these issues. Not only Osiander, but Professor Petrus Ramus of the University of Paris, had asserted that Copernicus's theory used hypotheses that were false. Ramus wrote: "The fiction of hypotheses is absurd . . . would that Copernicus had rather put his mind to the establishing of an astronomy without hypotheses." And he offered his chair at Paris "as the prize for an astronomy constructed without hypotheses." Kepler wrote in his Astronomia Nova of 1609 that had Ramus not died in the meantime, "I would of good right claim [his chair] myself, or for Copernicus." He also indignantly revealed that Osiander was the author of the anonymous preface to De Revolutionibus and asserted: "I confess it a most absurd play to explain the processes of nature by false causes, but there is no such play in Copernicus, who indeed himself did believe his hypotheses true . . . nor did he only believe, but also proved them true" (Blake 1960, p. 43). Kepler intended to proceed in the same realistic spirit: "I began this work declaring that I would found astronomy not upon fictive hypotheses, but upon physical causes" (Quoted in Westman 1971, p. 128). Astronomy "can easily do without the useless furniture of fictitious circles and spheres" (Kepler 1952, p. 964). In taking such a view Kepler was consciously aware of contributing to a revolution not only in the prevailing theories in astronomy but also in the prevailing view of the field's purposes. He described his work as involving "the unexpected transfer of the whole of astronomy from fictitious circles to natural causes, which were the most profound to investigate, difficult to explain, and difficult to calculate, since mine was the first attempt" (quoted in Gingerich 1973d, p. 304).

According to Kuhn, disagreement over the problems, aims, and methods of a field is one of the things that makes competing schools "incommensurable"—i.e., makes arguments for either of them circular, the choice a matter of "faith" or a "conversion experience" based, sometimes, on "personal and inarticulate aesthetic considerations" rather than on "rational" argument (1970, pp. 41, 94, 51, 158). But in fact Kepler did present rational (if not always decisive) arguments for the shift in astronomical aims that he advocated, grounds for asserting that these aims could and should be achieved. Most of these grounds were neither inarticulate nor merely personal, but were explicitly stated attempts to show that a heliostatic theory could meet the widely used criteria for realistic acceptance.

We saw [p. 416] that one such criterion, in this historical period and others, is progressiveness—prediction of novel facts. Thus we are not surprised to find Kepler arguing as follows in his *Mysterium Cosmographicum* (1596) for an essentially Copernican theory—i.e., one that has the planets somehow orbiting a stationary sun:

> My confidence was upheld in the first place by the admirable agreement between his conceptions and all [the objects] which are visible in the sky; an agreement which not only enabled him to establish earlier motions going back to remote antiquity, but also to predict future [phenomena], certainly not with absolute accuracy, but in any case much more exactly than Ptolemy, Alfonso, and other astronomers (quoted in Koyré, 1973, p. 129).

Kepler (*ibid*, p. 133) also echoed Copernicus's and Rheticus's appeals to criterion (6), well-testedness: "Nature likes simplicity and unity. Nothing trifling or superfluous has ever existed: and very often, one single cause is destined by itself to [produce] several effects. Now, with the traditional hypotheses there is no end

to the invention [of circles]; with Copernicus, on the other hand, a large number of motions is derived from a small number of circles" (1973, p. 133). As Koyré pointed out, this claim about numbers of circles is an overstatement which had become traditional among Copernicus and his followers. But we can accept the part of this argument alluding to the variety of evidence for the earth's motion.

We also saw [pp. 416–419] that realistic acceptance tended to be associated with belief and interest in the determinate values of the planetary distances that Copernicus's theory and data provided. There can be no doubt that Kepler had both belief and the most intense interest. In 1578 Kepler's teacher Michael Mästlin had published a theory of the motion of the comet of 1577 that asserted that it moved within the heliocentric shell of Venus, a theory that presupposed the Copernican arrangement of the inferior planets and his values for their distances: "I noticed that the phenomena could be saved in no other way than if . . . [the comet's radii] were assumed to be 8420 parts when . . . the semidiameter of the [earth's orbit] is 10,0900; and likewise, when the semidiameter of Venus' eccentric is 7193." Kepler wrote in 1596 that Mästlin's theory that the comet "completed its orbit in the same orb as the Copernican Venus" provided the "most important argument for the arrangement of the Copernican orbs" (quotations in Westman, 1972b, pp. 8, 22). . . .

A corollary of our principle (4) governing realistic acceptance [p. 412] is that a theory's failure to provide any means at all—let alone well-tested hypotheses—to determine some of its parameters counts against realistic acceptance. Kepler appealed to this corollary when he tried to show that Ptolemy believed his theory was more than a prediction-device: "to predict the motions of the planets Ptolemy did not have to consider the order of the planetary spheres, and yet he did so diligently[7] (Kepler, [1984]). Since the hypothesis from which

Ptolemy obtained the order (that it corresponds to increasing orbital period) was entirely untested, I do not say that the order was determinate, but only specified.

We have seen earlier that such writers as Proclus and Praetorius argued against realistic acceptance of any astronomical theory on the grounds that knowledge of the full truth of such a theory exceeds merely human capacities and is attainable only by God. Aware of this traditional instrumentalist argument, Kepler felt obligated to argue on theological grounds that there is no *hubris* in claiming to know the true geometry of the cosmos:

> Those laws [governing the whole material creation] are within the grasp of the human mind; God wanted us to recognize them by creating us after his own image so that we could share in his own thoughts. For what is there in the human mind besides figures and magnitudes? It is only these which we can apprehend in the right way, and . . . our understanding is in this respect of the same kind as the divine . . . (Letter of 1599, in Baumgardt 1951, p. 50).

To supplement his theological arguments, Kepler also attempted to undermine such support as astronomical scepticism received from the unobservability of the planets' orbits in physical space: "But Osiander . . . (i)f [you say that] this art knows absolutely nothing of the causes of the heavenly motions, because you believe only what you see, what is to become of medicine, in which no doctor ever perceived the inwardly hidden cause of a disease, except by inference from the external bodily signs and symptoms which impinge on the senses, just as from the visible positions of the stars the astronomer infers the form of their motion" (Kepler, 1984).

Another epistemological argument we saw was popular among astronomical instrumentalists asserts that since there are, or may be, alternative systems of orbits equally compatible with all observational data, no one system can

be asserted as physically correct. About twenty years after the Ptolemaic astronomer Clavius attacked the argument from observational equivalence, Kepler mounted his own attack from a Copernican viewpoint. First, he argued, sets of hypotheses—some true, some false—which have exactly the same observational consequences are found (if ever) far less frequently than those who use the argument from equivalence suppose:

> In astronomy, it can scarcely ever happen, and no example occurs to me, that starting out from a posited false hypothesis there should follow what is altogether sound and fitting to the motions of the heavens, or such as one wants demonstrated. For the same result is not always in fact obtained from different hypotheses, whenever someone relatively inexperienced thinks it is (Kepler, [1984]).

For example, Kepler argued, Magini attempted (1589) to produce a Ptolemaic theory agreeing with the *Prutenic Tables*, but failed to obtain Copernicus's prediction that Mars has a greater paralax than the sun. Kepler believed that whenever two conflicting hypotheses give the same results for a given range of phenomena, at least one of them can be refuted by deriving observational predictions from it in conjunction with new auxiliary hypotheses:

> "And just as in the proverb liars are cautioned to remember what they have said, so here false hypotheses which together produce the truth by chance, do not, in the course of a demonstration in which they have been applied to many different matters, retain this habit of yielding the truth, but betray themselves" (Kepler, [1984]).

Thus a false hypothesis may occasionally yield a true prediction, but only when it chances to be combined with an auxiliary hypothesis containing a compensatory error, as when Copernicus proposed a lunar latitude and a stellar latitude, both too small by the same amount, and thus obtained a correct prediction for an occultation of the star by the moon (Kepler, 1984). Conjoined with different auxiliary hypotheses, this one on the moon would certainly "betray itself." Kepler was arguing —exactly in accordance with (6) . . .—that we have good reason to accept a hypothesis realistically when it is supported by a variety of phenomena, where this means "in conjunction with many sets of auxiliary hypothesis." Moreover, he appealed to the rationale for this idea . . .—namely, that it reduces the chance of compensatory errors. . . .

When two hypotheses seem to be observationally indistinguishable, one way Kepler thought they could be distinguished is by relating them to what he called "physical considerations": "And though some disparate astronomical hypotheses may yield exactly the same results in astronomy, as Rothmann insisted . . . of his own mutation [geostatic transformation] of the Copernican system, nevertheless a difference arises because of some physical consideration" (Kepler, forthcoming). Physics, in this context, includes dynamics and cosmology—theories of the causes of motion and of the large-scale structure of the universe. . . .

. . . Kepler used physical considerations—specifically, about the causes of planetary motions—to argue in favor of his own theory, which was Copernican in using a moving earth, non-Copernican in using elliptical orbits. In ancient and medieval astronomy the problem of why the planets move had either not arisen, or had been solved in a very simple way. To the extent that hypothesized motions were viewed as mere computation-devices, the problem of explaining them dynamically did not arise. Motions that were considered physically real, such as those of the spheres carrying the stars or planets, were usually explained as due to the spheres' "nature" or to spiritual intelligences attached to them. But Kepler, in part because he thought that God created nothing haphazardly but followed a rational

plan knowable by man, sought to understand why the planets move as the do (Koyré 1973, pp. 120–122).

In accordance with principle (1)—consistency with the laws of physics counts in favor of realistic acceptance—the ideas of physical explanation and realistic interpretation of planetary orbits were intimately connected in Kepler's mind:

> Consider whether I have made a step toward establishing a physical astronomy without hypotheses, or rather, fictions, . . . The force is fixed in the sun, and the ascent and descent of the planets are likewise fixed according to the greater or lesser apparent emanation from the sun. These, therefore, are not hypotheses or (as Ramus calls them) figments, but the very truth, as the stars themselves; indeed, I assume nothing but this (quoted in Gingerich 1975, p. 271).
> . . . Astronomers should not be granted excessive license to conceive anything they please without reason: on the contrary, it is also necessary for you to establish the probable cause of your Hypotheses which you recommend as the true causes of Appearances. Hence, you must first establish the principles of your astronomy in a higher science, namely Physics or Metaphysics . . . (quoted in Westman, 1972a, p. 261).

In addition to the foregoing arguments based on criteria (1) and (4)–(7) . . . for realistic acceptance—criteria that had been used by earlier writers—Kepler formulated two criteria of his own. One of these might be called "explanatory depth": it counts in favor of realistic acceptance of a theory that

(8) it explains facts that competing theories merely postulate.

After asserting the superior accuracy of Copernicus's retrodictions and predictions, Kepler remarked: "Furthermore, and this is much more important, things which arouse our astonishment in the case of other(s) [astronomers] are given a reasonable explanation by Copernicus. . . ." In particular, Ptolemy merely postulated that the deferent motions of the sun, Mercury, and Venus have the same period (one year). Copernicus, in contrast, could explain this equality on the basis of his theory that the planets evolve around the sun. Transformed into an earth-centered system, this theory yields components of the sun's and each planet's motions that are, as Kepler put it, "projections of the earth's proper motion on to the firmament" (quoted in Koyré 1973, pp. 129, 136–137).

Second, Kepler argued that readers of Ptolemy should be astonished that the five planets, but not the sun and moon, show retrograde motion,[8] whereas Copernicus can explain these facts, specifically by saying the five planets have epicycles of such speeds and sizes as to produce retrograde motion but the sun and moon do not. Kepler presumably meant that Copernicus's theory, when transformed geostatically, yields these statements about epicycle. Using Copernicus's figures for the radii and periods of all the planets' heliostatic orbits, one can show that their geostatic transforms will contain combinations of circles producing retrogression. In contrast, the moon, since it shares the earth's heliocentric motion, does not have a component of its geostatic motion that mirrors the earth's orbit and thereby yields retrogression, as does the epicycle of a superior planet. Finally, Kepler argued, since the earth's heliostatic orbit is circular with constant speed, it follows that the sun's geostatic orbit shows no retrogression (Koyré 1973, pp. 136–137).

Kepler's third and fourth points are similar to ones made by Copernicus himself. The third is that Ptolemy postulates but cannot explain the relative sizes of the planets' epicycles, whereas their ratios can be obtained by transforming Copernicus's system into a geostatic one. The fourth is that Ptolemy postulates that,

but does not explain why, the superior planets are at the closest point on their epicycles (and hence brightest) when at opposition with the sun, whereas this fact too results from a geostatic transformation of Copernicus's system.

Kepler sometimes said these four arguments are designed to show Copernicus's theory is preferable to Ptolemy's (Koyré 1973, p. 136), and sometimes to unnamed "other" astronomers' (p. 129). It is worth noting, however, that arguments from explanatory depth do not establish the superiority of Copernicus's system to Tycho's. Either of these can explain anything (regarding relative motions within the solar system) asserted by the other, by means of the appropriate transformation. (This symmetric relation does not hold between Copernicus's theory and Ptolemy's, since a heliostatic transformation of the latter would yield few if any features of the former. For example, the transform would have the planets orbiting a moving earth.) Of all Kepler's arguments, it is only the dynamical ones considered above—that there is a plausible physical explanation why the planets should move around the sun, but not why the sun should move around the earth carrying the other planets' orbits with it—that favor Copernicus's theory over Tycho's.

The last argument by Kepler that I shall consider has a remarkably contemporary ring. One of Ursus's arguments against Tycho had been an induction on the falsity of all previous astronomical theories (Jardine 1979, p. 168). Kepler's reply was that despite the continuing imperfection of astronomical theories, cumulative progress had nonetheless been made at least since Ptolemy. Erroneous in other respects, Ptolemy's theory at least taught us that "the sphere of the fixed stars is furthest away, Saturn, Jupiter, Mars, follow in order, the Sun is nearer than them, and the Moon nearest of all. These things are certainly true. . . ." Tycho taught us at least that "the Sun is the centre of motivation of the five planets," Copernicus that the earth-moon distance varies less than

Ptolemy said, and unspecified astronomers established the "ratios of the diameters of the Earth, Sun and Moon. . . . Given that so many things have already been established in the realm of physical knowledge with the help of astronomy, things which deserve our trust from now on and which are truly so, Ursus' despair is groundless" (Kepler, 1984). Similarly, Kepler argued in favor of Copernicus that he "denied none of the things in the [ancient] hypotheses which give the cause of the appearances and which agree with observations, but rather includes and explains all of them" (quoted in Jardine 1979, pp. 157–158). This last statement is part of Kepler's reply to the objection that Copernicus's theory might be false even though it saves the phenomena.

Clearly, then, Kepler was appealing to a principle we have not previously come across: It counts in favor of realistic acceptance of a theory that

> (9) it agrees with some of the nonobservable claims of some previous theories purporting to explain the same observations.

I say "nonobservational" because the agreed-upon claims Kepler mentioned here were not observable phenomena such as brightness and angular positions, but unobservables such as the planets' orbits. The tacit assumption behind (9) seems to be that if the astronomical theories produced through history were merely a series of devices for predicting observations, there would be relatively little reason to expect them to contain any common nonobservational parts: whereas this is what we would expect if the sequence of principal theories contains a growing set of true descriptions of astronomical reality.

Contemporary Realisms

I said this argument sounds contemporary because it is echoed with little change in an argument Hilary Putnam has recently discussed, attributing it to R. Boyd[9] (forthcoming). According to this argument, a new and better theory in a given field of science usually implies "the *approximate truth of the theoretical laws of the earlier theories in certain circumstances.*" Further, scientists usually require this feature of new theories in part because they believe that (a) the "laws of a theory belonging to a mature science are typically approximately *true*"; and meeting this requirement is fruitful in part because this belief is true (Putnam 1978, pp. 20–21). Like Kepler, then, Boyd thinks that there is a degree of agreement in the nonobservational hypotheses of successive theories in a given field, and that this tends to show that these hypotheses are (partially or approximately) true and are not just prediction-devices. And like Kepler, Putnam (1978, p. 25) thinks that this consideration helps rescue contemporary science from the charge, based on induction from past theories, that it is probably false (1978, p. 25).

Boyd labels as "realism" the conjunction of (a) above with (b): "terms in a mature science typically *refer*" (Putnam 1978, p. 20). This essay is mainly about a quite different thesis also called "realism"—the thesis that *scientific theories in general are put forward as true, and accepted because they are believed to be true.* But we have just seen that our astronomical case study has at least some connection with Boyd's kind of realism as well. I should like to conclude with some remarks about the more general question of the relevance of this case-study to various versions of realism.

Let us call the version of realism I have mainly been discussing "purpose-realism," since it is based on a thesis about the purpose of any scientific theory, and identifies acceptance with belief that that purpose is fulfilled. This is the kind of realism stated (and criticized) by van Fraassen: "*Science aims to give us, in its theories, a literally true story of what the world is like; and acceptance of a scientific theory involves the belief that it is true*" (1980, p. 8). Van Fraassen's own opposing position, which he calls "constructive empiricism," is: "*Science aims to give us theories which are empirically adequate* [true regarding observables]; *and acceptance of a theory involves as belief only that it is empirically adequate.*" Now I claim to have shown above and in my 1979 paper that purpose-realism and constructive empiricism are both over-generalizations, and that each holds for some theories but not others. Neither of the theses stated by van Fraassen can accommodate the extensive historical evidence that scientists sometimes believe that a theory is true and sometimes only that it is empirically adequate, and that there are different sets of grounds for these two beliefs.

Consider now the question whether this case study has any further relevance for Boyd's thesis, which we might call "approximation-realism" because it appeals to the concept of approximate truth. We should note first that approximation-realism is very different from purpose-realism. It is one thing to talk about the purpose of scientific theories and what those who accept them therefore believe, and quite another to say when this aim has to some degree actually been accomplished. That this distinction is nonetheless insufficiently appreciated is clear from the fact that Boyd (1976) puts approximation-realism forward as a rival to an earlier version of van Fraassen's (1976) thesis, which refers to purpose. Another difference between the two theses is that although purpose-realism is sufficiently clear to be refuted, the obscurity of approximation-realism makes its assessment difficult and perhaps impossible. I leave aside the question of what might be meant by a "mature science," and say nothing of the vagueness of "typically." The more difficult question is whether it makes any sense to speak of a law or theory (Boyd 1976) as "approximately true." It certainly makes sense, although the statement is somewhat vague, to say that a particular *value* for a given magnitude is approximately correct—e.g., that "$\theta = 3.28$" is approximately true because in fact $\theta = 3.29$. But speaking of a *law* or *theory* as "approximately true" raises serious problems. Usually a law or theory refers to several

different magnitudes—their values and relations at various times and places. Given two theories, one may be more accurate with respect to some magnitudes, and the other theory more accurate with respect to some others. If this happens, it is quite unclear what it would mean to say that one theory is *on the whole* more accurate than another. Some weights would have to be assigned to the various quantities, and no general way to do this springs readily to mind. It might seem that this problem could be obviated at least in the special case in which, for theories, T_1 and T_2 and *every* common magnitude, T_1's predicted value is never further from (and is sometimes closer to) the true value than T_2's. But Miller (1975) has shown that uniformly greater accuracy in this sense is impossible—at least where the two predictions never lie on different sides of the true value. . . .

I conclude, then, that approximation-realism is too obscure to be assessed and is likely to remain so. (This stricture does not apply to Kepler's somewhat similar view, since he says only that there is a cumulatively growing set of truths upon which the principal astronomers up to any given time have agreed—and this does not presuppose a concept of approximate truth.)

I shall end this essay by considering two final "realistic" theses. Boyd remarks, "What realists really should maintain is that *evidence for a scientific theory* is evidence that both its theoretical claims and its empirical claims are . . . approximately true with respect to certain issues"[10] (Boyd 1976, pp. 633–634). Similarly, Glymour (1976) defines "realism" as "the thesis that to have good reason to believe that a theory is empirically adequate is to have good reason to believe that the entities it postulates are real and, furthermore, that we can and do have such good reasons for some of our theories." (Glymour has in mind van Fraassen's (1976) concept of empirical adequacy: roughly, that all measurement-reports satisfy the theory.) To avoid the difficulties just discussed, I shall ignore Boyd's use of "approximately" and define "empirical realism" as the thesis that *evidence for a theory's empirical adequacy is evidence for its truth.* This claim is logically independent of claims as to which theories are in fact approximately true, or as to what the purpose of science is, although it might have affinities to such claims. . . . I . . . claim to have shown above and in my 1979 paper that a given body of data may be regarded as good evidence for the empirical adequacy but not for the truth of a theory—as when the theory conflicts with physics, contains indeterminate quantities, lacks proven predictive capability, etc.

Perhaps Boyd would not be much bothered by this argument and would say that the main concern of a "realistically"-minded philosopher is to assert the less specific thesis, which I will call "evidential realism," that *we sometimes have evidence that a theory is true (and not just empirically adequate).* I claim to have shown that evidential realism is correct, and moreover to have spelled out at lest some of the reasons—criteria (1)–(9) above, and acceptability of explanatory basis (in my 1979 paper)—that scientists have counted in favor of a theory's truth over very long historical periods. If someone wants to say that what scientists have considered to be reasons are not really reasons, or are not good enough, I can only reply that such a claim clashes with what I take to be one of the purposes of the philosophy of science—to state explicitly, clearly, and systematically the principles of reasoning that have been and are used in actual scientific practice.

Notes

This material is based upon work supported by the National Science Foundation under Grants No. SOC 77-07691 and SOC 78-26194. I am grateful for comments on an earlier draft by Ian Hacking, Geoffrey Hellman, Roger Rosenkrantz, Robert Rynasiewicz and Ferdinand Schoeman.

1. a mathematical device developed to aid in the reconciliation of Ptolemaic astronomy with the results of accurate observation.
2. one of the mathematical devices used to explain the motion of the planets—editor
3. one of the mathematical devices used to explain the motion of the planets—editor
4. apparent motion of the stars over the course of a year—editor
5. precession of the equinoxes, that is, the occurrence of the equinoxes (times when the sun crosses the equator) earlier in each successive year—editor
6. the hypothesis, to the effect that there is no space, no emptiness, between planetary spheres (shells), that Ptolemy used to determine the distances of the planets from the earth—editor
7. I am grateful to Nicholas Jardine for allowing me to see and quote his unpublished draft translation. His final, published version may be different.
8. brief intervals of westward motion that occasionally interrupt the normal eastward motion of the planets—editor
9. I shall assume for the sake of argument that Putnam gives an accurate account of Boyd's thinking, or at least of some stage thereof.
10. From the context, and to avoid triviality, the phrase I have italicized has to be interpreted to mean "instances of (i.e., evidence for) a scientific theory's empirical adequacy."

References

Armitage, Angus, 1962, *Copernicus, The Founder of Modern Astronomy*, New York: A. S. Barnes.

Baumgardt, Carola, 1951, *Johannes Kepler: Life and Letters*, New York: Philosophical Library.

Bernardus de Virduno, 1961, *Tractatus super total Astrologiam*, Werl/Westf: Dietrich-Coelde-Verlag.

Blake, Ralph M., 1960, "Theory of Hypothesis among Renaissance Astronomers," in R. Blake (ed.), *Theories of Scientific Method,*. Seattle: University of Washington Press, pp. 22–49.

Bluck, R. S., 1955, *Plato's Phaedo*, London: Routledge & Kegan Paul.

Boyd, Richard, 1976, "Approximate Truth and Natural Necessity," *Journal of Philosophy*, 73:633–635.

———, Forthcoming. *Realism and Scientific Epistemology* Cambridge: Cambridge University Press.

Carnap, Rudolf. 1956, "The Methodological Character of Theoretical Concepts," *The Foundations of Science and the Concepts of Psychology and Psychoanalysis*, in Herbert Feigl and Michael Scriven (eds.), *Minnesota Studies in the Philosophy of Science*, vol. I. Minneapolis: University of Minnesota Press, pp. 33–76.

Copernicus, Nicolaus, 1976, *On the Revolutions of the Heavenly Spheres*, Trans. Alistair M. Duncan, New York: Barnes & Noble, Orig. ed. 1543.

Cornford, Francis M., 1957, *Plato's Cosmology*, Indianapolis: Bobbs-Merrill.

Dreyer, J. L. E., 1953, *A History of Astronomy from Thales to Kepler*, New York: Dover.

Duhem, Pierre, 1969, *To Save the Phenomena*, Trans. Stanley L. Jaki, Chicago: University of Chicago Press, Orig. ed. 1908.

Gardner, Michael R., 1979, "Realism and Instrumentalism in 19th-Century Atomism," *Philosophy of Science* 46:1–34.

———, 1982, "Predicting Novel Facts," *British Journal for the Philosophy of Science*, 33:1–15.

Gingerich, Owen, 1973a, "Copernicus and Tycho," *Scientific American* 229:87–101.

———, 1973b, "A Fresh Look at Copernicus," *The Great Ideas Today* 1973, Chicago: Encyclopaedia Brittanica, pp. 154–178.

———, 1973c, "From Copernicus to Kepler: Heliocentrism as Model and as Reality," *Proceedings of the American Philosophical Society* 117:513–522.

———, 1973d, Kepler, In *Dictionary of Scientific Biography*, ed. C. C. Gillespie, vol. 7, New York: Scribners, pp. 289–312.

———, 1975, "Kepler's Place in Astronomy," *Vistas in Astronomy*, ed. A. & P. Beer, vol. 18, Oxford: Pergammon, pp. 261–278.

Glymour, Clark, 1976, "To Save the Noumena," *Journal of Philosophy* 73:635–637.

Goldstein, Bernard, 1967, "The Arabic Version of Ptolemy's 'Planetary Hypotheses.'" *Transactions of the American Philosophical Society*, n.s. vol. 57, part 4:3–12.

Hamilton, Edith and Cairns, Huntington, 1963, *The Collected Dialogues of Plato*, New York: Bollinger Foundation.

Hanson, Norwood R., 1973, *Constellations and Conjectures*, Dordrecht: Reidel.

Hutchins, Robert M., 1952, *Great Books of the Western World*, vol. 16, Chicago: Encyclopaedia Britannica.

Jardine, Nicholas. 1979. "The Forging of Modern Realism: Clavius and Kepler against the Sceptics," *Studies in History and Philosophy of Science* 10:141–173.

Johnson, Francis R., 1937. *Astronomical Thought in Renaissance England*, Baltimore: Johns Hopkins Press.

Kepler, Johannes, 1952, *Epitome of Copernican Astronomy*, Trans. C. G. Wallis, Orig. ed. 1618–1621, In Hutchins, 1952, pp. 841–1004.

———, [1984], *A Defense of Tycho against Ursus*, Trans. Nicholas Jardin, Written about 1601.

Koyré, Alexander, 1973, *The Astronomical Revolution*, Trans. R. E. W. Maddison, Ithaca: Cornell University Press, Orig. ed. 1961.

Kuhn, Thomas S., 1957, *The Copernican Revolution*, Cambridge, Mass: Harvard University Press.

———, 1970, *The Structure of Scientific Revolutions*, Chicago: University of Chicago Press.

Lakatos, Imre, 1970, "Falsification and the Methodology of Scientific Research Programmes," In *Criticism and the Growth of Knowledge*, ed. Imre Lakatos and Alan Musgrave, pp. 91–195, London: Cambridge University Press [see this volume pp. 195].

Lakatos, Imre and Zahar, Elie, 1975, *Why Did Copernicus' Research Program Supersede Ptolemy's?* In Westman (1975c), pp. 354–383.

Lloyd, G. E. R., 1978, "Saving the Appearances," *Classical Quarterly* 28:202–222.

Miller, David, 1975, The Accuracy of Predictions, *Synthèse* 30:159–191.

Nagel, Ernest, 1961, *The Structure of Science*, New York: Harcourt, Brace and World.

Neugebauer, Otto, 1952, *The Exact Sciences in Antiquity*, Princeton: Princeton University Press.

Newton, Isaac, 1934, *Mathematical Principles of Natural Philosophy*, Trans. Andrew Motte and Florian Cajori, Berkeley: University of California Press, Orig. ed. 1687.

Pedersen, Olaf, 1974, *A Survey of the Almagest*, Odense: Odense University Press.

Proclus, 1903, *In Platonis Timaeum Commentaria*, Ed. E. Diehl, Leipzig.

———, 1909, *Hypotyposis Astronomicarum Positionum*, Ed. C. Manitius, Leipzig.

Ptolemy, Claudius, 1952, *The Almagest*, Trans. R. C. Taliaferro, In Hutchins 1952, pp. 1–478.

———, 1970. *Planetary Hypotheses*, In *Claudii Ptolemae: opera quae extant omnia, volumen II, opera astronomica minora*, ed. J. L. Heiberg, pp. 69–145, Leipzig: B. G. Teubneri.

Putnam, Hilary, 1978, *Meaning and the Moral Sciences*, London: Routledge & Kegan Paul.

Rosen, Edward, trans, 1959, *Three Copernican Treatises*, New York: Dover.

Rosenkrantz, Roger, 1976, "Simplicity," *Foundations of Probability Theory, Statistical Inference, and Statistical theories of Science*, ed. William A. Harper and C. Hooker, vol. I, pp. 167–203, Dordrecht: Reidel.

Samohursky, Samuel, 1962, *The Physical World of Late Antiquity*, London: Routledge & Kegan Paul.

Shapere, Dudley, 1969, "Notes Towards a Post-Positivistic Interpretation of Science," *The Legacy of Logical Positivism*, ed. Stephen Barker and Peter Achinstein, pp. 115–160, Baltimore: Johns Hopkins Press.

van Fraassen, Bas, 1976, "To Save the Phenomena," *Journal of Philosophy* 73:623–632.

———, 1980, *The Scientific Image*, Oxford: Clarendon.

Vlastos, Gregory, 1975, *Plato's Universe*, Seattle:

University of Washington Press.

Westman, Robert, 1971, *Johannes Kepler's Adoption of the Copernican Hypothesis*, Unpublished doctoral dissertation, Ann Arbor: University of Michigan.

———, 1972a, "Kepler's Theory of Hypothesis and the 'Realist Dilemma.'" *Studies in History and Philosophy of Science* 3:233–264.

———, 1972b, "The Comet and the Cosmos: Kepler, Mästlin and the Copernican Hypothesis," *The Reception of Copernicus' Heliocentric Theory*, ed. J. Dobrzycki, pp. 7–30, Dordrecht: Reidel.

———, 1975a, "The Melanchthon Circle, Rheticus, and the Wittenberg Interpretation of the Copernican Theory," *Isis* 66:165–193.

———, 1975b, *Three Responses to the Copernican Theory: Johannes Praetorius, Tycho Brahe, and Michael Maestlin*, In Westman (1975c), pp. 285–345.

———, 1975c, *The Copernican Achievement*, Berkeley: University of California Press.

Zahar, Elie, 1973, "Why Did Einstein's Research Programme Supersede Lorentz's?" *British Journal for the Philosophy of Science* 24:95–123, 223–262.

IAN HACKING

Experimentation and Scientific Realism

Experimental physics provides the strongest evidence for scientific realism. Entities that in principle cannot be observed are regularly manipulated to produce new phenomena and to investigate other aspects of nature. They are tools, instruments not for thinking but for doing.

The philosopher's standard "theoretical entity" is the electron. I will illustrate how electrons have become experimental entities, or experimenter's entities. In the early stages of our discovery of an entity, we may test hypotheses about it. Then it is merely a hypothetical entity. Much later, if we come to understand some of its causal powers and use it to build devices that achieve well-understood effects in other parts of nature, then it assumes quite a different status.

Discussions about scientific realism or antirealism usually talk about theories, explanation, and prediction. Debates at that level are necessarily inconclusive. Only at the level of experimental practice is scientific realism unavoidable—but this realism is not about theories and truth. The experimentalist need only be a realist about the entities used as tools.

A Plea for Experiments

No field in the philosophy of science is more systematically neglected than experiment. Our grade school teachers may have told us that scientific method is experimental method, but histories of science have become histories of theory. Experiments, the philosophers say, are of value only when they test theory. Experimental work, they imply, has no life of its own. So we lack even a terminology to describe the many varied roles of experiment. Nor has this one-sidedness done theory any good, for radically different types of theory are used to think about the same physical phenomenon (e.g., the

From *Philosophical Topics*, Vol. 13, No. 1, 1983, pp. 71–87. Reprinted by permission.

magneto-optical effect). The philosophers of theory have not noticed this and so misreport even theoretical enquiry.

Different sciences at different times exhibit different relationships between "theory" and "experiment." One chief role of experiment is the creation of phenomena. Experimenters bring into being phenomena that do not naturally exist in a pure state. These phenomena are the touchstones of physics, the keys to nature, and the source of much modern technology. Many are what physicists after the 1870s began to call "effects": the photoelectric effect, the Compton effect, and so forth.[1] A recent high-energy extension of the creation of phenomena is the creation of "events," to use the jargon of the trade. Most of the phenomena, effects, and events created by the experimenter are like plutonium: They do not exist in nature except possibly on vanishingly rare occasions.[2]

In this paper I leave aside questions of methodology, history, taxonomy, and the purpose of experiment in natural science. I turn to the purely philosophical issue of scientific realism. Simply call it "realism" for short. There are two basic kinds: realism about entities and realism about theories. There is no agreement on the precise definition of either. Realism about theories says that we try to form true theories about the world, about the inner constitution of matter and about the outer reaches of space. This realism gets its bite from optimism: We think we can do well in this project and have already had partial success. Realism about entities—and I include processes, states, waves, currents, interactions, fields, black holes, and the like among entities—asserts the existence of at least some of the entities that are the stock in trade of physics.[3]

The two realisms may seem identical. If you believe a theory, do you not believe in the existence of the entities it speaks about? If you believe in some entities, must you not describe them in some theoretical way that you accept? This seeming identity is illusory. *The vast majority of experimental physicists are realists about en-*

tities but not about theories. Some are, no doubt, realists about theories too, but that is less central to their concerns.

Experimenters are often realists about the entities that they investigate, but they do not have to be so. R. A. Millikan probably had few qualms about the reality of electrons when he set out to measure their charge. But he could have been skeptical about what he would find until he found it. He could even have remained skeptical. Perhaps there is a least unit of electric charge, but there is no particle or object with exactly that unit of charge. Experimenting on an entity does not commit you to believing that it exists. Only manipulating an entity, in order to experiment on something else, need do that.

Moreover, it is not even that you use electrons to experiment on something else that makes it impossible to doubt electrons. Understanding some causal properties of electrons, you guess how to build a very ingenious, complex device that enables you to line up the electrons the way you want, in order to see what will happen to something else. Once you have the right experimental idea, you know in advance roughly how to try to build the device, because you know that this is the way to get the electrons to behave in such and such a way. Electrons are no longer ways of organizing our thoughts or saving the phenomena that have been observed. They are now ways of creating phenomena in some other domain of nature. Electrons are tools.

There is an important experimental contrast between realism about entities and realism about theories. Suppose we say that the latter is belief that science aims at true theories. Few experimenters will deny that. Only philosophers doubt it. Aiming at the truth is, however, something about the indefinite future. Aiming a beam of electrons is using present electrons. Aiming a finely tuned laser at a particular atom in order to knock off a certain electron to produce an ion is aiming at present electrons. There is, in contrast, no present set of theories that one has to believe in. If realism about theories is a doctrine about the aims of science, it is a doctrine laden with certain kinds of values. If realism about entities is a matter of aiming electrons next week or aiming at other electrons the week after, it is a doctrine much more neutral between values. The way in which experimenters are scientific realists about entities is entirely different from ways in which they might be realists about theories.

This shows up when we turn from ideal theories to present ones. Various properties are confidently ascribed to electrons, but most of the confident properties are expressed in numerous different theories or models about which an experimenter can be rather agnostic. Even people in a team, who work on different parts of the same large experiment, may hold different and mutually incompatible accounts of electrons. That is because different parts of the experiment will make different uses of electrons. Models good for calculations on one aspect of electrons will be poor for others. Occasionally, a team actually has to select a member with a quite different theoretical perspective simply to get someone who can solve those experimental problems. You may choose someone with a foreign training, and whose talk is well-nigh incommensurable with yours, just to get people who can produce the effects you want.

But might there not be a common core of theory, the intersection of everybody in the group, which is the theory of the electron to which all the experimenters are realistically committed? I would say common lore, *not* common core. There are a lot of theories, models, approximations, pictures, formalisms, methods, and so forth involving electrons, but there is no reason to suppose that the intersection of these is a theory at all. Nor is there any reason to think that there is such a thing as "the most powerful nontrivial *theory* contained in the intersection of all the theories in which this or that member of a team has been trained to believe." Even if there are a lot of shared be-

liefs, there is no reason to suppose they form anything worth calling a theory. Naturally, teams tend to be formed from like-minded people at the same institute, so there is usually some real shared theoretical basis to their work. That is a sociological fact, not a foundation for scientific realism.

I recognize that many a scientific realism concerning theories is a doctrine not about the present but about what we might achieve, or possibly an ideal at which we aim. So to say that there is no present theory does not count against the optimistic aim. The point is that such scientific realism about theories has to adopt the Peircean principles of faith, hope, and charity. Scientific realism about entities needs no such virtues. It arises from what we can do at present. To understand this, we must look in some detail at what it is like to build a device that makes the electrons sit up and behave.

Our Debt to Hilary Putnam

It was once the accepted wisdom that a word such as "electron" gets its meaning from its place in a network of sentences that state theoretical laws. Hence arose the infamous problems of incommensurability and theory change. For if a theory is modified, how could a word such as "electron" go on meaning the same? How could different theories about electrons be compared, since the very word "electron" would differ in meaning from theory to theory?

Putnam saved us from such questions by inventing a referential model of meaning. He says that meaning is a vector, refreshingly like a dictionary entry. First comes the syntactic marker (part of speech); next the semantic marker (general category of thing signified by the word); then the stereotype (clichés about the natural kind, standard examples of its use, and present-day associations. The stereotype is subject to change as opinions about the kind are modified.) Finally, there is the actual referent of the word, the very stuff, or thing, it denotes if it denotes anything. (Evidently dictionaries cannot include this in their entry, but pictorial dictionaries do their best by inserting illustrations whenever possible.)[4]

Putnam thought we can often guess at entities that we do not literally point to. Our initial guesses may be jejune or inept, and not every naming of an invisible thing or stuff pans out. But when it does, and we frame better and better ideas, then Putnam says that, although the stereotype changes, we refer to the same kind of thing or stuff all along. We and Dalton alike spoke about the same stuff when we spoke of (inorganic) acids. J. J. Thomson, H. A. Lorentz, Bohr, and Millikan were, with their different theories and observations, speculating about the same kind of thing, the electron.

There is plenty of unimportant vagueness about when an entity has been successfully "dubbed," as Putnam puts it. "Electron" is the name suggested by G. Johnstone Stoney in 1891 as the name for a natural unit of electricity. He had drawn attention to this unit in 1874. The name was then applied to the subatomic particles of negative charge, which J. J. Thomson, in 1897, showed cathode rays consist of. Was Johnstone Stoney referring to the electron? Putnam's account does not require an unequivocal answer. Standard physics books say that Thomson discovered the electron. For once I might back theory and say that Lorentz beat him to it. Thomson called his electrons "corpuscles," the subatomic particles of electric charge. Evidently, the name does not matter much. Thomson's most notable achievement was to measure the mass of the electron. He did this by a rough (though quite good) guess at e, and by making an excellent determination of e/m, showing that m is about $1/1800$ the mass of the hydrogen atom. Hence it is natural to say that Lorentz merely postulated the existence of a particle of negative charge, while Thomson, determining its mass, showed that there is some such real stuff beaming off a hot cathode.

The stereotype of the electron has regularly changed, and we have at least two largely incompatible stereotypes, the electron as cloud and the electron as particle. One fundamental enrichment of the idea came in the 1920s. Electrons, it was found, have angular momentum, or "spin." Experimental work by O. Stern and W. Gerlach first indicated this, and then S. Goudsmit and G. E. Uhlenbeck provided the theoretical understanding of it in 1925. Whatever we think, Johnstone Stoney, Lorentz, Bohr, Thomson, and Goudsmit were all finding out more about the same kind of thing, the electron.

We need not accept the find points of Putnam's account of reference in order to thank him for giving us a new way to talk about meaning. Serious discussion of inferred entities need no longer lock us into pseudo-problems of incommensurability and theory change. Twenty-five years ago the experimenter who believed that electrons exist, without giving much credence to any set of laws about electrons, would have been dismissed as philosophically incoherent. Now we realize it was the philosophy that was wrong, not the experimenter. My own relationship to Putnam's account of meaning is like the experimenter's relationship to a theory. I do not literally believe Putnam, but I am happy to employ his account as an alternative to the unpalatable account in fashion some time ago. . . .

Interfering

Francis Bacon, the first and almost last philosopher of experiments, knew it well: The experimenter sets out "to twist the lion's tail." Experimentation is interference in the course of nature; "nature under constraint and vexed; that is to say, when by art and the hand of man she is forced out of her natural state, and squeezed and molded."[5] The experimenter is convinced of the reality of entities, some of whose causal properties are sufficiently well understood that they can be used to interfere *elsewhere* in nature. One is impressed by entities that one can use to test conjectures about other, more hypothetical entities. In my example, one is sure of the electrons that are used to investigate weak neutral currents and neutral bosons. This should not be news, for why else are we (nonskeptics) sure of the reality of even macroscopic objects, but because of what we do with them, what we do to them, and what they do to us?

Interference and interaction are the stuff of reality. This is true, for example, at the borderline of observability. Too often philosophers imagine that microscopes carry conviction because they help us see better. But that is only part of the story. On the contrary, what counts is what we can do to a specimen under a microscope, and what we can see ourselves doing. We stain the specimen, slice it, inject it, irradiate it, fix it. We examine it using different kinds of microscopes that employ optical systems that rely on almost totally unrelated facts about light. Microscopes carry conviction because of the great array of interactions and interferences that are possible. When we see something that turns out to be unstable under such play, we call it an artifact and say it is not real.[6]

Likewise, as we move down in scale to the truly unseeable, it is our power to use unobservable entities that makes us believe they are there. Yet, I blush over these words "see" and "observe." Philosophers and physicists often use these words in different ways. Philosophers tend to treat opacity to visible light as the touchstone of reality, so that anything that cannot be touched or seen with the naked eye is called a theoretical or inferred entity. Physicists, in contrast, cheerfully talk of observing the very entities that philosophers say are not observable. For example, the fermions are those fundamental constituents of matter such as electron neutrinos and deuterons and, perhaps, the notorious quarks. All are standard philosophers' "unobservable" entities. C. Y. Prescott, the initiator of the experiment described below, said in a recent lecture, that "of these fermions, only the t quark is yet unseen. The

failure to observe $t\bar{t}$ states in e^+e^- annihilation at PETRA remains a puzzle."[7] Thus, the physicist distinguishes among the philosophers' "unobservable" entities, noting which have been observed and which not. Dudley Shapere has just published a valuable study of this fact.[8] In his example, neutrinos are used to see the interior of a star. He has ample quotations such as "neutrinos present the only way of directly observing" the very hot core of a star.

John Dewey would have said that fascination with seeing-with-the-naked-eye is part of the spectator theory of knowledge that has bedeviled philosophy from earliest times. But I do not think Plato or Locke or anyone before the nineteenth century was as obsessed with the sheer opacity of objects as we have been since.

Making

Even if experimenters are realists about entities, it does not follow that they are right. Perhaps it is a matter of psychology: Maybe the very skills that make for a great experimenter go with a certain cast of mind which objectifies whatever it thinks about. Yet this will not do. The experimenter cheerfully regards neutral bosons as merely hypothetical entities, while electrons are real. What is the difference?

There are an enormous number of ways in which to make instruments that rely on the causal properties of electrons in order to produce desired effects of unsurpassed precision. I shall illustrate this. The argument—it could be called the "experimental argument for realism"—is not that we infer the reality of electrons from our success. We do not make the instruments and then infer the reality of the electrons, as when we test a hypothesis, and then believe it because it passed the test. That gets the time order wrong. By now we design apparatus relying on a modest number of home truths about electrons, in order to produce some other phenomenon that we wish to investigate.

That may sound as if we believe in the electrons because we predict how our apparatus will behave. That too is misleading. We have a number of general ideas about how to prepare polarized electrons, say. We spend a lot of time building prototypes that do not work. We get rid of innumerable bugs. Often we have to give up and try another approach. Debugging is not a matter of theoretically explaining or predicting what is going wrong. It is partly a matter of getting rid of "noise" in the apparatus. "Noise" often means all the events that are not understood by any theory. The instrument must be able to isolate, physically, the properties of the entities that we wish to use, and damp down all the other effects that might get in our way. *We are completely convinced of the reality of electrons when we regularly set to build—and often enough succeed in building—new kinds of device that use various well understood causal properties of electrons to interfere in other more hypothetical parts of nature.*

It is not possible to grasp this without an example. Familiar historical examples have usually become encrusted by false theory-oriented philosophy or history, so I will take something new. This is a polarizing electron gun whose acronym is PEGGY II. In 1978, it was used in a fundamental experiment that attracted attention even in *The New York Times*. In the next section I describe the point of making PEGGY II. To do that, I have to tell some new physics. You may omit reading this and read only the engineering section that follows. Yet it must be of interest to know the rather easy-to-understand significance of the main experimental results, namely, that parity is not conserved in scattering of polarized electrons from deuterium, and that, more generally, parity is violated in weak neutral-current interactions.[9]

Parity and Weak Neutral Currents

There are four fundamental forces in nature, not necessarily distinct. Gravity and electromagnetism are familiar. Then there are the strong and weak forces (the fulfillment of Newton's program, in the *Optics*, which taught that all nature would be understood by the interaction of particles with various forces that were effective in attraction or repulsion over various different distances, i.e., with different rates of extinction).

Strong forces are 100 times stronger than electromagnetism but act only over a minuscule distance, at most the diameter of a proton. Strong forces act on "hadrons," which include protons, neutrons, and more recent particles, but not electrons or any other members of the class of particles called "leptons."

The weak forces are only 1/10,000 times as strong as electromagnetism, and act over a distance 100 times greater than strong forces. But they act on both hadrons and leptons, including electrons. The most familiar example of a weak force may be radioactivity.

The theory that motivates such speculation is quantum electrodynamics. It is incredibly successful, yielding many predictions better than one part in a million, truly a miracle in experimental physics. It applies over distances ranging from diameters of the earth to 1/100 the diameter of the proton. This theory supposes that all the forces are "carried" by some sort of particle: Photons do the job in electromagnetism. We hypothesize "gravitons" for gravity.

In the case of interactions involving weak forces, there are charged currents. We postulate that particles called "bosons" carry these weak forces.[10] For charged currents, the bosons may be either positive or negative. In the 1970s, there arose the possibility that there could be weak "neutral" currents in which no charge is carried or exchanged. By sheer analogy with the vindicated parts of quantum electrodynamics, neutral bosons were postulated as the carriers in weak neutral interactions.

The most famous discovery of recent high-energy physics is the failure of the conservation of parity. Contrary to the expectations of many physicists and philosophers, including Kant,[11] nature makes an absolute distinction between right-handedness and left-handedness. Apparently, this happens only in weak interactions.

What we mean by right- or left-handed in nature has an element of convention. I remarked that electrons have spin. Imagine your right hand wrapped around a spinning particle with the fingers pointing in the direction of spin. Then your thumb is said to point in the direction of the spin vector. If such particles are traveling in a beam, consider the relation between the spin vector and the beam. If all the particles have their spin vector in the same direction as the beam, they have right-handed (linear) polarization, while if the spin vector is opposite to the beam direction, they have left-handed (linear) polarization.

The original discovery of parity violation showed that one kind of product of a particle decay, a so-called muon neutrino, exists only in left-handed polarization and never in right-handed polarization.

Parity violations have been found for weak *charged* interactions. What about weak *neutral* currents? The remarkable Weinberg-Salam model for the four kinds of force was proposed independently by Stephen Weinberg in 1967 and A. Salam in 1968. It implies a minute violation of parity in weak neutral interactions. Given that the model is sheer speculation, its success has been amazing, even awe-inspiring. So it seemed worthwhile to try out the predicted failure of parity for weak neutral interactions. That would teach us more about those weak forces that act over so minute a distance.

The prediction is: Slightly more left-handed polarized electrons hitting certain targets will scatter than right-handed electrons. Slightly more! The difference in relative frequency of the two kinds of scattering is 1 part in 10,000, comparable to a difference in probability between 0.50005 and 0.49995. Suppose one used the standard equipment available at the Standard Linear Accelerator Center in the early 1970s, generating 120 pulses per second, each pulse providing one electron event. Then you would have to run the entire SLAC beam for

twenty-seven years in order to detect so small a difference in relative frequency. Considering that one uses the same beam for lots of experiments simultaneously, by letting different experiments use different pulses, and considering that no equipment remains stable for even a month, let alone twenty-seven years, such an experiment is impossible. You need enormously more electrons coming off in each pulse—between 1000 and 10,000 more electrons per pulse than was once possible. The first attempt used an instrument now called PEGGY I. It had, in essence, a high-class version of J. J. Thomson's hot cathode. Some lithium was heated and electrons were boiled off. PEGGY II uses quite different principles.

PEGGY II

The basic idea began when C. Y. Prescott noticed (by chance!) an article in an optics magazine about a crystalline substance called gallium arsenide. GaAs has a curious property; when it is struck by circularly polarized light of the right frequencies, it emits lots of linearly polarized electrons. There is a good, rough and ready quantum understanding of why this happens, and why half the emitted electrons will be polarized, three-fourths of these polarized in one direction and one-fourth polarized in the other.

PEGGY II uses this fact, plus the fact that GaAs emits lots of electrons owing to features of its crystal structure. Then comes some engineering—it takes work to liberate an electron from a surface. We know that painting a surface with the right stuff helps. In this case, a thin layer of cesium and oxygen is applied to the crystal. Moreover, the less air pressure around the crystal, the more electrons will escape for a given amount of work. So the bombardment takes place in a good vacuum at the temperature of liquid nitrogen.

We need the right source of light. A laser with bursts of red light (7100 Ångstroms) is trained on the crystal. The light first goes through an ordinary polarizer, a very old-fashioned prism of calcite, or Iceland spar[12]—this gives linearly polarized light. We want circularly polarized light to hit the crystal, so the polarized laser beam now goes through a cunning device called a Pockel's cell, which electrically turns linearly polarized photons into circularly polarized ones. Being electric, it acts as a very fast switch. The direction of circular polarization depends on the direction of current in the cell. Hence, the direction of polarization can be varied randomly. This is important, for we are trying to detect a minute asymmetry between right- and left-handed polarization. Randomizing helps us guard against any systematic "drift" in the equipment.[13] The randomization is generated by a radioactive decay device, and a computer records the direction of polarization for each pulse.

A circularly polarized pulse hits the GaAs crystal, resulting in a pulse of linearly polarized electrons. A beam of such pulses is maneuvered by magnets into the accelerator for the next bit of the experiment. It passes through a device that checks on a proportion of polarization along the way. The remainder of the experiment requires other devices and detectors of comparable ingenuity, but let us stop at PEGGY II.

Bugs

Short descriptions make it all sound too easy; therefore, let us pause to reflect on debugging. Many of the bugs are never understood. They are eliminated by trial and error. Let me illustrate three different kinds of bugs: (1) the essential technical limitations that, in the end, have to be factored into the analysis of error; (2) simpler mechanical defects you never think of until they are forced on you; and (3) hunches about what might go wrong.

Here are three examples of bugs:

1. Laser beams are not as constant as science fiction teaches, and there is always an irre-mediable amount of "jitter" in the beam over any stretch of time.

2. At a more humdrum level, the electrons from the GaAs crystals are back-scattered and go back along the same channel as the laser beam used to hit the crystal. Most of them are then deflected magnetically. But some get reflected from the laser apparatus and get back into the system. So you have to eliminate these new ambient electrons. This is done by crude mechanical means, making them focus just off the crystal and, thus, wander away.

3. Good experimenters guard against the absurd. Suppose that dust particles on an experimental surface lie down flat when a polarized pulse hits it, and then stand on their heads when hit by a pulse polarized in the opposite direction. Might that have a systematic effect, given that we are detecting a minute asymmetry? One of the team thought of this in the middle of the night and came down next morning frantically using antidust spray. They kept that up for a month, just in case.[14]

Results

Some 10^{11} events were needed to obtain a result that could be recognized above systematic and statistical error. Atthough the idea of systematic error presents interesting conceptual problems, it seems to be unknown to philosophers. There were systematic uncertainties in the detection of right- and left-handed polarization, there was some jitter, and there were other problems about the parameters of the two kinds of beam. These errors were analyzed and linearly added to the statistical error. To a student of statistical inference, this is real seat-of-the-pants analysis with no rationale whatsoever. Be that as it may, thanks to PEGGY II the number of events was big enough to give a result that convinced the entire physics community.[15] Left-handed polarized electrons were scattered from deuterium slightly more frequently than right-handed electrons. This was the first convincing example of parity-violation in a weak neutral current interaction.

Comment

The making of PEGGY II was fairly nontheoretical. Nobody worked out in advance the polarizing properties of GaAs—that was found by a chance encounter with an unrelated experimental investigation. Although elementary quantum theory of crystals explains the polarization effect, it does not explain the properties of the actual crystal used. No one has got a real crystal to polarize more than 37 percent of the electrons, although in principle 50 percent should be polarized.

Likewise, although we have a general picture of why layers of cesium and oxygen will "produce negative electron affinity," that is, make it easier for electrons to escape, we have no quantitative understanding of why this increases efficiency to a score of 37 percent.

Nor was there any guarantee that the bits and pieces would fit together. To give an even more current illustration, future experimental work, briefly described later in this paper, makes us want even more electrons per pulse than PEGGY II can give. When the aforementioned parity experiment was reported in *The New York Times*, a group at Bell Laboratories read the newspaper and saw what was going on. They had been constructing a crystal lattice for totally unrelated purposes. It uses layers of GaAs and a related aluminum compound. The structure of this lattice leads one to expect that virtually all the electrons emitted would be polarized. As a consequence, we might be able to double the efficiency of PEGGY II. But, at present, that nice idea has problems. The new lattice should also be coated in work-reducing paint. The cesium-oxygen compound is applied at high temperature. Hence the aluminum tends to ooze into the neighboring layer of GaAs, and the pretty artificial lattice becomes a

bit uneven, limiting its fine polarized-electron-emitting properties.[16] So perhaps this will never work. Prescott is simultaneously reviving a souped-up new thermionic cathode to try to get more electrons. Theory would not have told us that PEGGY II would beat out thermionic PEGGY I. Nor can it tell if some thermionic PEGGY III will beat out PEGGY II.

Note also that the Bell people did not need to know a lot of weak neutral current theory to send along their sample lattice. They just read *The New York Times.*

Moral

Once upon a time, it made good sense to doubt that there were electrons. Even after Thomson had measured the mass of his corpuscles, and Millikan their charge, doubt could have made sense. We needed to be sure that Millikan was measuring the same entity as Thomson. Thus, more theoretical elaboration was needed, and the idea had to be fed into many other phenomena. Solid state physics, the atom, and superconductivity all had to play their part.

Once upon a time, the best reason for thinking that there are electrons might have been success in explanation. Lorentz explained the Faraday effect with his electron theory. But the ability to explain carries little warrant of truth. Even from the time of J. J. Thomson, it was the measurements that weighed in, more than the explanations. Explanations, however, did help. Some people might have had to believe in electrons because the postulation of their existence could explain a wide variety of phenomena. Luckily, we no longer have to pretend to infer from explanatory success (i.e., from what makes our minds feel good). Prescott and the team from the SLAC do not explain phenomena with electrons. They know how to use them. Nobody in his right mind thinks that electrons "really" are just little spinning orbs about which you could, with a small enough hand, wrap your fingers and find the direction of spin along your thumb. There is, instead, a family of causal properties in terms of which gifted experimenters describe and deploy electrons in order to investigate something else, for example, weak neutral currents and neutral bosons. We know an enormous amount about the behavior of electrons. It is equally important to know what does *not* matter to electrons. Thus, we know that bending a polarized electron beam in magnetic coils does not affect polarization in any significant way. We have hunches, too strong to ignore although too trivial to test independently: For example, dust might dance under changes of directions of polarization. Those hunches are based on a hard-won sense of the kinds of things electrons are. (It does not matter at all to this hunch whether electrons are clouds or waves or particles.)

When Hypothetical Entities Become Real

Note the complete contrast between electrons and neutral bosons. Nobody can yet manipulate a bunch of neutral bosons, if there are any. Even weak neutral currents are only just emerging from the mists of hypothesis. By 1980, a sufficient range of convincing experiments had made them the object of investigation. When might they lose their hypothetical status and become commonplace reality like electrons?—when we use them to investigate something else.

I mentioned the desire to make a better electron gun than PEGGY II. Why? Because we now "know" that parity is violated in weak neutral interactions. Perhaps by an even more grotesque statistical analysis than that involved in the parity experiment, we can isolate just the weak interactions. For example, we have a lot of interactions, including electromagnetic ones, which we can censor in various ways. If we could also statistically pick out a class of weak interactions, as precisely those where parity is not conserved, then we would possibly

be on the road to quite deep investigations of matter and antimatter. To do the statistics, however, one needs even more electrons per pulse than PEGGY II could hope to generate. If such a project were to succeed, we should then be beginning to use weak neutral currents as a manipulable tool for looking at something else. The next step toward a realism about such currents would have been made.

The message is general and could be extracted from almost any branch of physics. I mentioned earlier how Dudley Shapere has recently used "observation" of the sun's hot core to illustrate how physicists employ the concept of observation. They collect neutrinos from the sun in an enormous disused underground mine that has been filled with old cleaning fluid (i.e., carbon tetrachloride). We would know a lot about the inside of the sun if we knew how many solar neutrinos arrive on the earth. So these are captured in the cleaning fluid. A few neutrinos will form a new radioactive nucleus (the number that do this can be counted). Although, in this study, the extent of neturino manipulation is much less than electron manipulation in the PEGGY II experiment, we are nevertheless plainly using neutrinos to investigate something else. Yet not many years ago, neutrinos were about as hypothetical as an entity could get. After 1946 it was realized that when mesons disintegrate giving off, among other things, highly energized electrons, one needed an extra nonionizing particle to conserve momentum and energy. At that time this postulated "neutrino" was thoroughly hypothetical, but now it is routinely used to examine other things.

Changing Times

Although realisms and anti-realisms are part of the philosophy of science well back into Greek pre-history, our present versions mostly descend from debates at the end of the nineteenth century about atomism. Anti-realism about atoms was partly a matter of physics; the energeticists thought energy was at the bottom of everything, not tiny bits of matter. It also was connected with the positivism of Comte, Mach, K. Pearson, and even J. S. Mill. Mill's young associate Alexander Bain states the point in a characteristic way, apt for 1870:

> Some hypotheses consist of assumptions as to the minute structure and operation of bodies. From the nature of the case these assumptions can never be proved by direct means. Their merit is their suitability to express phenomena. They are Representative Fictions.[17]

"All assertions as to the ultimate structure of the particles of matter," continues Bain, "are and ever must be hypothetical. . . . The kinetic theory of heat serves an important intellectual function." But we cannot hold it to be a true description of the world. It is a representative fiction.

Bain was surely right a century ago, when assumptions about the minute structure of matter could not be proved. The only proof could be indirect, namely, that hypotheses seemed to provide some explanation and helped make good predictions. Such inferences, however, need never produce conviction in the philosopher inclined to instrumentalism or some other brand of idealism.

Indeed, the situation is quite similar to seventeenth-century epistemology. At that time, knowledge was thought of as correct representation. But then one could never get outside the representations to be sure that they corresponded to the world. Every test of a representation is just another representation. "Nothing is so much like an idea as an idea," said Bishop Berkeley. To attempt to argue to scientific realism at the level of theory, testing, explanation, predictive success, convergence of theories, and so forth is to be locked into a world of representations. No wonder that scientific anti-realism is so permanently in the race. It is a variant on "the spectator theory of knowledge."

Scientists, as opposed to philosophers, did, in general, become realists about atoms by 1910. Despite the changing climate, some anti-realist variety of instrumentalism or fictionalism remained a strong philosophical alternative in 1910 and in 1930. That is what the history of philosophy teaches us. The lesson is: Think about practice, not theory. Anti-realism about atoms was very sensible when Bain wrote a century ago. Anti-realism about *any* submicroscopic entities was a sound doctrine in those days. Things are different now. The "direct" proof of electrons and the like is our ability to manipulate them using well-understood low-level causal properties. Of course, I do not claim that reality is constituted by human manipulability. Millikan's ability to determine the charge of the electron did something of great importance for the idea of electrons—more, I think, than the Lorentz theory of the electron. Determining the charge of something makes one believe in it far more than postulating it to explain something else. Millikan got the charge on the electron; but better still, Uhlenbeck and Goudsmit in 1925 assigned angular momentum to electrons, brilliantly solving a lot of problems. Electrons have spin, ever after. The clincher is when we can put a spin on the electrons, and thereby get them to scatter in slightly different proportions.

Surely, there are innumerable entities and processes that humans will never know about. Perhaps there are many in principle we can never know about, since reality is bigger than us. The best kinds of evidence for the reality of a postulated or inferred entity is that we can begin to measure it or otherwise understand its causal powers. The best evidence, in turn, that we have this kind of understanding is that we can set out, from scratch, to build machines that will work fairly reliably, taking advantage of this or that causal nexus. Hence, engineering, not theorizing, is the best proof of scientific realism about entities. My attack on scientific anti-realism is analogous to Marx's onslaught on the idealism of his day. Both say that the point is not to understand the world but to change it. Perhaps there are some entities which in theory we can know about only through theory (black holes). Then our evidence is like that furnished by Lorentz. Perhaps there are entities which we shall only measure and never use. The experimental argument for realism does not say that only experimenter's objects exist.

I must now confess a certain skepticism, about, say, black holes. I suspect there might be another representation of the universe, equally consistent with phenomena, in which black holes are precluded. I inherit from Leibniz a certain distaste for occult powers. Recall how he inveighed against Newtonian gravity as occult. It took two centuries to show he was right. Newton's ether was also excellently occult—it taught us lots: Maxwell did his electromagnetic waves in ether, H. Hertz confirmed the ether by demonstrating the existence of radio waves. Albert A. Michelson figured out a way to interact with the ether. He thought his experiment confirmed G. G. Stoke's ether drag theory, but, in the end, it was one of the many things that made ether give up the ghost. A skeptic such as myself has a slender induction: Long-lived theoretical entities which do not end up being manipulated commonly turn out to have been wonderful mistakes.

Notes

1. C. W. F. Everitt suggests that the first time the word "effect" is used this way in English is in connection with the Peltier effect, in James Clerk Maxwell's 1873 *Electricity and Magnetism*, par. 249, p. 301. My interest in experiment was kindled by conversation with Everitt some years ago, and I have learned much in working with him on our joint (unpublished) paper, "Theory or Experiment, Which Comes First?"

2. Ian Hacking, "Spekulation, Berechnung und die Erschaffnung der Phänomenen," in *Versuchungen: Aufsätze zur Philosophie, Paul Feyerabends*, no. 2, ed. P. Duerr (Frankfort, 1981), 126–158.

3. Nancy Cartwright makes a similar distinction in her book, *How the Laws of Physics Lie* (Oxford:

Oxford University Press, 1983). She approaches realism from the top, distinguishing theoretical laws (which do not state the facts) from phenomenological laws (which do). She believes in some "theoretical" entities and rejects much theory on the basis of a subtle analysis of modeling in physics. I proceed in the opposite direction, from experimental practice. Both approaches share an interest in real life physics as opposed to philosophical fantasy science. My own approach owes an enormous amount to Cartwright's parallel developments, which have often preceded my own. My use of the two kinds of realism is a case in point.

4. Hilary Putnam, "How Not to Talk About Meaning," "The Meaning of 'Meaning,'" and other papers in *Mind, Language and Reality*, Philosophical Papers, Vol. 2 (Cambridge: Cambridge University Press, 1975).

5. Francis Bacon, *The Great Instauration*, in *The Philosophical Works of Francis Bacon*, trans. Ellis and Spedding, ed. J. M. Robertson (London, 1905), 252.

6. Ian Hacking, "Do We See Through a Microscope?" *Pacific Philosophical Quarterly* 62 (1981): 305–322.

7. C. Y. Prescott, "Prospects for Polarized Electrons at High Energies," SLAC-PUB-2630, Stanford Linear Accelerator, October 1980, p. 5.

8. "The Concept of Observation in Science and Philosophy," *Philosophy of Science* 49 (1982): 485–526. See also K. S. Shrader-Frechette, "Quark Quantum Numbers and the Problem of Microphysical Observation," *Synthàse* 50 (1982): 125–146, and ensuing discussion in that issue of the journal.

9. I thank Melissa Franklin, of the Standard Linear Accelerator, for introducing me to PEGGY II and telling me how it works. She also arranged discussion with members of the PEGGY II group, some of whom are mentioned below. The report of experiment E-122 described here is "Parity Nonconservation in Inelastic Electron Scattering," C. Y. Prescott et al., in *Physics Letters*. I have relied heavily on the in-house journal, the *SLAC Beam Line*, report no. 8, October 1978, "Parity Violation in Polarized Electron Scattering." This was prepared by the in-house science writer Bill Kirk.

10. The odd-sounding bosons are named after the Indian physicist. S. N. Bose (1894–1974), also remembered in the name "Bose-Einstein statistics" (which bosons satisfy).

11. But excluding Leibniz, who "knew" there had to be some real, natural difference between right- and left-handedness.

12. Iceland spar is an elegant example of how experimental phenomena persist even while theories about them undergo revolutions. Mariners brought calcite from Iceland to Scandinavia. Erasmus Bartholinus experimented with it and wrote it up in 1609. When you look through these beautiful crystals you see double, thanks to the so-called ordinary and extraordinary rays. Calcite is a natural polarizer. It was our entry to polarized light, which for three hundred years was the chief route to improved theoretical and experimental understanding of light and then electromagnetism. The use of calcite in PEGGY II is a happy reminder of a great tradition.

13. It also turns GaAs, a 3/4 to 1/4 left-hand/right-hand polarizer, into a 50-50 polarizer.

14. I owe these examples to conversation with Roger Miller of SLAC.

15. The concept of a "convincing experiment" is fundamental. Peter Gallison has done important work on this idea, studying European and American experiments on weak neutral currents conducted during the 1970s.

16. I owe this information to Charles Sinclair of SLAC.

17. Alexander Bain, *Logic, Deductive and Inductive* (London and New York, 1870), 362.